MACRO
ECONOMICS
FIRST CANADIAN EDITION

MACRO ECONOMICS
FIRST CANADIAN EDITION

RUDIGER DORNBUSCH
Massachusetts Institute of Technology

STANLEY FISCHER
Massachusetts Institute of Technology

GORDON R. SPARKS
Queen's University

McGRAW-HILL RYERSON LIMITED
Toronto   Montreal   Auckland   Bogota   Guatemala   Hamburg
Johannesburg   Lisbon   London   Madrid   Mexico   New Delhi
Panama   Paris   San Juan   São Paulo   Singapore   Sydney
Tokyo

MACROECONOMICS: First Canadian Edition

ISBN 0-07-548093-X

1 2 3 4 5 6 7 8 9 0   D   10 9 8 7 6 5 4 3 2

Printed and bound in Canada

Care has been taken to trace ownership of copyright material contained in this text. The publishers will gladly take any information that will enable them to rectify any reference or credit in subsequent editions.

Canadian Cataloguing in Publication Data

Dornbusch, Rudiger.
  Macroeconomics

Includes bibliographical references and index.
ISBN 0-07-548093-X

1. Macroeconomics. I. Fischer, Stanley. II. Sparks, Gordon R. III. Title.

HB171.5.D618 1981   339   C81-095132-0

CONTENTS

PREFACE

Our aim in writing this book has been to explain how modern macroeconomics is used in understanding important economic issues, and to help the reader analyze macroeconomic problems for her or himself. The book provides full coverage of basic macroeconomics, such as national income accounting, aggregate demand, and IS-LM analysis. It goes beyond the standard coverage in presenting also the theory of aggregate supply, the interesting and vitally important topics of inflation and unemployment, and a detailed treatment of basic open-economy macroeconomics. No important topic has been omitted because it is too difficult, but we have taken great pains to make nothing more difficult than it need be. The book is policy- and issue-oriented, and this is reflected in continual references to economic events, issues and dilemmas in the postwar economy, as we elucidate the relevance of the theoretical material.

Macroeconomics is less cut-and-dried than microeconomics. That makes it unsatisfying if you are looking for definite answers to all economic problems, but should also make it more interesting because you have to think hard and critically about the material being presented. We have not hesitated to indicate where we think theories are incomplete. We unfortunately cannot guarantee that you will not at some future time have to unlearn something you learned from this book, but we hope you will have been warned.

Because the state of macroeconomics is not settled, and because it is so intimately tied up with policy making, the field is often seen as one in which anything goes and in which opposing Monetarist and Keynesian schools contend on almost every point. That is simply untrue. There are substantial areas of agreement among almost all macroeconomists – but it is less interesting to discuss points of agreement once you have understood them than to argue about disagreements. However, we do not emphasize the Keynesian-Monetarist debate in this book, preferring to discuss substantive matters and mentioning alternative views where relevant. Some prepublication reviewers of the book labeled us Keynesians and others called us Monetarists. We are quite happy to be known as neither or both.

CHANGES IN THE CANADIAN EDITION

The Canadian edition has been prepared making use of the relevant theoretical analysis in the second American edition. This material has been revised and supplemented with the aim of meeting the needs of Canadian courses. Areas of major change include national income accounting in Chapter 2, the determination of the money supply in Chapter 8, fiscal policy and public finance in Chapter 10, inflation and unemployment in Chapter 14, the monctarist approach and Bank of Canada policy in Chapter 15, and macroeconomic policy in an open economy in

Chapters 17 and 18.

The general outline of the book remains similar. It begins with the more traditional material in Chapters 2 through 8, which develop the aggregate demand side of the economy in detail. Chapters 11-16 focus on the supply side and discuss policy issues in an aggregate supply-demand framework. Most of the open economy material remains in the last two chapters, but the presentation is structured so that the sections using the IS/LM model with trade and capital flows can be read in advance of the supply side chapters.

The second American edition incorporated substantial revisions in large part in response to comments and suggestions from users and to reflect our own experience with the book. For example, the discussion of aggregate supply in Chapter 11 was simplified and more emphasis was placed on supply shocks. The distinction between real and nominal interest rates was given more attention, particularly in Chapter 13. Chapter 10 was expanded to include a description and analysis of the Great Depression of the 1930s.

HOW TO USE THE BOOK

To the Student:

Because we have not shied away from important topics even if they are difficult, parts of the book require careful reading. There is no mathematics except simple algebra. Some of the analysis, however, involves sustained reasoning. Careful reading should therefore pay off in enhanced understanding. Chapter 1 gives you suggestions on how to learn from this book. The single most important suggestion is that you learn actively. Some of the chapters (such as Chapter 9) are suitable for bedtime reading, but most are not. Use pencil and paper to be sure you are following the argument. See if you can find reasons to disagree with arguments we make. Work the problem sets! Be sure you understand the points contained in the summaries to each chapter. Follow the economic news in the press, and see how it relates to what you are learning. Try to follow the logic of budgets or other economic measures brought before Parliament.

STATISTICS CANADA DATA SOURCES

General Economic Data

11-003 Canadian Statistical Review (monthly)
11-206 Annual Supplement to Section I, Canadian Statistical Review
11-505 Canadian Statistical Review — Historical Sumary 1970

National Accounts

13-201 System of National Accounts — National Income and Expenditure Accounts (annual)
13-531 System of National Accounts — National Income and Expenditures Accounts, Volume I, The Annual Estimates 1926-1974
13-533 Volume II, The Quarterly Estimates 1947-1974
13-549 Volume III, A Guide to the National Income and Expenditure Accounts — Definitions — Concepts — Sources — Methods

Prices

62-010 Consumer Prices and Price Indexes (monthly)

Labour Force

71-001 The Labour Force (monthly)
71-201 Historical Labour Force Statistics (annual)

Other Sources

Bank of Canada Review (monthly)
Department of Finance, *Economic Review* (annual, published in April)

ACKNOWLEDGMENTS

The debts incurred by authors are among the nicest there are, and we are fortunate to have acquired many in a short time. We have been delighted with the success of the American edition and are grateful to the many readers who have given us suggestions for improving the text. Since we have been unable to accept all their suggestions, none of them should be held responsible for the deficiencies — we hope they are few — contained in this edition.

A totally revised version of the *Instructor's Manual*, prepared by us, is available on request from McGraw-Hill.

A *Study Guide* prepared by Gordon Sparks and Richard Startz is available to accompany this edition. The *Study Guide* contains a wide range of questions, starting from the very easy and progressing in each chapter to material that will challenge the more advanced student. It is a great help in studying, particularly since active learning is so important.

Edie Franks, McGraw-Hill Ryerson Sponsoring Editor, provided invaluable support and assistance. It has been a pleasure to work with her and other members of the McGraw-Hill Ryerson staff. We are also grateful to Juanita Hamilton who provided typing assistance.

Rudiger Dornbusch
Stanley Fischer
Gordon Sparks

TO THE MEMORY OF
BALFOUR B. SPARKS

Part 1

Part 1

INTRODUCTION

Part 1

INTRODUCTION

Macroeconomics is concerned with the behaviour of the economy as a whole — with booms and recessions, the economy's total output of goods and services and the growth of output, the rates of inflation and unemployment, the balance of payments, and exchange rates. To study the overall performance of the economy, macroeconomics focusses on the economic policies and policy variables that affect that performance — on monetary and fiscal policies, the money stock and interest rates, the public debt, and the government budget. In brief, macroeconomics deals with the major economic issues and problems of the day.

Macroeconomics is interesting because it deals with important issues. But it is fascinating and challenging, too, because it reduces the complicated details of the economy to manageable essentials. *Those essentials lie in the interactions among the goods, labour, and assets markets of the economy.*

In dealing with the essentials, we have to disregard details of the behaviour of individual economic units, such as households and firms, or the determination of prices in particular markets, or the effects of monopoly on individual markets. These are the subject matter of microeconomics. In macroeconomics we deal with the market for goods as a whole, treating all the markets for different goods — such as the markets for agricultural products and for medical services — as a single market. Similarly, we deal with the labour market as a whole, abstracting from differences between the markets for, say, unskilled labour and doctors. We deal wth the assets markets as a whole, abstracting from the differences between the markets for provincial bonds and Rembrandt paintings. The cost of the abstraction is that omitted details sometimes matter. For example, agricultural price rises in early 1973 had a significant effect on inflation and unemployment, but few macroeconomists had paid attention to the details of agricultural development ments before that time. (But they have since!) The benefit of the abstraction is increased understanding of the vital interactions among the goods, labour, and assets markets.

Despite the contrast between macroeconomics and microeconomics,

3

there is no basic conflict between them. After all, the economy in the aggregate is nothing but the sum of its submarkets. The difference between micro- and macroeconomics is therefore primarily one of emphasis and exposition. In studying price determination in a single industry, it is convenient for microeconomists to assume that prices in other industries are given. In macroeconomics, where we study *the* price level, it is for the most part sensible to ignore changes in relative prices of goods among different industries. In microeconomics, it is convenient to assume the total income of all consumers is given and to ask how consumers divide their spending out of that income among different goods. In macroeconomics, by contrast, the aggregate level of income or spending is among the key variables to be studied.

The great macroeconomists, including Keynes, and modern American leaders in the field, like Milton Friedman of the University of Chicago, Franco Modigliani of MIT, and James Tobin of Yale, have all had a keen interest in the applications of macrotheory to problems of policy making. Developments in macrotheory are closely related to the economic problems of the day. Indeed, the study of macroeconomics does not yield its greatest rewards to those whose primary interest is theoretical. The need for compromise between the comprehensiveness of the theory and its manageability inevitably makes macrotheory a little untidy at the edges. And the emphasis in macro is on the manageability of the theory and on its applications. To demonstrate that emphasis, this book uses the theories we present to illuminate recent economic events from the early 1960s through the end of the 1970s. We also refer continually to recent economic events to elucidate the meaning and the relevance of the theoretical material.

Modern macroeconomics is often seen as the battleground for conflict between two implacably opposed schools of thought — monetarism, represented by its champion, Milton Friedman, and "Keynesianism," or nonmonetarism, or fiscalism, represented by economists such as Franco Modigliani and James Tobin. This view is seriously misleading. There are indeed conflicts of opinion and even theory between monetarists and nonmonetarists, but much more important, there are major areas of agreement: there is far more to macroeconomics than the topics on which monetarists and fiscalists disagree. We do not emphasize the monetarist-fiscalist debate in this book, preferring to discuss substantive matters while mentioning alternative views where relevant.

We shall now in Section 1-1 present an overview of the key concepts with which macroeconomics deals. Section 1-2 presents a diagrammatic introduction to aggregate demand and supply, and their interaction; it gives a very general perspective on the fundamentals of macroeconomics and the organization of this book. Then, in Section 1-3, we outline the approach of the book to the study of macroeconomics and macropolicy making, and present a preview of the order in which topics are taken up. Section 1-4 contains brief remarks on how to use the book.

1-1 KEY CONCEPTS

Gross National Product

Gross national product (GNP) is the value of all goods and services produced in the economy in a given time period. GNP statistics are prepared on a quarterly basis. Chart 1-1 shows two measures of GNP— *nominal* or *current dollar* GNP and *real* or *constant dollar* GNP.[1] Nominal GNP measures the value of output at the prices prevailing in the period the output is produced, while real GNP measures the output produced in any one period at the prices of some base year. At present, 1971 serves as a base year for real income measurement.

Chart 1-1 shows that *nominal* GNP was equal to $260 billion in 1979 and $95 billion in 1971. Nominal GNP grew at an average rate of 13.5 percent during that period. If we divide total GNP by population, we obtain *per capita* nominal GNP, which was $11,000 in 1979 and $4,400 in 1971. That is,

[1] Notice that the scale for GNP in Chart 1-1 is not linear. For example, the distance from 60 to 65 is bigger than the distance from 145 to 150. The scale is logarithmic, which means that equal ratios are represented by equal distances. For instance, the distance from 60 to 120 is the same as the distance from 75 to 150, since GNP doubles in both cases. On a logarithmic scale, a variable growing at a constant rate (e.g., 4 percent per annum) is represented by a straight line.

CHART 1-1   REAL AND NOMINAL GNP, 1965-1980
(*Source*: Statistics Canada, 13-201, 11-003)

Note: Real GNP is calculated using 1971 prices. The scale is logarithmic. The logarithmic scale is explained in footnote 1.

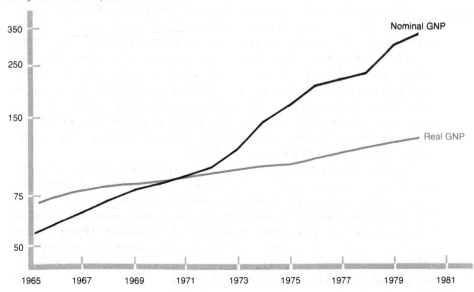

the average value of ouut produced in the Canadian economy in 1979 was $11,000 per member of the population. The chart shows that *real* GNP was $130 billion in 1979 and the same $95 billion in 1971,[2] implying an average annual growth rate of real GNP of about 4 percent over the period.

We will next consider, first, why nominal GNP has grown faster than real GNP, and second, the factors that cause real GNP growth. The difference between the growth rates of nominal and real GNP occurs because the prices of goods produced in the economy change over time. Real GNP calculates the value of goods produced at the prices that prevailed in the base year (1971, in this case), whereas nominal GNP values goods at the prices that prevail when they are produced. Since prices of nearly all goods have been rising, nominal GNP has risen faster — indeed, much faster — than real GNP. Price rises, or *inflation*, at the average rate of 9.5 percent per year for 1971-1979 account for the difference between the growth rates of real and nominal GNP.

With 1971 as the base year for the prices at which output is valued, we observe in Chart 1-1 two implications of the distinction between nominal and real GNP. First, in 1971 the two are equal because, in the base year, current and constant dollars are the same dollars. Second, with inflation, nominal GNP rises faster than real GNP, and therefore, after 1971, nominal GNP exceeds real GNP. The converse is of course true before 1971.

We turn next to reasons for the growth of real GNP. The first reason real GNP changes is that the available amount of resources in the economy may change. The resources are conveniently split into capital and labour. The labour force, consisting of people either working or looking for work, grows over time and thus provides one source of increased production. The capital stock, including buildings and machines, likewise has been rising over time, thereby making increased output possible. Increases in the availability of *factors of production* — the labour and capital used in the production of goods and services — thus account for part of the increase in real GNP.

The second source of change in real GNP is a change in the employment of the given resources available for production. Not all the capital and labour available are actually used at all times. In 1975, for example, the growth rate of real GNP slowed to 1.2 percent. With the labour force continuing to grow at a higher rate, *unemployment* rose above 7 percent. Given the available supply of factors of production, then, changes in factor utilization change real GNP.

The third reason for real GNP to change is that the *efficiency* with which factors of production work may change.[3] Over time, the same factors of

---

[2] Why are real and nominal GNP the same for 1971? Because we use 1971 prices to calculate real GNP. You may also want to calculate *real* per capita GNP for 1971 and 1979 from the numbers given in the text.

[3] These efficiency improvements are often called *productivity* increases. We use the word "efficiency" because productivity usually refers to what should be called "labour productivity," that is, output per person-hour of work.

production can produce more output. These increases in the efficiency of production result from changes in knowledge, including *learning by doing*, as people learn through experience to perform familiar tasks better.

Potential Output

One of the key macroeconomic policy concepts is *potential real GNP*, or *potential output*. Potential output is shown along with actual output in Chart 1-2. It is an estimate of the level at which real GNP would be if there were full employment.[4] The difference between potential and actual GNP is called the *GNP gap* and serves as a measure of economic slack or of the waste of productive resources due to insufficiently high levels of employment. As we see from the chart, there are large GNP gaps in the early 1960s and in the second half of the 1970s. More puzzling are the instances of a negative gap — for example, in 1966 and in 1973 when the economy was *overemployed* or in a *boom*.

How do we go about determining the economy's production potential, or potential GNP? The issue is a very important one because potential GNP

[4] For details on the construction of potential output series, see Economic Council of Canada, *Performance and Potential, mid-1950s to mid 1970s* (1970), and *Sixteenth Annual Review* (1979).

CHART 1-2 ACTUAL AND POTENTIAL GNP

(*Source*: E.A. Carmichael, *Reassessing Canada's Potential Economic Growth*, The Conference Board in Canada, 1979.

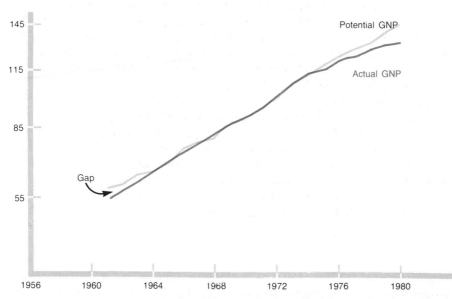

Note. The scale is logarithmic. Actual and potential GNP are in 1971 dollars.

TABLE 1-1 POTENTIAL GNP AND THE EQUILIBRIUM UNEMPLOYMENT RATE

| | GNP (billions of 1971 dollars) | | GNP gap | Equilibrium Unemployment Rate |
YEAR	POTENTIAL	ACTUAL	(percent)	(percent)
1961	59.0	54.7	7.3	4.1
1966	76.4	74.8	2.1	3.0
1971	95.4	94.5	1.0	5.2
1976	122.8	119.4	2.8	5.7
1978	132.3	126.0	4.7	6.4
1980	142.9	129.6	9.3	

Source: E.A. Carmichael, *Reassessing Canada's Potential Economic Growth*, The Conference Board in Canada, 1979.

serves as a guide for macroeconomic policies. The issue is also very controversial because throughout the 1970s, with changes in the composition of the labour force and shocks such as the oil price increases, measures of potential output have repeatedly been reassessed and revised downward. In the 1960s, an unemployment rate in the range of 3.5 to 4 percent of the labour force was thought to constitute full employment. Since the early 1970s, the *equilibrium* unemployment rate that is thought to constitute full employment has been revised upward and is now in excess of 5 percent, as shown in Table 1-1.

Potential output increases over time, as seen in Chart 1-2. The growth rate of potential output in the 1960s was close to 5 percent per year. In the seventies, it was successively revised downward and at present is only in the range of 3 to 4 percent per year. But what are the sources of potential or full-employment output growth? Potential output, or potential GNP, changes over time because the labour force grows and also because the average output of an employed person grows over time. The typical worker today produces more, in the same amount of time, than the typical worker of twenty years ago. This increase in output per worker is called *productivity increase*. There are two reasons for the increase in productivity. The first is that the typical workers have more capital — machines and factory space — with which to work now than they did then. The second is that there is *technical progress* — workers are better educated and machines are more sophisticated. (Think of pocket calculators!)

Growth and Unemployment

Growth in real GNP and the unemployment rate are widely watched as indicators of macroeconomic performance. High growth is viewed as a sign of strength in the economy. High and rising unemployment are seen as signs of weakness. In fact, there is a relationship between real GNP growth and the unemployment rate. Chart 1-3 provides an indication of that link.

We have already noted that changes in the employment of factors provide one of the sources of growth in real GNP. We would then expect high GNP growth to be accompanied by declining unemployment. That is indeed the case, as we observe from Chart 1-3. Periods where real GNP rises rapidly, such as the 1960s and 1971-1973, are periods where the unemployment rate declines. Conversely, when growth is sluggish as in the period 1977-1980, the unemployment rate increases.

A relationship between real growth and changes in the unemployment rate is known as *Okun's law*, named after its discoverer, the late Arthur Okun of the Brookings Institution, former chairperson of the U.S. Council of Economic Advisers. Okun's law says that for every two and a half percentage points growth in real GNP above the trend rate that is sustained for a year, the unemployment rate declines by one percentage point. This 2½-to-1 relationship, the status of which is somewhat exaggerated by calling it a law rather than an empirical regularity, provides a rule of thumb for

CHART 1-3 THE GROWTH RATE OF REAL OUTPUT AND
THE RATE OF UNEMPLOYMENT
(*Source:* Dept. of Finance, *Economic Review*)

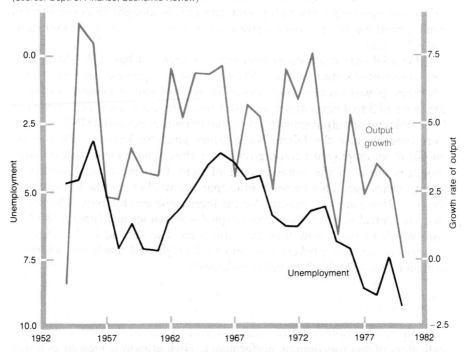

Note: Unemployment rate is on inverted scale.

see below

assessing the implications of real growth for unemployment.[5] While the rule is only approximate and will not work very precisely from year to year, it still does give a sensible translation from growth to unemployment.

The relation is a useful guide to policy because it allows us to ask how a particular growth target will affect the unemployment rate over time. Suppose we were in a deep recession with 9 percent unemployment. How many years will it take us to return to, say, 6 percent unemployment? The answer depends, of course, on how fast the economy grows in the recovery. One possible path is output growth of 5½ percent for three years. On this path, each year we are growing 2½ percent above a 3 percent trend and thus each year we take one percentage point off the unemployment rate. An alternative recovery strategy is front-loaded: Growth is high at the beginning and then slows down. Such a path might be one of growth rates equal to 6½, 5½, and 4½ percent, allowing a return to 6 percent unemployment in three years.

Aggregate Demand and Aggregate Supply

The central concerns of macroeconomics are the level of output and the price level or inflation rate. These are determined by the interaction of *aggregate demand* and *aggregate supply*. Under some conditions, employment depends only on total spending or aggregate demand. At other times, supply limitations are an important part of the policy problem and have to receive major attention. From the 1930s to the later 1960s, macroeconomics was very much demand-oriented. But in recent years the emphasis has shifted, and aggregate supply and *supply side economics* have gained in importance. This shift of emphasis and interest was no doubt fostered by the slow growth and high inflation experienced by the industrialized countries in the 1970s.

What are the relationships among aggregate demand and aggregate supply, output or employment, and prices? Aggregate demand is the relationship between spending on goods and services and the level of prices. If output limitations are not operative, increased spending or an increase in aggregate demand will raise output and employment with little effect on prices. In such conditions, such as those of the Great Depression of the thirties, it would certainly be appropriate to use expansionary aggregate demand policies to increase output.

But if the economy is close to full employment, increased aggregate demand will be reflected primarily in higher prices or inflation. The aggregate supply side of the economy has then to be introduced. The aggregate supply curve specifies the relationship between the amount of output firms produce and the price level. The supply side enters the picture

---

[5] The analysis of Canada's medium-term prospects shown in the Economic Council of Canada's *Sixteenth Annual Review* (1979) suggests a ratio of about 2 to 1.

not only in telling us how successful demand expansions will be in raising output and employment; it also has a role of its own. Supply disturbances or *supply shocks* can reduce output and raise prices as was the case when increases in the price of oil reduced the productive capacity of the economy. Conversely, policies that increase productivity, and thus the level of aggregate supply at a given price level, can help reduce inflationary pressures.

Inflation

Inflation is the rate of increase of prices. Expansionary aggregate demand policies tend to produce inflation, unless they occur when the economy is at high levels of unemployment. Protracted periods of low aggregate demand tend to reduce the inflation rate. Chart 1-4 shows one measure of inflation for the Canadian economy for the period since 1952. The inflation measure in the chart is the rate of change of the consumer price index, the cost of a given basket of goods, representing the purchases of a typical consumer.

The rate of inflation shown in Chart 1-4 fluctuates considerably. Just as we could tell much about the recent history of the economy from looking at Chart 1-2's picture of the course of actual and potential GNP, we can

---

CHART 1-4 THE RATE OF INFLATION (OF THE CONSUMER PRICE INDEX), 1952-1980 (*Source:* Statistics Canada, 11-003, 11-206)

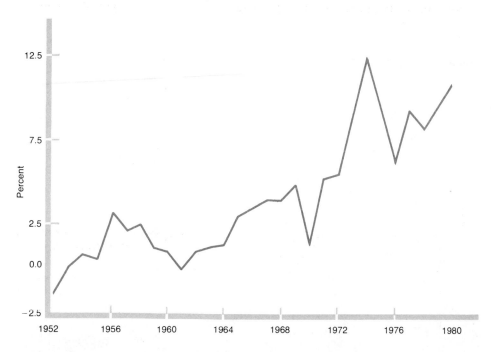

likewise see much of recent economic history in Chart 1-4. In particular, there is the long period of steady inflation from 1957 through 1964 when the inflation rate hovered around the 2 percent level. Then there is a slow climb in the inflation rate from 1965 to 1969, followed by a brief pause in 1970. Finally there are the inflationary bursts from 1971 through 1974 and 1977 to 1980 as the inflation rate rose to 12 percent and above.

Chart 1-4 presents the percentage *rate of change* of the consumer price index. It is interesting to ask how all those changes add up. Since 1952, consumer prices have more than tripled; in other words, the total increase in the price index since 1952 is over 200 percent. Much of that increase took place in the last few years.

Inflation, like unemployment, is a major macroeconomic problem. However, the costs of inflation are much less obvious than those of unemployment. In the case of unemployment, it is clear that potential output is going to waste, and therefore it is clear why the reduction of unemployment is desirable. In the case of inflation, there is no obvious loss of output. Nonetheless, policy makers have been willing to increase unemployment in an effort to reduce inflation — that is, to *trade off* some unemployment for less inflation.

Inflation-Unemployment Tradeoffs

The *Phillips curve* is a relationship between the rates of inflation and unemployment that has played a key role in macroeconomic policy discussions since its publication in 1958. Figure 1-1 presents a typical Phillips

FIGURE 1-1 A PHILLIPS CURVE

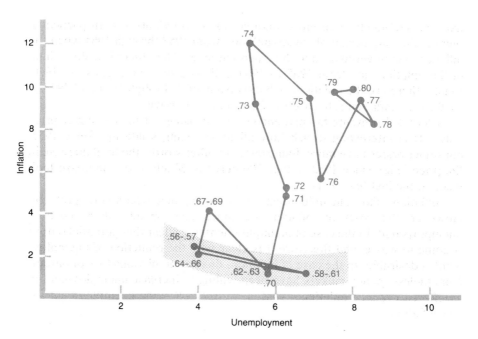

CHART 1-5 INFLATION AND UNEMPLOYMENT,
(*Source:* Statistics Canada, 11-003, 11-206, 11-505, 71-201)

curve, showing that high rates of inflation are accompanied by low rates of unemployment and vice versa. The curve suggests that less unemployment can always be attained by incurring more inflation and that the inflation rate can always be reduced by incurring the costs of more unemployment. In other words, the curve suggests there is a *tradeoff* between inflation and unemployment.

Chart 1-5 shows that the Phillips curve broadly describes Canadian experience in the period 1956-1966. However, we can see also that economic events of the last decade, particularly the combination of high inflation *and* high unemployment in 1974, are not consistent with the curve traced out in the earlier years.

Nonetheless, there remains a tradeoff between inflation and unemployment which is more sophisticated than a glance at Figure 1-1 would suggest, and which will enable us to make sense of Chart 1-5. In the short run, of say two years, there is a relation between inflation and unemployment of the type shown in Figure 1-1. That *short-run Phillips curve,* however, does not remain stable. It shifts as expectations of inflation change. In the long run, there is no tradeoff worth speaking about between inflation and unemployment. In the long run, the unemployment rate is basically independent of the long-run inflation rate.

The short- and long-run tradeoffs between inflation and unemployment are obviously a major concern of policy making and are the basic determinants of the potential success of stabilization policies.

Stabilization Policy

Policy makers have at their command two broad classes of policies with which to affect the economy. The first is *monetary policy*, which is controlled by the Bank of Canada. The instruments of monetary policy are changes in the stock of money, changes in the interest rate – the bank rate – at which the Bank of Canada lends money to banks, and some controls over the banking system. The second class of policies is *fiscal policy* under the control of Parliament, usually initiated by the government of the day. The instruments of fiscal policy are tax rates and government spending.

Monetary and fiscal policies affect the economy mainly through their effects on aggregate demand – these are *demand management* policies. Fiscal policy can also be used to some extent to affect aggregate supply through policies known as *supply management*.

One of the central facts of policy is that the effects of monetary and fiscal policy on the economy are not fully predictable, both in their *timing* and in the *extent* to which they affect demand. These two uncertainties are at the heart of the problems of *stabilization policy* — policies designed to moderate the fluctuations of the economy, and particularly the fluctuations of the rates of inflation, output, and unemployment. Chart 1-5 shows the recent fluctuations of the rates of inflation and unemployment, and suggests strongly that stabilization policy has not been fully successful in keeping them within narrow bounds. The failures of stabilization policy are due mostly to uncertainty about the way it works.

However, there are also questions of political economy involved in the way stabilization policy has been operated. The speed at which to proceed . in trying to eliminate unemployment, at the risk of increasing inflation, is a matter of judgment about both the economy and the costs of mistakes. Those who regard the costs of unemployment as high, relative to the costs of inflation, will run greater risks of inflation to reduce unemployment than will those who regard the costs of inflation as primary and unemployment as a relatively minor misfortune.

Political economy affects stabilization policy in more ways than through the costs which policy makers of different political persuasions attach to inflation and unemployment, and the risks they are willing to undertake in trying to improve the economic situation. There is also the so-called *political business cycle*, which is based on the observation that election results are affected by economic conditions. When the economic situation is improving and the unemployment rate is falling, there is an environment favourable to the government. There is thus the incentive to policy makers running for reelection, or who wish to affect the election results, to use stabilization policy to produce booming economic conditions before elections.

Stabilization policy is also known as *countercyclical* policy, that is, policy to moderate the trade cycle or *business cycle*, consisting of fairly regular cycles of booms, declines, recessions, and recoveries. Chart 1-2 shows that cycles in the last 25 years have been far from regular. The behaviour and even the existence of the trade cycle is substantially affected by the conduct of stabilization policy. Successful stabilization policy smooths out the cycle, while unsuccessful stabilization policy may worsen the fluctuations of the economy. Indeed, one of the tenets of monetarism is that the major fluctuations of the economy are a result of government actions rather than the inherent instability of the economy's private sector.

Monetarism, Nonmonetarism, and Activism

We noted above that there is some controversy over the existence of the tradeoff between inflation and unemployment. That controversy arose around 1967-1968 in the context of the debate in macroeconomics between monetarists and nonmonetarists, or fiscalists. We have already identified some of the major participants in the debate as Milton Friedman on the monetarist side and Franco Modigliani and James Tobin on the nonmone- tarist side. Among Canadian economists, prominent exponents of mone- tarism include Tom Courchene and David Laidler (University of Western Ontario) and their views have been vigorously challenged by Clarence Barber (University of Manitoba). However, macroeconomists cannot be neatly classified into one camp or the other. Instead, there is a spectrum of views. There are monetarists who make Friedman look like a fiscalist or Keynesian, and Keynesians who make Modigliani look like a monetarist. Not only that; there is no compelling unity in the views that are identified with monetarism, and the balanced economist is likely to accept some monetarist arguments and reject others. Nor is the debate one in which there is no progress. For example, both theory and empirical evidence have been brought to bear on the issue of the inflation–unemployment tradeoff, and it is no longer central to the monetarist-fiscalist debate.

Another major point of contention is the relation between *money* and *inflation*. *Monetarists* tend to argue that the quantity of money is the prime determinant of the level of prices and economic activity, and that excessive monetary growth is responsible for inflation and unstable monetary growth for economic fluctuations. Since they contend that variability in the growth rate of money accounts for variability of real growth, they are naturally led to argue for a monetary policy of low and constant growth in the money supply — a monetary growth rule. *Activists*, by contrast, point out that there is no close relationship between monetary growth and inflation in the short run and that monetary growth is only one of the factors affecting aggregate demand. They maintain that policy makers are — or at least can be — sufficiently careful and skillful to be able to use monetary and fiscal policy to control the economy effectively.

The skill and care of the policy makers are important because monetarists raise the issue of whether aggregate demand policies might not worsen the performance of the economy. Monetarists point to episodes, such as the overexpansionary policies followed by the Bank of Canada in 1971, to argue that policy makers cannot and do not exercise sufficient caution to justify using activist policy. Here the activists are optimists, suggesting that we can learn from our past mistakes.

A further issue that divides the two camps concerns the proper role of government in the economy. This is not really an issue that can be analyzed using macroeconomic theory, but it is difficult to follow some of the debate without being aware that the issue exists. Monetarists tend to be conservatives who favour small government and abhor budget deficits and a large public debt. They would favour tax cuts during recessions and cuts in public spending during booms with the net effect of winding up with a smaller share of government in the economy. Activists, by contrast, tend to favour an important and large role for government and are therefore not disinclined to use increased government spending and transfers as tools of stabilization policy. Differences between monetarists and activists must, therefore, be seen in a much broader perspective than their particular disagreements about the exact role of money in the short run.

1-2 AGGREGATE DEMAND AND SUPPLY

We have sketched the major issues and concepts we shall be discussing and using in the book. The key overall concepts are aggregate demand and aggregate supply. In this section we provide a brief preview of those concepts and of their interaction, with the aims of showing where we are heading and of keeping the material of Chapters 3 through 10 in perspective.

Figure 1-2 shows aggregate demand and supply curves. The vertical axis P is the price level, and the horizontal axis Y is the level of real output or income. Although the curves look like the ordinary supply and demand curves of microeconomics, a full understanding of them will not be reached until Chapter 12.

Aggregate demand is the total demand for goods and services in the economy. It depends on the aggregate price level, as shown in Figure 1-2. It can be shifted through monetary and fiscal policy. The aggregate supply curve shows the price level associated with each level of output. It can, to some extent, be shifted by fiscal policy. Aggregate supply and demand interact to determine the price level and output level. In Figure 1-2, P_0 is the equilibrium price level and Y_0 the equilibrium level of output. If the Y^d curve in this figure shifts up to the right, then the extent to which output and prices respectively are changed depends on the steepness of the aggregate supply curve.[6] If the Y^S curve is very steep, then a given change in aggregate

---

[6] Experiment with graphs like Figure 1-2 to be sure you understand this fact.

FIGURE 1-2 AGGREGATE DEMAND AND SUPPLY

demand mainly causes prices to rise and has very little effect on the level of output. If the Y^S curve is flat, a given change in aggregate demand will be translated mainly into an increase in output and very little into an increase in the price level.

One of the crucial points about macroeconomic adjustment is that the aggregate supply curve is not a straight line. Figure 1-3 shows that at low levels of output, below potential output Y_p, the aggregate supply curve is quite flat. When output is below potential, there is very little tendency for prices of goods and factors (wages) to fall. Conversely, for output above potential, the aggregate supply curve is steep and prices tend to rise continuously. The effects of changes in aggregate demand on output and prices therefore depend on the level of output relative to potential.

All these observations are by way of a very important warning. In Chapters 3 through 10 we focus on aggregate demand as the determinant of the level of output. We shall assume that prices are given and constant, and that output is determined by the level of demand — that there are no supply limitations. We are thus talking about the very flat part of the aggregate supply curve, at levels of output below potential.

The suggestion that output rises to meet the level of demand without a rise in prices leads to a very activist conception of policy. Under these circumstances, without any obvious tradeoffs, policy makers would favour very expansionary policies to raise demand and thereby cause the economy to move to a high level of employment and output. There are circumstances where such a policy view is altogether correct. The early 1960s are a case in point. Chart 1-2 shows that in those years output was substantially below

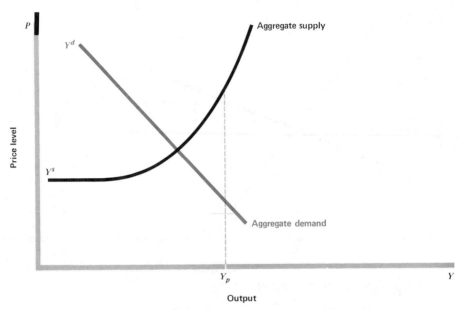

FIGURE 1-3 AGGREGATE DEMAND AND NONLINEAR AGGREGATE SUPPLY

potential. There were unused resources and the problem was a deficiency of demand. By contrast, in the late 1960s and early 1970s the economy was operating at full employment. There was no significant GNP gap. An attempt to expand output or real GNP further would run into supply limitations and force up prices rather than the production of goods. In these circumstances, a model that assumes that output is demand-determined and that increased demand raises output and *not* prices is simply inappropriate.

Should we think that the model with fixed prices and demand-determined output is very restricted and perhaps artificial? The answer is no. There are two reasons for this. First, the circumstances under which the model is appropriate — those of high unemployment — are neither unknown nor unimportant. Unemployment and downward price rigidity are continuing features of the Canadian economy. Second, even when we come to study the interactions of aggregate supply and demand in Chapter 12 and later, we need to know how given policy actions *shift* the aggregate demand curve at a given level of prices. Thus all the material of Chapters 3 through 10 on aggregate demand retains a vital part in the understanding of the effects of monetary and fiscal policy on the price level as well as output in circumstances where the aggregate supply curve is upward-sloping.

What, then, is the warning of this section? It is simply that the very activist spirit of macroeconomic policy under conditions of unemployment must not cause us to overlook the existence of supply limitations and price adjustment when the economy is near full employment.

1-3 OUTLINE AND PREVIEW OF THIS TEXT

We have sketched the major issues we shall be discussing in the book. We can now outline our approach to macroeconomics and the order in which the material will be presented. The key overall concepts, as already noted, are aggregate demand and aggregate supply. Aggregate demand is influenced by monetary policy, primarily via interest rates and expectations, and by fiscal policy. Aggregate supply is affected by fiscal policy and also by disturbances such as changes in the supply of oil.

Figure 1-4 presents a schematic view of the approach of the book to macroeconomics. Being schematic, the diagram is not comprehensive, but it does show the most important relationships we shall examine.

In broad outline, Chapters 3 and 4 are concerned with aggregate demand, Chapter 11 with aggregate supply, and Chapters 12 and 13 with the interactions between aggregate supply and demand. Chapters 5 through 10 present material which clarifies and deepens understanding of aggregate demand and of the ways in which monetary and fiscal policies affect the economy. Chapters 14 through 16 perform a similar service for aggregate supply and the interactions of aggregate supply and demand. Chapters 17 and 18 examine effects of international trade in goods and assets on the economy.

We now proceed to a chapter-by-chapter outline of the book. Chapter 2 is concerned with some definitions and relationships that arise in national income accounting. Many of these relationships, such as that between savings and investment, are used repeatedly in the rest of the book. Chapter

---

FIGURE 1-4 BASIC APPROACH TO MACROECONOMICS

3 is the first, rudimentary model of aggregate demand and the determination of real output. This simple model shows how aggregate demand determines the level of output. While it is decidedly simple, it nevertheless contains some of the essential elements of modern macroeconomics, and it is the backbone for some of the subsequent and more developed models. This rudimentary model enables us to give preliminary answers to questions about fiscal policy, such as: What is the effect on output of a 10 percent cut in taxes? What is the effect on output of an increase in government spending matched by an equal increase in taxes?

Chapter 3 abstracts entirely from monetary considerations in discussing income determination. Chapter 4 introduces those considerations. In that chapter, the simultaneous determination of output and interest rates is studied and emphasis is given to the interaction between the goods market — the market for goods and services — and assets or financial markets. A main point of that chapter is to study the role of money in the economy and to show how variations in the quantity of money, by changing interest rates, exert an effect on aggregate demand and thereby on the level of output.

Chapters 5 through 8 put flesh on the skeleton model which is used in Chapter 4 to study output determination and the channels through which monetary and fiscal policies affect the economy. Chapter 5 examines the determinants of consumption spending, which is the major component of aggregate demand. Chapter 6 discusses investment spending, which is important because it fluctuates a good deal and is significantly affected by monetary and fiscal policies. Chapter 7 examines the determinants of the demand for money, and Chapter 8 discusses the money supply process. Chapter 8 clarifies the role of the Bank of Canada in affecting and controlling the money supply and explains the mechanics of the way in which the Bank conducts monetary policy.

Chapters 9 and 10 are the first chapters discussing stabilization policy. Chapter 9 examines the problems of stabilization policy. It asks why it is not easier to apply the lessons of Chapters 3 through 8 to the control of the economy than the performance of the economy in recent years suggests it is. Chapter 10 briefly describes economic events of the Great Depression of the thirties, which still influence the structure of the Canadian economy and macroeconomic theories, and then reviews the Keynesian economic policies of the postwar years. This chapter illustrates the use of the tools acquired in earlier chapters. It also includes a discussion of the financing of government budget deficits and the issue of the burden of the public debt.

Chapter 11 begins the move over from the aggregate demand approach of the earlier chapters, which are of major relevance when the economy is operating at less than full capacity and prices can be taken to be more or less constant, to examine aggregate supply. Chapter 12 then combines the aggregate supply relationship with the aggregate demand apparatus, developed in Chapter 4, to study the joint determination of the levels of real output, interest rates, and prices.

Chapter 13 moves on from the determination of the price level and level of output to discuss inflation, output, and unemployment. The apparatus of Chapter 12 is useful in examining the effects of one-time changes in the money supply and fiscal policy on the economy, but quite unwieldy for the study of ongoing processes of inflation and changes in output over time. The model of Chapter 13 is well suited to discuss ongoing inflation along with output and unemployment.

Recent experience has made it quite obvious that interest rates and the inflation rate are related: interest rates are high when the inflation rate is high. This relationship was studied by Irving Fisher of Yale in the early part of the century. He concluded that interest rates rise with inflation to compensate lenders for the loss of purchasing power of money they lend that is implied by rising prices. The *Fisher relationship* between interest rates and inflation is also examined with the aid of the model of Chapter 13.

Chapter 14 returns to the inflation-unemployment tradeoff and the costs of inflation and unemployment. It examines the anatomy of unemployment in detail and draws the important distinction between anticipated and unanticipated inflation in discussing the costs of inflation. Chapter 15 then discusses the monetarist approach to policy. The adoption of a monetarist strategy by the Bank of Canada is reviewed and the success of its policy during the period 1975-1980 is considered.

Chapter 16 turns aside from the primarily short- and intermediate-run orientation of the book to examine long-term economic growth and the explanations for Canadian growth over the past century. In so doing, it essentially provides a detailed accounting of the development of potential output and the determinants of productivity growth that have, up to that point, not been carefully examined. In Chapter 16 we also examine the severe slowdown in productivity growth that has hit Canada and other industrialized economies in the last decade, and ask what supply side policies can be used to offset this adverse change.

Chapters 17 and 18 are devoted to international trade in goods and in assets. International trade is of major importance to the Canadian economy and the major economic shocks of the seventies — oil price increases — were trade-connected. Chapter 17 examines the ways in which trade affects GNP determination and the roles of monetary and fiscal policy under fixed exchange rates. This system, under which the external value of a country's currency is pegged within narrow bounds around a preannounced value, was adhered to by Canada during the period 1962-1970. During the 1950s and again in the period since 1970, a *flexible* or *floating* exchange rate has been used with the value of the Canadian dollar changing from day to day. Chapter 18 discusses trade and capital flows under flexible exchange rates, as well as the appropriate uses of monetary and fiscal policy in stabilizing an open economy.

1-4 PREREQUISITES AND RECIPES

In concluding this introductory chapter, a few words on how to use this book will be helpful. First, we note that there is no mathematical prerequisite beyond high school algebra. We do use equations whenever they appear helpful, but they are not an indispensable part of the exposition. Nevertheless, they can and should be mastered by any serious student of macroeconomics.

The technically harder chapters or sections are marked by an asterisk (*). They can be skipped or dipped into. Either they represent supplementary material, or we have provided sufficient nontechnical coverage to help the reader get on without them later in the book. The reason we do present more advanced material or treatment is to afford a complete and up-to-date coverage of the main ideas and techniques in macroeconomics. Even though you may not be able to grasp every point of a section marked by an asterisk on first reading — and should not even try to — these sections should certainly be read to get the main message and an intuitive appreciation of the issues that are raised.

The main problem you will encounter comes from the interaction of several markets and many variables. As Figure 1-4 already suggests, the direct and feedback effects in the economy constitute a quite formidable system. How can you be certain to progress efficiently and with some ease? The most important thing is to ask questions. Ask yourself, as you follow the argument, Why is it that this or that variable should affect, say, aggregate demand? What would happen if it did not? What is the critical link?

There is no substitute whatsoever for an *active form of learning*. Reading sticks at best for seven weeks. Are there simple rules for active study? The best way to study is to use pencil and paper and work the argument by drawing diagrams, experimenting with flowcharts, writing out the logic of an argument, working out the problems at the end of each chapter, and underlining key ideas. Another valuable exercise is to take issue with an argument or position, or to spell out the defence for a particular view on policy questions. Beyond that, if you get stuck, read on for half a page. If you are still stuck, go back five pages.

You should also learn to use the Index. Several concepts are discussed at different levels in different chapters. If you come across an unfamiliar term or concept, check the Index to see whether and where it was discussed earlier in the book.

As a final word, this chapter is designed for reference purposes. You should return to it whenever you want to check where a particular problem fits or where a particular subject matter is relevant. The best way to see the forest is from Chapter 1.

2

NATIONAL INCOME ACCOUNTING

Macroeconomics is ultimately concerned with the determination of the economy's total output, the price level, the level of employment, interest rates, and other variables discussed in Chapter 1. A necessary step in understanding how these variables are determined is *national income accounting*. The national income accounts provide both the actual measures of such macroeconomic variables as output and income and a conceptual framework for relating the various measures to one another.

We study national income accounting not only because it provides us with our basic measure of the performance of the economy in producing goods and services, but also because it highlights the relationships among three key macroeconomic variables: output, income, and spending. This chapter will introduce a few accounting relationships among output, income, spending, and components of spending, and in so doing, will advance us right into the subject of macroeconomics — because those accounting relationships involve some of the chief concepts with which we deal throughout the book.

Before we delve into the details of national income accounting, we briefly indicate the main relationships among the key variables. The central concept is gross national product (GNP), which measures the value of all final goods and services currently produced in the economy and valued at market prices. GNP is thus a measure, indeed the basic measure, of the total output produced in the economy in a given year.[1] GNP includes the value of goods, such as automobiles and eggs, produced, along with the value of services, such as haircuts or medical services.

Starting from the concept of GNP, it will be shown, first, that the value of output produced gives rise to the total income received by wage earners

---

[1] GNP suffers from some defects as a measure of the performance of the economy because it does not value certain economic activities that are hard to measure, such as the value of housespouses' services or the work of volunteers, and also because it does not deduct the cost of nuisance outputs, such as pollution, from the value of output. For a detailed discussion of the Canadian system of national accounts, see Statistics Canada, 13-549.

and the recipients of interest, profits, and dividends. Second, total spending on goods and services in the economy is equal to the value of output. And third, total spending is therefore also related to the value of all incomes received. The relationship between total spending and total income suggests, correctly, that spending on goods and services plays a role in determining the levels of income and production in the economy. The economics of the interactions between spending and the level of output constitutes the main theme of Chapter 3.

Although the three relationships we have just described appear simple, there is considerable complexity in the actual national income accounts in relating GNP to national income and to total spending. Those complexities arise in large part from the way in which indirect and direct taxes affect national income relative to GNP, but also involve the role of foreign trade. We investigate the details of the relationships among output, income, and spending in Sections 2-1 through 2-3, starting in Section 2-1 with a description of GNP.

In Section 2-4, we further expand on the distinction between *nominal* GNP, or output measured in current prices, and *real* GNP. The discussion is followed in Section 2-5, with a brief look at different price indexes. Here we distinguish the consumer price index from producer prices and the GNP deflator. In Section 2-6, we set out the national income relations formally, as a prelude to the economic analysis that begins in Chapter 3.

2-1 GROSS NATIONAL PRODUCT AND NET NATIONAL PRODUCT

Our aim in this section is to describe some important aspects of the measurements of GNP. This will set the scene for the discussion of the relationships among GNP, income, and spending, which were emphasized in the introduction and which will be examined in Sections 2-2 and 2-3.

As we noted earlier, GNP measures the value of all final goods and services produced in the economy during a given period. It includes the value of such goods produced as houses and beer, and the value of services, like brokers' services and economists' lectures. Each of these is valued at its market price and the values are added together to give GNP. In a simple economy that produces twenty bananas, each valued at 30 cents, and sixty oranges, each valued at 25 cents, GNP is equal to $21 [= (30 cents × 20) + (25 cents × 60)]. In the Canadian economy in 1979, the value of GNP was $260 billion.

There are a number of subtleties in the calculation of GNP that are important to keep in mind. First, we are talking about *final* goods and services. The insistence on final goods and services is simply to make sure that we do not double-count. For example, we would not want to include the full price of an automobile in GNP, and then also include the value of the tires that were sold to the automobile producer as part of GNP. The components of the car, sold to the manufacturers, are called *intermediate* goods, and their value is not included in GNP. Similarly, the wheat that goes into bread is an intermediate good, and we do not count the value of the wheat sold the miller and the value of the flour sold the baker, as well as the value of the bread, as part of GNP.

In practice, double-counting is avoided by working with *value added*. At each stage of the manufacture of a good, only the value added to the good at that stage of manufacture is counted as part of GNP. The value of the wheat produced by the farmer is counted as part of GNP. Then the value of the flour sold by the miller *minus* the cost of the wheat is the miller's value added. If we follow this process along, we will see that the sum of value added at each stage of processing will be equal to the final value of the bread sold.[2]

The second point is that GNP consists of the value of output *currently* produced. It thus excludes transactions in existing commodities such as old masters or existing houses. We count the construction of new houses as part of GNP, but we do not add trade in existing houses. We do, however, count the value of realtors' fees in the sale of existing houses as part of GNP. The realtor provides a current service in bringing buyer and seller together, and that is appropriately part of current output.

Third, GNP values goods at *market prices*. It is important to recognize that the market price of many goods includes indirect taxes such as the sales tax and various excise taxes, and thus the market price of goods is not the same as the price the seller of the good receives or the cost of production. The price net of indirect taxes is the *factor cost, which is the amount* received by the factors of production that manufactured the good. GNP is valued at market prices, and not at factor cost. This point becomes important when we relate GNP to the incomes received by the factors of production.

Valuation at market prices is a principle that is not uniformly applied because there are some components of GNP that are difficult to value. There is no very good way of valuing the services of housepersons, or a self-administered haircut, or, for that matter, the services of the police force or the government bureaucracy. Some of these activities are simply omitted from currently measured GNP, as, for instance, housepersons' services. Government services are valued at cost, so that the wages of government employees are taken to represent their contribution to GNP. There is no unifying principle in the treatment of these awkward cases, but rather a host of conventions is used, which we will not detail here.

Net national product (NNP) as distinct from GNP deducts from GNP the *depreciation* of the existing capital stock over the course of the period. The production of GNP causes wear and tear on the existing capital stock;

---

[2] How about the flour that is directly purchased by households for baking in the home? It is counted as a contribution toward GNP since it represents a final sale.

for example, a house depreciates over the course of time, or machines wear out as they are used. If resources were not used to maintain or replace the existing capital, GNP could not be kept at the current level. Accordingly, we use NNP as a better measure of the rate of economic activity that could be maintained over long periods, given the existing capital stock and labour force. Depreciation is a measure of the part of GNP that has to be set aside to maintain the productive capacity of the economy, and we deduct that from GNP to obtain NNP. In 1979, depreciation was $28 billion, or about 10 percent of GNP.

Now that we have defined the basic concept of the value of output or GNP in the economy, we shall proceed to develop the relationships described earlier, which centre around GNP. In particular, we will focus on the following three areas:

1 The production of GNP has as its counterpart the income of the factors of production. We will want to know what the breakdown of income is among wages and salaries, rents, interest, and profits.
2 Cutting across the categories of income described in point 1, we shall want to examine what part of GNP accrues to households, whether in the form of wages, or interest, or rental income, or profits. We are led to the concept of *personal disposable income*, the amount of income households have available for spending or saving. We shall want to see how that is related to GNP.
3 The production of GNP gives rise to a supply of goods and services that is purchased by the various sectors of the economy. When output is divided into expenditure categories, the total value is equal to GNP but is referred to as *gross national expenditure* (GNE). The expenditure side of the national accounts provides us with a breakdown of GNE into consumption, investment, government expenditure on goods and services, and net exports as components of the aggregate demand for output.

Points 1 and 2 are taken up in Section 2-2, and point 3 is analyzed in Section 2-3.

2-2 GNP AND INCOME

We now consider the relation between the value of output or GNP and the incomes that are generated in the production process. In this section we show that *income is equal to the value of output* because the receipts from the sale of output must accrue to someone as income. The purchaser of bread is indirectly paying the farmer, the miller, the baker, and the supermarket operator for the labour and capital used in production and is also contributing to their profits.

GNP and National Income

Our statement above equating the value of output and income is correct with two qualifications:

1 The first correction arises from depreciation. As already noted, part of GNP has to be set aside to maintain the productive capacity of the economy. Depreciation should not be counted as part of income, since it is a cost of production. As a rule, depreciation amounts to about 10 percent of GNP. Depreciation is usually referred to in the national income accounts as *capital consumption allowances*. After subtracting depreciation from GNP, we have NNP.

2 The second adjustment arises from indirect taxes, in particular, sales and excise taxes, that introduce a discrepancy between market price and prices received by producers. GNP is valued at market price, but the income accruing to producers does not include the sales and excise taxes that are part of market price, and thus falls short of GNP. Indirect taxes, along with some other items of the same nature, account for about 10 percent of GNP.

With these two deductions we can derive *national income* from GNP, as shown in Table 2-1, which gives the dollar figures for 1979. National income gives us the value of output at *factor cost* rather than market prices, which is GNP. It tells us what factors of production actually receive as income before direct taxes and transfers.

TABLE 2-1 GNP AND NATIONAL INCOME, 1979 (BILLIONS OF DOLLARS)

Gross national product (GNP)		260.3
Less:		
Capital consumption allowances	28.0	
Equals:		
Net national product (NNP)		232.3
Less:		
Indirect taxes less subsidies	28.2	
Residual error of estimate	−.2	
Equals:		
National income		204.3

Source: Statistics Canada, 11-003.

Factor Shares in National Income

We next ask how national income is split among different types of incomes, as shown in Table 2-2.

TABLE 2-2 NATIONAL INCOME AND ITS DISTRIBUTION, 1979 (BILLIONS OF DOLLARS)

National income		$204.3	100.0%
Wages, salaries and other labour income		145.9	71.4
Corporation profits	$34.3		
Less dividends paid to nonresidents	2.9		
Plus inventory valuation adjustment	−6.7	24.7	12.1
Interest and misc. investment income		18.9	9.3
Net income of unincorporated business			
Farm	4.4		
Nonfarm, including rent	10.4	14.8	7.2

Source: Statistics Canada, 11-003.

The most striking fact of Table 2-2 is the very large share of wages and salaries in national income. This accounts for over 71 percent. Dividends paid to nonresidents are deducted from corporation profits because national income is defined to include earnings of Canadian residents only.[3] The inventory valuation adjustment is made in order to exclude capital gains or losses on inventories that appear as part of profits measured under business accounting procedures but are not related to current production. Rental income includes not only rents received by landlords but also the *imputed* income of owner-occupied housing.[4]

The division of national income into various classes is not too important for our macroeconomic purposes. It reflects, in part, such questions as whether corporations are financed by debt or equity, whether a business is or is not incorporated, and whether the housing stock is owned by persons or corporations — which, in turn, are owned by persons.[5]

National Income and Personal Income

A considerably more important question from the macroeconomic view-point is how much the personal sector — households and unincorporated businesses — actually receives as income, inclusive of transfers. This quantity is measured by *personal income. Transfers* are those payments that do *not* arise out of current productive activity. Thus, welfare payments and

[3] The measurement of GNP and national income is based on the earnings of Canadian factors of production located in Canada or elsewhere. An alternative measure of output provided by Statistics Canada, called *gross domestic product*, measures production within the geographic boundaries of Canada using both Canadian and nonresident factors of production.

[4] GNP includes an estimate of the services homeowners receive by living in their homes. This is estimated by calculating the rent on an equivalent house. Thus the homeowner is treated as if she pays herself rent for living in her house.

[5] You might want to work out how Table 2-2 would be modified for each of the possibilities described in this sentence.

TABLE 2-3 NATIONAL INCOME AND PERSONAL INCOME, 1979
(BILLIONS OF DOLLARS)

National income		$204.3
Less:		
Corporation profits	24.7	
Other adjustments	.4	
Plus:		
Dividends and interest on government debt	4.3	
Transfers from government	26.4	
Other transfers	.8	
Equals:		
Personal income		210.7

Source: Statistics Canada, 11-003.

unemployment benefits are examples of transfer payments. The level of personal income is important because it is a prime determinant of household consumption and saving behaviour.

To go from national income to personal income, we have to remove the part of national income that accrues to the corporate sector and add back dividends paid out to Canadian residents. As shown in Table 2-3, we also add transfers from government which include such payments as unemployment insurance benefits, family allowances and old age pensions. Interest on government debt is also treated like a transfer payment. It is part of personal income, but is excluded from national income because much of the debt has been incurred to finance past government expenditure which does not contribute to current production of goods and services.

Although we have derived personal income in Table 2-3 by starting with national income and making adjustments, we should recognize that it is also possible to build up to an estimate of personal income by looking at its components in a way similar to that shown in Table 2-2. In particular, personal income consists of labour income, plus income of unincorporated business, plus interest and dividends, plus transfers.

Personal Disposable Income and Its Allocation

Not all personal income is available for spending by households. The amount available for spending, *personal disposable income*, deducts from personal income the personal tax payments and other transfers to government made by the household sector. The other transfers include such items as licence fees and traffic tickets.

Personal disposable income is then available for personal consumption expenditure, other transfers, and saving. By far the largest outlay is for personal consumption, as shown in Table 2-4.

TABLE 2-4 DISPOSITIONS OF PERSONAL INCOME, 1979 (BILLIONS OF DOLLARS)

Personal income		$210.7
Less:		
Personal taxes	36.1	
Other transfers to government	2.1	
Equals:		
Personal disposable income		172.5
Less:		
Personal consumption expenditure	150.5	
Other transfers	3.9	
Equals:		
Personal saving		18.1

Source: Statistics Canada, 11-003.

In summary, this section has shown the relation between GNP, which is a measure of productive activity in the economy, and income receipts that accrue to the household sector. The main steps in the long chain we have followed arise from taxes, transfers between sectors, depreciation, and corporation profits.

These intermediate steps remind us that there is an important difference between GNP as the value of output at market prices and the spendable receipts of the household sector. We could have a positive personal disposable income even if GNP were zero, provided there was someone to make the necessary transfer payments. Likewise, GNP could be large and disposable income small if the government sector took in a lot of taxes. The larger taxes are relative to government transfers, the smaller is disposable income relative to GNP.

Summary

We summarize here in a few identities (and in the accompanying Chart 2-1) the relationships reviewed in each table:

GNP − capital consumption allowances ≡ NNP (Table 2-1)   (1)
NNP − indirect taxes ≡ national income   (2)
National income ≡ labour income + corporation profits + interest + net income of unincorporated business (Table 2-2)   (3)
National income − corporation profits + dividends and interest on government debt + transfers ≡ personal income   (4)
Personal income − personal taxes and other transfers to government ≡ personal disposable income (Table 2-4)   (5)
Personal disposable income ≡ personal consumption expenditure and other transfers + personal saving (Table 2-4)   (6)

GNP				
	Depreciation			
	NNP	Indirect taxes		
		National income	Personal income = National income − Corporation profits + Dividends and interest on government debt + Transfers	Personal taxes and other transfers to government
				Personal disposable income

CHART 2-1 THE RELATION BETWEEN GNP AND PERSONAL DISPOSABLE INCOME

2-3 OUTPUT AND COMPONENTS OF DEMAND

In the previous section, we started with GNP and asked how much of the value of goods and services produced actually gets into the hands of households. In this section we present a different perspective on GNP by asking who buys the output, rather than who receives the income. More technically, we look at the demand for output and speak of the components of *gross national expenditure* (GNE). Total demand is made up of four components: (1) consumption spending by households; (2) investment spending by businesses; (3) government (federal, provincial and municipal) expenditure on goods and services; and (4) net foreign demand. We shall now look more closely at each of these components.

Table 2-5 presents a breakdown of gross national expenditure in 1979 by components of demand. The table illustrates that the chief component of demand is consumption spending by the personal sector. This includes anything from food to golf lessons but involves also, as we shall see in discussing investment, consumer spending on durable goods such as automobiles, spending which might be regarded as investment rather than consumption.

TABLE 2-5 COMPONENTS OF GROSS NATIONAL EXPENDITURE, 1979 (BILLIONS OF DOLLARS)

Personal consumption expenditure		$150.5	57.8%
Gross business investment		56.4	21.7%
Government expenditure on goods and services		59.0	22.6%
Net exports of goods and services			
Exports	76.6		
Less Imports	82.4	−5.8	−2.2%
Residual error of estimate		.2	.1%
Gross national expenditure (GNE)		$260.3	100.0%

Next in importance we have government expenditure on goods and services. Here we have such items as national defence expenditures, road paving by provincial and municipal governments, and salaries of government employees. It is important to note here that the government component of GNE is expenditure on *goods and services* and excludes transfer payments. For all levels of government in 1979 the transfer component of spending amounted to about $45 billion, so that total budgetary spending was about $105 billion.

Gross business investment is an item that requires some definitions. First, throughout this book, we will mean by investment additions to the physical stock of capital. As we use the term, investment does *not* include buying a bond or purchasing stock in General Motors. In practice, investment includes expenditure on machinery and equipment, nonresidential construction, residential construction, and additions to business inventories of goods. The classification of spending as consumption or investment remains to a significant extent a matter of convention. From the economic point of view, there is little difference between a household building up an inventory of peanut butter and a grocery store doing the same. Nevertheless, in the national income accounts, the individual's purchase is treated as a personal consumption expenditure, whereas the store's purchase is treated as investment in the form of inventory investment. Although these borderline cases clearly exist, we can retain as a simple rule of thumb that investment is associated with the business sector's adding to the physical stock of capital, including inventories.

Similar issues arise in the treatment of household sector expenditures. For instance, how should we treat purchases of automobiles by households? Since automobiles usually last for several years, it would seem sensible to classify household purchases of automobiles as investment. We would then treat the *use* of automobiles as providing consumption services. (We could think of imputing a rental income to owner-occupied automobiles.) However, the convention is to treat all household expenditures as consumption spending. This is not quite so bad as it might seem, since the accounts do separate out households' purchases of durable goods like cars and refrigerators from their other purchases. There is thus information in the accounts on those parts of household spending that, with considerable justification, could be categorized as investment spending. When consumer spending decisions are studied in detail, expenditures on consumer durables are usually treated separately.

The convention that is adopted with respect to the household sector's purchases of houses also deserves comment. The accounts treat the building of a house as investment by the business sector. When the house is sold to a private individual, the transaction is treated as the transfer of an asset, and not then an act of investment. Even if a house is custom-built by the owner, the accounts treat the builder who is employed by the owner as undertaking the act of investment in building the house. The investment is thus attributed to the business sector.

In passing, we note that in Table 2-5, investment is defined as "gross." It is gross in the sense that depreciation is not deducted. Net investment is gross investment minus depreciation. Thus NNP is equal to net investment plus the other categories of spending in Table 2-5.

The item net exports appears in Table 2-5 to show the effects of foreign trade on the demand for domestic output. Exports are added in as they represent demand by foreigners for our goods. Imports are subtracted out since they represent the part of domestic spending that is not for domestically produced goods. The practice in the national accounts is to include under consumption, investment and government expenditure all spending by Canadian residents both on domestically produced and foreign goods. To obtain total spending on domestically produced goods (GNE), imports are subtracted out.

The point can be illustrated with an example. Assume that instead of having spent $150 billion, the personal sector had spent $2 billion more. What would GNP have been? If we assume that government and investment spending had been the same as in Table 2-5, we might be tempted to say that GNP would have been $2 billion higher. That is correct if all the additional spending had fallen on our goods. The other extreme, however, is the case where all the additional spending falls on imports. In that event, consumption would be up $2 billion *and* net exports would be down $2 billion, with no net effect on GNP.

2-4 REAL AND NOMINAL GNE

Nominal GNE measures the value of output in a given period in the prices of that period or, as it is sometimes put, in *current dollars*. Thus 1980 nominal GNE measures the value of the goods produced in 1980 at the market prices that prevailed in 1980, and 1976 GNE measures the value of goods produced in 1976, at the market prices that prevailed in 1976. Nominal GNE changes from year to year for two reasons. The first is that the physical output of goods changes. The second is that market prices change. As an extreme and unrealistic example, one could imagine the economy producing exactly the same output in two years, between which all prices have doubled. Nominal GNE in the second year would be double nominal GNE in the first year, even though the physical output of the economy has not changed at all.

Real GNE is a measure that attempts to isolate changes in physical output in the economy between different time periods by valuing all goods produced in the two periods *at the same prices,* or in *constant dollars.* Real GNE is now measured in the national income accounts in the prices of 1971. That means that, in calculating real GNE, today's physical output is multiplied by the prices that prevailed in 1971 to obtain a measure of what today's output would have been worth had it been sold at the prices of 1971. We can return to the extremely simple example we used at the beginning of the chapter of an economy that produces only bananas and oranges, to illustrate the calculation of real GNE. The hypothetical outputs and prices of bananas and oranges in the two years are shown in the first two columns of Table 2-6. Nominal GNE in 1971 was $11.25 and nominal GNE in 1980 was $21.00, or an increase in nominal GNE of 87 percent. However, much of the increase in nominal GNE is purely a result of the increase in prices between the two years, and does not reflect an increase in physical output. When we calculate real GNE in 1980 by valuing 1980 output in the prices of 1971, we find real GNE equal to $13.80, which is an increase of 23 percent rather than 87 percent. The 23 percent increase is a better measure of the increase in physical output of the economy than the 87 percent increase.

We see from the table that the output of bananas rose by 33 percent, while the output of oranges increased by 20 percent from 1971 to 1980. We should thus expect our measure of the increase in real output to be somewhere between 20 percent and 33 percent, as it is. You will realize that the increase in real GNE that is calculated depends on the prices that are used in the calculation. If you have a calculator you might want to compare the increase in real GNE between 1971 and 1980 if the prices of 1980 are used to make the comparison. The ambiguities that arise in comparisons using different prices to calculate real GNE are an inevitable result of the attempt to use a single number to capture the increase in output of both

TABLE 2-6 REAL AND NOMINAL GNE, AN ILLUSTRATION

1971 nominal GNE		1980 nominal GNE		1980 real GNE*	
15 bananas @ 15¢	$ 2.25	20 bananas @ 30¢	$ 6.00	20 bananas @ 15¢	$ 3.00
50 oranges @ 18¢	$ 9.00	60 oranges @ 25¢	$15.00	60 oranges @ 18¢	$10.80
	$11.25		$21.00		$13.80

*Measured in 1971 prices.

CHART 2-2 REAL AND NOMINAL GNE*
(*Source*: Statistics Canada, 11-003, 11-206)

*Quarterly, seasonally adjusted at annual rates.

bananas and oranges when those two components did not increase in the same proportion. However, the ambiguity is not a major concern when there is inflation at any substantial rate, and that is precisely when we most want to use real (rather than nominal) GNE to study the performance of the economy.

Chart 2-2 shows the behaviour of real and nominal GNE over the past few years. It is particularly noteworthy that nominal GNE rose continuously during the period, even while real GNE fell as it did, for example, during 1974. It would clearly be a mistake to regard the increases in nominal GNE as indicating that the performance of the economy was improving during 1974 despite the fall in physical output. Real GNP is the better measure of the performance of the economy in producing goods and services, and it is the measure we should and do use in comparing output in different years.

2-5 PRICE INDEXES

The calculation of real GNE gives us a useful measure of inflation known as the GNE *deflator*. Returning to the hypothetical example of Table 2-6, we can get a measure of inflation between 1971 and 1980 by comparing the value of 1980 GNE in 1980 prices and 1971 prices. The ratio of nominal to real GNE in 1980 is 1.52(=21 ÷ 13.80). In other words, output is 52 percent higher in 1980 when it is valued using the higher prices of 1980, than when it is valued in the lower 1971 prices. We ascribe, accordingly, the 52 percent increase to price changes, or inflation, over the period 1971-1980. The GNE deflator is the ratio of nominal GNE in a given year to real GNE, and it is a measure of inflation from the period from which the base prices for calculating real GNE are taken, to the current period.

Since the GNE deflator is based on a calculation involving all the goods produced in the economy, it is a very widely based price index that is frequently used to measure inflation. It differs in four main ways from the other major index, the *consumer price index* (CPI), or cost of living index. First, it measures the prices of a much wider group of goods than the CPI, which is based on the market basket of goods purchased by an average consumer. Second, the CPI measures the cost of a given basket of goods, which is the same from year to year. The basket of goods included in the GNE deflator, however, differs from year to year, depending on what is produced in the economy in each year. The goods valued in the deflator in a given year are the goods that are produced in the economy in that year. When wheat production is high, wheat receives a relatively large weight in the computation of the GNE deflator. By contrast, the CPI measures the cost of a fixed bundle of goods that does not vary over time.[6] Third, the CPI directly includes prices of imports, whereas the deflator includes only prices of goods *produced* in Canada. The behaviours of the two main indexes used to compute inflation, the GNE deflator and the CPI, accordingly differ from time to time. For example, at times when the price of imported oil rises rapidly, the CPI is likely to rise faster than the deflator.

A third important price index is the industry selling price index. Like the CPI, this is a measure of the cost of a given basket of goods. It differs from the CPI partly in its coverage, which includes, for example, semifinished goods. It differs, too, in that it is designed to measure prices at an early stage of the distribution system. Whereas the CPI measures prices where urban households actually do their spending — that is, at the retail level — the industry selling price index is constructed from prices at the level of the first significant commercial transaction. This difference is important because it makes the latter a relatively flexible price index and one that signals changes in the general price level, or the CPI, some time before they actually materialize.

Table 2-7 shows the CPI, the industry selling price index, and the GNE deflator for the last 18 years. We note from the table that all three indexes have been increasing throughout the period. This is a reflection of the fact that

---

[6] Price indexes are, however, occasionally revised to change weights to reflect current expenditure patterns.

TABLE 2-7 THREE PRICE INDEXES (1971 = 100)

	Consumer Price Index	Industry Selling Price Index	GNE Deflator
1961	75.0	82.4	72.4
1966	83.5	88.7	82.6
1971	100.0	100.0	100.0
1976	148.9	161.6	160.2
1979	191.2	217.9	201.1
percent increase			
1961-1979	155%	164%	178%

Source: Statistics Canada, 11-003, 11-505.

the average price of goods has been rising, whatever basket we look at. We note, too, that the cumulative increase (price 1979/price 1961) differs across indexes. This difference occurs because the indexes represent the prices of different commodity baskets.

The mechanics of price indexes are illustrated with the help of the price index formula.[7] The CPI is a price index which compares the current and base year cost of a basket of goods of *fixed* composition. If we denote the base year quantities of the various goods by q_0^i and their base year prices by p_0^i, the cost of the basket in the base year is $\Sigma p_0^i q_0^i$, where the summation (Σ) is over all the goods in the basket. The cost of a basket of the *same* quantities but at today's prices is $\Sigma p_t^i q_0^i$, where p_t^i is today's price. The CPI is the ratio of today's cost to the base year cost, or

$$\text{Price index} = \frac{\Sigma p_t^i q_0^i}{\Sigma p_0^i q_0^i} \times 100$$

multiplied, as a matter of convention, by 100.[8] Table 2-7 thus shows that in 1979 the cost of the standard consumer basket had increased relative to 1971 by 91 percent. Similarly, the GNE deflator had risen relative to the base year by over 100 percent.

2-6 SOME IMPORTANT IDENTITIES

In this section we formalize the discussion of Sections 2-1 through 2-3 by writing down a set of relationships which will be used extensively in

---

[7] Detailed discussion of the consumer price index can be found in Statistics Canada, 62-010. See, too, problem 7 at the end of this chapter.

[8] The price index defined here is called a Laspeyres index. A Laspeyres index uses base year weights and in that respect differs from a Paasche index, which uses current year quantities as weights. The GNE deflator is a Paasche index. See problem 7.

Chapter 3. We introduce here some notation and conventions that we will follow throughout the book.

For analytical work in the following chapters, we will not use all the detail that comes up in national income accounting. Specifically, we will simplify our analysis by omitting the distinction between GNP and national income. For the most part we will disregard depreciation and thus the difference between GNP and NNP, as well as the difference between gross and net investment. We shall refer simply to investment spending. We will also disregard indirect taxes and nongovernment transfer payments. With these conventions in mind, *we refer to national income and GNP interchangeably as income or output*. These simplifications have no serious consequence and are made only for expositional convenience. Finally, and only for a brief while, we omit both the government and the foreign sector.

A Simple Economy

We denote the value of output in our simple economy, which has neither a government nor foreign trade, by Y. Consumption is denoted by C and investment spending by I. The first key identity we want to establish is that between output produced and output sold. Output produced is Y, which can be written in terms of the components of demand as the sum of consumption and investment spending. (Remember, we have assumed away the government and foreign sectors.) Accordingly, we can write the identity of output sold and output produced as[9]

$$Y \equiv C + I \qquad (7)$$

Now the question is whether Equation (7) is really an identity. Is it inevitably true that all output produced is either consumed or invested? After all, do not firms sometimes make goods that they are unable to sell? The answer to each of the questions is yes. Firms do sometimes make output that they cannot sell and that accumulates on their shelves. However, we count that accumulation of inventories as part of investment (as if the firms sold it to themselves), and, therefore, all output is either consumed or invested. Note that we are talking here about *actual* investment, which includes investment in inventories that firms might be very unhappy to make. Because of the way investment is defined, output produced is identically equal to output sold.

Identity (7) formalizes the basis of Table 2-5 (we are still assuming away

---

[9] Throughout the book we will be careful to distinguish identities from equations. Identities are statements that are *always* true because they are directly implied by definitions of variables or accounting relationships. They do not reflect any economic behaviour but are extremely useful in organizing our thinking. Identities, or definitions, will be shown with the sign ≡, and equations with the usual equality sign =.

the government and external sectors). The next step is to draw up a corresponding identity for Table 2-4 and identity (6), which examined the disposition of personal income. For that purpose, it is convenient to ignore the existence of corporations and consolidate or add together the entire private sector. Using this convention, we know that private sector income is Y, since the private sector receives as income the value of goods and services produced. Why? Because who else would get it? — there is no government or external sector yet. Now the private sector receives, as disposable income, the whole of income Y. How will that income be allocated? Part will be spent on consumption and part will be saved. Thus we can write[10]

$$Y \equiv S + C \tag{8}$$

where S denotes private sector saving. Identity (8) tells us that the whole of income is allocated to either consumption or saving.

Next, identities (7) and (8) can be combined to read:

$$C + I \equiv Y \equiv C + S \tag{9}$$

The left-hand side of Equation (9) shows the components of demand, and the right-hand side shows the allocation of income. The identity emphasizes that output produced is equal to output sold. The value of output produced is equal to income received, and income received, in turn, is spent on goods or saved.

The identity in Equation (9) can be slightly reformulated to look at the relation between saving and investment. Subtracting consumption from each part of Equation (9), we have

$$I \equiv Y - C \equiv S \tag{10}$$

Identity (10) is an important result. It shows first that in this simple economy, saving is identically equal to income less consumption. This result is not new, since we have already seen it in Equation (8). The new part concerns the identity of the left and right sides: Investment is identically equal to saving. One can think of what lies behind this relationship in a variety of ways. In a very simple economy, the only way the individual can save is by undertaking an act of physical investment — by storing grain or building an irrigation channel. In a slightly more sophisticated economy, one could think of investors financing their investing by borrowing from individuals who save. However, it is important to recognize that Equation (10) expresses the identity between investment and saving, and that some of

---

[10] Again ask yourself why Eq. (8) should be identically true. What could you do with your income other than consume or save it? There is no alternative.

the investment might well be undesired inventory investment, occurring as a result of mistakes by producers who expected to sell more than they actually do. The identity is really only a reflection of our definitions — output less consumption is investment, output is income, and income less consumption is saving. Even so, we will find that identity (10) will play a key role in Chapter 3.

Reintroducing the Government and Foreign Trade

We can now reintroduce the government sector and the external sector. First, for the government we shall denote expenditure on goods and services by G and all taxes by T. Transfers to the private sector (including interest) are denoted by R. Net exports (exports minus imports) are denoted by NX.

We return to the identity between output produced and sold, taking account now of the additional components of demand, G, and NX. Accordingly, we restate the content of Table 2-5 by writing

$$Y \equiv C + I + G + NX \tag{11}$$

Once more we emphasize that in Equation (11) we use actual investment in the identity and thus do not preclude the possibility that firms might not at all be content with the investment. Still, as an accounting identity, Equation (11) will hold.

Next we turn to the derivation of the very important relation between output and disposable income. Now we have to recognize that part of income is spent on taxes, and that the private sector receives net transfers R in addition to national income. Disposable income is thus equal to income plus transfers less taxes:

$$Y_d \equiv Y + R - T \tag{12}$$

We have written Y_d to denote disposable income. Disposable income, in turn, is allocated to consumption and saving, so that we can write

$$Y_d \equiv C + S \tag{13}$$

Combining Equations (12) and (13) allows us to write consumption as the difference between income, plus transfers minus taxes, and saving:

$$C + S \equiv Y_d \equiv Y + R - T \tag{14}$$

or

$$C \equiv Y_d - S \equiv Y + R - T - S \tag{14a}$$

Identity (14a) states that consumption is disposable income less saving, or alternatively, that consumption is equal to income plus transfers less taxes and saving. Now we use the right-hand side of Equation (14a) to substitute for C in identity (11). With some rearrangement we obtain

$$S - I \equiv (G + R - T) + NX \tag{15}$$

Identity (15) cannot be overemphasized. What it states is that the excess of saving over investment of the private sector ($S - I$) is equal to the *budget deficit* ($G + R - T$) plus the *trade surplus* (NX). On the right-hand side of Equation (15), the first term is the budget deficit of the government — government spending plus transfers (including interest payments) less tax collection. The second term on the right-hand side of Equation (15) shows net exports. Even without any behavioural content, Equation (15) is already useful because it suggests that there are important relations between the accounts of the domestic private sector $S - I$, the government budget $G + R - T$, and the external sector. Identity (15) states that if the private sector is in balance in the sense that saving equals investment, then any government budget deficit (surplus) is reflected in an equal external deficit (surplus).

Another perspective on this key identity is gained by singling out the government budget:[11]

$$T - R - G \equiv (I - S) + NX \tag{15a}$$

If the government has a budget surplus because government spending ($G + R$) is smaller than tax collection, then the counterpart is either an external surplus or an excess of private investment over saving. The principle can be generalized by noting that any imbalance in the budget or the balance between saving and investment must be reflected in a matching external deficit. If the domestic economy absorbs more resources than it produces — if investment exceeds savings and/or the budget is in deficit — then there is an external deficit. Conversely, if a country spends less than its income, there will be an external surplus. Individuals spending less than their income will each build up assets or claims on other people. For example, these assets could be money, or bonds, or stocks. A sector that spends less than its income accumulates claims on other sectors. Thus, if we have an excess of saving over investment, then the domestic private sector will be accumulating claims on either the government — if there is a budget deficit — or on the rest of the world — if there is an external surplus. One sector's deficit is always equal to another's surplus simply because one person's receipts are another person's expenditures.

[11] *Government* throughout this chapter means the federal government plus provincial and municipal governments. A breakdown by level of government can be found in Statistics Canada publications and Dept. of Finance, *Economic Review*.

2-7 SUMMARY

We conclude with a brief summary of the major points of this chapter.

1 Nominal GNP is the value of the economy's output of final goods and services measured at market prices.
2 Real GNP is the value of the economy's output measured in the prices of some base year. Real GNP comparisons, based on the same set of prices for valuing output, provide a better measure of the change in the economy's physical output than nominal GNP comparisons, which also reflect inflation.
3 National income is equal to GNP minus depreciation and indirect taxes.
4 National income is equal to the incomes received in the economy, valued at factor cost.
5 Gross national expenditure is conveniently divided into consumption, investment, government expenditure on goods and services, and net exports. The division between consumption and investment in the national income accounts is somewhat arbitrary at the edges.

CHART 2-3 THE BASIC MACROECONOMIC IDENTITY

I *NX*		*T − R*	*T − R*
G			
			S
C	*Y*	*Yd*	*C*

6 One sector's surplus is another sector's deficit. For example, the excess of the private sector's savings over investment is equal to the sum of the budget deficit and the foreign trade surplus.

7 For the remainder of the book we use a simplified model for expositional convenience. We assume away depreciation, indirect taxes, nongovernment transfer payments, and the difference between households and corporations. For this simplified model, Chart 2-3 and Equation (16) review the *basic macroeconomic identity*:

$$C + G + I + NX \equiv Y \equiv Y_d + (T - R) \equiv (T - R) + S + C \qquad (16)$$

The left-hand side is the demand for output by components which is identically equal to output supplied. Output supplied is equal to income. Disposable income is equal to income plus transfers less taxes. Disposable income is allocated to saving and consumption.

PROBLEMS

1 Show from national income accounting that:
   (a) An increase in taxes (while transfers remain constant) must imply a change in the trade balance, government purchases or the saving-investment balance.
   (b) An increase in disposable income must imply an increase in consumption or an increase in saving.
   (c) An increase in both consumption and saving must imply an increase in disposable income.
2 The following is information from the national income accounts for a hypothetical country:

GNP	240
Gross investment	40
Net investment	15
Consumption	150
Government expenditure on goods and services	48
National income	190
Wages and salaries	146
Net income of unincorporated business	16
Dividends	5
Interest income	13
Government budget surplus	−15
Interest on government debt	7
Government transfer payments	25

   What is:
   (a) NNP?
   (b) Net exports?
   (c) Indirect taxes?
   (d) Corporate profits?
   (e) Personal income?
   (f) Personal disposable income?
   (g) Personal saving?
3 What would happen to GNP if the government hired unemployed workers, who had been getting R in unemployment benefits, as government employees to do nothing, still giving them R? Explain.
4 What is the difference in the national income accounts between:
   (a) A firm's buying an auto for an executive and the firm's paying the executive additional income to buy himself a car?
   (b) Your hiring your spouse (who takes care of the house) rather than just having him or her do the work without pay?
   (c) Your deciding to buy a Canadian-made car rather than a German car?
5 Explain the following terms:
   (a) Value added
   (b) Factor cost
   (c) Inventory investment
   (d) GNE deflator
6 This question deals with price index numbers. Consider a simple economy where there are only three items in the CPI: food, housing, and entertainment

(fun). Assume in the base period, say 1971, the household consumed the following quantities at the then prevailing prices.

	Quantities	Prices per unit, dollars	Expenditure, dollars
Food	5	14	70
Housing	3	10	30
Fun	4	5	20
Total			120

(a) Consider what the CPI will be in 1980 if the prevailing prices have changed as follows: food, $30 per unit; housing, $20 per unit; and fun, $6 per unit. In making your calculations, use the formula for the CPI given in the text.

*(b) Show that the change in the CPI relative to the base year is a weighted average of the individual price changes where the weights are given by the base year expenditure shares of the various goods.

*7 Price indexes that use base year quantities are called Laspeyres indexes. By contrast, an index that uses current year quantities is called a Paasche index. A Paasche index, therefore, is defined by the formula:

$$\text{Price index} = \frac{\Sigma p_i^i q_0^i}{\Sigma p_i^i q_0^i} \times 100$$

You are asked to calculate both the Laspeyres and Paasche indexes for the information provided in Table 2-6. In addition, find the GNE deflator (base year 1971) appropriate for that table. How do the three indexes compare?

8 This question is a national income accounting puzzle. Consider an economy where personal disposable income is $1,000. Corporate profits are $120. Gross investment is $180, and net investment is $140. The government makes transfer payments to persons of $100. Indirect taxes are $190. The government collects $150 in personal income taxes. Dividends are $30 and interest on government debt is $35. Given this information, what is GNP?

9 Discuss the implications of the following events for national income and personal disposable income:
(a) The government increases the corporate income tax rate from 50 percent to 60 percent.
(b) Personal income taxes are increased.
(c) There is an increase in family allowance payments.
   In all these questions, assume that GNP remains unchanged.

10 Assume that GNP is $120, personal disposable income is $100, and the government budget deficit is $7. Consumption is $85 and the trade surplus is $2.
(a) How large is saving S?
(b) What is the size of investment I?
(c) How large is government spending?

3

AGGREGATE DEMAND AND EQUILIBRIUM INCOME AND OUTPUT

n Chapter 2 we studied the measurement of national income and output (GNP). With these fundamental concepts, we are now able to begin our study of the factors that determine the level of national income and product. Ultimately, we want to know why national income sometimes falls (and the rate of unemployment rises), as it did in 1974-1975 and 1980, and why at other times income rises very rapidly (and unemployment falls), as it did in 1971-1973. We also want to know what determines the rate of inflation. Why was it so high in 1974? Why did it rise from 1978 to 1980? We want to know whether public policies, such as changes in government spending and tax rates, or changes in the growth rate of the money supply, or changes in interest rates, can affect the level of income and the rates of inflation and unemployment, and if they can, we want to know how.

The study of those questions occupies the rest of the book. But we will proceed slowly. We begin in this chapter with a simplified model of the economy that isolates the crucial concept of *aggregate demand*, while still omitting both some factors that affect aggregate demand and considerations of aggregate supply. In later chapters we gradually introduce those other factors. By the time we have completed Chapter 13, we will be able to understand the behaviour of the key macroeconomic variables — the rates of unemployment and inflation, and the level of GNP.

Our discussion of the determination of the level of output in this chapter starts from the basic macroeconomic identities in Equation (16) of Chapter 2 and in Chart 2-3: First, net national product (NNP) is equal to total spending on goods and services, consisting of consumption C, net investment I, government expenditure on goods and services G, and net exports NX. Second, net national product is also equal to net income received in the economy.[1] Income, in turn, increased by transfers R and reduced by taxes T,

---

[1] Because net national product (or output) is equal to net income received in the economy, economists tend to use the terms *income* and *output* interchangeably when discussing the level of economic activity.

is allocated to consumption C and saving S. Thus:

$$C + I + G + NX \equiv Y \equiv S + (T - R) + C$$

In this chapter we go beyond that *accounting identity* to begin our study of the factors that determine the level of national product or output. In particular, we focus on the interactions between the level of output and aggregate demand. We shall see that there is a single level of *equilibrium* output at which the aggregate (total) demand for goods and services is equal to the level of output. To begin with, we simplify our task by discussing a hypothetical world without a government ($G \equiv T \equiv R \equiv O$) and without foreign trade ($NX \equiv O$. In such a world, the accounting identity simplifies to

$$C + I \equiv Y \equiv S + C \tag{1}$$

where Y denotes the real value of output and income. Further, we will remember that throughout this chapter a change in a macroeconomic aggregate is a change in its *real* value at constant prices. Thus, when we speak of a change in income or a change in consumption spending, we mean a change in real income or a change in real consumption spending.

We shall study in Section 3-1 the important concepts of *goods market equilibrium* and *equilibrium output*. In that section we assume, for expositional purposes, that aggregate demand is *autonomous* — that is, independent of the level of income. In fact, however, consumption spending is related to the level of income — that is, changes in consumption spending are *induced* by changes in income.[2] Accordingly, in Section 3-2 we recognize this point and discuss the factors that affect the level of consumption by introducing the *consumption function*. We derive an explicit formula for the equilibrium level of income and output. Section 3-3 studies the effects of changes in autonomous spending on equilibrium output. The effects of those changes are summarized by the *multiplier*, which is examined in detail in Section 3-3. The government sector is introduced in Section 3-4, which includes the first discussion of fiscal policy. The discussion of fiscal policy is extended to the government budget in Section 3-5, and Section 3-6 brings foreign trade into the analysis.

3-1 Equilibrium Output

In this chapter and the next we shall assume a world where all prices are given and constant. Such a world would exist if a sufficient level of

---

[2] The terms *autonomous* and *induced* are traditionally used to indicate spending that is independent of the level of income and dependent on the level of income, respectively. More generally, autonomous spending is spending that is independent of the other variables that are explained in a given theory.

unemployment of resources allowed firms, within the relevant range, to supply any amount of output without significantly affecting their unit costs.[3] In terms of Figure 1-1, we are dealing with a situation in which the aggregate supply curve is horizontal.

If firms could supply any amount of output at the prevailing level of prices, what would determine the level of output actually produced? Demand must enter the picture. We would expect firms to produce at a level just sufficient to meet demand. If output produced was in excess of demand, firms would find their inventories piling up, and conversely, if production fell short of demand, inventories would be running down or households would be unable to make the consumption purchases they had planned.

The preceding paragraph suggests a notion of equilibrium output as that level where demand equals supply, so that unintended changes in inventories are zero and households' actual consumption is equal to their planned consumption. Before exploring that notion further, we have to dispose of an unsettling issue that arises from the accounting identity in Equation (1), derived from our study of national income accounting. The identity in Equation (1) states that demand, $C + I$, is *identically* equal to supply Y, *whatever* the level of output. That seems to mean that demand equals supply at *any* level of output, so that any level of output could be the equilibrium level.

The issue is resolved by remembering that in Equation (1), investment is *actual* investment and consumption is *actual* consumption. The investment measured in Equation (1) includes involuntary, or unintended, inventory changes, which occur when firms find themselves selling more or less goods than they had planned to sell. Similarly, if households cannot buy all the goods they want, the consumption measured in Equation (1) will be different from planned consumption. By contrast, our concept of equilibrium output suggests a situation where unintended inventory changes are zero and consumption is equal to planned consumption. We clearly have to make a distinction between the *actual* aggregate demand that is measured in an accounting context and the relevant economic concept of *planned* (desired, intended) aggregate demand.

Actual aggregate demand $(C + I)$ is, by the accounting identity in Equation (1), equal to the level of output (Y). The output level is determined by firms. In deciding how much to produce, firms calculate how much investment, including inventory investment, they want to undertake. They also produce to meet the demand for consumption they forecast will be forthcoming from households. *Planned* aggregate demand consists of the amount of consumption households plan to carry out plus the amount of

[3] It is important to note that the assumption that prices are constant is made to simplify the exposition of Chapters 3 and 4. In later chapters, we use the theories developed in Chapters 3 and 4 to study the factors that determine the price level and cause it to change over time.

investment planned by firms.[4] If firms miscalculate households' consumption demands, planned aggregate demand does not equal actual aggregate demand. Suppose first that firms overestimate consumption demand. The firms find their inventories increasing by more than they had planned, because some of the goods they had planned to sell are not bought by consumers and have instead to be added to inventories. In that case, actual aggregate demand or output exceeds planned aggregate demand, and firms have unanticipated or unintended inventory investment. Similarly, if firms underestimate households' consumption demand, there is unintended inventory decumulation, and actual aggregate demand is less than planned aggregate demand. If we denote aggregate demand by A, the above discussion implies

$$I_{\text{unintended}} \equiv A_{\text{actual}} - A_{\text{planned}} \tag{2}$$

Now actual aggregate demand (A_{actual}) is equal to the level of output Y, and planned aggregate demand (A_{planned}) is the sum of consumption and intended investment $C + I_{\text{int}}$.[5] Thus, using Equation (2), we find

$$
\begin{aligned}
I_{\text{unintended}} &\equiv A_{\text{actual}} - A_{\text{planned}} \\
&\equiv Y - (C + I_{\text{int}})
\end{aligned}
\tag{3}
$$

The identity in Equation (3) can now be linked with the discussion of equilibrium output. We defined equilibrium output as the level of production such that actual aggregate demand is equal to planned aggregate demand. By Equation (3), this implies that unintended inventory accumulation is zero when output is at its equilibrium level.

We shall adopt the convention of using the term *aggregate demand* only in the sense of "planned" and reserve for it the notation A. Similarly, we shall use the term *investment demand* exclusively for planned investment spending — the amount firms plan to spend for investment and denote it by I. Unintended inventory changes will be denoted by I_u. With these conventions, we can rewrite Equation (3) as

$$I_u \equiv Y - A \equiv Y - C - I \tag{3a}$$

where we have used the fact that $A \equiv C + I$ (aggregate demand is the sum of consumption and investment demands).

So far, we have isolated a *concept* of equilibrium output. We have said that there is equilibrium when output supplied is equal to aggregate demand.

---

[4] From now on we shall assume that actual consumption is equal to planned consumption, so that all differences between actual and planned aggregate demand are reflected in unintended inventory changes. In practical terms, this means we are not considering situations where firms put "Sold Out" signs in their windows and customers cannot buy what they want.
[5] Recall that we are assuming actual consumption is equal to planned consumption.

We define that situation as equilibrium because then households find themselves consuming at the rate they planned, and firms find themselves investing at the rate they planned. We have also defined aggregate demand in terms of planned spending. To repeat, aggregate demand is the sum of the amounts households plan to spend on consumption goods and firms plan to spend on investment.

Now we want to go beyond the mere concept of equilibrium output and find out what the equilibrium level of output actually is. For that purpose we need to make an assumption about aggregate demand. The simplest assumption we can make is that aggregate demand is some constant level $\bar{A}$. Our simplest assumption thus makes the demands for consumption and investment independent of the level of income (or autonomous). With this aggregate demand function, it is easy to determine the equilibrium level of output. Recalling that the equilibrium condition is that output supplied equals aggregate demand, we have

$$Y \equiv \bar{A} \tag{4}$$

There are some insights to be gained even from this simple model. Turn to Figure 3-1, where we have plotted on the horizontal axis output Y and, on the vertical axis, aggregate demand A. The aggregate demand function $A \equiv \bar{A}$ is shown as the horizontal line with intercept $\bar{A}$. We show, too, a 45° line that serves as a reference line in that it translates any horizontal distance into an equal vertical distance. For any given level of Y on the horizontal axis, the 45° line gives the level of A on the vertical axis such that $Y = A$. Clearly, from Equation (4) and Figure 3-1, the equilibrium level of output is $Y_0 = \bar{A}$.

Consider now a level of output below Y_0, corresponding to a situation in which firms produce less than the equilibrium level of output. At any level of output below Y_0, aggregate demand $\bar{A}$ exceeds the level of output so that there is an *excess demand* — aggregate demand exceeds output. Consequently, inventories are run down, or unintended inventory reductions take place. The magnitude of unintended inventory changes is given by the vertical distance between the aggregate demand schedule $\bar{A}$ and the 45° line at each level of income, since, using (3a), $I_u \equiv Y - \bar{A}$. At a level of income above Y_0, by contrast, output exceeds aggregate demand, and inventories consequently pile up at a rate equal to the difference between the 45° line and the aggregate demand schedule. At Y_0, output exactly equals aggregate demand, and correspondingly there are no unintended inventory changes.

Will the economy actually reach the equilibrium output level, Y_0? It is reasonable to assume that firms cut production whenever an excess of output over aggregate demand causes inventories to pile up. Suppose now that output initially exceeds the equilibrium level, Y_0. Then firms are unable to sell all the goods they produce and find themselves with increasing inventories. As they find their inventories increasing, they reduce the level

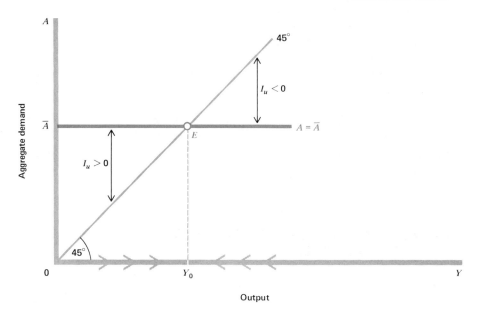

Output

FIGURE 3-1 EQUILIBRIUM WITH CONSTANT AGGREGATE DEMAND

of production so as to prevent a further buildup of inventories. Conversely, suppose that the level of output is below the equilibrium level, Y_0. Then firms find their inventories decreasing because demand exceeds their production.[6] Under those circumstances, they will increase output to meet the demand for goods. The arrows on the horizontal axis in Figure 3-1 are a convenient way of describing the behaviour of firms that we have discussed. The arrows show that the level of output is decreasing whenever output is above Y_0 and increasing whenever Y is less than Y_0. Accordingly, Y will move to the equilibrium level Y_0, which is precisely what our verbal discussion leads us to believe.[7]

We have now mastered both the concept and the mechanics of the determination of equilibrium output. There are three essential notions:

[6] Alternatively, if inventories are zero, firms find themselves having to turn away customers because goods are out of stock. This too would lead firms to increase their output.

[7] You may have noticed that the adjustment process we describe raises the possibility that output will temporarily exceed its new equilibrium level during the adjustment to an increase in aggregate demand. This is the *inventory cycle*. Suppose firms desire to keep on hand inventories which are proportional to the level of demand. When demand unexpectedly rises, inventories are depleted. In subsequent periods, the firms have to produce not only to meet the new higher level of aggregate demand, but also to restore their depleted inventories and to raise them to a higher level. While they are rebuilding their inventories and also producing to meet the higher level of demand, their total production will exceed the new level of aggregate demand.

- Aggregate demand determines the equilibrium level of output.
- At equilibrium, unintended changes in inventories are zero, and households consume the amount they have planned to consume.
- An adjustment process for output based on unintended inventory changes will actually move output to its equilibrium level.

Note, too, that the definition of equilibrium implies that actual spending on consumption and investment equals planned spending. In equilibrium, aggregate demand, which is planned spending, equals output. Since output identically equals income, we see also that in equilibrium, planned spending equals income.

3-2 THE CONSUMPTION FUNCTION AND AGGREGATE DEMAND

The preceding section studied the equilibrium level of output (and income) on the assumption that aggregate demand was simply a constant $\overline{A}$. In this section, we extend the discussion to a more realistic specification of aggregate demand and begin to examine the economic variables that determine it. We separate aggregate demand into its components, consumption and investment demand, and assume an explicit *consumption function.* The assumed consumption function relates consumption spending by households to the level of income. Planned investment is treated as constant at the level $\overline{I}$. Because consumption demand depends on the level of income, so too does aggregate demand. Aggregate demand is no longer constant, as in Section 3-1, and we shall have to modify Figure 3-1 accordingly. First, though, we examine the consumption function.

The Consumption Function

We assume that consumption spending is a linear function of income:[8]

$$C = \overline{C} + cY \qquad (5)$$

where

$$\overline{C} > 0 \quad \text{and} \quad 0 < c < 1$$

This consumption function is shown in Figure 3-2*a*. The *intercept* is $\overline{C}$ and the *slope* is *c*.

The fundamental notion underlying this consumption function is that an

---

[8] Note that because income is equal to output, we use the same symbol, *Y*, for both income and output.

individual's level of consumption is primarily determined by her income. The higher the income, the higher the level of consumption.

The consumption function [Equation (5)] implies that at low levels of income, consumption exceeds income, while at high levels of income, consumption falls short of income. This feature can be seen in Figure 3-2a, which includes a 45° line along which income is equal to consumption. At low levels of income, the consumption function lies above the 45° line, and consumption therefore exceeds income. As we shall see, that means that at low levels of income, the individual or household is dissaving. At high levels of income, the household saves, since consumption is less than income.

These relationships between income and consumption arise from the positive intercept, $\bar{C}$, in Equation (5), and the fact that the coefficient c is less than unity. The coefficient c is sufficiently important for us to have a special name for it. The coefficient c is called the *marginal propensity to consume*: it is the increase in consumption per unit increase in income. In our case, the marginal propensity to consume is less than unity, which implies that out of a dollar increase in income, only a fraction c is spent on consumption. For example, if c is 0.9, then, when income rises by $1, consumption increases by 90 cents.

Consumption and Saving

What happens to the rest, the fraction $1 - c$ that is not spent on consumption? Looking at the right-hand side of Equation (1) above (namely,

---

FIGURE 3-2a THE CONSUMPTION FUNCTION

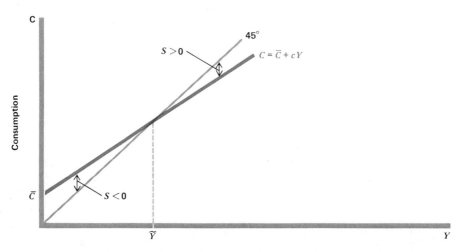

Income

$Y \equiv S + C$), we recognize that there is a relationship among income, consumption, and saving. Specifically, Equation (1) says that income that is not spent on consumption is saved, or

$$S \equiv Y - C \tag{6}$$

What Equation (6) tells us is that by definition, *saving is equal to income minus consumption*. This means that we cannot postulate, in addition to the consumption function, an independent saving function and still expect consumption and saving to add up to income.

The consumption function in Equation (5), together with Equation (6), which we call the *budget constraint*, implies a saving function. The saving function is the function that relates the level of saving to the level of income. Substituting the consumption function in Equation (5) into the budget constraint in Equation (6) yields the saving function

$$\begin{aligned} S &\equiv Y - C \\ &= Y - (\overline{C} + cY) \\ &= -\overline{C} + (1 - c)Y \end{aligned} \tag{7}$$

From Equation (7), saving is an increasing function of the level of income because the *marginal propensity to save, $s = 1 - c$*, is positive. Furthermore, the saving function is the mirror image of the consumption function. At low levels of income, saving is negative, thus reflecting the fact that consumption exceeds income. Conversely, at sufficiently high levels of income,

(*i.e. dividend*).

FIGURE 3-2*b*   THE SAVING FUNCTION

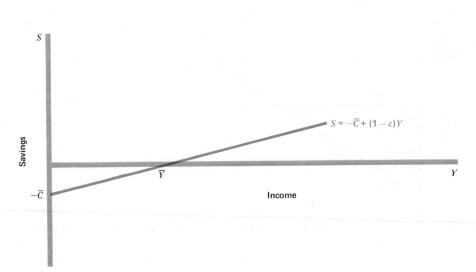

saving becomes positive and thus reflects the fact that not all income is spent on consumption.

The interrelationship between the consumption and saving functions, examined in Equation (7) can also be seen graphically in Figure 3-2*a*, where the vertical distance between the consumption function and the 45° line at each level of income measures saving. Figure 3-2*b* shows the saving function that is derived from the consumption function in Figure 3-2*a* by plotting the vertical distance between income and consumption spending at each level of income. Of course, Figure 3-2*b* is merely a representation of Equation (7). Note that the slope of the saving function in Figure 3-2*b* is the marginal propensity to save, $s = 1 - c$, as defined above.

Planned Investment and Aggregate Demand

We have now specified one component of aggregate demand, consumption spending. To complete the specification of aggregate demand, we must also consider the determinants of investment spending, or an *investment function*. We shall cut short the discussion for the present by simply assuming that planned investment spending is at a constant level $\overline{I}$.[9] Having specified each of the components of aggregate demand, we can now write the aggregate demand function as their sum:

$$A \equiv C + I \ intended$$

$$\equiv \overline{C} + cY + \overline{I} \tag{8}$$

Equilibrium Income and Output

The next step is to use this aggregate demand function to determine the equilibrium level of income and output. We therefore return to the *equilibrium condition* in the goods market:

$$Y = A \tag{9}$$

which states that in equilibrium, output supplied, or income, equals output demanded, or planned aggregate spending. The level of aggregate demand is specified in Equation (8), so that substituting for A in Equation (9), we have the equilibrium condition as

$$Y = \overline{C} + cY + \overline{I} \tag{10}$$

Since we have Y on both sides of the equilibrium condition in Equation (10), we can solve for the equilibrium level of income and output, denoted by Y_0,

[9] In Chapters 4 and 6, investment spending will become a function of the rate of interest and will gain an important place in the transmission of monetary policy.

in terms of the parameters of the aggregate demand function $(\bar{C}, \bar{I}, c)$. From Equation (10), we can write

$$Y - cY = \bar{C} + \bar{I}$$

or

$$Y(1 - c) = \bar{C} + \bar{I}$$

Thus the equilibrium level of income, at which aggregate demand equals output, is[10]

$$Y_0 = \frac{1}{1 - c}(\bar{C} + \bar{I}) \tag{11}$$

We have arrived rather quickly at Equation (11) for the equilibrium level of income and output. It is therefore worthwhile to retrace our steps and use Figure 3-3 to gain understanding of what is involved in the derivation. We plot the aggregate demand function shown in Equation (8). The intercept $\bar{A}$ — autonomous spending — is equal to $\bar{C} + \bar{I}$, and the slope is given by the

[10] As a convention, we use the subscript $_0$ to denote the equilibrium level of a variable.

FIGURE 3-3 DETERMINATION OF EQUILIBRIUM INCOME

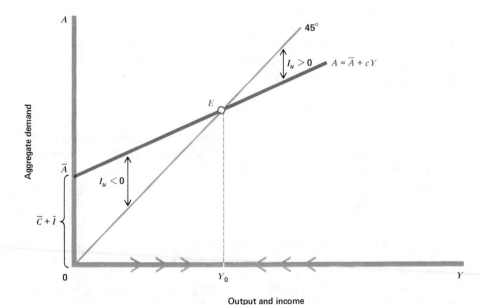

Output and income

marginal propensity to consume, c. This aggregate demand schedule shows the planned level of spending in the economy (consumption plus investment spending) that is associated with each level of income. As is apparent from the figure, aggregate demand increases as the level of income rises. In fact, Figure 3-3 differs from Figure 3-1 only in that the aggregate demand function of Figure 3-3 is upward-sloping rather than horizontal. This relation arises because consumption spending, a component of aggregate demand, increases as income increases.

Consider now the determination of the equilibrium level of income. Remember that the equilibrium level of income is such that aggregate demand equals output (which in turn equals income). The 45° line in Figure 3-3 shows points at which output and aggregate demand are equal. The aggregate demand schedule in Figure 3-3 cuts the 45° line at E, and it is accordingly at E that aggregate demand is equal to output (equals income). Only at E, and at the corresponding equilibrium level of income and output, Y_0, does aggregate demand exactly equal output. At that level of output and income, planned spending precisely matches production.

We also showed in Section 3-1 that at the equilibrium level of output, unintended inventory changes are zero. In Figure 3-3, unintended changes in inventories associated with each level of output are equal to the vertical distance between the aggregate demand function and the 45° line. At levels of income below Y_0, unintended inventory changes are therefore negative because aggregate demand exceeds output. Conversely, at levels of output above Y_0, involuntary inventory changes are positive because aggregate demand falls short of output. Only at the equilibrium level of income, Y_0, are unintended inventory changes equal to zero.

The arrows in Figure 3-3 indicate once again how we reach equilibrium. If firms expand production whenever they face unintended decreases in their inventory holdings, then they increase output at any level below Y_0, because, below Y_0, aggregate demand exceeds output and inventories are declining. Conversely, for output levels above Y_0, firms find inventories piling up and therefore cut production. This process will lead us to the output level Y_0, where current production exactly matches planned aggregate spending. Again, the arrows in Figure 3-3 represent the dynamic process by which the economy moves to the equilibrium level of output Y_0.[11]

Figure 3-3 sheds light, too, on the determinants of the equilibrium level of income calculated in Equation (11). The position of the aggregate demand schedule is characterized by its slope c and intercept $\bar{A}$. The intercept $\bar{A}$ is the level of autonomous spending, that is, spending that is independent of the level of income. For our aggregate demand function, Equation (8), autonomous spending is equal to $\bar{C} + \bar{I}$. The other determinant of the equilibrium level of income is the marginal propensity to consume, c, which

---

[11] Do you see that there is once more the possibility of an inventory cycle? Refer back to footnote 7.

is the slope of the aggregate demand schedule. Given the intercept, a steeper aggregate demand function — as would be implied by a higher marginal propensity to consume — implies a higher level of equilibrium income. Similarly, for a given marginal propensity to consume, a higher level of autonomous spending — in terms of Figure 3-3, a larger intercept — implies a higher equilibrium level of income. These results, suggested by Figure 3-3, are easily verified from Equation (11), which gives the formula for the equilibrium level of income.

Saving and Investment

A further perspective on equilibrium income can be gained from Figure 3-4. Here we have shown separately the consumption schedule and the aggregate demand function. The vertical distance between the two schedules represents the constant level of planned investment spending, $\bar{I}$. As we saw earlier, the equilibrium level of income is Y_0, because only at that level of output does aggregate planned spending equal income. The breakdown of aggregate spending into its consumption and investment components is useful to bring out an important relationship that holds in equilibrium in this simple economy without a government and foreign trade. Specifically, *in equilibrium, planned investment equals saving*.

We recall from Figure 3-2 that the vertical distance between the consumption schedule and the 45° line measures saving at each level of income. The vertical distance between the aggregate demand schedule and the consumption schedule measures planned investment spending. At the equilibrium level of income, these two distances coincide, and accordingly, saving equals (planned) investment.[12] By contrast, above the equilibrium level of income Y_0, saving (the distance between the 45° line and the consumption schedule) exceeds investment, while below Y_0, investment exceeds saving.

Now, is the equality between saving and investment at equilibrium an essential characteristic of the equilibrium level of income, or is it a mere curiosity? It is an essential characteristic of equilibrium. We can see that by starting with the basic equilibrium condition Equation (9), which states that in equilibrium, $Y = A$. If we subtract consumption from both Y and A, we realize that $Y - C$ is saving and $A - C$ is planned investment. In symbols,

$$Y = A$$
$$Y - C = A - C$$
$$S = \bar{I} \tag{12}$$

---

[12] Recall that we have agreed to mean "planned investment" when we use the term *investment*.

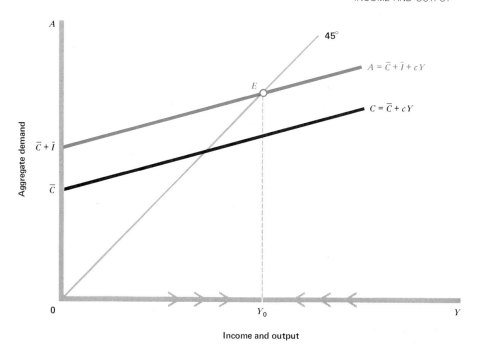

FIGURE 3-4 CONSUMPTION AND INVESTMENT AS COMPONENTS OF AGGREGATE
DEMAND

Thus, the definition of equilibrium, "aggregate demand is equal to output," is equivalent to the condition that saving equals investment. The condition $S = \bar{I}$ is merely another way of stating the basic equilibrium condition.[13]

Recall also that in equilibrium, unintended inventory accumulation is zero. The "saving equals investment" definition of equilibrium also implies that in equilibrium there is no unintended inventory investment. Saving is income less consumption. Given the equality of income and output, saving is therefore the excess of output over consumption. That excess must exactly equal planned investment spending for there to be no unintended inventory changes. But that says that saving has to be equal to planned investment if there are to be no unintended inventory changes.

There is also a diagrammatic derivation of the equilibrium level of income that corresponds to the statement of the equilibrium condition in Equation (12) as the balance between saving and investment. In Figure 3-5, we show the saving function that was derived in Figure 3-2. We have drawn, too, planned investment spending indicated by the horizontal line with

---

[13] In the problem set, we ask you to derive Eq. (11) for Y_0 by starting from $S = \bar{I}$ and substituting for S from Eq. (7).

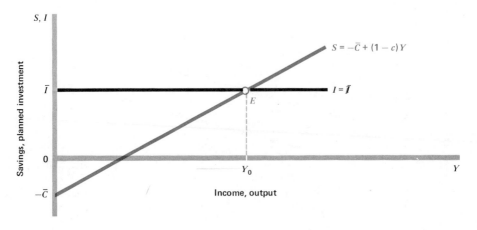

FIGURE 3-5 SAVINGS AND INVESTMENT

intercept $\bar{I}$. Equilibrium income is shown as the level Y_0. To complete the argument, remember that from Equation (3a) unintended inventory changes are defined as:

$$I_u = Y - C - \bar{I} \tag{3a}$$

Substituting the definition of saving $S \equiv Y - C$, we have

$$I_u = S - \bar{I} \tag{13}$$

Equation (13) shows us that when saving equals investment, the unintended inventory changes are zero, and thus serves as a check on Equation (12) as a statement of the equilibrium condition.

3-3 THE MULTIPLIER

In this section we develop an answer to the following question: By how much does a $1 increase in *autonomous* spending raise the equilibrium level of income?[14] There would appear to be a simple answer. Since, in equilibrium, income equals aggregate demand, it would seem that a $1 increase in (autonomous) demand or spending should raise equilibrium income by $1. That answer is wrong. Let us now see why.

---

[14] Recall that autonomous spending $\bar{A}$ is spending that is independent of the level of income. Note also that the answer to this question is contained in Eq. (11). Can you deduce the answer directly from Eq. (11)? This section provides an explanation of that answer.

Suppose first that output increased by $1 to match the increased level of autonomous spending. This output and income increase would in turn give rise to further *induced* spending as consumption rises because the level of income has risen. How much of the initial $1 increase in income would be spent on consumption? The answer to that question is given by the marginal propensity to consume, c. Out of an additional dollar of income, a fraction c is consumed. Assume then that production increases further to meet this induced expenditure, that is, that output and so income increase by $1 + c$. That will leave us with an excess demand because the very fact of an expansion in production and income by $1 + c$ will give rise to further induced spending. This story could clearly take a long time to tell. We seem to have arrived at an impasse where expansion in output to meet excess demand leads to a further expansion in demand without an obvious end to that process.

It helps to lay out the various steps in this chain more carefully. We start off in the first round with an increase in autonomous spending $\Delta\bar{A}$. Next we allow an expansion in production to exactly meet that increase in demand. Production accordingly expands by $\Delta\bar{A}$. This increase in production gives rise to an equal increase in income and, therefore, via the consumption function, $C = \bar{C} + cY$, gives rise in the second round to induced expenditures of size $c(\Delta A)$. Assume again that production expands to meet the increase in spending. The production adjustment this time is $c(\Delta\bar{A})$ and so is the increase in income. This gives rise to a third round of induced spending equal to the marginal propensity to consume times the increase in income $c(c\;\Delta\bar{A}) = c^2\;\Delta\bar{A}$. Careful inspection of the last term shows that induced expenditures in the third round are smaller than those in the second round. Since the marginal propensity to consume, c, is less than 1, the term c^2 is less than c.

If we write out the successive rounds of increased spending, starting with the initial increase in autonomous demand, we obtain

$$\Delta A = \Delta\bar{A} + c\;(\Delta\bar{A}) + c^2\;\Delta\bar{A} + c^3\;\Delta\bar{A} + \dots .$$
$$= \Delta\bar{A}(1 + c + c^2 + c^3 + \dots) \tag{14}$$

It is obvious that for $c < 1$, the successive terms in the series become progressively smaller. In fact, we are dealing with a geometric series the sum of which is calculated as

$$\Delta A = \frac{1}{1 - c}\Delta\bar{A} = \Delta Y_0 \tag{15}$$

From Equation (15), therefore, the cumulative change in aggregate spending is equal to a multiple of the increase in autonomous spending. This could also have been deduced from Equation (11).[15] The multiple $1/(1 - c)$ is

---

[15] If you are familiar with the calculus, you will realize that the multiplier is nothing other than the derivative of the equilibrium level of income, Y_0, in Eq. (11) with respect to autonomous spending. Use the calculus on Eq. (11) above and Eq. (26) below to check the statements of the text.

called the *multiplier*. It tells us by how much we have to multiply a given change in autonomous spending to obtain the corresponding changes in equilibrium income and aggregate demand. Because the multiplier exceeds unity, we know that a $1 change in autonomous spending increases equilibrium income and output by more than $1.[16] The concept of the multiplier is sufficiently important to create a new notation. Defining the multiplier as α, we have

$$\alpha \equiv \frac{1}{1-c} \tag{16}$$

Inspection of the multiplier in Equation (16) shows that the larger the marginal propensity to consume, the larger is the multiplier. With a marginal propensity to consume of 0.75, the multiplier is 4; for a marginal propensity to consume of 0.8, the multiplier is 5. The reason is simply that a high marginal propensity to consume implies that a large fraction of an additional dollar of income will be consumed. Accordingly, expenditures induced by an increase in autonomous spending are high and, therefore, so is the expansion in output and income that is needed to restore balance between income and demand (or spending).

Before proceeding further, we note that the relationship between the marginal propensity to consume, c, and the marginal propensity to save, s, allows us to write Equation (16) in a somewhat different form. Remembering from the budget constraint that saving plus consumption adds up to income, we realize that the fraction of an additional dollar of income consumed plus the fraction saved must add up to a dollar or

$$1 \equiv s + c$$

We can use the relation $s \equiv 1 - c$ and substitute in Equation (16) to obtain an equivalent formula for the multiplier in terms of the marginal propensity to save:

$$\alpha \equiv \frac{1}{s} \tag{16a}$$

---

[16] *Two warnings*: (1) The multiplier is necessarily greater than 1 in this very simplified model of the determination of income, but as we shall see in the discussion of "crowding out" in Chapter 4, there may be circumstances under which it is less than 1. (2) The term *multiplier* is used more generally in economics to mean the effect on some endogenous variable (a variable whose level is explained by the theory being studied) of a unit change in an exogenous variable (a variable whose level is not determined within the theory being examined). For instance, one can talk of the multiplier of a change in the income tax rate on the level of unemployment. However, the classic use of the term is as we are using it here — the effects of a change in autonomous spending on equilibrium output.

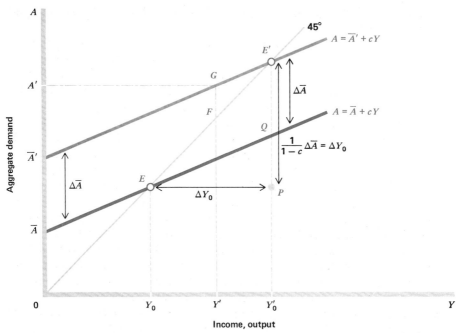

FIGURE 3-6 GRAPHICAL DERIVATION OF THE MULTIPLIER

Figure 3-6 provides a graphic interpretation of the effects of an increase in autonomous spending on the equilibrium level of income. The initial equilibrium is at point E with an income level Y_0. Consider next an increase in autonomous spending from $\overline{A}$ to $\overline{A}'$. This is represented by a parallel upward shift of the aggregate demand schedule where the shift is exactly equal to the increase in autonomous spending. The upward shift means that now, at each level of income, aggregate demand is higher by an amount $\Delta\overline{A} \equiv \overline{A}' - \overline{A}$.

At the initial level of income, Y_0, aggregate demand now exceeds income or output. Consequently, unintended inventory decumulation is taking place at a rate equal to the increase in autonomous spending, equal to the vertical distance $\Delta\overline{A}$. Firms will respond to that excess demand by expanding production, say to income level Y'. This expansion in production has two effects. First, it gives rise to induced expenditure, increasing aggregate demand to the level A'. Second, at the same time, it reduces the gap between aggregate demand and output to the vertical distance FG. Additional spending is induced because the marginal propensity to consume out of additional income is positive, while the gap between aggregate demand and output narrows because the marginal propensity to consume is less than 1. Thus, a marginal propensity to consume that is positive but less than unity implies that a sufficient expansion in output will restore the balance between aggregate demand and output. In Figure 3-6 the new equilibrium is indicated by point E' and the corresponding level of income is Y_0'. The change in income required is therefore, $\Delta Y_0 = Y_0' - Y_0$.

The magnitude of the income change required to restore equilibrium depends on two factors. The larger the increase in autonomous spending, represented in Figure 3-6 by the parallel shift in the aggregate demand schedule, the larger is the income change. Furthermore, the larger the marginal propensity to consume — that is, the steeper the aggregate demand schedule — the larger the income change.

As a further check on our results, we want to verify from Figure 3-6 that the change in equilibrium income in fact exceeds the change in autonomous spending. For that purpose, we simply use the 45° line to compare the change in income ΔY_0 ($= EP = PE'$) with the change in autonomous spending that is equal to the vertical distance between the new and old aggregate demand schedule (QE'). It is clear from Figure 3-6 that the change in income PE' exceeds the change in autonomous spending QE'.

Finally, there is yet another way of deriving the multiplier. The relationship between the change in equilibrium income and a change in autonomous spending can be directly derived from the concept of equilibrium. We remember that in equilibrium, aggregate demand equals income or output. From one equilibrium to another, it must therefore be true that the change in income ΔY_0 is equal to the change in aggregate demand ΔA:

$$\Delta Y_0 = \Delta A \qquad (17)$$

Next we split up the change in aggregate demand into the change in autonomous spending, $\Delta \bar{A}$, and the change in expenditure induced by the consequent change in income — that is, $c\,\Delta Y_0$.

$$\Delta A = \Delta \bar{A} + c\Delta Y_0 \qquad (18)$$

Combining Equations (17) and (18), we obtain the change in income as

$$\Delta Y_0 = \Delta \bar{A} + c\Delta Y_0$$

or

$$\Delta Y_0(1 - c) = \Delta \bar{A}$$

or

$$\Delta Y_0 = \frac{1}{1 - c}\Delta \bar{A} = \alpha\Delta \bar{A} \qquad (19)$$

There are three important points to remember from this discussion:

- An increase in autonomous spending raises the equilibrium level of income.
- The increase in income is a multiple of the increase in autonomous spending.
- The larger the marginal propensity to consume, the larger is the multiplier, arising from the relation between consumption and income.

As a check on your understanding of the material of this section, you should develop the same analysis, and the same answers, in terms of Figure 3-5.

3-4 THE GOVERNMENT SECTOR

So far, we have ignored the role of the government sector in the determination of equilibrium income. The government affects the level of equilibrium income in two separate ways. First, government expenditure on goods and services, G, is a component of aggregate demand. Second, taxes and transfers affect the relation between output and income, Y, and the *disposable income* — income that is available for consumption or saving — that accrues to the private sector, Y_d. In this section, we will be concerned with the way in which government purchases, taxes, and transfers affect the equilibrium level of income.

We start again from the basic national income accounting identities. The introduction of the government restores government purchases on the expenditure side of Equation (1) of this chapter, and taxes less transfers on the allocation of income side. We can, accordingly, rewrite the identity in Equation (1) as

$$C + I + G \equiv S + (T - R) + C \qquad (1a)$$

The definition of aggregate demand has to be augmented to include government expenditure on goods and services — the purchases of military equipment and services of bureaucrats, for instance. Thus we have

$$A \equiv C + \overline{I} + G$$

Consumption will no longer depend on income but rather on *disposable income*, Y_d. Disposable income, Y_d, is the net income available for spending by households after paying taxes to, and receiving transfers from, the government. It thus consists of income less taxes plus transfers, $Y + R - T$. The consumption function is now

$$C = \overline{C} + cY_d = \overline{C} + c(Y + R - T) \qquad (5a)$$

A final step is a specification of *fiscal policy*. Fiscal policy is the policy of the government with regard to the level of government spending and the tax structure. We assume that the government purchases a constant amount $\bar{G}$, that it makes a constant amount of transfers $\bar{R}$, and that it collects a fraction t of income in the form of taxes. For example, if t equals 0.2, there is an income tax equal to 20 percent of income.

$$G = \bar{G} \qquad R = \bar{R} \qquad T = tY \qquad (20)$$

With this specification of fiscal policy we can rewrite the consumption function, after substitution from Equation (20) for R and T in Equation (6a) as:

$$C = \bar{C} + c(Y + \bar{R} - tY)$$

$$C = (\bar{C} + c\bar{R}) + c(1 - t)Y \qquad (21)$$

We note from Equation (21) that the presence of transfers raises autonomous consumption spending by the marginal propensity to consume out of disposable income c times the amount of transfers.[17] The presence of income taxes, by contrast, lowers consumption spending at each level of income. That reduction arises because households' consumption is related to disposable income rather than income itself, and income taxes reduce disposable income relative to the level of income. While the marginal propensity to consume out of disposable income remains c, the marginal propensity to consume out of income now is $c(1 - t)$, where $1 - t$ is the fraction of income left after taxes.

Equilibrium Income

We are now set to study income determination when the government's role is included. We return to the equilibrium condition for the goods market, $Y = A$, and after substituting from Equation (21), we can write the equilibrium condition as:

$$Y = (\bar{C} + c\bar{R}) + c(1 - t)Y + \bar{I} + \bar{G}$$

$$= (\bar{C} + c\bar{R} + \bar{I} + \bar{G}) + c(1 - t)Y$$

$$= \bar{A} + c(1 - t)Y$$

---

[17] Note that we are assuming no taxes are paid on transfers from the government. As a matter of fact, taxes are paid on some transfers, such as interest payments on the government debt, and not paid on other transfers, such as welfare benefits.

We can solve this equation for Y_0, the equilibrium level of income, by collecting terms in Y:

$$Y[1 - c(1 - t)] = \overline{A}$$

$$Y_0 = \frac{1}{1 - c(1 - t)} \overline{A} \tag{22}$$

In comparing Equation (22) with Equation (11), we see that the government sector makes a substantial difference. It raises autonomous spending by the amount of government purchases, $\overline{G}$, and by the amount of induced spending out of net transfers, $c\overline{R}$. At the same time, income taxes lower the multiplier. As can be seen from Equation (22), if the marginal propensity to consume is 0.8 and taxes are zero, the multiplier is 5; with the same marginal propensity to consume and a tax rate of 0.25, the multiplier is cut in half to $1/[1 - 0.8(0.75)] = 2.5$. Income taxes reduce the multiplier because they reduce the induced increase of consumption out of changes in income. When there are no taxes, a dollar increase in income raises disposable income by exactly a dollar and induced consumption increases by c times the increase in disposable income. If there are taxes, however, a dollar increase in income raises disposable income by only $(1 - t)$ dollars. Induced consumption rises, therefore, only by $c(1 - t)$. In terms of Figure 3-2, the presence of transfers shifts the intercept of the aggregate demand schedule up by $c\overline{R}$. The slope, which is the marginal propensity to consume out of income, declines because of the presence of income taxes.

Effects of a Change in Government Purchases

We want now to consider the effects of changes in fiscal policy on the equilibrium level of income. We can distinguish three possible changes in fiscal variables: changes in government purchases, changes in transfers, and income tax changes. The simplest illustration is that of a change in government purchases. This case is shown in Figure 3-7, where the initial level of income is Y_0. An increase in government purchases represents a change in autonomous spending and therefore shifts the aggregate demand schedule upward in a parallel fashion by an amount equal to the increased government expenditure. At the initial level of output and income, the demand for goods exceeds output and, accordingly, firms expand production until the new equilibrium at point E' is reached. By how much does income expand? We remember that the change in equilibrium income will equal the change in aggregate demand, or

$$\Delta Y_0 = \Delta \overline{G} + c(1 - t)\Delta Y_0$$

where the remaining terms ($\overline{C}$, $\overline{R}$, and $\overline{I}$) are constant by assumption. Thus, the change in equilibrium income is

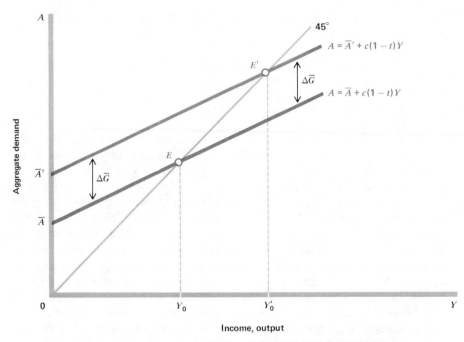

FIGURE 3-7 THE EFFECTS OF AN INCREASE IN GOVERNMENT PURCHASES

$$\Delta Y_0 = \frac{1}{1 - c(1 - t)} \Delta \overline{G} = \overline{\alpha} \Delta \overline{G} \qquad (23)$$

where we have introduced the notation $\overline{\alpha}$ to denote the multiplier in the presence of income taxes:

$$\overline{\alpha} \equiv \frac{1}{1 - c(1 - t)} \qquad (24)$$

From Equation (23) it is apparent that a $1 increase in government purchases will lead to an increase in income in excess of a dollar. Thus, as we have already seen, with a marginal propensity to consume of $c = 0.8$ and an income tax rate of $t = 0.25$, we would have a multiplier of 2.5: a $1 increase in government spending raises equilibrium income by $2.50.

Effects of Increased Transfer Payments

Consider next an increase in transfer payments. In terms of Figure 3-7, we again have an increase in autonomous spending, so that aggregate demand increases at each level of income. The parallel shift in the aggregate demand schedule will be equal to the marginal propensity to spend out of disposable income, c, times the increase in transfers, or $c\Delta\overline{R}$. Again, the demand for goods will exceed production at the initial level of income and output, and an expansion in output will take place to eliminate the excess demand. To calculate the change in equilibrium income, we again use the condition that the change in aggregate demand will equal the change in income. The change in aggregate demand in this case is the change in autonomous spending, $c\Delta\overline{R}$, plus induced spending $c(1 - t)\Delta Y$, so that we can write

$$\Delta Y_0 = c\Delta\overline{R} + c(1 - t\Delta Y_0$$

or

$$\Delta Y_0 = \frac{1}{1 - c(1 - t)}(c\Delta\overline{R}) = \bar{\alpha}\, c\Delta\overline{R} \tag{25}$$

Equation 25 shows that an increase in transfer payments will raise the equilibrium level of income. For plausible values of c and t, it furthermore remains true that we have a multiplier effect — that a dollar increase in transfers raises equilibrium income by more than a dollar. Thus, for $c = 0.8$ and $t = 0.25$, the multiplier for transfer payments is 2.0.

The multiplier for government purchases is higher than the multiplier for transfers because a dollar increase in government purchases translates into a dollar increase in autonomous spending, whereas a dollar increase in transfers results in an increase of only c (less than 1) dollars in autonomous spending.

The Effects of an Income Tax Change

The final exercise in fiscal policy is a reduction in the income tax rate. This is illustrated in Figure 3-8 by an increase in the slope of the aggregate demand function because that slope is equal to the marginal propensity to spend out of income, $c(1 - t)$. The figure shows that at the initial level of income, the aggregate demand for goods now exceeds output because the tax reduction gives rise to increased consumption. The new higher equilibrium level of income is indicated by Y_0'.

To calculate the change in equilibrium income, we equate the change in income to the change in aggregate demand. The change in aggregate demand has two components. First, we have the change in spending at the initial level of income that arises from the tax cut. This part is equal to the marginal propensity to consume out of disposable income times the change in disposable income due to the tax cut, $cY_0\Delta t$, where the term $Y_0\Delta t$ is the initial level of income times the change in the tax rate. The second component of the change in aggregate demand is the induced spending due to higher income. This is now evaluated at the new tax rate t' and has the

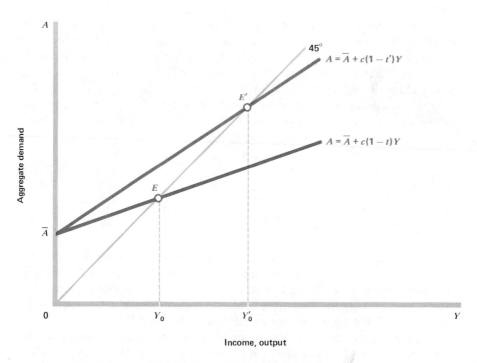

Income, output

FIGURE 3.8 THE EFFECTS OF A DECREASE IN THE TAX RATE

value $c(1 - t')\Delta Y_0$. We can therefore write.[18]

$$\Delta Y_0 = -cY_0\Delta t + c(1 - t')\, \Delta Y_0 \tag{26}$$

or

$$\Delta Y_0 = -\frac{1}{1 - c(1 - t')}cY_0\Delta t \tag{27}$$

An exercise will clarify the effects of an income tax cut. Assume initially a level of income equal to $Y_0 = 100$, a marginal propensity to consume $c = 0.8$, and a tax rate $t = 0.2$. Assume next a tax cut that reduces the income tax rate to $t' = 0.1$. At the initial level of income, disposable income therefore rises by $100\,(t - t') = \$10$. Out of the increase in disposable income of $10, a fraction $c = 0.8$ is spent on consumption so that aggregate demand, at the initial level of income, increases by $8. This corresponds to the first term on the right-hand side of Equation (26). The increase in aggregate demand gives rise to an expansion in output and income. Per dollar increase in income,

---

[18] You should check Eq. (27) by using Eq. (22) to write out Y_0 corresponding to a tax rate of t, and Y_0' corresponding to t'. Then subtract Y_0 from Y_0' to obtain ΔY_0 as given in Eq. (27).

disposable income rises by a fraction $(1 - t')$ of the increase in income. Furthermore, of the increase in disposable income, only a fraction, c, is spent. Accordingly, induced consumption spending is equal to $c(1 - t')\Delta Y_0$, which is the second term in Equation (26). How much does the income tax cut achieve in terms of output expansion? Substituting our parameters in Equation (27), we have

$$\Delta Y_0 = -\frac{1}{1 - 0.8(1 - 0.1)}(0.8)\,(100)\,(0.1 - 0.2) = (3.57)\,(8)$$

$$= 28.56 \tag{27a}$$

In our example, a cut in the tax rate, such that taxes fall by \$10 at the initial level of income, raises equilibrium income by \$28.56.

Note, however, that although taxes are initially cut by \$10, the government's total taxes received fall by less than \$10. Why? The reason is that the government receives 10 percent of the induced increase in income, or \$2.856, as taxes. Thus the final reduction in tax receipts by the government is not the initial \$10, but rather, \$7.144.[19]

Summary

1 Government purchases and transfer payments act like increases in autonomous spending in their effects on equilibrium income.

2 Income taxes reduce disposable income relative to the level of income and their effects on equilibrium income and output are thus the same as those resulting from a reduction in the propensity to consume.

As a final comment on the material of this section, we note that all the results we have derived can be obtained in a straightforward manner by taking the change in aggregate demand at the initial level of income times the multiplier. (Check this proposition for each of the fiscal policy changes we have considered.) You will want to consider, too, the effect on equilibrium income of an increase in government purchases combined with an equal reduction in transfer payments, $\Delta \bar{G} = -\Delta \bar{R}$.[20]

---

[19] We leave it to you to calculate the multiplier relating the change in equilibrium income to the total change in taxes received by the government. How does it compare with the multiplier for transfer payments at the new tax rate t'? Check Eqs. (27) and (25) to make sure your answer is correct.

[20] See problem 9 at the end of the chapter.

3-5 THE BUDGET

In this section we deal with the government budget. We start by defining the concept of the *budget surplus*, denoted by BuS. The surplus is the excess of the government's revenues, consisting of taxes, over its total spending, consisting of expenditure on goods and services and transfer payments:

$$\text{BuS} \equiv T - G - R \tag{28}$$

A negative budget surplus — an excess of government expenditure over revenues — is a *budget deficit*.

Since the budget surplus (and especially the deficit) receives much attention from politicians, economists, and the press, we want now to study the budget surplus in relation to the level of income. Substituting in Equation (28) the assumption of a proportional income tax that yields a tax revenue $T = tY$, gives us

$$\text{BuS} = tY - G - R \tag{28a}$$

In Figure 3-9 we plot the budget surplus as a function of the level of income for given $G = \bar{G}$, $R = \bar{R}$, and income tax rate t. At low levels of income, the budget is in deficit (the surplus is negative) because payments $\bar{G} + \bar{R}$ exceed income tax collection. For high levels of income, by contrast, the budget shows a surplus, since income tax collection outweighs expenditures in the form of government purchases and transfers.

Figure 3-9 shows immediately that the budget surplus can be changed by changes in income that derive from sources other than a change in fiscal policy. Thus, for example, an increase in income that arises because of increased autonomous investment spending will give rise to an increase in the budget surplus or a reduction in the budget deficit. Why? Because the increase in income raises income tax collection and, therefore, for a given level of government outlays, lowers the deficit. To make the same point in a somewhat different manner, a reduction in economic activity, given fiscal policy as summarized by the parameters $\bar{G}$, $\bar{R}$, and t, must lead to a reduction in the budget surplus, or an increase in the deficit.

This feature of the budget, or of fiscal policy, whereby taxes are automatically reduced when income falls, is called *automatic stabilization*. Its effects were described in Section 3-4 as a reduction in the multiplier due to income taxes. The presence of income taxation ensures that a given reduction in autonomous spending will lead to less of a decline in income than would occur in the absence of income taxes because the multiplier $\bar{\alpha}$ is smaller than the multiplier α. In general, *automatic stabilizers* are those elements in the economy that reduce the impact of changes in autonomous spending on the equilibrium level of income. Unemployment benefits, for example, are also an automatic stabilizer.

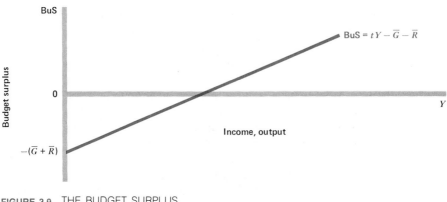

FIGURE 3.9 THE BUDGET SURPLUS

The Effects of Government Purchases and Tax Changes on the Budget Surplus

Next we want to inquire how various changes in fiscal policy affect the budget. In particular, we want to find out whether an increase in government purchases must reduce the budget surplus. At first sight, this would appear obvious because increased government purchases, from Equation (28), are reflected in a reduced surplus, or increased deficit. At further thought, it becomes apparent, however, that the increased government purchases will give rise to a (multiplied) increase in income and, therefore, to increased income tax collection. This raises the interesting possibility that tax collection might increase by more than government purchases.

A brief calculation will show that the first guess is right — increased government purchases reduce the budget surplus. From Equation (23) the change in income due to increased government purchases is equal to $\Delta Y_0 = \bar{\alpha} \Delta \bar{G}$. A fraction of that increase in income is collected in the form of taxes so that tax revenue increases by $t\bar{\alpha}\Delta\bar{G}$. The change in the budget surplus is therefore[21]

$$\begin{aligned}
\Delta \text{BuS} &= \Delta T - \Delta \bar{G} \\
&= t\bar{\alpha}\Delta\bar{G} - \Delta\bar{G} \\
&= \left[\frac{t}{1 - c(1 - t)} - 1 \right]\Delta\bar{G} \\
&= -\frac{(1 - c)(1 - t)}{1 - c(1 - t)}\Delta\bar{G}
\end{aligned} \tag{29}$$

which is unambiguously negative. We have, therefore, shown that an increase in government purchases will reduce the budget surplus, although

[21] We use Eq. (24) to substitute for $\bar{\alpha}$ in Eq. (29)

by considerably less than the increase in purchases. For instance, for $c = 0.8$ and $t = 0.2$, a dollar increase in government purchases will create a 44-cent reduction in the surplus.[22]

In the same way, we can consider the effects of an increase in the tax rate on the budget surplus. We know that the increase in the tax rate will reduce the level of income. It might thus appear that an increase in the tax rate, keeping the level of government spending constant, could reduce the budget surplus. In fact, an increase in the tax rate increases the budget surplus, despite the reduction in income that it causes.[23]

Finally, we can investigate the budgetary effects of simultaneous changes in income tax rates and government purchases. We will work through these cases by using a simple example. We assume that a fiscal policy is implemented that reduces the income tax rate from $t = 0.2$ to $t' = 0.1$. At an initial level of income of \$100, such a tax cut results in a loss of tax revenue of \$10. In combination with the tax cut, we implement a reduction of government purchases in the amount of \$10. What is the net effect on equilibrium income and the budget of the fiscal policy package, assuming a marginal propensity to consume of $c = 0.8$? With an income tax rate of $t' = 0.1$, the multiplier will be $\bar{\alpha} = 3.57$. A \$10 decrease in government purchases accordingly lowers income by \$35.70. The tax cut, in turn, will raise income by \$28.56 $= (0.8)(0.1)(100)(3.7)$. The net effect of the package on income is therefore a reduction in income of the order of \$7.14. What is the effect on the budget? Government purchases decline by \$10; tax revenue declines at the initial level of income by \$10, owing to the tax cut, and suffers a further reduction, due to the decline in income, of $(0.1)(7.14) = 0.71$. The net effect of this cut in government purchases, combined with a decrease in taxes that is equal, *at the initial level of income*, to the cut in government purchases, is therefore a slight increase in the budget deficit. The budget deficit changes because the level of income falls and taxes therefore fall more than they were reduced initially.

In this example, the combined tax decrease and government purchases decrease raised the budget deficit. What would happen to the level of income if government purchases and taxes changed by exactly the same amount, so that the budget surplus remained unchanged between the initial and final level of income? The answer to this question is contained in the famous *balanced budget multiplier* result. The result is that the balanced budget multiplier is exactly 1. That is, an increase in government purchases, accompanied by an equal increase in taxes, increases the level of income by exactly the amount of the increase in purchases.[24] This interesting result is derived in the appendix to this chapter.

---

[22] In this case, $\bar{\alpha} = 1/[1 - 0.8(0.8)] = 2.78$ (see p. 70). So $\Delta BuS = -2.78(0.2)(0.8) = -0.44$.

[23] The effects of an increase in the tax rate on the budget surplus are examined in detail in problem 7 at the end of this chapter.

[24] Note that the balanced budget multiplier may well be less than 1 in the more sophisticated models of Chapter 4, in which investment spending depends on the interest rate.

The major points of the preceding discussion are that a balanced budget cut in government purchases lowers equilibrium income and that a dollar increase in government purchases has a stronger impact on equilibrium income than a dollar cut in taxes. A dollar cut in taxes leads only to a fraction of a dollar's increase in consumption spending, the rest being saved, while government purchases are reflected dollar for dollar in a change in aggregate demand.[25]

The Full-Employment Budget Surplus

A final topic to be treated here is the concept of the *full-employment budget surplus*.[26] Recall that increases in taxes add to the surplus and that increases in government expenditures reduce the surplus. Increases in taxes have been shown to reduce the level of income, and increases in government purchases and transfers to increase the level of income. It thus seems that the budget surplus is a convenient, simple measure of the overall effects of fiscal policy on the economy. when government expenditure increases, the level of income rises and the budget surplus falls. When taxes increase, the level of income falls and the budget surplus rises.

However, the budget surplus by itself suffers from a serious defect as a measure of the direction of fiscal policy. The defect is that the surplus can change *passively* because of changes in autonomous private spending, as we have seen. Thus, if the economy moves into a recession, tax revenue automatically declines and the budget moves in to a deficit (or reduced surplus). Conversely, an increase in economic activity causes the budget to move into a surplus (or reduced deficit). These changes in the budget take place automatically for a given tax structure. This implies that we cannot simply look at the budget deficit as a measure of whether government fiscal policy is expansionary or deflationary. A given fiscal policy may imply a deficit if private spending is low and a surplus if private spending is high. Thus, it is important to note that increases in the budget deficit do not necessarily mean that the government has changed its policy in an expansionary direction in an attempt to increase the level of income.

Since we frequently want to measure the way in which fiscal policy is being *actively*, rather than *passively*, used to affect the level of income, we require some measure of policy that is independent of the particular position of the business cycle — boom or recession — in which we may find ourselves. Such a measure is provided by the *cyclically adjusted budget surplus*, which we shall denote by BuS*. BuS* measures the budget not at the actual level of income, but rather at the level of income that would prevail if the

---

[25] Rather than go through the analysis of changes in transfer payments, we will leave it to you to work through an example of the effects on the budget of a change in transfer payments in the problems at the end of the chapter.

[26] The concept of the full-employment surplus was first used by E. Cary Brown. "Fiscal Policy in the Thirties: A Reappraisal," *American Economic Review*, December 1956.

economy was growing at a steady rate with no cyclical fluctuations around the long-term trend. If an estimate of the full-employment level of income or potential output is used as a benchmark, BuS* is called the *full-employment budget surplus*. Using this concept, a given fiscal policy summarized by $\bar{G}$, $\bar{R}$, and t is assessed by the level of the surplus, or deficit, that is generated at full employment. Using Y_p to denote the full-employment level of income, we can write

$$\text{BuS*} = tY_p - \bar{G} - \bar{R} \tag{30}$$

In Figure 3-10 we replicate the budget surplus schedule from Figure 3-9 but add the full-employment level of income Y_p. The full-employment budget surplus is indicated by the corresponding point on the budget surplus schedule. To see the difference between the actual and the full-employment budget, we subtract the actual budget in Equation (28a) from Equation (30) to obtain

$$\text{BuS*} - \text{BuS} = t(Y_p - Y) \tag{31}$$

It is apparent that the only difference arises from income tax collection.[27] Specifically, if output is below full employment, the full-employment surplus exceeds the actual surplus. Conversely, if actual output exceeds full-employment (or potential) output, the full-employment surplus is less than the actual surplus.

Chart 3-1 shows the actual and cyclically adjusted surplus as a fraction of GNP for the years 1953 to 1979. In periods of rapid growth and relatively

[27] In practice, transfer payments, such as welfare and unemployment benefits, are also partly affected by the state of the economy, so that R also depends on the level of income. But the major cause of differences between the actual surplus and the full-employment surplus is the income tax.

FIGURE 3.10 THE ACTUAL AND FULL-EMPLOYMENT BUDGET SURPLUSES

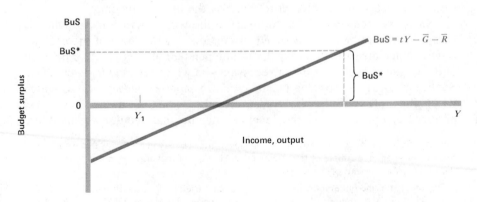

low unemployment, such as 1964-1969, the actual surplus rises above the adjusted one, while in recession years such as 1958, 1961, 1970 and 1975, the growth of tax revenues slows down and the actual surplus falls below the adjusted one. The emergence of large cyclically adjusted deficits in the period 1975-1979 reflects the expansionary fiscal policy adopted during that period in response to rising unemployment rates.

One final word of warning: The high-employment surplus is a better measure of the direction of active fiscal policy than the actual budget surplus. But it is not a perfect measure of the thrust of fiscal policy. The reason is that balanced budget increases in government purchases are themselves expansionary, so that an increase in government purchases matched by a tax increase that keeps the surplus constant leads to an increase in the level of income. Because fiscal policy involves the setting of a number of variables — the tax rate, transfers, and government purchases — it is difficult to describe the thrust of fiscal policy perfectly in a single number.[28] But the high-employment surplus is nevertheless a useful guide to the direction of fiscal policy.

---

[28] A very lucid discussion of the full-employment surplus and other measures — such as the weighted full-employment surplus — that attempt to adjust for the imperfections of the full-employment surplus measure is contained in Alan S. Blinder and Robert M. Solow, "Analytical Foundations of Fiscal Policy," in Alan S. Blinder et al. *The Economics of Public Finance* (Washington, D.C.: The Brookings Institution, 1974).

CHART 3-1 THE ACTUAL AND CYCLICALLY ADJUSTED BUDGET SURPLUS AS A FRACTION OF GNP (*Source*: Dept. of Finance, *Economic Review*)

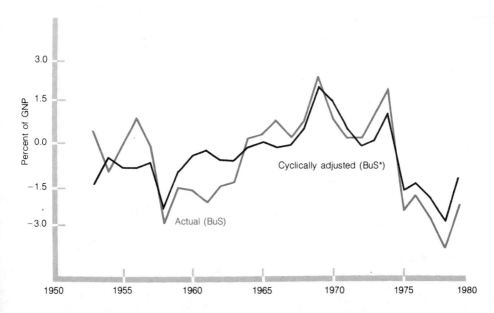

3-6 THE FOREIGN SECTOR

For a country like Canada that exports about one-quarter of its total output and spends a similar fraction of its income on imports, foreign trade plays an important role in the determination of equilibrium income. When foreign trade is taken into account, we return to the general case represented by the basic accounting identity given at the beginning of the chapter. Aggregate demand becomes:

$$A = C + I + G + NX$$

Denoting exports by X and imports by Q, we have

$$NX = X - Q$$

As in the case of planned investment and government spending, we assume that exports are fixed at a given level (denoted by $\bar{X}$). On the other hand, since imports represent part of domestic demand, they are assumed to depend on income. Using a linear relationship we have

$$Q = \bar{Q} + mY \tag{32}$$

where the slope m is called the *marginal propensity to import*.

To determine the equilibrium level of income, we use the equilibrium condition, $Y = A$ together with the consumption function (21) and the import function (32):

$$
\begin{aligned}
Y &= (\bar{C} + c\bar{R}) + c(1-t)Y + \bar{I} + \bar{G} + \bar{X} - \bar{Q} - mY \\
&= (\bar{C} + c\bar{R} + \bar{I} + \bar{G} + \bar{X} - \bar{Q}) \\
&\quad + [c(1 - t) - m]Y \\
&= \bar{A} + [c(1 - t) - m]Y
\end{aligned}
$$

Solving for the equilibrium level of income Y_0, we obtain:

$$Y_0 = \frac{1}{1 - c(1 - t) + m}\bar{A} \tag{33}$$

Comparing Equation (33) with Equation (11), we see that exports add to and imports subtract from autonomous spending. In addition, imports are similar to taxes in that they reduce the increases in demand for domestic output induced by increases in income, and thereby lower the multiplier. The higher is the marginal propensity to import, then, the lower is the multiplier.

3-7 SUMMARY

1 Output is at its equilibrium level when the aggregate demand for goods is equal to the level of output.

2 Aggregate demand consists of planned spending by households on consumption, firms on investment goods, and government on its expenditure on goods and services.

3 When output is at its equilibrium level, there are no unintended changes in inventories and all economic units are making precisely the purchases they had planned to. An adjustment process for the level of output based on the accumulation or decumulation of inventories leads the economy to the equilibrium output level.

4 The level of aggregate demand is itself affected by the level of output (equal to the level of income) because consumption demand depends on the level of income.

5 The consumption function relates consumption spending to income. Income that is not consumed is saved, so that the saving function can be derived from the consumption function.

6 The multiplier is the amount by which a one-dollar change in autonomous spending changes the equilibrium level of output. The greater the propensity to consume, the higher the multiplier.

7 Government purchases and government transfer payments act like increases in autonomous spending in their effects on the equilibrium level of income. A proportional income tax has the same effects on the equilibrium level of income as a reduction in the propensity to consume. A proportional income tax thus reduces the multiplier.

8 The budget surplus is the excess of government receipts over its expenditure. When the government is spending more than it receives, the budget is in deficit. The size of the budget surplus (deficit) is affected by the government's fiscal policy variables — government purchases, transfer payments, and tax rates.

9 The budget surplus is also affected by changes in taxes and transfers resulting from changes in the level of income occurring as a result of changes in private autonomous spending. The *cyclically adjusted* or *full-employment* (high-employment) budget surplus is accordingly frequently used as a measure of the active use of fiscal policy. The full-employment surplus measures the budget surplus that would exist if output were at its potential (full-employment) level.

10 When foreign trade is taken into account, exports add to and imports subtract from autonomous spending. The dependence of imports on income affects the size of the multiplier: the higher is the marginal propensity to import, the lower is the multiplier.

APPENDIX

This appendix considers the *balanced budget multiplier* result mentioned in the text. The balanced budget multiplier refers to the effects of an increase in government purchases accompanied by an increase in taxes such that, in the new equilibrium, the budget surplus is exactly the same as in the original equilibrium. The result is that the multiplier of such a policy change is unity. In other words, the balanced budget multiplier is 1. A multiplier of unity obviously implies that output expands by precisely the amount of the increased government purchases with no induced consumption spending. It is apparent that what must be at work is the effect of higher taxes that exactly offset the effect of the income expansion, and that thus maintain disposable income, and hence consumption, constant. With no induced consumption spending, output expands simply to match the increased government purchases.

We can derive this result by noting that the change in aggregate demand ΔA is equal to the change in government purchases plus the change in consumption spending. The latter is equal to the marginal propensity to consume out of disposable income, c, times the change in disposable income, ΔY_d, that is, $\Delta Y_0 - \Delta T$, where ΔY_0 is the change in output. Thus:

$$\Delta A = \Delta \bar{G} + c(\Delta Y_0 - \Delta T) \tag{A1}$$

Since from one equilibrium to another the change in aggregate demand has to equal the change in output, we have

$$\Delta Y_0 = \Delta \bar{G} + c(\Delta Y_0 - \Delta T)$$

or

$$\Delta Y_0 = \frac{1}{1 - c}(\Delta \bar{G} - c\Delta T) \tag{A2}$$

Next we note that by assumption the change in government purchases between the new equilibrium and the old one is exactly matched by a change in tax collection so that $\Delta \bar{G} = \Delta T$. It follows from this last equality, after substitution in Equation (A2), that with this particular restriction on fiscal policy we have

$$\Delta Y_0 = \frac{1}{1 - c}(\Delta \bar{G} - c\Delta \bar{G}) = \Delta \bar{G} = \Delta T \tag{A3}$$

so that the multiplier is precisely unity.

Another way of deriving the balanced budget multiplier result is by considering the successive rounds of spending changes caused by the government policy changes. Suppose each of government purchases and taxes increased by \$1. Let $c(1 - t)$, the induced increase in aggregate demand caused by a \$1 increase in income in the presence of taxes, be denoted by $\bar{c}$. Now Table A3-1 shows the spending induced by the two policy changes. The first column shows the changes in spending resulting from the change in government purchases and its later

TABLE A3-1 THE BALANCED BUDGET MULTIPLIER

| Spending round | Change in spending resulting from | | | |
	$\Delta \bar{G} = 1$	$\Delta T = 1$	Net this round	Total
1	1	$-\bar{c}$	$1 - \bar{c}$	$1 - \bar{c}$
2	$\bar{c}$	$-\bar{c}^2$	$\bar{c} - \bar{c}^2$	$1 - \bar{c}^2$
3	$\bar{c}^2$	$-\bar{c}^3$	$\bar{c}^2 - \bar{c}^3$	$1 - \bar{c}^3$
4	$\bar{c}^3$	$-\bar{c}^4$	$\bar{c}^3 - \bar{c}^4$	$1 - \bar{c}^4$
$\vdots$				
n	$\bar{c}^{2n-1}$	$-\bar{c}^n$	$\bar{c}^{n-1} - \bar{c}^n$	$1 - \bar{c}^n$

repercussions. The second column similarly gives the spending effects in successive rounds of the tax increase. The third column sums the two effects for each
spending round, while the final column adds all the changes in spending induced
so far. Since $\bar{c}$ is less than 1, $\bar{c}^n$ becomes very small as the number of spending
rounds, n, increases, and the final change in aggregate spending caused by the
balanced budget increase in governmental spending is just equal to $1.

Finally, the balanced budget multiplier can also be thought of from a
somewhat different perspective. Consider the goods market equilibrium condition
in terms of saving, taxes, investment, transfers, and government purchases

$$S + T - R = \bar{I} + G \tag{A4}$$

Now, using the definition of the budget surplus, $BuS \equiv T - R - G$,

$$BuS = \bar{I} - S \tag{A5}$$

If there is no change in the budget deficit, nor a change in investment, then the
equilibrium change in saving is zero. For saving not to change, disposable income
must remain unchanged. This says that $\Delta Y_d = \Delta Y - \Delta T = 0$, and hence shows once
more that the change in income equals the change in taxes. This in turn equals the
change in government purchases. Hence, the balanced budgt multiplier, or more
precisely the multiplier associated with an unchanging budget surplus or deficit, is
equal to unity. This perspective on the income determination process is very useful
because it emphasizes the fact that a change in the surplus or deficit of one sector
is matched by a corresponding change in the deficit or surplus of the remaining
sectors. If the government surplus is constrained by fiscal policy to be unchanged,
so too must be the private sector's surplus, $S - \bar{I}$.

PROBLEMS

1 Here we investigate a particular example of the model studied in Sections 3-2 and 3-3 with no government. Suppose the consumption function is given by $C = 100 + 0.8Y$ while investment is given by $\bar{I} = 50$.
   (a) What is the equilibrium level of income in this case?
   (b) What is the level of saving in equilibrium?
   (c) If for some reason output was at the level of 800, what would the level of involuntary inventory accumulation be?
   (d) If $\bar{I}$ were to rise to 100 (we will discuss what determines $\bar{I}$ in later chapters), what would be the effect on equilibrium income?
   (e) What is the multiplier, α, here?
   (f) Draw a diagram indicating the equilibria in both 1(a) and 1(d).

2 Suppose consumption behaviour were to change in problem 1 so that $C = 100 + 0.9Y$ while $\bar{I}$ remained at 50.
   (a) Would you expect the equilibrium level of income to be higher or lower than in 1(a)? Calculate the new Y_0' to verify this.
   (b) Now suppose investment increases to $\bar{I} = 100$ just as in 1(d). What is the new equilibrium income?
   (c) Does this change in investment spending have more or less of an effect on Y_0 than in problem 1? Why?
   (d) Draw a diagram indicating the change in equilibrium income in this case.

3 We showed in the text that the equilibrium condition $Y = A$ is equivalent to the $S = \bar{I}$, or saving = investment, condition. Starting from $S = \bar{I}$ and the saving function, derive the equilibrium level of income.

4 This problem relates to the so-called *paradox of thrift*. Suppose $I = \bar{I}$ is fixed, and that $C = \bar{C} + cY$.
   (a) What is the savings function, that is, the function that shows how savings is related to income?
   (b) Suppose individuals want to save more at every level of income. Show, using a figure like Figure 3-5, how the savings function is shifted.
   (c) What effect does the increased desire to save have on the new equilibrium level of savings? Explain the paradox.

5 Now let us look at a model which is an example of the one presented in Sections 3-4 and 3-5; that is, it includes government purchases, taxes, and transfers. It has the same features as the one in problems 1 and 2, except that it also has a government. Thus, suppose consumption is given by $C = 100 + 0.8Y_d$ and $\bar{I} = 50$, while fiscal policy is summarized by $\bar{G} = 200$, $\bar{R} = 64.5$, $t = 0.25$.
   (a) What is the equilibrium level of income in this more complete model?
   (b) What is the new multiplier $\bar{\alpha}$? Why is this less than the multiplier in problem 1e?

6 Using the same model as in problem 5 above:
   (a) What is the value of the budget surplus BuS when $\bar{I} = 50$?
   (b) What is BuS when $\bar{I}$ increases to 100?
   (c) What accounts for the change in BuS from 5a to 5b?
   (d) Assuming that the full-employment level of income Y_n is 1,200, what is the full-employment budget surplus BuS* when $\bar{I} = 50$? 100? (Be careful.)
   (e) What is BuS* if $\bar{I} = 50$ and $\bar{G} = 250$, with Y_n still equal to 1,200?

(f) Explain why we use BuS* rather than simply BuS to measure the direction of fiscal policy.

7 Suppose we expand our model to take account of the fact that transfer payments R do depend on the level of income Y. When income is high, transfer payments like unemployment benefits will fall. Conversely, when income is low, unemployment is high and so are unemployment benefits. We can incorporate this into our model by writing transfers as $R = \bar{R} - bY$, $b > 0$. Remembering that our equilibrium income is derived as the solution to $Y_0 = C + \bar{I} + \bar{G} = \bar{C} + cY_d + \bar{I} + \bar{G}$, where $Y_d = Y + R - T$ is disposable income.

(a) Derive the expression for Y_0 in this case, just as Equation (22) was derived in the text.

(b) What is the new multiplier now?

(c) Why is the new multiplier less than the standard one, $\bar{\alpha}$?

8 Now we look at the role taxes play in determining the equilibrium income. Suppose we have an economy of the type in Sections 3-4 and 3-5 described by the following functions:

$$C = 50 + 0.8Y_d$$
$$\bar{I} = 70$$
$$\bar{G} = 200$$
$$\bar{R} = 100$$
$$t = 0.20$$

(a) Calculate the equilibrium level of income and the multiplier in this model.

(b) Calculate also the budget surplus, BuS.

(c) Suppose now t is increased to 0.25. What is the new equilibrium income? The new multiplier?

(d) Calculate the change in the budget surplus. Would you expect the change in the surplus to be more or less if $c = 0.9$ rather than 0.8?

(e) Can you explain why the multiplier is 1 when $t = 1$?

9 Suppose the economy is operating at equilibrium with $Y_0 = 1,000$. If the government undertakes a fiscal change so that the tax rate t increases by 0.05 and government spending by 50, will the budget surplus go up or down? Why?

10 Suppose the government decides to reduce transfer payments (such as welfare), but to increase government purchases of goods and services by an equal amount. That is, it undertakes a change in fiscal policy such that $\Delta \bar{G} = -\Delta \bar{R} > 0$.

(a) Would you expect equilibrium income to rise or fall as a result of this change? Why? Check out your answer with the following example: Suppose initially $c = 0.8$, $t = 0.25$, and $Y_0 = 600$. Now let $\Delta \bar{G} = 10$, $\Delta \bar{R} = -10$.

(b) Find the change in equilibrium income, ΔY_0.

(c) What is the change in the budget surplus, ΔBuS? Why has BuS changed?

*11 We have seen in problem 10 that an increase in G accompanied by an equal decrease in R does not leave the budget unchanged. What would the effect on equilibrium income be if R and G change to leave the budget surplus BuS fixed?

Notice that BuS $= T - R - G$. We want ΔBuS $= \Delta t - \Delta R - \Delta G = 0(*)$ so $\Delta R = \Delta T - \Delta G$. Since t is constant, $\Delta T = t\Delta Y_0(**)$. We also know that $Y_0 = \bar{\alpha}(C +$

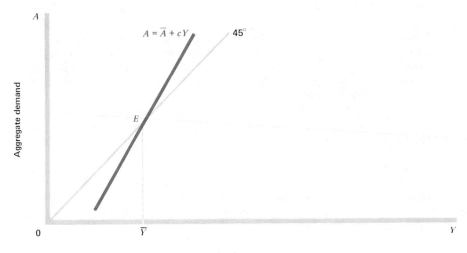

FIGURE 3A

$\bar{I} + \bar{G} + c\bar{R})$ and $\Delta Y_0 = \bar{\alpha}(\Delta\bar{G} + c\Delta\bar{R})$.

Substituting (*) and (**) into this last equation, derive an expression for ΔY in terms of ΔG. Simplify that expression, using the fact that $\bar{\alpha} = \{1/[1 - c(1 - t)]\}$, to obtain the balanced budget result in the case of changes in transfers and government spending.

*12 In the preceding appendix we derived the balanced budget multiplier result. It states that if $\Delta G = \Delta T$ from the initial to final equilibrium, then $\Delta Y = \Delta G$. Let us look at an example of this balanced budget multiplier in action. Consider the economy described by the following functions:

$$\begin{aligned} C &= 85 + 0.75Y_d \\ \bar{I} &= 50 \\ \bar{G} &= 150 \\ \bar{R} &= 100 \\ t &= 0.20 \end{aligned}$$

(a) Derive the multiplier $\bar{\alpha}$ and the level of autonomous spending $\bar{A}$.

(b) From 12(a) calculate the equilibrium level of income and the budget surplus.

(c) Now suppose G rises to 250 while t increases to 0.28. Repeat step 12(a) for the new fiscal policy.

(d) Calculate Y_0' and BuS', the new income and budget surplus.

(e) What are ΔT, ΔG, ΔY, ΔBuS?

(f) In view of this result and that of problem 10, what do you think the effect on income would be if we had a balanced budget change where $\Delta R = \Delta T$?

*13 Suppose the aggregate demand function is as drawn in Figure 3A. Notice that at Y_0 the slope of the aggregate demand curve is *greater* than 1. (This would happen if $c > 1$.) Complete this picture as is done in Figure 3-3 to include the arrows indicating adjustment when $Y \neq Y_0$ and show what I_u is for $Y < Y_0$ and $Y > Y_0$. What is happening in this example, and how does it differ fundamentally from Figure 3-3?

14 Let us look at the effect of the foreign sector by adding the following equations to the model in problem 8:

$$\overline{X} = 150$$
$$Q = 10 + .14Y$$

(a) Calculate the equilibrium level of income and the multiplier in this model.

(b) Why is the multiplier less than the one obtained in problem 8?

*(c) Derive an expression for the trade balance, NX, as a function of income and plot it in a diagram with Y on the horizontal axis.

*(d) Show the effect of a change in income on the trade balance, using your diagram. Show also the effect on the trade balance of a change in exports, given income.

*(e) Calculate the effect on equilibrium income and the trade balance of an increase in exports.

4

MONEY, INTEREST, AND INCOME

The stock of money, interest rates, and the Bank of Canada seemingly had no place in the model of income determination developed in Chapter 3. Clearly, though, we know that money has an important role to play in the determination of income and employment. Interest rates are frequently mentioned as an important determinant of aggregate spending and the Bank of Canada and monetary policy receive at least as much public attention as fiscal policy. This chapter introduces money and monetary policy, and builds an explicit framework of analysis in which the interaction of goods and assets markets can be studied.

The model we will study here, called the IS-LM model, is the core of modern macroeconomics. It maintains the spirit and, indeed, many details of the previous chapter. In particular, it remains true that aggregate demand determines the equilibrium level of output.

The model is broadened, though, by introducing the interest rate as an additional determinant of aggregate demand. In Chapter 3, autonomous spending and fiscal policy were the chief determinants of aggregate spending. Now we add the interest rate and argue that a reduction in the rate of interest raises aggregate demand. This seems a minor extension, which can readily be handled in the context of Chapter 3. This is not entirely correct, because we have to ask what determines the rate of interest. That question extends our model to include the markets for financial assets and forces us to study the interaction of goods and assets markets. Interest rates and income are jointly determined by equilibrium in goods and assets markets.

What is the payoff for that complication? The introduction of assets markets and interest rates serves three important purposes. First, we need the extension to understand how monetary policy works. Second, the analysis qualifies the conclusions of Chapter 3. To appreciate the latter point, consider Figure 4-1, which lays out the logical structure of the model. In Chapter 3, we looked at the submodel of autonomous spending and fiscal policy as determinants of aggregate demand and equilibrium income. Here the inclusion of assets markets — money demand and supply, as we shall see — introduces an additional channel. Thus, an expansionary fiscal policy, for

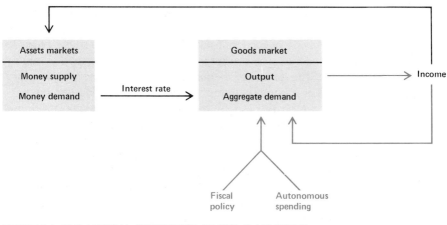

FIGURE 4-1 THE LOGICAL STRUCTURE OF THE IS-LM MODEL

example, would in the first place raise spending and income. That increase in income, though, would affect the assets markets by raising money demand and thereby raising interest rates. The higher interest rates in turn reduce aggregate spending and thus, as we will show, dampen the expansionary impact of fiscal policy. Indeed, under certain conditions, the increase in interest rates may be sufficiently important to *fully* offset the expansionary effects of fiscal policy. Clearly, such an extreme possibility is an important qualification to our study of fiscal policy in Chapter 3.

Third, even if the interest rate changes just mentioned only dampen (rather than fully offset) the expansionary effects of fiscal policy, they nevertheless have an important side effect. The composition of aggregate demand between investment and consumption spending will depend on the rate of interest. Higher interest rates dampen aggregate demand mainly by reducing investment. Thus, an expansionary fiscal policy would tend to raise consumption through the multiplier, but it would tend to reduce investment through the induced increase in interest rates. The side effects of fiscal expansion on interest rates and investment continue to be a sensitive and important issue in policy making. An influential view is that fiscal expansion should not be used as a tool for demand management because the increase in government spending takes place at the expense of private investment. Government spending crowds out, or displaces, private investment because it tends to raise interest rates.

These three reasons justify the more complicated model we study in this chapter. There is the further advantage that the extended model helps us to understand the functioning of financial markets.

We can use Figure 4-1 once more to lay out the structure of this chapter. We start in Section 4-1 with a discussion of the link between interest rates and aggregate demand. Here we use the model of Chapter 3 directly, augmented to include an interest rate as a determinant of aggregate demand. We will derive a key relationship — the IS curve — that shows combinations of interest rates and levels of income for which the goods markets clear. In Section 4-2, we turn to assets markets and, in particular, to the money market. We show that the demand for money depends on interest rates and income and that there is a combination of interest rates and income levels — the LM curve — for which the money market clears.[1] In Section 4-3, we combine the two schedules to study the joint determination of interest rates and income, as a brief glance ahead at Figure 4-10 will show. Section 4-4 lays out the adjustment process toward equilibrium. Monetary and fiscal policy are discussed in Sections 4-5 and 4-6. The political economy of monetary and fiscal policy is taken up in Section 4-7. We conclude the chapter with a formal statement of the model. An appendix discusses the relationship between interest rates, asset prices, and asset yields.

4-1 THE GOODS MARKET AND THE IS CURVE

In this section, we will derive a "goods market equilibrium schedule" — a combination of interest rates and levels of income such that the goods market is in equilibrium. That is the IS schedule, which is shown in Figure 4-2b. To derive the IS schedule, we start with the analysis of goods market equilibrium of Chapter 3, and modify it to take account of the relationship between investment spending and the interest rate.

In Chapter 3, we relied on an aggregate demand function of the form:

$$A = \bar{A} + \bar{c}Y \tag{1}$$

where $\bar{A}$ denotes autonomous spending and is equal to

$$\bar{A} \equiv \bar{C} + \bar{I} + \bar{G} + \bar{c}\bar{R} \tag{2}$$

and where we have introduced the shorthand notation $\bar{c} \equiv c(1 - t)$ to denote the marginal propensity to spend out of income.

Equilibrium in the goods market requires that output equals aggregate demand:

$$Y = A \tag{3}$$

and leads, by substitutions from Equation (1), to the equation

---

[1] The term IS and LM are shorthand representations respectively, of investment equals saving (goods market equilibrium) and money demand (L) equals money supply (M), or money market equilibrium. The classic article that introduced this model is J.R. Hicks, "Mr. Keynes and the Classics: A Suggested Interpretation," *Econometrica, 1937*, pp. 147-159. The article remains worth reading.

$$Y = \bar{A} + \bar{c}Y \tag{3a}$$

This can be solved for the equilibrium level of income:[2]

$$Y_0 = \frac{\bar{A}}{1 - \bar{c}} = \bar{\alpha}\bar{A} \tag{3b}$$

In Equation (3b) we have used the shorthand notation for the multiplier with taxes, $\bar{\alpha} \equiv 1/(1 - \bar{c})$.

The level of planned investment $\bar{I}$ in Equation (2) was treated as constant in Chapter 3. However, planned investment spending is influenced by the rate of interest, being inversely related to it. We explore the determinants of investment spending in depth in Chapter 6, but a simple argument will show why planned investment spending is negatively related to the interest rate. Investment is spending on additions to the capital stock. Such investment is undertaken with an eye to the profits that can be obtained in the future by operating machines and factories. Now, suppose firms borrow to buy the capital, in the form of machines and factories, that they use. Then the higher the interest rate, the more firms have to pay out in interest each year from the earnings they receive from their investment. Thus, the higher the interest rate, the less the profits to the firm after paying interest, and the less it will want to invest. Conversely, a low rate of interest makes investment spending profitable and is, therefore, reflected in a high level of planned investment.

Accordingly, we modify the assumption that investment spending is constant by specifying an investment spending function of the form:[3]

$$I = \bar{I} - bi \qquad b > 0 \tag{4}$$

where i is the rate of interest and b measures the interest response of investment. $\bar{I}$ now denotes autonomous investment spending, that is, investment spending that is independent of both income *and* the rate of

---

[2] To move from Eq. (3a) to Eq. (3b), we collect terms in Y to obtain $Y(1 - \bar{c}) = \bar{A}$. Then we divide both sides by $(1 - \bar{c})$ to yield Eq. 3b).

[3] Here and in other places in the book, we specify linear (straight-line) versions of behavioural functions. We use the linear specifications to simplify both the algebra and the diagrams. The linearity assumption does not lead to any great difficulties so long as we confine ourselves to talking about small changes in the economy. You should often draw nonlinear versions of our diagrams to be sure you can work with them. This would be particularly useful where, as in Figure 4-2, the position and shape of one curve (in this case, the IS curve) depend on the position and shape of another curve (the aggregate demand schedules in the upper panel, in this case).

interest.[4] Equation (4) states that the lower the interest rate, the higher is planned investment with the coefficient b measuring the responsiveness of investment spending to the interest rate.

We now modify the aggregate demand function Equation (1) to reflect the new planned investment spending schedule Equation (4). Aggregate demand still consists of the demand for consumption goods, investment, and government spending on goods and services. Only now investment spending depends on the interest rate. We have

$$\begin{aligned} A &\equiv C + I + G \\ &= \bar{C} + c\bar{R} + c(1 - t)Y + \bar{I} - bi + \bar{G} \\ &= \bar{A} + \bar{c}Y - bi \end{aligned} \tag{1a}$$

where

$$\bar{A} \equiv \bar{C} + c\bar{R} + \bar{I} + \bar{G} \tag{2a}$$

From Equation (1a) it is clear that an increase in the interest rate reduces aggregate demand at a given level of income because an interest rate increase reduces investment spending. Note that the term $\bar{A}$, which is the part of aggregate demand unaffected by either the level of income or the interest rate, does include part of investment spending, namely, $\bar{I}$. As noted earlier, $\bar{I}$ is the *autonomous* component of investment spending, which is independent of the interest rate (and income).

At any given level of the interest rate, we can still proceed as in Chapter 3 to determine the equilibrium level of income and output. As the interest rate changes, the equilibrium level of income changes. The relationship we shall now derive between the interest rate and the equilibrium level of income in the goods market is the *IS curve*.

Figure 4-2 is used to derive the IS curve. For a given level of the interest rate, say i_1, the last term of Equation (1a) is a constant (bi_1), and we can in Figure 4-2a draw the aggregate demand function of Chapter 3, this time with an intercept $\bar{A} - bi_1$. The equilibrium level of income obtained in the usual manner is Y_1 at point E_1. Since that equilibrium level of income was derived for a given level of the interest rate i_1, we can plot that pair (namely, i_1, Y_1) in the bottom panel as point E_1. We now have one point, E_1, on the IS curve.

Consider next a lower interest rate, i_2. At a lower interest rate, aggregate demand would be higher at each level of income because investment spending is higher. In terms of Figure 4-2a, that implies an upward shift of the aggregate demand schedule. The entire aggregate demand schedule

---

[4] In Chapter 3, investment spending was defined as autonomous with respect to income. Now that the interest rate appears in the model, we have to extend the definition of autonomous to mean independent of both the interest rate and income. To conserve notation, we continue to use $\bar{I}$ to denote autonomous investment, but recognize that the definition is broadened.

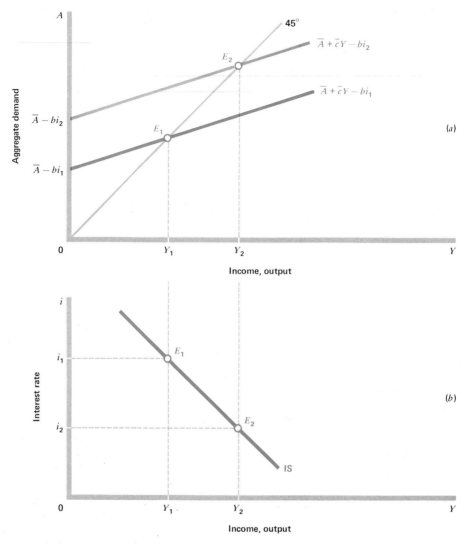

FIGURE 4-2 DERIVATION OF THE IS CURVE

shifts upward by $-b\Delta i$, where Δi, the assumed change in the interest rate, is negative. The curve shifts upward because the intercept $\bar{A} - bi$ has been increased. Given the increase in aggregate demand, we note that the equilibrium level of income rises to point E_2, with an associated income level Y_2. At point E_2, in the bottom panel, we record the fact that an interest rate i_2 implies an equilibrium level of income, Y_2 — equilibrium in the sense that the goods market is in equilibrium (or that the goods market *clears*). Point E_2 is another point on the IS curve.

We can apply the same procedure to all conceivable levels of the interest rate and thereby generate all the points which make up the IS curve. They have in common the property that they constitute combinations of interest rates and income (output) such that the goods market clears. We therefore refer to the IS curve as the *goods market equilibrium schedule*.

Figure 4-2 shows that the IS curve is negatively sloped, reflecting the increase in aggregate demand associated with a reduction in the interest rate. We can alternatively derive the IS curve by using the goods market equilibrium condition:

$$Y = A \tag{5}$$

Substituting from Equation (1a) for aggregate demand in Equation (5), we obtain

$$Y = \bar{A} + \bar{c}Y - bi \tag{6}$$

which can be simplified to

$$Y = \bar{\alpha}(\bar{A} - bi) \qquad \bar{\alpha} \equiv \frac{1}{1 - \bar{c}} \tag{6a}$$

From Equation (6a), we note that a higher interest rate implies a lower level of equilibrium income for a given $\bar{A}$, as Figure 4-2 shows. (Recall that $\bar{\alpha}$ is the multiplier of Chapter 3.)

The construction of the IS curve is quite straightforward and may even be deceptively simple. We can gain further understanding of the economics of the IS curve by asking and answering the following questions:

- What determines the slope of the IS curve?
- What determines the position of the IS curve, given its slope, and what causes the curve to shift?
- What happens when the interest rate and income are at levels such that we are not on the IS curve?

The Slope of the IS Curve

We have already noted that the IS curve is negatively sloped because a higher level of the interest rate reduces investment spending, therefore reduces aggregate demand, and therefore reduces the equilibrium level of income. The steepness of the curve depends on how sensitive investment spending is to changes in the interest rate, and also on the multiplier $\bar{\alpha}$ in Equation (6a).

Suppose that investment spending is very sensitive to the interest rate, so that b in Equation (6a) is large. Then, in terms of Figure 4-2, a given change in the interest rate produces a large change in aggregate demand, and thus shifts the aggregate demand curve in Figure 4-2a up by a large distance. A large shift in the aggregate demand schedule produces a correspondingly large change in the equilibrium level of income. If a given change in the interest rate produces a large change in income, the IS curve is very flat. Thus the IS curve is flat if investment is very sensitive to the interest rate, that is, if b is large. Correspondingly, with b small and investment spending not very sensitive to the interest rate, the IS curve is relatively steep.

Consider next the effects of the multiplier $\bar{\alpha}$ on the steepness of the IS curve. Figure 4-3 shows aggregate demand curves corresponding to different multipliers. The coefficient $\bar{c}$ on the darker aggregate demand curves is smaller than the corresponding coefficient $\bar{c}'$ on the lighter aggregate demand curves. The multiplier is accordingly larger on the lighter aggregate demand curves. The initial levels of income, Y_1 and Y'_1, correspond to the interest rate i_1 on the lower of each of the darker and lighter aggregate demand curves, respectively. A given reduction on the interest rate, to i_2, raises the intercept of the aggregate demand curves by the same vertical distance, as shown in the top panel. However, the implied change in income is very different. For the lighter curve, income rises to Y'_2, while it rises only to Y_2 on the darker line. The change in equilibrium income corresponding to a given change in the interest rate is accordingly larger as the aggregate demand curve is steeper; that is, the larger the multiplier, the greater rise in income. That should not be surprising since effectively the change in the interest rate and induced change in investment acts in the same way on the aggregate demand curves as a change in autonomous spending $\bar{A}$. As we see from Figure 4-3b, the smaller the multiplier, the steeper the IS curve. Equivalently, the larger the multiplier, the larger the change in income produced by a given change in the interest rate.

We have thus seen that the smaller the sensitivity of investment spending to the interest rate and the smaller the multiplier, the steeper the IS curve. This conclusion can be confirmed by using Equation (6a). We can turn Equation (6a) around to express the interest rate as a function of the level of income:

$$i = \frac{\bar{A}}{b} - \frac{1}{\bar{\alpha} b} \qquad (6b)$$

Thus, for a given change in Y, the associated change in i will be larger in size as b is smaller and $\bar{\alpha}$ is smaller.

Given that the slope of the IS curve depends on the multiplier, fiscal policy can affect that slope. The multiplier $\bar{\alpha}$ is affected by the tax rate:

$$\bar{\alpha} = \frac{1}{1 - c(1 - t)} \qquad (7)$$

FIGURE 4-3 EFFECTS OF THE MULTIPLIER ON THE STEEPNESS OF THE IS CURVE

An increase in the tax rate reduces the multiplier. Accordingly, the higher the tax rate, the steeper the IS curve.

The Position of the IS Curve

We now want to answer the question of what determines the position of the IS curve, and what causes it to shift that position. Figure 4-4 shows two different IS curves, the lighter one of which lies to the right and above the

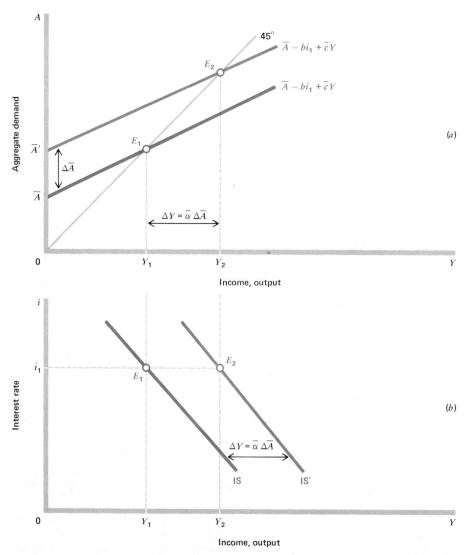

FIGURE 4-4 A SHIFT IN THE IS CURVE CAUSED BY A CHANGE IN AUTONOMOUS SPENDING

darker IS curve. What might cause the IS curve to be at IS′ rather than at IS in Figure 4-4? The answer is an increase in the level of autonomous spending.

In Figure 4-4a we show an initial aggregate demand curve drawn for a level of autonomous spending $\overline{A}$ and for an arbitrary interest rate i_1. Corresponding to the initial aggregate demand curve is the point E_1 on the IS curve in Figure 4-4b. Now, at the same interest rate, let the level of autonomous spending increase to $\bar{A}'$. The increase in autonomous spending increases the equilibrium level of income at the interest rate i_1. The point E_2 in Figure 4-4b is thus a point on the new goods market equilibrium schedule IS'. Since E_2 was an arbitrary point on the initial IS curve, we can perform the exercise for all levels of the interest rate and thereby generate our new curve IS'. We see that an increase in autonomous spending shifts the curve out to the right.

By how much does the curve shift? The change in income, as a result of the change in autonomous spending, can be seen from the top panel to be just the multiplier times the change in autonomous spending. That means that the IS curve is shifted horizontally by a distance equal to the multiplier times the change in autonomous spending, as can be seen from the fact that the distance between E_1 and E_2, in the lower panel, is the distance between Y_1 and Y_2 in the upper panel.

Now the level of autonomous spending is

$$\bar{A} \equiv \bar{C} + \bar{I} + \bar{G} + c\bar{R} \tag{2}$$

Accordingly, <u>an increase in government purchases or transfer payments will</u> <u>shift the IS curve out to the right, the extent of the shift depending on the</u> <u>size of the multiplier. A reduction in transfer payments or in government</u> <u>purchases shifts the IS curve to the left.</u>

Positions Off the IS Curve

We gain understanding of the meaning of the IS curve by considering points off the curve. Figure 4-5 reproduces Figure 4-2, along with two additional points — the *dis*equilibrium points E_3 and E_4. Consider first the question of what is true for points off the schedule, points such as E_3 and E_4. In Figure 4-5b, at point E_3 we have the same interest rate i_2 as at point E_2, but the level of income is lower than at E_2. Since the interest rate i_2 at E_3 is the same as at E_2 in Figure 4-5b, we must have the same aggregate demand function corresponding to the two points. Accordingly, looking now at Figure 4-5a, we find both points are on the same aggregate demand schedule. At E_2 on that schedule, aggregate demand exceeds the level of output. Point E_3 is therefore a point of *excess demand for goods*: the interest rate is too low or the output is too low for the goods market to be in equilibrium. Demand for goods exceeds output.

Consider next, point E_4 in Figure 4-5b. Here we have the same rate of interest i_1 as at E_1, but the level of income is higher. Given the interest rate i_1, the corresponding point in Figure 4-5a is at E_4 where we have an *excess supply of goods*, since output is larger than aggregate demand — that is, aggregate demand given the interest rate i_1 and the income level Y_2.

The preceding discussion can be generalized by saying that points above and to the right of the IS curve — points like E_4 — are points of excess supply

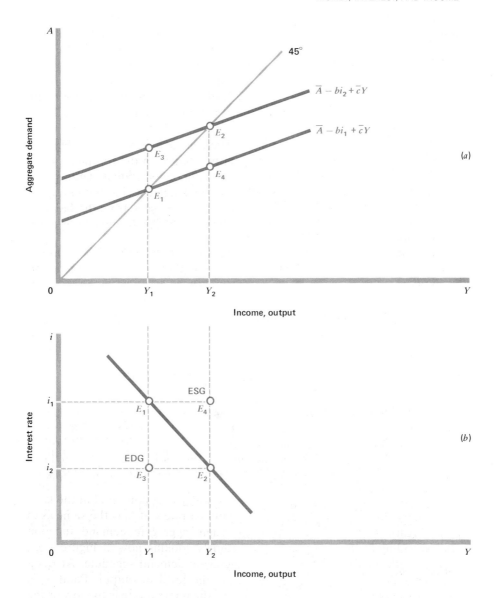

FIGURE 4-5 EXCESS SUPPLY (ESG) AND DEMAND (EDG) IN THE GOODS MARKET TO THE RIGHT AND LEFT, RESPECTIVELY, OF THE CURVE

of goods. This is indicated by ESG (excess supply of goods) in Figure 4-5b. Points below and to the left of the IS curve are points of excess demand for goods. At a point like E_3, the interest rate is too low and aggregate demand is therefore too high, relative to output. EDG (excess demand for goods) shows the region of excess demand in Figure 4-5.

Summary

The major points about the IS curve are:

1 The IS curve is the schedule of combinations of the interest rate and level of income such that the goods market is in equilibrium.
2 The IS curve is negatively sloped because an increase in the interest rate reduces planned investment spending and therefore reduces aggregate demand, thus reducing the equilibrium level of income.
3 The smaller the multiplier and the less sensitive investment spending is to changes in the interest rate, the steeper the curve.
4 The IS curve is shifted by changes in autonomous spending. An increase in autonomous spending, including an increase in government purchases, shifts the IS curve out to the right.
5 At points to the right of the curve, there is excess supply in the goods market, and at points to the left of the curve, there is excess demand for goods.

We turn now to examine behaviour in the assets markets.

4-2 THE ASSETS MARKETS AND THE LM CURVE

In the preceding section, we discussed aggregate demand and the goods market. In the present section, we turn to assets markets. The assets markets are the markets in which money, bonds, stocks, houses, and other forms of wealth are traded. Up to this point in the book, we have ignored the role of those markets in affecting the level of income, and it is now time to remedy the omission.

There is a large variety of assets, and a tremendous volume of trading occurs every day in the assets markets, but we shall simplify matters enormously by grouping all available financial assets into two groups, *money* and *interest-bearing assets*.[5] By analogy with our treatment of the goods market, where we proceeded as if there were a single commodity called output, we will proceed in the assets market as if there are only two assets, money and all others. It will be useful to think of the other assets as marketable claims to future income such as *bonds*.

---

[5] We shall be assuming in this section that certain assets, such as the capital that firms use in production, are not traded. That too is a simplification. A more complex treatment of the assets markets would allow for the trading of capital and would introduce a relative price for the capital operated by firms. This treatment is usually reserved for advanced graduate courses. For such a treatment of the assets market, see James Tobin, "A General Equilibrium Approach to Monetary Theory," *Journal of Money, Credit and Banking*, February 1969, pp. 15-29, and, by the same author, "Money, Capital and Other Stores of Value," *American Economic Review*, May 1961, pp. 26-37.

A bond is a promise to pay to its holder certain agreed-upon amounts of money at specified dates in the future. For example, a borrower sells a bond in exchange for a given amount of money today, say $100, and promises to pay a fixed amount, say $6, each year to the person who owns the bond, and to repay the full $100 (the principal) after some fixed period of time, such as three years, or perhaps longer. In this example, the interest rate is 6 percent, for that is the percentage of the amount borrowed that the borrower pays each year.

The Wealth Constraint

At any given time, an individual has to decide how to allocate his or her financial wealth between alternative assets. The more bonds held, the more interest is received on total financial wealth. The more money held the less likely the individual is not to have money available when he or she wants to make a purchase. The person who has $1,000 in financial wealth has to decide whether to hold, say, $900 in bonds and $100 in money, or rather, $500 in each type of asset, or even $1,000 in money and none in bonds. We refer to decisions on the form in which to hold assets as *portfolio decisions*.

The example makes it clear that the portfolio decisions on how much money to hold and the decision on how many bonds to hold are really the same decision. Given the level of financial wealth, the individual who has decided how many bonds to hold has implicitly also decided how much money to hold. There is thus a *wealth budget constraint* which implies that the sum of the individual's demands for money and bonds has to add up to that person's total financial wealth.

At this stage we have to reintroduce the crucial distinction between *real* and *nominal* variables. The nominal demand for money is the individual's demand for a given number of dollars, and similarly, the nominal demand for bonds is the demand for a given number of dollars' worth of bonds. By contrast, the real demand for money is the demand for money expressed in terms of the number of units of goods that money will buy: it is equal to the nominal demand for money divided by the price level. If the nominal demand for money is $100 and the price level is $2 per good — meaning that the representative basket of goods cost $2 — then the real demand for money is fifty goods. If the price level later doubles to $4 per good and the demand for nominal money likewise doubles to $200, the real demand for money is unchanged at fifty goods. Real money balances — real balances, for short — are the quantity of nominal money divided by the price level, and the real demand for money is often called *the demand for real balances*. Similarly, real bond holdings are the nominal quantity of bonds divided by the price level.

The wealth budget constraint in the assets market states that the demand for real balances, which we shall denote L, plus the demand for real bond holdings, which we denote V, must add up to the real financial wealth of the individual. Real financial wealth is, of course, simply nominal wealth W divided by the price level P:

$$L + V = \frac{W}{P} \tag{8}$$

Note, again, that the wealth budget constraint implies, given an individual's real wealth, that a decision to hold more real balances is also a decision to hold less real wealth in the form of bonds. This implication turns out to be both important and convenient. It will allow us to discuss assets markets entirely in terms of the money market. Why? Because, given real wealth, when the money market is in equilibrium, the bond market will turn out also to be in equilibrium. We shall now show why that should be.

The total amount of real financial wealth in the economy consists of real money balances and real bonds in existence. Thus, total real financial wealth is equal to

$$\frac{W}{P} \equiv \frac{M}{P} + V^s \tag{9}$$

where M is the stock of nominal money balances and V^s is the real value of the supply of bonds. Total real financial wealth consists of real balances and real bonds. The distinction between Equations (8) and (9) is that Equation (8) is a constraint on the amount of assets individuals *wish* to hold, whereas Equation (9) is merely an accounting relationship which tells us how much financial wealth there is in the economy. There is no implication in the accounting relationship in Equation (9) that individuals are necessarily happy to hold the amounts of money and bonds that actually exist in the economy.

Now we substitute Equation (8) into Equation (9) and rearrange terms to obtain

$$\left(L - \frac{M}{P}\right) + (V - V^s) = 0 \tag{10}$$

Let us see what Equation (10) implies. Suppose first that the demand for real balances L is equal to the existing stock of real balances M/P. Then, the first term in parantheses in Equation (10) is equal to zero, and therefore the second term in parantheses must also be zero. Thus, if the demand for real balances L is equal to the supply of real balances M/P, the demand for real bonds V must be equal to the supply of real bonds V^s.

Stating the same proposition in terms of "markets," we can say that the asset budget constraint implies that when the money market is in equilibrium so that $L = M/P$, so too is the bond market in equilibrium and therefore $V = V^s$. Similarly, when there is excess demand in the money market so that $L > M/P$, Equation (10) implies that there is an excess supply of bonds, $V < V^s$. We can therefore fully discuss the assets markets by concentrating our attention on the money market.

The Demand for Money

We can now proceed by concentrating on the money market, and initially on the demand for real balances.[6] The demand for money is a demand for *real* balances because the public holds money for what it will buy. The higher the price level, the more nominal balances a person has to hold to be able to purchase a given quantity of goods. If the price level doubles, then an individual has to hold twice as many nominal balances in order to be able to buy the same amount of goods.

The demand for real balances depends on the level of real income and the interest rate. It depends on the level of real income because individuals hold money to finance their expenditures, which, in turn, depend on income. This demand for money to finance regular spending on goods is known as the transactions demand for money. The demand for money depends also on the interest rate. The cost of holding money is the interest that is foregone by holding it rather than interest-bearing assets. The higher the interest rate, the more costly it is to hold money, rather than other assets, and accordingly, the less cash will be held at each level of income. Individuals can economize on their holdings of cash, when the interest rate rises, by being more careful in managing their money, by making transfers from money to bonds whenever their money holdings reach any appreciable magnitude. If the interest rate is 1 percent, then there is very little benefit from holding bonds rather than money. However, when the interest rate is 10 percent, one would probably go to some effort not to hold more money than needed to finance day-to-day transactions.

On these simple grounds, then, the demand for real balances increases with the level of real income and decreases with the interest rate.[7] The demand for real balances is accordingly written:[8]

$$L = kY - hi \qquad k>0 \qquad h > 0 \tag{11}$$

The parameters k and h reflect the sensitivity of the demand for real balances to the level of income and the interest rate, respectively. A \$5 increase in income raises money demand by $k \times \$5$. An increase in the

---

[6] The demand for money is studied in depth in Chapter 7; here we only briefly present the arguments underlying the demand for money.

[7] As we shall see in Chapter 7, there are other motives than transactions motives for holding money, and they too point to a negative relationship between the demand for money and the interest rate.

[8] Once again, we write the demand for real balances as a linear function of real income and the interest rate, though that cannot be true for all levels of the interest rate. The demand for real balances cannot be negative. The linear form of the demand function applies only over a limited range of values of income and the interest rate. You should experiment with a nonlinear form of the demand function in some of the diagrams below.

interest rate by one percentage point reduces real money demand by h dollars.

The demand function for real balances, Equation (11), implies that for a given level of income, the demand is a decreasing function of the rate of interest. Such a demand curve is shown in Figure 4-6 for a level of income Y_1. The higher the level of income, the larger the demand for real balances, and therefore the further to the right the demand curve. The demand curve for a higher level of real income Y_2 is also shown in Figure 4-6.

The Supply of Money, Money Market Equilibrium, and the LM Curve

Now that we have specified a demand function for money, we can study the equilibrium in the money market. For that purpose we have to say how the supply of money is determined. The nominal quantity of money M is controlled by the Bank of Canada, and we shall take it as given at the level $\bar{M}$. We are assuming the price level is constant at the level $\bar{P}$, so that the real money supply can be taken to be fixed at the level $\bar{M}/\bar{P}$.[9]

In Figure 4-7, we show combinations of interest rates and income levels such that the demand for real balances exactly matches the available supply.

[9] Since for the present we are holding constant the money supply and price level, we refer to them as exogenous and denote that fact by a bar.

FIGURE 4-6 THE DEMAND FOR REAL BALANCES AS A FUNCTION OF THE INTEREST RATE AND REAL INCOME

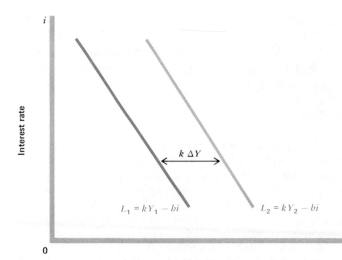

Demand for money

Starting with the level of income Y_1, we have the associated demand curve for real balances L_1, in Figure 4-7b. It is drawn, as in Figure 4-6, as a decreasing function of the interest rate. The existing supply of real balances $\bar{M}/\bar{P}$ is shown by the vertical line, since it is given and therefore independent of the interest rate. The interest rate i_1 has the property that it clears the money market. At that interest rate, the demand for real balances equals the supply. Therefore, point E_1 is an equilibrium point in the money market. That point is recorded in Figure 4-7a as a point on what we shall be calling the *money market equilibrium schedule*, or the *LM curve*.

Consider next the effect of an increase in income to Y_2. In Figure 4-7b, the higher level of income causes the demand for real balances to be higher at each level of the interest rate, so the demand curve for real balances shifts to the right to L_2. At the initial interest rate i_1, we now have an excess demand for money. Therefore, we require an increase in the interest rate to i_2 in order to maintain equilibrium in the money market at that higher level of income. Accordingly, our new equilibrium point is E_2. In Figure 4-7a, we record point E_2 as a point of equilibrium in the money market. Performing the same exercise for all income levels, we generate a series of points that can be linked up to give us the LM schedule, or the money market equilibrium schedule. Along the LM schedule, the demand for real balances is equal to the given real money supply.

Given the fixed supply of real balances, the LM curve is positively sloped. An increase in the interest rate reduces the demand for real balances. To maintain the demand for real balances equal to the fixed supply, the level of income has, therefore, to rise. Accordingly, money market equilibrium implies that an increase in the interest rate is accompanied by an increase in the level of income.

FIGURE 4-7 DERIVATION OF THE LM CURVE

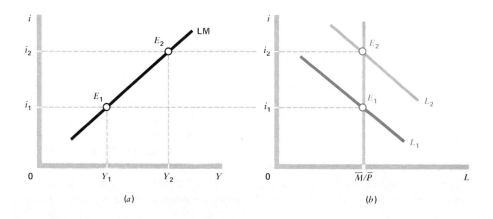

(a)

(b)

The LM curve can be obtained directly by combining the demand curve for real balances, Equation (11), and the fixed supply of real balances. For the money market to be in equilibrium, we require that demand equals supply, or that

$$\frac{\bar{M}}{\bar{P}} = kY - hi \tag{12}$$

Solving for the interest rate, we have

$$i = \frac{1}{h}\left(kY - \frac{\bar{M}}{\bar{P}}\right)$$

The relationship (12a) is the LM curve.

Next we ask the same questions about the properties of the LM schedule that we asked about the IS curve.

The Slope of the LM Curve

The larger the responsiveness of the demand for money to income, as measured by k, and the lower the responsiveness of the demand for money to the interest rate h, the steeper will be the LM curve. This point can be established by experimenting with Figure 4-7. It can also be confirmed by examining Equation (12a), where a given change in income ΔY has a larger effect on the interest rate i, the larger is k and the smaller is h. If the demand for money is relatively insensitive to the interest rate, so that h is close to zero, the LM curve is nearly vertical. If the demand for money is very sensitive to the interest rate, so that h is large, then the LM curve is close to horizontal. In that case, a small change in the interest rate is accompanied by a large change in the level of income to maintain money market equilibrium.

The Position of the LM Curve

The real money supply is held constant along the LM curve. It follows that a change in the real money supply will shift the LM curve. In Figure 4-8, we show the effect of an increase in the real money supply. In Figure 4-8b, we have drawn the demand for real money balances for a level of income Y_1. With the initial real money supply $\bar{M}/\bar{P}$, the equilibrium is at point E_1, with an interest rate i_1. The corresponding point on the LM schedule is E_1. Consider next the effect of an increase in the real money supply to $\bar{M}'/\bar{P}$, which is represented by a rightward shift of the money supply schedule. At the initial level of income and, hence, on the demand schedule L_1, we now have an excess of supply of real balances. To restore money market equilibrium at

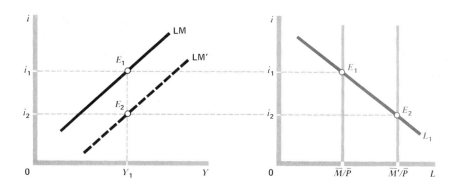

FIGURE 4-8 AN INCREASE IN THE SUPPLY OF MONEY FROM $\bar{M}$ TO $\bar{M}'$ SHIFTS THE LM CURVE TO THE RIGHT

the income level Y_1, the interest rate has to decline to i_2. The new equilibrium is, therefore, at point E_2. This implies that in Figure 4-8a, the LM schedule *shifts* to the right and down to LM'. At each level of income the equilibrium interest rate has to be lower to induce people to hold the larger real quantity of money. Alternatively at each level of the interest rate, the level of income has to be higher so as to raise the transactions demand for money and thereby absorb the higher real money supply. These points can be noted, too, from inspection of the money market equilibrium condition in Equation (12a).

Positions Off the LM Curve

Next we consider points off the LM schedule, to characterize them as points of excess demand or supply of money. For that purpose, we look at Figure 4-9, which reproduces Figure 4-7 but adds the disequilibrium points E_3 and E_4.

Consider first point E_1, where the money market is in equilibrium. Next assume an increase in the level of income to Y_2. This will raise the demand for real balances and shift the demand curve to L_2. At the initial interest rate, the demand for real balances would be indicated by point E_4 in Figure 4-9b, and we would have an excess demand for money — an excess of demand over supply — equal to the distance E_1E_4. Accordingly, point E_4, in Figure 4-9a, is a point of excess demand for money: the interest rate is too low and/or the level of income too high for the money market to clear. Consider next point E_3, in Figure 4-9b. Here we have the initial level of income Y_1, but an interest rate that is too high to yield money market equilibrium. Accordingly, we have an excess supply of money equal to the distance E_3E_2. Point E_3 in Figure 4-9a therefore corresponds to an excess supply of money.

More generally, any point to the right and below the LM schedule is a

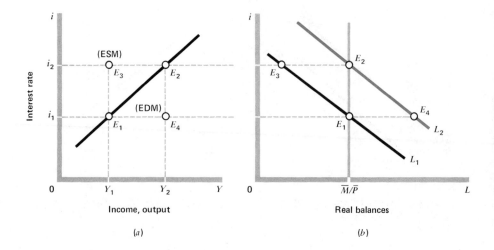

point of excess demand for money, and any point to the left and above the LM curve is a point of excess supply. That is shown by the EDM and ESM notations in Figure 4-9a.

Summary

The following are the major points about the LM curve.

1   The LM curve is the schedule of combinations of the interest rate and level of income such that the money market is in equilibrium.
2   When the money market is in equilibrium, so too is the bond market. The LM curve is, therefore, also the schedule of combinations of the level of income and the interest rate such that the bond market is in equilibrium.
3   The LM curve is positively sloped. Given the fixed money supply, an increase in the level of income, which increases the demand for money, has to be accompanied by an increase in the interest rate. This reduces the demand for money and thereby keeps the demand for money equal to the supply.
4   The LM curve is shifted by changes in the money supply. An increase in the money supply shifts the LM curve out to the right.
5   At points to the right of the LM curve, there is an excess demand for money, and at points to its left, there is an excess supply of money.

We are now ready to discuss the joint equilibrium of the goods and assets markets.

4-3 EQUILIBRIUM IN THE GOODS AND ASSETS MARKETS

We have so far studied the conditions that have to be satisfied for the goods and money markets, respectively, to be in equilibrium. These conditions are summarized by the IS and LM schedules. The task now is to determine how these markets are brought into *simultaneous* equilibrium. For simultaneous equilibrium, interest rates and income have to be such that *both* the goods market *and* the money market are in equilibrium. That condition is satisfied at point E in Figure 4-10. The equilibrium interest rate is therefore i_0, and the equilibrium level of income is Y_0, *given* the exogenous variables,[10] in particular, the real money supply and fiscal policy. At point E, *both* the goods market and the assets market are in equilibrium.

Now that we have moved rather quickly from the derivation of the IS and LM curves to the equilibrium of the economy that is implied by their intersection, it is worth stepping back to review our assumptions and the meaning of the equilibrium at E. The major assumption that we are making is that the price level is constant and that firms are willing to supply whatever amount of output is demanded at that price level. Thus, we assume the level of output Y_0, in Figure 4-10, will be willingly supplied by firms at the price level $\bar{P}$. We repeat again that this assumption is one that is

[10] Recall from Chapter 3 that exogenous variables are those whose values are not determined within the system being studied.

FIGURE 4-10 GOODS AND ASSETS MARKET EQUILIBRIUM

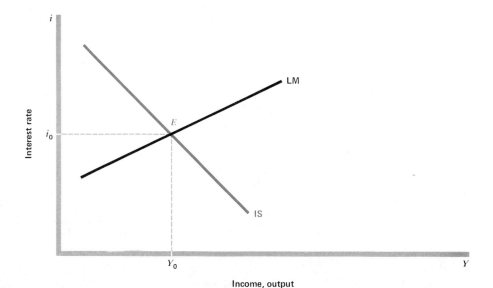

needed for the development of our analysis; it will be dropped in Chapter 11 when we begin to study the determinants of the price level.

At the point E, in Figure 4-10, the economy we are studying is in equilibrium, given the price level, because both the goods and money markets are in equilibrium. The demand for goods is equal to the level of output on the IS curve. And on the LM curve, the demand for money is equal to the supply of money. That also means the supply of bonds is equal to the demand for bonds, as our discussion of the wealth budget constraint showed. Accordingly, at point E, firms are producing the amount of output they plan to (there is no unintended inventory accumulation or decumulation), and individuals have the portfolio compositions they desire.

Changes in the Equilibrium Levels of Income and the Interest Rate

The equilibrium levels of income and the interest rate will change when either the IS or the LM curve shifts. Figure 4-11, for example, shows the effects on the equilibrium levels of income and the interest rate of an increase in autonomous consumption $\bar{C}$. Such an increase raises autonomous spending $\bar{A}$, and therefore shifts the IS curve out to the right. That results in a rise in the level of income and an increase in the interest rate.

We recall from Section 4-2 that a change in autonomous spending, equal

FIGURE 4-11 EFFECTS OF AN INCREASE IN AUTONOMOUS SPENDING ON INCOME AND THE INTEREST RATE

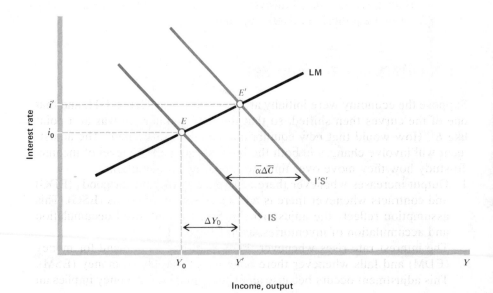

in this case to $\Delta\bar{C}$, shifts the IS curve to the right by the amount $\bar{\alpha}\Delta\bar{C}$, as we show in Figure 4-11. In Chapter 3, where we dealt only with the goods market, we would have argued that $\bar{\alpha}\Delta\bar{C}$ would be the change in the level of income resulting from the change of $\Delta\bar{C}$ in autonomous spending. But it can be seen in Figure 4-11 that the change in income here is only ΔY_0, which is clearly less than the shift in the IS curve $\bar{\alpha}\Delta\bar{C}$.

What explains the fact that the increase in income is smaller than the increase in autonomous spending, $\Delta\bar{C}$, times the simple multiplier, $\bar{\alpha}$? Diagrammatically, it is clear that it is the slope of the LM curve. If the LM curve were horizontal, there would be no difference between the extent of the horizontal shift of the IS curve and the change in income. If the LM curve were horizontal, then the interest rate would not change when the IS curve shifts. It will be recalled that we stated in Chapter 3 that we were assuming a fixed interest rate, so that the results of that chapter correspond to this case.

What is the economics of what is happening? The increase in autonomous spending does tend to increase the level of income. But an increase in income increases the transactions demand for money. With the supply of money fixed, the interest rate has to rise to ensure that the demand for money stays equal to the fixed supply. When the interest rate rises, investment spending is reduced because investment is negatively related to the interest rate. That means the total change in aggregate demand is less than $\bar{\alpha}\Delta\bar{C}$. Accordingly, the equilibrium change in income is less than the horizontal shift of the IS curve.

We have now provided an example of the uses of the IS-LM apparatus. That apparatus is most useful for studying the effects of monetary and fiscal policy on income and the interest rate, and we shall so use it in Sections 4-5 and 4-6. Before we do that, however, we want to ask how the economy moves from one equilibrium, like E, to another, like E'.

4-4 ADJUSTMENT TOWARD EQUILIBRIUM

Suppose the economy were initially at a point like E in Figure 4-11, and that one of the curves then shifted, so that the new equilibrium was at a point like E'. How would that new equilibrium actually be reached? The adjustment will involve changes in both the interest rate and the level of income. To study how they move over time, we make two assumptions:

1 Output increases whenever there is an excess demand for goods (EDG) and contracts whenever there is an excess supply of goods (ESG). This assumption reflects the adjustment of firms to undesired decumulation and accumulation of inventories, as in Chapter 3,

2 The interest rate rises whenever there is an excess demand for money (EDM) and falls whenever there is an excess supply of money (ESM). This adjustment occurs because an excess demand for money implies an

excess supply of other assets (bonds). In attempting to satisfy an excess demand for money, people sell off bonds and thereby cause their prices to fall or their yields (interest rates) to rise.

A detailed discussion of the relationship between the price of a bond and its yield is presented in the appendix to this chapter. Here we give only a brief explanation. For simplicity, consider a bond which promises to pay the holder of the bond $5 per year forever. The $5 is known as the bond *coupon*, and a bond which promises to pay a given amount to the holder of the bond forever is known as a *perpetuity*. If the yield available on other assets is 5 percent, the perpetuity will sell for $100 because at that price it too yields 5 percent (= $5/$100). Now suppose that the yield on other assets rises to 10 percent. Then the price of the perpetuity will drop to $50 because only at that price does the perpetuity yield 10 percent, that is, the $5 per year interest on a bond costing $50 gives its owners a 10 percent yield on their $50. This example makes it clear that the *price* of a bond and its *yield* are inversely related, given the coupon.

We discussed the way in which an excess demand for money causes asset holders to attempt to sell off their bonds, thereby causing their prices to fall and their yields to rise. Conversely, when there is an excess supply of money, people attempt to use their money to buy up other assets, raising their prices and lowering their yields.[11]

[11] We assume that the rate of adjustment in each market is proportional to the excess demand in that market.

FIGURE 4-12 DISEQUILIBRIUM AND DYNAMICS IN THE GOODS AND MONEY MARKETS

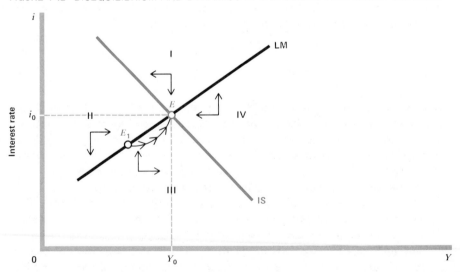

Income, output

In Figure 4-12 we use the analysis underlying Figures 4-5 and 4-9 to study the adjustment of the economy. Four regions are represented in Figure 4-12, and they are characterized in Table 4-1. We know from Figure 4-9 that there is an excess supply of money above the LM curve, and hence we show ESM in regions I and II in Table 4-1. Similarly, we know from Figure 4-5 that there is an excess demand for goods below the IS curve.

TABLE 4-1 DISEQUILIBRIUM REGIONS IN FIGURE 4-12

	Goods market	Money market
I	ESG($Y>A$)	ESM($L<M/P$)
II	EDG($Y<A$)	ESM($L<M/P$)
III	EDG($Y<A$)	EDM($L>M/P$)
IV	ESG($Y>A$)	EDM($L>M/P$)

Hence, we show EDG for regions II and III in Table 4-1. You should be able to fill in the remaining details of Table 4-1.

The adjustment directions specified in assumptions 1 and 2 above are represented by arrows. Thus, for example, in region IV we have an excess demand for money that causes interest rates to rise as other assets are sold off for money and their prices decline. The rising interest rates are represented by the upward-pointing arrow. There is, too, an excess supply of goods in region IV, and, accordingly, involuntary inventory accumulation to which firms respond by reducing output. Declining output is indicated by the leftward pointing arrow. The adjustments shown by the arrows will lead ultimately, perhaps in a cyclical manner, to the equilibrium point E. For example, starting at E_1 we show the economy moving to E, with income and the interest rate increasing along the *adjustment path* indicated.

For many purposes it is useful to restrict the dynamics by the reasonable assumption that the money market adjusts very fast and the goods market adjusts relatively slowly. Since the money market can adjust merely through the buying and selling of bonds, it is reasonable to think of the interest rate as adjusting rapidly and the money market effectively being always in equilibrium. Such an assumption will imply that we are always on the LM curve: any departure from the equilibrium in the money market is almost instantaneously eliminated by an appropriate change in the interest rate. In disequilibrium, we therefore move along the LM curve, as is shown in Figure 4-13. The goods market adjusts relatively slowly because firms have to change their production schedules, which takes time. For points below the IS curve, we move up along the LM schedule with rising income and interest rates, and for points above the IS schedule, we move down along the LM schedule with falling output and interest rates until point E is reached. The adjustment process is *stable* in that the economy does move to the equilibrium position at E.

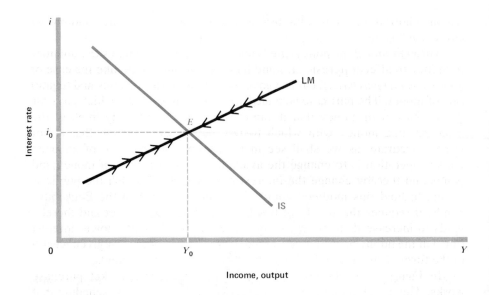

FIGURE 4-13 ADJUSTMENT TO EQUILIBRIUM WHEN THE MONEY MARKET ADJUSTS QUICKLY

The adjustment process shown in Figure 4-13 is very similar to that of Chapter 3. To the right of the IS curve, there is an excess supply of goods, and firms are therefore accumulating inventories. They cut production in response to their inventory buildup, and the economy moves down the LM curve. The difference between the adjustment process here and in Chapter 3 is that as the economy moves toward the equilibrium level of income here, with a falling interest rate, desired investment spending is actually rising as the interest rate falls.[12]

Now that we have established that the economy does adjust toward its equilibrium position, we turn to examine the effects of monetary and fiscal policy on equilibrium interest rate and level of income.

4-5 MONETARY POLICY

In this section we are concerned with the effect of an increase in the real quantity of money on the interest rate and level of income. We will break up that inquiry into two separate questions. First, what is the ultimate effect of the increase in the money supply when the new equilibrium is reached?

---

[12] In a more detailed analysis, one would want to allow for the possibility that desired investment would be cut back in response to excess inventories. This again raises the possibility of the *inventory cycle*, referred to in Chapter 3.

Second, how is the new equilibrium reached, or what is the *transmission mechanism*?

Through monetary policy, the Bank of Canada manipulates the quantity of money to affect interest rates and income. We shall here take the case of an *open market purchase*. That is a government purchase of bonds and (equal) sale of money. The purchase is made by the Bank of Canada, which pays for its purchase with money that it can create. One can usefully think of the Bank printing money with which to buy bonds, even though that is not strictly accurate, as we shall see in Chapter 8. The purpose of an open market operation is to change the available *relative* supplies of money and bonds and thereby change the interest rate or yield at which the public is willing to hold this modified composition of assets. When the Bank buys bonds, it reduces the supply of bonds available in the market and thereby tends to increase their price, or lower their yield. Only at a lower interest rate will the public be prepared to hold a larger fraction of their given wealth in the form of money, and a lower fraction in the form of bonds.

In Figure 4-14 we show graphically how the open market purchase works, The initial equilibrium at point E is on the initial LM schedule that corresponds to a real money supply, $\bar{M}/\bar{P}$. Consider next an open market operation that increases the nominal quantity of money, and given the price level, the real quantity of money. We showed in Section 4-2 that, as a

---

FIGURE 4-14 THE ADJUSTMENT PATH OF THE ECONOMY FOLLOWING AN INCREASE IN THE MONEY STOCK

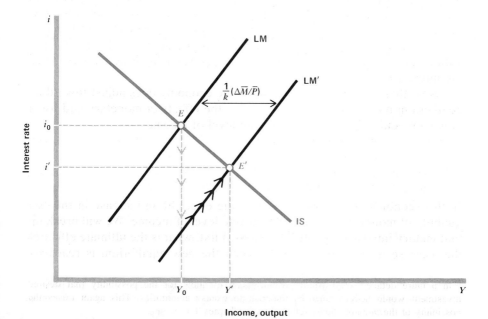

consequence, the LM schedule will shift to LM′. Therefore our new equilibrium will be at point E' with a lower interest rate and a higher level of income. The equilibrium level of income rises because the open market purchase reduces the interest rate and thereby increases investment.

As can be seen from Figure 4-14, the flatter the IS schedule, the larger will be the change in income. If money demand is very sensitive to the interest rate, then a given change in the money stock can be absorbed in the assets markets with only a small change in the interest rate. The effects of an open market purchase on investment spending would then be small. By contrast, if the demand for money is not very sensitive to the interest rate, a given change in the money supply will cause a large change in the interest rate and have a big effect on investment demand.[13] Similarly, if the demand for money is very sensitive to income, a given increase in the money stock can be absorbed with a relatively small change in income.

Consider next the adjustment process to the monetary expansion. At the initial equilibrium point E, the increase in the money supply creates an excess supply of money to which the public adjusts by attempting to reduce its money holdings by buying other assets. In the process, asset prices increase and yields decline. By our assumption that the assets markets adjust rapidly, we move immediately to point E_1, where the money market clears, and where the public is willing to hold the larger real quantity of money because the interest rate has declined sufficiently. (The lower the responsiveness of the demand for money to the interest rate, the larger the change in the interest rate that is required.) At point E_1, however, there is an excess demand for goods. The decline in the interest rate, given the initial income level Y_0, has raised aggregate demand and is causing inventories to run down. In response, output expands and we start moving up the LM schedule. Why does the interest rate rise in the adjustment process? Because the increase in output raises the demand for money and that increase has to be checked by higher interest rates.

The Transmission Mechanism

Two steps in the transmission mechanism — the process by which changes in monetary policy affect aggregate demand — are essential. The first is that an increase in real balances generates a *portfolio disequilibrium* — at the prevailing interest rate and level of income, people are holding more money than they want. This causes portfolio holders to attempt to reduce their money holdings by buying other assets, thereby changing asset yields. In other words, the change in the money supply changes interest rates. The

---

[13] In the problem set, we ask you to provide a similar explanation of the role of the slope of the IS curve – which is determined by the multiplier and the interest sensitivity of investment demand – in determining the effect of monetary policy on income.

second stage of the transmission process occurs when the change in interest rates affects aggregate demand.

These two stages of the transmission process are essential in that they appear in almost every analysis of the effects of changes in the money supply on the economy. The details of the analysis will often differ— some analyses will have more than two assets and more than one interest rate, some will include an influence of interest rates on categories of demand other than investment, and so on — but these two stages will be present.[14] For example, here is a description of the effect of an open market purchase by the Federal Reserve provided by Warren L. Smith:[15]

> The way in which monetary policy induces portfolio adjustments which will, in due course, affect income and employment may be described briefly as follows: A purchase of, say, Treasury bills by the Federal Reserve will directly lower the yield on bills and, by a process of arbitrage involving a chain of portfolio substitutions will exert downward pressure on interest rates on financial assets generally. . . .
>
> With the expected yield on a unit of real capital initially unchanged, the decline in the yields on financial assets, and the more favorable terms on which new debt can be issued, the balance sheets of households and businesses will be thrown out of equilibrium. The adjustment toward a new equilibrium will take the form of a sale of existing financial assets and the issuance of new debt to acquire real capital and claims thereto. . . . This stock adjustment approach is readily applicable, with some variations to suit the circumstances, to the demands for a wide variety of both business and consumer capital — including plant and equipment, inventories, residential construction, and consumer durable goods.

In studying the details of the transmission process, it is important to see how much influence money has at each stage. For instance, if the demand for money is very sensitive to changes in the interest rate, or if interest rate changes have only a small effect on aggregate demand,[16] then monetary policy tends to be relatively ineffective. Conversely, to obtain a large

[14] Some analyses also include a mechanism by which change in real balances have direct effect on aggregate demand through the *real balance effect*. Essentially, the argument is that wealth affects consumption demand (as we shall see in Chapter 5) and that an increase in real balances increases wealth and therefore consumption demand. This effect would not apply in the case of an open market purchase, which merely exchanges one asset for another (bonds for money) without changing wealth. The real balance effect is not very important empirically because the relevant real balances are only a small part of wealth.

[15] Warren L. Smith, "A Neo-Keynesian View of Monetary Policy," *Controlling Monetary Aggregates* (Boston: Federal Reserve Bank of Boston, 1969), pp. 105-117. The Federal Reserve is the American counterpart of the Bank of Canada.

[16] We refer to the responsiveness of aggregate demand — rather than investment demand — to the interest rate because consumption demand may also respond to the interest rate. Higher interet rates may lead to more saving and less consumption at a given level of income. Empirically, it has been difficult to isolate such an interest rate effect on consumption.

increase in income from a monetary increase, we require a low responsive-ness of money demand to the interest rate and a high responsiveness of aggregate demand to a change in the interest rate.

The Liquidity Trap

In discussing the effects of monetary policy on the economy, two extreme cases have received much attention. The first is the *liquidity trap*, a situation in which the public is prepared, at a given interest rate, to hold whatever amount of money is supplied. This implies that the LM curve is horizontal and that changes in the quantity of money do not shift it. In that case, monetary policy carried out through open market operations[17] has no effect on either the interest rate of level of income. In the liquidity trap, monetary policy is powerless to affect the interest rate.

There is a liquidity trap at a zero interest rate. At a zero interest rate, the public would not want to hold any bonds, since money, which also pays zero interest, has the advantage over bonds of being usable in transactions. Accordingly, if the interest rate ever, for some reason, got down to zero, increases in the quantity of money could not induce anyone to shift into bonds and thereby reduce the interest rate on bonds even below zero. An increase in the money supply in that case would have no effect on the interest rate and income, and the economy would be in a liquidity trap.

The belief that there was a liquidity trap at low positive (rather than zero) interest rates was quite prevalent during the forties and fifties. It was a notion associated with the Keynesian followers and developers of the theories of the great English economist John Maynard Keynes — although Keynes himself did state that he was not aware of there ever having been such a situation.[18] The importance of the liquidity trap stems from its presenting a circumstance under which monetary policy has no effect on the interest rate and thus on the level of real income. Belief in the trap, or at least the strong sensitivity of the demand for money to the interest rate, was the basis of the Keynesian belief that monetary policy has no effects on the economy. There is no strong evidence that there ever was a liquidity trap, and there certainly is not one now.

---

[17] We say "through open market operations" because an increase in the quantity of money carried out simply by giving the money away increases individuals' wealth and, through the real balances effect, has some effect on aggregate demand. An open market purchase, however, increases the quantity of money and reduces the quantity of bonds by the same amount, leaving wealth unchanged.

[18] J.M. Keynes, *The General Theory of Employment, Interest and Money* (New York: Macmillan, 1936), p. 207.

The Classical Case

The polar opposite of the horizontal LM curve — which implies that monetary policy cannot affect the level of income — is the vertical LM curve. The LM curve is vertical when the demand for money is unaffected by the interest rate. Under those circumstances, any shift in the LM curve has a maximal effect on the level of income. Check this by moving a vertical LM curve to the right and comparing the resultant change in income with the change produced by a similar horizontal shift of a nonvertical LM curve.

The vertical LM curve is called *classical*. It implies that the demand for money depends only on the level of income and not at all on the interest rate. This view was associated with the classical *quantity theory of money* which argues that the level of nominal income was determined solely by the quantity of money. We return to this view in Section 4-8. As we shall see, a vertical LM curve implies not only that monetary policy has a maximal effect on the level of income, but also that fiscal policy has no effect on income. The vertical LM curve, implying the comparative effectiveness of monetary policy over fiscal policy, is sometimes associated with the view that "only money matters" for the determination of output. Since the LM curve is vertical only when the demand for money does not depend on the interest rate, the interest sensitivity of the demand for money turns out to be an important issue in determining the effectiveness of alternative policies.

4-6 FISCAL POLICY

In this section we are concerned with the effects of fiscal policy on the economy. Specifically, we examine the effect of an increase in government spending, given the tax structure and the real quantity of money.

The effects of an increase in government spending can be determined from Figure 4-15. We start off at point E, where both markets clear. The increase in government spending creates an excess demand for goods at the initial point and therefore shifts the IS schedule to IS′. For goods market equilibrium we require at the initial interest rate a higher level of income, namely, the level indicated by point E_1, where the distance EE_1 is equal to the multiplier $\bar{\alpha}$ times the increase in government spending.

At the ultimate equilibrium position $E′$, we have a higher interest rate and a higher level of income than at E. Therefore, an increase in government spending is expansionary with respect to income. The expansion of income is, however, less than that indicated by the simple multiplier and point E_1. This is because the interest rate rises, reduces investment, and thereby somewhat offsets the multiplier effect on private aggregate demand. The higher interest rate is required in order to maintain monetary equilibrium at the higher level of income, as we discussed in Section 4-3.

The flatter the LM schedule, the larger is the increase in income that is generated by the increased government spending, as you can show by using

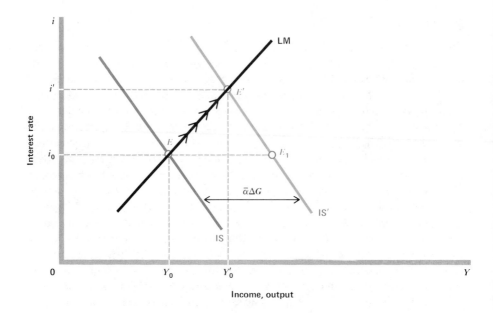

FIGURE 4-15 EFFECTS OF AN INCREASE IN GOVERNMENT SPENDING

the diagram. The increase in income is also larger, the bigger is the multiplier, $\bar{\alpha}$, as one would expect. Finally, the increase in income is smaller, the more responsive is aggregate demand to the interest rate — for the larger the response of aggregate demand to the induced increase in the interest rate, the more the initial expansionary multiplier effect is offset.

Consider next the adjustment process starting from the initial equilibrium at point E. We continue to assume that the money market clears fast and continuously, while output adjusts only slowly. This implies that as government spending increases, we stay initially at point E, since there is no disturbance in the money market. The excess demand for goods, however, causes output to be increased and that increase in output and income raises the demand for money. The resulting excess demand for money, in turn, causes interest rates to be bid up and we proceed up along the LM curve with rising output and rising interest rates until the new equilibrium at point E' is reached.

The fact that we do not have an increase in output to the full extent of the simple multiplier $\bar{\alpha}$ times the increase in government spending is entirely due to our now taking account of the assets markets. As income rises, the demand for money increases and people try to sell off other assets to acquire cash balances and, in doing so, cause asset prices to decline and interest rates to rise. This increase in interest rates, in turn, reduces investment spending and dampens the expansionary effect of increased government spending by reducing aggregate private demand relative to what it would have been at a constant interest rate.

The Liquidity Trap Again

In the analysis of fiscal policy, there has also been consideration of the two extreme cases we discussed in connection with monetary policy. If the economy is in the liquidity trap so that the LM curve is horizontal, then an increase in government spending has its full multiplier effect on the equilibrium level of income. There is no change in the interest rate associated with the change in government spending and thus no investment spending is cut off. There is therefore no dampening of the effects of the increased government spending on income.

You should draw your own IS-LM diagrams to confirm that if the LM curve is horizontal, monetary policy has no impact on the equilibrium of the economy and fiscal policy has a maximal effect on the economy. Less dramatically, if the demand for money is very sensitive to the interest rate, so that the LM curve is almost horizontal, fiscal policy changes have a relatively large effect on output, while monetary policy changes have little effect on the equilibrium level of output.

There is one other circumstance in which fiscal policy has its full multiplier effect on the level of income. So far, we have taken the money supply to be constant at the level $\bar{M}$. It is possible that the Bank of Canada might instead manipulate the money supply so as to keep the interest rate constant. In that case, we could talk of a money supply *function* which is very elastic with respect to the interest rate. More simply, the Bank increases the money supply whenever there are signs of an increase in the interest rate, and reduces the money supply whenever the interest rate seems about to fall. If the money supply function is very elastic with respect to the interest rate, the LM curve again becomes very flat and fiscal policy has large impacts on the level of output.

The Classical Case Again and Crowding Out

If the LM curve is vertical, then an increase in government spending has no effect on the equilibrium level of income. It only increases the interest rate. This case is shown in Figure 4-16, where an increase in government spending shifts the IS curve to IS' but has no effect on income. If the demand for money is not related to the interest rate, as a vertical LM curve implies, then there is a unique level of income at which the money market is in equilibrium, and fiscal policy cannot affect the level of income.

Given that an increase in government spending does not change the level of income when the LM curve is vertical, we know also that aggregate demand must be unchanged. Therefore, we have to ask what component of spending (investment or consumption) is reduced when government spending is increased but total aggregate demand remains unchanged. The answer

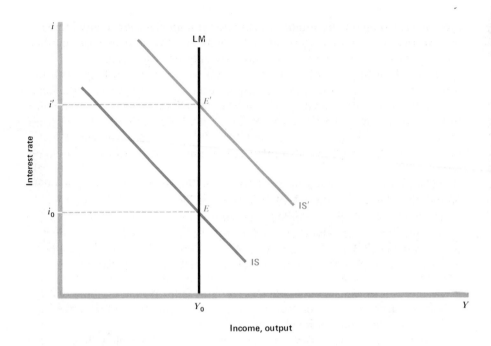

i

LM

i'

E'

Interest rate

i_0

E

IS'

IS

Y_0

Y

Income, output

FIGURE 4-16 THE VERTICAL LM CURVE AND CROWDING OUT

is that investment spending is reduced by an amount exactly equal to the increase in government spending. Consumption spending does not change because the level of income is unchanged and autonomous demand is unchanged. Thus we are assured that the increase in government spending is precisely offset by reduced investment spending. This phenomenon is known as *crowding out* — the government spending crowds out some other component of spending and has no effect on total spending. The crowding out argument is one which is frequently made in the press to suggest that government spending has no effects on output and employment.[19]

The view that government spending merely crowds out private spending is widely held by monetarist economists, such as Milton Friedman, who place primary emphasis on the role of the money stock in determining the level of income.[20] The monetarist emphasis on the stock of money is also implied by the LM curve being vertical, so that in the IS-LM context, monetarism is consistent with the view that the LM curve is vertical, or that the demand for money does not depend on the interest rate. However, there are other circumstances, such as a situation of full employment, in which

---

[19] Note again that, in principle, consumption spending could be reduced by increases in the interest rate, and then both investment and consumption would be crowded out.

[20] We discuss monetarism in Chapter 15.

there is crowding out. If output is at the full-employment level, any increase in government spending has to take place at the expense of another component of aggregate demand, and crowding out will occur.[21]

In brief, in the IS-LM context in which we are now working, with the price level given and the level of output responding to aggregate demand, monetarist views on crowding out and the major importance of money are fully consistent with the LM curve being vertical. Equivalently, they depend on the assumption that the demand for money does not depend on the interest rate. But there are also other conditions in which there is crowding out.

The extreme cases of a vertical LM curve or a flat LM curve represent boundaries that are useful for reference purposes. Beyond that, their use is quite limited, since any reasonable description for policy purposes will want to assume the intermediate case of an upward-sloping LM curve, so that both monetary and fiscal policy work. As we show in Chapter 7, the demand for real balances is definitely negatively related to the interest rate.

4-7 THE COMPOSITION OF OUTPUT

We have now seen that both monetary and fiscal policy can be used to expand aggregate demand and thus raise the equilibrium level of output. Since the liquidity trap and the classical case represent at best extremes useful for expositional purposes, it is apparent that policy makers can use either monetary or fiscal policy to affect the level of income.

In Figure 4-17 we address the policy problem of an economy that is in equilibrium at point E with an output level Y_0, below the full-employment level Y_p. What policy choices does that economy have? From the preceding analysis, it is obvious that we could use an expansionary monetary policy. By increasing the money supply, we could shift the LM curve down and to the right, lower interest rates, and raise aggregate demand until we reach E_2. Alternatively, we could use an expansionary fiscal policy to shift the IS curve up and to the right until we reach E_1. Finally, we can use a combination of monetary and fiscal policy. What package should we choose?

The choice of monetary and fiscal policy as tools of stabilization policy is an important and quite controversial topic. In Chapter 9 we will address some technical issues that deal with the flexibility and speed with which these policies can be implemented and can take effect. Here we do not

---

[21] Friedman has argued that his views do not depend on the demand for money not being a fucntion of the interest rate, making essentially the second argument above for crowding out. See Milton Friedman, "Interest Rates and the Demand for Money," in his *Optimum Quantity of Money* (Chicago: Aldine, 1969).

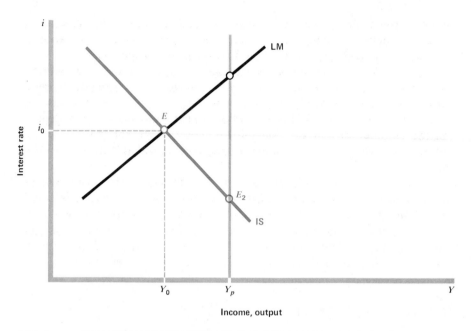

FIGURE 4-17 EXPANSIONARY POLICIES AND THE COMPOSITION OF OUTPUT

discuss speed and flexibility, but rather, look at what these policies do to the composition of aggregate demand.

Now, in that respect, there is a sharp difference between monetary and fiscal policy. Monetary policy operates by stimulating interest-responsive components of aggregate demand (primarily investment spending and, in particular, residential construction). There is strong evidence that the immediate and strongest effect of monetary policy is on residential construction. Fiscal policy, by contrast, operates in a manner that depends on precisely what goods the government buys or what taxes and transfers it changes. Here we might be talking of government expenditure on goods and services such as road paving, a reduction in the corporate profits tax, or in sales tax, or social insurance contributions. Each policy affects the level of aggregate demand and will cause an expansion in output, except that the type of output and the beneficiaries of the fiscal measures differ. A corporate tax cut affects both investment spending and, through distributed profits, personal consumption. An income tax cut has a direct effect on consumption spending. Given the quantity of money, all expansionary fiscal policies have in common that they will raise the interest rate.

Once we recognize that all the policies raise output but that they differ significantly in their impact on different sectors of the economy, we open up a problem of political economy. Given the decision of expanding aggregate demand, who should get the primary benefit? Should the expansion take place through a decline in interest rates and increased investment spending, or should it take place through a cut in taxes and increased personal spending, or should it take the form of an increase in the size of government?

Questions of speed and predictability of policies apart — these are taken up in Chapter 9 — the issues raised above have been settled by political preferences. Conservatives will argue for a tax cut any time. They will favour stabilization policies that in a recession cut taxes and in a boom cut government spending. Over time, given enough cycles, you wind up with a government sector that becomes very small, just as a conservative would want it to be. The counterpart view belongs to those who feel that there is much scope for government spending in education, environment, job training and rehabilition, and the like, and who, accordingly, favour expansionary policies in the form of increased government spending. Growth-minded people and the construction lobby finally argue for expansionary policies that operate through low interest rates.

What is the historical record? We study that question in more detail in Chapters 10 and 18, but we can already note that expansionary fiscal policies in the sixties were accompanied by expansionary monetary policies so as to achieve a balanced expansion. We shall also see, though, that there have been episodes in which very tight monetary policy was used to restrain aggregate demand. In those episodes, the major impact of the restrictive policies on aggregate demand occurred through reduced investment, particularly in housing.

The recognition that monetary and fiscal policy changes have different effects on the composition of output is important. It suggests that policy makers can choose a *policy mix* that will both get the economy to full employment and also make a contribution to solving some other policy problem. In later chapters we point out two other targets of policy which have been taken into account in setting monetary and fiscal policy — growth and balance of payments equilibrium.

*4-8 A FORMAL TREATMENT

So far, we have relied on a verbal and graphical treatment of the model, and we round off the discussion now by using the equilibrium conditions in Equations (6a) and (12a). To determine the equilibrium level of income, we want both the goods and money markets to clear. Repeating these equilibrium conditions here for convenience, we have:

Goods market:
$$Y = \bar{\alpha}(\bar{A} - bi) \tag{6a}$$

Money Market:
$$i = \frac{1}{h}\left(kY - \frac{\bar{M}}{\bar{P}}\right) \tag{12a}$$

Since we wish to have equilibrium simultaneously in both markets, we may solve these two equations simultaneously for the equilibrium interest rate and income level as functions of the exogenous variables. We proceed by substitution. Substituting Equation (12a) in Equation (6a) yields:

$$Y = \bar{\alpha}\left[\bar{A} - \frac{b}{h}\left(kY - \frac{\bar{M}}{\bar{P}}\right)\right] \tag{13}$$

or after collecting terms in Y,

$$Y_0 = \frac{h\bar{\alpha}}{h + kb\bar{\alpha}}\bar{A} + \frac{b\bar{\alpha}}{h + kb\bar{\alpha}}\frac{\bar{M}}{\bar{P}} \tag{13a}$$

where Y_0 is now the equilibrium level of income. The terms that multiply the exogenous variables $\bar{A}$ and $\bar{M}/\bar{P}$ can be thought of as more complicated multipliers that reflect the monetary repercussions that characterize this model and differentiate it from the simple Keynesian model. It is useful to rewrite Equation (13a) in a somewhat simplified form as:

$$Y_0 = \beta\bar{A} + \gamma\frac{\bar{M}}{\bar{P}} \tag{14}$$

where

$$\beta \equiv \frac{h\bar{\alpha}}{h + bk\bar{\alpha}} \tag{15}$$

and

$$\gamma \equiv \frac{b\bar{\alpha}}{h + bk\bar{\alpha}} \tag{16}$$

Here β and γ will be referred to as the *fiscal* and *money multipliers*, respectively.

The fiscal multiplier β tells us by how much an increase in government spending affects the equilibrium level of income, holding the real money supply constant. Examine Equation (13a) and consider the effect of an increase in government spending on income. The increase in government spending $\Delta\bar{G}$ is a change in autonomous spending, so that $\Delta\bar{A} = \Delta\bar{G}$. The effect of the change in $\bar{G}$ is given by:

$$\frac{\Delta Y_0}{\Delta\bar{G}} = \frac{h\bar{\alpha}}{h + bk\bar{\alpha}} \equiv \beta \tag{17}$$

We note that the expression in Equation (17) is zero if h becomes very small and will be equal to $\bar{\alpha}$ if h approaches infinity. This corresponds, respectively, to a vertical and horizontal LM schedule. Similarly, a large value of either b or k serves to reduce the effect on income of government spending. Why? A high value of k implies a large increase in money demand as income rises and hence, a large increase in interest rates in order to maintain money market equilibrium. In combination with a high b, this implies a large reduction in private aggregate demand. Equation (17) thus presents the algebraic analysis that corresponds to the graphical analysis of Figure 4-11.

Similarly, the money multiplier γ tells us by how much an increase in the real money supply affects the equilibrium level of income, keeping fiscal policy unchanged. Using Equation (13a) to examine the effects of an increase in the real money supply on income, we have

$$\frac{\Delta Y_0}{\Delta(\bar{M}/\bar{P})} = \frac{b\bar{\alpha}}{h + bk\bar{\alpha}} \equiv \gamma \tag{18}$$

The smaller h and k and the larger b and $\bar{\alpha}$ the more expansionary is the effect of an increase in real balances on the equilibrium level of income. Large b and $\bar{\alpha}$ corresponds to the graphical analysis presented in Figure 4-14.

The Classical Case and the Liquidity Trap

We return now to Equation (13a) to consider two extreme possibilities. One is the world of constant velocity. We define the *income velocity of money* as the ratio of income to money:

$$V \equiv \frac{Y}{M/P} \equiv \frac{PY}{M} \tag{19}$$

where PY is the level of nominal income. Income velocity V is thus the ratio of the level of nominal income to the nominal money stock. If the demand for money is unresponsive to the interest rate, then $h = 0$ and Equation (13a) reduces to

$$Y = \frac{1}{k} \frac{\bar{M}}{P} = \frac{V}{M/P} \tag{20}$$

where

$$V \equiv \frac{1}{k}$$

or

$$PY = VM \tag{20a}$$

This is the world of the *quantity theory of money* where nominal income PY is proportional to the nominal quantity of money, and changes in the nominal quantity of money are reflected in equiproportionate changes in nominal income. This is what we previously called the classical case. From Equation (20a) we see that, given the price level (say $\bar{P}$), and for fixed velocity, real income can change only if the nominal money supply changes. Fiscal policy is totally ineffective in this case.

The other extreme is represented by a world where h is infinite, so that money and other assets are effectively perfect substitutes. In such a world, Equation (13a) reduces to

$$Y = \bar{\alpha}\bar{A} \tag{21}$$

This is a "multiplier world" where autonomous spending entirely determines the level of real income. It occurs if the economy is in a liquidity trap.

4-9 SUMMARY

The IS-LM model presented in this chapter is a simplified, but useful model of the economy that lays particular stress on the channels through which monetary and fiscal policy affect the economy. The analysis proceeds by first studying equilibrium in the goods and money markets, respectively. The overall equilibrium of the model is achieved when the level of income and the interest rate are such that both markets are in equilibrium. If the money market is in equilibrium, then the other assets markets, represented here by the catch-all "bond market," are also in equilibrium. We have shown how the economy adjusts to changes and that under the reasonable dynamic assumptions made, the economy does move toward the equilibrium.

In Section 4-5, we saw how the monetary policy affects the economy, in the first instance, by disturbing the equilibrium in the assets markets and thus changing the interest rate, and then, through the effects of the interest rate on aggregate demand. Fiscal policy continues to affect the level of income as in Chapter 3, but the multiplier effects of fiscal changes on income are dampened by the effects of rising income on interest rates and thus on aggregate demand.

We also examined two extreme cases, In the liquidity trap, in which increases in the money supply affect neither the interest rate nor the level of income, only fiscal policy changes the level of income. Further because the interest rate is unchanged by the fiscal policy action, there is no induced reduction in investment spending and no dampening effect on output arising from falling investment. In the classical case, in which the demand for money does not depend on the interest rate, the level of income cannot change unless the supply of money changes. Fiscal policy changes affect only interest rates and the rate of investment while leaving total spending unchanged.

The extreme cases are of interest from a historical perspective, and useful for understanding the model, but neither is very helpful for understanding the current economy. There is much evidence that the demand for real balance is significantly related to the interest rate but not so strongly that we are in a liquidity trap.

And a final warning, which has already been mentioned: We are assuming here that any level of output that is demanded can be produced by firms at the constant price level. Price level behaviour, including inflation, will be discussed in substantially more detail in Chapters 11 to 13. Those chapters build on the analysis of the IS-LM model.

APPENDIX: INTEREST RATES, PRESENT VALUES, AND DISCOUNTING

In this appendix we deal with the relationships among bond coupons, interest rates and yields, and the prices of bonds. In doing so, we shall introduce the very useful concept of present discounted value (PDV).

Section 1

We start with the case of a perpetual bond, or perpetuity. Such bonds have been issued in a number of countries, including the United Kingdom, where they are called Consols. The Consol is a promise by the British government to pay a fixed amount to the holder of the bond every year and forever. Let us denote the promised payment per Consol by Q_c, the *coupon*.[22]

The *yield* on a bond is the return per dollar that the holder of the bond receives. The yield on a savings account paying 5 percent interest per year is obviously just 5 percent. Someone paying $25 for a Consol that has a coupon of $2.5 obtains a yield of 10 percent [($2.5/25) × 100].

The yield on a Consol and its price are related in a simple way. Let us denote the price of the Consol by P_c and the coupon by Q_c. Then, as the above example suggests, the yield i is just

$$i = \frac{Q_c}{P_c} \tag{A1}$$

which says that the yield on a perpetuity is the coupon divided by the price. Alternatively, we can switch Equation (A1) around to

$$P_c = \frac{Q_c}{i} \tag{A2}$$

which says that price is the coupon divided by the yield. So, given the coupon and the yield, we can derive the price, or given the coupon and the price, we can derive the yield.

None of this is a theory of the determination of the yield or the price of a perpetuity. It merely points out the relationship between price and yield. Our theory of the determination of the yield on bonds is, of course, presented in this chapter. The interest rate in this chapter corresponds to the yield on bonds, and we tend to talk interchangeably of interest rates and yields.

We shall return to the Consol at the end of this appendix.

---

[22] The *coupon rate* is the coupon divided by the face value of the bond, which is literally the value printed on the face of the bond. Bonds do not necessarily sell for their face value, though customarily the face value is close to the value at which the bonds are sold when they first come on the market.

Section 2

Now we move to a short-term bond. Let us consider a bond which was sold by a borrower for $100, on which the borrower promises to pay back $108 after one year. This is a one-year bond. The yield on the bond to the person who bought it for $100 is 8 percent. For every $1 lent, the lender obtains both the $1 principal and 8 cents extra at the end of the year.

Next we ask a slightly different question. How much would a promise to pay $1 at the end of the year be worth? If $108 at the end of the year is worth $100 today, then $1 at the end of the year must be worth $100/108, or 92.6 cents. That is the value today of $1 in one year's time. In other words, it is the *present discounted value* of $1 in one year's time. It is the present value because it is what would be paid today for the promise of money in one year's time, and it is discounted because the value today is less than the promised payment in a year's time.

Denoting the one-year yield or interest rate by i, we can write that the present discounted value of a promised payment Q_1, one year from now is

$$PDV = \frac{Q_1}{1 + i} \tag{A3}$$

Let us return to our one-year bond and suppose that the day after the original borrower obtained the money, the yield on one-year bonds rises. How much would anyone now be willing to pay for the promise to receive $108 after one year? The answer must be given by the general formula (A3). The bond is just a promise to pay $108 in one year's time, and if the yield on one-year bonds is i, then the present value of the promise is given by Equation (A3). That means that the price of the one-year bond will fall when the interest rate or yield on such bonds rises. Once again, we see that the price of the bond and the yield are inversely related, given the promised payments to be made on the bond.

As before, we can reverse the formula for the price in order to find the yield on the bond, given its price and the promised payment Q_1. Note that the price P is equal to the present discounted value (PDV), so that we can write

$$1 + i = \frac{Q_1}{P} \tag{A4}$$

Thus, given the price of the bond and the promised payment, we can find the yield.

Section 3

Next we consider a two-year bond. Such a bond would typically promise to make a payment, which we shall denote Q_1, of interest at the end of the first year, and then a payment of interest and principal (usually the amount borrowed) Q_2, at the end of the second year. Given the yield i on the bond, how do we compute its PDV, which will be equal to its price?

We start by asking first what the bond will be worth one year from now. At that stage, it will be a one-year bond, promising to pay the amount Q_2 in one year's time, and yielding i. Its value one year from now will accordingly be given by Equation

(A3) except that Q_1 in Equation (A3) is replaced by Q_2. Let us denote the value of the bond one year from now by PDV_1, and note that

$$PDV_1 = \frac{Q_2}{1 + i} \tag{A5}$$

To complete the PDV of the two-year bond, we can now treat it as a one-year bond, which promises to pay Q_1 in interest one year from now, and also to pay PDV_1 one year from now, since it can be sold at that stage for that amount. Hence, the PDV of the bond, equal to its price, is

$$PDV = \frac{Q_1}{1 + i} + \frac{PDV_1}{1 + i} \tag{A6}$$

or

$$PDV = \frac{Q_1}{1 + i} + \frac{Q_2}{(1 + i)^2} \tag{A6a}$$

As previously, given the promised payments Q_1 and Q_2, the price of the bond will fall if the yield rises, and vice versa.

It is now less simple to reverse the equation for the price of the bond to find the yield than it was before: that is because from Equation (A6), we obtain a quadratic equation for the yield, which has two solutions.

Section 4

We have now provided the outline of the argument whereby the present discounted value of *any* promised stream of payments for any number of years can be computed. Suppose that a bond, or any other asset, promises to pay amounts Q_1, Q_2, Q_3, ..., Q_n in future years, 1, 2, 3, ..., n years away. By pursuing the type of argument given in Section 4-3, it is possible to show that the PDV of such a payments stream will be:

$$PDV = \frac{Q_1}{1 + i} + \frac{Q_2}{(1 + i)^2} + \frac{Q_3}{(1 + i)^3} + \ldots + \frac{Q_n}{(1 + i)^n} \tag{A7}$$

As usual, the price of a bond with a specified payments stream will be inversely related to its yield.

Section 5

Finally, we return to the Consol. The Consol promises to pay the amount Q_c forever. Applying the formula, we can compute the present value of the Consol by:

$$PDV = Q_c \left[\frac{1}{(1 + i)} + \frac{1}{(1 + i)^2} + \frac{1}{(1 + i)^3} + \ldots + \frac{1}{(1 + i)^n} + \ldots \right] \tag{A8}$$

The contents of the parentheses on the right-hand side are an infinite series, the sum of which can be calculated as $1/i$. Thus:

$$\text{PDV} = \frac{Q_c}{i} \tag{A9}$$

This section casts a slightly different light on the commonsense discussion of Section 1 of this appendix. Equations (A8) and (A9) show that the Consol's price is equal to the PDV of the future coupon payments.

PROBLEMS

1 The following equations describe an economy. (Think of C, I, G, etc., being measured in billions and i as percent; a 5 percent interest rate implies $i = 5$.)

$$C = 0.8(1 - t)Y \qquad 1$$
$$t = 0.25 \qquad 2$$
$$I = 400 - 20i \qquad 3$$
$$\bar{G} = 500 \qquad 4$$
$$L = 0.25Y - 30i \qquad 5$$
$$\frac{\bar{M}}{\bar{P}} = 350 \qquad 6$$

   (a) What is the equation that describes the IS curve?
   (b) What is the general definition of the IS curve?
   (c) What is the equation that describes the LM curve?
   (d) What is the general definition of the LM curve?
   (e) What are the equilibrium levels of income and the interest rate?
   (f) Describe in words the conditions that are satisfied at the intersection of the IS and LM curves, and why this is an equilibrium.
2 Continuing with the same equations:
   (a) What is the value of $\bar{\alpha}$, which corresponds to the simple multiplier (with taxes) of Chapter 3?
   (b) By how much does an increase in government spending of $\Delta\bar{G}$ increase the level of income in this model, which includes the assets markets?
   (c) By how much does a change in government spending of $\Delta\bar{G}$ affect the equilibrium interest rate?
   (d) Explain the difference between your answers to 2(a) and 2(b).
   (e) Relate your answer to 2(d) to the question of *crowding out*.
   (f) What is the money multiplier in this system? (In other words, by how much does a change in the real money stock of $\Delta\bar{M}/\bar{P}$ affect the equilibrium level of income?)
3 (a) Explain in words how and why the multiplier $\bar{\alpha}$ and the interest sensitivity of aggregate demand affect the slope of the IS curve.
   (b) Explain why the slope of the IS curve is a factor in determining the working of monetary policy.
4 Explain in words how and why the income and interest sensitivities of the demand for real balances affect the slope of the LM curve.
5 (a) Why does a horizontal LM curve imply that fiscal policy has the same effects on the economy as we derived in Chapter 3?
   (b) What is happening in this case in terms of Figure 4-1?
   (c) Under what circumstances might the LM curve be horizontal?
6 We mentioned in the text the possibility that the interest rate might affect consumption spending. An increase in the interest rate could in principle lead to increases in saving and therefore a reduction in consumption given the level of income. Suppose that consumption were in fact reduced by an increase in the interest rate. How would the IS curve be affected?

7   Suppose that the money supply, instead of being constant, increased (slightly) with the interest rate.
      (a) How would this change affect the construction of the LM curve?
      (b) Could you see any reason why the Bank of Canada might follow a policy of increasing the money supply along with the interest rate?

8   (a) How does an increase in the tax rate affect the IS curve?
      (b) How does it affect the equilibrium level of income?
      (c) How does it affect the equilibrium interest rate?

9   Draw a graph of how i and Y respond over time (i.e., use time as the horizontal axis) to:
      (a) An expansion in the money supply
      (b) An increase in taxes
      You may assume that the money market adjusts much more rapidly than the goods market.

10   In Figure 4-17, the economy can move to full employment by an expansion in either money or the full-employment deficit. Which policy leads to E_1 and which to E_2? How would you expect the choice to be made? Who would most strongly favour moving to E_1? E_2? What policy would correspond to "balanced growth"?

11   "We can have the GNP path we want equally well with a tight fiscal policy and an easier monetary policy, or the reverse, within fairly broad limits. The real basis for choice lies in many subsidiary targets, besides real GNP and inflation, that are differentially affected by fiscal and monetary policies." What are some of the subsidiary targets referred to in the quote? How would they be affected by alternative policy combinations?

*12   (a) Nominal GNP in 1979 was about $260 billion, and the money supply was about $23 billion. What then was the income velocity of money?
      (b) We noted that if the demand for money is totally interest-insensitive, velocity V is just the inverse of the coefficient k of our money demand function, where k represents the income sensitivity of the demand for money. We can interpret k as the fraction of a year's income that people hold in the form of money. Using the numbers of (12a), what fraction of the year's income do people hold as money? How many weeks' income on average are people holding in the form of money?

*13   A bond promises to pay the holder $6 at the end of the first year and $106 at the end of the second year.
      (a) If the interest rate or yield is 6 percent, what is the value of the bond?
      (b) Without necessarily solving the arithmetic, write out an expression for how much the bond will be worth if the interest rate drops to 5 percent. Is this more or less than in 13(a)? Why?

Part 2

5

CONSUMPTION, INCOME, WEALTH, AND LAGS

The IS-LM model developed in Chapter 4 provides a framework which enables us to understand the interaction of some of the main macroeconomic variables. Now we retrace our steps to present a more detailed and more sophisticated treatment of the key equations in the IS-LM model. The present chapter deals with the consumption function. The following three chapters deal with investment, money demand, and money supply. As a unit, these chapters flesh out the behavioural equations of the IS-LM model and thus move us toward a more realistic and reliable understanding of the working of the economy.

Our starting point in examining consumption behaviour is the consumption function we have been using in the previous chapters. Thus far, we have been assuming that consumption is a linear function of disposable income:

$$C = \bar{C} + cY_d \qquad \bar{C} > 0, 1 > c > 0 \qquad (1)$$

Now what does the empirical evidence show? Do the data for the post-World War II period bear out the hypothesis of a consumption function such as Equation (1)? We plot consumption and disposable income (both in 1971 dollars) for each of the years from 1953 through 1979 in Chart 5-1. The diagram clearly reveals a close positive relationship between consumption and disposable income. To find numerical estimates of the intercept ($\bar{C}$) and the marginal propensity to consume (c) we "fit" a regression line to the observations. The regression line is fitted to the data using the method of least squares, which produces the linear equation that best characterizes the relation between consumption and disposable income contained in the data.[1]

---

[1] It is frequently useful to summarize a relationship, such as that of Chart 5-1, between consumption expenditures and disposable income by writing an equation such as Eq. (2), which has specific numerical values in it, rather than the more general form of Eq. (1), which does not specify numerical values of the coefficients $\bar{C}$ and c. The line drawn in Chart 5-1 is the line represented by Eq. (2). That line is calculated by minimizing the sum of the squares of the vertical distance of the points in Chart 5-1 from the line, and it provides a good description of the general relationship between the two variables. For further details on the fitting of such lines, called least-squares regression lines, see Robert S. Pindyck and Daniel L. Rubinfeld, *Econometric Models and Economic Forecasts* New York: McGraw-Hill, 1976.

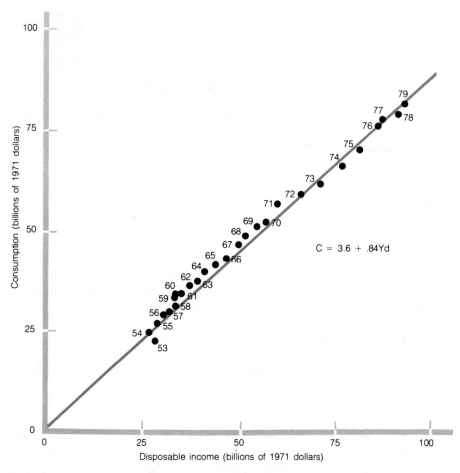

CHART 5-1 THE CONSUMPTION-INCOME RELATION 1953-1979

The estimated regression line is shown in Chart 5-1 as the solid line and is reported in Equation (2). The estimate of the intercept is $\bar{C}$ = 3.6 (3.6 billion 1971 dollars) and the estimate of the marginal propensity to consume is .84.

$$C = 3.6 + .84Y_d \qquad \text{(annual data 1953-1979)} \qquad (2)$$

Two characteristics of a consumption function such as Equation (1) are borne out by the empirical Equation (2). There is a positive intercept ($\bar{C}$ = 3.6), and the marginal propensity to consume (c = .84) is positive and less than unity.

If we divide through by Y_d in Equation (2), we obtain an equation that gives the average propensity to consume (C/Y_d) as a function of disposable income:

$$\frac{C}{Y_d} = \frac{3.6}{Y_d} + .84 \tag{3}$$

Equation (3) indicates that the average propensity to consume declines as disposable income rises. However, although the intercept, 3.6, is positive, it is small relative to disposable income, which was \$93 billion in 1979. If the intercept were actually zero, then we see from Equations (1) and (3) that consumption would be proportional to disposable income, with $C/Y_d = c$. The marginal and average propensities to consume would be equal. The relationship shown by Chart 5-1 and Equation (2) is close to one of proportionality, with the average and marginal propensities to consume out of disposable income equal to each other, at about .92.

Inspection of the regression line in Chart 5-1 suggests that the estimated equation fits well. There are no points far off the fitted line. As a first approximation, then, Equation (2) provides a reasonable summary of consumption behaviour. The next step is to ask whether there is reason to believe Equation (2) can be improved upon, and if so, to determine how.

Chart 5-2 shows the annual *changes* in consumption compared with the

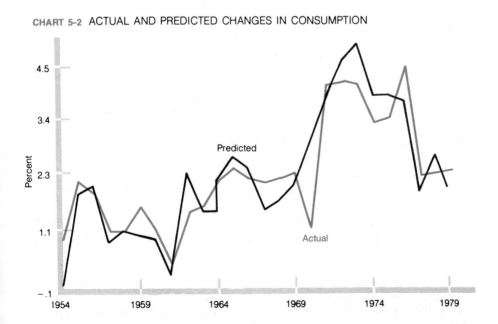

CHART 5-2 ACTUAL AND PREDICTED CHANGES IN CONSUMPTION

changes calculated from Equation (2). The derivations of the actual changes from the predicted ones raise questions about how well the equation predicts consumption behaviour. For example, in a number of years such as 1964, 1967 and 1973 the errors exceeded 20 percent of the actual change in consumption. In 1962 the percentage error was over 50 percent and in 1954 it was over 100 percent. In addition, the predicted change is above or below the actual change for some years at a time, for example, from 1967 to 1969, and 1972 to 1975. It appears that the simple consumption function Equation (2) can be improved upon.[2]

In this chapter, we shall explore three more sophisticated formulations of the consumption function than Equation (1). These are the *life-cycle theory of consumption, the permanent-income hypothesis*, and the *relative-income* formulation, described in Sections 5-2 through 5-4. Before we examine those theories, though, we outline in Section 5-1 an empirical puzzle about the consumption function that was historically important in leading to the new theories of the consumption function.

5-1 A CONSUMPTION FUNCTION PUZZLE

The puzzle we describe consists of two types of evidence that made their appearance in the late 1940s and that were apparently in conflict. The first type of evidence came from estimates of the standard consumption function, Equation (1), using annual U.S. data for the 1929-1941 period. (No earlier data were available then.) The estimated equation (in 1972 dollars) is

$$C = 47.6 + 0.73 \, Y_d \qquad \text{(annual data, U.S., 1929-1941)} \qquad (4)$$

Using Canadian data for the period 1926-1940, the estimated equation (in 1971 dollars) is

$$C = 3.0 + .69 \, Y_d \qquad \text{(annual data, Canada, 1926-1940)} \qquad (4a)$$

These equations clearly imply that the average propensity to consume falls as the level of income rises. They also have low marginal propensities to consume. If we used Equation (4a) to predict today's average propensity to consume in Canada, the estimate would be around .72, which of course is far off the actual ratio of about .88.

The second piece of evidence was the finding by Simon Kuznets, using averages of U.S. data over long periods — 10 and 30 years — that there was

---

[2] You should check the *Canadian Statistical Review* to see how well Equation (2) predicts consumption for 1980. Disposable income in 1971 dollars can be obtained by dividing the current dollar figure by the implicit price index (deflator) for personal consumption expenditure.

near proportionality between consumption and income.[3] This is consistent with the intercept term in Equation (1) being zero. The average propensity to consume that he found for three overlapping 30-year periods is shown in Table 5-1. The Kuznets results suggest, using long-term averages, that there is little variation in the ration of consumption to income and, in particular, that there is no tendency for the average propensity to decline.

TABLE 5-1 THE KUZNETS FINDING

	1869-1898	1884-1913	1904-1933
Average propensity	.867	.867	.879

Source: Simon Kuznets, National Income, A Summary of Findings, (New York: National Bureau of Economic Research, 1946), table 16.

There is clearly a conflict between the implications of the consumption function in Equations (4) and (4a) and Kuznets' findings. The Kuznets results suggest that the average propensity to consume is constant over long periods whereas Equations (4) and (4a) suggest it falls as income rises. It is also clear that the consumption function estimated in Equation (4a) on the basis of the prewar data is inconsistent with the same function estimated on the basis of postwar data, that is Equation (2).

The puzzle of the discrepancy between Kuznet's findings and Equation (4) was well known by the time the three alternative theories we outline below were developed. In resolving the puzzle, all three theories draw on the notion that consumption is related to a broader income measure than just current income. As already noted, the broader measures go under the names of *lifetime income, permanent income,* and *relative income*. These concepts have in common the recognition that consumption spending is maintained relatively constant in the face of fluctuations of current income. Consumption spending is not geared to what we earn today, but to what we earn on average. The important question obviously is what "average" means in this context.

The theories we present all imply that there is a difference between the marginal propensity to consume in the short run and the marginal propensity to consume in the long run. The short-run consumption function — the relationship between consumption spending and *current* disposable income — is indeed quite flat. However, this consumption function shifts upward over time. These shifts in the relationship between consumption and current disposable income bring into the discussion the roles of *wealth* and *perma-*

[3] Simon Kuznets, *National Product Since 1869,* and *National Income, A summary of Findings* (New York: National Bureau of Economics Research, 1946).

nent income in affecting consumer spending.[4] These considerations are taken up in the next two sections.

5-2 THE LIFE-CYCLE THEORY OF CONSUMPTION AND SAVING

The consumption function (1) is based on the simple notion that individuals' consumption behaviour in a given period is related to their income in that period. The life-cycle hypothesis views individuals, instead, as planning their consumption and saving behaviour over long periods, with the intention of allocating their consumption in a satisfactory way over their entire lifetimes. The life-cycle hypothesis views savings as resulting mainly from individuals' desires to provide for consumption in old age. As we shall see, the theory points to a number of unexpected factors affecting the savings rate of the economy; for instance, the age structure of the population is, in principle, an important determinant of consumption and savings behaviour.

To anticipate the main results of this section, we can already state here that we will derive a consumption function of the form:

$$C = a\frac{W}{P} + cY_d \tag{5}$$

where W/P is real wealth, a is the marginal propensity to consume out of wealth, and c is the marginal propensity to consume out of disposable income. We will show what determines the marginal propensities, why wealth should be an argument in the consumption function, and what the life-cycle consumption theory implies about the ratio of consumption to income, C/Y_d.

Consider now a woman who expects to live for L years, work and earn for N years, and be in retirement for $(L - N)$ years. The individual's consumption planning is assumed to start when she begins work, so that year 1 is the first year of work. We shall, in what follows, ignore any uncertainty about either life expectancy or the length of working life. We shall assume, too, that no interest is earned on savings, so that current

[4] The theories of the consumption function developed hereafter are also useful for explaining another empirical puzzle that we shall not go into in detail. In *cross-sectional* studies of the relationship between consumption and income — studies in which the consumption of a sample of families is related to their income — the marginal propensity to consume out of disposable income also appears to be lower than the average propensity to consume, with the average propensity to consume falling as the level of income rises. If you are interested in the reconciliation of this evidence with the long-run evidence of Kuznets, you should look at the ingenious explanation advanced by Milton Friedman through the permanent-income hypothesis. Follow up the reference given in footnote 10.

saving translates dollar for dollar into future consumption possibilities. With these assumptions, we can approach the saving or consumption decision with two questions. First we ask, What are the individual's lifetime consumption possibilities? Second, we are interested in the way this woman will choose to distribute her consumption over her lifetime. We shall now consider the consumption possibilities.

For the moment we ignore property income (income from assets) and focus attention on labour income. We denote the annual real labour income by Z. Given N years of working, *lifetime income* (from labour) is ZN, income per working year times the number of working years. Consumption over the individual's lifetime cannot exceed this lifetime income unless she is born with wealth, which we initially assume is not the case. Accordingly, we have determined the first part of the consumer's problem in finding the limit of lifetime consumption.

We assume the individual will want to distribute consumption over her lifetime so that she has a flat or even flow of consumption. Rather than consume a lot in one period and very little in another, the preferred profile is to consume exactly equal amounts in each period.[5] Clearly, this assumption implies that consumption is not geared to *current* income (which is zero during retirement) but rather to *lifetime income*.

Lifetime consumption equals lifetime income. This means that the planned level of consumption C, which is the same in every period, times the number of years in life L equals lifetime income:

$$CL = ZN \qquad (6)$$

Lifetime income is equal to ZN. Dividing through by L, we have planned consumption per year, C, that is proportional to labour income:

$$C = \frac{N}{L} Z \qquad (7)$$

The factor of proportionality in Equation (7) is N/L, the fraction of lifetime spent working. Accordingly Equation (7) states that in each year of

---

[5] Why? The basic reason is the notion of diminishing marginal utility of consumption. Consider two alternative consumption plans. One involves an equal amount of consumption in each of two periods, the other involves consuming all in one period and none in the other. The principle of diminishing marginal utility of income implies that, in the latter case, we would be better off by transferring some consumption from the period of plenty toward that of starvation. The loss in utility in the period of plenty is *more* than compensated by the gain in utility in the period of scarcity. And there is a gain to be made by transferring consumption so long as there is any difference in consumption between the two periods. The principle of diminishing marginal utility of consumption conforms well with the observation that most people choose stable life-styles – not, in general, saving furiously in one period to have a big bust in the next, but rather, consuming at about the same level from period to period.

life a fraction of labour income is consumed, where that fraction is equal to the proportion of working life in total life.

The counterpart of Equation (7) is the saving function. Remembering that saving is equal to income less consumption we have

$$S \equiv Z - \overline{C} = \frac{Z(L - N)}{L} \tag{8}$$

Equation (8) states that saving during the period in which the individual works is equal to a fraction of labour income, with that fraction being equal to the proportion of life spent in retirement.

Figure 5-1 shows the pattern of consumption, saving, and dissaving.[6] Over the whole lifetime, there is an even flow of consumption at the rate C, amounting in total to CL. That consumption spending is financed during working life out of current income. During retirement the consumption is financed by drawing down the savings that have been accumulated during working life. Therefore the shaded areas $(Z - C)N$ and $C(L - N)$ are equal, or equivalently, saving during working years finances dissaving during

[6] Figure 5-1 was developed by Franco Modigliani in "The Life Cycle Hypothesis of Saving, the Demand for Wealth and the Supply of Capital," *Social Research*, vol. 33, no. 2, 1966. Modigliani, together with Richard Brumberg and Albert Ando, formulated the life-cycle theory.

FIGURE 5-1 LIFETIME INCOME, CONSUMPTION, SAVINGS, AND WEALTH IN THE LIFE-CYCLE MODEL

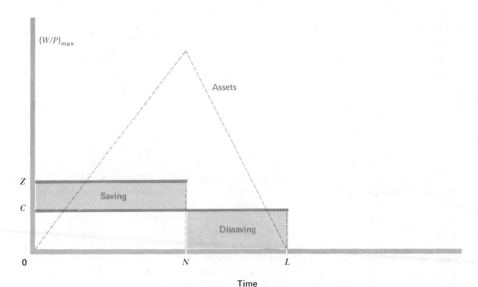

retirement. The important idea of lifetime consumption theory is apparent from Figure 5-1. It is that consumption plans are made so as to achieve a smooth or even level of consumption by saving during periods of high income and dissaving during periods of low income. That is, therefore, an important departure from consumption based on current income. It is an important difference because, in addition to current income, the whole future profile of income enters into the calculations of lifetime consumption. Before developing that aspect further, however, we return to Figure 5-1 to consider the role of assets.

During the working years, the individual saves to finance consumption during retirement. The savings build up assets, and we accordingly show in Figure 5-1 how the individual's wealth or assets increase over working life and reach a maximum at retirement age. From that time on, assets decline because the individual sells assets to pay for current consumption. We can briefly ask, What is the maximum level that assets reach? We remember that assets are built up to finance consumption during retirement. Total consumption during retirement is equal to $C(L - N)$. Further, since annual consumption is equal to $C = ZN/L$, the maximum stock of assets is $(W/P)_{max} = ZN(L - N)/L$, which is reached exactly at the point of retirement. From then on, assets decline until they reach precisely zero at the end of life.

Introducing Wealth

The next step is to extend this model and allow for initial assets or wealth, that is, assuming the individual is born to wealth.[7] We can simply draw on the previous insight that the individual consumer will spread any existing resources to achieve an even lifetime consumption profile. The individual who has assets in addition to labour income will plan to use these assets to add to lifetime consumption. An individual who is at some point T in life, with a stock of wealth W/P and labour income accruing for another $(N - T)$ years at the rate of Z, and with a life expectancy of $(L - T)$ years to go, will behave as follows. The person's lifetime consumption possibilities are

$$C(L - T) = \frac{W}{P} + (N - T)Z \tag{9}$$

where we have included wealth W/P along with lifetime labour income as a source of finance for lifetime consumption. From Equation (9), consumption in each period is equal to

$$C = a\frac{W}{P} + cZ \qquad a \equiv \frac{1}{L - T} \qquad c \equiv \frac{N - T}{L - T} \qquad N \geq T \tag{10}$$

[7] The individual may receive wealth early in life through gifts or bequests. In the fully developed life-cycle theory, the individual, in calculating life-time consumption, has also to take account of any bequests he or she may want to leave.

where the coefficients a and c are respectively the marginal propensities to consume out of wealth and labour income.

It is important to recognize from Equation (10) that the marginal propensities are related to the individual's position in the life cycle. The closer a person is to the end of lifetime, the higher the marginal propensity to consume out of wealth. Thus, a man with two more years of life will consume half his wealth in each of the remaining two years. The marginal propensity to consume out of labour income is related both to the number of years during which further income will be earned, $N - T$, and to the number of years over which these earnings are spread, $L - T$. It is quite clear from Equation (10) that an increase in either wealth or labour income will raise consumption expenditures. It is apparent, too, that lengthening working life relative to retirement will raise consumption simply because it increases lifetime income. The most basic point, however, is that Equation (10) shows both (lifetime) income and wealth as determinants of consumption spending.

To summarize where we have come so far, we note that in this form of the life-cycle model:

1 Consumption is constant over the consumer's lifetime.
2 Consumption spending is financed by lifetime income plus initial wealth.
3 During each year a fraction $1/(L - T)$ of wealth plus expected earnings will be consumed.
4 Current consumption spending depends on current wealth and lifetime income.

Extensions

The model as so far outlined makes very strong simplifying assumptions. It can be extended to remove most of the strong assumptions without affecting the underlying properties of Equation (10), that consumption is related to both income and wealth.

First, it is necessary to take account of the possibility that saving earns interest, so that a dollar not consumed today will provide more than a dollar's consumption tomorrow. Second, the analysis is little affected when it is extended to allow for the facts that individuals are uncertain of the length of their lifetimes, and also that they sometimes want to leave bequests to their heirs. In this latter case, they would not plan to consume all their resources over their own lifetimes. Similarly, the model has to be extended to take account of the composition of the family over time, so that some consumption is provided for children before they begin to work. But, to repeat, these extensions do not change the basic results contained in Equation (10).

A final extension is very important. In practice, one never knows exactly what one's lifetime labour income will be, and lifetime consumption plans have to be made on the basis of predictions of future labour income. This, of course, raises the issue of how income is to be predicted. We will not pursue this important issue here, but will leave it to the next section on permanent income, which is an estimate of lifetime income. However, expected lifetime labour income would be related to current disposable income, leading to a form of the consumption function like Equation (5), perhaps with other variables also included. Indeed, it is useful to think of the life-cycle and permanent-income theories as being fundamentally the same, with the life-cycle theory developing most carefully the implications of the model for the role of wealth and other variables in the consumption function,[8] and the permanent-income theory concentrating on the best way of predicting lifetime income.

Aggregate Consumption and Saving

The theory as so far outlined is strictly a theory about consumption and saving by single individuals over the course of their lifetimes. How does it relate to aggregate consumption, which is, after all, the focus of macroeconomic interest in consumption? Imagine an economy in which population and GNP were constant through time. Each individual in that economy would go through the life cycle of saving and dissaving outlined in Figure 5-1. The economy as a whole, though, would not be saving. At any one time, the saving of the working people would be exactly matched by the dissaving of retired people. However, if population were growing, there would be more young people than old, thus more saving in total than dissaving, and there would be net saving in the economy. Thus, aggregate consumption depends in part on the age composition of the population. It also depends on such characteristics of the economy as the average age of retirement and the presence or absence of old-age pensions. These surprising implications of the theory indicate the richness of the approach.

Implications

We want to return to Equation (5) to emphasize again the role of wealth. Note from (5) that if there were an increase in wealth, the ratio of consumption to disposable income would rise. This has a bearing on the puzzle described in Section 5-1, where the average propensity to consume seems, on the basis of Equation (4), to decline with income, and on the basis of Kuznets' findings, to remain constant on average over long periods.

If we divide through in Equation (5) by Y_d, we obtain

$$\frac{C}{Y_d} = a\,\frac{W/P}{Y_d} + b \qquad (11)$$

[8] The other variables indicated here will be discussed in the next paragraph.

Now, if the ratio of wealth to disposable income is constant, then Equation (11) shows that the ratio of consumption to disposable income will be constant. However, if the ratio of wealth to disposable income is changing, the average propensity to consume will be changing.

This suggests, as an explanation of the Kuznets puzzle, the possibility that the ratio of wealth to disposable income is roughly constant over long periods, and that it varied considerably during the 1930s to which period the consumption function, Equation (4), applies. Similarly, Equation (11) suggests that the variability of consumption in the short run, as seen in Chart 5-2, is explained in part by fluctuations in the ratio of wealth to disposable income. It is indeed true that the ratio of wealth to disposable income is reasonably constant in the long run, but fluctuates considerably in the short run.[9]

One further interesting implication of the life-cycle hypothesis is that it provides a route for the stock market to affect consumption behaviour. The value of stocks held by the public is part of wealth and should be — and is — included in W/P in Equation (5). When the value of stocks is high — when the stock market is booming — W/P is high and tends to increase consumption, and the reverse occurs when the stock market is depressed.

We continue now to the permanent-income theory of consumption, bearing in mind that we have not yet discussed the determinants of expected lifetime labour income in Equation (10) in any detail, and recalling that the two theories should be thought of as complementary rather than competing.

5-3 PERMANENT-INCOME THEORY OF CONSUMPTION

In the long run, the consumption-income ratio is very stable, but in the short run it fluctuates. The behaviour of the propensity to consume implied by the standard consumption function, Equation (1), appears to differ when the equation is fitted over different periods. The life-cycle approach explains these observations by pointing out that people want to maintain a smooth profile of consumption even if their lifetime income profile is uneven, and thus emphasizes the role of wealth in the consumption function. Another explanation, which differs in details but entirely shares the spirit of the life-cycle approach, is the permanent-income theory of consumption.

---

[9] The life-cycle theory also suggests why the simple consumption function of Eq. (2) would look different when estimated over different time periods, for example, 1953-1979 and 1926-1940. Equation (2) omits a variable, wealth, that should be in the consumption function. That means that the estimates we get for the intercept and the marginal propensity to consume will depend on how wealth changes in the period for which we are fitting the line. As a difficult problem, see whether you can show that the estimated average propensity to consume will be constant if the ratio of wealth to disposable income is constant, but is omitted from the equation when it is fitted. Similarly, show that when wealth is constant and is omitted when fitting Eq. (2), the estimated average propensity to consume will decline with income.

The theory, which is the work of Milton Friedman,[10] argues that people gear their consumption behaviour to their permanent or long-term consumption opportunities, not to their current level of income. A suggestive example provided by Friedman involves someone who is paid or receives her income only once a week on Fridays. We clearly do not expect that individual to concentrate her entire consumption on that one day on which income is received, with zero consumption on every other day. Again we are persuaded by the argument that individuals prefer a smooth consumption flow rather than plenty today and scarcity tomorrow or yesterday. On that argument, consumption on any one day of the week would be unrelated to income on that particular day but would rather be geared to average daily income — that is, income per week divided by the number of days per week. It is clear that in this extreme example, income for a period longer than a day is relevant to the consumption decision. Similarly, Friedman argues, there is nothing special about a period of the length of one quarter or one year that requires the individual to plan consumption within the period solely on the basis of income within the period; rather, consumption is planned in relation to income over a longer period.

The idea of consumption spending that is geared to long-term or average or permanent income is appealing and essentially the same as the life-cycle theory. It leaves two further questions. The first concerns the precise relationship between current consumption and permanent income. The second question is how to make the concept of permanent income operational, that is, how to measure it.

In its simplest form the permanent-income hypothesis of consumption behaviour argues that consumption is proportional to permanent income:

$$C = cY^P \qquad (12)$$

where Y^P is permanent (disposable) income. From Equation (12), consumption varies in the same proportion as permanent income. A 5 percent increase in permanent income raises consumption by 5 percent. Since permanent income should be related to long-run average income, this feature of the consumption function is clearly in line with the observed long-run constancy of the consumption-income ratio.

The next problem is how to think of, and measure, permanent income. Think of a person whose income has risen this year. She has to decide whether that income increase represents a permanent increase, or merely a *transitory* change, one that will not persist. In any particular case, the individual may know whether the increase is permanent or transitory. A government official who is promoted one grade will know that the increase in income is likely to be maintained. Or the worker who has exceptionally

---

[10] Milton Friedman, *A Theory of the Consumption Function* (Princeton, N.J.: Princeton University Press, 1957).

high overtime in a given year will likely regard that year's increased income as transitory. But in general, a person is not so certain about what part of any change in income is likely to be maintained, and is therefore permanent, and what part is not likely to be maintained, and is therefore transitory. Since the individual assumes that transitory income on average cancels out over the life span, being positive in some periods and negative in others, transitory income is assumed not to have any substantial effect on consumption.

The question of how to infer what part of an increase in income is permanent is resolved in a pragmatic way by assuming that permanent income is related to the behaviour of current and past incomes. To give a simple example, we might estimate permanent income as being equal to last year's income plus some fraction of the change in income from last year to this year:

$$
\begin{aligned}
Y^P &= Y_{-1} + \theta \, (Y - Y_{-1}) \qquad 0 < \theta < 1 \\
&= \theta \, Y + (1 - \theta) \, Y_{-1}
\end{aligned} \tag{13}
$$

where θ is a fraction and Y_{-1} is last year's income. The second line in Equation (13) writes permanent income as a *weighted average* of current and past income. The second formulation is of course equivalent to that in the first line. To understand Equation (13), assume we had a value of $\theta = 0.6$ and that this year's income was $Y = \$12,000$ and last year's income was $Y_{-1} = \$11,000$. The value of permanent income would be $Y^P = \$11,600$ ($= 0.6 \times \$12,000 + 0.4 \times \$11,000$). Thus, permanent income is an average of the two income levels. Whether it is closer to this year's or last year's income depends on the weight θ given to current income. Clearly, in the extreme with $\theta = 1$, permanent income is equal to current income.

An estimate of permanent income that uses only current and last year's income is an oversimplification. Friedman forms the estimate by looking at incomes in many earlier periods, as well as current income, but with weights that are larger for the more recent, as compared to the more distant, incomes.[11] There is no simple theory which would tell us what the relative magnitude of the weights on different incomes should be, except for two considerations. First, income in the distant past—say more than three years ago — should have less influence on permanent income than more recent incomes. Second, current income should have a weight that is less than 1, so that we look at both current and past incomes in forming our estimate. We should also repeat that we cannot expect a formula like Equation (13), based on the behaviour of income in the past, to include all the factors that influence a person's beliefs about future income. The discovery of a vast

---

[11] Friedman also adjusts permanent income by taking into account the growth of income over time.

amount of oil in a country, for instance, would raise the permanent incomes of the inhabitants of the country as soon as it was announced, even though a (mechanical) formula like Equation (13) based on past levels of income would not reflect such a change.

There are some special features of Equation (13) which deserve comment. First, if $Y = Y_{-1}$, that is, if this year's income is equal to last year's, then permanent income is equal to the income earned this year and last year. This guarantees that an individual who had always earned the same income would expect to earn that income in the future. Second, note that if income rises this year compared with last year, then permanent income rises by *less* than current income. The reason is that the individual does not know whether the rise in income this year is permanent. Not knowing whether the increase in income will be maintained or not, the individual does not immediately increase the expected or permanent income measure by the full amount of the actual or current increase in income.

Using equations (12) and (13), we can now rewrite the consumption function:

$$C = cY^P = c\theta Y + c(1 - \theta)Y_{-1} \tag{14}$$

The marginal propensity to consume out of *current* income is then just $c\theta$, which is clearly less than the long-run average propensity to consume, c. Hence, the permanent-income hypothesis implies that there is a difference between the short-run marginal propensity to consume and the long-run marginal (equal to the average) propensity to consume.

We shall see shortly that this implication is supported by the data. But first we explore it in more detail. The reason for the lower short-run marginal propensity to consume is that when current income rises, the individual is not sure that the increase in income will be maintained over the longer period on which she bases consumption plans. Accordingly, the person does not fully adjust consumption spending to the higher level that would be appropriate if the increase in income were permanent. However, if the increase turns out to be permanent, that is, if next period's income is the same as this period's, then the person will (next year) fully adjust consumption spending to the higher level of income. Note, though, that the adjustment here is completed in two years only because we have assumed, in Equation (13), that permanent income is an average of two years' income. Depending on how expectations of permanent income are formed, the adjustment could be much slower.

The argument is illustrated in Figure 5-2. Here we show the long-run consumption function as a straight line through the origin with slope c, which is the constant average and marginal propensity to consume out of permanent income. The lower flat consumption function is a short-run consumption function drawn for a given history of income which is reflected in the intercept $c(1 - \theta)Y_0$. The consumption function is therefore appropriate if last year's income was Y_0. Assume, in fact, that we start out in long-run equilibrium with actual and permanent income equal to Y_0 and consumption therefore equal to cY_0, as is shown at the intersection of long-run and short-run consumption functions at point E. Assume next that income increases to the level Y'. In the short run, which means during the current period, we revise our estimate of permanent income upward by θ times the increase in income and consume a fraction c of that increase in permanent income. Accordingly, consumption moves up along the short-run consumption function to point E'.

Note immediately that in the short run the ratio of consumption to income declines as we move from point E to E'. Going one period ahead and assuming that the increase in income persists so that income remains at Y', we get a shift in the consumption function. The consumption function shifts upward because, as of the given higher level of income, the estimate of permanent income is now revised upward to Y'. Accordingly, consumers want to spend a fraction of c of their new estimate of permanent income Y'. The new consumption point is E'', where the ratio of consumption to income is back to the long-run level. The example makes clear the point that in the short run, an increase in income causes a decline in the average propensity to consume because people do not anticipate that the increase in income will persist or be permanent. Once they do observe that the increase in income does persist, however, they fully adjust consumption to match their higher permanent income.

Like the life-cycle hypothesis, the permanent-income hypothesis has

FIGURE 5-2 THE EFFECT ON CONSUMPTION OF A SUSTAINED INCREASE IN INCOME

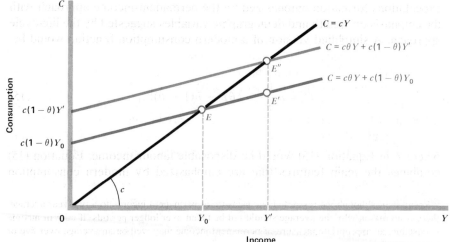

some other unexpected and interesting implications. Consider, for instance, the weight that should be given to current income in forming an estimate of permanent income as a function of the extent to which current income varies for a given individual. An individual whose income has been extremely unstable in the past will not give a large amount of weight to a change in income in any one year. The weight θ in Equation (14) for such an individual will be relatively small, and the marginal propensity to consume out of current income will accordingly be relatively small. On the other hand, an individual whose income has been very stable in the past will put a lot of weight on changes in current income and have a relatively large θ in Equation (14).[12] His marginal propensity to consume out of current income will therefore be relatively large. Friedman shows that this implication is borne out by the facts. Farmers, for instance, have very variable incomes and a low marginal propensity to consume out of current income.

To conclude this section, it is worth considering again the relationship between the life-cycle and permanent-income hypothesis briefly. The two hypotheses are not mutually exclusive. The life-cycle hypothesis pays rather more attention to the motives for saving than the permanent-income hypothesis does, and provides convincing reasons to include wealth as well as income in the consumption function. The permanent-income hypothesis, on the other hand, pays more careful attention to the way in which individuals form their expectations about their future incomes than the original life-cycle hypothesis does. Recall that current labour income entered the life-cycle consumption function to reflect expectations of future income. The more detailed analysis of the determinants of expected future income that is provided by the permanent-income hypothesis can be, and has been, included in the life-cycle consumption function.

Indeed, modern theories of the consumption function combine the expectations formation emphasized by the permanent-income approach with the emphasis on wealth and demographic variables suggested by the life-cycle approach. A simplified version of a modern consumption function would be

$$C = a\frac{W}{P} + b\theta Y + b(1 - \theta)Y_{-1} \tag{15}$$

where Y in Equation (15) would be disposable labour income. Equation (15) combines the main features that are emphasized by modern consumption

---

[12] Recall that, although we restricted our measure of permanent income to a two-year average, there is no reason why the average should not be taken over longer periods. If current income is unstable, an appropriate measure of permanent income may well be an average over five or more years.

theory.[13] It has a short-run marginal propensity to consume out of disposable labour income ($b\theta$) that is lower than the long-run marginal propensity (b). It also shows the role of wealth, which is an important influence on consumption spending.

Recent research on consumption has combined the two theories and has been aimed particularly at checking the implications of the permanent-income — and life-cycle — theory that transitory changes in income have little effect on consumption.[14]

We end this section by repeating a warning that is important enough for us to risk overstating. An equation like (15) performs quite well on average in predicting consumption. But it is always important to remember the underlying theory when using it. Equation (15) embodies the estimate of permanent income implied by Equation (13). If we have knowledge about some particular change in income — for example, that it is transitory — then we should use that knowledge in predicting consumption. For instance, a temporary one-year tax increase that reduced current disposable income would reduce current consumption by much less than a tax increase of the same size that was known to be permanent, even though Equation (15) does not show that.

5-4 THE RELATIVE-INCOME HYPOTHESIS

Modern theories of the consumption function have in common the objective of explaining short-run fluctuations in the ratio of consumption to disposable income combined with virtual constancy of the ratio of consumption to disposable income in the long run. Life-cycle and permanent-income theories explain this behaviour as an attempt to maintain a smooth flow of consumption that is geared to long-run consumption opportunities, as measured by lifetime income and wealth or by permanent income.

An earlier and influential theory along much the same lines is the relative-income hypothesis that was advanced by James Duesenberry.[15] The theory argues that current consumption depends not only on current income but also on the history of income. Individuals build up consumption standards that are geared to their *peak* income levels. If income declines relative to past income, then individuals will not immediately sacrifice the

---

[13] To fix ideas, you should draw a graph of Eq. (15) with consumption on the vertical axis and current disposable labour income on the horizontal axis. What is the intercept? How does the diagram differ from Figure 5-2? Show now the effects of (1) a transitory increase in income, (2) a sustained increase in income, and (3) an increase in wealth.

[14] See, for example, Robert E. Hall, "Stochastic Implications of the Life Cycle-Permanent Income Hypothesis: Theory and Evidence," *Journal of Political Economy*, December 1978. We should warn you that this is difficult reading.

[15] See James Duesenberry, *Income, Savings and the Theory of Consumer Behavior* (Cambridge, Mass.: Harvard University Press, 1952).

consumption standard they have adopted. There is a *ratchet effect*, and they will only adjust to a small extent to the decline in current income. However, there is an asymmetry because an increase in income relative to past peaks immediately raises the consumption level.

Figure 5-3 shows consumption behaviour according to the relative-income hypothesis. The dark line is the consumption function if current income is the peak level of income. Thus, if current income is Y_d^o and exceeds previous levels of income, then consumption would be at point E on the consumption function $C = cY$. If income declined from the level Y_d^o to Y_d', then consumption would adjust along the light schedule to E'. The peak level of income Y_d^o would continue to influence consumption because it determines the consumption standard that individuals seek to maintain. In the short run, therefore, saving adjusts so as to allow consumption to be maintained close to the habitual level. Assume next that income rose to the level Y_d''. This would be a new peak level of income, and consumption accordingly would rise to E''. If income were to decline back to Y_d^o, the new peak level Y'' would continue to influence consumption, so that we would find ourselves at point E'''.

The theory is very suggestive again of the attempt to smooth consumption in the face of income fluctuations. It has an intuitive appeal in its emphasis on consumption standards geared to peak income. It lacks, perhaps, the economic richness that the later theories of the life cycle and

FIGURE 5-3 THE RELATIVE-INCOME HYPOTHESIS

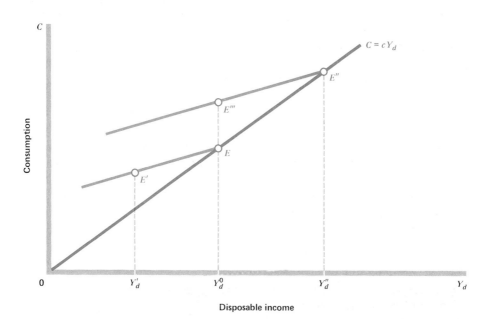

Disposable income

permanent income added. Its main shortcoming is the asymmetry that suggests that a current increase in income, if it exceeds a previous peak, immediately induces a new consumption standard. Here the alternative theories are more persuasive in that they suggest a partial adjustment for both an increase and a decrease in income. But the theory does suggest that, as the level of income rises over time, consumption will rise roughly in proportion, along the line $C = cY_d$.

*5-5 LAGS AND DYNAMICS

In this section we explore the implications of the permanent-income hypothesis for the adjustment of equilibrium output to changes in autonomous spending. Our theory of the consumption function implies that households only gradually adjust their consumption spending to a sustained change in income. What is the implication of such gradual adjustment of consumption, once we place the consumption function in the broader context of the determination of *equilibrium* income?

For example, suppose autonomous investment spending increases and that firms raise output to meet the increased demand. This, of course, raises income and evokes an increase in consumer spending which in turn induces a further rise in income. But the story does not stop here, because consumption only gradually rises to the full extent implied by the long-run consumption-income relation. Therefore the manner in which households form expectations about permanent income will affect the time path of consumption and thus the adjustment path of equilibrium income to an autonomous disturbance. We now examine these relations more carefully and, at the same time, use the opportunity to show the implications of permanent-income theory for saving behaviour. We assume throughout that individuals have no special knowledge about the permanence of changes in income, and thus use Equation (13) to form their estimates.

Permanent Income and Saving

Our permanent-income theory of consumption gave us in Equation (14) a consumption function with current and lagged income as determinants of current consumption spending. The consumption function of course implies a saving function which is derived using the definition of saving and substituting from (14) to obtain

$$S = Y - C = (1 - c\theta)Y - c(1 - \theta)Y_{-1} \tag{16}$$

The saving function has two important properties. First, if income is constant ($Y = Y_{-1}$), then saving is proportional to income. This is the long-run saving function shown in Equation (16a)

$$S = (1 - c)Y \tag{16a}$$

Second, the short-run propensity to save, given Y_{-1}, is equal to $s = 1 - c\theta$ and thus is larger than the long-run propensity.[16] This reflects the fact that consumers interpret a current change in income partly as transitory and do not adjust consumption fully; accordingly, a transitory increase in income leads to a relatively large increase in saving. If the increase in income is sustained, then, over time, consumption adjusts and savings declines to the long-run level implied by Equation (16a). In Figure 5-4, we show the long-run saving function that makes saving proportional to income. We also show the short-run saving function, drawn for a given level of past income, Y_{-1}. The two schedules intersect at the level of income $Y = Y_{-1}$ since, as argued above, if income is constant, we are on our long-run saving function. If current income, Y, exceeds last period's income, saving is above the long-run level, and if income is below the level of last period, the converse will be true. The figure clearly reflects the fact that the short-run propensity to save is higher than the long-run propensity.

Consider now using permanent-income saving behaviour in a more complete macroeconomic setting. Assume we look at the models of income determination in Chapter 3, where assets markets were disregarded. In that setting, the equilibrium level is determined by the equality of income and aggregate demand, or equivalently, by the equality of saving and investment.

---

[16] Remember θ is a fraction — say $\theta = .6$ — and hence $1 - c\theta$ is larger than $1 - c$.

FIGURE 5-4 SAVINGS AND INCOME IN THE SHORT AND LONG RUNS

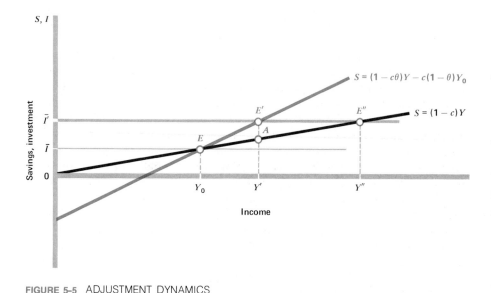

FIGURE 5-5 ADJUSTMENT DYNAMICS

(We disregard the government sector here). Using our saving function and treating investment as exogenous, we can write the equilibrium condition, $I = S$, as

$$\overline{I} = (1 - c\theta)Y - c(1 - \theta)Y_{-1} \qquad (17)$$

In Figure 5-5, we add the level of investment, $\overline{I}$, to the diagram. The initial equilibrium is at point E. At point E, saving — as given by the short-term saving function — is equal to investment, and thus the equilibrium condition in Equation (17) is satisfied. We also assume that we have reached a *full* equilibrium in that saving has fully adjusted to the level of income and we are saving according to permanent income. Hence, we are also on the long-run saving function.

The Adjustment Process

Suppose now that there is a permanent increase in investment to the level $\overline{I}'$. The investment schedule shifts upward. At the initial income level, Y_0, investment exceeds saving, there is an excess demand for goods, and accordingly, income expands until we reach a level Y'. At Y', short-run saving is equal to investment. Much of the increased income is saved, therefore freeing resources to meet the increased level of investment. But the equilibrium is only a short-run one because, as it persists, households recognize that the increase in income is not transitory. They adjust their permanent-income forecast and accordingly revise upward their consumption plans. The short-run saving schedule in the next period would shift downward (not drawn) through point A. The increased consumption would create excess demand for goods and thus lead to a further income expansion. The process of income expansion and revision of permanent income will continue over time until we reach point E''. Point E'' marks the new, long-run equilibrium or full equilibrium. Here, long-run saving is equal to investment. When we have reached that level of income, saving has fully adjusted and no more income changes take place.

There are two important implications of our analysis. The first is the distinction between short-run and long-run multipliers. In the short run, an increase in investment leads to an income expansion to point E'. The difference arises because the short-run propensity to consume is small — because income changes are taken as transitory rather than permanent — and hence there is relatively little induced spending. The second implication is that the adjustment process to a change in autonomous spending is a *dynamic* one. It is a process that occurs over time, rather than instantaneously, because only over time do households adjust their forecasts of permanent income and hence of planned saving and consumption. These adjustments in turn feed back to the equilibrium level of income and imply that output adjustment occurs over time.

FIGURE 5-6 THE INCOME ADJUSTMENT PROCESS

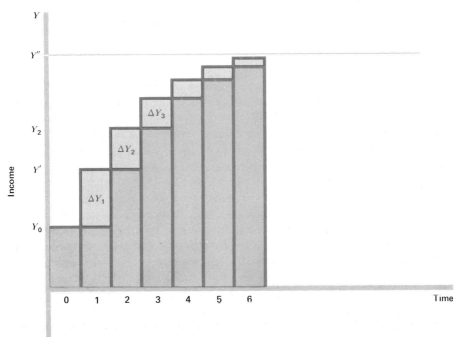

The dynamic adjustment of output to a change in autonomous spending can be represented in terms of Figure 5-5 as the movement from E to E' to E''. Over time, income increases from period to period and we can plot, as in Figure 5-6, each period's level of income. The initial disturbance immediately raises income from Y_0 to Y', or gives us a first-period increase in income of ΔY_1. In the second period, as households recognize the persistence of higher income, they raise their spending and thus induce a further rise in income to the level Y_2. The second-period rise in income, ΔY_2, is thus entirely due to the adjustment of consumption to the revision in permanent-income estimates. The same is true for the subsequent income adjustments. The time pattern of changes in income caused by the increases in $\overline{I}$ is called the *dynamic multiplier* of $\overline{I}$.

An exercise at the end of this chapter asks you to show that the period-to-period changes in income following the increase in autonomous investment get smaller and smaller, as is shown by the shaded areas in Figure 5-6. The fact that these changes occur over time and that the second, third, and subsequent period income changes may be quite sizable has important implications for policy, to which we turn now.

Policy Implications

Suppose we have a permanent decline in investment expenditure. With output demand determined, the decline in spending would of course lead to a fall in output and employment, occurring over a period of time.

Suppose the government wants to offset the reduction in aggregate demand by using tax cuts to keep income at the full-employment level. Since consumption adjusts only gradually to changes in income resulting from both the initial fall in investment and tax cuts, the policy maker who wants to stabilize output *over time* will have to know about the adjustment pattern of consumption so as not to overreact. The problems may be further complicated, as we discuss in Chapter 9, by the fact that frequently the policy maker too reacts only with a lag to changed circumstances.

In the short run, consumption does not respond fully to changes in income. Therefore it takes a relatively large tax cut to obtain a given change in consumption with which to offset the decline in investment. Over time, though, consumption adjusts to the change in disposable income and the tax cut that was initially just sufficient to offset reduced investment now turns out to be too generous. The compensating policy must therefore be one of a tax cut that is *front-loaded* and gradually phased down to the long-run level. The difference between the short-run and long-run tax cuts is determined by the relative size of the short-run and long-run tax multipliers.

It is important to bear in mind that we have assumed consumers have no special knowledge about the nature of the changes in income they experience as a result both of the initial change in investment and of subsequent tax adjustments. Remarkably enough, if consumers knew that the investment shift was permanent, and if they could be persuaded that the change in government policy was permanent, a one-time reduction in taxes, calculated using the long-run multiplier implied by the consumption function, would precisely stabilize income. For, in that case, the response to the fall in investment would recognize the permanent nature of the change, implying the long-run multiplier is relevant, and the response to the tax change would also recognize the permanent nature of the change. Consumption would adjust immediately, rather than gradually over the course of time.

The alternative theories of consumption we have presented in this chapter all include current disposable income among the factors that explain consumption behaviour. Each, however, points to other factors that also affect consumption. These other factors — wealth and lagged income — have to be taken into account when consumption spending is predicted for policy purposes. Large-scale econometric models do indeed embody more sophisticated consumption theories than the simple consumption function (1) of this and earlier chapters.

5-6 SUMMARY

This chapter has studied the consumption function in great detail.

1 The chapter starts out with the simple Keynesian consumption function:

$$C = 3.6 + .84Y_d \tag{2}$$

and finds that such a consumption function accounts well for observed consumption behaviour. The equation suggests that out of an additional dollar of disposable income, 84 cents are spent on consumption. The consumption function implies, too, that the ratio of consumption to income, C/Y_d, declines somewhat with the level of income.

2 Early empirical work on short-run consumption behaviour showed that the marginal propensity to consume was lower than that found in longer-period studies. The evidence revealed also that the average propensity to consume declined with the level of income. Postwar studies, by contrast, find a roughly constant average propensity to consume of about 0.9.

3 The evidence is reconciled by a reconsideration of consumption theory. Individuals will want to maintain relatively smooth consumption profiles over their lifetime. Their consumption behaviour is geared to their long-term consumption opportunities — permanent income or lifetime income plus wealth. With such a view, current income is only one of the determinants of consumption spending. Wealth and expected income play a role, too. A consumption function that represents this idea is:

$$C = a\frac{W}{P} + b\theta Y_d + b(1 - \theta)Y_{d-1} \tag{15}$$

which allows for the role of real wealth, W/P, current disposable income, Y_d, and lagged disposable income, Y_{d-1}.

4 The relative-income hypothesis argues that current consumption is related not only to current income, but also to previous peak income. The argument for this is that individuals find it difficult to reduce rates of consumption to which they have been accustomed.

5 Lagged adjustment of consumption to income results in a gradual adjustment of the level of income in the economy to changes in autonomous spending and other economic changes. An increase in autonomous spending raises income. But the adjustment process is spread out over time because the rising level of income raises consumption only gradually. This adjustment process is described by dynamic multipliers that show by how much income changes in each period following a change in autonomous spending (or other exogenous variables).

6 The dynamic adjustment of the economy to changes in policy variables, such as a change in government spending or transfers, creates a problem for policy making. The analysis of Section 5-4 shows that the policy maker needs detailed information about the dynamic responses of the economy, if policy is not to result in income levels that differ from the target levels. In a dynamic setting, the making of policy requires the policy maker to consider how much any particular policy action will affect income in each time period and to calculate *time paths* for policy variables that will bring about the desired performance.

PROBLEMS

1 What is the significance of the ratio of consumption to GNP in terms of the level of economic activity? Would you expect it to be higher or lower than normal during a recession (or depression)? Do you think the ratio would be higher in developed or undeveloped countries? Why?

The Life-Cycle Hypothesis

2 The text implies that the ratio of consumption to accumulated savings declines over time until retirement.
(a) Why? What assumption about consumption behaviour leads to this result?
(b) What happens to this ratio after retirement?
3 (a) Suppose you can earn just as much as your neighbour but are in much better health and expect to live longer than she does. Would you consume more or less than she does? Why? Derive your answer from Equation (7).
(b) According to the life-cycle hypothesis, what would the effect of the Canada Pension Plan be on your average propensity to consume out of (disposable) income?
(c) How would Equation (10) be modified for an individual who expects to receive $X per year of retirement benefits? Verify your result in 3b.
4 Give an intuitive interpretation of the marginal propensities to consume out of wealth and income at time T in the individual's lifetime in Equation (10).
* 5 In Equation (7), consumption in each year of working life is given by:

$$C = \left[\frac{N}{L} \right] Z \tag{7}$$

In Equation (10), consumption is given as

$$C = a\frac{W}{P} + cZ \qquad a \equiv \frac{1}{L - TL} \qquad c \equiv \frac{N - T}{L - T} \tag{10}$$

Show that Equations (7) and (10) are consistent for an individual who started life with zero wealth and has been saving for T years. (*Hint*: First, calculate the individual's wealth after T years of saving at rate $Z - C$. Then calculate the level of consumption implied by Equation (10) when wealth is at the level you have computed.)

Permanent-Income Hypothesis

6 In terms of permanent-income hypothesis, would you consume more of your Christmas bonus if:
(a) You knew there was a bonus every year.
(b) This was the only year such bonuses were given out.
7 Suppose the permanent-income is calculated as the average of income over the past five years; that is:

$$Y'' = \tfrac{1}{5}(Y + Y_{-1} + Y_{-2} + Y_{-3} + Y_{-4})$$

Suppose, further, that consumption is given by $C = 0.9Y''$.

(a) If you have earned $10,000 per year for the past ten years, what is your permanent income?

(b) Suppose next year (period $t + 1$) you earn $15,000. What is your new Y''?

(c) What is your consumption this year and next year?

(d) What is your short-run MPC? Long-run?

(e) Assuming you continue to earn $15,000 starting in period $t + 1$, graph the value of your permanent income in each period using the equation above.

8 Explain why good gamblers (and thieves) might be expected to live very well even in years when they don't do well at all.

* 9 The graph shows the lifetime earnings profile of a person who lives for four periods and earns incomes of $30, $60, and $90 in the first three periods of the life cycle. There are no earnings during retirement

(a) You are asked to determine the level of consumption, compatible with the budget constraint, for someone who wants an even consumption profile throughout the life cycle. Indicate in which periods the person saves and dissaves and what amounts.

(b) Assume now that, contrary to 9(a), there is no possibility for borrowing. The credit markets are closed to the individual. Under this assumption, what is the flow of consumption the individual will pick over the life cycle? In providing an answer, continue to assume that, if possible, an even flow of consumption is preferred.

(c) Assume next that the person described in 9(b) receives an increase in wealth or nonlabour income. The increase wealth is equal to $13. How will that wealth be allocated over the life cycle with and without access to the credit market? How would your answer differ if the increase in wealth were $23?

*10 Consider the consumption function in Equation (15). Assume autonomous investment spending in contrast, is in government spending. The economy is close to full employment and the government wishes to maintain aggregate demand precisely constant. In these circumstances, assume there is an increase in real wealth of $10 billion. What change in income taxes will maintain constant the equilibrium level of income in the present period? What further changes in taxes are required next year? The year after that?

*11 Assume the income tax rate is $t = 0.2$. Using Equation (15) and the information from Section 5-4, determine the size of the short-run and long-run multipliers.

12 Equation (15) shows consumption as a function of wealth, current and lagged disposable income. To reconcile that consumption function with permanent income expectations formation, you are asked to use Equation (13) and the consumption function:

$$C = a\frac{W}{P} + cY_d^P$$

to determine the magnitude of θ and $(1 - \theta)$ that is implied by Equation (15).

Adjustment and Dynamics

*13 Consider the equilibrium condition in Equation (17).

(a) Given the past level of income, Y_{-1} what is equilibrium current income? Give the answer both algebraically, solving for Y, and geometrically.

(b) Define the change in income $\Delta Y = Y - Y_{-1}$ and use this definition to rewrite Equation (17) as

$$\overline{I} = (1 - c)Y + c(1 - \theta)\Delta Y$$

or

$$\Delta Y = \frac{\overline{I} - (1 - c)Y}{c(1 - \theta)}$$

Show this equation in a diagram with ΔY and Y on the axes.

(c) Using your diagram developed in 13(b), what is the long-run level of income ($\Delta Y = 0$)?

(d) Consider now a permanent increase in investment to $\overline{I}'$. Use your diagram to show the change in income in the first period and in the long run.

(e) Assume $\overline{I} = 50$, $c = 0.8$, and $\theta = 0.75$. Calculate the initial full equilibrium value of income ($Y = Y_{-1}$). Next, consider an increase in investment to $\overline{I}' = 100$. Given Y_{-1} calculated before, what is the new level of income? What happens in the second period? What is the change in long-run income?

*14 Here is a challenge to your ability to develop diagrams. You are asked to show short-run and long-run income determination in the 45° diagram.

(a) Draw the short-run and long-run consumption functions and the aggregate demand schedule with $I = \overline{I}$.

(b) Show the initial full equilibrium.

(c) Show the short-run and long-run effects of increased investment on equilibrium income.

6

*INVESTMENT SPENDING

I n this chapter we continue our in-depth analysis of the macroeconomic relationships of the IS-LM model studied in Chapter 4. Chapter 5 moved beyond the simple consumption function of Chapter 3, paying particular attention to the role of lags and the precise way in which income enters the consumption function. Similarly, this chapter moves beyond the simple investment function of Chapter 4, in which investment was treated as a function of the interest rate. It provides a theoretical foundation for understanding how interest rates affect the level of investment. In addition, we will see how lags and variables other than interest rates — including tax rates — also affect the rate of investment.

Why study investment spending? In the first place, investment is a significant component of aggregate demand. The share of investment spending in GNP is shown in Chart 6-1. In 1979, it accounted for 21 percent of aggregate demand, and it was as high as 24 percent of aggregate demand in 1956. Clearly, investment spending constitutes a much smaller part of aggregate demand than consumption spending. Nonetheless, it plays an important role in the fluctuations of GNP over the course of the business cycle because it varies proportionately much more than consumption spending. Chart 6-1 also highlights the role of investment in relation to the business cycle. Gross investment as a percentage of ' GNP is plotted along with the unemployment rate (note that the scale for the unemployment rate is reversed). There is quite clearly a relationship between fluctuations in the level of economic activity, as indicated by the unemployment rate, and the share of investment spending in income. When unemployment is high, investment spending as a fraction of income is low, and vice versa. Indeed, this relationship goes back a long way. In 1933, during the Great Depression, investment spending was under 4 percent of GNP.

Second, investment is important because it is significantly affected by both monetary and fiscal policy. For instance, changes in the investment tax credit (to be described later) are a standard tool of fiscal policy, designed to affect investment spending. Monetary policy, too, has an important effect on investment, particularly on residential construction. Thus, changes in in-

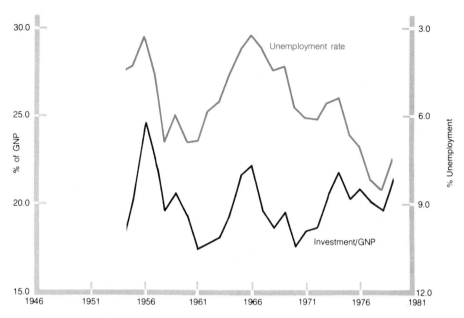

Note: The unemployment rate is on an inverted scale

CHART 6-1 GROSS INVESTMENT AS A PERCENTAGE OF GNP, AND THE UNEMPLOYMENT RATE (*Source*: Dept. of Finance, *Economic Review*)

vestment spending constitute one of the major channels by which monetary and fiscal policy affect aggregate demand.

One simple relationship is vital to the understanding of investment. *Investment is spending devoted to increasing or maintaining the stock of capital*. The stock of capital consists of the factories, machines, offices, and other durable products used in the process of production. The capital stock also includes residential housing as well as inventories. Investment is spending that adds to these components of capital stock. Recall the distinction drawn in Chapter 2 between *gross* and *net investment*. Gross investment represents total additions to the capital stock. Net investment subtracts depreciation — the reduction in the capital stock that occurs each period through wear and tear and the simple ravages of time — from gross investment. Net investment thus measures the increase in the capital stock in a given period of time.

In this chapter we disaggregate investment spending into three categories. The first consists of spending by business firms on productive capital in the form of *machinery and equipment* and *nonresidential construction*. The second is *residential construction* consisting of spending on houses and apartment buildings. These two categories comprise *fixed investment* as

TABLE 6-1 GROSS BUSINESS INVESTMENT, 1979 (BILLIONS OF DOLLARS)

Machinery and equipment	$20.5
Nonresidential construction	17.5
Residential construction	14.0
Total fixed investment	52.0
Change in inventories	4.4
Gross business investment	$56.4

Source: Statistics Canada, 11-003.

opposed to the third one, *inventory investment*, some elements of which were discussed in Chapter 3.

In 1979, investment spending in these categories was as shown in Table 6-1. Chart 6-2 shows the components of investment spending since 1954. Inventory investment and residential construction fluctuate more, as a share of GNP, than other fixed investment does. However, machinery and equipment and nonresidential construction account for over two-thirds of

CHART 6-2 COMPONENTS OF INVESTMENT SPENDING AS A PERCENTAGE OF GNP (*Source*: Dept. of Finance, *Economic Review*)

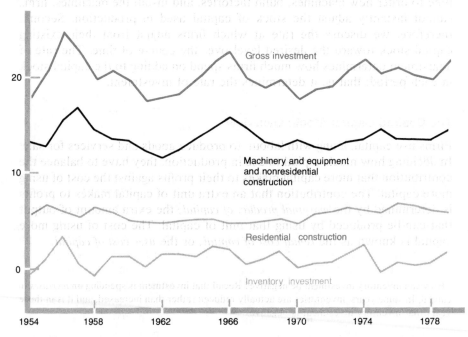

total investment spending. Note that the negative inventory investment in 1975 seen in Chart 6-2 is unusual, and that over most of the postwar period, inventory investment has been positive.[1]

In the remainder of this chapter, we develop theories and discuss evidence about the determinants of the rate of investment in each of the three major categories shown in Chart 6-2. We will develop what look like different models to explain each of the categories of investment spending. However, as we discuss in Section 6-4, the theories are essentially very similar, sharing a common view of the interaction between a desired capital stock and the rate at which the economy adjusts towards that desired stock.

6-1 BUSINESS FIXED INVESTMENT

The machinery, equipment, and structures used in the production of goods and services constitute the *stock* of business fixed capital. Our analysis of business fixed investment proceeds in two stages. First, we ask how much capital firms would like to use, given the costs and returns of using capital and the level of output they expect to produce. That is, we ask what determines the *desired capital stock*. The desired capital stock is the capital stock that firms would like to have in the long run, abstracting from the delays they face in adjusting their use of capital. However, because it takes time to order new machines, build factories, and install the machines, firms cannot instantly adjust the stock of capital used in production. Second, therefore, we discuss the rate at which firms adjust from their existing capital stock toward the desired level over the course of time. The rate of adjustment determines how much firms spend on adding to the capital stock in each period; that is, it determines the rate of investment.

The Desired Capital Stock: Overview

Firms use capital, along with labour, to produce goods and services for sale. In deciding how much capital to use in production, they have to balance the contribution that more capital makes to their profits against the cost of using more capital. The contribution that an extra unit of capital makes to profits is determined by the *marginal product of capital*, the extra amount of output that can be produced by using that unit of capital. The cost of using more capital is known as the *rental cost of capital*, or the *user cost of capital*.

---

[1] How can inventory investment be negative? Recall that investment is spending on *increases* in capital. In some years, inventories are actually reduced rather than increased, and it is in those years that inventory investment is negative.

To derive the rental cost of capital, we think of the firm as financing the purchase of the capital (whether the firm produces the capital itself or buys it from some other firm) by borrowing, at an interest cost i. In order to obtain the services of an extra unit of capital, in each period the firm must pay the interest cost i for each dollar of capital that it buys.[2] Thus the basic measure of the rental cost of capital is the interest rate. Later we shall go into much more detail about the rental cost of capital, but for the meantime we shall think of the interest rate as determining the rental cost.

In deciding how much capital they would like to use in production, firms compare the value of the marginal product of capital with the user or rental costs of capital. If the rental cost of capital is high, the marginal product of capital will have to be high for firms to be willing to pay the high cost of using the capital. If the rental cost of capital is low, firms will be willing to use capital even if its marginal product is low.

To give content to this relationship, we have to specify what determines the productivity of capital and what determines the user (rental) cost of capital. The marginal product of capital is examined next, and then we turn to the rental cost of the capital.

The Marginal Productivity of Capital

In understanding the marginal productivity of capital, it is important to note that firms can substitute capital for labour in the production of output. Different combinations of capital and labour can be used to produce a given level of output. If labour is relatively cheap, the firm will want to use relatively more labour, and if capital is relatively cheap, the firm will want to use relatively more capital.

The general relationship among the desired capital stock (K^*), the rental cost of capital (i_c), and the level of output is given by

$$K^* = g(i_c, Y) \tag{1}$$

Equation (1) indicates that the desired capital stock depends on the rental cost of capital and the level of output. The lower the rental cost of capital, the larger the desired capital stock. And the greater the level of output, the larger the desired capital stock. We will now explain in more detail the factors underlying Equation (1).

---

[2] Even if the firm finances the investment out of profits it has made in the past — retained earnings — it should still think of the interest rate as the cost of using the new capital, since it could otherwise have lent out those funds and earned interest on them, or paid them out as dividends to shareholders.

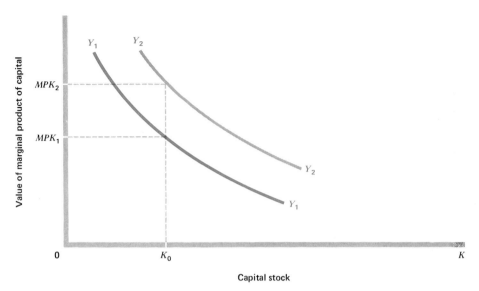

FIGURE 6-1 THE MARGINAL PRODUCT OF CAPITAL IN RELATION TO THE LEVEL OF OUTPUT AND THE CAPITAL STOCK

As the firm combines progressively more capital with relatively less labour in the production of a *given* amount of output, the marginal product of capital declines. This relation is shown in the downward-sloping schedules in Figure 6-1. Those schedules show how the marginal product of capital falls as more capital is used in producing a given level of output. The schedule Y_1Y_1 is drawn for a level of output Y_1. The schedule Y_2Y_2 is drawn for the higher output level Y_2. The marginal product of capital, given the capital stock, say K_0, is higher on the schedule Y_2Y_2 than on Y_1Y_1. That is because more labour is being used in combination with the given amount of capital K_0 to produce the level of output Y_2 than to produce Y_1.

Figure 6-1 shows the marginal product of capital in relation to the level of output and the amount of capital being used to produce that output. Figure 6-2 is a similar diagram which shows the desired capital stock as related to the rental cost of capital and the level of output. Given the level of output, say Y_1, the firm will want to use more capital, the lower the rental cost of capital — because at low rental costs of capital, it can afford to use capital even when its marginal productivity is quite low. If the rental cost of capital is high, the firm will be willing to use capital only if its marginal productivity is high — which means that the firm will not want to use very much capital. In producing a higher level of output, say Y_2, the firm will use

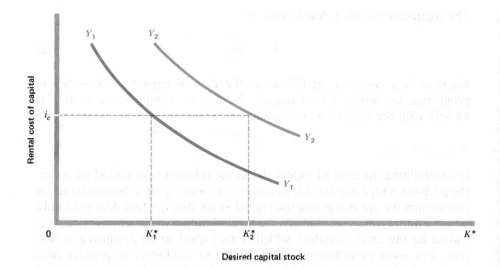

FIGURE 6-2 THE DESIRED CAPITAL STOCK
IN RELATION TO THE LEVEL OF OUTPUT
AND THE COST OF CAPITAL

both more capital and more labour, given the rental cost of capital.[3]
Therefore, at higher levels of output, the desired capital stock is higher.

The Cobb-Douglas Production Function

While Equation (1) provides the general relationship determining the desired
capital stock, a particular form of the equation, based on the Cobb-Douglas
production function, [4] is frequently used in studies of investment behaviour.

---

[3] Throughout this discussion, we have implicitly been assuming that the real wage paid to
labour is given and does not change as the rental cost of capital changes.

[4] The Cobb-Douglas production function is written in the form

$$Y = N^{1-a}K^a \qquad 1 > a > 0$$

where N is the amount of labour used. This production function is particularly popular beacuse
it is easy to handle, and also because it appears to fit the facts of economic experience quite
well. The coefficient a appearing in Eq. (2) is the same as the a of the production function. The
reader trained in calculus will want to show that a is the share of capital in total income.

The particular equation that is used is[5]

$$K^* = \frac{aY}{i_c} \tag{2}$$

where a is a constant. In this case, the desired capital stock varies in proportion to output. Given output, the desired capital stock varies inversely with the rental cost of capital.

Expected Output

In determining the desired capital stock, the relevant time period for which the decision on the capital stock applies, is obviously an important issue. In this section we are discussing the capital stock that the firm desires to hold at some future time. Accordingly, the level of output in Equations (1) and (2) should be the level of output which firms expect to be producing at that time. For some investments — such as that in machinery to produce hula hoops — the future time at which the output will be produced is a matter of months or only weeks. For other investments — such as that in airplane factories — the future time at which the output will be produced is years away.

This suggests that the notion of permanent income (in this case permanent output) is relevant to investment as well as consumption. For longer-lived investments, the firm's capital demand is governed primarily by its view on the level of output it will be producing on average in the future. The firm's long-run demand for business fixed capital, depending on the normal or permanent level of output, is thus relatively independent of the current level of output, and depends on *expectations* of future output levels. However, it is affected by current output to the extent that current output affects expectations of permanent output.[6]

---

[5] We draw attention here to a very subtle point. Equation (2) gives the marginal product of capital (MPK) when the *input of labour* is held fixed, while in Figures 1 and 2 we work with the MPK when labour is being adjusted so that *output* is kept fixed. The desired capital stock that corresponds to Figures 1 and 2 is

$$K^* = \left[\frac{aw}{(1-a)i_c} \right]^{1-a} Y$$

where w is the real wage.

Equation (2'), like Equation (2), implies that desired capital is proportional to Y and varies inversely with the rental cost of capital. We use (2) rather than (2') in the text because it is the form that has been used in empirical studies.

[6] The role of permanent income in investment has been emphasized by Robert Eisner. Much of his work is summarized in his book *Factors in Business Investment* (Cambridge, Mass.: Ballinger, 1978).

Summary on the Desired Capital Stock

It is worthwhile stepping back for a moment to summarize the main results so far

1   The firm's demand for capital—the desired capital stock K^*—depends on the rental cost of capital i_c and the expected level of output.
2   Firms balance the cost and benefits of using capital. The lower the rental cost of capital, the larger the optimal level of capital relative to output. This relation reflects the lower marginal productivity of capital when it is used relatively intensively. The intensive use of capital will be profitable only if the rental cost of capital is low.
3   The higher the level of output, the larger the desired capital stock.
4   The firm plans its capital stock in relation to expected future or permanent output.
5   Current output affects capital demand to the extent that it affects expectations about future output.

The Rental Cost of Capital Again

We have already introduced the notion of the rental or user cost of capital in determining the firm's desired capital stock. As a first approximation, we identified the rental cost of capital with the interest rate, on the argument that firms would have to borrow to finance their use of capital. Now we go into more detail on the costs per period of using capital.

To use capital for a single period, say a year, the firm can be thought of as buying the capital with borrowed funds and paying the interest on the borrowing. At the end of the year, the firm will still have some of the capital left. But the capital is likely to have depreciated over the course of the year. We shall assume that the firm intends to continue using the remaining capital in production in future years, and that its depreciation simply represents the using up of the capital in the process of production—physical wear and tear. We shall now examine the rental cost, taking into account interest costs and depreciation. Although taxes affect the cost to the firm of using capital, we shall for the meantime ignore taxes and return to them later.

Leaving aside taxes, we want now to examine the two elements in the rental cost of capital in more detail. For the moment, let us write the interest cost as i. Insofar as depreciation is concerned, we assume that a fixed proportion d of the capital is used up per period. The depreciation cost, per dollar of capital, is d.[7] The rental cost, or user cost, of capital, per dollar's worth of capital, which we denote by i_c, is therefore:

---

[7] Why is depreciation considered as a cost? We want to remind ourselves that the firm continues using the capital and therefore has to devote expenditures to maintaining the productive efficiency of capital and thus wear and tear. We are assuming that per dollar of capital, d dollars per period are required to maintain productive efficiency.

$$i_c \equiv i + d \qquad\qquad (3)$$

A simple numerical example should help in understanding Equation (3). Suppose the interest rate is 10 percent per year and the rate of depreciation is 15 percent. That means that by the end of the year, the firm will have to spend 15 cents per dollar of capital to maintain capital's production efficiency in the face of depreciation. The costs to the form of using the capital for the year are then the interest cost, 10 cents per dollar of capital, and the depreciation cost, 15 cents per dollar of capital. The cost of using capital for a year is thus 25 cents per dollar's worth of capital.

The Real Rate of Interest

It is time now to examine the interest component of the rental cost of capital in more detail. We have not, so far, distinguished between the *real* and the *nominal* rates of interest. The real rate of interest is the nominal rate of interest minus the rate of inflation. In general, someone borrowing at a stated nominal rate of interest, say 10 percent, does not know what the rate of inflation over the period of the borrowing will be. Accordingly, the real rate of interest relevant when a loan transaction is entered into is the *expected* real rate of interest — the stated nominal interest rate minus the rate of inflation expected over the period of the loan.

The notion of the real rate of interest is extremely important. Suppose that the nominal interest rate, the rate stated in the loan agreement, is 10 percent. Then suppose also that prices are rising at 10 percent. Someone borrowing $100 at the beginning of the year pays back $110 at the end of the year. But those dollars in which repayment is made buy less goods than the dollars lent at the beginning of the year when the loan was made. If the inflation rate is 10 percent, then the $110 paid at the end of the year buys the same amount of goods that could have been bought with the original $100 at the beginning of the year. In *real* terms, in terms of the goods which the money can buy, the lender has no more at the end than at the beginning of the year. Thus the *real* interest rate actually received was zero, even though the *nominal* interest rate was 10 percent. Putting things slightly differently, given the *nominal* interest rate, the higher the rate of inflation, the lower the *real* interest rate. In practice, nominal interest rates tend to be higher when inflation is higher.

Now, it is the *expected real* rate of interest that should enter the calculation of the rental cost of capital. Why? The firm is borrowing in order to produce goods for sale. On average, across all firms, it is reasonable to believe that the prices of the goods the firms sell will be rising along with the general price level. Thus the value of what the firm will be producing in the future will be rising with the price level, but the nominal amount of interest it has to pay back on account of its borrowings does not rise with the price level. The real value of the debt it has incurred by borrowing will be falling over time, as a result of inflation, and it should take that reduction in the real value of its outstanding debts into account in deciding how much capital to employ. To put it differently, the firm will be paying off its debts with dollars of lower real value than the dollars it borrowed.

Accordingly, we can be more precise in the way we write Equation (3) for the rental cost of capital. We write the rental cost of capital, taking account of expected inflation at the rate π^*, as

$$i_c \equiv i_r + d \equiv i - \pi^* + d \tag{4}$$

where i_r is the real interest rate, i the nominal interest rate, and

$$i_r \equiv i - \pi^* \tag{5}$$

Equation (5) states that the real rate of interest is the nominal interest rate minus the expected rate of inflation. Implicitly, Equation (5) refers to the expected real rate of interest. At the end of the period, when the rate of inflation is known, we can also state what the *actual* or realized real rate of interest for the period was — namely, the nominal interest rate i minus the actual rate of inflation.

To reiterate, it is important to note that the interest rate relevant to the firm's demand for capital is the *real* rate, and not the nominal rate. This makes it clear that the nominal rate of interest is not a good guide to the rental cost of capital. If the rate of inflation is zero and is expected to be zero, and the nominal interest rate is 5 percent, then the real interest rate is 5 percent. By contrast, if the nominal interest rate is 10 percent and inflation is at the rate of 10 percent, the real interest rate is zero. Other things equal, the desired capital stock in this example would tend to be higher than the nominal interest rate of 10 percent than with the nominal rate of 5 percent — because those rates correspond to real rates of zero and 5 percent respectively. As you have no doubt deduced, and as we shall show, investment spending tends to be higher when the rental cost of capital is lower. But, because of the distinction between real and nominal interest rates, that is *not* the same as saying that investment tends to be higher when the nominal rate of interest is lower.

Taxes and the Rental Cost of Capital

The rental cost of capital is affected by tax variables as well as by the interest rate and depreciation. The two main tax variables that affect the rental cost of capital are the corporate income tax and the investment tax credit. The corporate income tax is an essentially proportional tax on profits, whereby the firm pays a proportion, say t, of its profits in taxes. The investment tax credit allows firms to deduct from their taxes a certain fraction, say τ, of their investment expenditures in each year. For example, suppose the investment tax credit is 10 percent. Then a firm spending $1 million for investment purposes in a given year can deduct 10 percent of the $1 million, or $100,000, from the taxes it would otherwise have to pay the federal government.

We want to know what effects the corporate income tax and the investment tax credit have on the rental cost of capital. The easier case is the investment tax credit. Essentially, the investment tax credit reduces the price of a capital good to the firm by the ratio τ, since the government returns to the firm a proportion τ of the cost of each capital good. Equivalently, we can say that the rental cost is reduced by the factor τ. The investment tax credit therefore reduces the rental cost of capital.

The corporate income tax, surprisingly, has ambiguous effects on the desired stock of capital. The ambiguity stems from some complexities in the tax laws that we do not go into here. But the reason the complexities matter can be explained. In the presence of the corporate income tax, the firm will want to equate the *after-tax* marginal product of capital with the *after-tax* rental cost of capital in order to ensure that the marginal contribution of the capital to profits is equal to the marginal cost of using it.

Let us focus on the interest component of the rental cost. The basic point is that interest cost is treated as a deduction from revenues in the calculation of the corporation's taxes. Suppose there were no corporate income tax, no inflation, no depreciation, and an interest rate of 10 percent. The desired capital stock would be that level of the capital stock, say K^*_0, such that the marginal product of capital was 10 percent. Now suppose that the corporate income tax rises to 46 percent and the interest rate remains constant. At the capital stock K^*_0, the after-tax marginal product of capital is now 5.4 percent (since 46 percent of the profits are paid in taxes). But if the interest rate stays at 10 percent and the firm gets to deduct 46 percent of its interest payments from taxes, the after-tax cost of capital will be 5.4 percent too. In this case, the desired capital stock is unaffected by the rate of corporate taxation.

Thus, to a first approximation, ignoring all the complexities, the corporate income tax has no effect on the desired capital stock. The ambiguities arise when the special tax treatment of depreciation,[8] of inflation, and of investment financing other than through borrowing is taken into account.[9]

We conclude this section by noting its two main points. The investment

---

[8] For tax purposes depreciation is counted as a business expense, but these allowances follow complicated rules and are not generally equal to the depreciation that the capital stock actually undergoes.

[9] Some investment is financed through the sale of equities. Part of the return to equity holders typically takes the form of dividend payments. However, dividends are not treated as a deduction from profits in the calculation of corporate income taxes. Thus the basic argument presented in the case of interest payments, that the corporate income tax does not affect the desired capital stock, would not apply for equity financed investment.

tax credit reduces the rental cost of capital and increases the desired stock of capital. The corporate income tax has ambiguous effects on the desired stock of capital.

Summary and Effects of Fiscal and Monetary Policy on the Desired Capital Stock

We summarize, using Equation (1), which gives the desired capital stock as a function of the rental cost of capital and the expected level of output, and the preceding discussion of the rental cost of capital. From Equation (1) we note that the desired capital stock increases when the expected level of output rises and when the rental cost of capital falls.

The rental cost of capital falls when the real interest rate and the rate of depreciation fall. It likewise falls when the investment tax credit rises. Changes in the rate of corporate taxation have ambiguous effects on the desired capital stock.

The major significance of these results is their implication that monetary and fiscal policy affect the desired capital stock. Fiscal policy exerts an effect through both the corporate tax rate, t, and the investment tax credit rate, τ. Both these instruments are used to affect capital demand and thus investment spending. Since the effects of the investment tax credit are unambiguous, it receives the major attention as a fiscal means of affecting investment.

Monetary policy affects capital demand by affecting the market interest rate. The manner in which monetary policy affects capital demand is by changing the real market rate of interest relative to the marginal productivity of capital.[10] In that manner the profitability of owning and operating capital is affected, and thus the demand for capital is also influenced. A lowering of the nominal interest rate by the Bank of Canada (given the expected inflation rate), as reflected in a downward shift in the LM curve of Chapter 4, will induce firms to desire more capital. This expansion in capital demand in turn will affect investment spending, as we shall now see.

From Desired Capital Stock to Investment

We have now put more content into the general form of Equation (1) for the desired capital stock by discussing the rental cost of capital in detail. At any given time, the actual capital stock will almost certainly differ from the capital stock firms would like to have. How, then, do firms change their capital stocks in order to move toward the desired capital stock? In particular, is there any reason why firms do not attempt to move to their desired capital stocks immediately?

---

[10] We should note that the Bank of Canada is able to affect *nominal* interest rates directly by its sales and purchases of bonds. Its ability to control *real* interest rates is more limited.

Since it takes time to plan and complete an investment project, and because attempts to invest quickly are likely to be more expensive than gradual adjustment to the capital stock, it is unlikely that firms would attempt to adjust their capital stocks to the long-run desired level instantaneously. Very rapid adjustment of the capital stock would require crash programs by the firm which would distract management from its routine tasks and interfere with ongoing production. Thus, firms generally plan to adjust their capital stocks gradually over a period of time, rather than immediately.

The Flexible Accelerator

There are a number of hypotheses about the way in which firms plan to adjust their capital stock over time; we single out the *flexible accelerator hypothesis* here.[11] The basic notion behind the flexible accelerator hypothesis is that the larger the gap between the existing capital stock and the desired capital stock, the greater a firm's rate of investment. The hypothesis is that firms plan to close a fraction λ of the gap between the desired and actual capital stocks each period. Denote the capital stock at the end of last period by K_{-1}. The gap between the desired and actual capital stocks is $(K^* - K_{-1})$. The firm plans so that the capital stock at the end of the current period K will be such that

$$K - K_{-1} = \lambda(K^* - K_{-1}) \tag{6}$$

Equation (6) states that the firm plans to . .ave the capital stock at the end of the period be such that a fraction λ of the gap (between the desired capital stock K^* and the capital stock K_{-1} that existed at the end of last period) is closed. Rewriting Equation (6),

$$K = K_{-1} + \lambda(K^* - K_{-1}) \tag{6a}$$

In order to increase the capital stock from K_{-1} to the level of K indicated by Equation (6a), the firm has to achieve an amount of net investment, $I \equiv K - K_{-1}$, indicated by Equation (6). We can therefore write net investment as

$$I = \lambda(K^* - K_{-1}) \tag{7}$$

which is the flexible accelerator formulation of net investment. Notice that Equation (7) implies that investment is larger, the larger the gap between actual and desired capital stocks.[12]

[11] The flexible accelerator is a generalized form of the older *accelerator* model of investment, in which investment is proportional to the change in the level of GNP. The accelerator model is examined briefly in the appendix to this chapter.

[12] Gross investment, as opposed to net investment described in Eq. (7), includes, in addition, depreciation. Thus, gross investment is $I + dK_{-1}$, where d is again the rate of depreciation.

In Figure 6-3 we show the adjustment process of capital in a circumstance where the initial capital stock is K_1 and the given desired capital stock is K^*. The assumed speed of adjustment is $\lambda = 0.5$. Starting from K_1, . half the discrepancy between target capital and current actual capital is made up in every period. First-period net investment is therefore $0.5(K^* - K_1)$. In the second period, investment will be less because the previous period's investment will have raised the actual capital stock and thus reduced the size of the gap between actual and desired capital stock. Progressively, investment reduces the gap until the actual capital stock reaches the level of target capital. The speed with which this process allows actual capital to reach target capital is determined by λ. The larger is λ, the faster the gap is reduced.

In Equation (7), we have reached our goal of deriving an investment function that shows current investment spending determined by the desired stock of capital K^* and the actual stock of capital K_{-1}. According to the flexible accelerator hypothesis, any factor that increases the desired stock increases the rate of investment. Thus an increase in the expected output, or

FIGURE 6-3 ADJUSTMENT OF THE CAPITAL STOCK

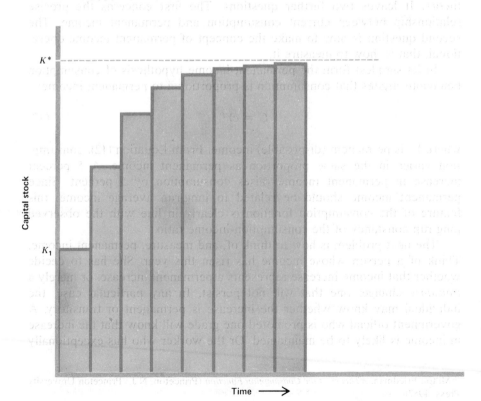

Time $\longrightarrow$

a reduction in the real interest rate, or an increase in the investment tax credit, will each increase the rate of investment. We thus have derived a quite complete theory of business fixed investment that includes many of the factors we should expect to affect the rate of investment. And the theory of investment embodied in Equation (7) also contains aspects of *dynamic behaviour* — that is, of behaviour that depends on values of economic variables in periods other than the current period.

There are two sources of dynamic behaviour in Equation (7). The first arises from expectations. The K^* term depends on the firm's estimate of future or permanent output. To the extent that the firm forms its estimates of permanent output as a weighted average of past output levels, there will be lags in the adjustment of the level of permanent output to the actual level of output. Accordingly, the desired capital stock will adjust only slowly over time to a change in the level of output. And in turn, investment will therefore also adjust slowly to a change in the level of output. The second source of dynamic behaviour arises from adjustment lags, in the specification that firms plan to close only a proportion of the gap between the actual and desired capital stocks each period, as shown in Figure 6-3. The adjustment lags produce lagged response of investment to changes in the variables that affect the desired capital stock.

Empiricial Results

At this point it is useful to ask how the investment model we have developed in Equation (7) performs empirically. To use Equation (7), it is necessary to substitute some specific equation for K^*, the desired capital stock. Frequently the much-used Cobb-Douglas form Equation (2), is chosen. Using Equation (2) in Equation (7) yields a (net) investment function of the form:

$$I = \lambda \left(\frac{aY}{i_c} - K_{-1} \right) \tag{8}$$

The rental cost of capital, i_c in Equation (8), is as in Equation (4), but also adjusted for taxes.

Empirical work, in particular that of Dale Jorgenson and his associates, shows that an investment function including the variables in Equation (8) provides a reasonable explanation of the behaviour of business fixed investment. However, the form shown in Equation (8) can be improved upon by allowing more scope for lagged or slow adjustment.[13] As it stands,

---

[13] See Dale W. Jorgenson, "Econometric Studies of Investment Behavior: A Survey," *Journal of Economic Literature*, December 1971, and Peter K. Clark, "Investment in the 1970's: Theory, Performance, and Prediction," *Brookings Papers on Economic Activity*, 1979. 1 (Washington, D.C.: The Brookings Institution, 1979). For an application of the theory with Canadian data, see G.O. Gaudet, J.D. May, and D.G. McFetridge, "Optimal Capital Accumulation: The Neoclassical Framework in a Canadian Context", *Review of Economics and Statistics*, August, 1976.

Equation (8), with the output variable not being explicitly permanent output, shows an immediate impact from a change in current output to investment spending. Moreover, Equation (8) implies that if the output increase were maintained, the first-period adjustment to the increase would be larger than the second-period adjustment, and so forth, as suggested by Figure 6-3. However, the empirical evidence suggests that the adjustment instead takes the bell-shaped form shown in Figure 6-4. The major impact of a change in output on actual investment occurs with a two-period (year) lag. The short-run impact on investment is less than the impact two years later. Investment spending, like consumption spending, adjusts only slowly over time.

There are two, not mutually exclusive, explanations for the behaviour shown in Figure 6-4, corresponding to the two sources of dynamic behaviour in Equation (7) that we discussed above. The first possibility is that the lag pattern of Figure 6-4 reflects the way in which expectations about future output, and thus the long-run desired capital stock, are formed. In that view, only a sustained increase in output will persuade firms that the capital stock should be increased in the long run. Figure 6-4 would then imply that it takes about two years for changes in the variables that determine the desired capital stock to have their major impact on expectations.

The second explanation relies less on expectations and more on the physical delays in the investment process. That interpretation would be that Figure 6-4 reflects the long time it takes for a change in the desired capital stock to be translated into investment spending. In industries in which

FIGURE 6-4 EFFECTS OF AN INCREASE IN OUTPUT IN PERIOD ZERO ON NET INVESTMENT IN SUBSEQUENT PERIODS

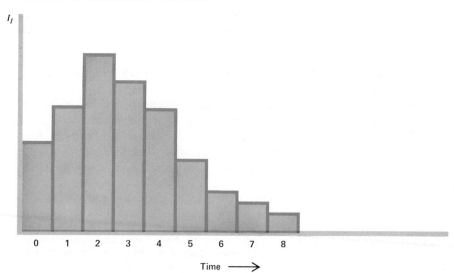

investment can be undertaken quickly, there may be some response within a year. But in the economy as a whole, the maximum impact on investment of a change in the desired capital stock happens only two years after the change in the desired stock.

In brief, the first explanation is that Figure 6-4 represents the slow adjustment of the desired capital stock to changes in the variables that, in the long run, determine that desired stock. The second explanation is that Figure 6-4 represents the long adjustment lags of investment in response to changes in the desired capital stock.

For many purposes, it does not matter which explanation of the form of Figure 6-4 is correct, and it is difficult to tell the explanations apart empirically. It is undoubtedly true that both explanations are relevant. The important point is that lags in the determination of the level of business fixed investment are long.

Sales and Profits as Determinants of Investment

Some studies of investment find either the level of sales or total profits to be factors explaining the level of investment. The level of sales could be interpreted as affecting expectations of future output and thus affecting the desired capital stock. Note that output and sales differ by the amount of inventory accumulation.

The role of profits can be interpreted similarly. High profits may provide an indication of future demand for the firm's product, and thus of future output. Alternatively, it is often argued that firms prefer to use retained profits to finance investment, rather than borrow. The preference might result from the expense of having to raise outside funds relative to using inside funds. However, it has to be remembered that in using its retained profits for investment, the firm has to consider the return that could be obtained on those funds by lending them out or by distributing them to the firm's owners.

The Timing of Investment and the Investment Tax Credit

The flexible accelerator model provides a useful summary of the dynamics of investment. But it does not sufficiently emphasize the *timing* of investment. Because investment is undertaken for the long run and often requires several years to complete, there is some flexibility in the dates on which the actual investment is undertaken. For example, suppose a firm wanted to have some machinery in place within three years. Suppose that it knew the investment tax credit would be raised substantially a year from now. The firm might be wise to delay the investment for a year and to make the machinery at a faster rate during the next two years, receiving the higher investment tax credit as the reward for waiting the extra year. Similarly, if a firm somehow knew that the cost of borrowing next year would be much lower than this year, it might wait a year to undertake its investment project.

The flexibility in the timing of investment leads to an interesting contrast between the effects of the investment tax credit and the income tax on investment and consumption respectively. We saw in Chapter 5 that a permanent change in the income tax has a much larger effect on consumption than a transitory change. However, the rate of investment *during the period* that a temporary investment tax credit is in effect would be higher than the rate of investment that would occur over the same period during which a permanent credit of the same magnitude was in effect. Why? If firms knew the investment tax credit was temporary, they would advance the timing of their planned investments in order to take advantage of the higher credit during the current period. If there were a permanent change in the investment tax credit, then the desired capital stock would rise, and there would on that account be more investment. But there would not also be a bunching of investment.

It is for this reason that temporary changes in the investment tax credit have been suggested as a highly effective countercyclical policy measure. However, this is not a simple policy tool, as expectations about the timing and duration of the credit might worsen the instability of investment.

Summary on Business Fixed Investment

The main conclusions of the theory of business fixed investment as developed here are:

1 Over time, net investment spending is governed by the discrepancy between actual and desired capital.
2 Desired capital depends on the rental (user) cost of capital and the expected level of output. Capital demand rises with expected output and the investment tax credit, and declines with an increase in *real* interest rates.
3 There is strong evidence that adjustment of actual to desired capital is a slow process. A sustained change in the profitability of capital or the level of income will not exert its maximum effect on investment for two years.
4 Although the adjustment of actual to desired capital is a slow process, what matters for aggregate demand management is the level of investment. From this perspective, monetary and fiscal policy do exert an effect on investment via the desired capital stock, although the short-run impact is likely to be minor. Over time, though, investment spending is more affected by monetary or fiscal policy. The lags with which these investment effects occur are important to bear in mind in shaping stabilization policy.
5 Investment theory, like consumption theory, emphasizes the role of expected or permanent income or output and other permanent variables as determinants of capital demand.

6-2 RESIDENTIAL CONSTRUCTION

We study residential construction separately from business fixed investment both because somewhat different theoretical considerations are relevant[14] and because institutional features of the economy make residential construction especially sensitive to changes in interest rates.

Chart 6-3 shows residential construction spending in constant (1971) dollars for the period 1954-1979. Residential construction declines in recession periods such as 1957, 1960-1961, 1970 and 1974-1975. There was also a decline in 1966 as a result of the tight monetary policy of that year.

Theory

Residential construction consists of the building of single-family and multi-family dwellings which we shall call housing. Housing is distinguished as an asset by its long life. Consequently, investment in housing in any one year tends to be a very small proportion of the existing stock of housing—about 3 percent. The theory of residential investment starts by considering the

---

[14] In the concluding section of this chapter, we explain why slightly different theoretical models are used in explaining business fixed investment and residential construction.

CHART 6-3 RESIDENTIAL CONSTRUCTION SPENDING (*Source*: Dept. of Finance, *Economic Review*)

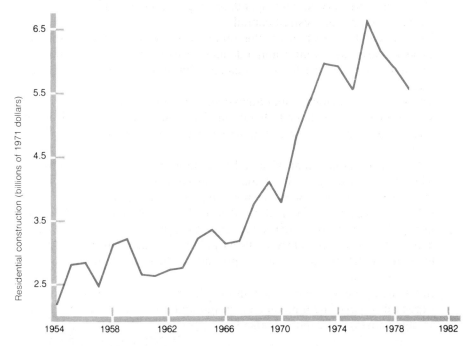

demand for the existing stock of housing. Housing is viewed as one among the many assets that a wealth holder can own.

In Figure 6-5a we show the demand for the stock of housing in the downward-sloping $D_0 D_0$ curve. The lower the price of housing (P_H), the greater is demand. The position of the demand curve itself depends on a number of economic variables: First, the greater is wealth, the greater is the demand for housing. The more wealthy individuals are, the more housing they desire to own. Thus an increase in wealth would shift the demand curve from $D_0 D_0$ to $D_1 D_1$. Second, the demand for housing as an asset depends on the real return available on other assets. If returns on other forms of holding wealth — such as bonds — are low, then housing looks like a relatively attractive form in which to hold wealth. The lower the return on other assets, the greater the demand for housing. A reduction in the return on other assets, such as bonds or common stock, shifts the demand curve from $D_0 D_0$ to $D_1 D_1$.

Third, the demand for the housing stock depends on the net real return obtained by owning housing. The gross return — before taking costs into account — consists of rent, if the housing is rented out, or the implicit return that the homeowner receives by living in the home, plus capital gains arising from increases in the value of the housing. In turn, the costs of owning the housing consist of interest cost, typically the mortgage interest rate, plus any real estate taxes, and depreciation. These costs are deducted from the gross return and, after tax adjustments, constitute the net return. An increase in the net return on housing caused, for example, by a reduction in

FIGURE 6-5 THE HOUSING MARKET: DETERMINATION OF THE ASSET PRICE OF HOUSING AND THE RATE OF HOUSING INVESTMENT the mortgage interest rate, makes housing a more attractive form in which to hold wealth and shifts up the demand curve for housing from D_0D_0 to D_1D_1.

The price of housing is determined by the interaction of this demand with the stock supply of housing. At any one time the stock supply is fixed – there is a given stock of housing that cannot be adjusted quickly in response to price changes. The supply curve of the stock of housing is the SS curve of Figure 6-5a. The equilibrium *asset price of housing*, P_H^0, is determined by the intersection of the supply and demand curves. The asset price of housing is simply the price of a typical house or apartment. At any one time, the market for the stock of housing determines the asset price of housing.

We now consider the determinants of the rate of investment in housing, and for that purpose turn to Figure 6-5b. The curve FS represents the supply of new housing as a function of the price of housing. This curve should be thought of in the same way as the regular supply curve of any industry. The supply curve, it will be recalled, represents the amount of a good that suppliers want to sell at the specified price. In this case, the good being supplied is new housing. The position of the FS curve is affected by the costs of factors of production used in the construction industry and by technological factors affecting the cost of building.

The curve FS is sometimes called the flow supply curve, since it represents the *flow* of new housing into the market in a given time period. In contrast, the *stock* supply curve SS represents the total amount of housing in the market at a moment of time.

Given the price of housing established in the asset market, P_H^0, building contractors supply the amount of new housing, Q_H^0, for sale at that price. The higher the asset price, the greater the supply of new housing. Now the supply of new housing is nothing other than gross investment in housing – total additions to the housing stock. Figure 6-5 thus represents our basic theory of the determinants of housing investment.

Any factor affecting the demand for the existing stock of housing will affect the asset price of housing, P_H, and thus the rate of investment in housing. Similarly, any factor shifting the flow supply curve FS will affect the rate of investment. We have already investigated the major factors shifting the DD demand curve for housing, but will briefly repeat that analysis.

Suppose the interest rate rises. Then the asset demand for housing falls and the price of housing falls; that in turn induces a decline in the rate of production of new housing, or a decline in housing investment. Or, suppose that the mortgage interest rate rises: once again there is a fall in the asset price of housing and a reduction in the rate of construction. Or let there be an increase in wealth that increases the demand for housing. The asset price of housing and the rate of construction – the rate of housing investment – both rise.

Because the existing stock of housing is so large relative to the rate of investment in housing, we can ignore the effects of the current supply of new housing on the price of housing in the short run. However, over time, the new construction shifts the SS curve of the left-hand panel to the right as it increases the housing stock. The long-run equilibrium in the housing industry would be reached, in an economy in which there was no increase in population or wealth over time, when the housing stock was constant. Constancy of the housing stock requires gross investment equal to depreciation, or net investment equal to zero. The asset price of housing would have to be at the level such that the rate of construction was just equal to the rate of depreciation of the existing stock of housing in long-run equilibrium. If population or income and wealth were growing at a constant rate, the long-run equilibrium would be one in which the rate of construction was just sufficient to cover depreciation and the steadily growing stock demand. In an economy subjected to continual nonsteady changes, that long-run equilibrium is not necessarily ever reached.

Minor qualifications to the basic theoretical structure arise chiefly because new housing cannot be constructed immediately in response to changes in P_H; rather, it takes a short time for that response to occur. Thus, the supply of new housing responds, not to the actual price of housing today, but to the price expected to prevail when the construction is completed. However, the lags are quite short; it takes less than a year to build a typical house. Another qualification stems from that same construction delay. Since builders have to incur expenses before they sell their output, they need financing over the construction period, and hence the position of the flow supply curve is affected by the interest rate.

An analysis of the housing market should also take into account the important role played by the mortgage interest rate and the availability of mortgages, since most houses are purchased with the aid of mortgage financing. Most of the funds obtained to finance new construction are provided by financial institutions, particularly life insurance companies, trust companies, mortgage loan companies, and chartered banks. When interest rates rise, the supply of mortgage funds is affected in two ways. First, the interest cost to financial institutions of attracting deposits rises as the return on alternative investments increases. Second, the proportion of their assets channelled into mortgages falls as the yields on other securities rise.

The impact of the cost and availability of mortgages on housing investment is strong, as can be observed by the fluctuations in residential investment shown in Charts 6-2 and 6-3. These impacts would be expected on the basis of the theory summarized in Figure 6-5. The general increase in interest rates increases the attractiveness of assets other than housing. The increase in mortgage rates and the unavailability of mortgages make housing more costly or difficult to hold. Each of these factors thus shifts the DD curve downward, reducing the asset price of housing. Then the unavailability of mortgages and the increased mortgage rate shift up the FS curve. Each of these shifts reduces the rate of housing investment.

6-3 INVENTORY INVESTMENT

Inventories consist of goods in the process of production and completed goods held by firms in anticipation of their sale. The ratio of inventories to monthly shipments in Canadian manufacturing has been in the range of 1.5 to 2.5 over the past 30 years.

The inventories of interest to us are those held to meet future demands for goods. Firms hold such inventories because goods cannot be instantly manufactured or obtained from the manufacturer to meet demand. Some inventories are held as an unavoidable part of the production process; there is an inventory of meat and sawdust inside the sausage machine during the manufacture of sausage, for example. Inventories are also held because it is less costly for a firm to order goods less frequently in large quantities than to order small quantities frequently — just as the average household finds it useful to keep several days' supplies on hand in the house so as not to have to visit the supermarket daily.

Firms have a desired ratio of inventories to final sales that depends on economic variables. The smaller the cost of ordering new goods and the greater the speed with which such goods arrive, the smaller the inventory-sales ratio. The more uncertainty about the demand for the firm's goods, given the expected level of sales, the higher the inventory-sales ratio. The inventory-sales ratio may also depend on the level of sales, with the ratio falling with sales because there is relatively less uncertainty about sales as sales increase. Finally, there is the interest rate. Since firms carry inventories over time, they must tie up money to buy and hold them. There is an interest cost involved in such inventory holding, and the desired inventory-sales ratio should be expected to fall with increases in the interest rate. However, such a link has been difficult to establish empirically.

The most interesting aspect of inventory investment lies in the distinction between anticipated and unanticipated investment. Inventory investment could be high in two circumstances. First, if sales are unexpectedly low, firms would find unsold inventories accumulating on their shelves; that constitutes unanticipated inventory investment. This is the type of inventory investment discussed in Chapter 3. Second, inventory investment could be high because firms plan to restore depleted inventories. The two circumstances obviously have very different implications for the behaviour of aggregate demand. Unanticipated inventory investment is a result of unexpectedly low aggregate demand. On the other hand, planned inventory investment can be a response to recent, unexpectedly high aggregate demand. That is, rapid accumulation of inventories could be associated with either rapidly declining aggregate demand or rapidly increasing aggregate demand.

The behaviour of inventory investment in the period since 1954 is shown in Chart 6-2. On the whole, inventory investment over the one-year periods of the chart has been closely tied to the behaviour of the business cycle as represented by the unemployment rate. Inventory investment has been low when unemployment has been high, and vice versa.

However, inventory behaviour over shorter time periods is more interesting and illuminating. Inventory behaviour over the business cycle is well illustrated in the 1974-1975 recession. In Chart 6-4, we show sales by Canadian manufacturing industries as measured by shipments and the ratio of inventories to shipments. As we move into the recession in the last quarter of 1974, the rate of growth of sales declines and becomes negative at the beginning of 1975. Initially, however, there is relatively little adjustment in production, so inventories are built up and the inventory-sales ratio increases. By the trough of the cycle in the first quarter of 1975, production is at a lower level and the inventory-sales ratio stops rising. As demand picks up again in the middle of 1975, increases in production lag behind, allowing the inventory-sales ratio to decline. Thus the inventory-sales ratio decreases as the economy moves out of the recession. The behaviour of inventories thus matches rather precisely the story of the adjustment

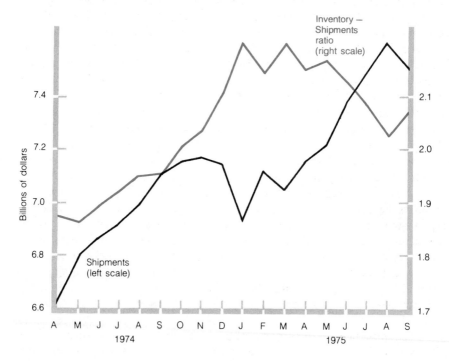

MANUFACTURING SHIPMENTS AND INVENTORY — SHIPMENTS RATIO
(*Source*: Statistics Canada, 11-003, 11-206)

process that we told in discussing the simple Keynesian model. In the initial phase of the downswing, inventories (passively) adjust to absorb the excess of production over demand. Subsequently, as involuntary inventory accumulation shows up in a high ratio of inventories to sales, firms cut production and thus actively restore the preferred ratio of inventories to sales.

As we noted in Chapter 3, the behaviour of inventories not only reflects fluctuations in the economy, but also contributes to those fluctuations through the so-called *inventory cycle*. When there is a fall in demand, inventories initially begin to increase, as can be seen in Chart 6-4, for example. When firms decide to reduce their inventories, they have to cut back their orders or reduce their own production for inventory, thus reducing demand by more than the initial fall in aggregate demand. This stage worsens the decline until inventories are back to their desired level and firms restore their inventory investment to a higher level again.

To make the point in a different way, we can consider the case of a hypothetical automobile dealer who sells, say, 30 cars per month, and holds an average of one month's sales — namely, 30 cars — in inventory. As long as sales stay steady at 30 cars per month, she will be ordering 30 cars per month from the factory. Now suppose sales drop to 25 cars per month, and it takes the dealer two months to respond to the change. During those two months her inventory will have climbed to 40 cars. In future she will want an inventory of only 25 cars on hand. Thus when she does respond to the fall in demand, she cuts her order from the factory from 30 to 15 in the third month, to get the inventory back to one month's sales. After the desired inventory-sales ratio has been restored, she will then order 25 cars per month from the factory. We see in this extreme case how the drop in demand of five cars, instead of leading to a simple drop in car output of five cars per month, causes a drop in output of fifteen cars in one month, followed by the longer-run drop in output of five cars per month.

6-4 CONCLUSIONS

In this chapter we have seen how investment fluctuates over the business cycle. We have broken investment spending down into the three categories of business fixed investment, residential construction, and inventory investment, and we have presented theories to explain the behaviour of each type of investment.

Slightly different theoretical considerations are relevant to the determination of each of the three categories of investment we have discussed. Nonetheless, there is a basic common element. That is the interaction, in each of the theories, of the demand for the stock of capital with the determinants of the rate of investment. The theory of business fixed investment started by examining the determinants of the desired capital stock, whereas the theory of residential construction looked at the demand for the stock of housing. The discussion of inventory investment started by examining the determinants of the desired inventory-sales ratio. Then, in each case, we went on to analyze or describe the determinants of the rate of that type of investment.

We come now to the question of why there is a difference between the theoretical models used to explain the level of business fixed investment and residential construction. The fundamental difference arises from the degree of standardization of the capital and the associated question of the existence of a good market for the used capital goods. Much of business fixed investment is in capital that is specifically designed for a given firm and is not of much use to other firms. It is, accordingly, difficult to establish a market price for the stock of that type of capital, and the theory used in discussing residential construction would be difficult to apply in that case. Although housing too varies a good deal, it is nonetheless possible to talk of a price of housing. Further, used housing is a very good substitute for new housing, whereas that is less often true for many capital goods.[15] If we disaggregated business fixed investment further than we have, we might well find that the model used to study housing investment is readily applicable for certain categories of business fixed investment, for which the capital good in question is relatively standard and has a good secondhand market.

Of the factors affecting the rate of investment, the real rate of interest is important because it affects both business fixed investment and housing investment. It does not appear to have strong effects on inventory spending. Fiscal policy affects the rate of business fixed investment by affecting the rental cost of capital.

Different variables affect the scale of each type of investment. The expected level of output is the major determinant of the overall scale of business fixed investment. Wealth is the major scale variable affecting the demand for housing and thus, ultimately, the rate of housing investment. The desired stock of inventory capital is related to the level of sales, but there is no simple relationship between the rate of inventory investment and changes in the level of output. A high rate of inventory investment may either be an addition to aggregate demand (if the investment is planned) or a

---

[15] The two models look very different. However, you may be able to see a way of casting the analysis of the housing market in terms of the theory used in discussing business fixed investment. You can define the desired capital stock of housing as that stock which the economy will eventually reach when the price of housing reaches a constant level. Then the level of investment will be an increasing function of the difference between that stock and the existing stock. Similarly, the model we have used for housing investment can be transformed into a model of business fixed investment. This is the so-called *Tobin's q* theory of investment. See James Tobin, "A General Equilibrium Approach to Monetary Theory," *Journal of Money, Credit and Banking*," February 1969.

reflection of a low level of aggregate demand (if the investment is unanticipated).

There are differences, too, in the stress placed on other factors affecting each category of investment. Lags in adjustment and lags arising from expectations that depend on past history are extremely important determinants of the rate of business fixed investment. Institutional arrangements, particularly those relating to the mortgage market, play an important role in affecting the rate of residential construction.

Total investment in the economy is simply the sum of investment spending in each of the three categories that we have studied separately in this chapter. Thus, each of the factors that affects the components of investment spending also affects the level of total investment. The real interest rate is thus one of the major factors that has an unambiguous effect on investment spending, as do the fiscal variables that influence the rental cost of capital. Monetary policy influences the level of investment by affecting the real rate of interest.

In brief, this chapter provides the theory that explains the role of the interest rate in the investment function of Chapter 4, while pointing out that the interest rate used there should be a *real* interest rate. It also showed that other variables, such as the level of output and the level of wealth, affect the rate of investment. Finally, it clarified the ways in which monetary and fiscal policy variables affect the rate of investment.

APPENDIX: THE ACCELERATOR MODEL OF INVESTMENT

The flexible accelerator model described in Section 6-1 is a substantial generalization of the original accelerator model of investment, which argued that the rate of investment is proportional to the *change* in GNP. To derive the accelerator model of investment, assume that there is complete adjustment of the capital stock to its desired level within one period (i.e., that $\lambda = 1$), so that $K = K^*$, that there is no depreciation so that $d = 0$, and that the desired capital output ratio is a constant, independent of the rental cost of capital:

$$K^* = \beta Y \tag{A1}$$

In Equation (A1), β is a constant which should not be confused with the β in any other chapter. Substituting Equation (A1) into Equation (9), setting $\lambda = 1$, and noting that $K_{-1} = K^*_{-1}$, we obtain

$$I = \beta(Y - Y_{-1}) \tag{A2}$$

which is precisely the original accelerator model of investment.

While the flexible accelerator model Equation (9) is indeed a considerable generalization of the simple accelerator model, the simpler model drives home the point that the rate of investment depends on the lagged, as well as the current, value of GNP. This means that any action taken this period to affect current investment and thus current GNP will also affect investment — and thus GNP — in subsequent periods. As we saw in our discussion of the permanent-income hypothesis, such a relationship presents considerable difficulties to policy makers.

PROBLEMS

1 We have seen in Chapters 5 and 6 that *permanent* income and output, rather than current income and output, determine consumption and investment.
   (a) How does this affect the IS-LM model built in Chapter 4?
   (b) What are the policy implications of the use of the "permanent" measures?
2 In Chapter 4 it was assumed that investment rises during periods of low interest rates. That, however, was not the case during the 1930s, when investment and interest rates were both very low. Explain how this can occur. What would have been appropriate fiscal policy in such a case?
3 According to the description of business fixed investment in this chapter, how would you expect a firm's investment decisions to be affected by a sudden increase in demand for its product? What factors would determine the speed of its reaction?
4 It is often suggested that investment spending is dominated by "animal spirits" — the optimism or pessimism of investors. Is this argument at all consistent with the analysis of Section 6-2?
5 Explain how the two panels of Figure 6-5 react together over time. What would happen if the demand for housing stock (DD) shifts up and to the right over time?
6 Trace carefully the step-by-step effects on the housing market (using Figure 6-5) of an increase in interest rates. Explain each shift and its long-run and short-run effects.
7 In the past, restrictive monetary policy hurt the housing industry in an effort to avoid excess aggregate demand.
   (a) What is the mechanism by which this happened?
   (b) Can you suggest ways in which this heavy burden can be spread out rather than be concentrated on the housing industry?
   (c) Should the burden be spread?
8 (a) Explain how final sales and output can differ.
   (b) Point out from Chart 6-4 the periods of planned and unplanned inventory investment.
   (c) During a period of slow but steady growth, how would you expect final sales and output to be related? Explain. Draw a hypothetical figure like Chart 6-4 for such a period.
9 Suppose that an explicitly temporary tax credit is enacted. The tax credit is at the rate of 10 percent and lasts only one year.
   (a) What is the effect of this tax measure on investment in the long run (say after four or five years)?
   (b) What is the effect in the current year and the following year?
   (c) How will your answers under 10(a) and 10(b) differ if the tax credit is permanent?
10 In Chart 6-4 we discuss the pattern of inventory adjustment during the 1974-75 recession. Use the seasonally adjusted data in Section 6, Table 1 of the *Canadian Statistical Review* to analyze the pattern of inventory investment during the 1980 recession.
11 For this question use the Cobb-Douglas production function, and the corresponding desired capital stock given by Equation (2). Assume that $a = 0.3$, $Y = 2.5$ billion, and $i_c = 0.15$.

(a) Calculate the desired capital stock K*.
(b) Now suppose that Y is expected to rise to 3 billion. What is the corresponding desired capital stock?
(c) Suppose that the capital stock was at its desired level before the change in income was expected. Suppose further that $\lambda = 0.4$ in the flexible accelerator model of investment. What will be the rate of investment in the first year after expected income changes? In the second year?
(d) Does your answer in (c) refer to gross or net investment?

7

THE DEMAND FOR MONEY

This chapter continues the process of filling in the details of the IS-LM model that we studied in Chapter 4. In Chapters 5 and 6, we took a closer look at theoretical and empirical aspects of the major private sector components of demand in the goods market — consumption and investment spending. In this chapter, we analyze the demand for money, and thus move from the goods market to the assets markets. In Chapter 8, we complete our discussion of the assets markets in the IS-LM framework by examining the determinants of the supply of money and the role of the Bank of Canada in the money markets.

We start discussing the topic of money demand with the concept of the demand for *real balances*, introduced in Chapter 4. One of the essentials of money demand is that individuals are interested in the purchasing power of their money holdings — the value of their cash balances in terms of the goods the cash will buy. They are not concerned with their *nominal* money holdings, that is, the number of dollar bills they hold. What this means in practice is that (1) *real* money demand is unchanged when the price level increases, but *all* real variables, such as the interest rate, real income, and real wealth, remain unchanged; and (2) *nominal* money demand increases in proportion to the increase in the price level, given the constancy of the real variables just specified.[1]

We have a special name for behaviour that is not affected by changes in the price level itself, all real variables remaining unchanged. We say that an individual is free from *money illusion* if a change in the level of prices, holding all real variables constant, leaves real behaviour, including real money demand, unchanged. By contrast, an individual whose real behaviour is affected by the price level is said to suffer from money illusion.

We shall see that empirical evidence supports the theoretical argument that the demand for money is a demand for real balances — or that the demand for nominal balances, holding real variables constant, is proportional to the price level. In Chapter 4, we also assumed that the demand for

[1] Be sure you understand that (1) and (2) say the same thing in slightly different ways.

money increases with the level of real income and decreases with the nominal interest rate. We shall see that, in this chapter, both theory and evidence support the type of demand for money function used in Chapter 4.

You will also recall that the demand for money is important in determining the effectiveness of fiscal policy in changing the level of income. Changes in fiscal variables, such as tax rates or government spending, affect the level of income if the demand for money is interest-elastic. If the demand for money is totally interest-inelastic — if it does not react at all to changes in the interest rate — increases in government spending totally *crowd out* private spending and leave the level of income unaffected.

The demand for money has been studied very intensively at both the theoretical and empirical levels. There is by now almost total agreement that the demand should, as a theoretical matter, increase as the level of real income rises and decrease as the nominal interest rate rises. Empirical work bears out these two properties of the demand for money function.

We start in Section 7-1 by examining the components of the stock of money in Canada. Then, in Section 7-2, we briefly review the traditional reasons for the use of money. Section 7-3, the longest of the chapter, presents the basic theory of the demand for money. Section 7-4 examines the evidence supporting the theoretical conclusions. Sections 7-5 and 7-6 discuss the *velocity* of money — a concept related to the demand for money — and the effects of anticipated inflation on the demand for money, respectively.

7-1 COMPONENTS OF THE MONEY STOCK

The money supply definitions currently provided by the Bank of Canada are shown in Table 7-1.[2] The money supply concept we shall be using in most of this chapter is M1 since it is used by the Bank of Canada in formulating monetary policy. It consists of currency and demand deposits and in June 1980 was equal to $23,634 million, of which about 40 percent was currency.

Currency consists of notes and coin in circulation outside the banking system, and demand deposits are chequing accounts in the chartered banks. Thus the M1 definition of money includes the major assets that serve as a *medium of exchange* or as the means of making payments. It does not, however, include all chequable deposits. When chequable savings deposits in chartered banks are added in, we obtain the money supply concept designated as M1B by the Bank of Canada. Both concepts include only deposits in the chartered banks and it could be argued that chequable deposits in other financial institutions such as trust companies and credit unions should also be included. Similarly, there is a question as to whether

---

[2] For a detailed description of the definitions, see *Bank of Canada Review*, Table 14 and the appended notes. historical data are given in the March 1981 issue.

TABLE 7-1 COMPONENTS OF THE MONEY STOCK, JUNE, 1980
(MILLIONS OF DOLLARS, AVERAGE OF WEDNESDAYS)

(1) Currency	9,313
(2) Demand deposits	14,321
(3) M1 = (1) + (2)	23,634
(4) Chequable savings deposits	7,387
(5) M1B = (3) + (4)	31,021
(6) Nonchequable personal savings deposits	63,477
(7) Nonpersonal notice deposits	2,083
(8) M2 = (5) + (6) + (7)	96,581
(9) Nonpersonal term deposits	35,532
(10) Foreign currency deposits of residents	10,781
(11) M3 = (8) + (9) + (10)	142,894

Source: Bank of Canada Review

credit cards should not be regarded as means of making payment. If so — and the argument is certainly compelling — we should probably count the amount that people are allowed to charge by using their credit cards as part of the money stock.

Historically, there have often been changes in the type of assets which can be used as means of payment, and simultaneous disagreements about what constitutes money in those circumstances. When cheques first began to be widely used in England early in the nineteenth century, there was a disagreement over whether demand deposits should be regarded as part of the money stock. Now that point is not disputed. We can expect there to be continuing changes in the financial structure over the years, with consequent changes in the definitions of the various money supply concepts.

Table 7-1 also shows the broader definitions of the money supply, M2 and M3. M2 adds a variety of nonchequable interest bearing savings accounts and notice deposits to M1B.[3] The components of M2 that are not part of M1 are in general less *liquid* than M1 in that they cannot immediately and conveniently be used for making payments. However, they are assets that are close to being money in the sense that they are available with only a little difficulty for making payments. M3 includes all Canadian dollar deposits in chartered banks and foreign currency deposits held by residents.

In summary, there is no unique set of assets which will always constitute the money supply. At present, there are arguments for using a broader

---

[3] A notice deposit is an account on which the bank reserves the right to require notice before a withdrawal can be made. Personal savings accounts have such a provision, but it is not normally enforced (look at the small print in your passbook!).

definition of the money stock than M1 and even arguments for using a less broad definition — should $1,000 bills be included, for example? Further, over the course of time, the particular assets that serve as a medium of exchange, or means of payment, will certainly change further.

7-2 THE FUNCTIONS OF MONEY

Money is so widely used that we rarely step back to think how remarkable a device it is. It is impossible to imagine a modern economy operating without the use of money or something very much like it. The essential role of money is to separate the acts of buying and selling goods. In a mythical barter economy in which there is no money, every transaction has to involve an exchange of goods (and/or services) on both sides of the transaction. The examples of the difficulties of barter are endless. The economist wanting a haircut would have to find a barber wanting to listen to a lecture on economics; the peanut farmer wanting a suit would have to find a tailor wanting peanuts, and so on. Without money, modern economies could not operate. In this context, money is a _medium of exchange_, and that is its essential function.

Money, as a medium of exchange, makes it unnecessary for there to be a "double coincidence of wants" in exchanges. By the double coincidence, we have in mind the above examples. The wants of two individuals would have to be identically matched for the exchange to take place. For instance, the man selling peanuts would have to find a buyer whose goods he wanted to buy (the suit) while, at the same time, the woman selling suits would have to find a buyer whose goods she wanted to buy (the peanuts).

There are four traditional functions of money, of which the medium of exchange is the first.[4] The other three are store of value, unit of account, and standard of deferred payment. These stand on a different footing from the medium of exchange function.

A _store of value_ is an asset that maintains value over time. Thus, an individual holding a store of value can use that asset to make purchases at a future date. If an asset were not a store of value, then it would not be used as a medium of exchange. Imagine trying to use ice cream as money, in the absence of refrigerators. There would hardly ever be a good reason for anyone to give up goods for money (ice cream) if the money were sure to melt within the next few minutes. And if the seller were unwilling to accept the ice cream in exchange for his or her goods, then the ice cream would not be a medium of exchange. But there are many stores of value other than money — such as bonds, stocks, and houses.

The _unit of account_ is the unit in which prices are quoted and books kept.

---

[4] See W.S. Jevons, _Money and the Mechanism of Exchange_, (London: Routledge, Kegan, Paul 1910).

Prices are quoted in dollars and cents, and dollars and cents are the units in which the money stock is measured. Usually, the money unit is also the unit of account, but that is not essential. In the German hyperinflation of 1922-1923, dollars were the unit of account for some firms, whereas the mark was the medium of exchange.

Finally, as a *standard of deferred payment*, money units are used in long-term transactions, such as loans. The amount that has to be paid back in five or ten years is specified in dollars and cents. Dollars and cents are acting as the standard of deferred payment. Once again, though, it is not essential that the standard of deferred payment be the money unit. For example, the final payment of a loan may be related to the behaviour of the price level, rather than being fixed in dollars and cents. This is known as an indexed loan.

The last two of the four functions of money are, accordingly, functions which money *usually* performs, but not functions that it *necessarily* performs. And the store of value function is one that many assets perform.

There are fascinating descriptions of different types of money that have existed in the past that we do not have room to review here, but there is one final point we want to emphasize.[5] *Money is whatever is generally accepted in exchange*. However magnificently a piece of paper may be engraved, it will not be money if it is not accepted in payment. However unusual the material of which it is made, anything that is generally accepted in payment is money. The only reason money is accepted in payment is that the recipient believes that it can be spent at a later time. There is thus an inherent circularity in the acceptance of money. Money is accepted in payment because it is believed that it will also be accepted in payment by others.

7-3 THE DEMAND FOR MONEY: THEORY

In this section we review the three major motives underlying the demand for money. In doing so, we will concentrate on the effects of changes in income and changes in the interest rate on money demand.

The three theories we are about to review correspond to Keynes' famous three motives for holding money:[6] (1) the transactions motive, which is the demand for money arising from the use of money in making regular payments; (2) the precautionary motive, which is the demand for money to meet unforeseen contingencies; and (3) the speculative motive, which arises from the uncertainties about the money value of other assets that an individual can hold. In discussing the transactions and precautionary

---

[5] See Paul Einzig, *Primitive Money* (New York: Pergamon Press, 1966).

[6] J.M. Keynes, *The General Theory of Employment, Interest and Money* (New York: Macmillan, 1936), chap. 13.

motives, we are mainly discussing M1, whereas the speculative motive refers more to M2 or M3, as we shall see.

Although we examine the demand for money by looking at the three motives for holding it, we cannot separate out a particular person's money holdings, say $500, into three neat piles of, say, $200, $200, and $100, that are being held for each motive. Money being held to satisfy one motive is always available for another use. The person holding unusually large balances for speculative reasons also has those balances available to meet an unexpected emergency, so that they also serve as precautionary balances. All three motives influence an individual's holdings of money, and, as we shall see, each leads to the prediction that the demand for money should fall as the interest rate on other assets increases.

This final point is worth emphasizing. Money (M1) generally earns no interest or less interest than other assets. Anyone holding money is giving up interest that could be earned by holding some other asset, such as a savings deposit or a bond. The higher the interest loss from holding a dollar of money, the less money we expect the individual to hold. The demand for money will thus be higher, the greater the interest rate on money itself if interest is paid on demand deposits, and will be lower, the higher the interest rate on alternative assets. In practice, we can measure the cost of holding money as the difference between the interest rate paid on money (perhaps zero) and the interest rate paid on the most nearly comparable other asset, such as a savings deposit or, for corporations, a term deposit or commercial paper.

For most of the remainder of the chapter, we shall assume that money earns no interest. This is in fact true of most of the M1 stock. Further, it is easy to modify the analysis to take account of the payment of interest on money. All that is necessary is to substitute the difference between the interest rate on the alternative asset and the interest rate on money in places we mention only the interest rate on the alternative asset.

The Transactions Demand

The transactions demand for money arises from the use of money in making regular payment for goods and services. In the course of each month, an individual makes a variety of payments for such items as rent or mortgage, groceries, the newspaper, and other purchases. In this section we examine how much money an individual would hold for such purchases.

In analyzing the transactions demand, we are concerned with a tradeoff between the amount of interest an individual forgoes by holding money and the costs and inconveniences of holding a small amount of money. To make the problem concrete, consider a man who is paid, say, $1,200 each month. Assume that he spends the $1,200 evenly over the course of the month, at the rate of $40 per day. Now at one extreme, the individual could simply leave his $1,200 in cash (whether currency or demand deposits) and spend it at the rate of $40 per day. Alternatively, on the first day of the month the individual could take his $40 to spend that day and put the remaining $1,160 in a daily-interest savings account. Then every morning he could go to the bank to withdraw that day's $40 from the savings account. By the end of the month he would have earned interest on the money he had each day in the savings account. This would be the *benefit* of keeping his money holdings down as low as $40 at the beginning of each day. The *cost* of keeping money holdings down is simply the cost and inconvenience of the trips to the bank to withdraw the daily $40. To decide on how much money to hold for transactions purposes, the individual has to weigh the costs of holding small balances against the interest advantage of doing so.

We now study the tradeoff in more detail and derive a formula for the demand for money. Suppose the nominal monthly income[7] of the individual is Y_N. We make the simplifying assumption that Y_N is paid in to his savings account, rather than his chequing account, each month. The money is spent at a steady rate over the course of the month. To spend it, the individual has to get it out of the savings account and into cash, which may be currency or a chequing account. If left in the savings accounts, the deposit earns interest at a rate of i per month. It earns zero interest as cash. The cost to the individual of making a transfer between cash and the savings account (which we henceforth call bonds for convenience) is $$b.[8] That cost may be the individual's time, or it may be a cost that he explicitly pays someone else to make the transfer. For convenience we refer to it as a broker's fee.

Although we are describing an individual's transactions demand, similar considerations are relevant for firms deciding how to manage their money. You should think of this model as applying equally well, with small changes in terminology and assumptions, to firms and households.

The analysis of the demand for money we are now outlining is known as an *inventory-theoretic approach*. Originally, the approach was developed to determine the inventories of goods a firm should have on hand. In that context, the amount Y_N would be the monthly sales of the good, b, the cost of ordering the good, and i the interest cost of carrying the inventory. The analogy between money as an inventory of purchasing power, standing ready to buy goods, and an inventory of goods, standing ready to be bought by customers, is quite close. The inventory-theoretic approach to the demand for money is associated with the names of William Baumol and James Tobin.[9] The most famous result of Baumol and Tobin's work is the

---

[7] As a reminder, nominal income Y_N is defined as real income Y times the price level P: $Y_N \equiv PY$.

[8] This b should not be confused with the b in earlier chapters; there are not sufficient letters of the alphabet for us to use each letter for only one concept.

[9] William Baumol, "The Transactions Demand for Cash: An Inventory Theoretic Approach," *Quarterly Journal of Economics*, November 1952; and James Tobin, "The Interest-Elasticity of Transactions Demand for Cash," *Review of Economics and Statistics*, August 1956.

square-root law of the demand for money, which is presented later in Equation (4).

The individual has to decide how many transactions to make between bonds and cash each month. If he makes just one transaction, transferring Y_N into cash at the beginning of the month, his cash balance over the course of the month will be as shown in Figure 7-1*a*. It starts at Y_N, is spent evenly over the month, and is down to zero by the end of the month, at which time a new payment is received by the individual and transferred into his chequing account. If he makes two withdrawals from the savings account, he first transfers $Y_N/2$ into cash at the beginning of the month, resulting in a cash balance that is run down to zero in the middle of the month, at which time another $Y_N/2$ is transferred into cash and spent evenly over the rest of the month.[10] Figure 7-1*b* shows the individual's cash holdings in that case.

We shall denote the size of a cash withdrawal from the bond portfolio (savings account) by Z,[11] and the number of withdrawals from the bond portfolio by n. Thus, n is the number of times the individual adds to his cash balance during the month. If he makes n equal-sized withdrawals during the month, transferring funds from his savings account to his chequing account, then the size of each transfer is Y_N/n, since a total of Y_N has to be transferred from the savings account into cash. For example, if Y_N is $1,200, and n, the number of transactions, is 3, then Z, the amount transferred to cash each time, is $400. Accordingly, we can write

$$nZ = Y_N \qquad (1)$$

[10] With simple interest being paid on the savings account, it is true that the individual's transactions between bonds and cash should be evenly spaced over the month. We leave the proof of that for the case where there are two transactions to the problem set.

[11] Please do not confuse Z in this chapter with Z in Chapter 5.

FIGURE 7-1   THE AMOUNT OF CASH HELD DURING THE MONTH RELATED TO THE NUMBER OF WITHDRAWALS

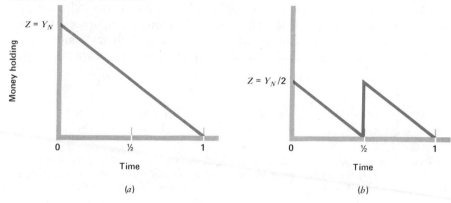

Suppose that the amount Z is transferred from bonds to cash at each withdrawal. What then is the *average* cash balance over the course of the month? We want to find the size of the average cash balance in order to measure the interest that is lost as a result of holding cash; if that amount were not held as cash, it could be held as interest-earning bonds. In Figure 7-1a, the average cash balance held during the month is $Y_N/2 = Z/2$, since the cash balance starts at Y_N and runs down in a straight line to zero.[12] In the case of Figure 7-1b, the average cash balance for the first half of the month is $Y_N/4 = Z/2$, and the average cash balance for the second half of the month is also $Z/2$. Thus, the average cash balance for the entire month is $Y_N/4 = Z/2$. Similarly, if three withdrawals were made, the average cash balance would be $Y_N/6 = Z/2$. In general, the average cash balance is $Z/2$, as you might want to confirm by drawing diagrams similar to Figure 7-1 for $n = 3$ or other values of n.

The interest cost of holding money is the interest rate times the average cash balance, or $iZ/2$. From Equation (1), that means the total interest cost is $iY_N/2n$. The other component of the cost of managing the portfolio is the brokerage cost, or the cost in terms of the individual's time and inconvenience in managing his money. That cost is just the number of withdrawals made, n, times the cost of each withdrawal, b, and is thus equal to nb. The total cost of managing the portfolio is the interest cost plus the total brokerage cost:

$$\text{Total cost} = nb + \frac{iY_N}{2n} \qquad (2)$$

Equation (2) shows formally that the brokerage cost nb increases as the number of withdrawals (transactions between bonds and money) rises, and that the interest cost decreases as the number of withdrawals increases. It thus emphasizes the tradeoff faced in managing money, and suggests that there is an optimal number of withdrawals the individual should make to minimize the total cost of holding money to meet transactions requirements for buying goods.

To derive that optimal point, we want to find the point at which the benefit of carrying out another withdrawal is less than, or just equal to, the cost of making another transaction between bonds and money. If the benefit of making another transaction were greater than the cost, then another withdrawal should be made, and the original point could not have been optimal. The cost of making another transaction is always equal to b. In Figure 7-2, we show the costs of making a further transaction by the marginal cost curve MC, which is horizontal at the level b. The financial benefit from making

---

[12] The average cash balance is the average of the amount of cash the individual holds at each moment during the month. For instance, if he held $400 for 3 days and zero for the rest of the month, the average cash balance would be $40, or one-tenth (3 days divided by 30 days) of the month times $400.

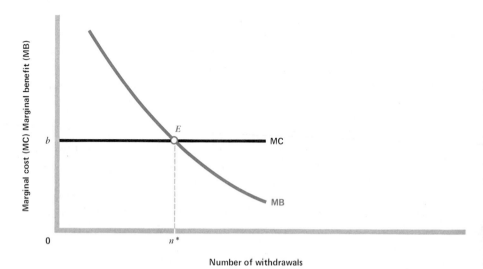

FIGURE 7-2 OPTIMAL CASH MANAGEMENT: DETERMINING THE OPTIMAL NUMBER OF WITHDRAWALS

another transaction is represented by the MB (marginal benefit) curve in Figure 7-2, which represents the interest *saved* by making another withdrawal and thus having a smaller cash balance on average during the month.

The more transactions between money and bonds an individual makes, the lower the total interest cost is. But the reduction of the interest cost that is obtained by making more transactions falls off rapidly as the number of withdrawals increases. There is a substantial saving in interest costs by making two withdrawals rather than one, but very little saving in interest costs by making 31 transactions rather than 30.

This suggests that the marginal benefit of making more withdrawals decreases as the number of withdrawals becomes large. The MB curve in Figure 7-2, is accordingly, downward-sloping.[13]

In Figure 7-2, the optimal number of transactions is given by n^*, the number at which the marginal benefit in terms of interest saved is equal to the marginal cost of making a transaction. Given the number of transactions and the individual's income, we also know the average cash balance M, using the relationship between average money holdings and the size of each transfer which we derived earlier:

[13] Two points about Figure 7-2: First, note that we have, for convenience, drawn the curves as continuous, even though you will recognize that it is only possible to make an integral number of transactions, and not, for example, 1.6 or 7.24 transactions. Second, if you can use the calculus, try to derive the equation of the marginal benefit curve from the component of costs in Eq. (2) that is due to interest lost.

$$M = \frac{Z}{2} = \frac{Y_N}{2n} \tag{3}$$

From Figure 7-2 we can see two of the important results of the inventory theory of the transactions demand for money. First, suppose the brokerage cost rises. That shifts the MC curve up, decreases the number of withdrawals n, and therefore [from Equation (3), where M is inversely related to n] increases the average holding of money. Second, an increase in the interest rate shifts up the MB curve, therefore increases n, and thus [again, from Equation (3)] reduces the holding of money: when the interest rate is higher, the individual is willing to make more trips to the bank to earn the higher interest now available. Figure 7-2 thus shows one of the key results we wanted to establish — that the demand for money is inversely related to the interest rate.

In the case of an increase in income, Figure 7-2 is unfortunately less useful. An increase in income shifts up the MB curve and thus increases the number of transactions. But from Equation (3), we see that an increase in the number of transactions accompanying an increase in income does not necessarily imply that the demand for money rises. If the number of transactions increases less than in proportion to the increase in income, then the income increase raises the demand for money. However, if the number of transactions increases more than in proportion to the increase in income, the increase in income could lower the demand for money. This second eventuality sounds strange; fortunately, as a more complete algebraic analysis of the individual's optimal behaviour would show, it is not possible under the assumptions we have made so far.

The famous square-root formula to which we referred earlier both makes the results of the graphical analysis of Figure 7-2 more precise and resolves the ambiguity about the effects of income on the demand for money. The formula gives the demand for money that is obtained as a result of minimizing the total costs in Equation (2) with respect to the number of withdrawals, and then using Equation (3) to derive the cash balance.[14] The formula is

$$M^* = \sqrt{\frac{bY_N}{2i}} \tag{4}$$

Equation (4) shows that the transactions demand for money increases with the brokerage fee, or the cost of transacting, and with the level of income. The demand for money decreases with the interest rate.

Equation (4) also shows that an increase in income raises the demand for money proportionately less than the increase in income itself. To put the same point somewhat differently, the ratio of income to money, Y_N/M, rises

---

[14] If you can handle calculus, try to derive Eq. (4).

with the level of income. A person with a higher level of income than another holds proportionately less money than the other person. This point is sometimes put in different words by saying that there are *economies of scale* in cash management.

Yet another way of saying the same thing is that the income elasticity of the demand for money is less than 1 [it is equal to $\frac{1}{2}$ in Equation (4)]. The income elasticity measures the percentage change in the demand for money due to a 1 percent change in income.[15]

Similarly, Equation (4) implies that the elasticity of the demand for money with respect to the brokerage fee is $\frac{1}{2}$, and the elasticity with respect to the interest rate is $-\frac{1}{2}$.

What accounts for the fact that people can somehow manage with less cash per dollar of spending as income increases? The reason is that cash management is more effective at high levels of income because the average cost per dollar of transaction is lower with large-size transactions. In turn, the lower average cost of transactions results from the fixed brokerage fee per transaction; it costs as much to transfer $10 as $10 million, so that the average cost per dollar transferred is lower for large transfers.

However, in the case of households, we should recognize that the "brokerage cost" b, the cost of making withdrawals from a savings account, is in part the cost of time and the nuisance of having to go to the bank. Since the cost of time to individuals is likely to be higher the higher their income, b may rise with Y_N. In that case, an increase in income would result in an increase in the demand for money by more than the income elasticity of $\frac{1}{2}$ indicates because b goes up together with Y_N.

The Demand for Real Balances

We started this chapter by emphasizing that the demand for money is a demand for real balances. It is worth confirming that the inventory theory of the demand for money implies that the demand for real balances does not change when all prices double (or increase in any other proportion). When all prices double, both Y_N and b in Equation (4) double — that is, both nominal income and the nominal brokerage fee double. Accordingly, the demand for nominal balances doubles, so that the demand for real balances is unchanged. The square-root formula does not imply any money illusion in the demand for money. Thus we should be careful when saying the income elasticity of demand for money implied by Equation (4) is $\frac{1}{2}$. The elasticity of the demand for *real* balances with respect to *real* income is $\frac{1}{2}$. But if

[15] The income elasticity of demand is $\dfrac{\Delta(M/P)}{M/P} \bigg/ \dfrac{\Delta Y}{Y}$.

Similarly, the interest elasticity is $\dfrac{\Delta(M/P)}{M/P} \bigg/ \dfrac{\Delta i}{i}$.

income rises only because all prices (including b) rise, then the demand for *nominal* balances rises proportionately.

*Integer Constraints

So far we have, in the text, ignored the important constraint that it is possible to make only an integral number of transactions, such as 1, 2, 3, etc., and that it is not possible to make 1.25 or 3.57 transactions. However, when we take account of this constraint, we shall see that it implies that many people do not make more than the essential one transaction between money and bonds within the period in which they are paid.[16] Consider our previous example of the person who received $1,200 per month. Suppose, realistically, that the interest rate per month on savings deposits is ½ percent. The individual cannot avoid making one initial transaction, since income initially arrives in the savings account. The next question is whether it pays to make a second transaction. That is, does it pay to keep half the monthly income for half a month in the savings account and make a second withdrawal after half a month? With an interest rate of ½ percent per month, interest for half a month would be ¼ percent. Half the income would amount to $600 and the interest earnings would, therefore, be $600 × ¼ percent = $1.50.

Now if the brokerage fee exceeds $1.50, the individual will not bother to make more than one transaction. And $1.50 is not an outrageous cost in terms of the time and nuisance of making a transfer from the savings to the chequing account. Thus, for many individuals whose monthly net pay is below $1,200, we do not expect the formula (4) to hold exactly. Their cash balance would instead simply be half their income. They would make one transfer into cash at the beginning of the month; Figure 7-1a would describe this cash balance. For such individuals, the income elasticity of the demand for money is 1, since their demand for money goes up precisely in proportion with their income. The interest elasticity is zero, so long as they make only one transaction, because they transfer all their income into cash immediately as they receive it.

The very strong restrictions on the income and interest elasticities of the demand for money of Equation (4) are not valid when the integer constraints are taken into account. Instead, the income elasticity is an average of the elasticities of different people, some of whom make only one transaction from bonds to money, and the elasticity is therefore between ½ and 1. Similarly, the interest elasticity is also an average of the elasticities across different individuals, being between − ½ and zero.[17] Because firms deal with larger amounts of money, they are likely to make a large number of

[16] If we had assumed that individuals were paid in cash, it would turn out that many people would not make any transactions between money and bonds in managing their transactions balances.

[17] See Robert J. Barro, "Integer Constraints and Aggregation in an Inventory Model of Money Demand," *Journal of Finance*, March 1976.

transactions between money and bonds, and their income and interest elasticities of the demand for money are therefore likely to be close to the $\frac{1}{2}$ and $-\frac{1}{2}$ predicted by Equation (4).

*The Payment Period

Once the integer constraints are taken into account, it can also be seen that the transactions demand for money depends on the frequency with which individuals are paid (the payment period). If one examines the square-root formula (4), the demand for money does not seem to depend on how often a person is paid, since an increase in the payments period increases both Y_N and i in the same proportion. Thus the demand for money appears unaffected by the length of the period. However, consider a woman, say, who makes only one transaction from bonds to money at the beginning of each month. Her money demand is $Y_N/2$. If such a person were paid weekly, her demand for money would be only one-quarter of the demand with monthly payments. Thus we should expect the demand for money to increase with the length of the payments period.

Summary

The inventory-theoretic approach to the demand for money gives a precise formula for the transactions demand for money: The income elasticity of the demand for money is $\frac{1}{2}$ and the interest elasticity is $-\frac{1}{2}$. When integer constraints are taken into account, the limits on the income elasticity of demand are between $\frac{1}{2}$ and 1, and the limits on the interest elasticity are between $-\frac{1}{2}$ and zero. We have outlined the approach in terms of an individual's demand for money, but a similar approach is relevant for firms.

Some of the assumptions made in deriving the square-root formula are very restrictive. People do not spend their money evenly over the course of the month, and they do not know exactly what their payments will be. Their cheques are not paid into savings accounts, and so on. It turns out, though, that the major results we have derived are not greatly affected by the use of more realistic assumptions. There is thus good reason to expect the demand for money to increase with the level of income and to decrease as the interest rate (or generally, the cost of holding money) increases.

The Precautionary Motive

In discussing the transactions demand for money, we focussed on transactions costs and ignored uncertainty. In this section, we concentrate on the demand for money that arises because people are uncertain about the payments they might want to, or have to, make.[18] Suppose, realistically, that

---

[18] See Edward H. Whalen, "A Rationalization of the Precautionary Demand for Cash," *Quarterly Journal of Economics*, May 1966.

an individual did not know precisely what payments he would be receiving in the next few weeks and what payments he would have to make. He might decide to have a hot fudge sundae, or need to take a cab in the rain, or have to pay for a prescription. If he did not have money with which to pay, he would incur a loss. The loss could be missing a fine meal, or missing an appointment, or having to come back the next day to pay for the prescription. For concreteness, we shall denote the loss incurred as a result of being short of cash by $c.[19] The loss clearly varies from situation to situation, but as usual we simplify.

The more money the individual holds, the less likely he is to incur the costs of illiquidity (that is, not having money immediately available). But the more money he holds, the more interest he is giving up. We are back to a tradeoff situation similar to that examined in relation to the transactions demand. Somewhere between holding so little money for precautionary purposes that it will almost certainly be necessary to forgo some purchase (or to borrow in a hurry), and so much money that there is little chance of not being able to make any payment that might be necessary, there must be an optimal amount of precautionary balances to hold. That optimal amount will involve the balancing of interest costs against the advantages of not being caught illiquid.

Once more, we write down the total costs of holding an amount of money M.[20] This time we are dealing with expected costs, since it is not certain what the need for money will be. We denote the probability that the individual is illiquid during the month by $p(M,\sigma)$. The function $p(M,\sigma)$ indicates that the probability of the person's being illiquid at some time during the month depends on the level of money balances M being held and the degree of uncertainty σ about the net payments that will be made during the month. The probability of illiquidity is lower, the higher is M, and higher, the higher is the degree of uncertainty σ. The *expected cost* of illiquidity is $p(M,\sigma)c$ — the probability of illiquidity times the cost of being illiquid. The interest cost associated with holding a cash balance of M is just iM. Thus, we have

$$\text{Expected costs} = iM + p(M,\sigma)c \qquad (5)$$

To determine the optimal amount of money to hold, we compare the marginal costs of increasing money holding by \$1 with the expected marginal benefit of doing so. The marginal cost is again the interest forgone, or i. That is shown by the MC curve in Figure 7-3. The marginal benefit of increasing money holding arises from the lower expected costs of illiquidity. Increasing precautionary balances from zero has a large marginal benefit, since that takes care of small, unexpected disbursements that are quite

---

[19] This c should not be confused with the marginal propensity to consume.
[20] This paragraph contains technical material that is optional and can easily be skipped.

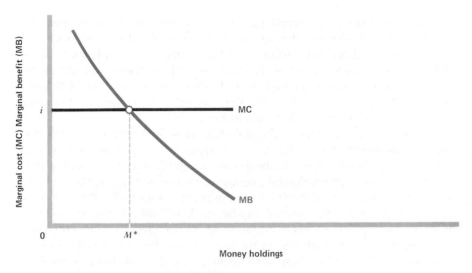

FIGURE 7-3 THE PRECAUTIONARY DEMAND FOR MONEY

likely. As we increase cash balances further, we continue to reduce the probability of illiquidity, but at a decreasing rate. We start to hold cash to insure against quite unlikely events. Thus, the marginal benefit of additional cash is a decreasing function of the level of cash holdings — more cash on hand is better than less, but at a diminishing rate. The marginal benefit of increasing cash holdings is shown by the MB curve in Figure 7-3.

The optimal level of the precautionary demand for money is reached where the two curves intersect. That level of money is shown as M^* in Figure 7-3. Now we can use Figure 7-3 to examine the determinants of the optimal level of the precautionary demand. It is, first, apparent that precautionary balances will be larger when the interest rate is lower. A reduction in the interest rate shifts the MC curve down and increases M^*. The lower costs of holding money makes it profitable to insure more heavily against the costs of illiquidity. An increase in uncertainty leads to increased money holdings because it shifts up the MB curve. With more uncertainty about the flow of spending, there is more scope for unforeseen payments and thus a greater danger of illiquidity. It therefore pays to insure more heavily by holding larger cash balances. Finally, the lower the costs of illiquidity, c, the lower is money demand. A reduction in c moves the MB curve down. Indeed, if there were no cost to illiquidity, no one would bother to hold money. There would be no penalty for not having it, while at the same time, holding it would mean a loss of interest.

The model of precautionary demand can be applied to goods other than money. It is a broad theory that applies to any commodity inventory that is held as insurance against contingencies. For instance, cars carry spare tires. You can work out circumstances under which one would want to have more than one spare tire in a car, and even circumstances in which zero would be the optimal number. The idea of the precautionary demand for money or for goods is quite general. So, too, are the determinants of the precautionary demand; the alternative cost in terms of interest forgone, the cost of illiquidity, and the degree of uncertainty that determines the probability of illiquidity.

The Speculative Demand for Money

The transactions demand and the precautionary demand for money emphasize the medium of exchange function of money, for each refers to the need to have money on hand to make payments. Each theory is more relevant to the M1 defintion of money than any other, though the precautionary demand could certainly explain part of the holding of savings accounts and other relatively liquid assets which are part of M2. Now we move over to the store of value function of money and concentrate on the role of money in the investment portfolio of an individual.

An individual who has wealth has to hold that wealth in specific assets. Those assets make up a *portfolio*. One would think an investor would want to hold the asset which provides the highest returns. However, given that the return on most assets is uncertain, it is unwise to hold the entire portfolio in a single *risky asset*. You may have the hottest tip that a certain stock will surely double within the next two years, but you would be wise to recognize that hot tips are far from infallible, and that you could lose a lot of money in that stock as well as make money. A prudent, risk-averse investor does not put all her eggs in one basket. Uncertainty about the returns on risky assets leads to a diversified portfolio strategy.

As part of that diversified portfolio, the typical investor will want to hold some amount of a safe asset as insurance against capital losses on assets whose prices change in an uncertain manner. The safe asset would be held precisely because it is safe, even though it pays a lower expected return than risky assets. Money is a safe asset in that its nominal value is known with certainty.[21]. In a famous article,[22] James Tobin argued that money would be held as the safe asset in the portfolios of investors. The title of the article, "Liquidity Preference as Behavior towards Risk," explains the essential notion. In this framework, the demand for money — the safest asset — depends on the expected yields, as well as on the riskiness of the yields, on other assets. The riskiness of the return on other assets is measured by the variability of the return. Using reasonable assumptions, Tobin shows that an increase in the expected return on other assets — an increase in the

---

[21] Of course, when the rate of inflation is uncertain, the real value of money is also uncertain, and money is no longer a safe asset. Even so, the uncertainties about the values of equity are so much larger than the uncertainties about the rate of inflation that money can be treated as a relatively safe asset.

[22] James Tobin, "Liquidity Preference as Behavior towards Risk," *Review of Economic Studies*, February 1958.

opportunity cost of holding money (that is, the return lost by holding money)—lowers money demand. By contrast, an increase in the riskiness of the returns on other assets increases money demand.

An investor's aversion to risk certainly generates a demand for a safe asset. The question we want to consider is whether that safe asset is money. That is, we want to ask whether considerations of portfolio behaviour do generate a demand for money. The relevant considerations in the portfolio are the returns and the risks on assets. From the viewpoint of the yield and risks of holding money, it is clear that savings and term deposits have the same risks as currency or demand deposits. However, they generally pay a higher yield. The risks in both cases are the risks arising from uncertainty about inflation. Given that the risks are the same, and with the yields on savings and term deposits higher than on currency and demand deposits, portfolio diversification explains the demand for assets such as savings and term deposits better than the demand for M1. We therefore regard the speculative demand as applying primarily to M2 and M3.

The implications of the speculative, or risk-diversifying, demand for money are similar to those of the transactions and precautionary demands. An increase in the interest rate on nonmoney assets, such as long-term bond yields or equity yields, will reduce the demand for M2 and M3. An increase in the rate paid on term deposits will increase the demand for term deposits, perhaps even at the cost of the demand for M1, as people take advantage of the higher yields they can earn on their investment portfolios to increase the size of those portfolios. One important difference between the speculative and the other two categories of demand is that here the level of wealth is clearly relevant to the demand for M2 and M3. The level of wealth determines the size of the total portfolio, and we expect that increases in wealth lead to increases in the demand for the safe asset, and thus in M2 and M3 demand.

One final point on the speculative demand. Many individuals with relatively small amounts of wealth will indeed hold part of that wealth in savings accounts in order to diversify their portfolios. But bigger investors are sometimes able to purchase other securities such as treasury bills which pay higher interest and also have fixed (i.e., risk-free) nominal values. For such individuals or groups, the demand for a safe asset is not a demand for money.

7-4 EMPIRICAL EVIDENCE

This section examines the empirical evidence — the studies made using actual data—on the demand for money. We noted in Chapter 4, and again at the beginning of Section 7-3, that the *interest elasticity* of the demand for money plays an important role in determining the effectiveness of monetary and fiscal policies. We then showed in Section 7-3 that there are good theoretical reasons for believing the demand for real balances should depend on the interest rate. The empirical evidence supports that view very strongly. Empirical studies have established that the demand for money is responsive to the interest rate. An increase in the interest rate reduces the demand for money.

The theory of money demand also predicts that the demand for money should depend on the level of income. The response of the demand for money to the level of income, as measured by the *income elasticity* of money demand, is also important from a policy viewpoint. The income elasticity of money demand provides a guide to the Bank of Canada as to how fast to increase the money supply to support a given rate of growth of GNP without changing the interest rate.

Suppose that the aim is for GNP growth of 10 percent, 6 percent real growth and 4 percent inflation. If the Bank of Canada wants to provide a sufficient growth rate of money to prevent interest rates from rising, it has to know the income elasticity of the demand for real balances. Suppose the real income elasticity is $\frac{1}{2}$. Then we would require monetary growth of 7 percent to prevent an increase in interest rates. Why? First, the demand for nominal money increases in proportion to the price level, since money demand is a demand for real balances. Thus 4 percent growth in money is needed to meet the increased demand from the 4 percent increase in the price level. The 6 percent growth in real income would increase the demand for real balances by 3 percent (= 6 percent $\times$ $\frac{1}{2}$), given the real income elasticity of $\frac{1}{2}$. Hence, the needed 7 percent (= 4 + 3) growth in the nominal money supply to meet the increased demand arising from the increase in income.

The empirical work on the demand for money has introduced one complication that we did not study in the theoretical section. That is that the demand for money adjusts to changes in income and interest rates *with a lag*. When the level of income or the interest rate changes, there is first only a small change in the demand for money. Then, over the course of time, the change in the demand for money increases, slowly building up to its full long-run change. Reasons for this lag are not yet certain. The two usual possibilities exist in this case too. The lags may arise because there are costs of adjusting money holdings, or they may arise because money holders' expectations are slow to adjust. If people believe that a given change in the interest rate is temporary, they may be unwilling to make a major change in their money holdings. As time passes and it becomes clearer that the change is not transitory, they are more willing to make a larger adjustment.

There are several published studies of the demand for money in Canada using postwar quarterly data.[23] The results of the most recent one are fairly

[23] See for example K. Clinton, "The Demand for Money in Canada, 1955-70," *Canadian Journal of Economics*, February, 1973; N. Cameron, "The Stability of Canadian Demand for Money Functions," *Canadian Journal of Economics*, May, 1979; S. Poloz, "Simultaneity and the Demand for Money in Canada," *Canadian Journal of Economics*, August, 1980.

TABLE 7-2 ELASTICITIES OF REAL MONEY DEMAND (M1)

	Y	i
Short run	0.22	−0.054
Long run	0.73	−0.18

Source: S. Poloz, "Simultaneity and the Demand for Money in Canada," Canadian Journal of Economics, August, 1980, p. 413.

typical and are summarized in Table 7-2. The table shows the elasticities of the demand for real balances with respect to real income Y (real GNP) and the rate on commercial paper i. This interest rate is relevant to the demand for money because commercial paper is an asset which is very liquid for corporations that hold it instead of money for short periods of time.

In the short run (one quarter), the elasticity of demand with respect to real income is 0.22. This means that a 1 percent increase in real income raises money demand by 0.22 percent, which is considerably less than proportionately. The table shows that the interest elasticity of money demand with respect to interest rates is negative: an increase in interest rates reduces money demand. The short-run interest elasticity is quite small. An increase from 8 percent to 10 percent, that is, a 25 percent increase (10/8 = 1.25), reduces the demand for money by only 1.35 percent (= 0.054 × 25 percent).

The long-run elasticities exceed the short-run elasticities by a factor of more than 3, as Table 7-2 shows. The long-run real income elasticity is 0.73, meaning that in the long run the increase in real money demand occurring as a result of a given increase in real income is only 73 percent as large as the increase in income. Real money demand thus rises less than proportionately to the rise in real income. The long-run interest elasticity is −0.18, meaning that an increase in i from 8 to 10 percent would reduce the demand for money by 4.5 percent.

How long is the long run? That is, how long does it take the demand for money to adjust from the short-run elasticities of Table 7-2 to the long-run

TABLE 7-3 DYNAMIC PATTERNS OF ELASTICITIES OF MONEY DEMAND WITH RESPECT TO REAL INCOME AND INTEREST RATES

Quarters elapsed	Y	i
1	0.22	−0.054
2	0.37	−0.092
3	0.48	−0.119
4	0.55	−0.138
8	0.69	0.172
Long run	0.73	−0.182

Source: Calculated using the elasticities shown in Table 7-2 and reported by Poloz, op. cit.

elasticities shown in the table? Actually, it takes forever for the full long-run position to be reached. Table 7-3, however, shows the elasticities of the demand for real balances in response to changes in the level of income and interest rates after one, two, three, four, and eight quarters. Three-fourths of the adjustment is complete within the first year, and over 90 percent of the adjustment is complete within the first two years.

In summary, we have so far described three essential properties of money demand:

1 The demand for real money balances responds negatively to the rate of interest. An increase in interest rates reduces the demand for money.
2 The demand for money increases with the level of real income. However, the income elasticity of money demand is less than 1 so that money demand increases less than proportionately with income.
3 The short-run responsiveness of money demand to changes in interest rates and income is considerably less than the long-run response. The long-run elasticities are estimated to be over three times the size of the short-run elasticities.

There is one more important question to be considered. This is the question of how money responds to an increase in the level of prices. Here a number of researchers have found strong evidence that an increase in prices raises nominal money demand in the same proportion. We can add, therefore, a fourth conclusion:

4 The demand for nominal money balances is proportional to the price level. There is no money illusion; in other words, the demand for money is a demand for *real* balances.

*7-5 THE INCOME VELOCITY OF MONEY

The *income velocity of money* is the number of times the stock of money is turned over per year in financing the annual flow of income. Thus in 1979 GNP was about $260 billion, the money stock (M1) was $23.1 billion, and velocity was therefore about 11.3. The average dollar of money balances financed $11.30 of spending on final goods and services, or the public held on average 9 cents of M1 per dollar of income.[24] While we usually calculate

---

[24] Why do we say income velocity and not plain velocity? There is another concept, transactions velocity, that is, the ratio of total transactions to money balances. Total transactions far exceed GNP for two reasons. First, there are many transactions involving the sale and purchase of assets that do not contribute to GNP. Second, a particular item in final output typically generates total spending on it that exceeds the contribution of that item to GNP. For instance, one dollar's worth of wheat generates transactions as it leaves the farm, as it is sold by the miller, as it leaves the baker for the supermarket, and then as it is sold to the household. One dollar's worth of wheat may involve several dollars of transactions before it is sold for the last time. Transactions velocity is thus higher than income velocity.

velocity for the economy as a whole, we can also calculate it for an individual. For instance, for someone earning $12,000 per year, who has average money balances during the year of $1,000, the income velocity of money holdings is 12.

Income velocity (from now on we shall refer to velocity rather than income velocity) is defined, as in Section 4-8, as

$$V \equiv \frac{Y_N}{M^S} \tag{6}$$

the ratio of nominal income to nominal money stock. If we rewrite (6) as

$$Y_N \equiv VM \tag{6a}$$

we see one of the major reasons economists have examined the behaviour of velocity. Given the nominal money stock and the velocity, we know the level of nominal income. Thus, if we can predict the level of velocity, we can predict the level of nominal income, given the money stock.

Further, *if* velocity were constant, changing the money supply would result in proportionate changes in nominal income. Any policies, including fiscal policies, that did not affect the money stock would not affect the level of income. You will probably now recognize that we have previously discussed a case of constant velocity. In Chapter 4, we discussed the effectiveness of fiscal policy when the demand for money is not a function of the interest rate and the LM curve is therefore vertical. That vertical LM curve is the same as the assumption of constant velocity.

The discussion of constant velocity suggests that the behaviour of velocity is closely related to the behaviour of the demand for money. Indeed, the notion of velocity is important because it is a convenient way of talking about money demand. For that reason, the term is frequently used in policy discussions. Discussions about monetary policy would be difficult to follow (or even more difficult to follow than they now are) without knowledge of the meaning of velocity.

We now examine the relationship between velocity and the demand for money. Let the demand for real balances be written $L(i,Y)$ consistent with Chapter 4. Recall that Y is real income. Then, when the supply of money is equal to the demand for money, we have

$$\frac{M}{P} = L(i,Y) \tag{7}$$

or $M = PL(i,Y)$. Now we can substitute for the nominal money supply into Equation (6) to obtain

$$V = \frac{Y_N}{PL(i,Y)} = \frac{Y}{L(i,Y)} \tag{6b}$$

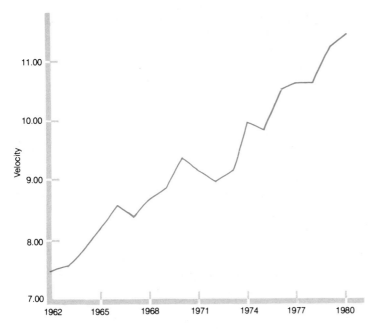

CHART 7-1 THE INCOME VELOCITY OF MONEY (M1)
(*Source: Bank of Canada Review*)

where we have recognized that Y_N/P is the level of real income. Income velocity is the ratio of the level of real income to the demand for real balances.

From Equation ($6b$) we note that velocity is a function of real income and the interest rate. Consider first the effects of a change in the interest rate on velocity. An increase in the interest rate reduces the demand for real balances and therefore increases velocity: when the cost of holding money increases, money holders make their money do more work, and thus turn it over more often.

The way in which changes in real income affect velocity depends on the income elasticity of the demand for money. If the income elasticity of the demand for real balances were 1, then the demand for real balances would change in the same proportion as income. In that case, changes in real income would not affect velocity. For, suppose that real income Y increased by 10 percent. The numerator Y in Equation ($6b$) would increase by 10 percent as would the denominator, and velocity would be unchanged. However, we have seen that the income elasticity of the demand for money is less than 1. That means that velocity *increases* with increases in real income. For example, suppose that real income rose 10 percent, and the demand for real balances increased only by 7.3 percent ($= .73 \times 10$ percent), as Poloz's results suggest. Then the numerator of Equation ($6b$) would increase by more than the denominator, and velocity would rise.

The empirical work reviewed in Section 7-4 makes it clear that the demand for money and, therefore, also velocity do react systematically to changes in interest rates and the level of real income. The empirical evidence therefore decisively refutes the view that velocity is unaffected by changes in interest rates and that fiscal policy is, accordingly, incapable of affecting the level of nominal income. In terms of Equation (6b), and using the analysis of Chapter 4, expansionary fiscal policy can be thought of as working by increasing interest rates, thereby increasing velocity, and thus making it possible for a given stock of money to support a higher level of nominal GNP.

The empirical evidence we reviewed in Section 7-4 is useful in interpreting the behaviour of velocity shown in Chart 7-1. The chart shows a striking and steady increase in velocity. The velocity of M1 has increased from under 8 in the early sixties to over 11 in 1980. The average dollar finances one-and-a-half times the income flow now that it did in the early sixties. This increase in velocity can of course be explained by the same factors that explain the demand for money. Velocity has risen because income has risen (since the income elasticity of demand is less than 1) and because interest rates have risen.

7-6 VELOCITY AND INFLATION

We begin to discuss inflation systematically only in Chapter 13, but we can take up here an important and fascinating aspect of inflation. The question is: How does inflation affect the demand for money? It is especially important to distinguish here between the demand for *nominal* and *real* money balances. Earlier in the chapter we have seen that (1) an increase in the price level, all real variables remaining unchanged, leaves the demand for real balances unchanged and increases the demand for nominal balances in proportion to the increase in the price level, and (2) an increase in the rate of interest increases the cost of holding money and reduces the demand for real balances.

These two points are relevant in discussing the effects of expected inflation — expected continuing increases in prices — on the demand for real balances. We have seen that a one-time increase in the price level, all real variables remaining unchanged after this increase, leaves the demand for real balances unaffected. But now assume that prices increase and that the public interprets the price increases as merely the prelude to further continuing price increases. That is, the public anticipates inflation. Inflation reduces the purchasing power of money. Thus, inflation at the rate of 5 percent reduces the real value of a nominal dollar that is held for a period of one year by 5 percent. Inflation acts as a tax on real balances.[25] Someone,

---

[25] We explore the notion of inflation as a tax on real balances in more detail in Chapter 13.

holding $100 for a year during which inflation is 5 percent, in effect pays $5 for holding that money during the year. If she held less money, she would pay a smaller tax; if she reduced her cash holdings to $50, the tax would be only $2.50. There is thus an incentive, when increased inflation is expected, to try to reduce holdings of real balances and, instead, hold assets whose value is not as adversely affected by inflation. It is precisely this consideration that causes the public to reduce the demand for real balances when inflation is expected.

The effects of expected inflation on the demand for real balances have a strong influence on the behaviour of the price level when money supply growth increases. Suppose the money supply has been growing at 5 percent, that real income was constant, and that the inflation rate had been a steady 5 percent. Then let the money supply start growing more rapidly, say at 10 percent. Ultimately, prices will increase at a 10 percent rate as well. But with 10 percent inflation expected, the demand for real balances is lower than when the expected inflation rate is only 5 percent. That means that at some stage during the process by which the economy adapts from an inflation rate of 5 percent to a rate of 10 percent, real balances have to be reduced. The only way real balances can fall is for prices to increase more rapidly than the money supply. Accordingly, at some point during the adjustment process, prices have to increase more rapidly than at 10 percent, which is the rate at which the nominal money supply is growing. That means that an increase in the growth rate of money to a new higher level produces, at some point, a rate of inflation higher than the rate of growth of money. The adjustment of real balances during an inflationary period will imply that prices increase more rapidly than the nominal money stock.

How does this observation link up with evidence on money demand during inflationary periods? Phillip Cagan of Columbia University studied the demand for real balances during *hyperinflations* — extremely rapid inflations in an interesting and famous article.[26] His evidence shows that the demand for real balances declines dramatically as inflation reaches very high levels. As we noted earlier, expected inflation reduces the demand for money because it is a cost of holding money. For instance, during the Austrian hyperinflation in 1922-1923, the *monthly* rate of inflation rose from roughly zero to more than 80 percent. This extraordinary increase in inflation brought about a decline in real money demand to *one-fifth* the level that had been held at zero inflation. Velocity increased by a factor of 5. The evidence for other countries is, if anything, even more striking.

Cagan's evidence raises the question of how real money demand, or velocity, can be so flexible. How do people manage to reduce their money holdings per dollar, or crown, of income by so much? As inflation increases, the public takes more care in how it manages its cash balances. Money is spent more rapidly after it is received. Firms begin to pay their workers more

[26] Phillip Cagan, "The Monetary Dynamics of Hyperinflation," in Milton Friedman (ed.), *Studies in the Quantity Theory of Money* (Chicago: The University of Chicago Press, 1956).

frequently. Money becomes like a hot potato, with people anxious to pass it on rapidly. One can almost see the velocity of circulation increasing as people scurry to get rid of cash. These changes in payments patterns and shopping habits do impose costs on money holders that are the major cost of expected inflation, as we shall see in Chapter 14.

The adjustment of the demand for money to expected inflation is, in principle, no different from the adjustment to changes in the interest rate, which also increase the cost of holding money. Indeed, in countries with sufficiently well-developed capital markets, expected inflation is reflected in nominal interest rates. When inflation is expected, borrowers know that they will repay their debts in money that has lower purchasing power than the money they originally borrowed, and lenders know that too. Lenders, accordingly, become more reluctant to lend at any given level of the nominal interest rate, and borrowers become more anxious to borrow at a given nominal interest rate. The result is that the *nominal* interest rate rises when inflation is expected, thus compensating lenders for the loss of purchasing power of money.

The rise in the nominal interest rate that we are talking about reminds us of the distinction between *real* and *nominal* interest rates made in Chapter 6. When the expected rate of inflation rises, nominal interest rates — interest rates which specify how many dollars have to be repaid — increase. The real interest rate — the nominal interest rate minus the expected rate of inflation — need not rise and may even fall. Undoubtedly, one of the major reasons for the increase in nominal interest rates since the fifties is the increase in the expected rate of inflation. This relationship will be investigated in more detail in Chapter 13. In some Latin American countries where inflation rates have reached 100 percent per year or more, no one is surprised by bank loan rates of, say, 80 percent.

In talking about both the expected rate of inflation itself and nominal interest rates, we raise the question of whether each is a separate influence on the demand for money. In well-developed capital markets, in which interest rates are free to move to reflect expected inflation, the nominal interest rate is the relevant opportunity cost of holding money. That is because individuals could make investments at that interest rate. In markets where interest rates are controlled and rates do not rise to reflect expected inflation, individuals begin to think of the alternative of buying goods rather than holding money when the expected rate of inflation rises. The expected inflation rate itself then becomes a separate influence on the demand for money. Franco Modigliani has offered the following useful rule of thumb to decide whether the nominal interest rate or the expected rate of inflation should be included as determining the demand for money: If the nominal interest rate exceeds the expected rate of inflation, the nominal interest rate should be thought of as the cost of holding money. If the expected inflation rate exceeds the nominal interest rate, think of the expected inflation rate as the cost of holding money.

7-7 SUMMARY

1 The demand for money is a demand for real balances. It is the purchasing power, not the number, of their dollar bills that matters to holders of money.

2 The money supply (M1) is made up of currency and demand deposits. M2 and M3 are broader measures that include savings accounts and term and notice deposits.

3 The chief characteristic of money is that it serves as a means of payment.

4 There are two broad reasons why people hold money and thus forgo interest that they could earn by holding alternative assets. These reasons are transactions costs and uncertainty.

5 Transactions costs are an essential aspect of money demand. If it were costless to move (instantaneously) in and out of interest-bearing assets, nobody would hold money. Optimal cash management would involve transfers from other assets (bonds or saving deposits) just prior to outlays, and it would involve immediate conversion into interest-bearing form of any cash receipts. The existence of transactions costs — brokerage costs, fees, and time costs — makes it optimal to hold some money.

6 The inventory-theoretic approach shows that an individual will hold a stock of real balances that varies inversely with the interest rate but increases with the level of real income and the cost of transactions. The income elasticity of money demand is less than unity, so that there are economies of scale.

7 Transactions costs, in combination with uncertainty about payments and receipts, give rise to a precautionary demand for money. Money holdings provide insurance against illiquidity. Optimal money holdings are higher, the higher the variability of net disbursements and the higher the cost of illiquidity. Since money holdings involve forgoing interest, the optimal money holding will vary inversely with the rate of interest.

8 Portfolio diversification involves the tradeoff between risk and return. Saving deposits form part of an optimal portfolio because they are not risky — their nominal value is constant. Saving deposits dominate currency or demand deposits, which are also safe nominal assets, because they bear interest. Thus the speculative portfolio demand for money is a demand for savings deposits.

9 The empirical evidence provides strong support for a negative interest elasticity of money demand and a positive income elasticity. Because of lags, short-run elasticities are much smaller than long-run elasticities. The long-run income elasticity is about 0.7, and the long-run interest elasticity is about -0.2.

10 The income velocity of money is defined as the ratio of income to

money or the rate of turnover of money. Since the sixties, velocity has increased to a level in excess of 11.

11 The empirical evidence implies that an increase in real income raises velocity, as does an increase in the rate of interest. At higher levels of income or at higher interest rates, there is a lower demand for money in relation to income. Higher interest rates lead people to economize on cash balances.

12 Inflation implies that money loses purchasing power, and inflation thus creates a cost of holding money. The higher the rate of inflation, the lower the amount of real balances that will be held. Hyperinflations provide striking support for this prediction. Under conditions of very high expected inflation, money demand falls dramatically relative to income. Velocity rises as people use less money in relation to income.

PROBLEMS

1 To what extent would it be possible to design a society in which there was no money? What would the problems be? Could currency at least be eliminated? How? (Lest all this seems too unworldly, you should know that some people are beginning to talk of a "cashless economy" in the next century.)

2 Evaluate the effects of the following changes on the demand for M1 and M2. Which of the functions of money do they relate to?

   (a) "Instant cash" machines which allow 24-hour withdrawals from savings accounts at banks
   (b) The employment of more tellers at your bank
   (c) An increase in inflationary expectations
   (d) Widespread acceptance of credit cards
   (e) Fear of an imminent collapse of the government
   (f) A rise in the interest rate on nonchequable savings deposits

*3 The assumption was made in the text that in the transactions demand for cash model, it is optimal to space transactions evenly throughout the month. Prove this as follows in the case where $n = 2$. Since one transaction must be made immediately, the only question is when to make the second one. For simplicity, call the beginning of the month $t = 0$, and the end of the month $t = 1$. Then consider a transaction strategy which performs the second transaction at time t_0. If income is Y_N, then this will require moving $t_0 Y_N$ into cash now, and $(1 - t_0)Y_N$ at time t_0. Calculate the total cost incurred under this strategy, and try various values of t_0 to see which is optimal. (If you are familiar with calculus, prove that $t_0 = \frac{1}{2}$ minimizes total cost.)

*4 For those students with calculus, derive Equation (4) from Equation (2) by minimizing total costs with respect to n.

5 (a) Determine the optimal strategy for cash management for the person who earns $1,600 per month, can earn 0.5 percent interest per month in a savings account, and has a transaction cost of $1.
   (b) What is the individual's average cash balance?
   (c) Suppose her income rises to $1,800. By what percentage does her demand for money rise? (Pay attention to the integer constraints.)

6 Discuss the various factors that go into an individual's decision regarding how many traveler's cheques to take on a vacation.

7 In the text, we said that the transactions demand-for-money model can also be applied to firms. Suppose a firm sells steadily during the month and has to pay its workers at the end of the month. Explain then how it would determine its money holdings.

8 This chapter emphasizes that the demand for money is a demand for real balances. At the same time, inflation causes the real demand to fall. Explain how these two assertions can both be correct.

9 "Muggers favour deflation." Comment.

8

THE MONEY SUPPLY PROCESS

We have so far taken the money supply to be given and determined by the Bank of Canada. By and large, the Bank is indeed able to determine the money supply quite accurately, but it does not set it directly. In this chapter we study the way in which the actions of the Bank of Canada, the chartered banks, and the public interact in determining the stock of money.

In conducting monetary policy, the Bank of Canada pays attention to the behaviour of both interest rates and the money supply. We will show that the Bank of Canada cannot simultaneously set both the money supply and the interest rate at whatever levels it wants, though it can set either the money supply or the interest rate. In addition, we shall examine in some detail the way in which the Bank of Canada operates monetary policy.

8-1 DEFINITIONS

We noted in Chapter 7 that the money supply measure M1 is the sum of demand deposits, DD, plus currency held by the public CU.

$$M1 = DD + CU \tag{1}$$

A broader measure of the money supply is M2, which adds personal savings and nonpersonal notice deposits, SD, to M1:

$$M2 = M1 + SD \tag{2}$$

Chart 8-1 shows the history of these aggregates and their components. Savings deposits have been growing more rapidly than the other components of the money supply, and M2 has accordingly been growing more rapidly than M1. Over the 1970-79 period, M1 grew at 10.4 percent per

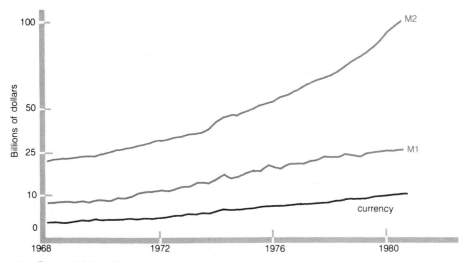

Note: The scale is logarithmic.

CHART 8-1 MONETARY AGGREGATES (*Source: Bank of Canada Review*)

annum and M2 at 13.7 percent. The 10.4 percent growth rate of M1 from 1970 to 1979 is well above the average rate of growth of M1 of 4.2 percent from 1960 to 1969.

Table 8-1 reproduces Table 7-1 and shows the June 1980 components of the money stock. M1 is about $23.6 billion, about 40 percent of that consisting of currency. The difference between M2 and M1 of $72.9 billion is composed chiefly of personal savings deposits.

For simplicity, we shall now ignore the distinction between demand and savings deposits and consider the money supply process as if there were only a uniform class of deposits D. Using that simplification, we define money as deposits plus currency:

TABLE 8-1 COMPONENTS OF THE MONEY STOCK, JUNE 1980
(MILLIONS OF DOLLARS, AVERAGE OF WEDNESDAYS)

(1)	(2)	(3)	(4)	(5)
			Personal savings	
Currency	Demand deposits	M1 = (1) + (2)	and nonpersonal notice deposits	M2 = (3) + (4)
9,313	14,321	23,634	72,947	96,581

Source: Bank of Canada Review

$$M \equiv CU + D \qquad\qquad (3)$$

Starting from Equation (3), we now begin to develop the details of the process of money stock determination. It is apparent from Equation (3) that both the public and the chartered banks have an influence on the determination of the money supply. The public has a role because its demand for currency affects the currency component CU. The banks have a role because the other component of the money stock, deposits D, is a liability of the banks, that is, a debt the banks owe their customers. We know too that the Bank of Canada has a part (the most important) in determining the money supply. The interactions among the actions of the public, the chartered banks, and the Bank of Canada determine the money supply, and we shall summarize their behaviour in the money supply process by three separate variables.

From the viewpoint of money supply determination, the variable on which we concentrate as representing the behaviour of the public, is the *currency-deposit ratio*, that is, the ratio of the public's holdings of currency to its holdings of deposits. We denote the currency-deposit ration CU/D, by cu.

The behaviour of the chartered banks is summarized by the *reserve-deposit ratio*. Cash reserves are assets held by the banks to meet (1) the demands of their customers for currency and (2) payments their customers make by cheques which are deposited in other banks. Cash reserves consist of notes held by the chartered banks — *till money* — and also of deposits held by the chartered banks at the Bank of Canada. This latter reserve category deserves some attention. The chartered banks have bank accounts at the Bank of Canada which they can use to make payments among themselves. Thus, when my bank has to make a payment to your bank because I paid you with a cheque drawn on my bank account, it makes the payment by transferring money from its account to your bank's account at the Bank of Canada. Cash reserves thus consist of till money to meet customers' demands for currency and deposits at the Bank of Canada to make payments to other banks. We examine the determinants of the banks' demand for reserves, RE, in more detail in Section 8-3, but in the meantime we summarize that behaviour by the reserve-deposit ratio, $RE/D \equiv r$. The reserve ratio is less than 1, since banks hold assets other than reserves, such as loans they make to the public and securities in their portfolios.

The Bank of Canada's behaviour is summarized by the stock of *high-powered money*, or the *monetary base*, H. High-powered money consists of currency and deposits of the chartered banks at the Bank of Canada. Part of the currency is held by the public and the remainder is held by the chartered banks as till money. The notes that constitute most of the outstanding stock of currency are issued by the Bank of Canada, and the cash reserves held by chartered banks as Bank of Canada deposits are a liability of the Bank of Canada — that is, a debt of the Bank of Canada to the chartered banks.

8-2 THE MONEY MULTIPLIER

In this section we develop a simple diagrammatic approach to money stock determination. The approach is organized around the demand for, and supply of, high-powered money. The demand — the public's demand for currency and the banks' demand for reserves — and the supply, determined by the Bank of Canada, interact to determine the equilibrium money stock.

We start with the demand for high-powered money, or the monetary base (the terms are interchangeable). The demand for high-powered money, H^d, arises from currency demand by the public, CU, and cash reserve demand by the chartered banks RE:

$$\checkmark H \equiv CU + RE \tag{4}$$

The right-hand side of Equation (4) can be developed to express the demand for high-powered money in terms of the ratios cu and r, as well as the money stock M. Consider first the currency holdings of the public, which can be expressed in terms of the money stock M and the currency deposit ratio cu:

$$CU = \frac{CU}{M} M = \left(\frac{CU}{D + CU} \right) M \tag{5}$$

or

$$CU = \left(\frac{cu}{1 + cu} \right) M \tag{5a}$$

In Equation (5) we have simply multiplied and divided by the money supply M and then substituted the definition of the money stock, $M \equiv D + CU$. In moving from Equation (5) to Equation (5a), we have divided numerator and denominator of the term in parentheses by deposits D, and then substituted the definition of the currency-deposit ratio, $cu \equiv CU/D$.

Equation (5a) gives us an expression for currency demand in terms of the currency-deposit ratio and the money stock. The equation says that the public wants to hold a fraction $cu/(1 + cu)$ of its money balances in the form of currency. The higher cu, the higher the fraction of money balances the public wants to hold in the form of money, and the lower the fraction to be held in the form of deposits. (That latter fraction is $1/(1 + cu)$)

We can proceed in a manner parallel to Equation (5) in deriving an expression for cash reserves in terms of the money stock and the reserve ratio r. Here we write reserves as

$$RE = \left(\frac{RE}{M} \right) M = \left(\frac{RE}{D + CU} \right) M \tag{6}$$

Dividing both numerator and denominator of the term in parentheses by D and using the definitions $cu \equiv CU/D$ and $r \equiv RE/D$,

$$RE = \left(\frac{r}{1 + cu}\right)M \qquad (6a)$$

Equation $(6a)$ states that reserve demand is equal to a fraction $r/(1 + cu)$ of the money stock. The fraction is larger, the higher the reserve ratio r. It is lower, the higher the currency-deposit ratio cu.[1]

We now have developed expressions for both cash reserves and currency in terms of money and the cu and r ratios. Substituting Equations $(5a)$ and $(6a)$ as the total demand for high-powered money in Equation (4), we obtain

$$H^d = \frac{cu}{1 + cu}M + \frac{r}{1 + cu}M$$

$$H^d = \left(\frac{cu + r}{1 + cu}\right)M \qquad (4a)$$

Equation $(4a)$ shows the relation between the demand for high-powered money H^d, the reserve and currency ratios, and the money supply.

The demand for high-powered money derived in Equation $(4a)$ is shown graphically in Figure 8-1 by the positively sloped line. Note that the slope of the demand for high-powered money line in this figure is less than 1, since r is less than 1 — banks hold assets other than cash reserves in their portfolios. Equation $(4a)$ reflects the *portfolio preferences* of the public and the banks. The way in which the public wants to divide its portfolio between currency and demand deposits and the preferences of the chartered banks between holding cash reserves and holding other assets determine cu and r respectively.

The supply of high-powered money is determined by the Bank of Canada. We denote the stock of high-powered money by $\bar{H}$, and show the supply in Figure 8-1 by the horizontal line at the level $\bar{H}$. Equating the supply of and demand for high-powered money, we have

$$\bar{H} = H^d = \left(\frac{cu + r}{1 + cu}\right)M \qquad (7)$$

Now we can turn Equation (7) around to read

---

[1] We could have derived Eq. $(6a)$ directly by remembering that $RE = rD$ and that deposits are a fraction $1/(1 + cu)$ of the money supply $D = M/(1 + cu)$. Substituting that expression for deposits, we have $RE + rD = [r/(1 + cu)]M$.

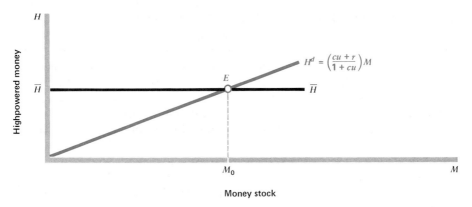

FIGURE 8-1 MONEY STOCK DETERMINATION

$$M = \left(\frac{1 + cu}{cu + r}\right)\overline{H} \qquad (8)$$

In terms of Figure 8-1, the equilibrium money stock, M, in Equation (8), is determined by the intersection of the supply and demand curves for high-powered money, which occurs at point E. The equilibrium money stock implied by Equation (8) is shown in Figure 8-1 as M_0.

Underlying the determination of the equilibrium money stock are the portfolio preferences of the public and banks, reflected in the slope of the H^d line in Figure 8-1, and the actions of the Bank of Canada, represented by the position of the $\overline{H}$ line. In equilibrium the money stock is such that, first, the public and banks have their preferred composition of portfolios (cu and r), and second, the demand for high-powered money is equal to the supply.

FIGURE 8-2 AN INCREASE IN THE MONETARY BASE

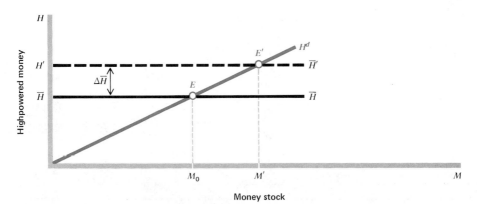

The next step is to use Figure 8-1 and Equation (8) to study the effects of changes in $\bar{H}$, cu, and r on the money stock. We examine first an increase in the stock of high-powered money, as seen in Figure 8-2. An increase in the supply of the monetary base (high-powered money) shifts the $\bar{H}\bar{H}$ schedule upward by $\Delta\bar{H}$. At the initial level of the money stock, the supply of high-powered money exceeds the demand. The money supply thus expands until we reach point E', where the new equilibrium money stock is M'. The adjustment process by which this new equilibrium stock is achieved will be discussed in Section 8-6.

Note from Figure 8-2 that the increase in the equilibrium money stock exceeds the increase in the monetary base. A $1 increase in high-powered money increases the money stock by a multiple of $1. This is the reason the monetary base is referred to as high-powered money. The precise relationship between the increase in the monetary base and the increase in the equilibrium money stock depends on the slope of the H^d schedule. The flatter the slope, the larger is the increase in the money stock for a given change in monetary base. To examine this relationship in more detail, it is useful to rewrite Equation (8) more simply as

$$M = m\bar{H} \tag{8a}$$

where

$$m \equiv \left(\frac{1 + cu}{cu + r} \right) \tag{9}$$

In Equation (9), m is the *money multiplier*, which tells us how much the money stock increases when the stock of high-powered money is increased by $1. Note from Equation (7) that the money multiplier is just the inverse of the slope of the H^d schedule in Figure 8-2.

It is clear from Equation (9) that the multiplier is larger, the lower are cu and r. The lower the increase in demand for high-powered money (currency plus reserves) per dollar increase in the money stock, the larger the increase in the money stock we require to absorb an increased monetary base.

TABLE 8-2 THE MONEY MULTIPLIER, JUNE 1980

	(1) Currency	(2) Reserves	(3) Deposits	cu	r	$m = \dfrac{1+cu}{r+cu}$
	(millions of dollars)			= (1)/(3)	= (2)/(3)	$= \dfrac{(1)+(3)}{(1)+(2)}$
M1	9,313	6,495	14,321	.650	.454	1.5
M2	9,313	6,495	87,268	.107	.074	6.1

Source: Bank of Canada Review

Conversely, an increase in *cu* increases the demand for high-powered money at any given level of *M*, and therefore causes the H^d curve to rotate up to the left and reduce the equilibrium money stock, while an increase in the reserve ration, *r*, decreases the money stock, given $\bar{H}$.

Table 8-2 shows the calculation of the multiplier for M1 and M2 using figures for June, 1980. In the case of M1, a $1 increase in high-powered money leads to an expansion of the money stock of 1.5. Why? The reason is that an increase in the money stock of $1 raises the demand for high-powered money only by a fraction. In our example, using Equation (4a), it raises the demand for the monetary base by 67 cents. To raise demand for high-powered money by $1 and equate it with the increased supply, the money stock must increase by $1.50 (= 1/.67).

The behaviour of the money multipliers over the period 1968 to 1980 is shown in Chart 8-2. A glance at this chart shows that they are far from constant. Since the Bank of Canada controls $\bar{H}$, it would be able to control *M* exactly if the multiplier were constant or fully predictable. However, the money multiplier varies, not entirely predictably, and the Bank of Canada cannot always set the money supply at precisely the level it wants. In the rest of this chapter we take a closer look at the reasons the money multiplier varies.

In summary, the money stock is bigger, the larger the stock of high-pow-

CHART 8-2 THE MONEY MULTIPLIERS, 1968-1980 (*Source*: Bank of Canada Review)

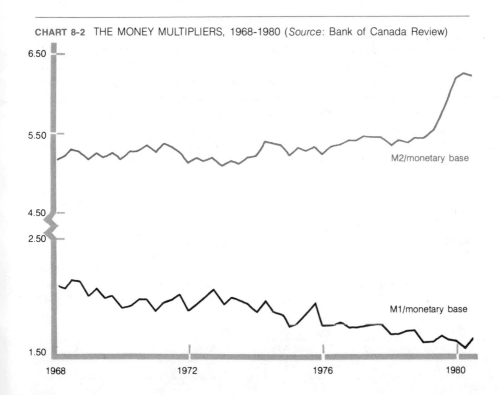

ered money, $\bar{H}$, and the larger the money multiplier, m. The money multiplier, in turn, is larger, the smaller are the currency-deposit ratio, cu, and the reserve-deposit ratio, r.

8-3 THE STOCK OF HIGH-POWERED MONEY

Table 8-3 shows the balance sheet of the Bank of Canada. The components of the monetary base appear on the liability side and high-powered money is created when the Bank of Canada acquires assets or reduces its liability in the form of Government of Canada deposits.

The major means by which the Bank of Canada changes the monetary base is *open market operations*. We will examine the mechanics of an open market *purchase*, an operation in which the Bank of Canada buys, say, $1 million of government bonds from individuals or businesses which comprise the nonbank private sector. The accounting for the open market purchase is shown in Table 8-4. The Bank of Canada's holdings of government securities rise by $1 million and the nonbank private sector's holdings fall by the same amount. How does the Bank of Canada pay for the bonds? It writes a cheque on itself and the seller deposits the cheque in a chartered bank which in turn sends the cheque to the Bank of Canada. Thus, chartered bank reserves held in the form of Bank of Canada deposits increase by $1 million. The Bank of Canada owns more government securities, and the stock of high-powered money has been increased by the amount of the open market purchase. That increase in high-powered money shows up as an increase in chartered bank deposits at the Bank of Canada. Later, as the money stock increases, the demand for currency will rise, and part of the increase in $\bar{H}$ will show up on the Bank of Canada's balance sheet as currency. Chartered bank deposits will fall by the amount that currency rises on the ("Liabilities") side of Table 8-4. You should now trace the way in which an open market sale reduces the stock of high-powered money.

The only strange part of the story of the open market purchase is that the Bank of Canada can write cheques on itself. The cheque instructs the

---

TABLE 8-3 BALANCE SHEET OF THE BANK OF CANADA, JUNE, 1980 (MILLIONS OF DOLLARS)

Assets		Liabilities	
Government of Canada securities	$13,869	Notes in circulation:	
		Held by chartered banks	$ 1,520
Advances to chartered banks	—	Other	8,343
		Chartered bank deposits	5,001
Net foreign currency assets	848	Government of Canada deposits	10
Other assets, net	157		
Total assets	$14,874	Total Liabilities	$14,874

TABLE 8-4 EFFECTS ON BALANCE SHEETS OF AN OPEN MARKET
PURCHASE FROM THE NONBANK PRIVATE SECTOR

Nonbank private sector		
Assets		**Liabilities**
Government securities	−1	
Deposits	+1	

Chartered Banks		
Assets		**Liabilities**
Cash reserves	+1	Deposits	+1

Bank of Canada		
Assets		**Liabilities**
Government securities	+1	Chartered bank deposits	+1

Bank to pay $1 million to the order of the seller of the bond. The payment is made by giving the eventual owner of the cheque a deposit at the Bank of Canada. That deposit can be used to make payments to other banks, or it can be exchanged for currency. Just as the ordinary deposit holder at a chartered bank can obtain currency in exchange for deposits, the chartered bank deposit holder at the Bank of Canada can acquire currency in exchange for its deposits. When the Bank of Canada pays for the bond with a deposit, it creates high-powered money with a stroke of the pen. Further, since it is the issuer of currency, it also creates high-powered money with the printing press. In either event, the Bank of Canada can create high-powered money at will merely by buying assets, such as government bonds, and paying for them with its liabilities.

We have assumed so far that the open market purchase is made from the nonbank private sector. What will happen if the seller is a chartered bank? This case is illustrated in Table 8-5. The chartered bank receives a cheque from the Bank of Canada and exchanges it for a deposit. Thus chartered bank cash reserves and the stock of high-powered money increase as in the

TABLE 8-5 EFFECTS ON BALANCE SHEETS OF AN OPEN MARKET
PURCHASE FROM A CHARTERED BANK

Chartered Banks		
Assets		**Liabilities**
Government Securities	−1	
Cash reserves	+	

Bank of Canada		
Assets		**Liabilities**
Government securities	+1	Chartered bank deposits	+1

previous case, but the transaction has no direct effect on the nonbank private sector.

Government of Canada Deposits and the Base

As shown in Table 8-3, the Government of Canada maintains deposits with the Bank of Canada and it uses this account for government receipts and payments. If this were the only bank account maintained by the government, fluctuations in government revenues and expenditures would be reflected in fluctuations in the stock of high-powered money. For example, in a period in which the government receives more than it spends, there would be a transfer of deposits from the chartered banks to the government's account at the Bank of Canada so that cash reserves would be reduced. To avoid these effects, the Government of Canada maintains deposits with the chartered banks as well as with the Bank of Canada. Transfers of these deposits between the chartered banks and the Bank of Canada can then be used to offset the effects of government transactions and provide an alternative means of controlling the stock of high-powered money.

Borrowed Reserves

The chartered banks can increase their cash reserves by borrowing from the Bank of Canada at a rate of interest known as the *bank rate*. This arrangement is designed to provide a "lender of last resort" and advances are made to the chartered banks only occasionally (as can be seen in Table 8-3, there were no advances outstanding in June, 1980). Rather than relying on advances from the Bank of Canada, the chartered banks typically meet their cash requirements by varying the amount of *day-to-day loans* they make available to a group of investment dealers who carry inventories of Government of Canada securities. When necessary, these dealers can in turn obtain financing from the Bank of Canada under *purchase and resale agreements (PRA)*; that is, they can sell securities to the Bank of Canada with an agreement to repurchase them within a stated maximum time period. Thus, when the chartered banks reduce their day-to-day loans they may induce an increase in PRA, so that the end result is the same as if the banks had borrowed from the Bank of Canada directly. Of the $13,869 million of government securities held by the Bank of Canada in June 1980 (see Table 8-3), $258 million were held under PRA.

8-4 THE SIZE OF THE MONEY MULTIPLIER

The next element in the money supply formula (8) is the currency-deposit ratio, which reflects the behaviour of the public. The currency-deposit ratio is determined primarily by payment habits and has a strong seasonal pattern; it is highest around Christmas. The ratio increases when the ratio of consumption to GNP increases, since currency demand is more closely linked to consumption than GNP, while deposit demand is more closely linked to GNP. The ratio of cuurency to demand deposits has shown a rising trend and this accounts for some of the decline in the M1 multiplier shown in Chart 8-2.

The banking system affects the supply of money through the reserve-deposit ratio r. The major determinants of this ratio are the *minimum required cash reserve ratios* prescribed under the Bank Act. Beginning in 1968 the ratios were set at 12 percent for demand deposits and 4 percent for notice deposits. Over the period 1981 to 1984, the ratios are to be reduced in stages to 10 percent and 3 percent respectively. Given different reserve ratios for the two classes of deposits, the ratio of reserves to total deposits will depend on the proportions of demand and notice deposits in the total. Since M1 includes only demand deposits, the multiplier for M1 reflects not only the ratio of reserves to total deposits but also the ratio of demand deposits to total deposits. The fall in the M1 multiplier and the rise in the M2 multiplier shown in Chart 8-2 reflect the fact that notice deposits grew at a faster rate than demand deposits over the period 1968 to 1980.

A second factor affecting the reserve-deposit ratio is the amount of *excess cash reserves* held by the chartered banks beyond the level of required cash reserves. In deciding how much excess reserves to hold, a bank's economic problem is very similar to the problem of the individual in deciding on a precautionary demand for money. Banks hold reserves to meet demands on them for currency or payments to other banks. The opportunity cost of holding excess cash reserves is the interest foregone and in principle we might expect the demand to depend on the rate of interest. However, since chartered bank holdings of excess cash reserves are typically very small (less than one-tenth of one percent of total deposits) this relationship is not of much importance in determining the money multiplier.

8-5 BANK CREDIT AND THE ADJUSTMENT PROCESS

This section extends the discussion of chartered banks to explore the relationship between *bank credit* and the money stock, and to show how the money stock adjusts toward its equilibrium value when the monetary base $\bar{H}$ is changed.

Bank Credit

Bank credit consists of the loans and investments made by the chartered banks. The amount outstanding in June, 1980 is shown in the balance sheet of the chartered banks in Table 8-6. Ignoring Government of Canada

TABLE 8-6 BALANCE SHEET OF THE CHARTERED BANKS, JUNE 1980
(BILLIONS OF DOLLARS)

Assets		Liabilities	
Bank of Canada deposits	$ 6.5	Demand deposits	$ 14.3
and notes		Personal savings deposits	70.7
Loans and investments		Nonpersonal term and	
Government of Canada		notice deposits	38.3
securities	9.7	Government of Canada	
Loans	110.8	deposits	1.9
Other securities	7.7	Other liabilities, net	10.0
Total Canadian dollar	$134.7	Total	$134.7
Major assets			

deposits and net other liabilities, we have that bank credit BC, plus reserves RE, equals deposits D:

$$BC + RE \equiv D \tag{10}$$

or, equivalently, that bank credit is equal to deposits less reserves:

$$BC \equiv D - RE \tag{10a}$$

Adding and subtracting currency on the right-hand side yields

$$BC \equiv (D + CU) - (RE + CU) \tag{11}$$

or

$$BC \equiv M - \bar{H} \tag{11a}$$

where we have substituted the definition of the money supply and high-powered money into Equation (11) to obtain Equation (11a).

Equation (11a) states that bank credit is equal to the money supply less high-powered money. In Figure 8-3, this is shown by introducing a 45° line into the diagram so that we can measure the money supply M_0 by the vertical distance to that line. Accordingly, with a money supply M_0 and a stock of high-powered money $\bar{H}$, the equilibrium supply of bank credit is given by the distance AE, the difference between M and $\bar{H}$, as in Equation (11a).

The relationship (11a) between the money stock and the bank credit can be understood by thinking of how a bank creates credit. When banks expand credit by making loans or purchasing securities, they pay for the assets they acquire by creating deposits. A bank that makes a loan to a customer does not give the customer currency, but rather gives the loan in the form of a

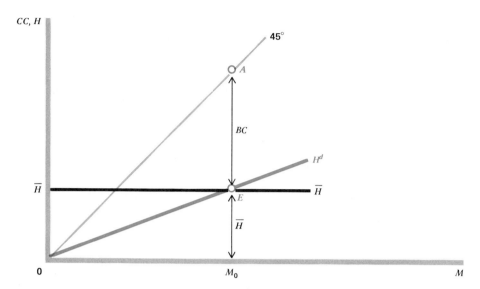

FIGURE 8-3   THE EQUILIBRIUM MONEY STOCK AND BANK CREDIT

deposit at the bank and allows the customer to draw on the deposit. The customer is obviously free to draw down the account by taking out currency or else to write a cheque on the account and make payments in that manner.

The important aspect of credit creation is that it leads automatically to money creation. A bank creates a deposit in making a loan. Deposits are part of our definition of the money supply and, therefore, bank credit creation implies money creation. Even if the loan customer collected the loan entirely in the form of currency, it is still true that the money supply would have increased by the increase in the public's holding of currency.[2]

It is apparent, too, that an increase in high-powered money, as in Figure 8-3, would increase bank credit, as would a reduction in either cu, or r. The diagram is useful in another respect. It emphasizes the makeup of the money supply in terms of the credit and high-powered money components. The higher the reserve ratio—the more nearly the H^d schedule coincides with the 45° line — the larger the high-powered money component of the money supply and the smaller the fraction that has as its counterpart bank credit.

The Adjustment Process

Here we briefly describe the adjustment process toward the equilibrium money stock shown in Figure 8-3. We use Table 8-7 to clarify the

---

[2] You are asked to explain this in the problem set.

TABLE 8-7 MULTIPLE EXPANSION OF BANK DEPOSITS, BANK CREDIT, AND THE MONEY MULTIPLIER

Increase in H	Increase in currency	Increase in deposits	Increase in reserves	Increase in bank credit	Stage
1	$\dfrac{cu}{1+cu}$	$\dfrac{1}{1+cu}$	$\dfrac{r}{1+cu}$	$\dfrac{1-r}{1+cu}$	Round 1
	$\dfrac{cu}{1+cu}\left(\dfrac{1-r}{1+cu}\right)$	$\dfrac{1}{1+cu}\left(\dfrac{1-r}{1+cu}\right)$	$\dfrac{r}{1+cu}\left(\dfrac{1-r}{1+cu}\right)$	$\dfrac{1-r}{1+cu}\left(\dfrac{1-r}{1+cu}\right)$	Round 2
	$\dfrac{cu}{1+cu}\left(\dfrac{1-r}{1+cu}\right)^2$	$\dfrac{1}{1+cu}\left(\dfrac{1-r}{1+cu}\right)^2$	$\dfrac{r}{1+cu}\left(\dfrac{1-r}{1+cu}\right)^2$	$\dfrac{1-r}{1+cu}\left(\dfrac{1-r}{1+cu}\right)^2$	Round 3
	$\dfrac{cu}{1+cu}\left(\dfrac{1-r}{1+cu}\right)^n$	$\dfrac{1}{1+cu}\left(\dfrac{1-r}{1+cu}\right)^n$	$\dfrac{r}{1+cu}\left(\dfrac{1-r}{1+cu}\right)^n$	$\dfrac{1-r}{1+cu}\left(\dfrac{1-r}{1+cu}\right)^n$	Round $n+1$
	$\dfrac{cu}{1+cu}\,SU$	$\dfrac{1}{1+cu}\,SU$	$\dfrac{r}{1+cu}\,SU$	$\dfrac{1-r}{1+cu}\,SU$	Total*
	$\dfrac{cu}{cu+r}$	$\dfrac{1}{cu+r}$	$\dfrac{r}{cu+r}$	$\dfrac{1-r}{cu+r}$	After substituting for SU from Equation (12)

*SU is defined by Eq. (12).

description, which provides another way of thinking about the money multiplier.

Suppose the stock of high-powered money has been increased by \$1, say through an open market purchase. We start by considering an individual man who sold the Bank of Canada a bond for \$1. He deposited the cheque with which he was paid at his bank. But he, like all other portfolio holders, is assumed to have a currency deposit ratio of cu. Therefore, of the \$1 increase in his money holdings, he will want to keep the fraction $(cu/1 + cu)$ in currency and the remaining $(1/1 + cu)$ in deposits. These reactions are shown in the first row, Round 1, of Table 8-7.

At this stage the bank has increased deposits of $(1/1 + cu)$. Its portfolio preference is to keep the fraction r of its increased deposits as reserves. The remaining fraction $(1 - r)$ is available to the bank to extend credit either by making a loan or by buying securities. These reactions are shown in columns 3 and 4 of the first row of Table 8-7.

Round 2 starts with the individual who has received a loan of $[(1 - r)/1 + cu]$ (the amount shown in the fourth column, row 1) from the bank, or who has sold it that amount of securities. He too wants to hold the fraction $(cu/1 + cu)$ of his increased money holdings as currency and the remaining fraction of $(1/1 + cu)$ as deposits. Once again the bank at which he makes his deposit, not necessarily the same bank, will hold some of the increased deposits as reserves and extend credit with the remainder of the deposit. These procedures are summarized by the second row, Round 2, in Table 8-7.

The table shows also Round 3, the logic of which you can now fill in for yourself. Obviously, this process continues to infinity.[3]

We can now add up the increases in currency, deposits, reserves, and bank credit occurring over all the rounds together, that is, during the entire process. As in the appendix to Chapter 4, we are now dealing with the sum of an infinite series, denoted here as SU. That sum is given by[4]

$$SU = 1 + \left(\frac{1 - r}{1 + cu}\right) + \left(\frac{1 - r}{1 + cu}\right)^2 + \left(\frac{1 - r}{1 + cu}\right)^3 + \ldots$$

$$= \frac{1 + cu}{cu + r} \tag{12}$$

We use Equation (12) in arriving at the bottom row of Table 8-7, which shows that currency increases by the fraction $(cu/cu + r)$ of \$1 following the increase in H of \$1, that deposits increase by $(1/cu + r)$, that reserves increase by $r/cu + r)$, and finally, that credit increases by $[(1 - r)/cu + r]$.

Adding the increases in currency and deposits, we discover that the two together have risen by the amount $[(1 + cu)/cu + r]$, which is nothing other than the money multiplier. Table 8-7 thus provides another way of thinking about the money multiplier. The table also shows how, and by how much, the banking system creates credit when the Bank of Canada increases high-powered money.

Table 8-7 illustrated the process known as the *multiple expansion of bank deposits*. It shows how an increase in deposits leads to further deposits and therefore how the money multiplier works. There is one further aspect of the results shown in Table 8-7 to which we draw attention. It is possible to say that the banking system creates money in the sense that if there were not a banking system, a \$1 increase in H would increase the money stock only by \$1. With the banking system, the \$1 increase in H leads to more than

---

[3] Of course, we could not get through an infinite number of steps in real life, but in practice, after a few, say ten, steps, most of the adjustment is complete.

[4] Technical note: The formula for the sum of a geometric series, which can in general be written, as

$$SU = 1 + a + a^2 + a^3 + \ldots +$$

where a is a number between minus and plus 1, is

$$SU = \frac{1}{1 - a}$$

If you have not met geometric series before, you may want to take an example, say $a = \frac{1}{4}$, and start adding the terms in the first formula in the footnote. You will soon find your answer coming close to 4/3, which is the answer given by the second formula in the footnote.

a \$1 increase in M. The interesting point is that, at each stage of the process, no one bank believes it is, or can be said to be, creating money. At each stage, each bank in the process is only lending out money that has been deposited with it. The bank manager would rightly, and no doubt vehemently, deny that the bank is creating money. The system as a whole, though, is creating money through the successive rounds of loans and subsequent further bank deposits.

8-6 EQUILIBRIUM IN THE MONEY MARKET

We can now combine the money supply function in Equation ($8a$) with the money demand function developed in Chapter 7 to study money market equilibrium. For that purpose we will continue to assume, as we generally have so far that the price level is given at the level $\bar{P}$. Furthermore, for the purpose of this section, we will take the level of real income as given, $Y = Y_0$. With both the price level and level of income fixed, money demand will depend only on the interest rate, while the money supply depends on the arguments in Equation (9). The money market equilibrium will determine the equilibrium interest rate and quantity of money for given $\bar{P}$ and Y_0.

The equilibrium condition in the money market is that the real money supply M/P equals the demand for real balances, or

FIGURE 8-4 EQUILIBRIUM IN THE MONEY MARKET

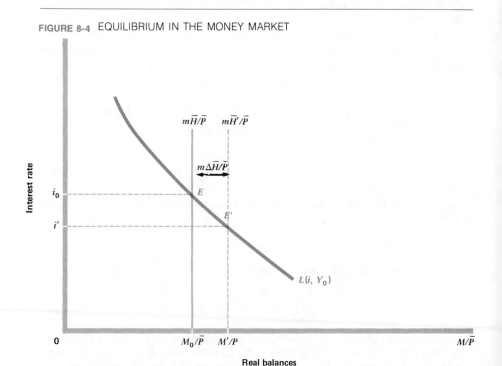

$$\frac{M}{P} = L(i,Y) \tag{13}$$

Substituting the expression (8*a*) for M in the money market equilibrium condition (13), and noting $P = \bar{P}$ and $Y = Y_0$ by assumption, we obtain

$$\frac{\bar{H}}{\bar{P}} = L(i,Y_0) \tag{13a}$$

We now have the money market equilibrium condition in terms of the interest rate and the other variables affecting the supply of, and demand for, money.

In Figure 8-4 we show the real money demand function as a downward-sloping schedule, drawn for a given level of real income. The real money supply (given $\bar{P}$, cu, and r) is represented by a vertical line and is drawn for a given stock of high-powered money $\bar{H}$. The equilibrium interest rate is determined at point E.

Figure 8-4 can be used to study the effects of monetary policy on interest rates, given the price level and the level of income. In terms of the LM curve of Chapter 4, we will ask how the LM curve shifts, given the level of income, when monetary policy changes. Figure 8-5 shows the initial curve, LM_0, corresponding to the stock of high-powered money $\bar{H}$. As we saw in Section 8-2, an open market purchase increases the stock of high-powered money and therefore shifts the supply of money in Figure 8-4 to the right by the money multiplier times the increase in the base $m\Delta\bar{H}/P$. The supply of money shifts

FIGURE 8-5 EFFECTS OF MONETARY POLICY ON THE LM CURVE

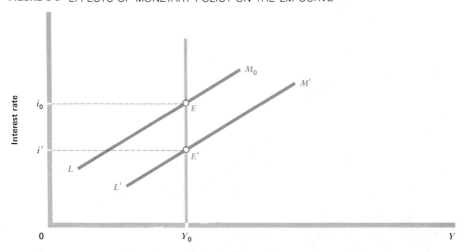

Income, output

to the position shown by the broken line, corresponding to the larger stock of high-powered money $\bar{H}'$. Given the level of income, the increase in the base via an open market purchase raises the real money supply from $M_0/\bar{P}$ to $M'/\bar{P}$ and reduces the interest rate from i_0 to i'. Corresponding to the increase in the base, the LM curve in Figure 8-5 shifts down and to the right to $L'M'$.

Control of the Money Stock and Control of the Interest Rate

We make a simple but important point in this section: The Bank of Canada cannot simultaneously set both the interest rate and the stock of money at any given target levels that it may choose. If the Bank of Canada wants to achieve a given interest rate target, such as 8 percent, it has to supply the amount of money that is demanded at that interest rate. If it wants to set the money supply at a given level, say $40 billion in the month of June 1982, it has to allow the interest rate to adjust to equate the demand for money to that supply of money.

Figure 8-6 illustrates the point. Suppose that the Bank of Canada for some reason, decides that it wants to set the interest rate at a level $i*$ and the money stock at the level $M*$, but that the demand for money function is as shown in $L(i, Y_0)$. The Bank is able to move the money supply around, as in Figure 8-4, but it is not able to move the money demand function around. It therefore has to accept that it can set only the combinations of the interest

---

FIGURE 8-6 CONTROLLING THE MONEY STOCK AND INTEREST RATES

Real money stock

rate and the money supply that lie along the money demand function. At the interest rate i^*, it can have the money supply $M_0/\bar{P}$. At the target money supply $M^*/\bar{P}$, it can have the interest rate i_0. But it cannot have both $M^*/\bar{P}$ and i^*.

The point is sometimes put more dramatically as follows. When the Bank of Canada decides to set the interest rate at some given level and keep it fixed — a policy known as *pegging* the interest rate — it loses control over the money supply. It has to supply whatever amount of money is demanded at that interest rate. If the money demand curve were to shift, because of income growth, say, the Bank would have to increase the stock of high-powered money to increase the money supply.

As an operational matter, the Bank of Canada in its day-to-day operations can more easily control interest rates exactly than it can control the money stock exactly. The Bank buys and sells government securities — primarily treasury bills — on a regular basis. If the Bank of Canada wants to raise the price of government securities (lower the interest rate), it can buy the securities at the price it wants. If it wants to reduce the price of government securities (raise the interest rate), it can sell a sufficient amount of securities from its large portfolio. Thus, on a day-to-day basis, the Bank can determine interest rates quite accurately.

8-7 OTHER INSTRUMENTS OF MONETARY POLICY

The above discussion has focussed on the operation of monetary policy through control of the monetary base using open market operations. The Bank of Canada also makes use of changes in the bank rate and *secondary reserve requirements* to influence credit markets.

Changes in the Bank Rate

As indicated in Section 8-3 above, the bank rate is the rate of interest at which the Bank of Canada makes advances to the chartered banks. During the period 1956-1962 and more recently beginning in March, 1980, the Bank of Canada has used a floating bank rate system under which the rate is automatically set each week at ¼ of one percent above the rate of interest on 91-day treasury bills. At other times the bank rate has been fixed at the discretion of the Bank of Canada.

In principle, an increase in the bank rate can affect the money supply by raising the chartered banks' demands for excess cash reserves. Banks might be induced to maintain a larger cushion in view of the higher cost of borrowing if they suffer a loss of cash and are forced to seek accommodation from the Bank of Canada to meet their reserve requirements. It is not likely that this mechanism is of much importance in Canada, since the chartered banks rarely borrow from the Bank of Canada. On the other hand, the bank rate still plays an important role as a signal of the Bank's views concerning the appropriate level of interest rates and its intentions with regard to monetary tightness or ease. The "announcement effects" of bank rate changes are frequently used to reinforce the effects of changes in monetary policy.

Secondary Reserve Requirements

At times when the Bank of Canada is attempting to restrain inflationary forces, it may wish to dampen expenditures not only through higher interest rates but also through some form of direct control over the expansion of bank loans. Restricting the supply of cash reserves will not restrain the banks from extending credit if they have substantial quantities of liquid assets that can be sold off to finance new loans. The Bank of Canada is empowered to restrict the ability of the chartered banks to expand their loans through the imposition of a required minimum secondary reserve ratio within the range of 0 to 12 percent of deposits. Secondary reserves are defined as holdings of treasury bills, day-to-day loans, and excess cash reserves. A required minimum ratio of 8 percent was in effect during the period 1972 to 1974. In 1975 and 1976 it was lowered in stages to 5 percent and it has remained at that level since.

*8-8 SHORT-RUN CONTROL OF THE MONEY SUPPLY

The discussion of bank deposit expansion given above neglected some institutional features of reserve requirements that influence the short-run response of the banking system to changes in the supply of high-powered money.[5]

Reserve Averaging Period

An individual bank is subject to erratic day-to-day fluctuations in its cash position as cheques are cleared and deposits are transferred from one bank to another. In view of this, the required reserve ratios apply not to each day's holdings of cash reserves, but to the average level over some specified period. Since 1969, this reserve averaging period has been two weeks. Thus, banks do not need to adjust to changes in their cash reserves on a particular day unless they are approaching the end of a two-week period with an average level of reserves below the minimum requirement.

Furthermore, the level of required cash reserves in effect at any time is not based on the current volume of deposits, but rather on the average volume of deposits during the *preceding* month. Thus, an expansion of loans and deposits will not affect total excess reserves during the current month,

---

[5] For a detailed description of the requirements under the Bank Act, see *Bank of Canada Review*, notes to Table 9.

but will increase the level of required reserves that must be held in the following month. Of course, to the extent that the banks are not all expanding their loans at the same rate, deposits and cash will be redistributed, so that the faster growing banks will tend to lose reserves to the slower growing ones.

Chartered bank holdings of Bank of Canada notes that can be counted towards reserve requirements are also calculated as an average over the preceding month. This means that changes in the public's demand for currency have no effect on a bank's reserve position in the current month unless they induce the bank to reduce or replenish its till money by respectively increasing or running down its deposits at the Bank of Canada.

Actual Versus Desired Excess Cash Reserves

Under the circumstances described above, the Bank of Canada can control not only the total base, but also the reserve component of the base. Further, since required cash reserves are determined by deposits in the preceding month, effective control can be exercised over the excess cash reserves of the chartered banks.

The method by which the Bank of Canada induces changes in the money supply is to cause the actual level of excess reserves to diverge from the level which the banks find it desirable to maintain.[6] Suppose that the Bank of Canada wishes to bring out a contraction of the money supply. By setting the level of excess cash reserves below the level regarded by the banks as a minimum acceptable one, it will induce the banks to sell liquid assets in an attempt to increase their holdings of cash. However, the banking system as a whole will be frustrated in this attempt, since the assets it sells will be paid for by cheques drawn on the banks; assets and deposits will fall but cash reserves will remain the same. In addition, interest rates will rise since the banks will have to offer increased yields to induce nonbank investors to increase their holdings of securities at the expense of their holdings of bank deposits. As long as the supply of excess cash reserves is kept below the level desired by the banks, the money supply will continue to fall and interest rates will continue to rise.

Thus, if the Bank of Canada wishes to reduce the money supply by some target amount, it keeps the banks in a tight cash position until the target is achieved, and then restores the supply of cash reserves to the level desired by the banks. Similarly, an increase in the money supply is brought about by injecting additional cash into the banking system and inducing the banks to bid for additional liquid assets. In practice, this control of the money supply through cash reserve management by the Bank of Canada is a

---

[6] For a detailed discussion of this mechanism, see J.F. Dingle, G.R. Sparks and M.A. Walker, "Monetary Policy and the Adjustment of Chartered Bank Assets," *Canadian Journal of Economics*, Nov., 1972.

process of successive approximation, because the level of cash desired by the banks varies and cannot easily be predicted. By testing the reaction of the banks to a particular supply of cash, the Bank of Canada can estimate the target levels of cash that the banks are attempting to achieve and adjust the supply accordingly.

8-9 SUMMARY

1 The nominal money supply is determined by the actions of the public through the currency-deposit ratio, the chartered banks through the reserve-deposit ratio, and by the Bank of Canada.

2 The reserve-deposit ratio depends on the required minimum ratios, the banks' demand for excess reserves and the proportions of demand and notice deposits.

3 The Bank of Canada affects the money supply primarily through open market operations which control the monetary base, or high-powered money.

4 The Bank of Canada cannot set both the interest rate and the stock of money at whatever target levels it chooses. If it controls the interest rate, it gives up control over the money supply, and vice versa.

5 Other instruments of monetary policy are changes in the bank rate and secondary reserve requirements.

6 Since required cash reserves depend on average deposits in the preceding month, the Bank of Canada can exercise control over the money supply in the short run by setting the supply of excess cash reserves. Changes in the money supply are induced by purchases or sales of liquid assets by the chartered banks in response to deviations of actual cash reserves from the desired level.

PROBLEMS

1 Use Figure 8-3 to show the equilibrium amounts of currency and deposits.

2 Show the effects on the balance sheets of the Bank of Canada and the chartered banks of a change in the monetary base brought about by a transfer of government deposits from the chartered banks to the Bank of Canada.

3 Table 8-4 shows the initial impact on the Bank of Canada's balance sheet of an open market purchase. As noted in the text, at the end of the process both currency and chartered bank deposits at the Bank of Canada rise. What is the final increase in currency? Use the ratios cu and r in arriving at your answer.

4 "All money is credit." Discuss.

5 "All credit is money." Discuss.

6 A proposal for "100 percent banking" involves a reserve-deposit ratio of unity. Such a scheme has been proposed in order to enhance control over the money supply. Indicate (a) why such a scheme would help monetary control and (b) what bank balance sheets would look like under this scheme. (c) How would banking remain profitable, under 100 percent money?

7 Suppose a bank has excess reserves and makes a loan to someone who immediately withdraws the deposit the bank has given him and holds it as currency. Why does the bank's granting of the loan increase the money supply?

8 Discuss the impact of credit cards on the money multiplier.

9 This problem extends the analysis of the chapter by further distinguishing between M1 and M2. Assume a currency-demand deposit ratio cu and a desired ratio of demand to notice deposits of the public, $d = DD/ND$. Assume, too, that banks have reserve preferences, described by r_d and r_n, with respect to demand and notice deposits, where the reserve ratio for notice deposits r_n is lower than that for demand deposits r_d.

   (a) Use the definition of M1 and the ratios d, r_d and r_n to derive an expression for the equilibrium stock of M1.

   (b) Use the definition of M2 and the ratios to derive an expression for the equilibrium stock of M2.

   (c) Show the effects of an increase in the demand-notice deposit ratio on credit.

10 By using Figures 8-1, 8-4, and 8-5, show the effect of an increase in required reserves on:

   (a) The equilibrium money supply

   (b) Interest rates

   (c) The equilibrium level of income

11 The Canada Deposit Insurance Corporation insures chartered bank deposits against bank default. Discuss the implications of that deposit scheme for the money multiplier.

12 Assume required reserves were zero. Would banks hold any reserves?

9

PROBLEMS OF STABILIZATION POLICY

This chapter discusses the problems of macroeconomic policy making. An understanding of the general difficulties of carrying out successful stabilization policies — policies to reduce the fluctuations of the economy — helps explain economic performance over the past 30 years. Chart 9-1, which shows the unemployment rate over the last 50 years, gives the clear impression that stabilization policy has left something to be desired.

The reason for discussing the problems of stabilization policy here is that the preceding chapters have laid out a clear body of theory that seems to show exactly the policy measures that can be used to maintain full employment. We saw that high unemployment, or a large GNP gap, can be reduced by an expansion in aggregate demand. An increase in aggregate demand in turn can be achieved by expansionary monetary or fiscal policies: an increase in the money supply, a reduction in taxes, an increase in government spending, or an increase in transfers. Similarly, a boom can be contained by restrictive monetary or fiscal policies.

The policies needed to prevent the fluctuations in unemployment shown in Chart 9-1 accordingly appear to be simple and obvious. How, then, did the fluctuations occur? The answer obviously is that policy making is far from simple. Part of the difficulty of policy making arises from the possible *conflict between the maintenance of full employment and the target of low inflation*. That important issue is discussed in the second of the two general chapters on the problems of policy making, Chapter 14. In this chapter we discuss in detail three problems that suggest why policy should not be expected to achieve its targets, such as full employment, at all times. The three *handicaps of policy making* are:

1 *Lags* in the effects of policy
2 The role of *expectations* in determining private sector responses to policy
3 *Uncertainty* about the effects of policy

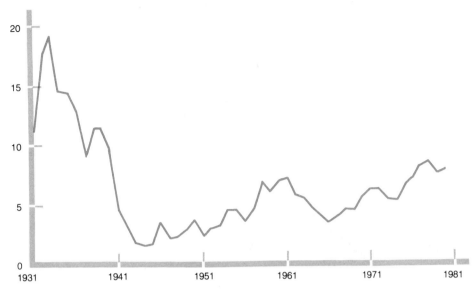

CHART 9-1 UNEMPLOYMENT RATE IN CANADA, 1931–1980
(*Source*: Statistics Canada, 11-505; Dept. of Finance, *Economic Review*)

In a nutshell, we are going to argue that a policy maker who (1) observes a disturbance, (2) does not know whether it is permanent or not, (3) takes time to develop a policy which (4) takes still more time to affect behaviour and (5) has uncertain effects on aggregate demand is very poorly equipped to do a perfect job of stabilizing the economy.

9-1 ECONOMIC DISTURBANCES

Before identifying in detail the obstacles in the way of successful policy making, we discuss *economic disturbances* in terms of their sources, persistence, and importance for policy. Disturbances are shifts in aggregate demand or aggregate supply, or shifts in money demand or supply, that cause output, interest rates, or prices to diverge from the target path.

We return to the IS-LM model as the framework for the discussion of economic disturbances in this chapter. In Figure 9-1 we show the IS and LM schedules and also the full-employment level of output, Y_p. The economy is initially at full employment at point E. Now what disturbances might cause the economy to move away from full employment? Obviously, anything that shifts the IS and/or LM curves would disturb the economy and move it away from E.

In terms of overall economic impact, the major disturbances to the

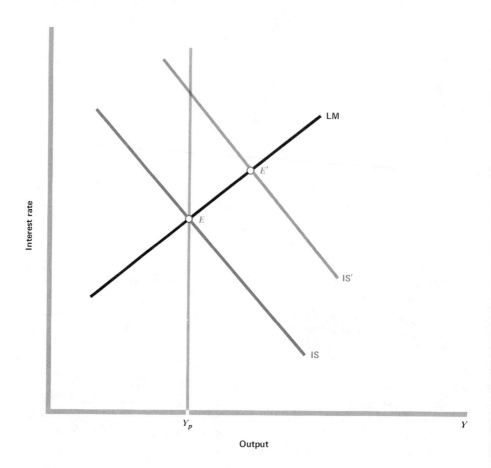

FIGURE 9-1 AN AGGREGATE DEMAND DISTURBANCE

economy — the forces moving the IS and LM curves — have been wars. The effects of the increases in government spending associated with World War II and the Korean War can be seen in Chart 9-1 in the very low unemployment rates in those periods. Of these, World War II had the largest impact on the economy. At the height of the war, in 1944, federal government spending exceeded 40 percent of GNP.

As shown in Figure 9-1, an increase in government spending would shift the IS schedule upward and therefore lead to an excess demand for goods. To contain aggregate spending to the full-employment level of output, increased government spending would have to be offset by a reduction in private demand, that is, a reduction in investment and/or consumption spending. Investment spending can be reduced by allowing the interest rate to rise, and consumption spending can be reduced by increasing income taxes. These conventional economic policies may not be sufficient in wartime, however. In World War II more direct methods of reducing investment and consumption were used. A system was set up in which investment projects had to be approved. That system served to reduce the overall rate of private investment and also to direct investment toward areas helpful for the war effort. There was also some rationing of consumption goods, which reduced consumption expenditure as some of the rationed demand spilled over into increased saving rather than being diverted toward other goods. Thus, the aggregate level of consumption spending was reduced by using rationing to reduce the consumption of various goods essential for the war effort (gasoline, tires, shoes, etc,).[1]

Changes in government spending or tax policies not connected with wars may also constitute economic disturbances. Government spending or taxes may be increased or reduced for reasons which have to do with the government's view of desirable social policies. Those changes too may affect the level of aggregate demand if not accompanied by appropriate monetary and fiscal policies. In a country like Canada that is heavily dependent on foreign trade, changes in foreign demand for our exports may be an important source of disturbances.

Other economic disturbances that lead to changes in aggregate demand, which originate in the private sector, are shifts in the consumption or investment function. If consumers decide to consume more out of their disposable income at any given level of income, the IS curve of Figure 9-1 shifts upward, tending to increase the level of income. If there is no economic explanation for the shift in the consumption function, then it is attributed to a change in the tastes of consumers between consumption and saving. In such a case, we describe the shift as a disturbance.

Similarly, if investment spending increases for no apparent economic reason, then we attribute the increase to an unexplained change in the optimism of investors about the returns from investment. Again, we regard that change in investment behaviour as a disturbance to the system. Changes in the optimism of investors are sometimes described as changes in their *animal spirits* — a term that suggests that there may be little rational basis for those spirits.[2] Some shifts in the investment function are caused by new inventions that require large amounts of investment for their successful marketing, such as the development of the railways in the nineteenth century and the spread of the automobile in the 1920s.

Shifts in the demand for money may affect the interest rate, and thus

---

[1] In passing, it is worth considering for a moment why partial rationing might work as a macroeconomic policy, that is, as a policy reducing aggregate demand. The reason must be that part of the expenditure that is precluded by rationing does not shift to other goods, but, instead, increases saving, that is, future consumption.

[2] Keynes, in particular, argued that shifts in the investment function were a major cause of fluctuations in the economy. See J.M. Keynes, *The General Theory of Employment, Interest and Money* (New York: Macmillan, 1936), chap. 22.

indirectly affect the rate of investment; they, too, constitute a possible source of private sector economic disturbances.

Disturbances that we have not yet incorporated in our basic theoretical framework also affect the level of income. These include changes in supply conditions, such as the oil embargo of 1973-1974, which will affect the level of income and are discussed in Chapter 11. In Chapter 13, we also discuss the possibility that the behaviour of wages may constitute a source of economic disturbances.

Finally, there is the interesting possibility that disturbances may be caused by the policy makers themselves. There are two different arguments concerning this possibility. First, since policy making is difficult, it is entirely possible that the attempts of policy makers to stabilize the economy could be counterproductive. Indeed, a forcefully stated and influential view of the causes of the Great Depression[3] argues that an inept monetary policy in the United States was chiefly responsible for the severity of the depression. The argument of Friedman and Schwartz is basically that the officials in charge of the American central bank in the early 1930s did not understand the workings of monetary policy and therefore carried out a policy that made the depression worse rather than better.

The second argument that policy makers themselves may be responsible for economic disturbances arises from the relationship between election results and economic conditions in the period before the election.[4] If it appears that incumbents tend to be reelected when economic conditions, primarily the unemployment rate, are improving in the year before the election, it is tempting for them to try to *improve* economic conditions in the period before the election; their efforts may involve tax reductions or increases in government spending. It is now quite common to talk of the *political business cycle*, meaning that business fluctuations are significantly affected by government economic policies undertaken for political reasons.

It has been argued that election results are significantly affected by the growth rate, rather than the level, of income, in the year leading up to an election. If that is so, then it is tempting indeed for governments to start an expansion in an election year. Despite the difficulties of policy making, it is always easy to start an economic expansion in the short run — though not to control it later when its inflationary consequences appear. While there is some evidence to support the notion of a political business cycle, the argument should be regarded as tentative because the link between economic conditions and election results is not yet firmly established.

We proceed next to discuss the three factors that make the task of policy

[3] See Milton Friedman and Anna J. Schwartz, *The Great Contraction* (Princeton, N.J.: Princeton University Press, 1965). We review the argument in Chapter 10.

[4] See, for example, Edward R. Tufte, *Political Control of the Economy* (Princeton, N.J.: Princeton University Press, 1978).

makers far more difficult than an overliteral interpretation of the simple IS-LM model in Figure 9-1 might suggest.

9-2 LAGS IN THE EFFECTS OF POLICY

Suppose that the economy was at full employment and has been affected by an aggregate demand disturbance that raises the equilibrium level of income above full employment in Figure 9-1 toward point E'. Suppose further that there was no advance warning of this disturbance and that, consequently, no policy actions were taken in anticipation of its occurrence. Policy makers now have to decide *whether at all* and *how* to respond to the disturbance.

The first concern — and the first difficulty — should be over the permanence of the disturbance and its subsequent effects. Suppose the disturbance is only transitory, such as a one-period reduction in consumption spending. When the disturbance is transitory so that consumption rapidly reverts back to its initial level, the best policy may be to do nothing at all. Provided suppliers or producers do not mistakenly interpret the increase in demand as permanent but, rather, perceive it as transitory, they will absorb it by production and inventory changes rather than capacity adjustments. The disturbance will affect income in this period but will have very little permanent effect. Policy actions generally do not affect the economy immediately. Any policy actions taken to offset the disturbance this period, for example, a tax increase, will have their impact on spending and income only over time. In later periods, however, the effects of the initial rise in demand on the level of income will be very small, and without the policy action the economy would tend to be very close to full employment. The effects of a tax increase therefore would be to lower income in later periods and move it away from the full-employment level. Thus, if the disturbance is temporary and it has no long-lived effects and policy operates with a lag, then the best policy is to do nothing.

Figure 9-2 illustrates the main issue. Assume an aggregate demand disturbance reduces output below potential, starting at time t_0. Without active policy intervention output declines for a while but then recovers and reaches the full-employment level again at time t_2. Consider next the path of GNP under an active stabilization policy, but one that works with the disadvantage of lags. Thus, expansionary policy might be initiated at time t_1 and start taking effect some time after. Output now tends to recover faster as a consequence of the expansion and, because of poor dosage and/or timing, actually overshoots the full-employment level. By time t_3, restrictive policy is initiated, and some time after, output starts turning down toward full employment and may well continue cycling for a while. If this is an accurate description of the potency or scope of stabilization policy, then the question must seriously arise whether it is worth trying to stabilize output or whether

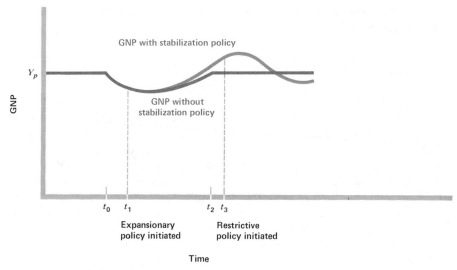

FIGURE 9-2 LAGS AND DESTABILIZING POLICY

the effect of stabilization policy is, in fact, to make things worse. Stabilization policy may actually *destabilize* the economy.

One of the main difficulties of policy making is in establishing whether or not a disturbance is temporary. It was clear enough in the case of World War II that a high level of defence expenditures would be required for some years. However, in the case of the Arab oil embargo of 1973-1974, it was not clear at all how long the embargo would last or whether the high prices for oil that were established in late 1973 would persist. At the time, there were many who argued that the oil cartel would not survive and that oil prices would soon fall – that is, that the disturbance was temporary. That did not turn out to be true. Let us suppose, however, that it is known that the disturbance will have effects that will last for several quarters, and that the level of income will, without policy, be below the full-employment level for some time. What lags do policy makers encounter?

We now consider the steps required before a policy action can be taken after a disturbance has occurred, and then the process by which that policy action affects the economy. There are delays, or lags, at every stage. It is customary and useful to divide the lags into an *inside* lag, which is the time period it takes to undertake a policy action — such as a tax cut, or an increase in the money supply — and the *outside* lag, which describes the timing of the effects of the policy action on the economy. The inside lag in turn is divided into *recognition, decision,* and *action* lags.

The Recognition Lag

The recognition lag is the period that elapses between the time a disturbance occurs and the time the policy makers recognize that action is required. This lag could in principle be *negative* if the disturbance could be predicted and appropriate policy actions considered *before* it even occurs. For example, we know that seasonal factors affect behaviour. Thus it is known that at Christmas the demand for currency is high. Rather than allow this to exert a restrictive effect on the money supply, the Bank of Canada will accomodate this seasonal demand by an expansion in high-powered money. In other cases the recognition lag has been positive, so that some time has elapsed between the disturbance and the recognition that active policy was required.

The major reason that there is any recognition lag at all, apart from the delay in collecting statistical data, is that it is never certain what the consequences of a disturbance will be. That uncertainty in turn is a result of economists' lack of knowledge of the workings of the economy (which is discussed in Section 9-4 below) as well as political uncertainties.

The Decision and Action Lags

The recognition lag is the same for monetary and fiscal policy. The Bank of Canada and the Department of Finance are in constant contact with one another and share their predictions about the future course of the economy. For the decision lag — the delay between the recognition of the need for action and a policy decision — by contrast there is a difference between monetary and fiscal policy. Once the need for a policy action has been recognized by the Bank of Canada, the decision lag for monetary policy is short. Further, the action lag — the lag between the policy decision and its implementation — for monetary policy is also short.

However, fiscal policy actions are less rapid. Once the need for a fiscal policy action has been recognized, the government has to prepare legislation for that action. Next, the legislation has to be considered and approved by Parliament before the policy change can be made. Even after the legislation has been approved, the policy change has still to be put into effect. If the fiscal policy takes the form of a change in tax rates, it may be some time before the changes in tax rates begin to be reflected in paycheques — that is, there may be an action lag.

The existence of the inside lag of policy making focusses attention on the *built-in* or *automatic stabilizers* that we discussed in Chapter 3. One of the major benefits of automatic stabilizers is that their inside lag is zero. Recall from Chapter 3 that the most important automatic stabilizer is the income tax. It stabilizes the economy by reducing the multiplier effects of any disturbance to aggregate demand. The multiplier for the effects of changes in autonomous spending on GNP is inversely related to the income tax rate. The higher the tax rate, the smaller the effects of any given change in autonomous demand on GNP. Similarly, unemployment compensation is another automatic stabilizer. When workers become unemployed and re-duce their consumption, that reduction in consumption demand tends to have multiplier effects on output. Those multiplier effects are reduced when a worker receives unemployment compensation because her disposable income is reduced by less than the loss in earnings.

Although built-in stabilizers have desirable effects, they cannot be carried too far without also affecting the overall performance of the economy. The multiplier could be reduced to 1 by increasing the tax rate to 100 percent, and that would appear to be a stabilizing influence on the economy. But with 100 percent marginal tax rates, the desire to work and consequently the level of GNP, would be reduced. Thus there are limits on the extent to which automatic stabilizers are desirable. Nonetheless, automatic stabilizers play an important role in the economy; it has been argued that the absence of significant unemployment compensation in the 1930s was one of the major factors making the Great Depression so severe, and that the existence of the stabilizers alone makes the recurrence of such a deep depression unlikely.

The Outside Lag

The inside lag of policy is a *discrete* lag in which policy can have no effect on the economy until it is implemented. The outside lag is generally a *distributed* lag: once the policy action has been taken, its effects on the economy are spread over time. There is usually a small immediate effect of a policy action, but other effects occur later.

The idea that policy operates on aggregate demand and income with a distributed lag is shown in Figure 9-3a and b. Suppose that we are considering a once-and-for-all increase in high-powered money in period 1, as shown in Figure 9-3a. This increase in high-powered money, by affecting interest rates and therefore aggregate spending, changes the level of income in subsequent quarters by the amounts indicated in Figure 9-3b. The height of the bars shows the amount by which GNP exceeds the level that it would have had in the absence of the policy change. Figure 9-3b is thus a *dynamic multiplier*, as discussed in Chapter 5. The main point to be made is that monetary or fiscal policies taken now affect the economy over time, with most of the effects typically not occurring in the first quarter. Thus, in Figure 9-3, a given increase in high-powered money in the short run raises GNP by only a small amount although, over the full adjustment period, the increase in GNP is substantial.

Figure 9-3 makes it clear that the impact of an increase in high-powered money (corresponding to an open market purchase by the Bank of Canada) is initially very small, and that it continues to increase over a long period of time. Thus, if it were necessary to increase the level of employment rapidly to offset a demand disturbance, a large open market purchase would be necessary. But in later quarters, the larger initial open market purchase would build up large effects on GNP, and those effects would probably overcorrect the unemployment, leading to inflationary pressures. It would then be necessary to reverse the open market purchase and conduct open

FIGURE 9-3a TIME PATH OF HIGH-POWERED MONEY

FIGURE 9-3b DYNAMIC MULTIPLIERS FOR THE EFFECTS OF THE CHANGE IN HIGH-POWERED MONEY ON GNP

market sales to avoid the inflationary consequences of the initial open market purchase.

It should thus be clear that when policy acts slowly, with the impacts of policy building up over time, considerable skill is required of policy makers if their own attempts to correct an initially undesirable situation are not to lead to problems that themselves need correcting. Recall also that we have been talking here about the *outside* lag, and that the policy action we are considering would be taken only six months after the initial disturbance if the inside lag is six months long.

Why are there such long inside lags? We have already discussed some of the reasons for these lags in Chapter 5 on the consumption function, where current consumption depends on lagged income, and also in Chapter 6 on investment, where the accelerator models imply that investment depends on lagged and current income. Similar lags are also present in the financial sector of the economy, where the demand for money depends on lagged income. Each of these sources of lags creates an outside lag, and their interaction generally produces longer lags than each of the underlying lags.

Because the point is so important, let us describe in more detail how the lags of monetary policy arise. Suppose the Bank of Canada conducts an open market purchase. Because aggregate demand depends heavily on lagged values of income, interest rates, and other economic variables, the open market purchase initially has effects mainly on short-term interest rates and not on income. Short-term interest rates, such as the treasury bill rate, affect long-term interest rates with a lag. The long-term interest rates in turn affect investment with a lag, and also affect consumption by affecting the value of wealth.[5] Then when aggregate demand is affected by the initial open market purchase, the increase in aggregate demand itself produces lagged effects on subsequent aggregate demand through the fact that both consumption and investment depend on past values of income. So the effects of an initial open market purchase will be spread through time, as in Figure 9-3.

Monetary and Fiscal Policy Lags

Ths discussion of the previous paragraph suggests that fiscal policy and certainly changes in government spending, which act directly on aggregate demand, may affect income more rapidly than monetary policy. This is indeed the case. However, the fact that fiscal policy acts faster on aggregate demand than monetary policy must not lead us to overlook the fact that fiscal policy has a considerably longer inside lag. Moreover, the inside lag for government spending is longer than that for taxes because, when the government purchases goods and services, it has to decide what goods to buy, have bids for the sale of those goods submitted by the private sector, and then decide on the award of the contracts. In summary, therefore, fiscal policy is attractive because of the short outside lag, but that advantage is more than offset by a potentially long inside lag.

Our analysis of lags indicates clearly one difficulty in undertaking stabilizing short-term policy actions: it takes time to set the policies in action, and then the policies themselves take time to affect the economy. But that is not the only difficulty. Further difficulties considered in Sections 9-3 and 9-4 arise from uncertainty about the exact timing and magnitude of the effects of policy. The dynamic multiplier of Figure 9-3 itself is not unchanging, and we do not know for sure how a particular policy will affect income in subsequent periods.

---

[5] Recall that in Chapter 5 we discussed the life-cycle model of consumption demand, in which consumption is affected by the level of wealth. Part of wealth is the value of stock market assets; the value of stock market assets rises when the long term interest rate falls. Thus, interest rates affect consumption through a wealth effect.

9-3 THE ROLE OF EXPECTATIONS

We have discussed the two basic sources of lags in economic behaviour in earlier chapters. The first source is the costs of rapid adjustment. For example, in Chapter 6 we showed how the costs of adjusting the actual capital stock to the desired capital stock led to lags in the investment function. The second source of lags is expectations. In this section we focus on expectations, their formation, and the effects they have on policy and its effectiveness.

While it is undoubtedly true that the past behaviour of a variable influences expectations about its future behaviour, it is also true that consumers and investors will sometimes use more information than is contained in the past behaviour of a variable when trying to predict its future behaviour. Consider, in particular, forecasts of permanent income — long-run average income. In Chapter 5, as in Friedman's original work on the consumption function, permanent income is estimated as an average of income in the recent past. Suppose, however, that you were a resident of a small country that had just discovered vast gold deposits. You would then take the information about the gold discovery into account in forming an estimate of your permanent income. You would *immediately* estimate a permanent income substantially higher than your historical average income. Or, suppose that you have been estimating the expected rate of inflation as an average of past rates of inflation, at a time when the inflation rate is high and a new government is elected on a strictly anti-inflationary platform. Then you would lower your estimate of the inflation rate; that is, you would use more information in predicting it than is contained solely in its past behaviour. It should be clear that it is in general very difficult to incorporate *all* relevant information that is used by economic agents within a simple economic model. That means there will inevitably be errors in what the models predict for the consequences of various policy actions, meaning in turn that it is difficult to control the economy precisely.

It is particularly important to consider the effects of a given policy action itself on expectations, since it is possible that a new type of policy will affect the way in which expectations are formed.[6] Suppose that the Bank of Canada announced a new monetary policy designed to stabilize the average level of income and avoid booms and recessions. The new policy would be to reduce the money supply whenever the income level rose and to increase the money supply whenever the income level fell. Such a *countercyclical rule* has implications for expectations. Clearly, it would be entirely

---

[6] The role of expectations in economics and the interaction between policy and expectations in particular have been the subject of much recent research. See, for example, Thomas J. Sargent and Neil Wallace, "Rational Expectations and the Theory of Economic Policy," *Journal of Monetary Economics*, April 1976. See also our discussion in Chapter 15.

inappropriate in the presence of such monetary policy to use an expectations mechanism that implies that an increase in income will persist. The monetary policy rule implies that the money supply would be reduced following an increase in income, and one expects the reduction in money to exert at least a dampening effect on income. While correct expectations mechanisms must therefore use information about policy responses to disturbances, such care is difficult to apply in practice. Most expectations mechanisms embodied in econometric models of the economy and used for the assessment of policies assume that expectations affecting consumption and investment spending are based entirely on past values.

This section has made two important points about the role of expectations in explaining the difficulties of policy making. First, the general point is that the difficulties of modeling the way in which expectations are formed will inevitably lead to errors in economists' forecasts of the effects of particular policy actions on the economy. The second point, a particular point, is that expectations themselves are likely to be affected by policy measures, and that failure to take account of the effects of policy on expectations will lead to mistaken predictions of the effects of those policies.

9-4 UNCERTAINTY

In Sections 9-2 and 9-3 we discussed the difficulties created for stabilization policy by uncertainty about lags and the nature of private sector expectations. In Section 9-1 we described uncertainty about the nature and permanence of the disturbances affecting the economy. These sources of uncertainty make it impossible to predict the effects of any given policy action exactly. In this section we point to other uncertainties complicating the task of policy making.

First, though, we want to extend the discussion of economic disturbances of Section 9-1. In that section we considered major disturbances to the economy. However, there are countless minor disturbances, of the same general nature as the major disturbances outlined in Section 9-1, that continually affect the economy. The weather and other natural phenomena affect the level of output and employment. Consumption and investment are subject to changes resulting from changes in tastes and animal spirits. Strikes — which have important economic causes, but probably also some noneconomic causes — take place, and affect the level of output temporarily. Political events affect the economy. New inventions lead to economic changes. Disturbances of these sorts occur all the time, and need not be major, but they do mean that there will always be uncertainty about the future behaviour of the economy.

In addition, there remain major uncertainties about the structure of the economy. It is convenient to distinguish between uncertainty about the correct model of the economy and uncertainty about the precise values of the parameters or coefficients within a given model of the economy, even though the distinction is not watertight. First, there is considerable uncertainty about the correct model of the economy. There is disagreement among economists on some of the behavioural functions of the economy. For example, we discussed a number of models of consumption. As yet, there has not been decisive evidence clearly demonstrating that one and only one of these models is correct. Accordingly, different economists use different models of consumption. Of course, the models have much in common, but they are not identical. There are also minor disagreements, for example, on the demand-for-money function, and those disagreements in turn lead to different predictions about the effects of policy.

Reasonable economists can and do differ about what theory and empirical evidence suggest are the correct behavioural functions of the economy. Generally, each economist will have reasons for favouring one particular form, and will use that form. But, being reasonable, the economist will recognize that the particular formulation being used may not be the correct one, and will thus regard its predictions as subject to a margin of error. Policy makers in turn will know that there are different predictions about the effects of a given policy, and will want to consider the range of predictions that are being made in deciding on policy.

Second, even within the context of a given model, there is uncertainty about the numerical values of the parameters of the model. Suppose for a moment that all economists agree that the life-cycle model of consumption, precisely as specified in Chapter 5, is the only correct model of consumption behaviour. On the basis of the historical evidence that we have, it is still not possible to measure the values of the marginal propensities to consume out of labour income and wealth in that consumption function without error. We stated in Chapter 5 that the propensity to consume out of income is about 0.84. However, we cannot be certain that the number is 0.84 and not 0.95, say, because the statistical evidence is not strong enough to enable us to specify the number exactly. The statistical evidence does enable us to say something about the likely range of the parameters,[7] so that we could be relatively certain that the true coefficient is between, say, 0.75 and 0.95, but at present, and for the forseeable future, we would not know it exactly. That uncertainty about the exact values of parameters in our models again means that the effects of policy cannot be predicted with accuracy.

This type of uncertainty has been called *multiplier uncertainty* to emphasize the fact that policy makers will not know the correct magnitude of policy actions, such as tax cuts, because they do not know what the multiplier is. Thus, with a marginal propensity to consume of 0.7, the multiplier would be 3.3 ($= 1/1 - 0.7$), while a marginal propensity to

---

[7] We are discussing here *confidence intervals* about estimates of parameters; see Robert S. Pindyck and Daniel L. Rubinfeld, *Econometric Models and Economic Forecasts* (New York: McGraw-Hill, 1976), p. 28, for further discussion.

consume of 0.6 would imply a multiplier of 2.5. If the GNP gap were estimated at, say, $30 billion, a multiplier of 3.3 would call for a $9 billion increase in spending while a multiplier of 2.5 would require $12 billion. If 3.3 were the true multiplier but policy makers erroneously picked 2.5, they would find themselves overshooting their target by $6 billion.

What is optimal behaviour in the face of such multiplier uncertainty? The more precisely policy makers are informed about the relevant parameters, the more activist the policy can afford to be. Conversely, if there is a considerable range of error in the estimate of the relevant parameters – in our example, the multiplier – then policy should be more modest. With poor information, very active policy runs a large danger of introducing unnecessary fluctuations in the economy.

9-5 ACTIVIST POLICY

We started this chapter asking why there are any fluctuations in the economy when the policy measures needed to iron out those fluctuations seem to be so simple. The list of difficulties in the way of successful policy making that we have outlined may have raised a different question: Why should one believe that policy can do anything to reduce fluctuations in the economy?

Indeed, considerations of the sort spelled out in the previous three sections have led Milton Friedman and others to argue that there should be no use of active countercyclical monetary policy,[8] and that monetary policy should be confined to making the money supply grow at a constant rate. The precise value of the constant rate of growth of money, Friedman suggests, is less important than the fact that monetary growth be constant and that policy should *not* respond to disturbances. At various times, he has suggested growth rates for money of 2 percent or 4 percent or 5 percent. As Friedman has expressed it, "By setting itself a steady course and keeping to it, the monetary authority could make a major contribution to promoting economic stability. By making that course one of steady but moderate growth in the quantity of money, it would make a major contribution to avoidance of either inflation or deflation of prices."[9]

In discussing the desirability of active monetary and fiscal policy, we want to distinguish between policy actions taken in response to major disturbances to the economy and fine tuning in which policy variables are continually adjusted in response to small disturbances to the economy. We see no case for arguing that monetary and fiscal policy should not be used actively in the face of major disturbances to the economy. Most of the

---

[8] See Milton Friedman, *A Program for Monetary Stability* (New York: Fordham University Press, 1959).

[9] Milton Friedman, "The Role of Monetary Policy," *American Economic Review*, March 1968.

considerations of the previous three sections of this chapter indicate some uncertainty about the effects of policy, but there are still clearly definable circumstances in which there can be no doubt that the appropriate policy is expansionary or contractionary. A government coming to power in 1933 should not have worried about the uncertainties associated with expansionary policy that we have outlined. The economy does not move from 25 percent unemployment to full employment in a short time (precisely because of those same lags that make policy difficult). Thus, expansionary measures, such as a rapid growth of the money supply, or increased government expenditures, or tax reductions, or all three, would have been appropriate policy since there was no chance they would have an impact only after the economy was at full employment. Similarly, contractionary policies for private demand are called for in wartime. In early 1977, with unemployment over 8 percent and rising rapidly and forecasts of unemployment for the next two years being very high, policies designed to reduce unemployment were appropriate.[10] In the event of large disturbances in the future, active monetary and/or fiscal policy should once again be used.[11]

Fine tuning presents more complicated issues. The basic question is whether policy variables should be adjusted at frequent intervals to attempt to smooth out minor disturbances to the economy. For example, should an increase of 0.5 percent in the unemployment rate lead to a small tax reduction, or a small increase in the rate of growth of the money supply, or should policy simply not respond to such disturbances? One possibility is that the initial increase in the unemployment rate is transitory and that policy action is therefore inappropriate; the other is that the initial disturbance is permanent and perhaps even the first sign of a major disturbance, in which case a policy reaction is suitable. If the disturbance is permanent, the appropriate policy response to a small disturbance is a small change in the course of policy. Thus, even if it turned out that the policy action was inappropriate because the disturbance was transitory, the (undesirable) consequences of the policy action would be limited because only a small adjustment had been made. Accordingly, we believe that fine tuning is appropriate provided that policy responses are always kept small in response to small disturbances.

However, we should emphasize that the argument for fine tuning is a controversial one. The major argument against it is that in practice policy makers cannot behave as suggested — making only small adjustments to small disturbances. Rather, it is argued they tend to try to do too much, if

---

[10] Because the inflation rate was high in 1977, policy making then required some judgment about the costs of inflation compared with those of unemployment, a topic discussed in Chapter 14. Policy in 1977 was thus more difficult than policy in 1933.

[11] Interestingly, Friedman argues for the use of active policy in the face of major disturbances in the article cited in footnote 13.

allowed to do anything. Instead of merely trying to offset disturbances, they attempt to keep the economy always at full employment and therefore undertake inappropriately large policy actions in response to small disturbances.

The major lesson of the previous three sections of this chapter is not that policy is impossible, but that policy that is too ambitious in trying to keep the economy always at full employment (with zero inflation) is impossible. The lesson is to proceed with extreme caution, always bearing in mind the possibility that policy itself may be destabilizing. We see no reason why the Bank of Canada should try to keep the money supply always growing at the same rate; we believe, on the contrary, that the stability of the economy would be improved by its following a careful countercyclical policy. Similarly, if fiscal policy were not subject to a long inside lag, we would believe it possible for cautiously used fiscal policy to be stabilizing.

Rules versus Discretion

Finally, in this chapter, we want to discuss an issue that has perhaps had more attention in the economics literature than it deserves. This is the issue of "rules versus discretion." The issue is whether the monetary authority and also the fiscal authority should conduct policy in accordance with a preannounced rule that describes precisely how their policy variables will be determined in all future situations, or whether they should be allowed to use their discretion in determining the values of the policy variables at different times. One example is the rule establishing the constant growth rate — say, at 4 percent — for monetary policy. The rule is that *no matter what happens*, the money supply will be kept growing at 4 percent. Another example would be a rule that the money supply growth rate will be increased by 2 percent per year for every 1 percent unemployment in excess of, say, 5 percent. Algebraically, such a rule would be expressed as

$$\frac{\Delta M}{M} = 4.0 + 2(u - 5.0) \tag{1}$$

where the growth rate of money $\Delta M/M$ is at an annual percentage rate and u is the percentage unemployment rate.

The activist monetary rule of Equation (1) is shown in Figure 9-4. On the horizontal axis, we show the unemployment rate, and on the vertical axis, the growth rate of the money stock. At 5 percent unemployment, monetary growth is 4 percent. If unemployment rises above 5 percent, monetary growth is *automatically* increased. Thus, with 7 percent unemployment, monetary growth would be 8 percent. Conversely, if unemployment dropped below 5 percent, monetary growth would be lowered below 4 percent. The rule therefore gears the amount of monetary stimulus to an indicator of the business cycle. By linking monetary growth to the unem-

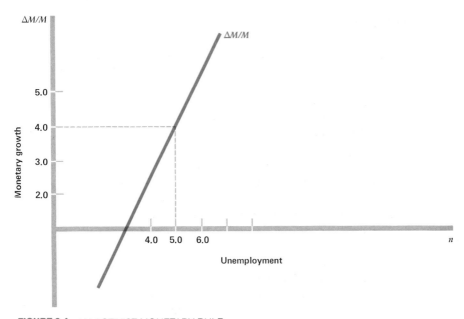

FIGURE 9-4 AN ACTIVIST MONETARY RULE

ployment rate, an activist, anticyclical monetary policy is achieved, but this is done without any discretion.

The issue of rules versus discretion has been clouded by the fact that most proponents of rules have been nonactivists, whose preferred monetary rule is a constant growth rate rule.[12] Consequently, the argument has tended to centre on whether activist policy is desirable or not. The fundamental point to recognize is that we can design *activist rules*. We can design rules that have countercyclical features without at the same time leaving any discretion in their actions to policy makers. The point is made by Equation (1), which is an activist rule because it expands money when unemployment is high and reduces it when unemployment is low. It leaves no room for policy discretion and in this respect is a rule.

Given that the economy and our knowledge of it are both changing over time, there is no case for stating permanent policy rules that would tie the hands of the monetary and fiscal authorities permanently. The practical issue in rules versus discretion then becomes that of whether the policy makers should announce in advance what policies they will be following for the forseeable future. This would seem to be a desirable development in that it would aid private individuals in forecasting the future course of the economy.

[12] An assessment of the issues is provided in Arthur Okun, "Monetary-Fiscal Activism: Some Analytical Issues," *Brookings Papers on Economic Activity,* 1972:1 (Washington, D.C.: The Brookings Institution, 1972).

9-6 SUMMARY

1 Despite the apparent simplicity of policies needed to maintain continuous full employment, the historical record of the behaviour of unemployment, shown in Chart 9-1, implies that successful stabilization policy is difficult to carry out.

2 Many of the complications in the execution of stabilization policy are a result of the tradeoff between inflation and unemployment in the short run. This important topic is deferred to Chapter 14. The present chapter concentrates on other sources of difficulty for stabilization policy.

3 The potential need for stabilizing policy actions arises from economic disturbances. Some of these disturbances, such as changes in money demand, consumption spending, or investment demand, arise from within the private sector. Others, such as wars, may arise for non-economic reasons.

4 Inappropriate economic policy may also tend to move the economy away from full employment. Policy may be inappropriate because policy makers make mistakes or because policy is manipulated for political reasons, leading to the political business cycle.

5 The first difficulty of carrying out successful stabilization policy is that policy works with lags. The *inside* lag — divided into recognition, decision, and action lags — is the period between which an action becomes necessary and when it is taken. The *outside* lag is the period between which a policy action is taken and when it affects the economy. The outside lag is generally a distributed lag: the effects of a policy action build up over the course of time.

6 The behaviour of expectations is a further source of difficulty for policy making. First, it is difficult to know exactly what determines expectations and to capture those factors in a simple formula. Second, policy actions themselves are likely to affect expectations.

7 More generally, there is always uncertainty about the effects of a given policy action on the economy. Economists are not agreed on the "correct" model of the economy, and evidence is not likely to be at hand soon to settle decisively disagreements over some behavioural functions — such as the consumption function. And even if we did know the form of the behavioural functions, the statistical evidence would be insufficient to pinpoint the values of the relevant parameters.

8 There are clearly occasions on which active monetary and fiscal policy actions should be taken to stabilize the economy. These are situations in which the economy has been affected by major disturbances.

9 Fine tuning — continuous attempts to stabilize the economy in the face of small disturbances — is more controversial. If fine tuning is undertaken, it calls for small policy responses in an attempt to moderate the economy's fluctuations, rather than to remove them entirely. A very

active policy in response to small disturbances is likely to destabilize the economy.

10 The real issue in rules versus discretion is whether policy actions should be announced as far in advance as possible. Such announcements are desirable in that they aid private individuals in forecasting the future behaviour of the economy.

10

FISCAL POLICY AND PUBLIC FINANCE

T his chapter is intended to serve two purposes. The first is to review the experience of the 1930s and the postwar period. The Great Depression is worth studying for purely historical interest, but of equal importance is the fact that the thirties and the war that followed molded many of the institutions and views of the modern economy. The role of government expanded markedly, and it was the experience of the thirties that led to the view, now taken for granted in practice, that the government has primary responsibility for satisfactory economic performance.

The second purpose of the chapter is to discuss a number of questions connected with the budget, government spending and taxes. In Section 10-3 we describe the financing of the federal government budget deficit — that is, how the government pays for the excess of its spending over its income from taxes. The issue of the burden of the debt is taken up at the conclusion of the chapter.

10-1 THE GREAT DEPRESSION

In this section we describe the experience of the 1930s and review the controversy over the causes of the depression. Data describing the performance of the Canadian economy are shown in Chart 10-1 and Table 10-1. As can be seen from the chart, between 1929 and 1933, real GNP fell by 30 percent and the price level fell by 20 percent. Investment collapsed; indeed, *net* investment was negative from 1932 to 1936. The unemployment rate rose to nearly 20 percent in 1933 and remained above 11 percent through the thirties, with the exception of 1937 when it dipped close to 9 percent. By 1933 the stock market had fallen almost to one-third of its 1929 value.

Events in Canada closely mirrored those in the United States and the economic collapse in the U.S. was a major cause of the decline in Canada.

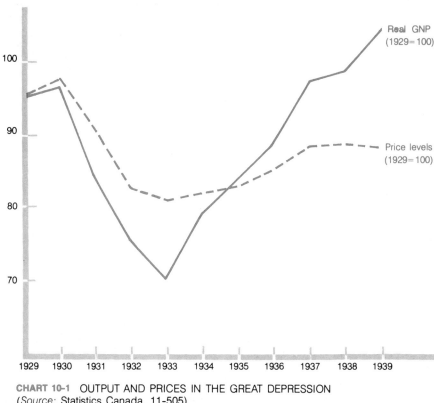

CHART 10-1 OUTPUT AND PRICES IN THE GREAT DEPRESSION
(*Source*: Statistics Canada, 11-505)

The sharp fall in our exports, shown in Table 10-1 resulted from the fall in income in the U.S. and other countries and the psychological impact was an important factor in the collapse of investment. In view of this it is necessary to examine events in the U.S. in order to obtain clues as to the causes of the depression.

American Experience in the 1930s

The depression and the stock market crash of October 1929 are popularly thought of as almost the same thing. In fact, the U.S. economy started turning down before the stock market crash. The peak of the business cycle is estimated to have been in August 1929, and the stock market itself peaked in September 1929. Using September 1929 as the base period, Standard & Poor's composite stock price index fell from 100 in September to 66 in November. It rose again through March 1930, but then the collapse continued until the index fell to 15 in June 1932.

By early 1931, the U.S. economy was suffering from a very severe

TABLE 10-1 THE GREAT DEPRESSION IN CANADA

	GNP	Govt. Exp.	Exports	GNE Deflator	Gross Investment	Budget Surplus	Unemployment Rate	Stock Market Index
	(billions of 1961 dollars)			(1961=100)	(% of GNP)		(%)	(1961=100)
1929	12.24	1.70	3.10	50.2	22.2	.2		49.0
1930	11.71	1.93	2.70	48.8	18.9	−3.9		35.0
1931	10.23	1.94	2.41	45.9	15.5	−6.6	11.6	21.9
1932	9.17	1.79	2.24	41.6	8.8	−7.3	17.6	14.2
1933	8.56	1.47	2.26	40.8	6.8	−5.0	19.3	17.6
1934	9.59	1.58	2.55	41.4	7.7	−4.7	14.5	22.1
1935	10.34	1.68	2.81	41.6	8.6	−4.0	14.2	23.6
1936	10.80	1.67	3.38	42.9	10.0	− .7	12.8	30.7
1937	11.89	1.79	3.46	44.1	11.8	− .6	9.1	32.6
1938	11.98	1.93	3.12	44.0	11.3	−2.8	11.4	26.8
1939	12.87	2.02	3.44	43.7	10.3	− .8	11.4	25.8

Source: Statistics Canada, 11-505

depression, but not one that was out of the range of the experience of the previous century.[1] It was in the period from early 1931 until Franklin Roosevelt became President in March 1933 that the Depression became "Great."

What was economic policy doing during this period? The money stock fell from 1929 to 1930, and then fell rapidly in 1931 and 1932 and continued falling through March 1933. At the same time, the composition of the money stock changed. In March 1931 the currency-demand deposit ratio was 18.5 percent; two years later, it was 40.7 percent. The fall in the money stock was accompanied by three waves of bank failures, in which banks closed because they were unable to pay cash to their depositors. The bank failures culminated in the bank holiday of March 1933, a measure imposed by the new president's closing all banks in the country for a week. Many of the closed banks never reopened. It was the bank failures that reduced depositors' confidence and led them to increase the currency-demand deposit ratio. The American central bank, commonly referred to as the Fed (Federal Reserve System), took very few steps to offset the fall in the money supply; for a few months in 1932 it did undertake a program of open market purchases, but otherwise seemed to acquiesce in bank closings and certainly failed to understand that the central bank should act vigorously in

[1] Milton Friedman and Anna Schwartz, in *A Monetary History of the United States* (Princeton, N.J.: Princeton University Press, 1963), give a very detailed account of the Great Depression, comparing it with other recessions and emphasizing the role of the Fed. For a more general economic history of the period, see Robert A. Gordon, *Economic Instability: The American Record* (New York: Harper & Row, 1974), chap. 3.

a crisis to prevent the collapse of the financial system.[2]

Fiscal policy too was not vigorous. The natural impulse of politicians then was to balance the budget in times of trouble, and much rhetoric was devoted to that proposition. The presidential candidates in 1932 campaigned on balanced budget platforms. In fact, the federal government ran enormous deficits, particularly for that time, averaging 2.5 percent of GNP from 1931 to 1933, and even more later. The belief in budget balancing was more than rhetoric, however, for state and local governments raised taxes to match their expenditures, as did the federal government, particularly in 1932 and 1933. President Roosevelt tried seriously to balance the budget — he was no Keynesian. The full-employment surplus which we introduced in Chapter 3 shows fiscal policy (combined state, local, and federal) as most expansionary in 1931, and moving to a more contractionary level from 1932 to 1934. In fact, the full-employment surplus was positive in 1933 and 1934, despite the actual deficits. Of course, the full-employment surplus concept had not been invented in the 1930s.

Economic activity recovered in the period from 1933 to 1937, with fiscal policy becoming more expansionary and the money stock growing rapidly. The growth of the money stock was based on an inflow of gold from Europe which provided an increase in high-powered money. This period also saw a program of legislative action to aid recovery known as the *New Deal*.

The 1937-1938 recession was very sharp, and it followed the tightening of *both* monetary and fiscal policy. The increase in the full-employment surplus was equal to 2.9 percent of GNP, the biggest change in the decade. On the monetary side, the Fed acted in 1936 and 1937 to reduce the excess reserves held by the banking system. From 1929 to 1937, banks had been increasing their holdings of reserves over and above those required by the Fed. The Fed feared that if it ever wanted to control the money supply by an open market sale, the banks would have excess reserves sufficiently large that they would not have to reduce their total assets, but would instead, merely reduce their reserve ratio.[3] Since the reserves were excess, the Fed decided to eliminate them merely by increasing required reserves.

When the Fed increased required reserves, the banks reacted by reducing their outstanding credit and maintaining the excess reserves. That is, it became clear that the excess reserves were assets the bank really wanted to hold. The reasons are fairly obvious. First, many banks had collapsed for lack of readily realizable assets just a few years before, and it was wise to be able to avoid that problem. And second, interest rates were so low at the time that it was cheap to hold excess reserves. The effect of the Fed's action was to reduce the money supply by nearly 3 percent from early

---

[2] Friedman and Schwartz speculate on the reasons for the Fed's inaction; the whodunnit or "Who didn't do it" on pp. 407-419 of their book (cited in footnote 1) is fascinating.

[3] Check back to Chapter 8 to see how a reduction in the reserve ratio can offset the effects of a change in the monetary base (H) on the money stock.

1937 to mid-1938. Thereafter, the money supply resumed growth, fiscal policy became less contractionary, and the recovery proceeded.

What Caused the Great Depression?

As for the causes of the Great Depression, there are essentially two hypotheses. These are (1) an autonomous decline in aggregate demand or (2) a monetary contraction. Within the "autonomous demand" camp (1), most claim that investment demand declined,[4] while some view consumption demand as having decreased autonomously. We now review these hypotheses.

We start with the autonomous demand reduction hypotheses. Growth in the twenties, in this view, was based on the mass production of the automobile and radio, and was fueled by a housing boom. The collapse of growth in the thirties resulted from the drying up of investment opportunities and a downward shift in investment demand. The collapse of investment combined with poor fiscal policy fits this picture. As can be seen in Table 10-1, fiscal policy followed a similar course in Canada, thereby making little contribution to offsetting the decline in investment and exports. Government expenditure fell between 1931 and 1934 and the sharp rise in the budget deficit reflected primarily falling revenues rather than deliberate countercyclical policy.

What does the autonomous demand view have to say about the monetary collapse? The Fed argued in the thirties that there was little it could have done to prevent the Depression, because interest rates were already as low as they could possibly go. A variety of sayings of the type, "You can lead a horse to the water but you can't make it drink," were used to explain that further reductions in interest rates would have had no effect if there was no demand for investment. Investment demand was thought to be very unresponsive to the rate of interest—implying a very steep IS curve. At the same time, the LM curve was believed to be quite flat, though not necessarily reaching the extreme of a liquidity trap. In this situation, as we saw in Chapter 4, monetary expansion would be relatively ineffective in stimulating demand and output.

It was also widely believed that the experience of the Depression showed that the private economy was inherently unstable in that it could self-depress with no difficulty if left alone. The experience of the thirties, implicitly or explicitly, was the basis for the belief that an active stabilization policy was needed to maintain good economic performance.

The view that monetary policy in the thirties had been impotent was sharply challenged in 1963 by Friedman and Schwartz in their *Monetary History*. They argued that the Depression, far from showing that money does

---

[4] This view is argued, for example, in Robert A. Gordon, *Economic Instability and Growth: The American Record* (New York: Harper & Row, 1974), chap. 3.

not matter, "is in fact a tragic testimonial to the importance of monetary factors."[5] They argued, with skill and style, that the failure of the Fed to prevent bank failures and the decline of the money stock from the end of 1930 to 1933 was largely responsible for the recession being as serious as it was. This monetary view in turn came close to being accepted as the orthodox explanation of the Depression.

A challenge to the monetary view has recently been issued by Peter Temin,[6] who focusses on the comparatively narrow question of what actually caused the Depression, rather than on whether it could have been avoided. Temin argues that the decline in the money stock was a *result* of the decline in economic activity, not a cause. The cause, he contends, was a fall in consumption (rather than investment) spending that set off a fall in income, which then in turn affected the monetary sector. Reinforced by the Fed's incompetence, this led to a dramatic reduction in money that aggravated the Depression. In terms of IS-LM schedules, Temin sees an initial, moderate leftward shift of the IS schedule in Figure 10-1.

[5] Friedman and Schwartz, op. cit., p. 300.

[6] Peter Temin, *Did Monetary Forces Cause the Great Depression?* (New York: Norton, 1976).

FIGURE 10-1 COMPETING EXPLANATIONS OF THE GREAT DEPRESSION

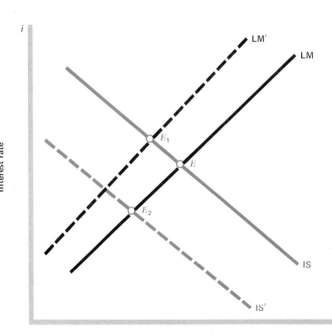

Output

But what about the reduction in the money stock? Should that not have caused the LM curve to move to the left simultaneously? Here we have to recognize that the IS and LM curves in Figure 10-1 are drawn for a given price level. But the aggregate price level was falling through this period, so that the LM curve would not necessarily have shifted to the left. The fall in the money supply was tending to make it move left, but the fall in the price level was offsetting that leftward shift. What, then, was the role of the bank failures? Temin argues that they were *caused* by the decline in income and the shift in the IS curve, since with a falling price level, low interest rates, and declining output, the *nominal* stock of money had to fall if the demand for real balances was to stay equal to supply. Bank failures were merely the mechanism that reduced the money supply.

The same interpretation could be made of the Canadian experience. There was little scope for monetary policy in Canada during the early years of the Depression as there was no central bank (the Bank of Canada began operations in 1935). As in the U.S., the money supply fell sharply after the 1929 crash, but for quite different reasons. There was no bank failures in Canada but the monetary base fell. This resulted from the institutional arrangements at the time under which the volume of bank reserves was determined primarily at the initiative of the chartered banks through a form of borrowing.[7] With the onset of the Depression, the demand for loans by credit-worthy borrowers collapsed and the chartered banks responded by contracting their operations.

How would one choose between the monetary and autonomous demand hypotheses? Temin focusses on the behaviour of interest rates. A leftward shift of the LM curve would have caused interest rates to rise, (point E_2), whereas a downward shift of the IS curve would have caused them to fall (point E_2). In fact, interest rates fell suggesting the IS curve shifted down. Proponents of the monetary view criticize this test for failing to distinguish between real and nominal interest rates. We shall have to wait until Chapter 13 to obtain a full understanding of this point, but the argument is that although the nominal interest rate in the thirties seems low, the *real* rate, the nominal rate minus the expected rate of inflation, could have been high. How? Because prices were falling at the time, supporters of the monetary view maintain that people must have been expecting deflation. Hence, despite the low nominal rate, the real interest rate was high. And that, they argue, is consistent with the Friedman-Schwartz view. The controversy will continue for some time.

As is often the case, there is more agreement here among economists than there seems to be. A careful reading of the Friedman-Schwartz book will show that they are really quite agnostic about what started the Depression in 1929. The main thrust of their argument relates to the question: Could the Depression have been avoided? And here they argue

[7] See T.J. Courchene, "An Analysis of the Canadian Money Supply: 1925-1934", *Journal of Political Economy*, May/June, 1969.

vigorously that expansive monetary policy, particularly in 1930 but also in the following years, would have prevented the Depression from being more than a serious recession. Temin is chiefly interested in what started the recession — which, on the basis of econometric evidence, he blames mainly on a downward shift in the consumption rather than the investment function. He would probably agree that better policy, monetary and fiscal, would have made the Depression much less severe.

There is general agreement then that the Great Depression could have been avoided. Both monetary and fiscal policy were so inept that they contributed significantly to making the recession into the worst depression for which we have data. If there had been prompt, strong, expansive monetary and fiscal policy, the economy would have suffered a recession, but not the trauma it did.

On the other hand, there remains considerable controversy between Friedman-Schwartz and Temin over the question, What caused the Depression? The reason is that the thirties are seen as the period that set the stage for massive government intervention in the economy. Those opposed to an active role for government have to explain away the debacle of the economy in the thirties. If the Depression occurred because of, and not despite, the government, the case for an active government role in economic stabilization is weakened. Further, the thirties are a period in which the economy behaved in such an extreme way that competing theories have to be subjected to the test of whether they can explain that period. Those are the main reasons the dispute over the causes of the Great Depression continues to be so lively more than 50 years after it began.

10-2 FISCAL POLICY IN THE POSTWAR PERIOD

The experience of the Great Depression and World War II resulted in a fundamental change in the role of government expenditures and taxes as instruments of government policy. The 1945 White Paper on Employment and Income established the principle that the federal government had a responsibility to maintain high and stable levels of employment and income. Since then, consideration of the desired degree of fiscal stimulus or restraint has become an important element in the budgets presented to Parliament.

Both the achievements and failures of economic policy in the postwar period can be seen in Chart 10-2. In comparison with earlier eras, the fifties and sixties were years of prosperity and steady growth. The first prolonged slump occurred during the years 1958 to 1961 when the unemployment rate reached a peak of 7.1 percent. By 1965, the economy was operating at or near potential, but in retrospect, it appears that policy makers misjudged the situation. As can be seen in Chart 10-3, rising income had moved government budgets into a surplus position, but some of the restraining effects of the built-in stabilizers were offset by tax cuts introduced in the federal budget of April, 1965. As a result, the cyclically adjusted federal budget

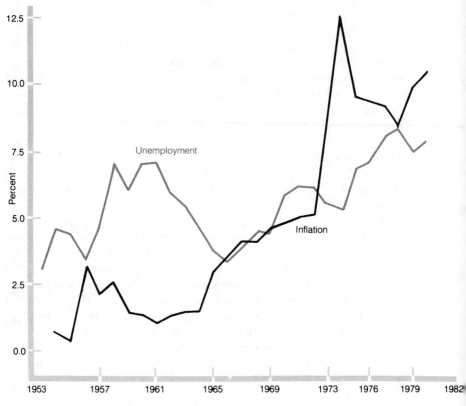

CHART 10-2 INFLATION AND UNEMPLOYMENT, 1953-1980
(*Source*: Statistics Canada, 11-206, 11-505, 71-201)

moved to a deficit position. Tax increases and some expenditure cuts were imposed in the years 1966-1968, but fiscal restraint came too late to prevent the entrenchment of inflationary forces. The rate of inflation had crept up steadily during the sixties and by 1969 had reached 4.6 percent.

Perspectives on economic policy in the sixties appear to differ widely. It was a period in which faith in the efficiency of activist fiscal policy reached a peak. Although the analytical approach consisted basically of the Keynesian tools we have outlined in Chapters 3 through 7, fiscal activism became known as the "New Economics" in the United States.[8] In one view, the period was one of high employment and prosperity, thanks to the activist

[8] One of the chief architects of U.S. policy in the sixties was Walter Heller, now a professor at the University of Minnesota. He was chairman of the Council of Economic Advisers which attracted as members and staff a succession of distinguished American economists. Among these were James Tobin of Yale, Gardener Ackley of the University of Michigan, Robert Solow of MIT, Otto Eckstein of Harvard, Kenneth Arrow of Stanford, and the late Arthur Okun, then of Yale and afterwards at the Brookings Institution, to name only a few.

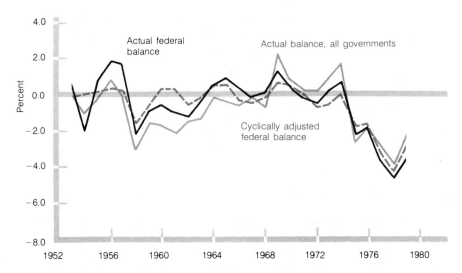

CHART 10-3 ACTUAL AND CYCLICALLY ADJUSTED BUDGET BALANCE AS A PERCENTAGE OF GNP
(*Source*: Dept. of Finance, Economic Review)

stance of policy. An alternative view is that overexpansionist policies in that period were responsible for the inflation that was to prove to be the economic policy problem of the seventies. Actually, both views are correct. Policy in the early sixties was indeed successful, and economic policy in the second half of the period was overexpansionary or, equivalently, not sufficiently contractionary, in the face of increases in spending to a large extent related to the Vietnam war. Government spending in the U.S. rose rapidly, and rising income in the U.S. stimulated demand for Canadian exports, thereby contributing to inflationary pressure in Canada.

The decade of the 1970s began with the federal government in a surplus position, but there was a shift to an expansionary policy in view of the steep rise in unemployment that had occurred. With an unemployment rate in excess of 6 percent during most of 1971 and 1972, the federal budget was maintained in a deficit position. In 1974 the emphasis shifted to moderating the inflationary pressures that were building up. At midyear the unemployment rate was down around 5 percent and the consumer price index was rising at a rate in excess of 10 percent. However, toward the end of the year there was a significant worsening of the outlook. Slower growth and rising unemployment occurred in Canada while the United States experienced a substantial *decline* in real GNP. In view of these conditions, an expansionary budget was brought down late in the year which provided for a reduction in personal income taxes of about $1.5 million in 1975.

As can be seen from Chart 10-3, the federal budget moved to a substantial deficit position in 1975 and 1976. This resulted from both the automatic response of tax revenues and unemployment insurance benefits to relatively low levels of economic activity, and the effects of discretionary policy as reflected in the cyclically adjusted federal balance. Further tax cuts were introduced in 1977 and 1978 in response to rising unemployment rates, but policy decisions were complicated by the emergence of a major dilemma. Although the unemployment rate rose above 8 percent for the first time since the 1930s, the rate of inflation continued at an unacceptably high level. This coexistence of high unemployment and a high inflation rate came to be called *stagflation*, and the question of its causes and cures is taken up in Chapter 15.

Government Revenue and Expenditure in the 1970s

Table 10-2 shows the pattern of federal government revenues and expenditures during the 1970s. Revenues grew faster than GNP during the early years, reaching a peak of 20.3 percent of GNP in 1974. Thereafter revenues grew more slowly than GNP as a result of a slowing down in income growth and the introduction of various tax reductions. As estimated by the

TABLE 10-2 FEDERAL GOVERNMENT REVENUE AND EXPENDITURE (BILLIONS OF DOLLARS)

	1970	1974	1978	1979	Average annual growth rate 1969-1979
Revenue					
Personal income taxes	6.41	11.13	13.25	15.97	11
Other personal direct taxes	1.02	2.41	4.09	3.90	15
Corporate income taxes	2.28	5.01	5.54	7.25	12
Sales and excise taxes and customs duties	4.03	8.50	9.71	10.34	10
Other revenue	1.78	2.93	5.05	5.81	14
Total revenue	15.52	29.98	37.64	43.27	11.6
(percent of GNP)	(18.1)	(20.3)	(16.3)	(16.6)	
Expenditure					
Goods and Services	5.01	8.38	13.27	13.62	11
Transfers to persons	4.06	8.71	14.62	14.70	15
Transfers to provinces and municipalities	3.40	6.16	10.86	11.79	16
Interest on the public debt	1.86	2.96	6.41	8.09	18
Other transfers	.93	2.66	3.84	4.24	18
Total expenditure	15.26	28.87	49.00	52.44	14.6
(percent of GNP)	(17.8)	(19.6)	(21.3)	(20.1)	

Source: Dept. of Finance, *Economic Review*

Department of Finance, the cumulative effect of the tax changes made in the budgets over the period 1972-1978 was a reduction in 1979 revenue of over $14 billion or about 25 percent of total revenue.[9]

Expenditures grew more rapidly than revenues over the decade leading to the sharp rise in the budget deficit shown in Chart 10-3. The most rapid rates of growth occurred in interest on the public debt and other transfers. The sharp rise in the latter category reflects primarily the growth of subsidies under the oil import compensation program. Under this program the federal government subsidizes users of imported oil to compensate them for the difference between the world price and the controlled domestic price. With the rapid increase in world oil prices in 1979, this difference widened to more than $17 per barrel, equivalent to more than half the price of imported oil delivered at Montreal. As a result, subsidy payments exceeded $1 billion in 1979,[10] and were projected to rise above $3 billion in the 1980-81 fiscal year.

Table 10-3 shows the budgetary position of the provincial and municipal

[9] See Dept. of Finance, *Economic Review*, April 1980, p. 113.

[10] Part of this subsidy is paid for by a tax on exports of crude oil. Revenue from this tax was $700 million in 1979.

TABLE 10-3 PROVINCIAL AND MUNICIPAL REVENUE AND EXPENDITURE (BILLIONS OF DOLLARS)

	1970	1974	1978	1979	Average annual growth rate 1969-1979
Revenue					
Own sources	15.10	26.47	45.94	51.11	14.3
Federal cash transfers	3.40	6.16	10.86	11.79	15.8
Total revenue	18.50	32.63	56.80	62.90	14.5
(percent of GNP)	(21.6)	(22.1)	(24.7)	(24.1)	
Expenditure					
Goods and services	14.74	24.88	42.23	46.14	13.9
Transfers to persons	2.82	4.68	8.91	9.76	14.5
Interest on the public debt	1.39	2.46	4.49	5.00	15.5
Other transfers	.20	.69	1.18	1.27	22.4
Total expenditure	19.15	32.71	56.81	62.17	14.3
(percent of GNP)	(22.3)	(22.2)	(24.7)	(23.9)	
Budget Balance					
Sask., Alberta and B.C.	−.07	.80	2.53	3.28	
Other provinces	−.58	−.88	−2.54	−2.55	
Total	−65	−.08	−.01	.73	

Source: Dept. of Finance, *Economic Review*.

governments. Although their expenditures grew at about the same rate as federal outlays during the 1970s, their revenues grew at a faster rate. As a result their budget balance improved, particularly in the second half of the decade. One of the principal contributions to the growth of revenues has been natural resources royalties. In 1979 these accounted for 7.3 percent of total revenues, as compared with 1.8 percent in 1970. Most of this increase has occurred since 1974 as a result of rapid increases in crude oil and natural gas prices and increased provincial royalty rates. About 90 percent of this revenue is received by the province of Alberta and almost all of the remainder goes to Saskatchewan and British Columbia. As can be seen in Table 10-3, the small surplus for provincial and municipal governments in 1979 represents the net effect of a substantial surplus in the three western-most provinces and a substantial deficit in the remaining provinces.

10-3 THE MECHANICS OF FEDERAL GOVERNMENT SPENDING AND FINANCING

In this section we examine how the federal government finances its spending. We are particularly interested in the relationship between the federal government's deficit and changes in the stocks of money and government debt.

How does the government pay for its spending? Directly, it pays for most of its spending with cheques, drawn on the Bank of Canada. Aside from the fact that the cheque is drawn on a bank in which private individuals do not have accounts, a payment made by the government looks much like a cheque payment made by anyone else. Like an individual, the federal government must have funds in the account on which it writes cheques. So the question of how the federal government finances its spending is the same as the question of how it makes sure that it has funds in the bank account (at the Bank of Canada) on which it writes its cheques.

The federal government receives the bulk of its revenues from taxes and in some years taxes are less than expenditures. Those are the years in which the federal government runs a budget deficit, as in the period 1975 to 1980. Total government expenditures consist of purchases of goods and services, G, and transfers, R. Denoting taxes by T and the deficit by BuD, with all variables measured in real terms, we know that

$$\text{BuD} \equiv (G + R) - T \equiv -\text{BuS} \tag{1}$$

Equation (1) reminds us that the budget deficit, BuD, is just the negative of the budget surplus, BuS. Thus in 1979, the deficit was $9 billion, or the surplus was minus $9 billion.

Now, how does the government make payments when its tax receipts are insufficient to cover its expenditures? The answer is that it has to borrow either from the public or from the Bank of Canada. When the government borrows from the private sector, it sells securities or debt to the private sector. In return, it receives cheques from individuals and firms (including banks) in exchange for the securities it sells them. These cheques are deposited in government accounts at the chartered banks or at the Bank of Canada, and can then be spent in the same way as tax receipts.

Alternatively, the government can borrow from the Bank of Canada by selling securities to the Bank. However, there is a major difference between government borrowing from the public and the Bank of Canada. When the Bank of Canada lends to the government by buying securities, it pays for them by giving the government a cheque on the Bank of Canada — that is, by creating high-powered money. When the government spends the deposit it has received at the Bank of Canada in exchange for its debt, it leaves the private sector with larger holdings of high-powered money. By contrast, when the government borrows from the public, it receives and then spends high-powered money, thus leaving the amount of high-powered money in the hands of the public unchanged — except for a brief transition period between the sale of securities and expenditures by the government. Since the stock of high-powered money is an important macroeconomic variable, the distinction between selling debt to the public and selling it to the Bank of Canada is in fact essential.

The distinction can be further clarified by noting that sales of securities to the Bank of Canada are referred to as *monetizing the debt*, meaning that the Bank creates (high-powered) money to finance the debt purchase. Yet another way of looking at the difference between sales to (borrowing from) the Bank of Canada and the public is to ask: What is the net change in the private sector's portfolio after the government has made *and* financed its expenditures? Consider first the case of borrowing from the public or selling debt to the public. In this case, the public holds more debt and an unchanged quantity of high-powered money, since the government spends the money it obtains from the debt sale to cover its deficit. Consider next the case where the deficit is financed by sale of debt to the Bank of Canada. In this event, the private sector's debt holding is unchanged while its holding of high-powered money is increased. The reason is that expenditures were financed by the creation of high-powered money by the Bank of Canada.

The government deficit can thus be financed in two ways: by sales of securities, or debt, to the private sector, and by borrowing from the Bank of Canada. Let ΔB_p be the change in the number of government bonds (securities) held by the private sector, ΔB_f be the change in the number of bonds held by the Bank of Canada, and P_b be the price in dollars paid for one bond. Let H be the stock of high-powered money. We have just seen that[11]

---

[11] As we saw in Chapter 8, the stock of high-powered money may change for reasons other than open market operations. For that reason we use the symbol for "approximately equal to" ($\simeq$) in Eq. (2). The change in the central bank's holdings of government bonds is only approximately equal to the change in high-powered money.

$$P \cdot \text{BuD} = P_b \cdot \Delta B_j \cdot \Delta B_p \simeq \Delta H + P_b \cdot \Delta B_p \tag{2}$$

Equation (2) is called the government's *budget constraint*. It states that the nominal budget deficit is financed by borrowing either from the Bank of Canada ($P_b \Delta B_j$) or from the private sector ($P_b \Delta B_p$). The change in Bank of Canada holdings of debt causes a corresponding change in high-powered money (ΔH), so that we can say that the budget deficit is financed either by selling debt to the public or by increasing the stock of high-powered money. It is in this sense that the Bank of Canada "monetizes" the debt.[12]

The view that the deficit is financed either by selling debt to the public or by increasing the stock of high-powered money looks at the government sector as a whole, including or "consolidating" the Bank of Canada along with the government in the government sector. When one thinks of the government sector as a whole, relative to the private sector, the transactions in which the Bank of Canada buys debt from or lends to the government are seen as mere bookkeeping entries within the government sector.

Although this consolidation is useful for some purposes, it is important to recognize that the institutional arrangements provide for a clear division of responsibility under which the Bank of Canada determines the division of the total deficit BuD, in Equation (2), between the change in high-powered money and the change in government debt held by the private sector. There is no *necessary* association between the size of the government deficit in Canada and increases in the stock of high-powered money. If the Bank of Canada does not purchase securities when the government is borrowing, the stock of high-powered money is not affected by the deficit. On the other hand, there will be a more or less automatic association between Bank of Canada purchases of securities and government borrowing if the Bank of Canada commits itself to maintaining interest rates on government bonds at a constant level. As we saw in Chapter 4, an increase in the government deficit tends to increase the interest rate. If the Bank of Canada wishes to prevent this it must intervene in the market and purchase securities.

Prior to 1975, the Bank of Canada's policy focussed primarily on target interest rates — which could change from time to time — so that there was a link between deficits and Bank of Canada purchases of securities. More recently the Bank has shifted to a policy which concentrates on the behaviour of the money supply. A commitment to bringing about a given money stock breaks the link between government deficits and the creation of high-powered money. Now the Bank of Canada creates high-powered money at a rate that should result in money's growing at the target rate, and the change in the stock of high-powered money is therefore not directly associated with the size of the government deficit.

[12] Note that the government budget constraint (2) also shows that for a given value of the deficit, changes in the stock of high-powered money are matched by offsetting changes in the public's holdings of government debt. A positive ΔH matched by a negative $P_b \Delta B_p$ is nothing other than an open market purchase.

Summary

Five main points have been made in this section.

1 Federal government spending is financed through taxes and through borrowing, which is necessary when the budget is in deficit.
2 Borrowing may be from the private sector or from the Bank of Canada.
★3 Lending to the government by the Bank of Canada changes the stock of high-powered money, whereas lending by the private sector to the government to finance the deficit does not affect the stock of high-powered money.
4 The stock of claims held by the Bank of Canada and the private sector against the government — the national debt — changes with the budget deficit. The national debt increases when there is a budget deficit and decreases when there is a budget surplus.
★5 Because the deficit can be financed in two ways, there is no *necessary* connection between the budget deficit and changes in the stock of high-powered money. Equation (2), the government budget constraint, says only that the *sum* of changes in the stock of debt and changes in high-powered money is approximately equal to the budget deficit.

The National Debt

We return now to Equation (2) which implies that when the budget is not balanced, the government changes the net amount of *claims* on it held by the private sector and the Bank of Canada. Those claims are the securities sold to the private sector and the Bank of Canada, and they represent claims for future interest payments. The total stock of such claims constitutes the *national debt*[13]. When the budget is in deficit, the national debt increases — the stock of claims against the government increases. When the budget is in surplus, the national debt decreases. The government takes in more taxes than it pays out, and can use the excess to retire (or buy back) previously issued debt.

The national debt is a direct consequence of past deficits in the federal budget. The national debt increases when there is a budget deficit and decreases when the budget is in surplus. The way the national debt is divided between private sector claims on the government and high-powered money depends on past monetary policy. If the Bank of Canada has financed only a small part of each deficit in the past, then the ratio of high-powered money to national debt is small.

The government sells securities more or less continuously. There is, for instance. a weekly treasury bill auction, at which prospective buyers of

[13] Note that we are not counting in the national debt those claims that are held by government agencies other than the Bank of Canada. We regard those claims as cancelling out within the government sector.

treasury bills (lenders to the federal government) submit sealed bids specifying how much they are prepared to lend at different interest rates. The government sells the amount of treasury bills it has offered at the auction to the bidders who offer the highest prices, or the lowest interest rates.[14] Longer-term debt issues are less frequent. Issues of government debt are not all made for the purpose of financing the budget deficit. Most debt issues are made to refinance parts of the national debt that are maturing. For example, the government has to pay the amount it borrowed to a treasury bill holder when the treasury bill matures. Six months after a 180-day treasury bill is issued, the government has to pay the face amount of the treasury bill to the holder. Typically, the government obtains the funds to make those payments by further borrowing. The process by which the government (with the help and advice of the Bank of Canada) finances and refinances the national debt is known as *debt management*. Only part of debt management is concerned with financing the current budget deficit. Most of it is concerned with the consequences of past budget deficits.

[14] Technically, there is no interest paid on treasury bills. Instead, a treasury bill is a promise to pay a given amount on a given date, say $100 on June 30. Before June 30, the treasury bill sells for a *discount* at less than $100, with the discount implying a rate of interest. For instance, if the treasury bill just described sold for $97.50 on January 1, the holder of the bill for six months would earn a little more than 5 percent per annum, or 2.5 percent for six months.

CHART 10-4 THE NATIONAL DEBT
(*Source: Bank of Canada Review*)

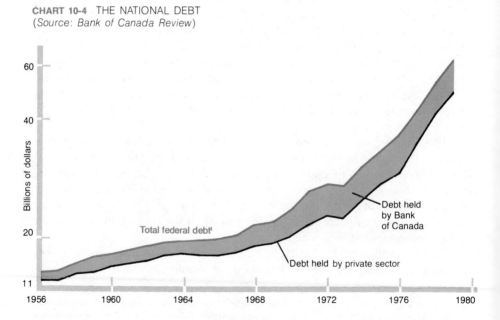

¹Excludes debts held in Government of Canada Accounts

Chart 10-4 shows the growth of the national debt over the past 25 years. Although the amount of debt has been steadily rising, it grew at a slower rate than GNP until the late 1970s. This is reflected in the decline in the ratio of debt to GNP shown in Chart 10-5. As a result of large federal deficits, the debt to GNP ratio began to move up in 1976, but it is still below the level of the early sixties.

To what extent is the national debt a burden? It must be recognized of course that corresponding to the liability that we all have as our share of the national debt, there are assets in the form of government securities held by Canadians. With the exception of debt held by foreigners, we owe the national debt to ourselves. Each individual shares in the public debt, but many individuals own claims on the government that are the other side of the national debt. If there is a debt for individuals taken together, it arises from prospective taxes to pay off the debt. The taxes that different individuals would pay to retire the debt would also vary among the population. To a first approximation, one could think of the liability that the debt represents as cancelling out the asset that the debt represents to the individuals who hold claims on the government.[15]

The question at issue then is whether the debt is counted as part of wealth for the population as a whole. It is not certain whether individuals take into

[15] For an eclectic, but difficult, view of this argument, see Robert J. Barro, "Are Government Bonds Net Wealth?" *Journal of Political Economy*, December 1974.

CHART 10-5 THE NATIONAL DEBT AS A PERCENTAGE OF GNP
(*Source*: Dept. of Finance, *Economic Review*)

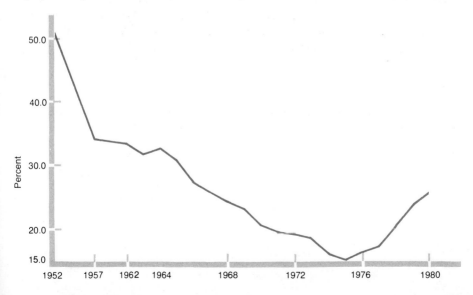

account the future tax liabilities connected with paying off the debt. There certainly does not seem to be any argument that the liability represented by some possible paying off of the debt at some unknown future time outweighs the value of the assets that individuals hold at present. At this level, then, there is no persuasive argument that the debt is a burden in the sense that the economy as a whole regards the national debt as a reduction in its wealth.

The only factor ignored in the previous paragraph is that part of the debt is owned by foreigners. In that case, for the Canadian economy as a whole, part of the asset represented by the debt is held by foreigners, while the future tax liability accrues entirely to residents. Then that part of the debt held by foreigners might represent a net reduction in the wealth of Canadian residents.

Although the debt is not a burden in the fairly crude sense in which one asks whether individuals regard themselves as being poorer because of the existence of the debt (leaving aside the part of the debt owned by foreigners), there are more sophisticated senses in which it might be a burden. The most important sense in which there is a possible burden arises from the potential long-run effects of the debt on the capital stock. Since debt financing increases the interest rate and reduces investment, the capital stock would be lower with debt financing than otherwise. If individuals regard the debt as part of their wealth, then they tend to increase their consumption at a given level of income, which results in a smaller proportion of GNP being invested.[16]

In the long run, that would result in a lower capital stock and thus a lower level of real output. In that sense, then, the debt could be a burden. Secondly, the debt might be a burden because debt servicing in the long run could require higher tax rates. If those tax rates have adverse effects on the amount of work that individuals do, then real output would be reduced. But it is far from certain that higher tax rates in fact reduce the amount of work that individuals do. Thus we conclude that the major sense in which the national debt may be a burden is that it may lead to a decline in the capital stock in the long run.

[16] For articles dealing with the burden of the debt, see J.M. Ferguson (ed.), *Public Debt and Future Generations* (Chapel Hill: University of North Carolina Press, 1964).

PROBLEMS

1 Using IS-LM curves, describe the competing "autonomous spending" and "monetary" explanations for the Great Depression.

2 Explain why many people believe the inflationary problems of the 1970s have their roots in the 1960s. How can this be so? What would be the cause? What could have been done to avoid such "heating up" of the economy, in this view?

3 Government budget deficits are often a source of public concern. What would be the implications for stabilization policy of a commitment to a balanced budget every year?

4 Discuss the notion of the monetary-fiscal policy mix. What determines the mix that is chosen. Illustrate, using a IS-LM diagram, how the effects of the mixes of 1966 and 1970 differ, given the information below. (Assume the level of income was the same.)

	1966	1970
cyclically adjusted federal deficit (% of GNP)	−.3	.6
increase in the treasury bill rate (percent)	.88	−2.94

5 What effect does a federal government surplus have on the stock of money and the stock of debt? Explain in detail the mechanics of how the stocks of money and bonds are affected.

6 Suppose the government issues $1 billion in treasury bills which are bought by the public. Then the Bank of Canada conducts open market purchases of $300 million. Effectively, how has the debt been financed?

7 Under what circumstances are fiscal and monetary policy related rather than existing as two completely independent instruments in the hands of the government?

8 Some people say that a huge government debt is a burden while others point out that a large debt means individuals own large amounts of government securities and thus are wealthier. Who is right?

Part 3

11

AGGREGATE SUPPLY

U p to this point we have discussed the determination of output on the assumption that prices are given and that firms supply all the output that is demanded at the current price level. But of course the aggregate price level changes over time, and changes in aggregate demand are likely to result in changes in both prices and output. We are now ready to begin our study of the determinants of the aggregate price level and its changes over time — that is, the rate of inflation. This chapter and the next develop the formal apparatus that enables us to study the simultaneous determination of the levels of output and prices.

Our analysis combines the theory of *aggregate demand* developed so far with a theory of *aggregate supply*. Aggregate demand and supply jointly determine the levels of output or income, and prices. The theory of aggregate supply will be developed in this chapter and combined with the theory of aggregate demand in Chapter 12.

Section 11-1 presents an intuitive preview and outline of the analysis of aggregate supply contained in the rest of the chapter. It is designed to be read by those interested in obtaining the essentials of the theory without necessarily going into details. Sections 11-2 through 11-6 develop the analysis of aggregate supply at a deeper level. Sections 11-7 and 11-8 contain further developments and refinements of interest to the more advanced student.

11-1 AGGREGATE DEMAND AND SUPPLY: A PREVIEW

In Chapter 4 we studied the aggregate demand side of the economy on the assumption that firms meet any level of demand at the prevailing level of prices, say P_0. The IS-LM framework allowed us to determine equilibrium output and spending as a function of fiscal and monetary policy variables. Monetary policy was represented by a given nominal money stock, M_0. In combination with the given price level, the nominal money stock implied a *real* money stock, M_0/P_0. The equilibrium level of spending was then a function of fiscal variables (and autonomous spending) and the level of real balances, or

$$Y^d = \beta \bar{A} + \gamma \frac{M}{P} \qquad \beta, \gamma > 0 \tag{1}$$

In Equation (1), Y^d denotes the equilibrium level of spending determined by the intersection of IS and LM curves. Equilibrium income or spending is written as a function of autonomous spending and fiscal variables, collected in the term $\bar{A}$, and as a function of the real money stock, M/P. The terms β and γ were developed as multipliers in Chapter 4 but need not concern us further until Chapter 12. From Equation (1) we note that an increase in the real money stock raises the equilibrium level of income. In terms of the analysis of Chapter 4, we have a rightward shift in the LM schedule and therefore a decline in equilibrium interest rates that leads to an increase in investment spending and hence to a rise in equilibrium income.

Suppose now that the nominal money stock is given and equal to M_0. What happens to aggregate demand if the price level declines? This raises the real money stock, lowers the interest rate, and raises real spending or aggregate demand. Conversely, if the price level increases, real balances will fall, interest rates will increase, and aggregate demand will fall. There is thus a relationship between the level of aggregate demand and the price level, *given the nominal money stock*. The higher the price level, the lower the level of aggregate demand, given the nominal money stock.

We show this relationship between the equilibrium level of real spending and the price level as the *aggregate demand schedule*, Y^d in Figure 11-1. The schedule slopes downward to reflect the fact that at a lower price level, the real money stock is higher, interest rates are lower, and aggregate demand is therefore higher. We will derive the schedule and study its properties at greater length in Chapter 12. For the present, we need retain only the fact that the schedule, representing Equation (1), is drawn for a given nominal money stock and given levels of autonomous spending and fiscal variables.[1]

Figure 11-1 also shows the aggregate supply schedule, Y^s. As we have drawn it, the schedule shows that increased output will be supplied only at a higher level of prices. Why does the schedule slope up? We will argue that firms base their prices on costs, primarily labour costs. When they expand their supply of output, firms also expand their input of labour. Using more labour will inevitably bid up wages somewhat — whether because overtime is necessary or because new workers have to be hired. Therefore the prices

---

[1] We use the term "*demand schedule*" in obvious analogy with microeconomics, where the demand for an individual commodity is negatively related to its price. The word "aggregate" qualifies the analysis and reminds us that we are talking about the demand for *all* goods and services in the economy and the general level of prices, rather than about the relative price of an individual commodity.

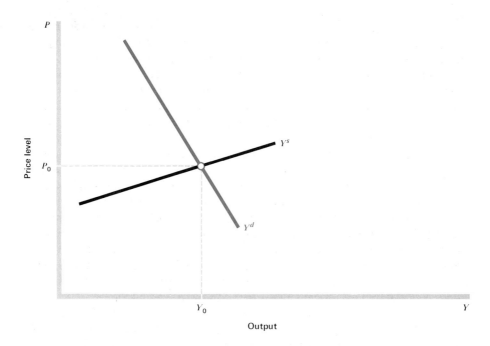

P

Price level

P_0

Y^s

Y^d

Y_0

Y

Output

FIGURE 11-1 AGGREGATE DEMAND AND SUPPLY

charged by firms will rise. We accordingly have an upward-sloping relationship between output and cost or prices. The slope of the aggregate supply
curve reflects the increase in labour use and labour cost (and other costs)
required to produce the increased output.

We will also develop in detail the important distinction between the
short-run aggregate supply curve — a relatively flat schedule as drawn in
Figure 11-1 — and the long-run aggregate supply curve, which we will argue
is vertical. Why are the short-run and long-run aggregate supply curves
different?

The distinction between short-run and long-run supply mirrors the
behaviour of factor prices in responding to over- or underemployment of
factors. (We can think of overemployment for the moment as substantial use
of overtime.) Clearly, factor prices would rise and keep rising as firms bid for
the overemployed factors, or they would keep falling if factors were
underutilized. The important point, though, and an empirical one, is that
factor prices and, in particular, wages, move slowly in response to unemployment or overemployment.

In the short-run, an increase in employment can be obtained at a
relatively small increase in wages. Similarly, a reduction in employment and
the resulting unemployment will lead to a relatively small decrease in

wages.[2] Over time, though, overemployment will mean constantly rising wages and unemployment will imply falling wages. With firms passing on changes in costs into changes in prices, the implication is that the only position of stable prices is at the level of output corresponding to the full employment of labour.[3] At that level of employment, wages — and thus, prices — will neither be falling because of unemployment nor rising because of overemployment. The long-run aggregate supply curve is thus vertical at the full employment level of output.

The distinction between the short- and long-run supply curves arises because wages respond slowly to changes in labour demand. In the short run — of, say, a few months — we move along a given aggregate supply curve like Y^S in Figure 11-2. At an employment level such as that corresponding to the output level Y' in Figure 11-2, the wage rate is higher than it is at output level Y_0. But, because there is overemployment at Y', the wage is not only higher than at Y_0 but is also rising. Thus, in the next period some months later, wages at any given level of output, say Y_0, will be higher than they were in the previous period. Hence, the whole supply curve shifts up over time as long as the economy remains in a condition of overemployment.

Consider now an application of the model. We start with Figure 11-1, which shows that equilibrium output and prices are determined by the intersection of aggregate demand and supply. We assume until further notice that this demand-supply equilibrium is achieved instantaneously. Now turn to Figure 11-2, which again shows the aggregate demand schedule, Y^d, and the short-run aggregate supply schedule, Y^S. It also shows the long-run aggregate supply curve, which is vertical at the level of potential output, Y_p. We start from a position of full equilibrium at point E.

Suppose that autonomous spending increases or, in terms of Chapter 4, that we have an upward shift of the IS schedule. For a given level of real balances, the shift implies an increase in equilibrium income or spending. In Figure 11-2 this is shown as a rightward shift of the aggregate demand schedule: at each level of prices and hence level of real balances, spending increases. At the initial level of prices, there is now excess demand leading firms to expand output. As firms hire more labour to produce the increased output, wages and labour costs rise and firms therefore charge higher prices. The new short-run equilibrium is at point E'. Both prices and output are higher at E' than at E. This is the first important point implied by the model:

---

[2] Indeed, we will argue in Chapter 14 that the response of wages to overemployment is likely to be greater than the response to unemployment, or that wages are less flexible downward than upward. This would imply that the aggregate supply curve would be flatter below the current level of output.

[3] In Chapter 13 we will introduce to the analysis the very important factor of expectations of inflation that will suggest that wages could be changing even at the full-employment level in order to maintain *real* wages — nominal wages divided by the price level — constant in the face of expected inflation. The verticality of the long-run aggregate supply curve can then be reinterpreted, as is shown in Chapter 13.

- Changes in aggregate demand lead in the short-run to changes in both output and prices in the same direction. The extent to which the aggregate price level rises depends on the slope of the aggregate supply curve.

Inspection of Figure 11-2 will show that the change in short-run equilibrium output, from Y_0 to Y', falls short of the horizontal shift in demand. The increase in prices dampens the expansion of output since it reduces the level of real balances, raises interest rates, and thereby lowers spending. The extent of this damping effect obviously depends on the steepness of the aggregate supply curve, that is, on the extent to which an output expansion and the expansion of employment that lies behind it raise wages (and other costs) and prices. If, in the short-run, wages and other costs do not respond at all to increased employment, the aggregate supply curve will be essentially flat and an increase in aggregate demand will in the short-run be met by increased output. Point 2 is then the following:

- The extent to which changes in demand are met by changes in output as opposed to prices depends on the response of costs to an expansion in output and employment. If wage costs are very unresponsive in the short-run, the supply curve is quite flat and shifts in demand are met at essentially constant prices.

FIGURE 11-2 EFFECTS OF AN INCREASE IN AGGREGATE DEMAND

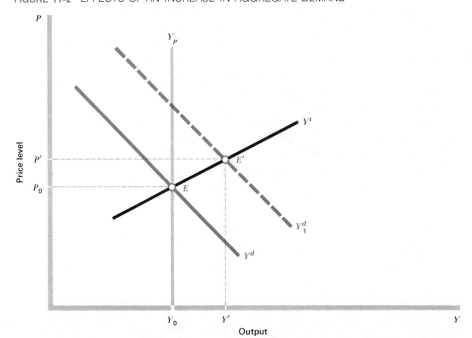

Consider next the adjustment process. The short-run equilibrium at point E' in Figure 11-2 is one of overemployment. Wages are consequently increasing and firms' costs are rising. To supply the same level of output without reducing profits, firms will charge higher prices. This is shown in Figure 11-3 as an upward shift of the aggregate supply schedule to Y_1^s. The increase in costs resulting from overemployment leads to a new short-run equilibrium at point E''. The price level has increased and equilibrium output has fallen, although it still exceeds the full-employment level. Thus, point E'' is only another short-run equilibrium and the process of wage and cost increases and the resulting upward shift in the supply curve will continue. Accordingly, we move, with a continually upward-shifting supply curve, along the aggregate demand schedule as indicated by the arrows. The process of cost and price increases continues until prices have risen sufficiently to reduce the level of real balances and hence of aggregate demand to the full-employment level, Y_p. Once Y_p is reached, there is no further tendency for wages to rise. At point E''', costs remain constant and the economy has reached a new long-run equilibrium. Accordingly, we have point 3:

- An expansion of output above normal will bring about overemployment

---

FIGURE 11-3 DYNAMIC ADJUSTMENT TO AN INCREASE IN AGGREGATE DEMAND

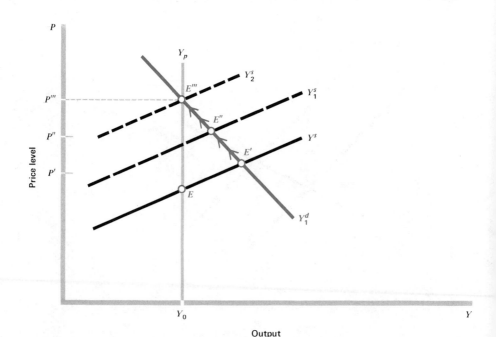

and therefore rising wages and costs. Firms will pass on these cost increases into higher prices. The aggregate supply schedule shifts upward, thereby raising equilibrium prices and reducing equilibrium output along the aggregate demand schedule. The process continues until output declines back to the level of full employment.

There is, of course, a parallel story for a decline in demand.

The last point, already implicit in our analysis, is made by describing the adjustment mechanism that leads us from a position of short-run over- or underemployment back to full employment. The adjustment mechanism operates through changes in the levels of wages, costs, and prices on the real money stock. Changes in the *real* money stock in turn change interest rates and therefore real spending. The last point, then, can be put as follows:

• Adjustment from positions of over- or underemployment takes place through changes in the level of prices and real balances. Overemployment leads to higher prices and lower real balances, and hence to a contraction in demand, while underemployment leads to a fall in prices, increasing real balances, and therefore an expansion in demand.

We have now sketched the essential elements of the aggregate demand and supply framework. The remaining task is to make these elements more precise. On the aggregate demand side, we will look, in Chapter 12, at the exact way in which monetary and fiscal policy determine the position of the aggregate demand schedule. We will ask questions such as: By how much does a tax cut shift the aggregate demand schedule? Or, by how much does an increase in the *nominal* money stock shift the aggregate demand schedule?

In the rest of this chapter, we flesh out the theory of aggregate supply. The analysis starts in Section 11-2 with a frictionless *neoclassical* model of factor markets and output supply. In this idealized economy, factor and goods prices are fully flexible and adjust instantly to changes in demand. In such an economy, the aggregate supply curve is vertical in the short-run as well as the long-run, and output is always at the full-employment level. Aggregate demand changes affect the level of prices but not output. The neoclassical model provides a background against which it is easier to understand the development of the theory of aggregate supply in the rest of the chapter.

The basic theory rests on three elements: (1) the determination of the firm's level of employment, studied in Section 11-4; (2) wage behaviour; and (3) pricing behaviour. The last two elements are studied in Section 11-5. Short-run and long-run aggregate supply curves are examined in Section 11-6. The theory is then extended and made more realistic by a discussion of supply shocks and materials prices in Section 11-7. Section 11-8 discusses the cyclical behaviour of productivity, prices, and the real wage.

11-2 THE FRICTIONLESS NEOCLASSICAL MODEL

The relationships between output and employment and between output and prices will be studied here in an idealized frictionless case. That is the case where wages and prices are flexible, where there are no costs either to workers in finding jobs or to firms in increasing or reducing their labour force, and where firms behave competitively and expect to sell all they produce at prevailing prices. That case will serve as a benchmark for the discussion of more realistic cases, but it also allows us to introduce such useful concepts as the production function and the demand for labour. Throughout, we will assume that labour is the only variable factor of production in the short run.

The Production Function

A production function provides a relation between the quantity of factor inputs, such as the amount of labour used, and the maximum quantity of output that can be produced using those inputs. The relation reflects only technical efficiency. In Equation (2) we write the production function

$$Y = F(N, \ldots) \tag{2}$$

where Y denotes real output, N is labour input, and the dots denote other cooperating factors (capital, for example) that are in short-run fixed supply. The production function is shown in Figure 11-4. It exhibits *diminishing returns*, which means that output increases proportionately less than labour input.

Diminishing returns are shown in the production function by the fact that it is not a straight line through the origin (constant returns) or an upward-curling line (increasing returns). Diminishing returns are explained by the fact that as employment increases and other inputs remain constant, each labourer on the job has fewer machines with which to work and therefore becomes less productive. Thus, increases in the amount of labour progressively reduce the addition to output that further employment can bring. An increase in the labour force will always raise output, but progressively less so as employment expands. The marginal contribution of increased employment is indicated by the slope of the production function, $\Delta Y/\Delta N$. It is readily seen that the slope flattens out as we increase employment, thus showing that increasing employment makes a positive but diminishing contribution to output.

Labour Demand

From the production function we can proceed to the demand for labour. We are asking how much labour a firm would want to hire. The rule of thumb is

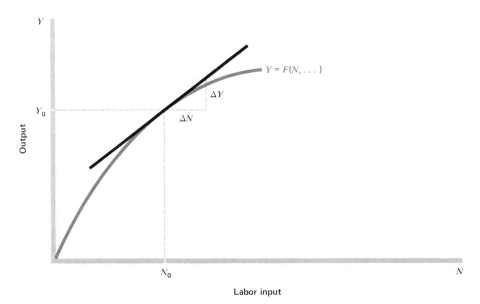

FIGURE 11-4 THE PRODUCTION FUNCTION AND THE MARGINAL PRODUCT OF LABOUR

to continue hiring additional labour and expand production as long as the increase in the value of output exceeds the increase in the wage bill. A firm will hire additional workers as long as they will bring in more in revenue than they cost in wages. The contribution to output of additional labour is called the marginal product of labour and has already been identified in Figure 11-4 with the slope of the production function. That marginal product, as we have seen, is both positive — additional labour is productive — and diminishing, which means that additional employment becomes progressively less productive. We also noted that a firm will employ additional labour as long as the marginal product of labour, MPN for short, exceeds the cost of additional labour. The cost of additional labour is given by the real wage, that is, the nominal wage divided by the price level. The real wage measures the amount of real output the firm has to pay each worker. Since hiring one more worker results in an output increase of MPN and a cost to the firm of the real wage, firms will hire additional labour if the MPN exceeds the real wage. This point is formalized in Figure 11-5, which looks at the labour market.

The downward-sloping schedule in Figure 11-5 is the demand for labour schedule which is the MPN schedule; firms hire labour up to the point at which the MPN is equal to the real wage. The MPN schedule shows the contribution to output of additional employment. It follows from our reasoning that the MPN is positive but that additional employment reduces it, so that the MPN schedule is negatively sloped.

Now consider a firm that currently employs a labour force, N_1, and assume the real wage is $(w/P)_0$, where w is the money wage and P the price of output. At an employment level N_1 in Figure 11-5, the firm is clearly employing too much labour since the real wage exceeds the MPN at that level of employment. What would happen if the firm should reduce employment? The reduction in employment would decrease output by the MPN times the change in employment, $MPN \cdot \Delta N$, and therefore reduce revenue to the firm. On the other side of the calculation, we have the reduction in the wage bill. Per unit reduction in employment, the wage bill would fall at the rate of the real wage, (w/P). The net benefit of a reduction in the employment level is thus equal to the vertical excess of the real wage over the MPN in Figure 11-5. It is apparent that at the level of employment N_1, that excess is quite sizable, and it pays the firm to reduce the employment level. Indeed, it pays to reduce employment until the firm gets to point N_0. Only at that point does the cost of additional labour — the real wage — exactly balance the benefit in the form of increased output.

The same argument applies to the unemployment level N_2. Here employment is insufficient because the contribution to output of additional employment, MPN_2, exceeds the cost of additional employment, and it therefore pays to expand the level of employment. It is readily seen that the only level of employment that precisely balances the costs and benefits is the level N_0. Therefore, given *any* real wage, the firm's demand for labour is shown by the MPN curve.

FIGURE 11-5 THE OPTIMAL EMPLOYMENT CHOICE FOR A GIVEN REAL WAGE

Equilibrium in the Labour Market

We have now developed the relation between output and employment (the production function) and the optimal employment choice for a given real wage that is implied by the demand for labour. It remains to consider the determination of the real wage as part of labour market equilibrium. What we have not yet dealt with is the supply of labour.

We will make a quite simple assumption concerning labour supply. We will assume that the supply of labour is fixed at $\bar{N}$ and that it is independent of the real wage.[4] This is shown in Figure 11-6 as the vertical schedule, $\bar{N}\bar{N}$. The equilibrium real wage is clearly $(w/P)_0$.

How would the labour market get to that equilibrium? Suppose that the real wage fell whenever there was an excess supply of labour and that it rose whenever there was an excess demand. In terms of Figure 11-6, this would mean that the real wage would decline whenever it was above $(w/P)_0$. At $(w/P)_1$, for example, labour demand is only N_1 and thus falls short of labour supply. This would put downward pressure on the real wage, cause the real wage to fall, and make it profitable to expand employment. Exactly the reverse argument holds for real wages lower than $(w/P)_0$, where there is an excess demand for labour.

[4] The exposition of this chapter would be little affected if we assumed that labour supply increased as the real wage increased. The major change then would be that the full-employment level of employment would depend on the level of the real wage. You might want to experiment with an upward-sloping labour supply curve as you continue reading. Figure 11-7 summarizes the complete equilibrium in the labour market and the corresponding level of *full-employment output* Y_p, which is the level of output associated with employment equal to the given labour supply.

FIGURE 11-6 EQUILIBRIUM IN THE LABOUR MARKET

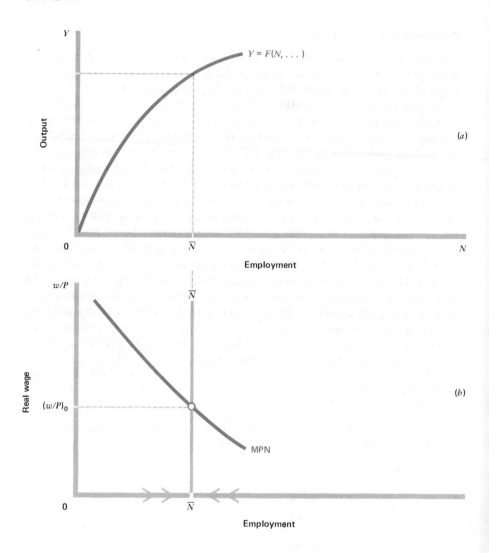

FIGURE 11-7 EQUILIBRIUM IN THE LABOUR MARKET AND FULL-EMPLOYMENT OUTPUT

From Figure 11-6 we see that adjustment of the real wage would bring the labour market into full-employment equilibrium at a real wage $(w/P)_0$ and an employment level equal to the given labour supply $\bar{N}$. Figure 11-7 summarizes the complete equilibrium in the labour market and the corresponding level of *full-employment output* Y_p, which is the level of output associated with employment equal to the given labour supply.

Neoclassical Goods and Labour Market Equilibrium

We have now derived the full-employment supply of output and have to complete the neoclassical model by asking how *money* wages and prices are determined. How can we be sure that goods produced can be sold? Here we make two important assumptions: (1) goods prices will rise or fall instantaneously to clear the goods market, and (2) money wages will instantaneously rise or fall to clear the labour market. How will that adjustment work?

In the labour market, the flexibility of money wages ensures that at each price level the money wage rises or falls to achieve the necessary level of the real wage. We are therefore continuously in labour market equilibrium and, whatever the level of prices, firms will employ the full-employment labour force $\bar{N}$ and supply the corresponding level of output Y_p. This is shown in Figure 11-8 in the aggregate supply curve Y_pY_p. The aggregate supply schedule is vertical to show that the equilibrium level of output supplied — when the labour market is in equilibrium — is independent of the price level. If prices rose relative to wages, firms would be making profits. In an attempt to secure even larger profits, they would attempt individually to expand their employment level at the going money wage. In the aggregate, though, all they would do would be to compete for the given labour force and drive up the money wage until it had risen in proportion to the increase in prices, thus leaving real output unchanged.

FIGURE 11-8 THE INTERACTION OF AGGREGATE SUPPLY AND DEMAND IN THE DETERMINATION OF THE EQUILIBRIUM PRICE LEVEL

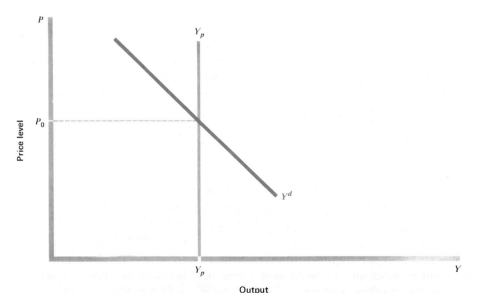

Figure 11-8 includes an aggregate demand curve, Y^d, along with the vertical neoclassical aggregate supply function.[5] Aggregate demand and supply jointly determine the equilibrium price level, P_0. We need not be concerned yet with a full understanding of the details of the adjustment process of the price level in response to shifts in aggregate supply or demand. We need only recognize that it is plausible that the economy will converge to a full-employment equilibrium with all markets in equilibrium. Given the equilibrium price level P_0, the nominal wage will adjust so that the real wage is $(w/P)_0$. Furthermore, *if* wages and prices adjust rapidly, and *if* firms respond rapidly in their production decisions to changing conditions, and *if* labour moves rapidly between jobs as some firms expand and others contract, we would expect to be in equilibrium continuously. Any disturbance, such as an increase in the nominal money supply or an improvement in technology, would immediately be reflected in changes in wages and prices that would restore the full-employment equilibrium.

The neoclassical full equilibrium is a useful reference point for the study of more realistic descriptions of macroeconomics. We should expect to converge to the neoclassical equilibrium in the long run. But in the short run, problems of transactions costs and information problems associated with finding and taking jobs, together with simple stickiness of wages and prices due to contractual arrangements, will affect the adjustment process. If, for example, prices do not fall fast enough in response to a decline in the nominal quantity of money, we would expect to get transitory disequilibrium and unemployment. Such unemployment would not occur in the neoclassical model. It is exactly the range of issues such as short-run adjustment and unemployment with which the macroeconomics of the short run is concerned. We therefore retain the neoclassical analysis as a reference point and turn next to a discussion of the adjustment process under less ideal conditions.

The more realistic theory of aggregate supply we are about to develop differs from the neoclassical theory in three important respects. (1) Because it is costly to hire and fire workers, firms do not stay precisely on their neoclassical demand function for labour, as in Figure 11-6. Rather, they look ahead in making their hiring decisions, which are based on both the expected real wage and the level of output they expect to produce in the future. (2) The money wage adjusts only slowly. It takes unemployment to reduce the money wage or overemployment to increase it. (3) The prices charged by firms are based mainly on their costs of production. Since costs are largely wages, which respond slowly to demand, prices too respond slowly to demand. Thus the supply curve is relatively flat in the short run.

In the short run, changes in aggregate demand therefore have relatively little impact on prices. As William Nordhaus of Yale has put it: "After three

---

[5] Recall from Section 1 that the aggregate demand curve slopes downward because increases in the price level reduce real balances, increase the interest rate, and reduce aggregate demand.

decades, the major intellectual problem continues to be the fact that so little response to demand shifts comes through prices and wages."[6]

11-3 OUTPUT AND PRODUCTIVITY

The neoclassical analysis of the previous section suggests that the *average productivity of labour* — the level of output per unit of labour — should vary inversely with the level of output. Figure 11-4 implies that output per unit of labour falls as the level of output rises.[7] In fact, though, productivity varies procyclically, as can be seen in Chart 11-1. The rates of growth of output and output per man-hour both fell in the 1970 recession and both rates of

[6] William Nordhaus, "Inflation Theory and Policy," *American Economic Review*, May 1976, p. 62.
[7] Be sure you can see from Figure 11-4 that the ratio Y/N falls as Y rises.

CHART 11-1 OUTPUT AND PRODUCTIVITY, PERCENT CHANGE
(*Source*: Dept. of Finance, *Economic Review*)

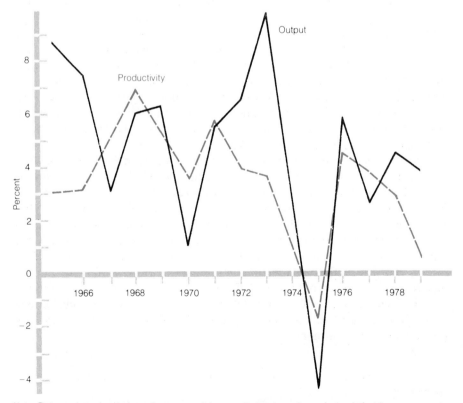

Note: Data are based on indexes for commercial nonagricultural goods-producing industries. Productivity is measured by output per man-hour.

growth dropped to negative values in 1975. The facts do not support the implication of Figure 11-4 for the behaviour of productivity. It is thus clear that at least some element of the neoclassical analysis of Section 11-2 has to be amended.

The essential modification of the neoclassical analysis we shall make is to recognize that in the short run, firms will not necessarily be on their marginal product of labour schedule, MPN. As we argue in this section and the next, a firm need not react to changes in demand by changing its labour force or even its level of production. Even without changing its labour force, a firm has two ways of meeting a change in demand. The first is to change its stock of inventories,[8] and the second is to adjust the rate at which the labour force works. In particular, if an increase in demand is viewed as *transitory* or temporary, the firm is likely to respond either by selling some goods held in inventory, by working its given labour force somewhat harder, perhaps including overtime, or by doing both. Similarly, in the face of a transitory decline in demand, the firm will retain its employees rather than lay them off, and it may therefore reduce hours of work or allow its inventories to build up.

The fact that variations in demand and sales may be seen as transitory suggests that we should analyze the firm's production decision separately from its employment decision, and that we should recognize that sales of goods can be made out of inventory without requiring production changes. To anticipate somewhat: If there are significant costs of hiring and firing labour, firms will want to have a relatively stable labour force but may still vary output as the demand for their goods varies.[9] Similarly, if there are significant costs to changing production rates, firms may want to stabilize production relative to sales, and thus allow inventories to fluctuate to meet very short-run movements in demand.[10]

We have now pointed to three possible adjustments a firm can make to a change in demand. It can adjust its inventory level, the rate at which its labour force works, or the size of its labour force. In the very shortest run, it is likely to respond to a change in demand by adjusting inventories. But inventories cannot be run down for very long, nor would firms want to keep accumulating them, and the adjustment of the rate at which the labour force works is likely to occur in the short run too. Then, over a slightly longer period, the firm will start adjusting its labour force as well. The rate of adjustment using each method will of course depend on how much information the firm has about the nature of the change in demand — the adjustment of the labour force will be made more quickly if the firm knows that the demand change is permanent.

---

[8] Of course, inventories can be used in this way only in those industries where it is possible to store output.

[9] An early article drawing attention to the importance of costs of adjusting the labour force is that of Walter Oi, "Labor as a Quasi-Fixed Factor," *Journal of Political Economy*, October 1962.

[10] However, we do not examine inventory adjustment explicitly in the rest of this chapter.

We can return now to the productivity behaviour shown in Chart 11-1. Why should labour productivity vary procyclically? The reason is simply that when output expands, firms have more work for their labour force to do, and labour works harder each hour that it is on the job.[11] Conversely, when output declines but firms are reluctant to lay off workers because the output decline may be temporary, the ratio of output to employment declines. Thus measured productivity — the ratio of output to employment — moves procyclically, or in the same direction as output. It is common to refer to firms' practice of not laying off workers in the face of a decline in demand as *labour hoarding*.

The major point of this section has been that the link between the firm's labour force and its output level is not automatic. In the presence of costs of adjusting the labour force — costs of hiring and firing labour and training new labour — the firm will not adjust its labour force completely in response to short-run changes in demand. Instead, the firm will adjust its labour force with a view to the level of output it will be producing over a longer period.

11-4 DETERMINATION OF THE LEVEL OF EMPLOYMENT

We now examine in more detail the firm's choice of employment level. How closely will employment move with output? We have already seen that firms can vary output as of a given employment level by using the labour force more or less intensively.[12] That is an efficient short-run adjustment, but it is clearly not a reasonable long-run strategy. A firm that expects a doubling in its output can achieve that output at much lower cost by increasing its labour force than by increasing the overtime work of its existing employees.

We have also argued that, unlike the neoclassical firms of Section 11-2, an actual firm will experience significant costs in changing employment in the short run. These costs arise from advertising, screening and interviewing new employees, and having to train those employees. Given these costs of changing employment, firms, in making their employment decisions, will look ahead to the levels of output they expect to be producing in the future.

What determines the average output the firm expects to produce over a longer period, such as a year or two, on which its present hiring decisions will in part be based? We refer to this output level as expected *normal* output. We can think of the typical firm as being a *monopolistic competitor* in the medium run of a year or two with which we are now concerned. The firm does not believe that it will be able to sell as much as it wants at the market

---

[11] Another reason that labour productivity rises in the short run when output increases is that the firm has certain overhead labour — such as management — that is needed to keep the firm operating at all but that is not expanded with output.

[12] In this section, we will not be discussing inventory adjustment explicitly, although, as noted above, it is one way of meeting short-run changes in demand.

price that will prevail for the industry, as the neoclassical firm of Section 11-2 believes. Rather, it believes that it will be faced by a downward sloping demand curve for its output and will set its own price.[13]

Given the demand curve the firm believes it will face over the next year or two, it will choose the price and the corresponding level of output at which it expects to operate over the period. The choice will be made with the aim of maximizing profits. The firm will undoubtedly also take a longer view than just the next year or two, since it will take into account the effects of the prices it charges in the near future on demand in later periods, and also the possibility that high prices will attract competitors into the industry.[14]

The amount of labour the firm will want to have on hand to meet

---

[13] Actually, the monopolistic competition model is flexible enough to incorporate as an extreme case the assumption that the firm is a perfect competitor, and at the other extreme, that there is a fixed maximum amount it will be able to sell in the future — the case of a *sales constraint.*

[14] Considerations of potential competition have been emphasized by Paolo Sylos-Labini and Joe S. Bain. For an exposition, see Franco Modigliani, "New Developments on the Oligopoly Front," *Journal of Political Economy*, June 1958.

FIGURE 11-9 REDUCED OUTPUT EXPECTATIONS DECREASE THE DEMAND FOR LABOUR AT EACH REAL WAGE expected normal output will depend on both the firm's expected level of output and the real wage it expects to pay for labour. If the real wage is high, the firm will plan to use relatively little labour and more other factors to meet demand.

The implied labour demand curve is shown in Figure 11-9 as the downward-sloping schedule. At a real wage $(w/P)_0$, the firm (or firms in the aggregate) will want to have on hand an amount of labour N_0, given that they hold output expectations Y_0. A reduction in expected output shifts the demand curve for labour to the left. With expected output $Y_1 < Y_0$, the quantity of labour demanded at the real wage $(w/P)_0$ declines to N'.

A reduction in the real wage below $(w/P)_0$ would raise labour demand because firms would find it profitable to use more labour and undertake less investment to meet expected demand. However, in the period of a year or two for which the concept of expected normal output is relevant, we should not expect to see any substantial shifts in the level of the overall capital stock, and thus the demand curve for labour in Figure 11-9 would be quite steep.

In summary, we have argued that (1) the aggregate demand for labour and employment depends on output expectations and the expected real wage; (2) increased output expectations increase the employment level; and (3) a reduction in the expected real wage increases labour demand and employment.

These considerations raise two questions: First, how do firms form their expectations about future output and real wages? Second, how do they respond to a change in demand they consider transitory?

We can start with the second question, which turns out to have a relatively obvious answer. If a firm faces a transitory increase in the demand for its output, but if at the same time it is costly to hire and fire additional labour, the firm will not expand employment substantially but, rather, will meet the increased demand out of inventories and through overtime. Obviously, though, the longer the increase in demand is expected to persist (or the less transitory it is) and the larger the increase in demand, the more likely it is that the firm will want to expand employment.

Next we turn to the always difficult question of expectations. We assume that firms expect the current level of real wages to persist. For output, we adopt a different convention. Here we recognize that if current demand is very low, firms do not believe that it will be low indefinitely. On the contrary, they expect demand to improve. Conversely, if demand is currently very high, firms anticipate some decline. Whether current demand is very high or low must obviously be judged relative to some benchmark. We take full-employment output Y_p to be the bench mark. The expectations formation we have just described can be formalized as

$$Y^e = \alpha Y + (1 - \alpha)Y_p, \qquad 0 \le \alpha \le 1 \qquad (3)$$

where Y^e is expected normal output.[15]

Equation (3) shows expected normal output Y^e as an average of full-employment output Y_p and current output Y. We treat the weight α in Equation (3) as given. If all disturbances causing the level of output to diverge from the full-employment level are believed to be entirely temporary, then α should be close to zero and changes in current output have almost no effect on expected output and therefore on employment. Conversely, if disturbances are expected to persist, and if it is believed that the economy takes a long time to move toward the full-employment level, then the weight α should be close to unity. Current output should receive a larger weight in the formation of expected output, and current employment would be more closely linked to current output.

In summary, the aggregate employment decision, taking all firms together, depends on expected output and the real wage. We can write a labour demand curve that is appropriate for the short run:

$$ N = N\left(Y^e, \frac{w}{P}\right) = N\left(Y_p, Y, \frac{w}{P}\right) \tag{4} $$

The labour demand function shows that the total level of employment depends on expected output and the real wage. Expected output, in turn, depends on both potential output and the current level of output. At a given real wage, the higher the output, the higher the demand for labour. And, given the level of output, the lower the real wage, the higher the demand for labour.

11-5 WAGE AND PRICE SETTING

This section continues the derivation of the aggregate supply schedule by discussing wage and price setting. We will examine the relationship between the level of employment and wages, and then between wages and prices. Then, linking output to employment, employment to wages, and wages to prices, we will finally derive the aggregate supply schedule.

It is also worth recalling that we expect the aggregate supply schedule to be flat in the short run—unlike the neoclassical schedule in Figure 11-7—but

---

[15] As we have noted frequently, modeling expectations with simple formulas is always difficult. You might want to consider the implications of an alternative formulation such as

$$ Y^e = \alpha Y + (1 - \alpha)Y_p + \lambda(Y_{-1} - Y_p) \qquad 0 < \lambda < 1 $$

as you continue reading. Is this formula a reasonable representation of how expectations might be formed?

we expect the long-run aggregate supply schedule to resemble the vertical neoclassical supply function.

We will start in this section by examining the link between wage behaviour and the level of employment. As for most of the elements of the theory of aggregate supply, empirical evidence on wage behaviour is not yet conclusive. Most existing empirical evidence is related to the famous Phillips curve, introduced in Chapter 1 and reviewed in greater depth in Chapters 13 and 14. In the late fifties, the Phillips curve was treated as a relationship between the rate of unemployment and the rate of increase of *nominal* wages.[16] Wages would increase when (measured) unemployment was very low, and would stay constant and perhaps even fall if unemployment was very high. Later, the argument was modified to take account of the effects of expected changes in the price level on nominal wages,[17] but we defer that important modification to the later chapters on the Phillips curve.

For the purposes of this chapter, it is sufficient to take the view that the state of the labour market determines the rate of change of money wages. Whenever employment is abnormally high, wages will be rising. Conversely, whenever employment is low, wages will be falling. This notion is consistent with the neoclassical view outlined in Section 11-2. But, in practice, the adjustment of the money wage to unemployment is not immediate, as assumed in the neoclassical analysis. Instead, wages move only slowly in response to labour market disequilibrium. In the short run, overemployment and underemployment are quite possible — even though the economy tends to move toward full employment in the absence of disturbances to aggregate demand and supply.

Once wage behaviour has been studied, we move over to price behaviour. The prices firms charge for their output are based mainly on the costs of producing output and in particular, on the most important of those costs, the money wage, or the cost of labour. Accordingly, there will be a link between the unemployment rate and the behaviour of the price level.

Wage Setting

The notion that the state of the labour market determines the behaviour of money wages is formalized in Figure 11-10 where we show a demand for labour curve (*NN*), drawn for the expected full-employment level of output,

[16] We should also note that the Phillips curve designation is now often used as we use it below: to describe a relationship between the rate of change of prices and the unemployment rate, rather than the wage-unemployment relation.

[17] Expected changes in the price level should affect nominal wages because labour and firms are both concerned with real wages. If the nominal wage for which labour contracts to sell its services remains fixed for, say, a year, then labour would be concerned with how the price level would change over the contract year, since the price level changes affect the real wage to be received. Hence, expected changes in the price level should affect the nominal wage.

Y_p. We show, too, the supply of labour $\bar{N}$. If the real wage were initially at a level such as $(w/P)_0$, there would be unemployment of labour equal to the distance $N_0\bar{N}$. That unemployment would in turn cause wages to start declining — this is precisely the insight of the Phillips curve. Given the price level — the behaviour of which we shall examine later — real wages would decline, adding to employment. However, the effect might be very slow because money wages might fall only slowly.

Now we will develop the simple notion illustrated in Figure 11-10 more formally. First, we have to explain that in this chapter we are abstracting from *frictional* unemployment — the unemployment that results from the rate at which people normally change jobs, and from the fact that it takes new workers some time to find their first job. This frictional unemployment is studied in detail in Chapter 14 under the name of the *natural rate of unemployment*, which can also be called the "full-employment rate of unemployment." Once we recognize that some unemployment is normal because of frictions in the labour market, we realize that overemployment is possible as well as underemployment. From now on we shall take $\bar{N}$ to be the level of employment that would exist at normal full employment. If the employment level is $\bar{N}$, we shall say that there is zero unemployment, even though the unemployment statistics, measuring also frictional unemployment, would report the actual unemployment rate at around 5 to 6 percent. Employment can exceed $\bar{N}$, in which case we say in this chapter that there is negative unemployment.

FIGURE 11-10 ADJUSTMENT IN THE LABOUR MARKET

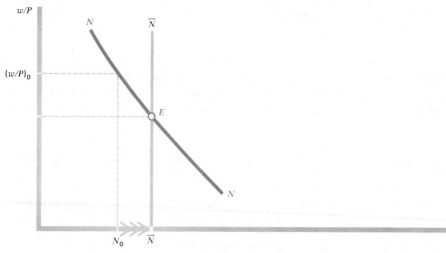

Employment

Wages respond to unemployment. If employment is below N, nominal wages will decline. Conversely, if employment is above $\bar{N}$ — or unemployment is negative — wages will increase. This idea is formalized in Equation (5):

$$w = w_{-1}(1 - \epsilon u) \qquad 0 < \epsilon < 1 \tag{5}$$

where u is the unemployment rate and ϵ measures the responsiveness of wages to unemployment. Consider first the case where unemployment is zero, $u = 0$. In that case current wages w are equal to last period's wages, w_{-1}, so wages neither rise nor fall. Next we look at the case where there is some unemployment, $u > 0$. Now the term in parentheses is less than 1, and accordingly, current wages are less than last period's wages. Therefore, Equation (5) reflects the fact that unemployment causes wages to decline.

To emphasize the percentage rate of change of wages — or wage inflation — we can rewrite Equation (5):[18]

$$\frac{w - w_{-1}}{w_{-1}} = -\epsilon u \tag{5a}$$

The unemployment rate u in Equation (5) or (5a) is defined as the fraction of the full-employment labour force $\bar{N}$ that is not employed:

$$u \equiv \frac{\bar{N} - N}{\bar{N}} \tag{6}$$

Thus, if the full-employment labour force is equal to 100 people of whom 94 are employed, the unemployment rate is $u = (100 - 94)/100 = 6$ percent.[19] Using the definition of the unemployment rate in Equation (6), we can rewrite the *wage equation* as

$$w = w_{-1}\left[1 - \epsilon\left(1 - \frac{N}{\bar{N}}\right)\right] \tag{5b}$$

From Equation (5b) it is apparent that the current wage depends on two elements. One is last period's wage. Other things equal, the current wage is

[18] To get from Eq. (5) to Eq. (5a), we divide both sides by w_{-1} and subtract 1 from both sides of the equation to obtain $w/w_{-1} - 1 = -\epsilon u$, which can be rewritten as Eq. (5a).

[19] Recall that we are defining $\bar{N}$ as the full-employment labour force so that N can exceed $\bar{N}$. This also means that the unemployment rate as defined in Eq. (6) is not the same as the unemployment rate that is announced each month. The published unemployment rate measures unemployment as a fraction of the labour force. Problem 9 at the end of this chapter asks you to relate the unemployment rate as measured in Eq. (6) to the published unemployment rate. Of course, our measure of u increases when the published unemployment rate increases, and vice versa.

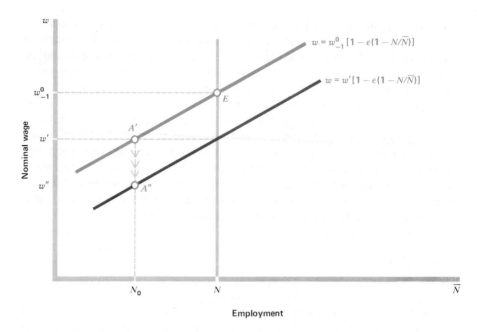

Nominal wage

$w = w^0_{-1} [1 - \epsilon(1 - N/\bar{N})]$

$w = w'[1 - \epsilon(1 - N/\bar{N})]$

FIGURE 11-11 THE WAGE EQUATION AND WAGE ADJUSTMENT IN RESPONSE TO LABOUR MARKET CONDITIONS

last period's wage. The other determinant of wages is employment, or more particularly, employment relative to the full-employment labour force $N/\bar{N}$. When employment exceeds the supply of labour, wages are rising, and when employment falls short, wages are falling.

In Figure 11-11 we show the current wage as a function of the level of employment, given the past wage w_{-1}. In studying the upper wage schedule, we first observe that when employment is equal to the full-employment labour supply $\bar{N}$, the current wage is equal to the past wage, or $w = w^0_{-1}$. Next we note that deviations from full employment affect the wage rate. An increase in employment, relative to $\bar{N}$, raises the wage and a reduction in employment lowers the wage.

In Figure 11-11 we also make the point that if employment were somehow kept below the full-employment level, then the money wage would keep on falling. To see that, we start at point E with full employment. Then we have a decline in employment because firms' output expectations decline. The decline in employment takes us to the employment level N_0, and the corresponding decline in money wages lowers the wage rate relative to last period. The money wage rate is now at w', having fallen from w^0_{-1}. The next step is to recognize that as we move ahead one period, unemployment is still the same, so there continues to be downward pressure on wages.

The new wage equation is based on the most recent money wage w'. It is shown as the lower schedule, crossing the $\bar{N}$ schedule at a wage rate $w_{-1} = w'$. The low employment level this period also exerts downward pressure on wages and we therefore move to point A'' with a further decline in wages. The process will continue in this manner until the falling money wages lower costs and prices sufficiently to expand aggregate demand and thereby raise output and employment.

In summary, we have said that wages are set on the basis of last period's money wage with an adjustment for the state of the labour market. When labour markets are tight, $N > \bar{N}$, wages are increasing. Conversely, when there is unemployment, $N < \bar{N}$, wages are falling. The slope of the wage equations in Figure 11-12 indicates the impact of a change in employment on the money wage rate. A steep schedule means that a change in current employment has a large impact on current money wages.

Price Setting

In the neoclassical framework of Section 11-2 it was assumed that prices are somehow adjusted by the "market." Now we shall instead assume that firms set prices, and that they set their prices on the basis of the costs of production. If a firm experiences an increase in costs, it will pass on that

FIGURE 11-12 THE AGGREGATE SUPPLY CURVE

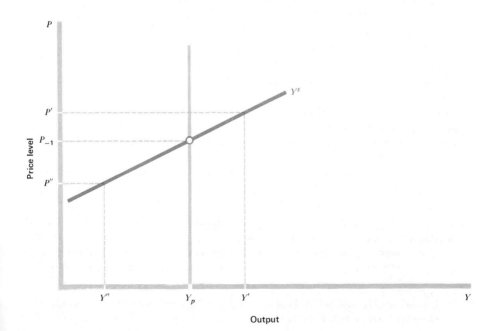

cost increase in the form of higher prices.[20]

We will proceed with two simplifying assumptions. First, labour costs are for the moment assumed to be the only variable cost. Second, prices are assumed to be based on wages, with a *markup* that allows for profits. Accordingly, increases in wages are assumed to be passed on into prices. With these simplifying assumptions, we can write the price level as

$$P = bw \qquad b > 1 \tag{7}$$

where b is a constant, the markup of prices over wages.[21]

We now have a relationship between prices and wages or labour cost. To go from here to an aggregate supply schedule, we have to use two further relations. One is the wage equation in (5) that links current wages to past wages and unemployment. Substituting for w in Equation (5) thus gives us

$$P = bw_{-1}(1 - \epsilon u) \tag{8}$$

In the present form, our price equation states that the level of prices set by firms will depend on last period's level of wages, w_{-1}, and on the unemployment rate. Prices are set higher, the higher were wages last period and the lower is current unemployment. The equation can be simplified by noting that last period's prices were proportional to the then prevailing wages, or

$$P_{-1} = bw_{-1} \tag{9}$$

We can thus substitute on the right-hand side of (8) to obtain a price equation in terms of past prices rather than wages:

$$P = bw_{-1}(1 - \epsilon u) = P_{-1}(1 - \epsilon u) \tag{10}$$

---

[20] For some evidence on wage-price behaviour, see Otto Eckstein (ed.), *The Econometrics of Price Determination* (Washington: Board of Governors of the Federal Reserve, 1972). See also George L. Perry, "Slowing the Wage–Price Spiral: The Macroeconomic View," *Brookings Papers on Economic Activity*, 1978:2 (Washington, D.C.: The Brookings Institution, 1978).

[21] We discuss four features of Eq. (7) later in the chapter. First, it simplifies by assuming labour is the only variable factor. We return to this point in Section 11-7. Second, it assumes that wages are passed on immediately into prices. In practice, an increase in wages is likely to be passed on slowly into prices, as firms initially respond to a cost increase by absorbing part of the change in costs so as not to lose customer goodwill. Problem 12 asks you to show that the slow pass-through of wages makes the aggregate supply curve flatter. Third, Eq. (7) implies that the real wage, w/P, is constant, and equal to $1/b$. Fourth, Eq. (7) does *not* assume that price is based on the current average cost of production at each level of output. Since the productivity of labour increases with the level of output, average costs of production fall at a given wage rate as output rises. Rather, Eq. (7) implicitly assumes that price is based on the cost of production at some given level of output, particularly expected normal output. We return to points 3 and 4 in Section 11-8.

In this form we recognize the role of current unemployment in determining the movement of prices over time. If there is unemployment, wages and prices will have fallen relative to last period. Conversely, if there is overemployment ($u < 0$), firms will raise prices relative to the past level.

So far, we have a relation only between prices, past prices, and the level of unemployment. The aggregate supply schedule we are looking for, though, is a relation between prices and current output. To establish that link, we assume that the GNP gap — the excess of potential over actual output — is proportional to the unemployment rate.[22] That relation is summarized in (11):

$$u = h\frac{Y_p - Y}{Y_p} \qquad h > 0 \tag{11}$$

where h is a constant discussed in connection with Okun's law in Chapter 1. It remains for us to substitute the GNP gap in place of the unemployment rate in (10) to obtain

$$P = P_{-1}\left(1 - \epsilon h[1 - \frac{Y}{Y_p}]\right) \tag{12}$$

11-6 THE AGGREGATE SUPPLY CURVE

Equation (12) is precisely the relationship we have been aiming to derive — the short-run aggregate supply schedule. Since we have come some distance in doing so, we should review the route. First, we studied the factors determining firms' hiring decisions, arguing that firms base their hiring decisions on the level of expected normal output, which responds only slowly to changes in current output. Second, we discussed wage behaviour, noting that wages respond only slowly to changes in the demand for labour. Thus, changes in aggregate demand affect hiring only slowly, and that in turn affects wages only slowly. Finally, we examined price-setting behaviour, maintaining that prices are set mainly on the basis of costs. Making the simplifying assumptions that prices are proportional to wages and that wage changes are passed on directly into prices, we were able to derive Equation (12).

We can explore the properties of Equation (12) using Figure 11-12. First, suppose output is at the full-employment level, or $Y/Y_p = 1$. We note from

---

[22] Equation (11) is essentially *Okun's law*, mentioned in Chapter 1. The basic notion underlying Eq. (11) is the obvious one that unemployment is lower when output is higher.

(12) that in this case prices are at the level of the previous period, having neither risen nor fallen. Thus the aggregate supply schedule intersects the vertical schedule representing potential output at the price level P_{-1} that prevailed in the previous period. To supply a higher level of output, say Y_1, the firm has to increase employment above normal, raising wages (perhaps through overtime) relative to their previous level. With increased labour costs, the firm will pass on these increased costs in the form of higher prices. Accordingly, for an output level Y_1', we have the supply price $P' > P_{-1}$. The converse is true for a decline in output below normal. If output declines, employment falls below normal, wages decline, and accordingly, firms charge a lower price, such as P'' at an output level Y''.

The Long-run Aggregate Supply Curve

An important point about the aggregate supply curve, already made in the introduction to this chapter, is that the schedule does not stay put over time. Rather, wage and cost changes induced by over- or underemployment are passed on into higher or lower prices. In the long run, therefore, the aggregate supply curve will be vertical, as we now show.

Consider first Figure 11-13, where we again show a short-run aggregate supply schedule, Y^S, drawn for a given level of past wages, and therefore prices, P_{-1}^0. Suppose now that firms choose to supply a higher level of output Y', say because demand increases. At what price will that output be supplied? In the short run, the supply price is P', only a modest increase over the previous period's price. What happens next? The decline in unemployment implied by the output and employment expansion means that wages will increase [see Eq. (5)] and that therefore firms will charge higher prices. The aggregate supply schedule shifts upward to Y_1^S and the new price is P''. (Note the upward shift of the Y^S schedule is such that in the second period the supply schedule cuts the $Y_{,,}$ schedule at the price P'). As long as output is maintained above potential, wages will be rising and therefore prices will be rising or the supply schedule will keep shifting up.

The very important point, then, is that a level of output above full employment will be accompanied by ever-increasing prices. Conversely, if output were sustained below normal levels, wages and prices would keep falling. This is precisely the neoclassical adjustment process described earlier with the one exception that we think of it as spread out over time.

Over time the supply curve of Figure 11-13 will keep shifting unless output is at the full-employment level. We can thus conclude that the long-run aggregate supply curve is vertical – in the long run the price level can be constant only if output is at the full-employment level.

We shall now make this argument more formally, and in the process derive the Phillips curve implied by Equation (12). The rate of inflation can be determined from (12) by dividing both sides by P_{-1} and subtracting unity from both sides to obtain

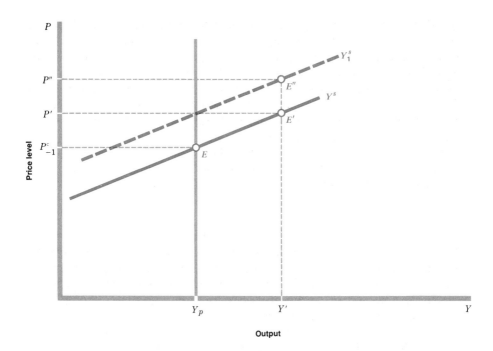

FIGURE 11-13 THE RESPONSE OF THE AGGREGATE SUPPLY CURVE TO OVEREMPLOYMENT

$$\frac{P - P_{-1}}{P_{-1}} = h\epsilon\left(\frac{Y}{Y_p} - 1\right) \tag{13}$$

Equation (13) shows that if output is above normal, the rate of inflation is positive, and conversely, if output is below normal, prices will be falling or there is deflation. The price level keeps changing unless $Y = Y_p$.

We can write the inflation rate equation similarly using Equation (14), which is stated in terms of the unemployment rate rather than the GNP gap:

$$\frac{P - P_{-1}}{P_{-1}} = -\epsilon u \tag{14}$$

This is of course the Phillips curve written here as a relation between unemployment and the rate of inflation.[23] The relation is shown in Figure 11-14. When unemployment is positive, prices are falling because wages are

---

[23] As noted earlier, the original Phillips curve was a relationship between the rate of change of *wages* and unemployment. The term is now used interchangeably to refer to equations like (5a) or (14).

falling. Conversely, when there is overemployment — u is negative — prices are rising, reflecting the rising wage costs that are brought about by excess demand in the factor markets. The inflation unemployment Phillips curve of Figure 11-14 will play a major role in the dynamic theory of aggregate supply we present in Chapter 13. However, recall that we have here abstracted from the effects of the expected price level on the current wage rate. In Chapter 13 we will augment the Phillips curve of Figure 11-14 to take account of expected changes in the price level.

Figure 11-14 shows that the price level will keep changing unless $u = 0$. Therefore only at $u = 0$, or $Y = Y_p$, can the price level be constant. The long-run aggregate supply curve, showing the level of output consistent with a given price level in the long run, is therefore vertical at the level of potential output, Y_p.

We have now completed the derivation of the aggregate supply curve. Although we have had to simplify at every stage, and although the theory of aggregate supply is still in an unsettled state, the basic derivation we have presented is quite robust. Modifying it to take account of variable costs other than wages, of the slow pass-through of costs into prices, of possible variations in the markup, and so forth, will not change the basic outline of a supply curve that shows prices rising relatively little with output in the short run, and that is vertical in the long run. These are the essentials that are brought out by the analysis.

FIGURE 11-14 THE INFLATION-UNEMPLOYMENT PHILLIPS CURVE

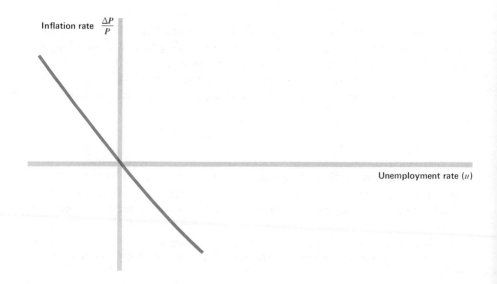

*11-7 MATERIALS PRICES AND SUPPLY SHOCKS

In this section we extend the aggregate supply framework to discuss an important analytical and practical issue: the treatment of materials prices and *supply shocks*. A supply shock is a disturbance to the economy arising on the supply side of the economy — as, for instance, the increase in food prices in 1973-1974, and, of primary importance, the increases in oil prices in 1973-1974 and 1979. The issue we have to discuss now is how to introduce materials prices — the prices of commodities like oil, zinc, or copper — into the analysis of aggregate supply. Our treatment of this issue makes a few critical simplifying assumptions, but even so, it will capture the essence of a supply shock.

The first step in introducing materials explicitly into the analysis is to recognize that materials are part of costs and that firms will take these costs into account in setting their prices. Next we note that as a matter of fact, materials prices are considerably more volatile than prices of finished goods and, in particular, that they rise relative to finished goods prices in expansions and fall during contractions. We represent this behaviour of material prices in Equation (15):

$$P_m = vP + vP\left(\frac{Y}{Y_p} - 1\right) \tag{15}$$

The equation states that materials prices are proportional to the general price level, P, but that they contain a cyclical element. When output is above normal, material prices rise relative to the price level, and when there is a contraction in output, they fall relative to the price level. The full-employment level of material prices is $P_m = vP$.[24]

Our discussion of the pricing behaviour of firms in the preceding sections already noted that firms base pricing decisions on normal costs, absorbing cyclical fluctuations in productivity. We will assume the same for materials prices, namely that firms base their pricing decisions on the average or cyclically adjusted price of materials, which we denote P_m' and which can be seen in Equation (15) to equal $P_m' = vP$.

The extended pricing rule by firms thus is based on labour cost and *normal* material costs:

$$P = bw + cP_m' \tag{16}$$

Substituting for the normal or full-employment material price, we obtain

$$P = bw + cvP \qquad cv < 1 \tag{17}$$

[24] The *real* price of materials, P_m/P, is: $P_m/P = vY/Y_p$. Thus the real price of materials exceeds or falls short of v depending on whether output is above or below normal.

or

$$P = \frac{b}{1 - cv} w \qquad (17a)$$

In the price equation the term c reflects the average use of materials per unit output and is taken as given in the short run. In the long run, though, it may well be a crucial parameter as an economy adjusts its technology to, for example, a change in the real price of oil.

From the revised pricing equation in (17), it is apparent that we are back to an equation like (7), provided the term $b/(1 - cv)$ remains constant. As long as that term is given, we can go ahead and substitute for wages and derive our aggregate supply schedule, the upward slope of which will reflect the cyclical movement of wages. Thus material prices will not make a fundamental difference to the aggregate supply schedule as long as two conditions are met. First, there is the assumption that firms absorb cyclical fluctuations in materials prices and price their goods on the basis of normal material costs. That assumption could easily be modified to allow for a cyclical effect of materials costs on prices. All the modification would do is make the aggregate supply schedule steeper (and nonlinear), as now both material prices and money wages rise during an expansion and fall in a contraction.[25] Second is the assumption that v remains constant, which we now modify.

An interesting application of our model concerns the case where there is an exogenous and permanent change in the real price of materials. The case in point is, of course, the oil price increase. How would we represent such a price increase in terms of our model? First we look at Equation (15) that shows material prices. An increase in the *real* price of materials implies that at each price level P, the price of materials is higher. Thus we can represent the increase in real materials prices as a rise in the factor of proportionality, v.[26]

The next step is to consider firms' adjustment to the increased real materials price. Since the materials price increase is considered permanent rather than transitory, firms will pass on the cost increase in the form of higher prices. In terms of Equation (17), we have an upward shift of the supply schedule at each level of wages.

In Figure 11-15 we show the effect of a materials price increase. We start at full employment with a price level P_0. Now a permanent increase in the real price of materials occurs. What happens to the aggregate supply schedule? At each level of output (and therefore of wages), costs rise and firms pass on the increased costs in the form of higher prices. Supply costs rise and therefore

---

[25] The interested student can verify this by substituting P_m as shown in Eq. (15) in place of P_m' in the price equation. Solving for the price level P will yield an expression that is more strongly cyclical than Eq. (17a).

[26] Check Eq. (15) to make sure an increase in v indeed raises P_m/P at any given level of (Y/Y_p).

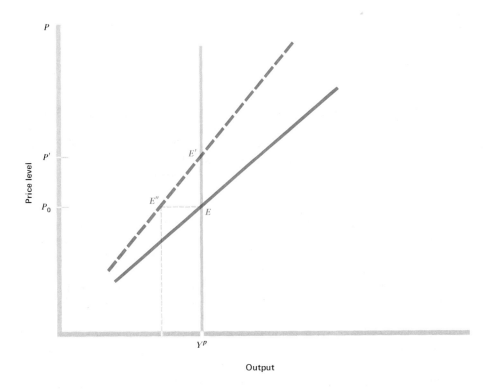

FIGURE 11-15 AN INCREASE IN THE PRICE OF MATERIALS

the whole aggregate supply schedule shifts upward. In addition, the supply curve becomes steeper.

A particularly interesting question, as we shall see in Chapter 15, is the policy choice for an economy faced with a supply shock such as the material price increase that shifts upward the aggregate supply schedule. One possibility is to attempt to maintain full employment at the cost of increased prices. This would correspond to an attempt to reach point E', and it would require an expansionary aggregate demand policy to accommodate the higher price level. Alternatively, there might be a strong preference for price stability and thus a point like E'' might be chosen. At E'', prices are held constant but output declines. Price stability is achieved by a recession sufficient to cut wage costs enough to offset the higher materials prices.

In either case the material price increase lowers real wages. This follows from Equation (17a) which can be rewritten as

$$\frac{w}{P} = \frac{1 - cv}{b} \tag{17b}$$

The important macroeconomic question is whether this *inevitable* fall in the real wage can be achieved with essentially stable prices or whether it takes inflation and recession — *stagflation* — to bring about the decline in real wages.

One conceivable adjustment to a materials price increase that is accepted as permanent is to have an offsetting reduction in domestic money wages so that the full-employment price level remains unchanged. (This also requires the use of aggregate demand policy, as we shall see in Chapter 12.) Alternatively, as already shown in Figure 11-15, we might have no change in money wages and therefore a rise in the level of prices.

11-8 PRODUCTIVITY, WAGES, AND PRICES

In this section we take up the issues of the effects of changes in productivity on prices in the short and long runs, and the behaviour of the profit rate.

We saw in Section 11-3 that productivity varies procyclically. The question then arises of whether prices should not reflect productivity changes. When output is low, productivity is low, and the cost of production per unit of output is therefore high. Similarly, when there are transitory decreases in productivity because of weather or other disturbances, would prices not be increased? The empirical evidence here is that firms base their pricing decisions on *normal* or *standard unit labour cost*, not on actual or current unit labour cost. That means that firms look at average or cyclically adjusted costs in setting prices. The pricing rule in Equation (7), $P = bw$, thus does not reflect movements in costs arising from productivity changes in the short run. These transitory fluctuations in costs are largely absorbed by firms. Prices are more stable than unit labour costs.

The stability of prices relative to unit labour costs holds for the aggregate price level. However, when we look at the structure of different markets, we find that the prices of some goods, such as agricultural products and raw materials, are very flexible and move more than unit costs. The prices of manufactured products tend to be much more stable. The reason for their stability is presumably the concern of the manufacturers for retaining customer goodwill. The distinction between the behaviour of prices in competitive and customer markets has been made by a number of economists, if not in exactly those words, and particularly by Arthur Okun.[27] The distinction is useful in thinking about the behaviour of the prices of different goods during the trade cycle, and in understanding the stickiness of some prices.

The response of prices to long-run changes in productivity is different from the response to short-run changes. Productivity grows over time as a

---

[27] Arthur Okun, "Inflation: Its Mechanics and Welfare Costs," *Brookings Papers on Economic Activity*, 1975:2 (Washington, D.C.: The Brookings Institution, 1975).

result of capital accumulation, learning, and new technology. The growth of productivity implies that as of given wages, costs per unit of output decline — with labour being more productive, it takes fewer hours to produce a unit of output. These permanent or trend increases in productivity do affect prices, since they change standard unit labour cost, as of a given nominal wage. But care is necessary here, since the wage itself is likely to adjust to the change in productivity. With labour being more productive, the neoclassical demand curve for labour in Figure 11-7 is likely to shift out to the right and the real wage will rise over time — as it has historically.[28]

We turn now to the third point in this section — the behaviour of the profit rate during the trade cycle. In particular, it is well known that profits tend to rise as the economy expands and to fall as the economy contracts. The behaviour of the profit rate is in fact fully consistent with the nonneoclassical theory of supply in this chapter. For we have noted that firms base their prices on normal unit costs. When there is an upswing, the productivity of labour increases and actual unit costs fall. But the prices firms charge change relatively little. Therefore their profits rise. Conversely, on the downswing, unit labour costs rise relative to prices and firms have reduced profits.

We make one further point here. As we noted, the term b in Equation (7) is the markup of prices on wages, or more generally, on variable costs. It might seem plausible that firms would increase the markup as the demand for their output increases, and decrease markup as demand falls. That would imply that the real wage would fall as output expands (because P is increasing relative to w). However, evidence on the behaviour of real wages during the trade cycle and of the markup is not yet definitive, and it is safest to say that there is no widely agreed-upon empirical evidence that the markup varies systematically with the cycle.[29]

11-9 SUMMARY

This chapter has covered a lot of very hard ground. The major point to be established was that output variations along the short-run aggregate supply schedule are accompanied by only moderate price increases. In the short run, the price level varies little with the level of output. Over time, however, wages, costs, and prices will keep rising if output is above normal and keep falling if output is below normal.

We summarize now the contents of the chapter.

1   The neoclassical theory of the demand for labour relates labour demand

---

[28] Chapter 16 will discuss the historical behaviour of productivity.

[29] See Robert J. Gordon, "Inflation in Recession and Recovery," *Brookings Papers on Economic Activity*, 1975:3 (Washington, D.C.: The Brookings Institution, 1975).

only to the real wage, given the quantity of other factors the firm is using. Competitive firms that are free to change the quantity of labour they use, costlessly and immediately, will hire labour up to the point where the real wage is equal to the marginal product of labour (MPN).

2   With wages and prices freely flexible, the equilibrium level of employment is determined in the labour market. The labour market is continuously in equilibrium at the full-employment level, and aggregate supply will therefore be the amount of output which that amount of labour produces. Given that the labour market is in equilibrium, the aggregate supply curve is vertical at the level of potential output – the aggregate supply is independent of the price level.

3   The aggregate supply theory we present starts from the recognition that it is costly for the firm to change the level of employment. In deciding how much labour to employ today, firms look ahead to the output level they expect to be producing in the future.

4   Firms accommodate temporary changes in demand largely by changing the amount of overtime their existing labour force works and by adjusting inventories.

5   The employment decision depends on both the real wage and the expected level of output. The expected level of output in turn depends on the full-employment level of output and the current level of output. Increases in expected output lead to increases in employment, and increases in the real wage reduce employment.

6   Current output affects current employment by affecting the expected level of output.

7   Nominal wages change in accordance with the state of excess demand in the labour market. When there is unemployment, wages fall, and when there is negative unemployment, wages rise. In this connection, it should be recalled that we abstract in this chapter from the existence of frictional unemployment.

8   Firms base the prices they charge on their costs of production. Thus, when wages rise because the level of employment is above the full-employment level, prices are increased too.

9   To assemble these elements: An increase in output is accompanied by an increase in prices. An increase in output resulting, say, from an increase in aggregate demand affects expected output, leading to an increase in employment. The increase in employment increases the nominal wage, which leads to some increase in the prices firms charge.

10 The full impact of changes in aggregate demand on prices occurs only over the course of time. A permanent increase in aggregate demand feeds slowly into an increased demand for labour, which in turn means wages rise slowly, which in turn means that prices are adjusted only over the course of time. If employment is somehow held above the full-employment level, wages and prices will continue to rise without end.

11   Material prices, along with wages, are a determinant of costs and prices. Firms base prices on normal or cyclically adjusted costs. Transitory changes in material prices are absorbed in profits. Permanent changes are passed on into changes in prices and therefore changes in real wages. Material price changes have been an important source of aggregate supply shocks.

12   Supply shocks, such as a material price increase, pose a difficult problem for macroeconomic policy. They can be accommodated through an expansionary aggregate demand policy with the effect of increased prices but stable output. Alternatively, they can be offset so that prices remain stable because of deflationary aggregate demand policy, but then output falls.

PROBLEMS

1   Using Figure 11-1, analyze the effects of an increase in the money stock on the price level and the level of output.

2   In problem 1, what happens to the level of real balances as a result of the increase in the nominal money stock?

3   Suppose a new method of production is invented which increases the marginal product of labour at each level of employment.
   (a) What effect does this have on the (neoclassical) demand for labour?
   (b) What effect does it have on the equilibrium real wage if the supply of labour is fixed and independent of the real wage?
   (c) How would your answer to 3(b) be affected if the supply of labour increased with the real wage?

4   Suppose that the new method of production increases the average product of labour at each level of employment as well as the marginal product, and revert to the assumption that labour supply is independent of the real wage.
   (a) What effect does the invention have on the equilibrium level of real output?
   (b) What effect does the invention have on the equilibrium price level? (You will have to use the aggregate demand diagram here.)
   (c) What effect does the invention have on the *nominal* wage?
   (d) How are your answers to 4(a), 4(b), and 4(c) affected if the supply of labour increases with the real wage?

5   What effect does a rightward shift in the supply curve of labour have on the aggregate supply curve, the equilibrium real wage, and the price level?

We move over now to the nonneoclassical aggregate supply curve developed in Sections 11-4 through 11-6.

6   (a) How do you account for the short-run behaviour of labour productivity?
   (b) What does the neoclassical model imply about the short-run behaviour of labour productivity, if one assumes that short-run fluctuations in output are accompanied by movements along a stable demand for labour curve of the sort presented in Figure 11-5?

7   (a) Given expected output, why does the real wage affect employment?
   (b) In the theory of aggregate supply presented in this chapter, how does the

real wage behave (does it go up or down?) when there is an increase in output?

8 Suppose that all firms believed that the current level of output Y, whatever its level, was the long-run level of output Y^e, so that the weight α in Equation (3) was one.

(a) How would that affect the slope of the aggregate supply curve? Be careful.

(b) Explain for what particular aspect of the behaviour of the economy in the short run the value of α in Equation (3) matters. Choose from (i) the slope of the aggregate supply curve, (ii) the behaviour of the real wage, (iii) the behaviour of labour productivity in the short run, and (iv) the behaviour of the money wage in the short run. Explain your answer.

9 Suppose the natural rate of unemployment is 5 percent. How would the rate of unemployment u, defined in Equation (6), be related to the officially published unemployment rate, u_f, that includes frictional unemployment?

10 (a) How does the variable ϵ affect the slope of the aggregate supply curve?
(b) How does the markup b affect the slope of the supply curve? Explain.

*11 How does an increase in materials prices P_m affect the aggregate supply curve?

*12 Assume, as in Section 11-5, that wages are the only variable cost. However, now assume that wages are passed on slowly into prices, so that Equation (7) is replaced by

$$P = b[cw + (1 - c)w_{-1}] \qquad 0 < c < 1 \qquad (7a)$$

Use Equation (7a) together with the other equations to derive the aggregate supply curve. Note that the position of the supply curve will depend on the lagged wage rate. How does the slope of the aggregate supply curve compare now with the case in the text, for which $c = 1$?

12

INCOME, PRICES, AND UNEMPLOYMENT

I n this chapter we combine aggregate supply, studied in Chapter 11, with aggregate demand, as studied in Chapter 4 and outlined in Chapter 11. The resulting analysis leads to the simultaneous determination of most of the important macroeconomic variables — the level of output, the price level, interest rates, and (un)employment.[1] This chapter, therefore, extends the analysis of Chapter 4 by explicitly introducing the price level as one of the variables to be determined. Recall that throughout Chapter 4 we took the price level P to be fixed. The price level is, of course, far from constant. The extension of the IS-LM analysis to examine the determination of the price level is therefore an extremely important step.

The analysis in this chapter further differs from the IS-LM framework in that it is essentially dynamic. The discussion of the supply side in the previous chapter introduced the distinction between the short-run and the long-run aggregate supply curves. That distinction is important in this chapter because it is the basis on which we distinguish between the short-run, intermediate-run, and long-run effects of monetary and fiscal policies on output and prices.

12-1 AGGREGATE DEMAND

In this section we derive the *aggregate demand function* in more detail than in Chapter 11. The aggregate demand function is a relationship between the planned level of real spending or demand for goods and the level of prices, *given* the quantity of money and fiscal policy. Since it is a relationship between the quantity of goods demanded and the price level, and since it will be seen to be downward-sloping, it looks like the regular demand curve of microeconomics. In this case, however, we consider the *aggregate*

---

[1] The only important macroeconomic variable that is not studied explicitly in this chapter is the inflation rate; its behaviour is analyzed in detail in Chapter 13.

demand for all goods and services as a function of the *aggregate* price level rather than the demand for a single good as a function of its (relative) price. Further, as we noted in Chapter 1, there is a lot behind the aggregate demand curve. It summarizes the equilibrium of both goods and assets markets.

In Chapter 4 we saw how the level of aggregate demand is determined by autonomous spending and the money stock. More formally, we can use the aggregate demand function, introduced in Equation (14) in Chapter 4:

$$Y = \beta\bar{A} + \gamma\frac{\bar{M}}{P} \tag{1}$$

$$\beta \equiv \frac{h\bar{\alpha}}{h + bk\bar{\alpha}} \qquad \gamma \equiv \frac{b\bar{\alpha}}{h + bk\bar{\alpha}}$$

where the terms β and γ are respectively the "multipliers" associated with fiscal and monetary policy and incorporate the interaction between goods and money markets. The term $\bar{A}$ denotes autonomous spending, including fiscal variables, $\bar{M}/P$ is the quantity of real balances, and Y is measured in *real* terms.

Equation (1) expresses the *joint* equilibrium of the goods and assets markets. It summarizes the basic results of Chapter 4: First, that the higher the level of autonomous spending (the further out to the right the *IS* curve), the higher the equilibrium level of income; and, second, that the higher the real money supply (the further to the right the LM curve), the higher the equilibrium level of income.

In deriving Equation (1), we explicitly assumed that any level of real output that was demanded could be produced, at the given price level. We thus ignored any constraints that might exist on aggregate supply. In this chapter, we shall explicitly consider the interaction of supply and demand. Accordingly, we do not treat Equation (1) as determining the level of output, but only as determining the level of demand *at a given price level*. If demand does not equal supply at that price level, then the price level is not an equilibrium price level and output is not at the equilibrium level either. The interaction of supply and demand determines the equilibrium levels of prices and real output, as shown in Chapter 11.

We shall now use Equation (1), together with the IS-LM analysis on which it is based, to study the relationship between the level of spending — the demand for goods — and the price level, given the nominal quantity of money and autonomous spending. It is obvious from inspection of Equation (1) that a higher price level implies lower real balances and therefore a lower equilibrium level of income and spending. This relationship is shown as the $Y^d(F,M/P)$ curve in Figure 12-1, where F represents the term $\beta\bar{A}$ in Equation (1).[2] To understand the relationship between aggregate demand and the price

---

[2] We use the symbol F to emphasize that fiscal variables affect the position of the aggregate demand curve by affecting the term $\beta\bar{A}$.

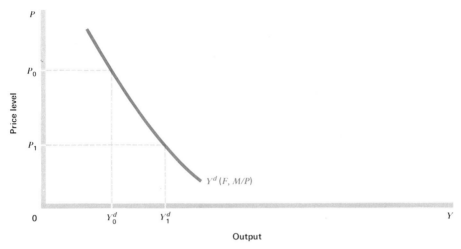

FIGURE 12-1 THE AGGREGATE DEMAND CURVE

level that is shown in Figure 12-1, we turn to the IS and LM curves that underlie that relationship.

In the upper panel of Figure 12-2 we show the familiar IS and LM schedules. In the lower panel we show the aggregate demand schedule. Consider first a price level P_0. Given fiscal policy, we have an IS curve. A given nominal quantity of money together with the price level P_0 will imply a quantity of real balances M/P_0 and an associated LM_0 curve. The equilibrium level of income is Y_0^d. Accordingly, we show point E_0 in the lower panel as one point on the aggregate demand schedule, or one combination of price and output levels such that both the goods market and money market are in equilibrium.

Consider next a lower price level P_1. Given the nominal quantity of money, the decline in the price level raises *real* balances to M/P_1, and therefore shifts the LM schedule to the right to LM'. The LM schedule shifts down and to the right because in order to induce the public to hold a larger quantity of real balances, income would have to be higher or interest rates would have to be lower. The new equilibrium level of income and spending is Y_1^d, and we record E_1 as another point on the aggregate demand schedule in the lower panel. The schedule of points on the aggregate demand curve in the lower panel is obtained by considering all possible price levels. It is the schedule generated by the intersection of the IS and LM curves as the price level changes, namely, $Y^d(F,M/P)$ in Figure 12-1, that we refer to as the aggregate demand schedule. It is clear from the way we have derived the schedule that we can think of it as a *market equilibrium* schedule — the locus of points along which *both* the money market and the goods market are in equilibrium, given the value of autonomous spending and the nominal money supply.

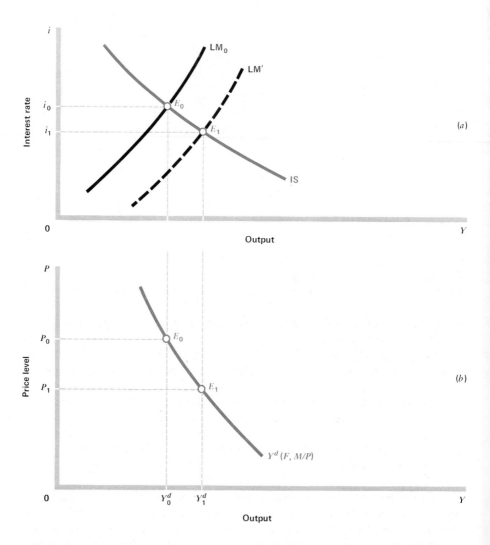

FIGURE 12-2 THE AGGREGATE DEMAND CURVE AS DERIVED FROM THE IS AND LM CURVES

Before we conclude this section, we want to give an economic interpretation of the aggregate demand relationship. Suppose that the goods and money markets are initially in equilibrium, so that we are at a point on the aggregate demand curve. Then let the price level increase. The higher price level reduces real balances and thereby creates an excess demand for real money balances at the given level of income. The excess demand for real balances raises interest rates. The increase in interest rates in turn reduces real spending by discouraging investment, and therefore leads to a decline in the equilibrium level of income. Thus the initial price increase leads to a decline in demand, so that the aggregate demand curve is negatively sloped.

There are two critical points to remember about the aggregate demand curve. The first is that autonomous spending and the nominal money supply are held constant as we move along the schedule. The second point can be seen by noting that the interest rate at E_1 in Figure 12-2 is lower than the interest rate at E_0 — the point is that the interest rate declines as the level of income rises along the aggregate demand curve. The declining interest rate derives from the fact that with a given *nominal* quantity of money, a decline in the price level implies an increase in *real* balances. This increase in real balances lowers interest rates. The lower interest rate in turn raises investment spending and has an expansionary effect on aggregate demand and income. Thus, as we move down the aggregate demand curve, a falling rate of interest accompanies a rising level of real demand and a falling price level.

12-2 PROPERTIES OF THE AGGREGATE DEMAND SCHEDULE

There are two sets of questions we look at here: First, what determines the slope of the aggregate demand schedule? Second, how does the aggregate demand schedule shift in response to changes in fiscal policy and the nominal money supply?

The Slope of the Aggregate Demand Curve

The answer to the first question is fortunately very easy. We can draw on considerations developed in the discussion of monetary policy in Chapter 4. We asked there what determines the effectiveness of monetary policy — the increase in income associated with an increase in the money supply. We studied that question by increasing the money supply at a given price level, that is, by increasing the real money supply. The slope of the aggregate demand schedule in Figure 12-2 reflects the answer to exactly the same question. The reason that the question is the same is that Figure 12-2 relates a change in the real money supply to the resulting change in the equilibrium level of income and spending. However, this time the real money supply changes because the price level changes. The amount by which a given change in prices, and therefore in the real money supply changes the equilibrium level of income and spending depends primarily on the response of money demand to the interest rate and the response of aggregate spending to the interest rate.

A low interest response of money demand and a high interest response of aggregate spending ensure a large effect of real money changes on output. The reason, as will be remembered from Chapter 4, is that a low interest response of money demand implies that a given change in real balances brings about a large change in interest rates. Given a change in interest rates, a large interest response of aggregate spending serves to translate the interest reduction into a large increase in spending. It follows, therefore, that the aggregate demand schedule is relatively flat — large changes in income and spending are associated with small changes in the price level — if monetary policy is very effective, that is, if the interest response of money demand is low and the interest response of spending is high.

The slope of the aggregate demand curve depends also on the multiplier $\bar{\alpha}$. Other things equal, a given reduction in the price level and an increase in real balances give rise to a larger increase in income and spending, the larger the multiplier or the larger the marginal propensity to spend. Accordingly, a large multiplier serves to flatten the aggregate demand function.[3]

The Effects of Monetary and Fiscal Policy Changes on the Aggregate Demand Curve

We turn now to the second question, which asks about the effects of changes in fiscal policy and the nominal money supply on the location of the aggregate demand curve. We are now examining the effects of variables that cause the entire aggregate demand curve to *shift*. In Section 12-1, by contrast, we were considering only movements along a *given* aggregate demand curve on which fiscal variables and the nominal money supply are kept constant. Before we proceed to a detailed graphical examination of the effects of an increase in the nominal money stock or expansionary fiscal policy on the aggregate demand curve, it is worth stepping back for a moment to ask what we expect to find.

We already know from Chapter 4 and Equation (1) that an increase in the nominal money supply increases aggregate demand as of a fixed price level. Thus we should expect an increase in the nominal money supply to shift the aggregate demand curve of Figure 12-1 outward, reflecting the increase in the demand for goods at a given price level that is caused by the change in the money stock. Similarly, we know that expansionary fiscal policy, such as an increase in government spending or a reduction in taxes, increases aggregate demand at a given price level. Accordingly, expansionary fiscal policy should also be expected to shift the aggregate demand curve outward.

We will now examine the effect of the policy changes in more detail. In Figure 12-3 we show the effects on the aggregate demand curve of an increase in the nominal quantity of money. Similarly, in Figure 12-4 we show the effects of an increase in government spending.

Consider first an increase in the nominal quantity of money. We are asking the following question: What is the effect of an increase in the nominal quantity of money on the equilibrium level of income and spending

---

[3] It will be useful for you to show the above propositions on the slope of the aggregate demand curve using Figure 12-2. See problem 2 at the end of the chapter.

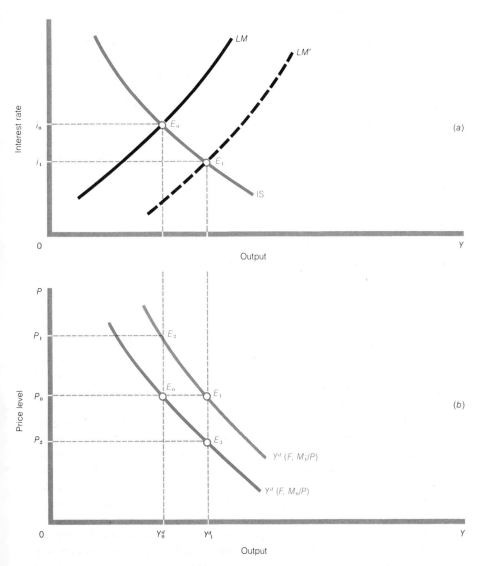

FIGURE 12-3 THE SHIFT IN THE AGGREGATE DEMAND CURVE DUE TO AN INCREASE IN THE NOMINAL MONEY SUPPLY ($M_1 > M_0$)

at a given price level P_0? The answer to that question will be the shift in the aggregate demand schedule. We know that for a given price level, an increase in the nominal quantity of money implies an increase in the real quantity of money. There is, therefore, a rightward shift in the LM curve to LM', as in the upper panel of Figure 12-3. As a consequence, the equilibrium level of income rises to Y_1^d. What happens is that at a given level of prices P_0, the higher nominal quantity of money implies a higher real quantity of money and therefore lower interest rates and higher equilibrium income and spending. We record this fact in the lower panel of Figure 12-3 by noting that point E_1 is a point on the new aggregate demand schedule.

The initial equilibrium price level was chosen arbitrarily. We could have started with any price level and thereby shown that the entire aggregate demand schedule shifts to the right.

There is an alternative and important way of recognizing the same point. When the nominal money supply increases, we could ask by how much the equilibrium price level would have to rise, at each level of income and spending, in order for aggregate demand to remain unchanged. It is clear from Equation (1) that aggregate demand would remain unchanged if the real money supply remained unchanged. Given an increase in the nominal money supply, we would therefore require prices to increase in such a way that M/P remains constant. In terms of Figure 12-3, this implies that an increase in the nominal money supply shifts the aggregate demand schedule up in exactly the same proportion as the increase in the nominal money stock. Thus the ratio P_1/P_0 in Figure 12-3 is the same as the ratio P_0/P_2, and each ratio is equal to M_1/M_0. This upward shift reflects an essential characteristic of aggregate demand. namely, that an equiproportionate increase in money and prices leaves the real money supply and therefore interest rates and real spending unchanged.[4]

Consider next the effect of an expansionary fiscal policy on the aggregate demand schedule. In Figure 12-4 we show that an expansionary fiscal policy in the form of increased government purchases or reduced taxes leads to an upward shift of the IS curve and a resulting increase in real income. At a given price level P_0, the fiscal expansion raises the equilibrium level of income and spending. In the lower graph this fact is recorded by point E_1 as a point on the new aggregate demand schedule. Since we could have started with any price level and corresponding LM curve in the upper panel, it is immediately apparent that, corresponding to the easier fiscal policy, we have a new aggregate demand schedule that lies everywhere to the right of the initial schedule. In fact, the rightward shift of the aggregate demand schedule at each price level, $\beta\Delta\bar{A}$, is related to the multiplier β in the equation for equilibrium aggregate demand, Equation (1). From the definition of β, it is apparent that the shift in the aggregate demand curve is larger, the larger the interest response of money demand, the lower the interest response of aggregate spending, and the smaller the income response of money demand.

Before proceeding, we summarize here the main points about aggregate

---

[4] As a technical point, we refer to this property of the aggregate demand function as *homogeneity* of degree zero in money and prices. This means that an equiproportionate increase in money and prices leaves *real* demand unchanged.

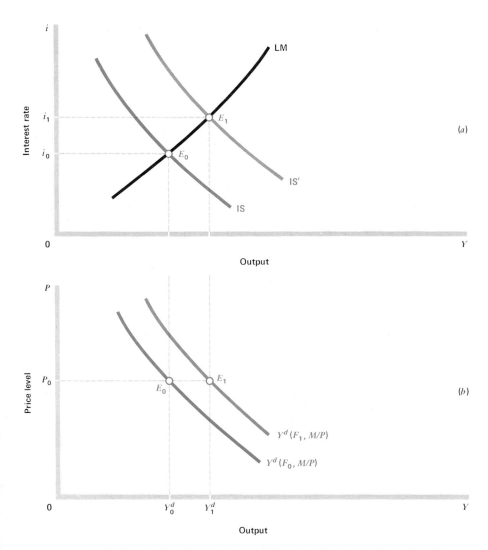

FIGURE 12-4 A SHIFT IN THE AGGREGATE DEMAND SCHEDULE DUE TO INCREASED GOVERNMENT SPENDING ($F_1 > F_0$)

demand: (1) The concept of aggregate demand provides a relation between equilibrium level of income and spending and the level of prices. (2) The aggregate demand schedule is negatively sloped because a reduction in the price level raises real balances, reduces interest rates, and thereby raises the equilibrium level of income and spending. (3) An increase in the nominal quantity of money, or an expansionary fiscal policy, shifts the aggregate demand schedule up and to the right; equivalently, an expansionary monetary or fiscal policy raises the equilibrium level of income and spending at each level of prices.

12-3 THE INTERACTION OF AGGREGATE DEMAND AND AGGREGATE SUPPLY

As in Chapter 11, we now combine aggregate demand and supply to derive the full equilibrium of the system, including supply constraints. In Figure 12-5, we draw the aggregate demand schedule corresponding to a given fiscal policy and nominal quantity of money. The short-run aggregate supply curve was derived in Chapter 11. Its positive slope reflects the sluggish adjustment of wages to output changes.[5] The long-run supply curve is vertical and corresponds to the vertical Y_pY_p line at the level of potential output.

As we have drawn it, the initial equilibrium at E is one of underemployment. Output is below the level of potential output and, accordingly, the level of unemployment is above normal. How does the economy adjust over time from the equilibrium at point E? The high level of unemployment at E will imply declining wages. Declining wages in turn reduce costs and shift the supply schedule down and to the right over time. The downward shift in

[5] Recall that the aggregate supply curve developed in Chapter 11 explicitly does *not* take account of the role of expected inflation in affecting wages. We examine the very important role of expected inflation in Chapter 13.

FIGURE 12-5 THE INTERACTION OF AGGREGATE DEMAND AND SUPPLY

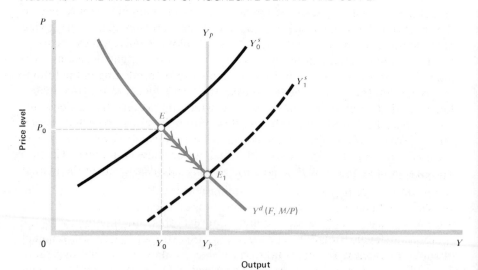

the supply schedule in turn causes equilibrium prices to decline, real balances to rise, interest rates to fall, and aggregate spending to increase. The adjustment process is therefore one of falling prices and increasing aggregate spending. The process of adjustment is represented by the arrows along the aggregate demand curve in Figure 12-5, which you will recognize as equivalent to Figure 11-3. This *automatic* process will continue until prices have declined sufficiently (and wages also declined sufficiently) for aggregate demand to support the full-employment level of output Y_1, at point E_1.

There is a critical lesson here. The point is that the levels of output and employment depend on aggregate demand which in turn depends on the real money supply, as we have seen in Equation (1). If wages are sluggish in the short run, then the real money supply (given the nominal supply of money) cannot rise fast enough to support full employment. Only over time and with protracted unemployment will wages decline to lower prices and raise real balances sufficiently to support full employment. In a world of perfect wage and price flexibility, we would always be at full employment. With sluggish wages and prices, by contrast, there is no assurance that we are always at full employment. Consequently, monetary and fiscal stabilization policy may be called upon to improve the macroeconomic performance implied by this *automatic* adjustment process.

Specifically, if aggregate demand, *at the current level of prices*, is insufficient to support the full-employment level of output as at point E in Figure 12-5, an expansion in aggregate demand is called for. As we saw earlier an expansion in the nominal quantity of money, or expansionary fiscal policy, would, by shifting the aggregate demand schedule, raise equilibrium income and spending at each level of prices. Expansionary aggregate demand policies can therefore be used to support full employment at the prevailing level of wages. In terms of Figure 12-5, expansionary policies shift the $Y^d(F, M/P)$ curve up and to the right. We have seen how the economy can undergo deflation to adjust the level of wages and prices to the prevailing quantity of money to reach the equilibrium at E_1. Alternatively, we may use monetary and fiscal policy to shift the aggregate demand curve to the right and thus move output to its full-employment level at the given wage rate.

There is a compelling logic to the argument that we should adapt the level of the nominal quantity of money to the prevailing level of wages and prices, rather than use unemployment or inflation to adapt wages and prices to whatever is the quantity of money. In the next two sections we shall study in considerably more detail how monetary policy and fiscal policy work in this more complete model. In particular, we are interested in the distinction between short-run and long-run effects of policies. The crucial point we shall make is that in the short run, both monetary and fiscal policy can be expansionary. In the long run, neither is expansionary, although fiscal policy retains some important real effects.

12-4 MONETARY POLICY

In this section, we examine the effects of an increase in the money stock. In Figure 12-6, we show the effect of an increase in the nominal quantity of money from M_0 to M_1 as a rightward shift in the aggregate demand schedule. As was shown in Figure 12-3, the aggregate demand schedule shifts upward in the same proportion as the increase in the nominal quantity of money. In Figure 12-6, we start with equilibrium at E, where output is at its potential level. In the short run, the increase in the money supply creates excess demand for goods at the initial price level. The excess demand in turn gives rise to an expansion in output and an increase in prices. The position of short-run equilibrium is at point E_1, where aggregate demand equals short-run supply. E_1 is also a point at which output exceeds potential output.

It is important to go behind the schedules for a moment to examine again the factors that account for the change in *real* output as a consequence of a change in the *nominal* quantity of money. On the supply side, the basic factor is the slow adjustment of nominal wages. The more sluggish the wages, the flatter the aggregate supply schedule and, accordingly, the larger the short-run expansion in output. Thus we retain the result from the supply side that sluggish wages imply that an increase in prices allows an expansion in real output.

FIGURE 12-6 THE EFFECTS OF MONETARY EXPANSION IN THE AGGREGATE DEMAND AND SUPPLY MODEL

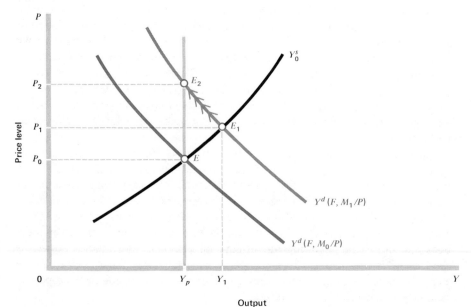

On the aggregate demand side, we note that an increase in the nominal money stock also increases the real money stock *provided* prices do not rise to offset fully the increase in the nominal money supply. We recall from Section 12-2 that the increase in the nominal money supply shifts the aggregate demand schedule up in the same proportion as the increase in the money stock. Thus $(P_2 - P_0)/P_0$ in Figure 12-6 is the proportionate increase in the money stock. Since in the short run prices increase by only $(P_1 - P_0)/P_0$, we clearly have an increase in real balances. The increase in real balances causes a reduction in interest rates and, therefore, an increase in real aggregate demand. The fact that prices increase proportionately less than nominal money accounts for the expansion in real demand that sustains the higher level of output. At point E_1, therefore, we have a lower interest rate than at E, and that decline in the interest rate accounts for the higher level of real aggregate demand.

However, the short-run equilibrium at point E_1 is only transitory. The process of the shifting of the supply curve, caused by rising wages induced by overemployment, sets in, as in Figure 12-5. How long will the process continue? Wages will continue rising as long as output is above potential. So the supply schedule will keep shifting until point E_2 is reached. At that point, output has returned to normal: wages, prices, and the nominal quantity of money *all* have increased in the same proportion. All real variables, including output and interest rates, have returned to their initial equilibrium.

The property of the economy whereby changes in the nominal quantity of money affect only nominal variables (the price level and wages), leaving all real variables unchanged, is referred to as the *neutrality of money*. We have just seen that money is neutral in the long run for an economy starting at full employment. We saw in Section 12-3 that when the economy is not initially at full employment, it adjusts over time until full employment is reached. Thus, even if the economy does not start at full employment, an increase in the money stock is neutral in the long run since it has no long-run effects on real variables. While it should be well understood that money is neutral in the long run, it should also be understood that monetary expansion causes an increase in output in the short run. Thus, money is not neutral in the short run. Accordingly, monetary policy can be used as a tool of stabilization policy to affect the behaviour of real variables, such as the levels of output and unemployment.

12-5 FISCAL POLICY

Consider next the effects of an expansionary fiscal policy. Referring to Figure 12-7, we again start with a full employment equilibrium at point E with output at its potential level Y_p. An expansion in government purchases or a cut in taxes will shift the aggregate demand schedule to the right and thus create an excess demand for goods at the initial level of prices. The resulting increase in output and prices serves to clear markets and establish

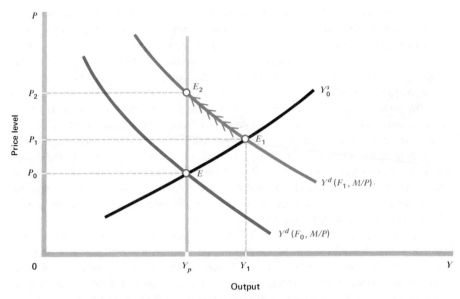

FIGURE 12-7 THE EFFECTS OF EXPANSIONARY FISCAL POLICY

a short-run equilibrium at point E_1. On the supply side, as in the discussion of monetary policy, we note that the sluggishness of wages allows an expansion in output and employment when prices rise. On the aggregate demand side at point E_1, a higher level of real spending is sustained by a higher level of government spending, or higher autonomous private spending due to tax cuts.

An important question concerns the interest rate at point E_1. Unlike the case of a monetary expansion, the interest rate at point E_1 is actually higher than at point E. It has increased to maintain balance between the demand for and supply of real balances. To establish that point, we observe that the increase in prices between E and E_1 implies that we have a lower quantity of real balances. Further, the expansion in output causes an increase in real money demand. To reduce the demand for real money to the new lower level of real supply, we clearly require a higher interest rate.

In the short run, a fiscal expansion raises output and employment. As in the case of monetary expansion, it will be more expansionary the flatter the aggregate supply curve — equivalently, the lower the responsiveness of costs to an expansion in output. Now consider again the adjustments that arise from the reduction in unemployment below normal. The resulting wage pressure will raise costs and thereby shift up the supply schedule. Again, the resulting price increase will reduce the real money supply, raise interest rates, and reduce real spending. In consequence, we will move up and along the aggregate demand schedule from E_1 to E_2 until output has returned to the potential level.

The next question to ask is, what will have happened once we return to the potential output level at E_2? It is apparent from Figure 12-7 that prices will have risen. The higher level of prices, given money, will have raised interest rates just sufficiently to reduce private real spending by exactly the increase in government spending. It is therefore true that, with long-run output given, increased purchases (absorption) of goods by the government leave fewer resources available for private purchases. The process by which the private sector is *crowded out*[6] in the long run is through higher prices and therefore higher interest rates.

The fact that, in the long run, private sector spending is displaced by increased government spending is entirely a consequence of the assumption that long-run output is fixed, so that if the government absorbs more, less is left to the private sector. This long-run crowding-out feature does not imply, however, that in the short run, government spending is ineffective in expanding output and aggregate demand. Again, it is critical to bear in mind that the long-run equilibrium is primarily an indication of a position to which the economy will adjust, given enough time. It should not be thought of as the point toward which the economy moves as the immediate short-run consequence of expansionary fiscal policy. It is true that the long-run interpretation of this model confirms the view that increased government spending always occurs at the expense of private real spending. While this

[6] Crowding out was defined in Chapter 4. As an exercise, show the effect of a tax cut on the long-run level and composition of private spending.

FIGURE 12-8 THE LONG-RUN EFFECT OF FISCAL EXPANSION ON INTEREST RATES

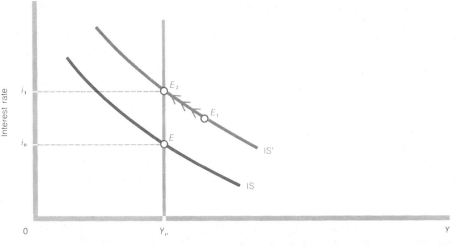

view may be correct in the long run,[7] it does not establish the case against active fiscal policy as a tool of short-run stabilization.

The relationship between fiscal policy and interest rates can be inferred too from Figure 12-8, which includes the familiar IS curve. We have drawn in the initial IS schedule and the IS' schedule corresponding to the increase in government spending. We also include a vertical line indicating potential output. Starting from the initial equilibrium at point E, the fiscal expansion first raises output and interest rates to some point like E_1. Subsequently, the rising prices cause the LM schedule (not drawn) to shift up and to the left so that the equilibrium moves along the IS' schedule until potential output is reestablished. At that point, the interest rate will have risen just enough to restore goods market equilibrium at the initial level of output.

12-6 THE BUDGET AND MACROECONOMIC EQUILIBRIUM

In Chapter 10, we considered the government's budget constraint and noted that a deficit can be financed either by borrowing from the private sector or by increasing the stock of high-powered money through the sale of debt to the Bank of Canada. In this section we consider the effects on the economy of the two alternative methods of financing an increase in government spending or reduction in taxes.

In this context it is important to distinguish between a temporary or transitory deficit and a continuing or permanent one. Here we confine our analysis to transitory deficits. The case of a permanent deficit is taken up in Chapter 13 where we deal with the process of continuing inflation.

Deficit Finance by Money Creation

The case of a transitory budget deficit financed by money creation is illustrated in Figure 12-9. The effect is to permanently raise the price level, even though the increase in government spending does not persist. Government spending by assumption reverts to its initial level after one period. However, that transitory government spending is financed by creation of money and that increase in the money stock is permanent. As we saw in Section 12-4, an increase in the stock of money permanently raises the long-run price level.

Now consider the argument in more detail, using Figure 12-9 and starting from full equilibrium at point E. The initial increase in government spending will shift the aggregate demand schedule out and to the right to Y_1^q because the demand for goods and services is raised. The effect of increased

---

[7] We say "may be" because we have here disregarded the effects of fiscal policy on the rate of investment and thus on the capital stock. See the problem set in Chapter 16 for further discussion.

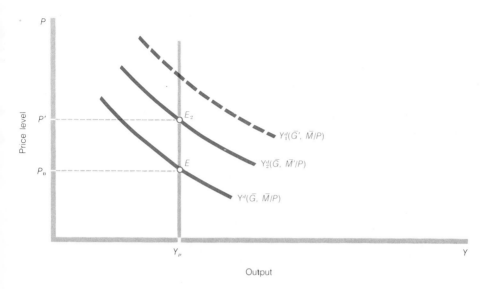

FIGURE 12-9 THE EFFECT OF A MONEY-FINANCED TRANSITORY INCREASE IN GOVERNMENT SPENDING

spending in the short run is to raise output and prices.[8] If we ignored the financing of the deficit, we would conclude that the economy returns to point E once government spending declines to its initial level. In fact, however, the government spending, when financed by money creation, gives rise to an increase in the stock of money that will remain even after the government spending falls back to the initial level. The effect of that increase in the money stock, with government spending back at the initial level $\bar{G}$, is shown by the aggregate demand schedule Y_2^d. We are not concerned here with the adjustment process but, rather, with the long-run effects. These can be directly inferred from Figure 12-9 by recognizing that output in the long run will be unaffected by the money-financed transitory government spending. Accordingly, with output at the level Y' the long-run effect of the financing is to raise prices to the level P'. A transitory money-financed deficit thus leads to a permanent increase in the level of prices. Note that the analysis implies that fiscal and monetary policy are interrelated through the financing of deficits.

Private Sector Financing of the Deficit

The case of a transitory budget deficit financed by borrowing from the

---

[8] The levels of output and prices in the short run would be given by the intersection of the Y_1^d curve and a short-run aggregate supply curve (not shown).

private sector is illustrated in Figure 12-10. We shall refer to this method as debt financing.

The initial effect of an increase in government spending is to move the aggregate demand curve out to Y_1^d from its initial position at Y^d. The extra government spending is financed by selling debt to the private sector. Thus the private sector accumulates government debt over the period during which government spending is at its higher level. Now, what effect does that higher stock of government debt held by the private sector have on aggregate demand?

Individuals holding government bonds regard those bonds as part of their wealth. Thus it would seem that, given the level of income, aggregate demand should rise when the stock of government bonds rises, because individuals holding those bonds have higher wealth. The higher wealth increases consumption demand.[9] Accordingly, the aggregate demand curve would shift out to the right as a result of the increase in privately held wealth. Hence, we show the final aggregate demand curve — after government spending has returned to its original level — at Y_2^d, above the initial curve Y^d. The difference between the two aggregate demand schedules Y^d

[9] Recall the discussion of wealth as a factor in consumption spending in Chapter 5.

FIGURE 12-10 EFFECT OF A TEMPORARY INCREASE IN GOVERNMENT SPENDING FINANCED BY BORROWING FROM THE PUBLIC and Y_2^d arises from the higher stock of government bonds $\bar{B}'$, compared to $\bar{B}$ on the initial aggregate demand curve. Since the effects of the higher wealth in consumption demand are likely to be small, we show the final aggregate demand curve Y_2^d below the aggregate demand curve Y_1^d.

There are two complications to this analysis. The first is that the existence of the higher stock of debt raises the amount of interest payments in the federal budget. If the budget was originally balanced at point E, it may not be balanced at E_2. Of course, since the price level at E_2 is higher than at E, tax receipts may have risen at E_2 compared with E, and perhaps the budget would be balanced. But it need not be. If it were not, then further financing of the deficit would have to be undertaken, and that would have subsequent effects on the equilibrium. We postpone the discussion of a permanent deficit to Chapter 13.

The second complication was discussed in Chapter 10. As was pointed out there, it is possible that individuals in the economy calculate their wealth taking into account the tax payments they will have to make in the future. Suppose that everyone believed that the national debt would eventually be paid off. Then everyone would know that at some point in the future, the federal government would have to run a surplus. Individuals might think the federal government would at some future date have to raise taxes in order to pay off the debt. To that extent an increase in the debt would increase their wealth and at the same time suggest to them that their taxes would be higher in the future. The net effect on aggregate demand might then be zero. The issue raised by this argument is sometimes posed by the question, "Are government bonds wealth?"

There is another way of looking at this argument. Now, instead of concentrating on wealth, we concentrate on disposable income. An increase in the debt raises disposable income for the private sector because it raises the interest payments the private sector receives. The federal government has to finance those interest payments in some way. Suppose that it financed them by raising taxes or reducing other transfer payments. Then disposable income would be unaffected, despite the higher debt. Consumption demand in this case would be little affected by the increase in the national debt. With such a combined change in the debt and taxes that leaves the budget balanced in the long run, the aggregate demand curve would return to its initial position at Y^d. There would be no (or little) long-run effect from the higher debt if the higher debt did not result in an unbalanced budget.

The theoretical and empirical issue of whether an increase in the national debt increases aggregate demand is not yet settled. It is difficult to isolate the effects of changes in the debt on consumption demand in empirical studies of consumption. The theoretical arguments we have are not conclusive. We are not certain whether individuals do take account of their future tax liabilities when they calculate their wealth. Thus we have to leave this question in an unresolved state.

There is one important difference between debt financing and money financing of a given short-run budget deficit. Money financing of the deficit tends to reduce the interest rate in the short run compared with debt financing. That is because money financing increases the nominal money stock, whereas debt financing does not. In the short run, then, debt financing reduces the level of investment compared with money financing. That is one of the issues connected with the crowding-out question that we studied in Chapter 4.

We want also to compare the effects on the price level of money and debt financing of a temporary increase in government spending. There is no question that the price level is higher with money financing than with debt financing. There are two reasons. First, money financing increases the money stock and debt financing does not. The higher the money stock, the greater the aggregate demand at any given price level. Second, we attributed a price level rise in the case of debt financing to the wealth effect of a greater stock of debt on consumption. While there is some argument about whether bonds are wealth, there is no question that money is wealth. So the wealth effect on consumption is larger in the case of money financing than debt financing. That, too, means that aggregate demand at any given price level will be higher with money than with debt financing.

We now summarize the effects of a temporary budget deficit financed by debt creation. Such financing probably increases aggregate demand but, because of the possible effects of anticipated future tax liabilities on consumption, that is not certain. Debt financing, starting from a balanced budget and if not compensated for by higher taxes or reductions in other transfer payments, leads to a permanent deficit in the budget. Debt financing raises the interest rate and reduces investment in the short run as compared with the effects of money financing.

12-7 DISTURBANCES, POLICY RESPONSE, AND SUPPLY MANAGEMENT

The preceding discussion prepares us for an analysis of macroeconomic disturbances and policy responses. Now that we have extended the IS-LM framework to include aggregate supply as well as aggregate demand, we can consider disturbances that arise either on the supply or the demand side of the economy. On the demand side, we can consider disturbances such as autonomous changes in money demand or shifts in the consumption or investment functions. Each such change will shift the aggregate demand function and therefore disturb the macroeconomic equilibrium. On the supply side, we can look at disturbances, such as exogenous increases in materials costs or changes in taxes on goods or labour, that shift the supply schedule.

The extension of our basic IS-LM framework to include supply considerations allows us to discuss the new interest in fiscal policy as a tool of *supply management*. This view holds that fiscal policy in the form of variations in indirect taxes or payroll taxes can be used to offset supply disturbances, while both monetary and fiscal policy can be used to maintain aggregate demand at the full-employment level of output.

We will now go through the effects of an increase in payroll taxes on aggregate supply. The analysis will show that the supply side effects of such a policy are to *increase* prices and *reduce* output. Accordingly, a *cut* in payroll taxes can be used as a stimulative, and relative to other tax cuts, noninflationary stabilization policy.

To explore this view of fiscal policy effects on aggregate supply, we consider the case of an increase in payroll taxes, that is, taxes on wages. When there is a tax on wages, the wage paid to workers is less than the wage paid by employers. We assume that the wage paid to workers adjusts only with changes in the unemployment rate. More technically, we assume that in the short run the *incidence* of the payroll tax is on employers. Accordingly, an increase in labour costs due to payroll taxes will lead firms to pass on that cost increase in the form of higher prices. It follows that the supply schedule shifts up and to the left at each level of output. In Figure 12-11, we show that an increase in payroll taxes causes the economy to move from its initial equilibrium at point E to a new equilibrium at point E_1 with higher prices and lower output. An increase in payroll taxes raises prices because it raises costs, given the wage rate. Output declines because the cost and price increases reduce the real money supply, raise interest rates, and therefore reduce real spending.

FIGURE 12-11 THE SUPPLY EFFECT OF A PAYROLL TAX INCREASE

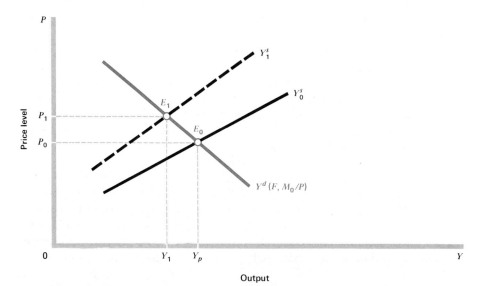

Output

In Figure 12-11, we have *not* considered a second aspect of the payroll tax increase that operates on the aggregate demand side. A payroll tax increase obviously reduces disposable income at each level of output, since the government now collects more taxes. As a result, aggregate demand declines at each level of output unless this deflationary effect is offset by increased transfers or increased government spending. In the absence of such compensating policies, the aggregate demand schedule would therefore shift to the left in Figure 12-11 and further add to the output reduction, but at the same time make the effect on the price level ambiguous.

The preceding discussion suggests two questions about the choice of fiscal policies. First, there is the question of comparing payroll taxes, which have both supply and demand effects, with other fiscal policy instruments, such as changes in government spending or transfers. Second, there is the question of determining what type of disturbances would be best countered by policies that have supply effects and what type of disturbances should be countered mainly by aggregate demand policies.

The answers to these questions must rely on the general principal that policies should be geared as closely as possible to the disturbances they are supposed to offset. Thus, for aggregate demand disturbances, say an autonomous reduction in investment, the appropriate response is an aggregate demand policy. These policies, if timely and precisely set up, will maintain aggregate demand close to full employment and keep the price level constant. They therefore prevent the need to adjust output and prices to a transitory change in aggregate demand. We note also that in the case of aggregate demand variations, policies that mainly affect aggregate supply are inappropriate. They are inappropriate because they may stimulate output in the right direction but they do so at the cost of changing prices.

Consider next a disturbance that arises entirely on the supply side. Assume a temporary increase in raw material prices that raises costs and thus shifts the aggregate supply schedule upward. In the absence of policy changes, we would experience both an increase in prices and a reduction in equilibrium output, as shown in Figure 12-11. An appropriate policy response would be, for example, a cut in payroll taxes. The payroll tax cut would exert an offsetting effect by reducing costs, thus leaving the supply schedule unaffected. Again we remember, however, that the payroll tax cut reduces tax revenue and therefore exerts an expansionary effect on aggregate demand. To neutralize this side affect of the tax cut, we would require an offsetting cut in government spending or a cut in transfers.

It is clear from the preceding discussion that certain fiscal policy measures may be useful in coping with supply disturbances. This potential role in offsetting supply disturbances has led to the suggestion that supply management be used as a systematic part of macroeconomic stabilization policy. Fiscal policy changes in the form of payroll and indirect tax changes could, according to this new policy view, be used to offset inflationary supply shocks, while aggregate demand policies would continue to be used to maintain full employment.[10]

It is fair to say that there has been relatively little experience with fiscal policy as a tool of price and supply management. Nevertheless, the concept is intriguing.[11] Because there are at least three macroeconomic policy targets — full employment, price stability, and growth — successful stabilization policy may well require the use of fiscal policies that operate on aggregate supply as well as monetary and fiscal policies that affect both the level and composition of aggregate demand.

Yet another aspect of the new *supply side economics* emphasizes the impact of taxes on labour supply, capital formation, and productivity and hence on potential output. This aspect is taken up in chapter 16.

12-7 SUMMARY

1   The aggregate demand function describes the equilibrium relationship between aggregate spending and the price level. The equilibrium in question is the simultaneous equilibrium of the goods and assets markets.

2   The aggregate demand curve slopes downward because an *increase* in the price level reduces real balances, increases the interest rate, and thereby *reduces* aggregate spending.

3   The aggregate demand curve is shifted up and to the right by an increase in the money stock or expansionary fiscal policy. At a given level of output, the aggregate demand curve shifts up in exactly the same proportions as the nominal money supply increases.

4   The short-run equilibrium of the economy is determined by the intersection of the short-run aggregate supply curve and the aggregate demand curve.

5   An increase in the money stock increases both output and the price level in the short run. In the long run, the aggregate supply curve shifts in response to positive or negative unemployment so that output moves back to its potential level.

6   In the long run, money is *neutral*, meaning that an increase in the money stock results only in an equiproportionate increase in prices.

7   Expansionary fiscal policy increases the levels of output and prices in the short run, but in the long run only increases prices. In the long run, expansionary fiscal policy mainly *crowds out* other expenditures and has no effect on output.

---

[10] A special issue of *Brookings Papers on Economic Activity*, 1978:2 (Washington, D.C.: The Brookings Institution, 1978), is devoted to supply management.

[11] See, too, our further discussions in Chapters 13 and 15.

8   A temporary increase in government spending financed by an increase in the stock of high-powered money increases the price level permanently. If it is financed by debt creation there will be a smaller permanent increase in the price level.

9   *Supply management policies* are attempts to move the aggregate supply curve, for example, by changes in payroll taxes. There is, as yet, little experience with such policies. Conventional monetary and fiscal policies which move the aggregate demand curve are called *demand management policies*.

10 In deciding what policies to use in response to disturbances, the general rule is to use policies that most directly offset the effects of the disturbance. A shift in demand should be countered by a demand management policy and a supply shift should be offset by supply management policy.

PROBLEMS

1 (a) Explain why the aggregate demand curve slopes down.
   (b) What happens to interest rates as we move down along this schedule, and why?
   (c) What happens to the nominal stock of money as we move down along the aggregate demand curve? To the real money stock?

2 The text states that a higher multiplier $\bar{\alpha}$ would flatten out the aggregate demand curve.
   (a) Give an economic interpretation of this fact.
   (b) Use Equation (1) to prove this, noting that

$$\gamma \equiv \frac{b\bar{\alpha}}{h + bk\bar{\alpha}}$$

   (If $\bar{\alpha}$ increases, what happens to γ? How is γ related to the slope of the aggregate demand curve?

3 (a) What would be the effect on the aggregate demand curve of a cut in transfer payments?
   (b) Would this effect be greater or smaller if the multiplier $\bar{\alpha}$ were higher?
   (c) Verify this answer using Equation (7) and the fact that

$$\beta \equiv \frac{h\,\bar{\alpha}}{h + bk\bar{\alpha}}$$

   *(d) Can you calculate $\Delta Y^d/\Delta R$ at a *fixed* level of price in terms of the variables we have already introduced? (Recall that R is transfer payments.)

4 Is it true that in the short run, expansionary fiscal or monetary policy can only increase output by also raising prices? Explain.

5 Suppose the aggregate supply curve were vertical. (Do you remember from Chapter 11 what would cause this?)
   (a) What would be the effects of expansionary fiscal and monetary policy in the short run on output, prices, and interest rates?
   (b) In the long run?

6 In the text it is noted that monetary policy is neutral in the long run even if the economy is not initially at full employment, as in Figure 12-6. Draw a diagram which demonstrates this fact and comment on the economic implications of this result. Does it seem to be a plausible one to you?

7 (a) Draw a diagram like Figure 12-7, indicating the effects of a tax increase in both the short and long runs.
   (b) In what way is such a change in fiscal policy not neutral in the long run?

8 Suppose investors suddenly become more optimistic than in the past and decide to invest more at given levels of income and interest rates. Trace the effects of such a shift through the IS and LM curves to see its effect on equilibrium income as derived with the aggregate supply and demand curves. Explain the effects of the change in optimism on interest rates, prices, and income.

*9 A sales tax at the rate of 1 percent is imposed on all final goods. At the same time, income taxes are cut so as to maintain the budget in balance at the initial equilibrium. GNP initially is $150 billion.

(a) What is the size of the income tax cut?

(b) What is the short-run effect of the policy package on output and prices?

(c) What is the long-run effect on output and prices?

*10 Analyze the difference in the impact on the interest rate, investment, and the price level of a temporary change in government spending, financed by money creation and borrowing, respectively.

13

INFLATION, OUTPUT, AND UNEMPLOYMENT

This chapter studies the behaviour of inflation, unemployment, output, and interest rates. It is a direct extension of our work in Chapter 12, differing in only three respects. First, rather than focus on the level of prices, we look at its rate of change, the rate of inflation. Second, we give more explicit attention to dynamics, the question of how the economy moves from one period to the next in the adjustment process. Third, we introduce one element so far omitted from our theoretical model, inflationary expectations.

Our major aim is to develop a realistic framework to understand the behaviour of the economy and to analyze such questions as: Why do inflation and unemployment sometimes increase together? Is inflation explained by lax monetary and fiscal policies? Can monetary and fiscal policies be used to raise the level of output permanently? Is it true that "inflation is always and everywhere a monetary phenomenon"?[1] Do high interest rates imply that monetary policy is tight?

Chart 13-1 points to the basic questions that we want to answer. The chart suggests that no extremely simple explanation — such as the view that unemployment declines when inflation increases — can account for the inflation-unemployment experience of the last two decades. In some periods, such as 1976-1977 and 1979-1980, inflation and unemployment move in the same direction. In other periods, for example, in 1974-1976 and 1977-1978, they move in opposite directions.

Chart 13-2 raises a second set of questions that will be dealt with in this chapter. Inflation and interest rates have both been rising since the 1950s. What relationship between inflation and interest rates accounts for this pattern?

The major element in explaining the unemployment-inflation and interest rate-inflation relations shown in the charts is inflationary expectations.

---

[1] See Milton Friedman, *Dollars and Deficits* (Englewood Cliffs, N.J.:Prentice-Hall, 1968), p.39.

Note: Inflation is the rate of change over the year of the Consumer Price Index.
CHART 13-1 INFLATION AND UNEMPLOYMENT
(*Source*: Statistics Canada, 11-003, 11-206, 11-505, 71-201)

We will show their place in the aggregate demand and supply framework and will demonstrate that the manner in which expectations are formed plays a crucial role in macroeconomic dynamics. The first place where inflationary expectations make their appearance is the Phillips curve — the relation between inflation and unemployment. In this chapter we will introduce an *expectations-augmented* Phillips curve. Inflationary expectations will also appear in the linkage between assets markets and goods markets. We introduce once again the relation between *nominal* and *real interest rates* and discuss the *Fisher relation*,[2] which argues that the real interest rate is unaffected by inflation in the long run, but may change in the short run as the economy adjusts to changes in the inflation rate.

This chapter is written in two parts. The first sets out the basic results in an informal and intuitive manner. In Section 13-1, we introduce the long-run relation between monetary growth and inflation, the cornerstone of monetarism. We show that in the long run, inflation is indeed a monetary phenomenon. From that long-run perspective we turn next to the much more controversial question of the short-run determinants of inflation. In Section 13-2, we show that in the short run, inflation is determined not only by monetary policy but also by the stance of fiscal policy, by the behaviour

[2] Irving Fisher (1867-1947), no relation, was one of the great American economists, a health freak, an entrepreneur, and a poor stock market speculator.

CHART 13-2 INTEREST RATES AND INFLATION
(*Source: Bank of Canada Review*)

Note: Interest rate is the yield on 3-month Treasury bills. Inflation rate is the growth rate of the seasonally adjusted Consumer Price Index excluding food.

of autonomous spending, inflationary expectations, and supply shocks. This section thus previews the major results that are developed in the rest of the chapter.

13-1 MONEY AND INFLATION IN THE LONG RUN

In this section we look at the long-run relationship between money and the inflation rate. We consider a situation in which the money stock is growing at a constant rate, and in which inflation has settled down to a constant rate. Everybody is aware of the inflation, has adjusted to it, and expects it to continue. To begin with, we discuss an economy in which the growth rate of potential output is zero, and in which output has adjusted to its potential level. The long-run equilibrium we describe, with a constant rate of inflation and a constant output level, is also called a *steady state*. Later we shall modify our analysis to account for the possibility that potential output is growing over time.

In an economy with a constant growth rate of money, a constant level of output, and with everyone fully adjusted to the presence of inflation, there is a very simple relationship between the growth rate of money and the inflation rate. In such an economy, prices will rise at exactly the rate at which the nominal money stock is increasing.

We can formalize this relationship by denoting the *growth rate* of money by $m \equiv \Delta M/M$ *and the rate of inflation by* $\pi \equiv \Delta P/P$:

$$\pi = m \qquad\qquad (1)$$

Equation (1), which we will derive and discuss in detail below, is a central statement in macroeconomics. It points out that, in the long run, or on average, there is a link between monetary growth and inflation. More precisely, in a *stationary* economy — an economy where real income is constant — the rate of inflation is equal to the growth rate of the nominal quantity of money.

Before explaining Equation (1) in more detail, we look briefly at some evidence. Chart 13-3 shows the rate of inflation and the growth rate of money for Canada over the past twenty years. The chart suggests that the growth rate of money and the inflation rate do tend to move together, but the realtionship is not exact. In part, this lack of an exact relationship reflects the role of other factors — such as fiscal policy changes, aggregate demand and supply disturbances, and shifts in money demand. A second factor making the relationship inexact is trend growth in output. We shall see later that the relationship, Equation (1), between the growth rate of the money

CHART 13-3 INFLATION AND MONETARY GROWTH
(*Source: Bank of Canada Review*)

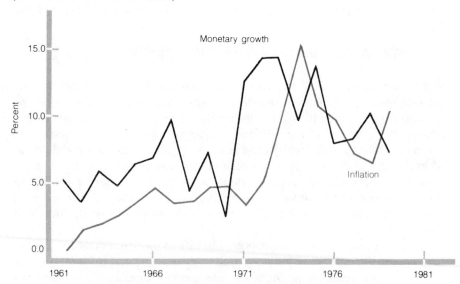

Note: Inflation and monetary growth are annual rates of the GNE deflator and of *M*1.

stock and the inflation rate has to be modified to take account of the long-run growth in output.

Now we return to Equation (1) to establish the long-run relation between inflation and monetary growth. For that purpose, we turn to the equilibrium condition in the money market, familiar from the LM curve:

$$\frac{M}{P} = L(i,Y) \tag{2}$$

or

$$M = PL(i,Y) \tag{2a}$$

Equations (2) and (2a) state that monetary equilibrium requires that money demand equals money supply. Equation (2) states this equilibrium condition in terms of real money demand and supply; Equation (2a) states the condition in terms of nominal money demand and supply.

Now consider long-run equilibrium where, by definition, all adjustments have taken place and, therefore, output and interest rates are constant. With output and interest rates constant, the demand for real money balances is constant. Therefore, to maintain the equality between the supply and demand for money, changes in the nominal money supply must be matched by corresponding changes in prices. For instance, if the stock of money were increasing by 5 percent per year, prices would have to be rising at the rate of 5 percent per year so as to maintain constant the real money supply M/P and thus maintain equilibrium in the money market. We have therefore established that in long-run equilibrium, money and prices must grow at the same rate.[3] That is precisely the message of Equation (1).

The argument that "inflation is always and everywhere a monetary phenomenon" is thus entirely correct as a description of long-run equilibrium. It is simply an implication of monetary equilibrium. The real money supply that yields monetary equilibrium is equal to the real money demand. To maintain a constant real money supply, an increasing nominal money stock has to be matched by rising prices. Thus, if the growth rate of the nominal money stock is 5 percent, the rate of inflation will be 5 percent. If the nominal money stock grows at the rate of 1000 percent, as it has in some

---

[3] The same point can be made starting from Eq. (2a). With constant real output and constant interest rates there will be a given, constant *real* demand for money L. Looking at Eq. (2a), we see that if the left-hand side — the nominal quantity of money — is increasing at some rate, the right-hand side — the demand for nominal balances — must be increasing at the same rate. But in the steady state, the only factor changing on the right-hand side is the price level, since $L()$ is constant. Therefore the price level must be increasing at the same rate as the nominal money stock.

hyperinflations, then the rate of inflation will be 1000 percent in long-run equilibrium.

Now we have to step back for a moment to ask how reasonable it is to look at the long run. After all, the economy is really never in long-run equilibrium. There is always some disturbance that upsets equilibrium and causes inflation and output to be different from their long-run values. That point is well taken and indeed reduces the interest we would otherwise have in long-run equilibrium. But there is a different way of looking at long-run equilibrium which makes it a less precise but much more powerful concept. This alternative is to think of the long-run equilibrium as the *average* behaviour of the economy over long time periods. To give an example, if on average over a five-year period the money stock had grown at 10 percent per year, with some variation, say, between 8 and 12 percent, we would expect the inflation rate to be about 10 percent. It might be a bit lower or higher depending on economic disturbances during the period, but it would be roughly 10 percent. The reason this average interpretation of the long run is powerful is that we are not trying to be more precise than is reasonable. We wind up with only a rule of thumb, but it is a very sturdy one.

Output Growth and Long-Run Inflation

The relationship (1) between monetary growth and inflation requires a minor correction to account for output growth. It is clear that growth in real income raises real money demand, and that, therefore, the assumption of a constant demand for real balances is not appropriate when output is growing. How should we account for the effects of output growth on the relationship between monetary growth and inflation? For example, how does the average growth rate of real income of about 4 percent in Canada in the post-World War II period affect Equation (1)?

In studying money demand in Chapter 7, we introduced the income elasticity of money demand. We noted there that the income elasticity of money demand is 0.7, which means that a 1 percent increase in real income raises real money demand by about 0.7 percent. Thus, if real income grows at the average rate of 4 percent and if the income elasticity of money demand is 0.7, then real money demand grows at the average rate of 2.8 percent (= 4 percent × 0.7) per year.

If real money demand is rising — say, at the rate of 2.8 percent per year — as a result of income growth, then monetary equilibrium requires that the real money supply increases at that same rate. The growth rate of the real money supply is just the difference between the growth rate of the nominal money stock and the rate of inflation. For instance, if the nominal money stock is increasing at 10 percent and the rate of inflation is 6 percent, the real money supply is growing at 4 percent. If the real money supply has to be growing at 2.8 percent to maintain monetary equilibrium, then the rate of inflation has to be 2.8 percent less than the rate of monetary growth, or, in symbols:

$$\pi = m - 2.8 \qquad (1a)$$

Equation (1a) states that the rate of inflation is equal to the growth rate of money *less* an adjustment arising from real income growth.

Equation (1a) partially explains why, in Chart 13-3, there is some discrepancy between the average rate of monetary growth and the rate of inflation. We observe from the chart that monetary growth usually exceeds the inflation rate. and Equation (1a) explains that fact by the growth in real money demand that results from real income growth.

Summary

Here we briefly summarize the long-run or average relation between inflation and monetary growth:

1 Inflation in the long run is a monetary phenomenon. By this we mean that increases in the growth rate of money are in the long-run reflected one for one in the rate of inflation.
2 The higher the growth rate of the nominal money supply, the higher the rate of inflation.
3 The rate of inflation is lower, the higher the growth rate of real money demand. This means that inflation is lower, the faster the growth rate of output, and the more real money demand rises with increased real income or output.

The simple long-run relationship between monetary growth and inflation contains one extremely important lesson. If a country wants to reduce its average inflation rate, it has somehow to reduce the average growth rate of the money stock.

13-2 INFLATION AND OUTPUT IN THE SHORT RUN: AN OVERVIEW

Chart 13-3 suggests that the short-run link between money and inflation is weaker than the long-run relationship. The absence of a close link between the growth rate of money and the inflation rate in the short run suggests that there are other factors accounting for inflation in the short run. We now turn our attention to those factors. At the same time, we are interested in short-run fluctuations in output and unemployment in the economy and the relationship between these output fluctuations and inflation. Chapter 12 has already suggested that the behaviour of the price level and the behaviour of output are closely related in the short run, and we will again find that to be true.

In this chapter we reformulate the theory of Chapter 12 to include expectations of inflation. The expected rate of inflation affects both aggregate supply and aggregate demand. On the aggregate supply side, nominal wages adjust not only to unemployment, but also to expected inflation. Nominal wages adjust to expected inflation because both firms and workers are concerned with the *real* wages they will be paying or receiving over the course of their labour contracts. If prices are expected to increase at, say, 10 percent during the course of a labour contract, then nominal wages will tend, for that reason, to increase at a rate of 10 percent over the course of the contract. Wage rises are passed on into price rises, and the inflation rate thus reflects expected inflation.

On the aggregate demand side, expectations of inflation are important because different interest rates are relevant for spending decisions and for portfolio choices, for equilibrium in the goods and markets. The expected *real* interest rate is relevant to the IS curve because, as we emphasized in Chapter 6, investment demand is affected by the expected real rate. However, as stressed in Chapter 7, the nominal interest rate is the cost of holding money, and it is therefore the nominal rate that is relevant to the LM curve. Since the difference between the expected real and nominal rates of interest is the expected inflation rate, and since aggregate demand is determined by the interaction of the goods and asset markets (IS and LM curves), the expected rate of inflation will affect aggregate demand. How? We will see that an increase in the expected rate of inflation *increases* aggregate demand. The essential reason is that an increase in the expected rate of inflation makes it more attractive to hold a real asset, such as capital, rather than a non-interest bearing asset like money. The desired capital stock and investment demand increases and therefore, so does aggregate demand.

Preview

This preview gives an idea, although not a complete understanding, of what is to come. We start in Section 13-3 with the aggregate supply side, which establishes the link between actual inflation, expected inflation, and output. We develop the aggregate supply curve

$$\pi = \pi^* + h\epsilon\left(\frac{Y}{Y_p} - 1\right) \tag{3}$$

Equation (3) states that the actual inflation rate π is equal to the expected inflation rate π^*, plus a term that depends on the difference between actual and potential output. The second term is already familiar from the development of aggregate supply in Chapter 11. When output is high relative to potential output, unemployment is low and wages are therefore rising and being passed on into price increases. The first element, the expected rate of inflation, means that there is a potential for inflation even at full employment. Wages, and therefore prices, will rise when output is at the full-employment level if inflation is expected and nominal wages adjust accordingly. Thus, on the supply side, the level of output (relative to potential) and the expected rate of inflation are the determinants of the inflation rate.

On the aggregate demand side, we develop Equation (4):

$$Y^d = Y^d_{-1} + \gamma f + \phi(m - \pi) + \eta(\pi^* - \pi^*_{-1}) \tag{4}$$

Equation (4) states that current real aggregate demand is equal to last period's aggregate demand, *plus* the increase that results from a change in fiscal policy, f, *plus* the increase that results from growth in real balances, $m - \pi$, plus the increase resulting from increases in the expected rate of inflation, $\pi^* - \pi^*_{-1}$.

Each of Equations (3) and (4) is a relationship between the inflation rate and the level of output, and we can, therefore, draw Equation (3) as the aggregate supply curve and Equation (4) as the aggregate demand curve. Their intersection will determine the short-run inflation rate and level of output. Their movements over time determine how the inflation rate and output adjust to changes in monetary and fiscal policy variables.

Using the aggregate supply and demand curves, we will establish the following results:

1 In the long run, increases in the growth rate of money affect *only* the inflation rate, and not output, which returns to its potential level, Y_p.
2 The short-run equilibrium of the economy is determined by the current and last period's expected inflation rates, π^* and π_{-1}, last period's output, Y^d_{-1}, fiscal policy, f, and the growth rate of the money stock, m.
3 The short-run response to an increase in the growth rate of money is typically a rise in both output and inflation. The response to an expansionary change in the fiscal policy variable, f, is similar.
4 The behaviour of expectations is crucial to the dynamic adjustment of the economy to changes in monetary and fiscal policy.

We are also interested in the behaviour of real and nominal interest rates. The major results here are:

5 In the long run, an increase in the growth rate of money increases the nominal interest rate by the same amount as the money growth rate increases, leaving the real interest rate unchanged.
6 The short-run effects of an increase in the growth rate of money on interest rates depend on the behaviour of expectations. If money growth increases and the expected inflation rate does not adjust, both the real and nominal interest rates fall initially. Then as expected inflation increases, both the real and nominal interest rates rise, with the nominal rate rising faster.
7 Fiscal policy can affect the real interest rate in both the short and long runs.

*13-3 AGGREGATE SUPPLY: THE EXPECTATIONS-AUGMENTED PHILLIPS CURVE

This section develops the relation between inflation, aggregate supply, and inflationary expectations shown in Equation (3). Our starting point is the theory of aggregate supply developed in Chapter 11. We showed there (in Eq. (11), page 319) that wage and price adjustment in response to the level of over- or underutilization of labour and other resources implies a positive relation between inflation and the GNP gap. If output is above normal, wages and costs in general will be rising and firms will pass on these increasing costs into higher prices. Conversely, when output is below normal, declining costs lead to falling prices.

The equation

$$\pi = h\epsilon\left(\frac{Y}{Y^p} - 1\right) \tag{3a}$$

implied by Equation (13) on page 321, summarizes the effect on cost and price inflation of deviations of output from normal. The coefficient $h\epsilon$ in Equation (3a) captures on one hand the effect of unemployment on wages and on the other the relation between unemployment and the GNP gap that is known as Okun's law. Thus we can look behind Equation (3a) and interpret wage behaviour related to unemployment as the source of inflationary pressure or deflationary pressure as the economy deviates from full employment.

In Figure 13-1 we show Equation (3a) — still leaving aside inflationary expectations. The schedule labelled AS_0 shows the inflation rate associated with each level of output. At full employment, inflation is zero. With actual output above potential, wages and prices are rising, or there is inflation. With output below normal, there is deflation, or wages and prices are falling.

The extent to which the GNP gap affects inflation is summarized by the slope of the aggregate supply schedule or the term $h\epsilon$ in Equation (3a). This term reflects the relation between unemployment and the GNP gap h, and the sensitivity of money wages to unemployment ϵ. The higher either of these parameters, the higher the rate of inflation that is associated with a given level of the gap, or, in other words, the steeper the aggregate supply schedule, the more adverse the *inflation-output tradeoff*; that is, the more inflation we get from a given expansion in output and employment.

We will show presently that the position of the aggregate supply schedule shown in Figure 13-1 will be affected by the expected rate of inflation in a more complete model. Before we turn to that point, we discuss the concept and role of inflationary expectations.

Expectations

The role of inflationary expectations in influencing wage formation and

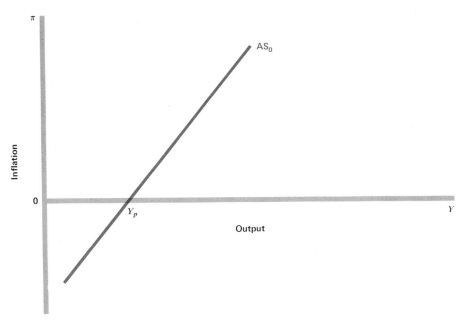

FIGURE 13-1 THE AGGREGATE SUPPLY SCHEDULE

therefore costs and prices is central to an understanding of the inflation process. Because labour contracts fix nominal wages for a given period ahead, labour will be concerned about its real wage over the period of the contract. A given money wage rate negotiated today will have less purchasing power two years from now if the inflation rate is 10 percent than if it is zero. Labour and firms, when they set current wages, will therefore look ahead to the inflation they expect over the period of the contract.

Typically, the environment is not one where the inflation rate has been constant for a long period and can be accurately predicted. More likely, the inflation rate in the recent past has varied somewhat and future inflation cannot be predicted with great accuracy. Given that uncertainty, we would assume expectations of inflation to be based in part on inflation rates actually experienced in the recent past. Labour would seek wage increases equal to the "habitual" rate of inflation that has recently been experienced, and thus find some insurance against the expected price increases.

Before proceeding to discuss how expectations are formed, we briefly reemphasize the critical role of inflationary expectations in the inflation process. Expectations are so critical because the simple fact that people expect inflation causes inflation. When wages increase because inflation is expected, costs increase and produce inflationary pressure as firms seek to pass on cost increases into higher prices.

When inflationary expectations are slow to adjust, monetary and fiscal policies will have quite large effects on the level of output and relatively small effects on the inflation rate. Two instances from recent economic history are relevant here. First, in the sixties, aggregate demand kept rising but inflation was very slow to develop, largely because the long period of moderate inflation of the late fifties and early sixties kept down expected inflation. Second, repeated attempts in the seventies to reduce existing inflation by restrictive monetary policy proved largely ineffective, resulting in unemployment rather than lower inflation. Expectations of inflation did not come down fast, and therefore actual inflation could not be reduced without substantially increasing unemployment.

Now we return once more to expectations formation. There is no generally accepted way in which to model inflationary expectations.[4] Traditionally, inflationary expectations have been regarded as some average of past inflation rates, but any information that is available about the future course of monetary and fiscal policies would also be relevant to inflationary expectations. For the purpose of the next few sections, we will make the simplifying assumption that the expected rate of inflation is equal to last period's rate of inflation:

$$\pi^* = \pi_{-1} \tag{5}$$

We adopt this oversimplified formulation only because it is easy to manipulate. Taking a long-run average over several years is more appropriate and important as a practical matter but really does not change the theory. All it does is to draw out the adjustment process over time and make for longer lags.

Later we will substitute for Equation (5) an alternative *perfect foresight* assumption which assumes individuals predict the inflation rate correctly:

$$\pi^* = \pi \tag{5a}$$

While Equation (5a) is difficult to believe as a literal description, it will help us see how important expectations are to the dynamic behaviour of the economy. It will also bring out aspects of the *rational expectations approach* to macroeconomics, to be discussed in Section 13-6, and in Chapter 15.

Inflationary Expectations and Aggregate Supply

We now turn to the aggregate supply Equation (3), which includes inflationary expectations. Because both firms and workers are concerned with *real* wages, nominal wages adjust for expected inflation through the π^* term, as well as in response to the state of the labour market through the

[4] See Robert M. Solow, "Down the Phillips Curve with Gun and Camera," in David A. Belsley et al. (eds.), *Inflation, Trade and Taxes* (Columbus: Ohio State University Press, 1976).

second term in (3), repeated here for convenience. The wage increases are then passed on into prices.

$$\pi = \pi^* + h\epsilon\left(\frac{Y}{Y_p} - 1\right) \tag{3}$$

Figure 13-2 shows the role of expectations in aggregate supply. We have reproduced the aggregate supply schedule AS_0, drawn for a zero expected inflation rate from Figure 13-1. An increase in the expected rate of inflation from zero to, say, $\pi^* = 5$ percent, will shift up the aggregate supply schedule so that now at full employment we would have a 5 percent rate of inflation. This is shown by the aggregate supply schedule AS_1. Conversely, a reduction in expected inflation below zero — the expectation of deflation — will shift the aggregate supply schedule downward to AS_2. The schedule AS_2, drawn in Figure 13-2, reflects the expectation of prices falling at the rate of 2 percent. For higher rates of expected deflation, the aggregate supply schedule would shift down further.

Embodying inflationary expectations in the aggregate supply schedule completes the picture of inflation and output on the supply side. Inflation depends on the state of the labour market, here measured by the GNP gap, and on inflationary expectations. Inflation is higher, the higher is actual output

FIGURE 13-2 AGGREGATE SUPPLY AND EXPECTED INFLATION

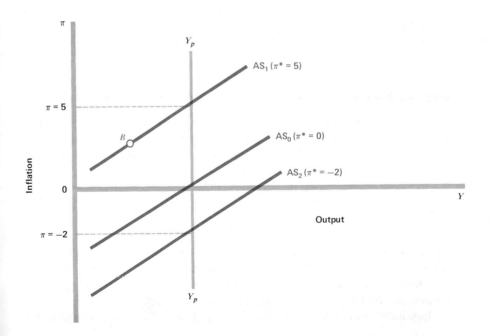

relative to potential output and the higher is expected inflation.

It is quite possible to have both inflation and unemployment (point *B*). That possibility arises when the expectation of inflation causes wages and prices to rise and unemployment does not exert sufficient dampening pressure on wage settlements to restore full employment. Clearly, this is the combination of facts observed in the seventies where persistent unemployment appeared together with inflation.

In concluding this section, we comment on a critical aspect of the aggregate supply schedule: In the long run, the aggregate supply schedule is vertical at the full-employment level. The long-run aggregate supply schedule is the schedule $Y_p Y_p$. In the long run, the level of output is independent of the rate of inflation, as is the rate of unemployment. The reason for these strong results — sometimes referred to as the *long-run vertical Phillips curve* — is that expectations will ultimately adjust to the existing rate of inflation. Thus, by Equation (3), equality of actual and expected inflation implies that output is at the full-employment level whatever the rate of inflation. Deviations of output from the full-employment level require expectational errors or deviations of the inflation rate from its habitual level. In the long run, by definition, there are no errors in expectations and therefore output is at the full-employment level.

*13-4 AGGREGATE DEMAND AND EXPECTED INFLATION

The preceding section showed that aggregate supply theory can be extended in a simple way to link output and the rate of inflation, taking account of inflationary expectations. In this section, we develop the link between aggregate demand and inflation, also taking inflationary expectations into account.

Aggregate Demand, Expected Inflation, and Interest Rates

In Chapters 11 and 12, we saw that aggregate demand depends on autonomous spending, including fiscal variables, and the real quantity of money. Taking explicit account of the fiscal variables, we can write aggregate demand as a function of fiscal and monetary variables:

$$Y^d = Y^d\left(F, \frac{M}{P}\right) \qquad (6a)$$

Here *F* is a measure of fiscal policy, which we take to be represented by the full-employment budget deficit. In the aggregate demand function in Equation (6a), an increase in the full-employment deficit increases aggregate demand, as does an increase in the real money supply.

Equation (6a) omits the effects of expected inflation on aggregate demand. The importance of expected inflation arises from the distinction between real and nominal interest rates. The interest rate relevant to goods market equilibrium (the IS curve) is the expected real rate, and the interest rate relevant to money market equilibrium (the LM curve) is the nominal rate. Since the two rates differ by the expected rate of inflation, changes in the expected rate of inflation will affect aggregate demand.

We will now extend Equation (6a) to include inflationary expectations and the distinction between real and nominal interest rates. We will show that the extended aggregate demand function can be written

$$Y^d = Y^d\left(F, \frac{M}{P}, \pi^*\right) \tag{6}$$

and that increases in the expected rate of inflation increase aggregate demand.

For that purpose, we go back to the IS and LM curves of Chapter 4. In Figure 13-3, we show the LM schedule. On the vertical axis, we have the *nominal* rate of interest relevant for the choice between money and other financial assets.

In the goods market, however, the *real* interest rate is relevant since it determines the level of investment. In particular, we showed in Chapter 4, Equation (6a), that we can write the IS schedule as

$$Y = (\bar{\alpha}(\bar{A} - bi_r) \tag{7}$$

where $\bar{A}$ denotes autonomous spending, $\bar{\alpha}$ is the multiplier, and i_r denotes the real rate of interest. If there are inflationary expectations, nominal and real interest rates will differ and we have to think about a way to introduce the IS schedule into Figure 13-3.

The critical step in reformulating the IS-LM model to include inflationary expectations is the realtion

$$i_r = i - \pi^* \tag{8}$$

which states that the (expected) real rate of interest is the nominal rate less the expected rate of inflation. We can use Equation (8) to substitute for the real interest rate in (7) to obtain the following equation:

$$Y = \bar{\alpha}(\bar{A} - bi + b\pi^*) \tag{9}$$

In this form we recognize that equilibrium output in the goods market depends on both the nominal interest rate *and* the expected rate of inflation. In particular, for a given nominal interest rate, i, an increase in expected inflation will increase equilibrium output. What is the mechanism? Increased inflationary expectations, *given the nominal interest rate*, imply a

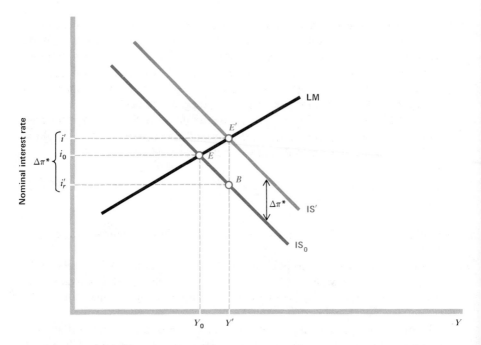

FIGURE 13-3 EFFECTS OF AN INCREASE IN THE EXPECTED INFLATION RATE ON THE REAL INTEREST RATE AND AGGREGATE DEMAND

lower real interest rate. This results in an increased incentive to invest, a rise in demand, and therefore a higher equilibrium output.

We also observe from Equation (9) that for a given rate of expected inflation, say π_0^*, we can draw the IS schedule as a function of the nominal interest rate. With given inflationary expectations, changes in the nominal interest rate correspond, one for one, to changes in the real rate. Accordingly, we draw in Figure 13-3 the schedule IS_0 corresponding to a given rate of expected inflation π_0^*. It is also clear that a change in expected inflation will shift the IS schedule. Increased inflationary expectations will shift the IS schedule up and to the right, since at each nominal interest rate they imply reduced real rates and hence an increased incentive to invest.

We can be more precise about the way in which changes in expected inflation shift the IS schedule. Note that since investment depends on the real rate, investment, and so equilibrium income, will remain unchanged if changes in inflationary expectations are precisely offset by changes in nominal interest rates. When inflationary expectations are up by two percentage points, demand and equilibrium income are unchanged only if nominal interest rates increase by the same amount. This implies, in terms of Figure 13-3, that a change in inflationary expectations, $\Delta\pi,^*$ shifts the IS schedule upward by exactly the same amount, $\Delta i = \Delta\pi^*$.

We can now use our modified IS-LM model to show the effect of increased inflationary expectations on the equilibrium levels of income, nominal and real interest rates. Suppose then, as shown in Figure 13-3, that there is an increase in the expected rate of inflation. At the initial equilibrium nominal interest rate and income level, the money market remains in equilibrium. In the goods market, however, there is now an excess demand. The increased inflationary expectations have reduced the real interest rate at point E, investment spending increases, and accordingly, the IS curve shifts up by $\Delta\pi^*$ to IS'. At E the excess demand for goods causes an income expansion. As the economy moves to the new equilibrium at E', income rises. This rise in income raises money demand and hence equilibrium nominal interest rates. We thus have shown that an increase in inflationary expectations will raise equilibrium income and spending or aggregate demand, as shown in Equation (6).

What can we say about the impact of increased inflationary expectations on interest rates? Figure 13-3 allows us to describe the effect on both nominal and real interest rates. We already see that the nominal interest rate will rise to i'. But we also see that the nominal interest rate rises by less than the full increase in inflationary expectations, that is, $i' - i_0 < \Delta\pi^*$. This of course implies that the equilibrium real interest rate, i_r, corresponding to the equilibrium at point E', must have declined.

In fact, from the definition of the real rate — the nominal rate less the expected inflation — it is apparent that the new real rate is the interest rate corresponding to point B and shown as i_r' on the vertical axis. The increased inflationary expectations thus drive a wedge between nominal and real interest rates: Nominal rates rise and real rates fall.

How much does the real interest rate change? That clearly depends on the slopes of the IS and LM curves. At one extreme, we could have a flat IS curve, indicating extreme sensitivity of investment demand to the real interest rate. Then an increase in the expected rate of inflation would have little effect on the equilibrium real rate of interest and would affect the nominal rate almost one for one. The increase in aggregate demand is correspondingly large. Alternatively, the steeper the LM curve, the smaller the change in the real rate. In the extreme classical or quantity theory world in which the LM curve is vertical, the change in the expected rate of inflation again does not affect the real rate and only changes the nominal rate. In this case, though, income does not change either.

We defer further examination of interest rate behaviour to Section 13-7. For the next few sections, we concentrate on the determination of output and inflation.

The Aggregate Demand Curve

We now use Equation (6) to derive an aggregate demand curve that relates the level of aggregate demand to the rate of inflation, as does Equation (4) in Section 13-2. From Equation (6), aggregate demand increases when the full-employment budget deficit expands, when real balances increase, and when the expected rate of inflation increases.

$$\Delta Y^d = \gamma f + \phi(m - \pi) + \eta \Delta \pi^* \tag{10}$$

In Equation (10), the change in aggregate demand depends on the *change* in fiscal policy, f, on the *change* in the expected rate of inflation ($\Delta \pi^* = \pi^* - \pi_{-1}$) and on the growth rate of real balances, $m - \pi$.[5] The growth rate of real money balances is equal to the growth rate of nominal balances less the rate of inflation. The terms γ and ϕ translate changes in the full-employment deficit and in real balances into changes in income, and therefore are related to the fiscal and monetary multipliers studied before. The term η summarizes the effects of expected inflation on aggregate demand, and thus depends on the slopes of the IS and LM curves.

Now, what is the interpretation of Equation (10)? If fiscal policy is expansionary, aggregate demand will rise. Thus an increase in the full-employment deficit, resulting from increased government spending or reduced taxes, raises aggregate demand. Similarly, aggregate demand rises if the real money supply grows (because nominal money grows faster than prices) or if the expected rate of inflation increases. These three factors will each raise aggregate demand relative to last period. We can underline that fact by writing aggregate demand this period, Y^d, as output (aggregate demand) last period, Y_{-1}, plus the change in demand arising from the three factors in Equation (10):[6]

$$Y^d = Y_{-1} + \gamma f + \phi(m - \pi) + \eta \Delta \pi^* \tag{10a}$$

where we have substituted $\Delta Y^d \equiv Y^d - Y_{-1}$.

We immediately recognize from Equation (10a) that we now have a relationship between aggregate demand and the rate of inflation. Given last period's income, expectations, the change in fiscal policy, and the growth

---

[5] Technical note: Equation (10) would follow from Equation (6) if (6) took the form

$$Y_d = \gamma F + \phi \, ln(M/P) + \gamma \pi^*$$

where ln stands for the natural logarithm.

$$\begin{aligned} Y^d - Y^d_{-1} \equiv \Delta Y^d &= \gamma (F - F_{-1}) + \phi\{ln(M/P) - ln(M_{-1}/P_{-1})\} + \gamma(\pi^* - \pi^*_{-1}) \\ &= \gamma f + \phi\{ln(M/M_{-1}) - ln(P/P_{-1})\} + \gamma (\pi^* - \pi_{-1}) \\ &= \gamma f + \phi(m - \pi) + \gamma(\pi^* - \pi^*_{-1}) \end{aligned}$$

In the last step we use the fact that $ln(M/M_{-1})$ is very close to $(M - M_{-1})/M_{-1} = m$ for moderate values of m. If Eq. (6) did not take this particular form, Eq. (10) could be looked on as a convenient approximation.

[6] In going from Eq. (10) to Eq. (10a), we substitute Y_{-1} in place of Y^d_{-1}. This is justified because, as we shall see below, last period's output was equal to last period's aggregate demand.

rate of money (Y_{-1}, $\Delta\pi^*$, f, and m), we are left with a relationship between current demand and the current rate of inflation. Equation (10a) shows that the higher the rate of inflation, the lower is the level of aggregate demand (again, *given* Y_{-1}, $\Delta\pi^*$, f, m). There is a very simple explanation for this relationship. Given the growth rate of money m, the higher the rate of inflation, the lower is the growth rate of real money balances, and therefore the smaller the increase in aggregate demand. Indeed, with inflation in excess of the growth rate of money, $m - \pi < 0$, real balances are declining and therefore real (and nominal) interest rates are increasing. In this case, current demand falls short of last period's demand because inflation has cut down the real money supply and thereby raised interest rates.

In Figure 13-4 we plot the aggregate demand schedule on the assumption that current changes in fiscal policy and expectations are zero ($f = 0$ and $\Delta\pi^* = 0$). The aggregate demand schedule is downward-sloping. Given the growth rate of money, a lower rate of inflation implies that real balances are higher and that therefore the interest rate is lower and spending is higher. The negative slope results from this connection between lower inflation and higher spending.

Given the negative slope of the curve, what determines its location? We observe from Equation (10a) (remember that we assume $f = 0$ and $\Delta\pi^* = o$) that when $m = \pi$, current aggregate demand equals last period's output, $Y^d = Y_{-1}$. Thus the aggregate demand schedule passes through point B in Figure 13-4 where, at an inflation rate equal to the monetary growth rate, we have no change in real balances and therefore no change in spending. For a lower rate of inflation, current spending exceeds last period's. Conversely, for a

---

FIGURE 13-4 THE AGGREGATE DEMAND SCHEDULE

FIGURE 13-5 THE EFFECT OF INCREASED MONETARY GROWTH ON AGGREGATE DEMAND

higher rate of inflation, current spending falls short of last period's.

The aggregate demand schedule in Figure 13-4 is drawn on the assumption of a given growth rate of money m and zero change in fiscal policy and expectations. We now briefly ask how changes in these variables would affect aggregate demand. In Figure 13-5 we show that an increase in monetary growth to m' will shift upward the aggregate demand schedule to pass through point C. With higher monetary growth, we need higher inflation if real balances and therefore aggregate demand are to remain constant over time. From Equation $(10a)$ it is apparent that an expansionary fiscal policy or an increase in the expected rate of inflation will likewise shift the aggregate demand schedule up and to the right. For each growth rate of nominal money and the rate of inflation, these changes provide extra expansionary force (over and above that from changing real balances) and therefore raise aggregate demand. Conversely, a move toward fiscal tightness or reduction in the expected rate of inflation shifts the aggregate demand schedule down and to the left.

In summary:

1 Current aggregate demand depends on past aggregate demand and the current stimulus that comes from fiscal expansion, growth in real balances, or increased expectations of inflation.
2 The aggregate demand curve is a downward-sloping relationship between the inflation rate and the level of output.

3   The position of the aggregate demand curve depends on last period's output (Y_{-1}), the growth rate of money (m), changes in the full-employment deficit (f) and changes in the expected rate of inflation ($\Delta\pi^*$). Increases in any of Y_{-1}, m, f, or $\Delta\pi^*$ increase aggregate demand and shift the aggregate demand curve upward.

*13-5 DETERMINING THE INFLATION RATE AND OUTPUT LEVEL IN THE SHORT RUN

To determine the inflation rate and the level of output in the short run, we put together our aggregate demand and supply curves. This is done in Figure 13-6. The intersection of the aggregate supply and demand curves at point E determines the inflation rate and the level of output this period, π_0 and Y_0, respectively.

Now, on what do the current rate of inflation and the level of output depend? They clearly depend on the positions of the aggregate supply and demand curves. Thus, changes in any of the variables that shift the aggregate supply and demand curves will affect the current inflation and output levels.

In Figure 13-6 we also show the consequences of an upward shift in the aggregate demand curve from AD_0 to AD_1. The equilibrium of the economy shifts from E to E_1, at which point both the inflation rate and the level of output are higher than they were at E. Upward shifts in the aggregate

---

FIGURE 13-6   THE DETERMINATION OF THE INFLATION RATE AND OUTPUT IN THE SHORT RUN, AND THE SHORT-RUN EFFECTS OF A SHIFT IN AGGREGATE DEMAND

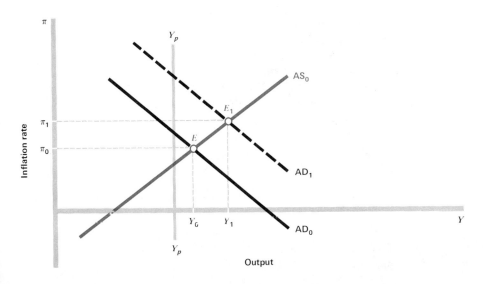

demand curve therefore result in increases in both the level of output and the inflation rate in the short run. We have already seen what determines the position of the AD curve and therefore what causes it to shift. The higher the lagged level of income Y_{-1}, the higher the aggregate demand curve; the greater the change in the full-employment budget deficit f, the greater the increase in expected inflation; and the higher the growth rate of money, the higher the AD curve. Therefore, both the inflation rate and the level of output are higher in the short run, the higher last period's income, the greater the change in the full-employment budget deficit, the greater the increase in expected inflation, and the greater the growth rate of money. Because the expected rate of inflation affects both aggregate supply and demand (even though in the latter case it is the *change* in expected inflation that is relevant), movements in the aggregate supply curve will in general be accompanied by shifts in the aggregate demand curve. Figure 13-7 shows the effects of an increase in the expected rate of inflation. The aggregate supply curve shifts up to AS_1, by the full amount of the increase in the expected rate of inflation, but the aggregate demand curve is shown shifting up less (to AD_1). The actual inflation rate rises and the level of output falls. The actual inflation rate rises by less than the expected inflation rate.

The result shown in Figure 13-7 clearly depends on the aggregate supply

FIGURE 13-7 THE EFFECTS OF AN INCREASE IN EXPECTED INFLATION ON OUTPUT AND INFLATION IN THE SHORT RUN

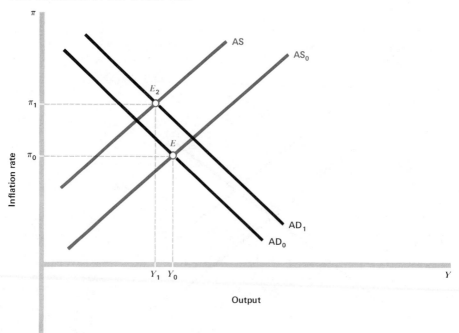

curve shifting more than the aggregate demand curve.[7] How reasonable is it that the aggregate demand curve should shift up by less than the increase in the expected rate of inflation? On careful examination, the condition depends essentially on the demand for real balances not being very interest-elastic. But we shall simply assume the condition is met because it is required if our aggregate supply-demand model is to be stable.[8]

Our preliminary analysis of aggregate supply and demand, in Figures 13-6 and 13-7, points to five factors affecting the inflation rate and the level of output in the short run: the expected rate of inflation, which determines the location of the aggregate supply curve, and the four other variables that determine the location of the aggregate demand curve. The four are the expected rate of inflation this period and last, the change in the full-employment budget surplus, the growth rate of nominal money, and the level of income last period. If policy makers want to change the behaviour of the inflation rate, in the short run, they have to try to affect the expected inflation rate, the change in the full-employment budget surplus, or the growth rate of the money supply. The level of income and expected inflation last period are not variables that can be changed by policy makers today.

The analysis in this section, like that of Chapter 12, points to the potential role of *supply management*. If policy makers want to reduce the inflation rate in the short run, then they can use *demand management* policies which shift the AD curve downward. But such policies will tend to reduce output along with the inflation rate. If policies could be found to shift the AS curve downward, they would make it possible to reduce the inflation rate without reducing the level of income.

We now turn to the analysis of the effects of monetary and fiscal policy on the rate of inflation and the level of output in the short and long runs.

*13-6 THE ADJUSTMENT OF OUTPUT AND INFLATION TO AN INCREASE IN MONETARY GROWTH

We have now looked at the short-run impact of shifts in the aggregate demand and supply schedules, and can proceed to study the adjustment process that links short-run and long-run equilibria. In this section, we examine the adjustment to an increase in the growth rate of money.

[7] Be sure you can see this. Experiment with your own version of Figure 13-7.

[8] It is clear that if the aggregate demand curve shifts up by more than the increase in the expected rate of inflation, an increase in the expected rate of inflation will cause an even larger increase in the actual rate of inflation. If this higher inflation feeds back in turn into higher expected inflation, the potential for instability becomes clear. We thus assume henceforth, that an increase in the expected rate of inflation shifts the aggregate demand curve up by less than the increase in the expected rate of inflation, as in Figure 13-8. The condition is satisfied if η in Eq. (10) is less than ϕ. Use of the IS and LM curves shows that this condition is more likely to be satisfied, the smaller is the coefficient h in the LM curve.

We start by using the expectations equation (5) in which the expected rate of inflation is the rate of inflation that occurred last period. Substituting that assumption about expectations into the aggregate supply curve, Equation (3), we have

$$\pi = \pi_{-1} + h\epsilon\left(\frac{Y}{Y_p} - 1\right) \tag{11}$$

as the aggregate supply curve. In this section we shall assume that the full-employment deficit is kept constant ($f = 0$), so that aggregate demand curve is described by Equation (10b):

$$Y^d = Y_{-1} + \phi(m - \pi) + \eta\Delta\pi^* \tag{10b}$$

The point of departure of our analysis is the long-run equilibrium at point E in Figure 13-8. What does long-run equilibrium imply in the model shown by Equations (10b) and (11)? Long-run equilibrium implies that (1) the economy is at full employment, $Y = Y_p$; (2) actual and expected inflation are equal, $\pi = \pi^*$; (3) the rate of inflation is equal to the growth rate of money, $\pi = m_0$; (4) aggregate demand equals aggregate supply, $Y^d = Y$; and (5) aggregate demand remains constant over time, $Y^d = Y_{-1}$.

These conditions are a full description of the equilibrium, but they are not all independent. Start with Equation (11) and note that equality of the actual and expected inflation rates implies that output is at the full-employment level.

Next consider Equation (10b) and note that equality of the growth rate of money and the rate of inflation, $\pi = m$, together with constancy of π^*, imply that current output equals past output. In other words, over time, aggregate demand remains constant. Finally, the condition that demand equals supply ensures that aggregate demand is equal to full-employment

FIGURE 13-8 LONG-RUN EQUILIBRIUM

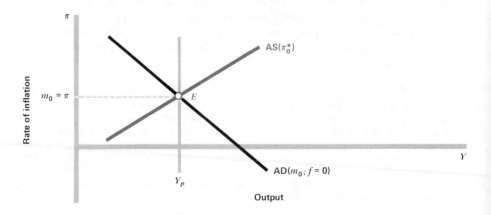

equals supply ensures that aggregate demand is equal to full-employment output.

Diagrammatically, in long-run equilibrium, the supply and demand curves intersect at point E in Figure 13-9. At E, the inflation rate is equal to the growth rate of money [by condition (3)], and output is at its potential level [by condition (1)].

Now starting from a position of full equilibrium at point E in Figure 13-9, the growth rate of money rises from m_0 to m' and stays at that higher level indefinitely. In this figure the increased monetary growth is shown by an upward shift of the aggregate demand schedule to AD_1. The impact effect, with as yet unchanged expectations and therefore an unchanged supply schedule, is to raise both the rate of inflation and real output. Inflationary expectations, because they are sticky, keep down the actual rate of inflation and prevent it from responding fully to the increased monetary growth. Consequently, the real money supply expands and real output rises to meet the increased demand for goods. This takes us to point E_1. However, the

FIGURE 13-9 SHORT-RUN ADJUSTMENT TO A CHANGE IN THE GROWTH RATE OF MONEY

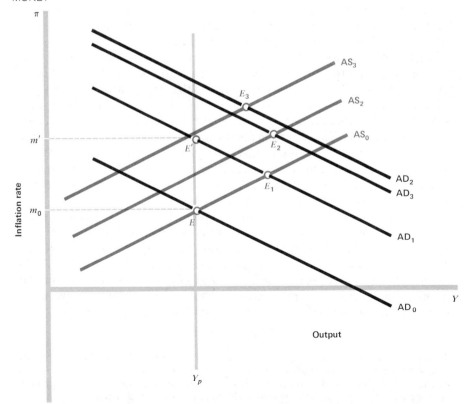

economy will not remain at point E_1. The increased rate of inflation will be reflected in higher inflationary expectations and therefore in upward shifts of the aggregate supply and demand schedules. Similarly, the expansion in real output is reflected in a further upward shift of the aggregate demand schedule.

Accordingly, in period 2, the period after the rise in the growth rate of money, both the aggregate supply and demand curves shift. The aggregate supply curve shifts because the expected rate of inflation has increased — and π^* has increased because the inflation rate at E_1 is higher than the inflation rate at E. We can tell precisely how the supply curve shifts by looking at Equation (11). The new aggregate supply curve AS_2 crosses the Y_p line at precisely the inflation rate that occurred in period 1. The aggregate demand curve shifts up because both lagged output and the expected inflation rate have risen, as can be seen from Equation (10b).

In period 2 the inflation rate and level of output are determined at E_2. The inflation rate is undoubtedly higher than it was at E_1, and we have shown the output level at E_2 also to be higher than in the previous period. However, it is possible that output could be less in period 2 than in period 1, depending on the slopes of the aggregate supply and demand curves and the extent to which the aggregate demand curve shifts from AD_1 to AD_2.

The two curves continue to shift in subsequent periods. As long as the inflation rate keeps rising, the aggregate supply curve will keep rising, since the actual inflation rate last period determines today's expected rate of inflation. The position of the aggregate demand curve is determined by the *level* of lagged output and the *change* of the expected inflation rate, $\Delta\pi^*$. Once $\Delta\pi^*$ is lower than $\Delta\pi^*$ last period (and that can happen even while the inflation rate is increasing)[9] and the level of output begins falling (that is, Y_{-1} is less than Y_{-2}), the aggregate demand curve will certainly fall. Either falling output or a decrease in the change in the inflation rate will tend to cause the aggregate demand curve to fall. In Figure 13-9 we show the equilibrium in period 3 with a higher inflation rate and lower level of output than in period 2. In fact, in both periods 2 and 3, the rate of inflation is even higher than it will eventually be in the long-run equilibrium at E'.

It is not worth following the shifts of the aggregate supply and demand curves during the adjustment process in much further detail. Figure 13-10 shows the pattern of adjustment as the economy moves from E_1, its first-period equilibrium, to the eventual long-run equilibrium at E'. We do not include the shifting supply and demand curves that underlie the pattern of adjustment shown so as to keep the diagram clear. And we have, for convenience, smoothed the time path of adjustment. The first few points E_1,

---

[9] Remember that we are referring to $\Delta\pi^* = \pi^* - \pi^*_{-1}$. Suppose that in three successive periods the expected inflation rate is 5, 8, and 9 percent respectively. Then $\Delta\pi^*$, which in part determines the position of the AD curve, is 3 percent in the second period and only 1 percent in the third period, even though the expected inflation rate itself is still rising.

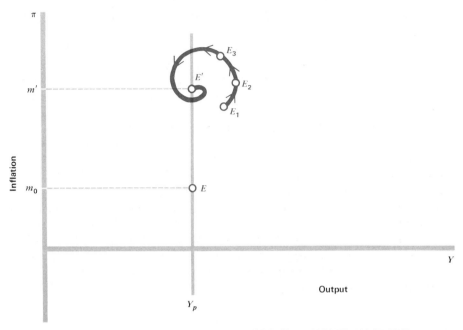

FIGURE 13-10 THE ADJUSTMENT PATH TO AN INCREASE IN MONETARY GROWTH

E_2, and E_3 that we traced in Figure 13-9 are also shown in Figure 13-10.

There are two special features of the adjustment process that deserve comment and that can be seen in Figure 13-10. First, given the expectations assumption (5), the economy does not proceed directly to the point of long-run equilibrium E'. Rather, the level of output will fall below Y_p at some stages in the adjustment process as a result of shifts in the aggregate supply and demand curves, and will, at other times, be above Y_p, as it is at E_1, E_2, and E_3. Similarly, the rate of inflation will sometimes be above its long-run equilibrium level m', as it is at E_2, and sometimes below it, as at E_1. Eventually, the economy settles down to its long-run rate of inflation m' and output level Y_p.

The *overshooting* of the inflation rate above its steady-state level during the adjustment process is not accidental or a result of our particular expectations assumptions. Rather, it is a common feature of the adjustment process of the economy to an increase in the growth rate of money. Why? At the new steady state, E', the level of output is the same as it was at E, but the inflation rate is higher. We would expect, and will show in Section 13-7, that the nominal interest rate is higher at E' than at E. That means the demand for, and level of, real balances is lower at E' than at E. The stock of real balances had to fall during the adjustment from E to E'. But real balances can fall only if the inflation rate exceeds the growth rate of money. Since money grew at the rate m' throughout the adjustment process, the inflation rate at some stage had to have exceeded m'. And this is precisely the overshooting feature.

The second important feature of the adjustment process is that in the course of the adjustment, there are times at which output decreases, while the inflation rate increases. For instance, between E_2 and E_3, in Figures 13-9 and 13-10, the inflation rate increases while output decreases. This inverse relationship between output and inflation is a result of the shifts of the supply curve caused by changes in the expected rate of inflation.

The inverse relationship between the rate of inflation and the level of output at some stages of the adjustment process predicted by our theory is significant, for it often occurs in practice. However, it is widely believed that the Phillips curve implies that there cannot be such an inverse relationship. If one ignores the role of expected inflation in the Phillips curve, it is easy to conclude that periods in which the inflation rate and output move in opposite directions—and particularly periods in which output is falling while the inflation rate is rising — cannot be explained by economics. In fact, during the period 1973-1980 when inflation and unemployment were frequently observed to rise together, there were complaints in the press that the laws of economics no longer seemed to be working. There is no law of economics that says the inflation rate and the level of output move in the same direction at all times. We should not be surprised if the level of output and the inflation rate move in opposite directions at some stages of the adjustment process. That is one of the major lessons of this section; it is the phenomenon of *stagflation* — stagnation with inflation.

The other major lesson, which we have mentioned several times, is that the details of the adjustment process depend on the formation of expectations. In a general way, it is easy to see that the details of the economy's adjustment must depend on the formation of expectations, since changing expectations are responsible for the way in which the aggregate supply curve shifts. We shall make the point more specifically now, however, by using the expectation assumption (5a), namely, that expectations show perfect foresight.

Perfect Foresight Expectations

The analysis so far has assumed that expected inflation is equal to last period's actual rate of inflation. This was taken up as a simple representation of expectations based on an average of past inflation rates. Now we change the expectations assumption quite radically. Specifically, we assume in Equation (5a) that people correctly foresee the inflation rate

$$\pi^* = \pi \qquad (5a)$$

This expectations assumption, combined with the aggregate supply function Equation (3), has an extremely powerful implication. We repeat Equation (3) here:

$$\pi = \pi^* + h\epsilon\left(\frac{Y}{Y_p} - 1\right) \tag{3}$$

Now if we substitute Equation (5a) into Equation (3), we see that we obtain

$$Y = Y_p \tag{12}$$

The implication of Equations (3) and (5a) together is that output is always at the potential level, which is what Equation (12) says.

Why? If we reexamine Equation (3), we will see that it says that output is at the potential level unless the expected and actual rates of inflation differ. By assuming perfect foresight expectations, we remove any differences between actual and expected inflation. What is the underlying economic story? The simple notion is that workers and firms in making their wage bargains plan to reach full employment, so that if their expectations turn out to be correct, there will be labour market equilibrium. Consequently, output will be at the potential level.

In particular, this means that the level of output is unaffected by expected changes in the growth rate of money, provided there is perfect foresight. Perfect foresight expectations are a special case of *rational expectations*, expectations which on average are right, and certainly not systematically wrong. The rational expectations notion, when used in a model like that of this section, indeed implies that monetary policy is ineffective, and members of the rational expectations school do take the view that monetary policy cannot be used systematically to affect output.[10]

We will not go into the details of the process of adjustment of the inflation rate to a change in the growth rate of money when there is perfect foresight. But it will be found that the inflation rate overshoots the steady-state inflation rate in the first period as a result of the effect of the increase in expected inflation on aggregate demand.

How reasonable is the result of the perfect foresight assumption that changes in the growth rate of money affect only the inflation rate and not the level of output? One possible objection should be disposed of, namely, that it is absurd to think that anyone can correctly predict the inflation rate. It is undoubtedly true that expectations will never be exactly correct, but the point is that if expectations are approximately correct, monetary policy will have little effect on output.

The more serious objection to the reasonableness of the result in Equation (12) criticizes the assumption underlying Equation (3). This is that

---

[10] The implications of perfect foresight and rational expectations for policy are being intensively studied by economists. We discuss the rational expectations school in more detail in Chapter 15. See Thomas J. Sargent and Neil Wallace, "Rational Expectations and the Theory of Economic Policy," *Journal of Monetary Economics*, April 1976, for an introduction to the approach.

the labour market works so smoothly that, in the short run, full employment will be attained if expectations of inflation are correct. In a context such as that of Chapter 11, in which prices do not adjust instantly to demand changes, monetary changes can have real effects through channels other than errors in expectations. If wage increases are passed on only slowly into price changes, as they were in Chapter 11, then a change in the growth rate of money would only slowly be passed through into prices. This means the aggregate supply curve would move up only slowly in response to a change in monetary growth, and output should, as a consequence, increase. Realistically, stickiness of wage and price adjustment remains an essential feature of the adjustment process of the economy. We return to this point in Chapter 15, in connection with the further discussion there of the implications of rational expectations.

The major implication of the alternative expectations hypotheses is that the dynamic behaviour of the economy is crucially affected by the way in which expectations are formed. With perfect foresight, changes in the rate of monetary growth leave output unaffected and cause the inflation rate to overshoot its steady-state level immediately. When expectations are formed on the basis of the lagged inflation rate, as in Equation (5), both output and inflation adjust slowly to the change in money growth. In this latter case, both output and inflation will at times be above, and at other times below, their steady-state levels during the adjustment process.

Summary

The main points made in this section were:

1 If inflationary expectations are based in a simple way on the past behaviour of the inflation rate, an increase in the rate of growth of the money stock increases both the inflation rate and the level of output in the short run. Both the rate of inflation and the level of output continue to fluctuate thereafter, tending eventually to move to the long-run equilibrium of the economy.
2 There are stages in the adjustment process of the economy to a change in the growth rate of money at which the level of output and the rate of inflation move in opposite directions. This occurs as a result of shifts in the aggregate supply curve caused by changes in expectations.
3 If expectations show perfect foresight, the response of the simple economy studied in this section to a change in the growth rate of money is very different. Output remains at its potential level throughout and the change in the growth rate of money affects only the inflation rate and not real income.
4 Even if expectations do show perfect foresight, changes in the growth rate of money can have effects on the level of real output if prices adjust only slowly to changes in demand. Such a mechanism was included in Chapter 11 and is omitted here only to keep the analysis relatively simple.

*13-7 FISCAL POLICY CHANGES

In the long run, the full-employment budget deficit is constant, and therefore f, the change in the full-employment deficit, is zero. Hence the inflation rate is in the long run independent of fiscal policy and is determined solely by the growth rate of money, as we saw in Section 13-1.

Fiscal policy may affect the level of potential output but not through channels we have been considering in this chapter. The route through which fiscal policy can affect the level of potential output is by affecting the mix of investment and consumption. If fiscal policy encourages investment, then the capital stock and level of potential output are likely to be higher in the long run. In this chapter, though, we have not included sufficient detail to study that allocative (between consumption and investment) role of fiscal policy. Instead, we treated fiscal policy as simply a method of affecting aggregate demand — and that is the way we shall continue to treat it in examining its short-run effects.

We will now consider what happens when there is an increase in the full-employment budget deficit, so that f, our measure of the *change* in the full-employment deficit, becomes positive in period 1. Thereafter, it reverts to zero. We assume the growth rate of money is constant at m_0. In the long run, we know, there are no effects of the fiscal policy change on either the inflation rate or the level of output.

Figure 13-11 is used for the analysis of the short-run effects of the increase in the full-employment deficit. The initial increase in the deficit moves the aggregate demand curve up from AD_0 to AD_1. We shall assume here that the expected rate of inflation is equal to last period's rate of inflation.[11] That ensures that the aggregate supply curve does not shift in the first period. The first-period equilibrium is, accordingly, at E_1, with both output and the inflation rate above their long-run levels.

Next period, both the supply and demand curves shift. The aggregate supply curve shifts up from AS_0 to AS_2 as a result of the change in the expected rate of inflation, which is now equal to last period's inflation rate. The aggregate demand curve is affected by the increases in lagged output and expected inflation, tending to cause the curve to shift upward, and by the fall in f, which is now back to zero, tending to cause the curve to shift downward. The net effect of these three factors on the aggregate demand curve is ambiguous, but we assume that the curve shifts down in period 2 from AD_1 to AD_2. As a result of these two shifts, we show the level of output at E_2 as lower than at E_1. However, if the aggregate demand curve shifts up, the level of output could be higher in the second period than in the first. Similarly, the inflation rate at E_2 may be either higher or lower than at E_1. Note that after period 2 the full-employment deficit is no longer changing.

---

[11] In the problem set, we ask you to carry out this analysis under the alternative expectations assumption that the expected inflation rate is equal to the growth rate of money.

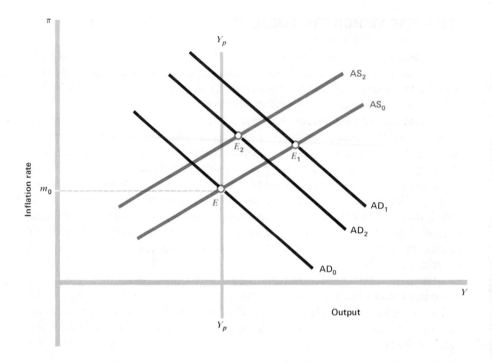

FIGURE 13-11 SHORT-RUN EFFECTS OF FISCAL POLICY

In subsequent periods, the rate of inflation and the level of output both continue to change, moving eventually to their long-run equilibrium levels. During the process of adjustment, the inflation rate and the output rate move both above and below their long-run equilibrium levels.

The analysis of both this section and the last makes it very clear that quite complicated patterns of adjustment of the economy can result from very simple assumptions about the ways in which expectations adjust and in which aggregate demand is determined. We have simplified greatly here; for example, we have assumed that aggregate demand is determined solely by the current fiscal policy and current real balances, rather than also by lagged fiscal policy and real balances. We simplified the dynamics of the Phillips curve by omitting the influence of lagged unemployment rates. We used a very simple model of expectation formation. And even so, we do not get to tell a very simple story about how the economy adjusts to policy changes — or, for that matter, to other disturbances. This reinforces the message of Chapter 9 about the difficulties of stabilization policy, for it is precisely the dynamics of the response of the economy to changes in policy that policy makers have to be able to predict if they are to carry out successful policy.

*13-8 THE FISHER RELATION:
REAL AND NOMINAL INTEREST RATES

We now return to the behaviour of real and nominal interest rates, particularly during the adjustment process to an increase in the growth rate of money. We show that the real interest rate is, in the long run, unaffected by changes in the growth rate of money and consequent changes in the inflation rate, but that the real interest rate may change in the short run. This is fundamentally the argument made by Irving Fisher.[12] Correspondingly, the nominal interest rate adjusts one for one with the inflation rate in the long run, but not in the short run.

Our analysis combines the IS curve, Equation (7), with the diagrammatic apparatus of the previous sections. In particular, it will be convenient to use Figure 13-10 to study real interest rate behaviour in response to a change in the growth rate of money. We recall that underlying Figure 13-10 is the assumption that the expected rate of inflation is equal to last period's inflation rate.

Now Equation (7) is

$$Y = \bar{\alpha}(\bar{A} - bi_r) \tag{7}$$

In Figure 13-12 we reproduce Figure 13-10 in the top panel. In the bottom panel we draw the IS curve, Equation (7), with the real interest rate, i_r, on the vertical axis. We see immediately from both Equation (7) and the diagram that there is a unique real interest rate corresponding to each level of income. Thus, to study the real interest rate during the adjustment process, we concentrate on the behaviour of real income.

Note first the long-run constancy of the real rate. Given fiscal policy, represented by $\bar{A}$ in Equation (7), there is a unique real interest rate corresponding to each level of income, and particularly to the level of potential output, Y_p. Since income in the long run is equal to Y_p, the real interest rate is in the long run equal to i_r^*.

Second, we consider the dynamic adjustment of the real interest rate following an increase in the growth rate of money. The real interest rate will decrease as long as income rises and increase as income falls. Thus, the real rate falls from i_r to i_r' as the economy moves from E to E_1 following the increase in the growth rate of money. The real rate continues to fall until income stops rising. The real rate then starts rising and continues to rise to above its steady-state level until income again turns around and begins to rise, at point B in Figure 13-12.

Figure 13-13 shows the time path of adjustment of the real rate to the change in monetary growth. Note particularly that the initial response of the

[12] Irving Fisher, *The Theory of Interest*, New York: A.M. Kelly, Publishers, 1965). Reprint of 1930 edition.

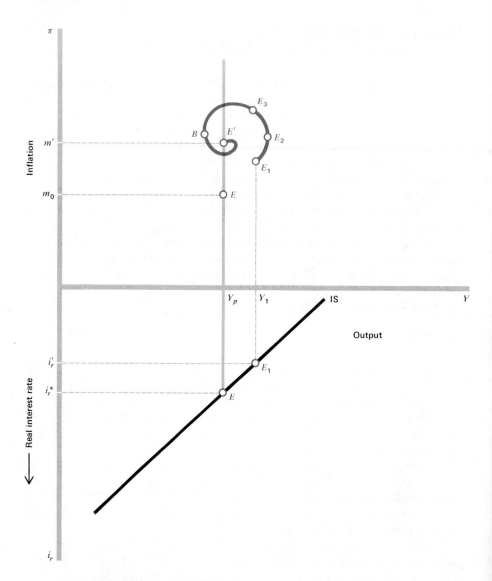

FIGURE 13-12 ADJUSTMENT OF OUTPUT, INFLATION, AND THE REAL INTEREST RATE TO AN INCREASE IN MONETARY GROWTH

real rate is to fall as the increase in the money stock reduces the nominal rate and expectations of inflation have not yet adjusted. Indeed, the fall in the real rate is the means by which monetary policy succeeds in increasing aggregate demand and output. Then later, as the inflation rate and price level rise, real balances fall, putting pressure on the nominal rate. At the same time, as expectations adjust, the real rate also rises.

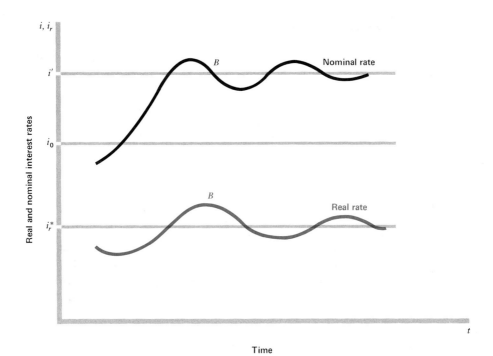

FIGURE 13-13 TIME PATHS OF THE REAL AND NOMINAL INTEREST RATES

Figure 13-13 also shows the behaviour of the nominal interest rate. In the first period, the nominal rate falls from its initial i_0 level, since the expected rate of inflation has not yet changed. Then, in subsequent periods, the nominal rate rises relative to the real rate as the expected rate of inflation (equal in this analysis to last period's inflation rate) rises. The nominal rate starts falling before the real rate.[13] Then the nominal rate fluctuates around its new long-run equilibrium level, i'.

What mechanisms are at work in affecting the behaviour of the nominal rate? Initially, the nominal rate falls when the money supply increases, prices rise less, and real balances therefore increase. Later, as the level of income rises and the expected rate of inflation increases, the demand for money rises and the nominal rate increases.

What would be the adjustment pattern of real and nominal interest rates if there were perfect foresight? Then the real rate should not change at all,

---

[13] Do you see why this is true? It is possible to read the nominal rate off Figure 13-12. The expected rate of inflation each period is last period's inflation rate. Therefore, add to the current real rate the inflation rate last period to find the current nominal rate. You should experiment with this method, which we do not present formally since it clutters up the diagram.

since the level of output does not change. The behaviour of the nominal rate would be exactly parallel to that of the inflation rate, initially rising by more than the growth rate of money increases, and then reaching a new steady state where it has risen by exactly the same amount as the growth rate of money.

We now see that there is good reason for nominal interest rates to have risen during the postwar period, as shown in Chart 13-2. Those increases can be attributed to increases in the expected rate of inflation, which would cause an increase in investment demand if nominal rates remained at their initial level. However, the analysis has shown that, in the long run, the real rate is invariant to changes in the inflation rate.

Next, we want briefly to consider the effects of an increase in the full-employment deficit on real and nominal interest rates. We will not carry out the complete analysis, leaving that for you. But we should note that the IS curve in the lower panel of the diagram would shift out to the right and up. The impact effect of the increased full-employment deficit is to increase both the real and nominal interest rates. Then, during the adjustment process, both interest rates fluctuate around their new higher steady-state levels. In the long run, the real interest rate is increased, as is the long-run nominal rate.

We have three final brief comments. First, what is the connection between the analysis of Chapter 4, which showed that an increase in the money supply would reduce the interest rate, and the dynamic analysis of this section? Chapter 4, of course, did not include expectations of inflation and thus did not distinguish real from nominal interest rates. In addition, the price level was fixed in Chapter 4. We should regard the analysis of that chapter as indicating the *short-run* effects of an increase in the money stock on interest rates. With unchanged expectations, we do see from Figure 13-13 that both real and nominal rates fall in the short run when the growth rate of the money stock is increased. Then the implications of price flexibility and expectations of inflation begin to affect interest rates, and the results of Chapter 4 become inapplicable. Of course, the analysis of that chapter remains valuable, since we still use the basic IS-LM framework to study interest rate behaviour in this chapter.

Second, we should note that the constancy of the real rate of interest discussed here should not be taken literally. We have omitted from the analysis any disturbances or shifts in the behavioural functions underlying the IS curve in the lower panel of Figure 13-12 and the aggregate supply and demand curves in the upper panel. Increases in investment demand or consumption demand would increase the real rate. Shifts in money demand would affect real and nominal rates in the short run, given the growth rate of money, as would other disturbances. There also are subtleties involving taxes that could upset the Fisher relation. But there is indeed a tendency for the real rate to be constant over long periods.

Third, historical data suggest that the average real interest rate has been surprisingly low. In the period 1926-1978, the *ex post* real interest rate on U.S. Treasury Bills averaged only 0.0 percent. Even the *ex post* real rate on long-term government bonds averaged only 0.6 percent.[14] The real return on common stocks over the same period averaged 6.1 percent.

Summary

1   An increase in the growth rate of money leaves the real interest rate unaffected in the long run and increases the nominal interest rate one for one.

2   An increase in the growth rate of money typically reduces both the real and nominal rates in the short run. Thereafter, the rates fluctuate around their steady-state values as the economy settles down to a new steady state.

3   Expansionary fiscal policy increases real and nominal interest rates in the short and long runs. Again, interest rates fluctuate around their steady-state values during the adjustment process.

4   The adjustment pattern for interest rates is heavily affected by the behaviour of expectations of inflation.

*13-9 INFLATION AND THE GOVERNMENT DEFICIT

In Chapter 12 we considered the effect of financing a temporary deficit by either money creation or borrowing from the private sector. The long-run effect in both cases was seen to be a permanent increase in the prive level. Here we analyze the effect on the rate of inflation of a permanent deficit fixed in real terms.

Consider first the case of debt finance. An attempt to run a permanent real deficit financed by debt must imply reductions in other transfer payments or increases in taxes. As the debt accumulates over time, interest payments on the debt increase. Without changes in other variables affecting the deficit, the deficit would continue to increase through the increasing interest payments. Such a policy cannot be maintained forever because eventually government spending and other transfers would be reduced to zero and taxes would have to continue to increase forever. That cannot be done forever without having adverse effects on the level of output. Therefore we conclude that attempts to finance a given real deficit purely

[14] These data are presented in Robert G. Ibbotson and Rex A. Sinquefield, *Stocks, Bonds, Bills, and Inflation: Historical Returns (1926-1978)* (New York: Financial Analysts Research Foundation, 1979).

through debt financing cannot be viable in the long run in an economy that is not growing.[15]

Consider next the effects of a small *permanent* budget deficit financed by money creation. We assume a "small" real deficit because we shall argue presently that there is a maximum deficit that can be financed by money creation. Attempts to go beyond that maximum deficit lead to uncontrolled inflation. Assume that the government increases its spending. That results in an increase in the full-employment deficit which shifts the aggregate demand curve AD in Figure 13-14 out to the right. In addition the growth rate of the nominal money stock increases and shifts the aggregate demand curve further out for that reason. These two factors shift the aggregate demand curve from AD_0 to AD_1 and move the economy from an equilibrium at E to E_1. Both the inflation rate and growth rate of output rise. Eventually, the aggregate demand curve shifts back to the left somewhat, as a result of the fact that the full-employment deficit is no longer increasing. However, because the money stock has to grow (at a higher rate) to finance the deficit, the aggregate demand curve remains permanently higher than it was

[15] The long-run effects of debt-financed changes in government spending are analyzed in a widely discussed paper by Alan Blinder and Robert Solow, "Analytical Foundations of Fiscal Policy," in A.S. Blinder et al., *The Economics of Public Finance* (Washington, D.C.: The Brookings Institution, 1974).

FIGURE 13-14 EFFECTS OF A PERMANENT INCREASE IN THE DEFICIT FINANCED BY MONEY CREATION

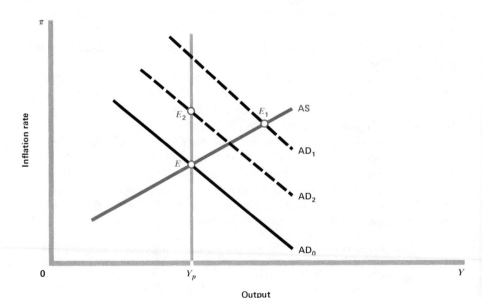

initially, and the inflation rate at the new long-run equilibrium E_2 is permanently higher than it was initially at E.

The Inflation Tax

In discussing the effects of a permanent real deficit, we said that it was possible that a deficit of given size could not be financed by money creation. To establish that fact, it is useful to think of inflation as a tax on the holdings of real money balances. To simplify the exposition, we shall talk only of equilibrium long-run inflation, in which the expected rate of inflation is equal to the actual rate of inflation.[16]

Inflation is a tax on the holdings of real balances because anyone who holds money when there is inflation loses part of the value of that money, owing to the inflation. A man starting the year with $100 will have to add $5 to his money holdings during the year merely to maintain their real value or purchasing power constant if there is 5 percent inflation. Alternatively, if he keeps his nominal money holdings constant at $100 over the year, he loses 5

---

[16] Inflation is often rhetorically described as "the cruelest tax of all." This statement does not refer to the analysis we are about to carry out of inflation as a tax on real balances in the long run with the actual inflation equal to expected inflation. Instead, it applies to the effects of unexpected inflation on those who have saved in nominal assets — such as savings deposits — for their retirement. Such individuals are obviously adversely affected by inflation. If the inflation is unexpected, they will find themselves with assets of lower real value than they had expected to have, and with a lower standard of living than they had planned.

FIGURE 13-15 THE DEMAND FOR REAL BALANCES AS A FUNCTION OF THE EXPECTED RATE OF INFLATION percent of the value of the money, owing to inflation. The effect of the inflation is thus the same as the effect of a tax on the holding of the money.

Let us spell out the argument more carefully. The value of the inflation tax is the amount that individuals have to add to their cash balances every year to maintain the real value of their cash balances constant. Let ΔM be the amount of nominal balances added to cash balances and P be the price level. Denote the real value of the inflation tax by T_I. Then

$$T_I = \frac{\Delta M}{P} \tag{3}$$

Now we can multiply and divide in Equation (3) by M to obtain

$$T_I = \frac{\Delta M}{M} \cdot \frac{M}{P} = \pi \cdot \frac{M}{P} \tag{3a}$$

In the absence of growth, and in the long run, $\Delta M/M$, the growth rate of the money stock, is equal to the rate of inflation π. Hence the inflation tax can be thought of as the inflation rate times holdings of real balances. In the long run, real balances are constant in the absence of growth, so that M/P is constant in the long run.

Now, how does the inflation tax behave as the inflation rate changes? At first glance, it might seem from Equation (3a) that the total inflation tax rises with the rate of inflation π. However, we know that holdings of real balances depend on the costs of holding real balances, and thus should be expected to fall as increases in the expected rate of inflation cause the nominal interest rate, the cost of holding money, to rise. Figure 13-15 draws a demand curve for real balances (LL) as a function of the expected inflation rate, holding the real interest rate and real income constant. Since the real interest rate is constant, the LL curve in effect shows the demand for money as a function of the nominal interest rate. The LL curve is therefore downward-sloping.

In long-run equilibrium, in which the expected rate of inflation is equal to the actual rate, $\pi = \pi^*$, the inflation tax is given by the area of the rectangle shown in Figure 13-15. The tax from Equation (3a) is the product of the inflation rate and the level of real balances or the "tax base" and that is precisely given by the area of rectangles such as that shown, with sides of length π_0^* and $(M/P)_0$.

For the demand curve shown in Figure 13-15, the inflation tax as a function of the inflation rate is shown in Figure 13-16. As the inflation rate rises from zero, the total tax rises. Eventually though, increases in the inflation rate drive down the demand for money so much that the total tax revenue falls. T_I^* is the maximum inflation tax revenue. At a zero inflation rate, there is no tax and so no tax revenue. Thus, increases in the inflation rate from zero will increase total revenue from the inflation tax. Eventually, though, the tax rate becomes high enough to drive demand down to the point

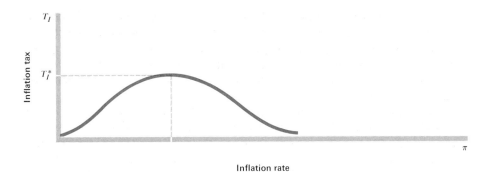

FIGURE 13-16 THE INFLATION TAX AS A FUNCTION OF THE RATE OF INFLATION

where total revenue begins to decline.[17] There is nothing special about a tax on real balances as opposed to a tax on any other commodity in this regard.

Inflation is not referred to as a tax merely because individuals find that the real value of their money balances is reduced by inflation. The counterpart of the public's payment of the inflation tax — additions to nominal money balances so as to keep their purchasing power constant and thus offset the effect of inflation — is the government's receipt of the inflation tax. Thus the government collects the tax by buying goods and services from the private sector with the money the private sector adds to its nominal balances. This budgetary aspect of the inflation tax completes the reason why inflation can be thought of as a tax collected from money holders and accruing to the government. Furthermore, it is this tax aspect of money-financed deficits that has led some to argue that there are only two ways the deficit can be financed, taxation or borrowing from the public. The third way, borrowing from the Bank of Canada and corresponding money creation, it is argued, is in fact a form of taxation.[18]

Now, what does all this have to do with the budget and macroeconomic adjustment? The major point of this part is that, in long-run equilibrium, there is a maximum amount of revenue that can be raised through the inflation tax. If the government attempts to raise more revenue than the maximum it can obtain through issues of high-powered money, and if it prints more high-powered money whenever it finds itself unable to cover its

[17] Can you show that the elasticity of demand for real balances with respect to the expected rate of inflation is one at the point of maximum revenue? Note that the "Laffer curve," which shows that income tax revenue first rises as the income tax rate rises and then falls as the tax rate reaches very high levels, is essentially the same as Figure 14-4.

[18] It should be noted that in Canada and most other countries, only part of the money supply — high-powered money — is issued by the government. The inflation tax collected by the government is based on its "sales" of high-powered money, and not on the change in the total money supply.

expenses, the rate of inflation will continue increasing. The public and the government will be competing for goods with the government printing money and the public trying to get rid of it. Eventually the economy will experience an extremely rapid inflation or a *hyperinflation*. For instance, in the German hyperinflation of 1922-1923, the average rate of inflation was 322 percent *per month*.

Keynes, in a masterful description of the hyperinflation process in Austria after World War I, tells of how people would order two beers at a time because they grew stale at a rate slower than their price was rising.[19] Other stories include those of a woman who carried her (worthless) currency in a basket and found that, having set down the basket for a moment, it was stolen, but the money had been left.

To return now to the budget deficit, we see why the government could not finance a deficit in excess of the maximum revenue from the inflation tax by borrowing from the central bank. In other words, there are real deficits that simply can not, in the long run, be financed by borrowing from the central bank, that is, by the issuing of high-powered money. Attempts to finance in that way would lead to hyperinflation. The fear that hyperinflation will result from large budget deficits may be one of the arguments in the minds of those most concerned over the budget deficit. But it is foolish to assume that any budget deficit, however small, will lead to a hyperinflation, even if it is financed by borrowing from the Bank of Canada.

The analysis of the inflation tax is not of great importance for Canada, with its well-functioning tax system and central bank. In other countries, with less well-developed tax systems, the printing of money may be one of the few ways the government has of obtaining resources. To put it differently, in some countries, large parts of government spending are financed by borrowing from the central bank and thus by inflation.

13-10 SUMMARY

1   Using the aggregate supply-demand framework of Chapter 12, we can draw aggregate supply and demand curves relating the level of output to the inflation rate rather than the price level.

2   The short-run aggregate supply curve is upward-sloping — higher inflation rates are associated with higher levels of output, in the short run. The slope of the aggregate supply curve is greater, the more unemployment reacts to changes in output (the larger is h) and the more rapidly wages respond to changes in unemployment (the larger is ϵ).

---

[19] See John Maynard Keynes, *A Tract on Monetary Reform* (New York: Macmillan, 1923), which remains one of the most readable accounts of inflation. See also Phillip Cagan, "The Monetary Dynamics of Hyperinflation," in Milton Friedman (ed.), *Studies in the Quantity Theory of Money* (Chicago: The University of Chicago Press, 1956).

The position of the aggregate supply curve depends on the expected rate of inflation.

3 The long-run aggregate supply curve is vertical.

4 The short-run aggregate demand curve is downward-sloping. It is steeper, the less sensitive is aggregate demand to changes in real balances (the smaller is ϕ). The position of the aggregate demand curve depends on lagged output, the rate of change of the full-employment deficit, changes in expected inflation, and the growth rate of the money stock.

5 In the short run, the rate of inflation and the level of output are determined by the current and lagged expected rates of inflation, the lagged level of output, the change in the full-employment surplus, and the growth rate of the money stock. An increase in the expected rate of inflation increases the actual rate of inflation and reduces output. Increases in the last three variables increase both the rate of inflation and output.

6 In the long run, the level of output is equal to potential output. The rate of inflation is equal to the growth rate of the money stock.

7 In the short run, an increase in the growth rate of money produces increases in output and inflation if expectations are based on the past behaviour of inflation. At stages during the adjustment process of the economy to the increased money growth, output and inflation will be moving in opposite directions.

8 If expectations show perfect foresight and if prices adjust immediately to wage changes, then output stays at its potential level when the growth rate of money rises.

9 In the short run, an increase in the full-employment deficit increases both output and the inflation rate. A one-time increase in the full-employment deficit has no permanent effects on the rate of inflation and the level of output.

10 The Fisher relation, that the real interest rate is independent of the inflation rate in the long run but varies during the adjustment process, is confirmed by the analysis of this chapter. Correspondingly, in the long run the nominal interest rate rises one for one with the inflation rate.

11 The behaviour of output, unemployment, inflation, and interest rates is heavily affected by the way in which expectations are formed.

12 A permanent increase in government spending financed by money creation results in a permanent increase in the inflation rate.

13 Inflation can be regarded as a tax on real balances. The federal government collects the tax through the quantity of high-powered money that it provides during inflation to meet the increased demand for high-powered money. There is a maximum revenue that can be raised through the inflation tax.

PROBLEMS

* 1 (a) Explain how the size of h and the size of ϵ affect the slope of the aggregate supply curve. Be sure to provide an intuitive explanation along with any other explanation.

  (b) Why is it the *product* $h\epsilon$ (rather than, for example, the sum $h + \epsilon$) that determines the slope of the AS curve?

  2 Explain in words why the expected rate of inflation affects the position of the aggregate supply curve.

  3 Suppose we have an economy where real output grows at the rate of 6 percent per year. The nominal quantity of money grows at the rate of 5 percent. The income elasticity of money demand is 0.5.

  (a) What is the rate of inflation in long-run equilibrium?

  (b) What is the growth rate of nominal income? (Remember that nominal income can grow because prices increase, real output rises, or both.)

  (c) How would your answers to 3(a) and 3(b) change if the income elasticity of money demand was unity?

  4 Suppose that the rate of inflation is 3 percent, that real wages are rising by 2 percent, and real balances are rising by 4 percent. What is:

  (a) The rate of increase of nominal wages?

  (b) The rate of growth of the nominal money stock?

* 5 How far *upward* does the aggregate demand curve, Equation (10a), shift at a given level of income for:

  (a) A 1 percent increase in the growth rate of the money stock?

  (b) An increase of one unit in f?

  (c) A one-unit increase in Y_{-1}?

  (d) A 1 percent increase in the expected rate of inflation.

  Explain why increases in each of those variables shift the AD curve up, and also try to explain the extent to which the curve is shifted in each case — 5(a), 5(b), 5(c), and 5(d).

* 6 (a) How does the *slope* of the aggregate demand curve determine the short-run effects on the rate of inflation and output of an increase in the growth rate of money — assuming that the expected rate of inflation is unaffected by the change in monetary growth?

  (b) How does the slope of the AS curve affect the way in which a change in the growth rate of money changes the rate of inflation and output in the short run? Provide a verbal explanation along with any diagrams you draw in both cases.

  7 (a) Suppose that there is a one-time increase in $Y_{,,}$ which thereafter remains constant. How does that affect the *long-run* inflation rate?

  (b) Suppose that $Y_{,,}$ began to grow steadily at a rate $\bar{x}$. How would that affect the long-run rate of inflation?

* 8 Draw an aggregate supply-demand diagram like Figure 13-9, but with a very flat aggregate supply curve. Then, assuming that $\pi^* = \pi_{-1}$, allow the growth rate of money to increase and show how the supply and demand curves shift in the first two periods. Show what happens to the rate of inflation and the level of output in these periods, starting from the period in which the growth rate of money increases. Compare your results with those of Figure 13-9 and explain the reasons for any differences.

* 9 Using the aggregate supply-demand diagrams of Chapter 12,
  (a) Show how in steady state the aggregate supply and demand functions would be shifting up over time in such a way as to keep output constant.
  (b) Analyze the *first-period* impact of an increase in monetary growth that does not affect expectations.

*10 Suppose the growth rate of money changes unexpectedly and that expectations are given by $\pi^* = m_{-1}$. Expectations are based on last period's money growth. Analyze the short- and long-run effects of the changed money growth on output, inflation, and the real and nominal interest rates.

*11 In analyzing the effects of a change in f in one period, we assumed that the expected rate of inflation was given by Equation (5). Now use the alternative assumption that $\pi^* = m$, that people believe the inflation rate is determined exclusively by monetary growth.
  (a) Analyze the dynamic consequences of a one-time increase in f.
  (b) Does this expectations assumption show perfect foresight?

*12 Explain in words the mechanism whereby the nominal interest rate adjusts to inflation in the long run.

 13 At the beginning of the chapter, in discussing Chart 13-1, we said that we wanted to be able to explain behaviour such as that shown in the chart. How does the analysis of this chapter explain that behaviour, particularly the periods when the unemployment rate and the inflation rate were increasing together?

*14 In Figure 13-3 we showed the effect of increased inflationary expectations on the equilibrium interest rate and level of output. In that figure we conducted the analysis with the nominal interest rate (i) on the vertical axis. Now show the same effects in a diagram that has the real interest rate on the vertical axis.
  (a) Express the LM curve in terms of the nominal interest rate and expected inflation, using the relation, $i_r = i - \pi^*$.
  (b) Draw the IS and LM schedules corresponding to the initial equilibrium.
  (c) Consider the increase in inflationary expectations. Which schedules shift and by how much?
  (d) Show in your diagram the change in the real interest rate.

 15 In some countries there is virtually no capital market in which the government can borrow, and only a rudimentary tax system, so that taxes produce only very small revenues.
  (a) What is the relationship between monetary and fiscal policy in such countries?
  (b) What does the inflation tax analysis imply about the ability of the government in such a country to spend a large share of GNP permanently?

*16 Recall that the elasticity of demand for real balances with respect to the expected inflation rate (see Figures 13-15 and 13-16) is defined as

$$\frac{\Delta(M/P)}{\Delta\pi^*} \cdot \frac{\pi^*}{(M/P)}$$

Prove that if $(\pi_0^*, (M/P_0)$ is the point in Figure 13-15 where T_I is maximized, then at π_0^* this elasticity is 1.

*17 Analyze the effects on the economy of a permanent increase in the level of government spending financed by money creation.

*18 Trace the path the economy follows when there is a permanent increase in government spending that is financed by borrowing from the public. Take account of the size of the deficit in each period. (Do not follow this sequence of events for more than three periods.)

14

THE PHILLIPS CURVE AND THE TRADEOFFS BETWEEN INFLATION AND UNEMPLOYMENT

I n mid-1979, all economic forecasters were predicting the 1980 recession. The inflation rate was running above 9 percent. Some argued strongly for a tax cut to try to head off the coming recession, while others felt that it was more important to try to reduce the inflation rate and refused to support a tax cut. These policy choices reflect an assessment of the relative costs of inflation and unemployment. They certainly reflect the judgment that there is a cost to inflation, and that this cost is sufficiently important to warrant a period of unemployment in order to reduce inflation. The policies imply, too, the belief that inflation can be reduced in the long run without the cost of a permanently higher rate of unemployment. This chapter investigates the premises of such policy choices. We address the questions of the costs of inflation and of unemployment, the meaning of unemployment, and the *tradeoff* between inflation and unemployment.

You will find that the problems in this chapter do not have definite answers. These problems are among the most lively and controversial in current economic research. Furthermore, the inflation-unemployment problem is the key issue in political economy. Although the answers in this area are few, it is well worth laying out the relevant considerations and analyzing the areas of agreement and controversy.

This chapter starts by revisiting the Phillips curve of Chapter 13 and investigating the tradeoff between inflation and unemployment. In Chapter 13 we argued that in the short run while the expected inflation rate is constant, the Phillips curve is relatively flat. This implies a short-run tradeoff between inflation and unemployment: in the short run, the unemployment rate can be reduced at the cost of higher inflation. By contrast, we argued that in the long run, the unemployment rate is equal to the natural rate. This indicates that there is no long-run tradeoff between inflation and unemployment, or alternatively, that the long-run Phillips curve is vertical. That view is not universally held. It has been argued that lower unemployment can be bought *in the long run* at the cost of higher inflation. We examine the arguments and evidence about the slope of the long-run Phillips curve in Section 14-1.

In Section 14-2 we study the structure of Canadian unemployment, emphasizing the flows in and out of the unemployment pool. The natural rate of unemployment is the focus of Section 14-3. We discuss the concept, some estimates of the natural rate, and methods of lowering the rate. Sections 14-4 and 14-5 explore the costs of unemployment and inflation respectively. Section 14-6 examines alternative strategies — steady but slow versus cold turkey — for ending inflation.

14-1 IS THE LONG-RUN PHILLIPS CURVE VERTICAL?

In Figure 14-1 we show two long-run Phillips curves. The vertical long-run curve P_VP_V was introduced in Chapter 13. Its essential property is the implication that in the long run, the unemployment rate is independent of the rate of inflation, and equal to the *natural rate*, u. The downward-sloping long-run curve, P_NP_N, by contrast, implies that in the long run, there is a *tradeoff* between inflation and unemployment. According to the negatively sloped curve, the economy can in the long run operate either with a high rate of inflation and low rate of unemployment, say at point A, or with a low rate of inflation and high rate of unemployment, at a point like B.

FIGURE 14-1 VERTICAL AND NEGATIVELY SLOPED LONG-RUN PHILLIPS CURVES

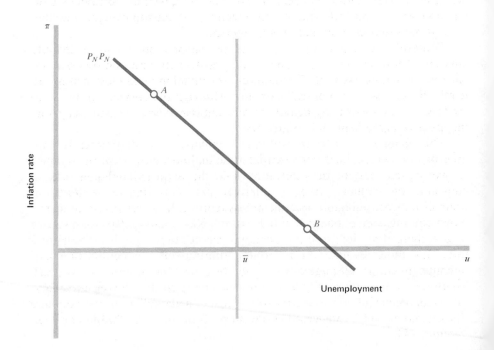

If there is a long-run tradeoff, as along the $P_N P_N$ curve, then policy makers must make the important choice between running a high-pressure economy in which inflation is high but there is little unemployment and jobs are easy to find and a low-pressure economy in which prices are stable but jobs are difficult to find. If the long-run curve is vertical, such as $P_V P_V$, there is no such choice. Indeed, if the long-run curve is vertical but policy makers mistakenly think there is a chice, they will be tempted to increase the inflation rate to try to reduce the unemployment rate, as $P_N P_N$ suggests they can. But all they will get in the long run is more inflation and no less unemployment, as indicated by the $P_V P_V$ curve. The issue is clearly important.

The view that there is a long-run tradeoff was widely accepted in the sixties, but does not now command much support. In the remainder of this section, we consider (1) why the view that there is a long-run tradeoff was held, and (2) what the implications of a long-run vertical Phillips curve are.

The main reason the long-run tradeoff view was accepted in the sixties was that it seemed to fit the facts. The original Phillips curve, estimated by Phillips on the basis of almost a century's data, was negatively sloping. Since a century is quite long enough to be the long run, it looked as though there was a negative long-run relationship. Similarly, you will see if you go back to Chart 1-5 on page 13, that in the fifties and sixties the inflation and unemployment rates in Canada were negatively related, as on $P_N P_N$. And even a decade is long enough to be the long run.

Of course, experience in Canada and other countries since then does not suggest that there is a negative long-run Phillips curve, as a further look at Chart 1-5 will confirm. Indeed, if anything, the long-run relationship looks positively sloped.[1]

At a theoretical level, the downward-sloping curve was initially accepted because the role of expectations of inflation was ignored. In terms of the Phillips curve used in Chapter 13

$$\pi = \pi^* - \epsilon(u - \bar{u}) \tag{1}$$

the expected rate of inflation, π^*, was omitted from early formulations of the curve.

Since the late fifties and early sixties were periods of low and relatively constant inflation, ignoring expectations of inflation did little harm to predictions made using the Phillips curve. The important change in ideas came in the late sixties and early seventies when the Phillips curve seemed to be shifting. It was apparent in 1971 that the 5 percent inflation then being experienced along with a 6 percent unemployment rate was inconsistent with the Phillips curve fitted on data from the fifties and sixties. It became clear that a Phillips curve without expectations was unstable.

---

[1] Milton Friedman, in his Nobel Prize lecture, argued that the long-run curve is positively sloped. See "Inflation and Unemployment," *Journal of Political Economy*, June 1977.

At that time, and even a little earlier, concentration shifted to the role of expectations of inflation in the process of wage bargaining. The suggestion was that when inflation was expected, labour would want its wage agreements to reflect the expected inflation, and firms would be willing to go along with the proposals since the prices they would expect to charge would also rise with expected inflation. The argument was advanced originally by Milton Friedman and Edmund Phelps,[2] and it leads to the *expectations-augmented Phillips curve*, Equation (1).

What are the implications of a Phillips curve, such as Equation (1), that is vertical in the long run? There is, first, the implication that there is no long-run tradeoff between inflation and unemployment. However, Equation (1) does suggest that there could be a short-run tradeoff, as long as the expected rate of inflation does not adjust to actual inflation. The idea here is that the public takes time to catch on to the rate of inflation, and that by the time it has recognized an inflation rate say, of 5 percent, the government could already have moved the rate of inflation up to 6 percent. Then, by the time the public has begun to expect 6 percent inflation, the actual rate of inflation could be moved to 7 percent — and so on. However, it is hard to believe that the public would not eventually come to understand that the inflation rate was accelerating. One can then argue that the acceleration of the inflation rate could be ever-increasing, but again, the public should ultimately catch on. Thus, even if it is possible to affect the unemployment rate through aggregate demand policy in the short run, it is not possible to do so in the long run.

Second, there is the implication of Equation (1), seen in Chapter 13, that if expectations are *rational*, that is, if people are on average right about expected inflation even in the short run, aggregate demand policy cannot be used systematically to affect unemployment in the short run either. This is *not* necessarily an implication of the long-run Phillips curve's being vertical, even though it is an implication of Equation (1). For example, suppose wages adjust slowly to changed expectations and prices in turn adjust slowly to wages. Under these conditions, aggregate demand policy can be used to affect unemployment in the short run even if expectations are rational, since then we are essentially in the fixed price or slowly adjusting price economy studied in Chapter 4. However, in the long run, as prices fully adjust, the Phillips curve would be vertical.

The vertical long-run Phillips curve generated controversy in the sixties since it seems to suggest that *nothing* can be done about long-run unemployment, which will settle down to the natural rate $\bar{u}$ whatever aggregate demand policies are followed. However, whether the long-run Phillips curve is vertical or downward-sloping, it may be possible to reduce the natural rate $\bar{u}$ through labour market policies. These are policies designed to make

---

[2] See Milton Friedman, "The Role of Monetary Policy," *American Economic Review*, March 1968, and Edmund Phelps, *Inflation Policy and Unemployment Theory* (New York: Norton, 1973).

the labour market more efficient. In terms of Figure 14-1, labour market policies would imply a leftward shift of the vertical long-run Phillips curve by reducing $\bar{u}$. Indeed, the idea of shifting the Phillips curve was discussed long before the issue of long-run vertical versus downward-sloping curves arose.

While there is now considerable agreement on a long-run vertical Phillips curve, that agreement is not unanimous.[3] Nor, for that matter, do we feel completely confident that the Phillips curve is vertical at *all* rates of inflation. Therefore we would not be surprised to see that the long-run Phillips curve has a shape such as that shown in Figure 14-2. At positive rates of inflation (to which our actual experience since 1945 is essentially limited), the curve is for all practical purposes vertical. At negative rates of inflation, it may well be practically horizontal. Even high unemployment will not cause prices to fall rapidly. The basis for the Phillips curve of Figure 14-2 is the suggestion that money wage behaviour is asymmetrical. Wages rise in the face of excess demand for labour or expected inflation, but do not fall at the same rate in the event of even heavy unemployment or expected

[3] See, for example, Robert Solow, "Down the Phillips Curve with Gun and Camera," in David A. Belsley et al. (eds.), *Inflation, Trade and Taxes* (Columbus: Ohio State University Press, 1976), and James Tobin, "Inflation and Unemployment," *American Economic Review*, March 1972.

FIGURE 14-2 THE LONG-RUN PHILLIPS CURVE WITH MONEY WAGES THAT ARE STICKY DOWNWARD

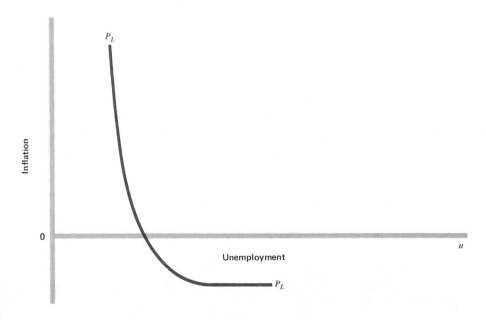

deflation.[4] There is some evidence for that view, and, if it is correct, the long-run Phillips curve might well be kinked, as in Figure 14-2.

What practical conclusions can we draw from our discussion of the Phillips curve here and in Chapters 11 and 13? The first important point is that the short-run Phillips curve with given expectations and/or sticky wages and prices may well be quite flat — large reductions in unemployment can be achieved with little increase in inflation. The next proposition is that expectations adjust and shift the Phillips curve up after an expansion of aggregate demand and reduction of unemployment. The expectations adjustment certainly raises the inflation cost of sustaining a lower unemployment level. The last proposition is that there is no *usable* long-run inflation-unemployment tradeoff in the economy. This means that for all practical purposes, the long-run Phillips curve is vertical and that expansionary aggregate demand policies cannot be used to reduce long-run unemployment. In the short run, though, increases in aggregate demand can be used as a means of reducing unemployment.

14-2 THE ANATOMY OF UNEMPLOYMENT

It is time to take a closer look at unemployment, now that we have reviewed the inflation-unemployment tradeoff. We will emphasize three central facts about unemployment:

1 There are substantial flows of individuals in and out of unemployment each month, and most people who become unemployed in any given month remain unemployed for only a short time.
2 Much of the unemployment is constituted of people who will be unemployed for quite a long time.
3 There is considerable variation of unemployment rates across different regions and groups in the labour force.

The first and second facts may seem contradictory. A numerical example should make it clear that there is no necessary contradiction. Suppose that the labour force consists of 100 people, and that five people become unemployed each month. Suppose that four of those people are unemployed for precisely one month, and one person will be unemployed for six months. Suppose also that the economy is in a steady state, so that this situation has repeated itself every month for years.

---

[4] In fact, money wages might not fall at all but simply remain constant. In that event, the rate of decline in prices would at most be equal to the rate of productivity growth. This is so because the rate of change of prices is approximately equal to the rate of change of wages less the growth rate of productivity. Accordingly, with money wages constant, productivity growth puts a floor under the rate of deflation.

We ask first how many people are unemployed at any one time, say September 30. There will be five people who became unemployed September 1, one person who became unemployed August 1 (and who has been unemployed for two months), and so on, back to the person who became unemployed April 1, and whose six months of unemployment will end the next day, on October 1. In total, there will be ten people unemployed. So the unemployment rate is 10 percent. Of the ten, six will suffer a six-month spell of unemployment before they again become employed. This is consistent with the second fact. But, remember that we started with five people becoming unemployed each month, four of whom remain unemployed for only a month. And that is consistent with the first fact, that most people who become unemployed within a given month remain so for only a short time. We shall return to this example later in this section.

The third fact, variation of unemployment rates across different groups or regions in the labour force, can be examined using the relationship between the overall unemployment rate, u, and the unemployment rates, u_i, of groups within the labour force. The overall rate is a weighted average of the unemployment rates of the groups:

$$u = w_1 u_1 + w_2 u_2 + \ldots + w_n u_n \tag{2}$$

The weights, w_i, are the fraction of the labour force that falls within the specific group, say, teenagers.

Equation (2) makes it clear that the overal unemployment rate either could be made up of unemployment rates that are much the same for different groups in the labour force, or else could conceal dramatic differences in unemployment rates among regions or among groups categorized, say, by age and sex. Fact 3 is that the aggregate rate does conceal substantial differences in unemployment rates. For instance, in 1979, the aggregate unemployment rate was 7.5 percent. For the age group 15-24 the rate was 13.0, while for the group aged 25 and over it was 5.4. In terms of Equation (2), we have

$$7.5\% = (0.28)13.0\% + (0.72)5.4\%$$

where the shares of the two groups in the labour force are 28 percent and 72 percent respectively.

We now turn to a more detailed examination of the three central facts about the anatomy of unemployment.

Flows In and Out of Unemployment

An unemployed person is defined as one who is out of work *and* who (1) has either actively looked for work during the previous four weeks, or (2) is waiting to be recalled to a job after having been laid off, or (3) is waiting to report to a new job within four weeks.[5]

Figure 14-3 shows how people enter and leave the *unemployment pool*. A person may become unemployed for one of four reasons: (1) The person may be a new entrant into the labour force, looking for work for the first time or else be a reentrant — someone returning to the labour force after not having looked for more than four weeks. (2) A person may leave a job in order to look for other employment and be counted as unemployed while searching. (3) The person may be laid off. A *layoff* means that the worker was not fired but rather, will return to the old job if demand for the firm's product recovers. A firm will typically adjust to a decline in produce demand by laying off some labour. A firm may also rotate layoffs among its labour force so that the individual laid-off worker may expect a recall even before product demand has fully recovered. (4) A worker may lose a job to which there is no chance of returning, either because he is fired or because the firm closes down.

These sources of inflow into the pool of unemployment have a counterpart in the outflow from the unemployment pool. There are essentially three ways of moving out of the pool of unemployment. (1) A person may be hired

[5] For a detailed description of the definitions used and the data collection procedures, see notes at the end of Statistics Canada, 71-001.

FIGURE 14-3 FLOWS IN AND OUT OF THE UNEMPLOYMENT POOL

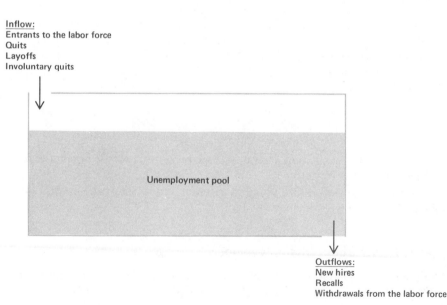

Inflow:
Entrants to the labor force
Quits
Layoffs
Involuntary quits

Unemployment pool

Outflows:
New hires
Recalls
Withdrawals from the labor force

TABLE 14-1 FLOWS INTO UNEMPLOYMENT, 1979

	Number (thousands)	Percent of labour force
Job losers	392	3.5
Job leavers	183	1.6
New entrants	52	.5
Reentrants	212	1.9
	838	7.5

Source: Statistics Canada, 71-001.

into a new job. (2) Someone laid off may be recalled. (3) An unemployed person may stop looking for a job and thus, by definition, leave the labour force. Such a person may plan to look for a job again soon.

Table 14-1 shows the breakdown of the average flow into unemployment in 1979. Notice that a substantial fraction is accounted for by reentrants into the labour force. There is also a substantial flow from the unemployment pool out of the labour force. In 1979 there were on average 475,000 persons not in the labour force who had lost their jobs or had been laid off. This suggests that the distinction between being unemployed and being out of the labour force is not a very sharp one, and that individuals move quite easily in both directions — between being unemployed (meaning essentially that they looked for a job in the last four weeks) and not employed (out of the labour force).

The data in Table 14-2 illustrates the fact that there are substantial flows of individuals in and out of unemployment. On average in 1978 there were 10,882,000 persons in the labour force and an average of 8.4 percent were unemployed. However, this unemployment rate does not represent a constant group of individuals who were unemployed for the whole year. Of the

TABLE 14-2 UNEMPLOYMENT RATE AND INCIDENCE OF UNEMPLOYMENT, 1978

Labour force and unemployment, annual average	
Total labour force (thousands)	10,882
Unemployed (thousands)	911
Unemployment rate (percent)	8.4
Incidence of unemployment	
In labour force at some time (thousands)	12,353
Unemployed at some time (thousands)	2,687
Incidence (percent)	21.8

Source: Statistics Canada, 71-001, July, 1980.

12,353,000 individuals who were in the labour force at some time during the year, 21.8 percent experienced a spell of unemployment with a duration that averaged less than a year.

Consideration of the *duration* of spells of unemployment provides an alternative way of looking at flows in and out of unemployment. Given the unemployment rate, the shorter the average spell of unemployment — the time the individual is unemployed — the larger are the flows. For instance, in the example at the beginning of this section we had a 10 percent unemployment rate with five people becoming unemployed each month. We could also have a 10 percent unemployment rate if ten people became unemployed each month and each one remained unemployed for exactly one month. In the earlier example, the average spell is longer than a month, since four out of five spells end in a month, but one out of five lasts six months. (The average spell is thus two months.) The shorter the average duration, the larger the flows of labour through the unemployment pool, given the overall unemployment rate.

Table 14-3 shows the distribution of unemployment by duration in 1977. About one half of those surveyed had been unemployed for less than nine weeks but over one-third had been unemployed for 14 weeks or more and 15 percent had been unemployed for more than six months. These data establish that despite the substantial flows in and out of unemployment, much of aggregate unemployment is accounted for by people who remain unemployed for a substantial time. Thus, if one believes that unemployment is a more serious problem when it affects only a few people intensely, rather than many people a little, these data suggest that unemployment is a more severe problem than the aggregate unemployment rate indicates. The next set of data we review, those on the distribution of unemployment by age and region support that view.

TABLE 14-3 DURATION OF UNEMPLOYMENT, 1977

	Number (thousands)	Percent
4 weeks or less	263	31.6
5-8 weeks	150	18.0
9-13 weeks	117	14.0
14-26 weeks	175	21.1
27-52 weeks	101	12.2
more than 52 weeks	26	3.1
	832	100.0

Note: Duration here does not refer to completed spells of unemployment but rather duration up to the end of the week of the survey.

Source: Statistics Canada, 71-001, May, 1978.

The Distribution of Unemployment

The third important fact about the anatomy of unemployment is that unemployment is distributed very unevenly across the population. Table 14-4 shows unemployment rates by age and sex. Unemployment is considerably higher in the age group 15-24 years, and in the age group 25 years and over it is higher among women. Table 14-5 and Chart 14-1 show unemployment rates by region. The Atlantic provinces have consistently shown the highest unemployment rates. In recent years, as a result of the oil and gas boom, the prairie provinces have experienced the lowest rates.

TABLE 14-4 UNEMPLOYMENT RATES BY AGE AND SEX, 1979

	Both sexes	Men	Women
15-24 years	13.0	13.3	12.7
25-44 years	6.0	4.9	7.8
45 years and over	4.5	4.0	5.4
Total	7.5	6.6	8.8

Source: Statistics Canada, 71-001.

CHART 14-1 UNEMPLOYMENT RATES BY REGION
(*Source: Bank of Canada Review*)

TABLE 14-5 UNEMPLOYMENT RATES BY PROVINCE, 1979

Newfoundland	15.4	British Columbia	7.7
Prince Edward Island	11.3	Ontario	6.5
New Brunswick	11.1	Manitoba	5.4
Nova Scotia	10.2	Saskatchewan	4.2
Quebec	9.6	Alberta	3.9

Source: Statistics Canada, 11-003.

14-3 THE NATURAL RATE OF UNEMPLOYMENT

The *natural rate of unemployment* is also called the full-employment level of unemployment, or the long-run equilibrium level of unemployment. In this section, we first discuss the determinants of the natural rate of unemployment and then examine estimates of changes in the natural rate since the fifties.

Figure 14-3 points to the factors causing the unemployment rate to change. Increases in the rate of entry to the labour force, or quits, or layoffs, or other job losses cause the unemployment rate to rise. Increases in hiring, or recalls, or withdrawals from the labour force, cause the unemployment rate to fall. Each of these factors is in part determined by economic variables, such as the level of aggregate demand and the actual and expected real wage rate. When aggregate demand rises (at a given real wage), firms increase their hiring. When aggregate demand falls, firms lay off workers. Thus there is an immediate link between the factors emphasized in Figure 14-3 and aggregate demand. However, it should be noted that the relationship between aggregate demand and the variables affecting the rate of unemployment is not unambiguous. For instance, an increase in the demand for labour increases quits at the same time as it reduces layoffs. A man thinking of leaving his job to search for another would be more likely to quit when the job market is good and demand is high than when there is heavy unemployment and the prospects of finding a good job quickly are low. When the unemployment rate is constant, flows in and out of unemployment just balance each other and these flows can match at any level of unemployment. The *natural rate of unemployment*, however, is that rate of unemployment at which flows in and out of unemployment just balance,[6] *and* at which expectations of firms and workers as to the behaviour of prices and wages are correct.

[6] We should recognize that when the labour force is growing and the unemployment rate is constant, the pool of unemployed grows over time. For example, with a labour force of 8 million and 5 percent unemployment, total unemployment is 400 thousand people. With a labour force of 10 million and 4.5 percent unemployment, there are 450 thousand unemployed, and the unemployment pool has grown by 50 thousand people.

The determinants of the natural rate of unemployment can be thought of in terms of the duration and frequency of unemployment. The *duration* of unemployment is the average length of time a person remains unemployed. That depends on (1) the organization of the labour market, in regard to the presence or absence of employment agencies, youth employment services, etc., (2) the demographic makeup of the labour force; (3) the ability and desire of the unemployed to keep looking for a better job; and (4) the availability and types of jobs. If all jobs are the same, an unemployed person will take the first one offered. If some jobs are better than others, it is worthwhile searching and waiting for a good one. If it is very expensive to remain unemployed, say, because there are no unemployment benefits, an unemployed person is more likely to accept a job offer than to continue looking for a better one. If unemployment benefits are high, then it may be worthwhile for the unemployed person to continue looking for a better job rather than to accept a poor job when one is offered.

The behaviour of workers who have been laid off is also important when considering the duration of unemployment. Typically, a worker who has been laid off returns to the original job and does not search for another job. The reason is quite simple: once a worker, say, has been with a firm for a long time, she has special expertise in the way that firm works which makes her valuable to that firm but is not of great benefit to another employer. In addition, she may have built up seniority rights, including a pension. That means that such an individual could not expect to find as good a job if she searched for a new one. Her best course of action may be to wait to be recalled.

There are two basic determinants of the *frequency* of unemployment. The first is the variability of the demand for labour across different firms in the economy. The second is the rate at which new workers enter the labour force. Even when aggregate demand is constant, some firms are growing and some are contracting. The contracting firms lose labour and the growing firms hire more labour. The greater this variability of the demand for labour across different firms, the higher the unemployment rate. Further, the variability of aggregate demand itself will affect the variability of the demand for labour. Second, the more rapidly new workers enter the labour force — the faster the growth rate of the labour force — the higher the natural rate of unemployment.

The four factors affecting duration and the two factors affecting frequency of unemployment are the basic determinants of the natural rate of unemployment.

You should note that the factors determining the level of the natural rate of unemployment are not immutable. The structure of the labour market and the labour force can change. The willingness of workers to remain unemployed while looking for, or waiting for, a new job can change. The variability of the demand for labour by different firms can shift. As Edmund Phelps has noted, the natural rate is not "an intertemporal constant, something like the speed of light, independent of everything under the sun."[7] Indeed, the natural rate is difficult to measure, and estimates of it have changed over the last few years from about 4 percent in the 1960s to 5.5 to 6 percent in the early eighties.

Estimates of the Natural Rate of Unemployment

Estimates of the natural rate of unemployment typically try to adjust for changes in the composition of the labour force, and perhaps for changes in the natural rate of unemployment of the various groups in the labour force. We can write an equation very similar to Equation (2) for the natural rate, $\bar{u}$;

$$\bar{u} = w_1\bar{u}_1 + w_2\bar{u}_2 + \ldots + w_n u_n \qquad (2b)$$

Equation $(2b)$ says that the natural rate is the weighted average of the natural rates of unemployment of the subgroups in the labour force.

Chart 14-2 shows the natural rate of unemployment as estimated in a

[7] See E. Phelps, "Economic Policy and Unemployment in the Sixties," *Public Interest*, Winter 1974.

CHART 14-2 THE NATURAL RATE OF UNEMPLOYMENT, 1957-1978
(*Source*: P. Fortin and L. Phaneuf, "Why Is the Unemployment Rate So High in Canada?" Paper presented at the meetings of the Canadian Economics Association, 1979.)

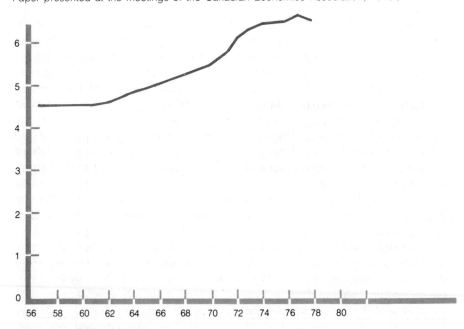

study by P. Fortin and L. Phaneuf, who consider four labour force groups on the basis of age and sex.[8] Table 14-6 shows the changing structure of the labour force as reflected by the data for these groups. Over the period 1966 to 1975, the proportion of younger persons in the labour force grew and this is reflected in a rise in the overall natural rate of unemployment since this group has consistently experienced higher unemployment. The proportion of women in the labour force has grown steadily over the past 15 years as a result of growth in the female *participation rate* (the fraction of women who are in the labour force). Since the unemployment rate for females aged 25 and over has also been rising, the increase in the participation rate for this group has contributed to the growth in the overall natural rate.

The sharp increase in the natural rate of unemployment in 1972 and 1973 reflects the estimated effects of liberalization of the benefits payable to the unemployed under the Unemployment Insurance Act. The provision of a high level of unemployment benefits makes it less urgent for an unemployed

[8] See P. Fortin and L. Phaneuf, "Why Is the Rate So High in Canada?" Paper presented at the meetings of the Canadian Economic's Association, May, 1979.

TABLE 14-6 THE CHANGING STRUCTURE OF THE LABOUR FORCE AND UNEMPLOYMENT, 1955-80

	MALES			FEMALES			TOTAL
	Total	15-24	25+	Total	15-24	25+	
Proportion of Total Labour Force							
1966	68.7	13.7	55.0	31.3	10.5	20.8	100.0
1970	66.4	14.2	52.2	33.6	11.2	22.4	100.0
1975	63.1	14.9	48.2	36.9	12.2	24.7	100.0
1980	60.0	14.5	45.5	40.0	12.3	27.7	100.0
Participation Rates							
1966	79.8	64.1	84.9	35.4	48.4	31.2	57.3
1970	77.8	62.4	83.3	38.3	49.4	34.5	57.8
1975	78.4	68.8	81.9	44.3	56.8	40.0	61.1
1980	78.3	72.0	80.5	50.3	62.6	46.2	64.0
Average Unemployment Rate							
1966-1970	4.3	8.3	3.3	4.4	6.4	3.4	4.3
1971-1975	5.5	11.2	3.9	7.0	9.8	5.5	6.0
1976-1980	6.9	14.1	4.7	8.9	13.0	7.0	7.7

Source: Statistics Canada, 71-001, 71-201.

person to obtain a job. Further, the fact that a laid-off worker will not suffer a large loss from being unemployed makes it more attractive for an employer to lay off workers temporarily than to attempt to keep them on the job.

There seems to be little doubt that unemployment compensation does add to the natural rate of unemployment. This does not imply, though, that unemployment compensation should be abolished. What is appropriate is a scheme that will create less incentive for firms to lay off labour while at the same time ensuring that the unemployed are not exposed to economic distress. This is obviously a difficult trick to carry off.

14-4 THE COSTS OF UNEMPLOYMENT

The costs of unemployment are so obvious that this section might seem superfluous. Society on the whole loses from unemployment because total output is below its potential level. The unemployed as individuals suffer both from their income loss while unemployed and from the low level of self-esteem that long periods of unemployment cause.[9]

This section provides some estimates of the costs of forgone output resulting from unemployment, and clarifies some of the issues connected with the costs of unemployment and the potential benefits from reducing unemployment. We distinguish between cyclical unemployment, associated with short-run deviations of the unemployment rate from the natural rate and "permanent" unemployment that exists at the natural rate.

Cyclical Unemployment

The fundamental cost of cyclical unemployment is the short-run loss of output. Are there any other costs of unemployment or, for that matter offsetting benefits? It is possible to imagine offsetting benefits. We do not discuss here the benefit arising from a temporary reduction in the inflation rate accompanying a temporary increase in unemployment, but rather, focus on the costs of unemployment taken by itself. A possible offsetting benefit occurs because the unemployed are not working and have more leisure. However, the value that can be placed on that leisure is small. In the first place, much of it is unwanted leisure.

Second, there is a fairly subtle issue that we shall have to explore. If a person were free to set her hours of work, she would work up to the point at which the marginal value of leisure to her was equal to the marginal return from working an extra hour. We would then be able to conclude that if her

---

[9] See Robert J. Gordon, "The Welfare Cost of Higher Unemployment," *Brookings Papers on Economic Activity*, 1973:1 (Washington, D.C.: The Brookings Institution, 1973); and Edmund S. Phelps, *Inflation Policy and Unemployment Theory* (New York: Norton, 1972).

workday were slightly reduced, the overall loss to her would be extremely small. The reason is that she acquires extra leisure from working less, at the cost of having less income. But she was previously at the point where the marginal value of leisure was equal to the after-tax marginal wage, so that the benefit of the increased leisure almost exactly offsets the private loss of income. However, the net marginal wage is less than the value of the marginal product of an employed person to the economy. The major reason is that society taxes the income of the employed person, so that society as a whole takes a share of the marginal product of the employed person. When the employed woman in our example stops working, she loses for herself only the *net* of tax wage she has been receiving. But society also loses the taxes she has been paying. The unemployed person values her leisure at the net of tax wage, and that value is smaller than the value of her marginal product for society as a whole. Therefore, the value of increased leisure provides only a partial offset to the cost of cyclical unemployment.

Note that we do not count both the individual's personal loss of income and the foregone output as part of the cost of unemployment. The reason is that the foregone output implicitly includes the individual's own loss of income — it estimates the total loss of output to the economy as a whole as a result of the reduction of employment. That loss could in principle be distributed across different people in the economy in many different ways. For instance, one could imagine that the unemployed person continues to receive benefit payments totalling close to her or his previous income while employed, with the benefit payments financed through taxes on working individuals. In that case, the unemployed person would not suffer an income loss from being unemployed, but society would still lose from the reduction in total output available.

However, the effects of an increase in unemployment are, in fact, borne heavily by the unemployed themselves. There is thus an extra cost to society of unemployment that is very difficult to quantify. The cost arises from the uneven distribution of the burden of unemployment across the population. Unemployment tends to be concentrated among the poor, and that makes the distributional aspect of unemployment a serious matter. It is not one we can easily quantify, but it should not be overlooked. Further, there are many reports of the adverse psychic effects of unemployment that, again, are not easy to quantify but should not be ignored.[10]

"Permanent" Unemployment

The benefits of reducing the natural rate of unemployment are more difficult to estimate than the costs of cyclical unemployment. We cannot use the short-run output-employment relationship since the increase in output

---

[10] See Harry Maurer, *Not Working* (New York: Holt, Rinehart and Winston, 1979), and Kay L. Schlozman and Sidney Verba, *Injury to Insult* (Cambridge: Harvard University Press, 1979).

associated with cyclical changes in unemployment results in part from the fact that the labour put back to work in the short run is able to use capital that had not been fully utilized when unemployment was high. However, in the long run, which is relevant when considering a reduction in the natural rate of unemployment, it would be necessary to invest to provide for the capital with which the newly employed would work.

The available estimates of the social benefits of a reduction in long-run unemployment cannot be narrowed down to very solid numbers. Even more difficult is the estimate of an "optimal" long-run unemployment rate. Here we ask the question whether any — and, if so, how much — unemployment is desirable in the long run. A first guess at the answer to that question is that all unemployment is wasteful, since the unemployed labour could usefully be employed. However, that answer is not totally persuasive. Those people who are unemployed in order to look for a better job are performing a valuable service not only for themselves. They are also performing a service for society by attempting to put themselves into a position in which they earn the most and are the most valuable. Because the composition of demand shifts over time, we can expect always to have some firms expanding and some contracting. This is true even with a stable level of aggregate demand. Those who lose their jobs will be unemployed and they benefit both society and themselves by not taking the very first job that comes along, but rather, searching for the optimal employment. Accordingly, we can conclude that some unemployment is a good thing in an economy in which the composition of demand changes over time. It is one thing to recognize this and quite another to pin down the optimal rate of unemployment numerically.

14-5 THE COSTS OF INFLATION

The costs of inflation are much less obvious than those of unemployment. There is no direct loss of output from inflation, as there is from unemployment. In studying the costs of inflation, we again want to distinguish the short run from the long run. In the case of inflation, though, the relevant distinction is between inflation that is *perfectly anticipated* and taken into account in economic transactions, and *imperfectly anticipated*, or unexpected inflation. We start with perfectly anticipated inflation because that case provides a useful bench mark against which to judge unanticipated inflation.

Perfectly Anticipated Inflation

Suppose that an economy has been experiencing a given rate of inflation, say 5 percent, for a long time, and that it is correctly anticipated that the rate of inflation will continue to be 5 percent. In such an economy, all contracts would build in the expected 5 percent inflation. Borrowers and lenders will both know and agree that the dollars in which a loan will be repaid will be worth less than the dollars which are given up by the lender when making the loan. Nominal interest rates would be 5 percent higher than they would be in the absence of inflation. Long-term wage contracts will increase wages at 5 percent per year to take account of the inflation, and then build in whatever changes in real wages are agreed to. Long-term leases will take account of the inflation. In brief, any contracts in which the passage of time is involved will take the inflation into account. Inflation has no real costs in such an economy, except for a minor qualification to be noted below.

That qualification arises because the interest rate that is paid on money might not adjust to the inflation rate. No interest is paid on currency — notes and coin — throughout the world, and no interest is paid on demand deposits in many countries. It is very difficult to pay interest on currency, so that it is likely that the interest rate on currency will continue to be zero, independent of the perfectly anticipated inflation rate. Interest can be, and in some cases is already, paid on demand deposits. Thus it is reasonable to expect that in a fully anticipated inflation, interest would be paid on demand deposits, and the interest rate paid on demand deposits would adjust to the inflation rate. If so, the only cost of perfectly anticipated inflation is that the inflation makes it more costly to hold currency.

The cost to the individual of holding currency is the interest forgone by not holding an interest-bearing asset. When the inflation rate rises, the nominal interest rate rises, the interest lost by holding currency increases, and the cost of holding currency therefore increases. Accordingly, the demand for currency falls. In practice, this means that individuals economize on the use of currency by carrying less in their wallets and making more trips to the bank to cash smaller cheques than they did before. The costs of these trips to the bank are often described as the "shoe-leather" costs of inflation. They are related to the amount by which the demand for currency is reduced by an increase in the anticipated inflation rate, and they are trivial.

We should add that throughout this discussion, we are assuming inflation rates that are not too high to effectively disrupt the payments system. This disruption was a real problem in some instances of hyperinflation, but it need not concern us here. We are abstracting, too, from the cost of "menu change." This cost arises simply from the fact that with inflation — as opposed to price stability — people have to devote real resources to marking up prices and changing pay telephones and vending machines as well as cash registers. These costs are there, but one cannot get too excited about them. On balance, the costs of fully anticipated inflation are trivial.

The notion that the costs of fully anticipated inflation are trivial does not square well with the strong aversion to inflation reflected in policy making and politics. The most important reason for that aversion is probably that inflations in Canada have not been steady, and that our inflationary experience is one of imperfectly anticipated inflation, the costs of which are substantially different from those discussed in this section.

There is a further line of argument that explains the public aversion to inflation, even of the fully anticipated, steady kind we are discussing here. The argument is that such a state is not likely to exist, that it is a mirage to believe that policy makers could and would maintain a steady inflation rate at any level other than zero. The argument is that policy makers are reluctant to use restrictive policy to compensate for transitory increases in the inflation rate. Rather than maintain a constant rate of inflation in the face of inflation shocks, the authorities would accommodate these shocks and therefore validate them. Any inflationary shock would add to the inflation rate rather than being compensated by restrictive policy. In this manner, inflation, far from being constant, would, in fact, be rising as policy makers validate any and every disturbance rather than use policy to rigidly enforce the inflation target. Zero inflation, it is argued, is the only target that can be defended without this risk.[11]

Although there are many examples of countries with long inflationary histories, there does not appear to be any tendency for the inflation rate of those countries to increase over time. The argument thus seems weak. However, it is true that the inflation rate has been more stable in countries with low rates of inflation than in countries with inflation rates that are on average higher,[12] perhaps providing a germ of validity to the notion.

Indexation of the Tax System

The contracts that would have to be adjusted for inflation to avoid distortion include the tax laws. For example, personal income tax rates are normally progressive and fixed in relation to nominal income so that taxes rise as a proportion of income as income increases. Consider the taxpayer shown in Table 14-7 in which we are comparing an initial situation with a price level of 100 and pretax nominal income of $20,000 with a later situation in which both the price level and pretax nominal income have doubled. Initially, taxes of $7,000 are paid on nominal income of $20,000. After the price level doubles, a higher proportion of nominal income, namely $20,000, is paid in taxes. That is because the income tax is progressive. That means that the real value of after-tax income falls with the price level and that the real value of taxes paid to the government rises with the price level — taxes increase from $7,000 to $20,000 in Table 14-7. In terms of the initial price level, taxes increase in real value by $3,000. Thus, with tax rates unchanged and a progressive tax system, inflation tends to raise real taxes.

[11] See William J. Fellner, introductory essay in William J. Fellner (ed.), *Contemporary Economic Problems* (Washington, D.C.: American Enterprise Institute, 1973).

[12] Arthur M. Okun, "The Mirage of Steady Inflation," *Brookings Papers on Economic Activity,* 2:1971 (Washington, D.C.: The Brookings Institution, 1971).

TABLE 14-7 EFFECTS OF INFLATION ON AFTER-TAX INCOME

Price Level	Pretax income, nominal	Taxes, nominal	After-tax income, nominal	After-tax income, real
100	$20,000	$ 7,000	$13,000	$13,000
200	40,000	20,000	20,000	10,000

To alleviate this problem, the federal government introduced in the budget of February 1973 a system for *indexing* the personal income tax. Since then the basic exemptions and tax brackets have been adjusted each year in proportion to the price level so that changes in the price level do not affect real taxes.[13] For the taxpayer in Table 14-7, the nominal taxes would only double from $7,000 to $14,000 with doubling of the price level.

The major economic argument against indexation of the tax system is that a progressive tax system in nominal terms provides an automatic stabilizer for the economy in response to changes in the price level. We recall the role of automatic stabilizers from Chapter 3. The argument there was that a proportional income tax would reduce the marginal propensity to spend out of income and therefore would reduce the size of the multiplier. The argument here is that with progressive taxation of nominal income — that is, taxes that increase as a proportion of income as nominal income rises — we would have further stabilizing effects. With progressive taxation of nominal income, an increase in the price level such as would arise from an aggregate demand disturbance would be dampened because tax rates rise with the increase in nominal income and thus reduce multipliers. While a simple proportional tax system provides for a built-in stabilizer, the further benefits of progressive taxation for built-in stabilizer purposes are small. Thus the economic argument against indexation of the tax system is weak.

Imperfectly Anticipated Inflation

The idyllic scene of full adjustment to inflation painted here does not describe economies that we actually know. Modern economies include a variety of institutional features representing different degrees of adjustment to inflation. Economies with long inflationary histories, such as those of Brazil and Israel, have made substantial adjustments to inflation through the

---

[13] This scheme does not make the personal income tax fully neutral. For example, full indexing would require the taxation of interest to be on the *real* (after-inflation) return on assets. A rough allowance for this was made in the budget of November 1974 by permitting $1,000 of interest income tax free.

use of indexing. Others in which inflation has been episodic, such as the Canadian economy, have made only small adjustments for inflation.

One of the important effects of inflation is to change the real value of assets fixed in nominal terms. A doubling of the price level, such as Canada experienced in the period from 1965 to 1977, cuts the purchasing power of all claims or assets fixed in money terms in half. Thus, someone who bought a 15-year government bond in 1965 and expected to receive a principal of, say, $100 in constant purchasing power at the 1980 maturity date, actually winds up with a $100 principal that has purchasing power of less than $50 in 1965 dollars. The more than doubling of the price level has effectively reduced the real value of the asset by over one-half. It has transferred wealth from creditors — holders of bonds — to debtors. This effect operates with respect to all assets fixed in nominal terms, in particular, money, bonds, savings accounts, insurance contracts, and some pensions. Obviously, it is an extremely important effect since it can certainly wipe out the purchasing power of a lifetime's saving that is supposed to finance retirement consumption.

These facts by themselves seem to explain the public concern over inflation. There appears to be a lot riding on each percentage-point change in the price level. That impression is slightly misleading. Many individuals are both debtors and creditors in nominal assets. Almost everyone has some money, and is thus a creditor in nominal terms. Many own housing, financed through mortgages whose value is fixed in nominal terms. Such individuals benefit from inflation because it reduces the real value of their mortgage. Other individuals have borrowed in nominal terms to buy consumer durables, such as cars, and to that extent have their real indebtedness reduced by inflation.

Table 14-8 shows the estimated impact of inflation on the relative net asset positions of households classified by age and income. Over the period 1969 to 1975, the young gained in relation to the old because they typically had much larger debts. The middle-income groups gained because they typically has assets in the form of real estate financed by mortgage debt. Fewer poor families had the means to buy property or to incur debt, while wealthier families naturally had a larger fraction of their wealth in financial assets.

In addition to the redistribution among households shown in Table 14-8, inflation brings about transfers among the household, corporate and government sectors. However, the gains and losses from these wealth transfers basically cancel out over the economy as a whole. When the government gains from inflation, the private sector may have to pay lower taxes later. When the corporate sector gains from inflation, owners of corporations benefit at the expense of others. If we really did not care about the distribution of wealth among individuals, the costs of unanticipated inflation would be negligible. Included in the individuals of the previous sentence are those belonging to different generations, since the current owners of the

TABLE 14-8 IMPACT OF INFLATION ON RELATIVE NET ASSET POSITIONS OF
HOUSEHOLDS, 1969-1975

Age group in 1969					
Under 25	25-34	35-44	45-54	55-64	65 and over
(Percent)					
21.1	14.5	4.4	-7.2	-10.8	-11.6

Income group			
Less than $4,000	$4,000-7,999	$8,000-14,999	$15,000 and over
(Percent)			
-10.8	5.1	10.9	-10.0

Source: Economic Council of Canada, Thirteenth Annual Review, p. 22.

national debt might be harmed by inflation — to the benefit of future
taxpayers.

Inflation redistributes wealth between debtors and creditors because
changes in the price level change the purchasing power of assets fixed in
money terms. There is room, too, for inflation to affect income positions by
changing the distribution of income. A popular line of argument has always
been that inflation benefits capitalists or recipients of profit income at the
expense of wage earners. Unanticipated inflation, it is argued, means that
prices rise faster than wages and therefore allow profits to expand. For
Canada in the postwar period, there is no persuasive evidence to this effect.
There is evidence that the real return on common stocks — that is, the real
value of dividends and capital gains on equity — is reduced by unanticipated
inflation. Thus, equity holders appear to be adversely affected by unanticipated inflation.[14]

The fact that unanticipated inflation acts mainly to redistribute wealth,
the net effects of which redistribution should be close to zero, has led to
some questioning of the reasons for public concern over inflation. The
gainers, it seems, do not shout as loudly as the losers. Since some of the
gainers (future taxpayers) have yet to be born, this is hardly surprising.
There is also a notion that the average wage earner is subject to an illusion
when both the nominal wage and the price level increase. Wage earners are

[14] See Charles R. Nelson, "Inflation and Rates of Return on Common Stocks," Journal of
Finance, May 1976. See also Franco Modigliani and Richard Cohn, "Inflation, Rational
Valuation and the Market," Financial Analysts Journal, March-April 1979, for a controversial
view of the reasons why inflation affects the stock market.

thought to attribute increases in nominal wages to their own merit rather than to inflation, while the general inflation of prices is seen as causing an unwarranted reduction in the real wage they would otherwise have received. It is hard to know how to test the validity of this argument.

It does appear that the redistributive effects of unanticipated inflation are large, and that, accordingly, some parts of the population could be seriously affected by unanticipated inflation. It is difficult to be more precise in discussing this complicated question, which, like others in this chapter, remains the subject of ongoing research.

1-6 SUMMARY

1 The long-run Phillips curve is essentially vertical. In the long run, there is no inflation-unemployment tradeoff.
2 The short-run Phillips curve is flatter than the long-run schedule because expectations are sticky and wages and prices are slow to adjust. But the Phillips curve shifts over time as expectations adjust to the actually realized rate of inflation.
3 The anatomy of unemployment for Canada reveals frequent and short spells of unemployment. Nonetheless, a substantial fraction of unemployment is accounted for by those who are unemployed for quite a long time.
4 There is considerable variation of unemployment rates across different regions and groups in the labour force.
5 The concept of the natural rate of unemployment singles out that part of unemployment which would exist even at full employment. The unemployment arises in part because of a high frequency of job changes. The natural rate of unemployment is hard to conceptualize and even harder to measure. It has recently been estimated to be about 6 percent compared with 4.5 percent in the fifties.
6 The cost of unemployment is the psychic and financial distress of the unemployed as well as the loss of output. The loss of output is not compensated by the unemployed's enjoying leisure. For one thing, a large part of unemployment is involuntary. For another, the social product of labour exceeds the wage rate because of income taxes.
7 The economy can adjust to perfectly anticipated inflation by moving to a system of indexed taxes and to nominal interest rates that reflect the expected rate of inflation. Thus there are no important costs to perfectly anticipated inflation. The only costs are those of changing price tags periodically and the cost of suboptimal holdings of currency.
8 Imperfectly anticipated inflation has important redistributive effects among sectors. Unanticipated inflation benefits monetary debtors and hurts monetary creditors. The government gains real tax revenue, and the real value of government debt declines.

PROBLEMS

1   In 1969, the Prices and Income Commission was established in an effort to improve the Phillips curve relationship through the use of voluntary wage-price guidelines. How would such a policy reduce inflation? Would you expect it to work in the short run? In the long run? What factors determine its effectiveness?

2   One frequently hears of the wage-price spiral. The underlying idea is that wage increases cause price increases, and these in turn cause more wage increases. These feed on one another in a never-ending spiral. Can the economy get caught in such a spiral? How would it get in? Out? Explain this notion in terms of the Phillips curve.

3   Discuss strategies whereby the government could reduce unemployment in or among:
    (a) Depressed industries
    (b) Unskilled workers
    (c) Depressed geographical regions
    (d) Teenagers
    Include comments on the *type* of unemployment you would expect in these various groups (i.e., relative durations of unemployment spells).

4   Discuss how the following changes would affect the natural rate of unemployment. Comment also on the side effects of these changes.
    (a) Elimination of unions
    (b) Increased participation of women in the labour market
    (c) Larger fluctuations in the *level* of aggregate demand
    (d) An increase in unemployment benefits
    (e) Elimination of minimum wages
    (f) Larger fluctuations in the *composition* of aggregate demand

5   Discuss the difference in unemployment and participation rates between men and women in view of Table 14.6. What do you think are the causes of these differences?

6   Some people say that inflation can be reduced in the long run without an increase in unemployment, and so we should reduce inflation to zero. Others say a steady rate of inflation at, say, 6 percent is not so bad, and that should be our goal. Evaluate these two arguments and describe what, in your opinion, are good long-run goals for inflation and unemployment. How would these be achieved?

7   In the past ten years, awareness of inflation has increased markedly.
    (a) Suppose people now adjust their expectations more rapidly than earlier because of this experience. What are the implications in terms of the effects of policy?
    (b) Suppose, instead, that people now take the view that inflation is going to be 6 percent no matter what the government does. What would this do to government efforts to reduce inflation below that figure? Explain.

* 8   How would the model in Chapter 13 be affected if a long-run Phillips curve like the one in Chart 14-1 were used, rather than a vertical long-run Phillips curve? Trace the short- and long-run effects of a decrease in the full-employment surplus in such a model.

9   Use the *Canadian Statistical Review* to find the unemployment data for the years 1969, 1975, and 1979. Use, as labour force groups, males and females,

15 to 24 years of age and 25 and over (that is, four groups). Then calculate what 1975 and 1979 unemployment would have been if each group in 1975 and 1979 had the unemployment rate of the group in 1969. What does the answer tell you?

10 What would be the effect of inflation on real income taxes if income taxation was:

(*a*) Regressive?

(*b*) Proportional?

(*c*) Indexed?

15

STABILIZATION POLICY:
THE PROBLEMS OF INFLATION
AND UNEMPLOYMENT

I n this chapter we focus on both the policy issues of the 1970s and the theories of economic policy that help explain the policy choices that were made and their failure or success. The use of active discretionary policy was increasingly questioned during the period. The view that active use of stabilization policy might be destabilizing was discussed in Chapter 9, and had long been argued by adherents of *monetarism*. Monetarist views were influential in the formulation of policy in the early part of the period. In the latter part of the 1970s, a more sophisticated critique of discretionary policy, developed by the *rational expectations school*, gained influence.

We begin with a discussion of monetarism and then consider alternative strategies for bringing down the rate of inflation by lowering the rate of growth of the money supply. The adoption of a monetarist approach by the Bank of Canada is then reviewed and its success or failure is considered. We conclude with a discussion of supply management and of the rational expectations approach to macroeconomics, which provides a possible explanation for the emergence of persistent high inflation.

15-1 MONETARISM

Milton Friedman and monetarism are almost synonymous. Monetarism appears, however, in many shades and covers quite a spectrum from a harder monetarism than the Friedman variety to eclectic Keynesianism. In that spectrum one would include distinguished economists such as Karl Brunner of the University of Rochester and Allan Meltzer of Carnegie-Mellon, Thomas Mayer of the University of California at Davis, Phillip Cagan of Columbia University, and David Laidler and Michael Parkin of the University of Western Ontario, to name only some of the most prominent. Monetarism is not confined to academic economists. Indeed, the Federal

Reserve Bank of St. Louis has long been a haven of a monetarist perspective on macroeconomics. If monetarism admits of some diversity, it nevertheless comes down to the proposition that money is extremely important for macroeconomics, that money is more important than other things such as fiscal policy, and, in some variants, that money is virtually *all* that matters.

Friedman's views on macroeconomics have been laid out in a series of scholarly articles, books, and popular writing.[1] Outstanding among his publications is *A Monetary History of the United States, 1867-1960*, a book written jointly with Anna J. Schwartz of the National Bureau of Economic Research. Despite its length, the *Monetary History* is an absorbing book that skilfully relates the behaviour of the economy to the behaviour of the stock of money. The book generally attributes changes in the level of prices and in economic activity — including the Great Depression — to movements in the stock of money.

What are the main features of monetarism?

Emphasis on the Stock of Money

Monetarism emphasizes the importance of the behaviour of the money stock in determining (1) the rate of inflation in the long run and (2) the behaviour of real GNP in the short run. Friedman has said:[2]

> I regard the description of our position as "money is all that matters for changes in *nominal* income and for *short-run* changes in real income" as an exaggeration but one that gives the right flavor of our conclusions.

The view that the behaviour of the money stock is crucial for determining the rate of inflation in the long run is consistent with the analysis of Chapter 13, as we noted there. The view that the behaviour of the money stock — by which Friedman usually means the *growth rate* of the money stock — is of primary importance in determining the behaviour of nominal and real GNP in the short run is not one we have accepted. Our treatment so far has given emphasis to *both* monetary and fiscal variables in determining the short-run behaviour of nominal and real GNP. But there is no doubt that monetary variables play an important role in determining nominal and real GNP in the short run.

An important part of monetarism is the insistence that changes in the growth rate of money — accelerations and decelerations — account for

[1] Some of Freidman's major articles are reprinted in *The Optimum Quantity of Money* (Chicago: Aldine, 1969). See also his book *A Program for Monetary Stability* (New York: Fordham University Press, 1959), and Milton Friedman and Anna J. Schwartz, *A Monetary History of the United States, 1867-1960* (Princeton, N.J.: Princeton University Press, 1963).

[2] "A Theoretical Framework for Monetary Analysis," *Journal of Political Economy*, March/April 1970, p. 217.

changes in real activity. Instability in monetary growth is mirrored in variability in economic activity. Thus Friedman argues:[3]

> Why should we be concerned about these gyrations in monetary growth? Because they exert an important influence on the future course of the economy. Erratic monetary growth almost always produces erratic economic growth.

Friedman's view of the primary importance of money is based in part on his careful historical studies, in which he was able to relate the booms and recessions of United States economic history to the behaviour of the money stock. In general, it appeared that increases of the growth rate of money produced booms and inflations, and decreases in the money stock produced recessions and sometimes deflations. In part, his view of the primary importance of money is based on a theoretical analysis of the effects of fiscal policy, as discussed in Chapter 12's analysis of the different methods of financing the government budget deficit. We showed there that a money-financed deficit has a larger permanent effect on the price level than a debt-financed deficit.

These permanent effects are long-run effects. It is less clear why Friedman places primary emphasis on monetary policy — as opposed to fiscal policy — in affecting the behaviour of real and nominal GNP in the short run.

Long and Variable Lags

Monetarism has emphasized that although the growth rate of money is of prime importance in determining the behaviour of GNP, the effects of changes in the growth rate of money on the subsequent behaviour of GNP occur with long and variable lags. On average, it takes a long time for a change in the growth rate of money to affect GNP, so the lag is long. In addition, the time it takes for this change to affect GNP varies from one historical episode to another — the lags are variable. These arguments are based on empirical and not theoretical evidence. Friedman estimates the lags may be as short as six months and as long as two years.

The Monetary Rule

Combining the preceding arguments, Friedman argues against the use of active monetary policy. He suggests that because the behaviour of the money stock is of critical importance for the behaviour of real and nominal GNP, and because money operates with a long and variable lag, monetary policy should not attempt to "fine-tune" the economy. The active use of

---

[3] "Irresponsible Monetary Policy," *Newsweek*, Jan. 10, 1972. Reprinted in Friedman's collection of public policy essays, *There's No Such Thing as a Free Lunch* (La Salle, Ill.: Open Court Publishing, 1975), p. 73.

monetary policy might actually destabilize the economy, because an action taken in 1980, say, might affect the economy at any of various future dates, such as in 1981 or 1982. By 1982, the action taken in 1980 might be inappropriate for the stabilization of GNP. Besides, there is no certainty that the policy will take effect in 1982 rather than in 1981. For example, suppose that the economy is currently in a recession, and that the money supply is increased rapidly today to increase the growth rate of real GNP. Today's increase in the growth rate of money might affect GNP within six months, and achieve its purpose. However, it might work only in two years, by which time GNP might well already have increased without the aid of the monetary policy action. And if the expansionary monetary policy affects an economy by then close to full employment, inflation will result.

Thus Friedman reaches the conclusion that although monetary policy has powerful effects on GNP, it should not be actively used lest it destabilize the economy. Accordingly, he argues that the money supply be kept growing at a constant rate, to minimize the potential damage that inappropriate policy can cause.[4]

The Unimportance of Interest Rates

In the IS-LM model of Chapter 4, changes in the money stock affect the economy primarily by affecting interest rates, which in turn affect aggregate demand and thus GNP. Accordingly, the level of interest rates seems to provide a guide to the effects of monetary policy on the economy. When interest rates are low, monetary policy seems to be expansionary, encouraging investment and thus producing a high level of aggregate demand. Similarly, high interest rates seem to indicate contractionary policy. Further, the central bank is able to control interest rates through open market operations. For instance, when it wants to reduce interest rates, it carries out open market purchases, buying bonds and raising their price. Since it can control the level of interest rates, and since interest rates provide a guide to the effects of monetary policy on the economy, it seems perfectly sensible for the central bank to carry out monetary policy by controlling interest rates. When it judges aggregate demand should be expanded, it lowers interest rates, and when it judges aggregate demand should be reduced, it raises interest rates. Through the 1950s and most of the 1960s, central banks did carry out monetary policy by attempting to set the level of interest rates.

Friedman and monetarism brought two serious criticisms of the procedure of attempting to set interest rates as the basis for the conduct of monetary policy. The first is that the behaviour of nominal interest rates is not a good guide to the direction — whether expansionary or contractionary

---

[4] For a concise statement, see Milton Friedman, "The Case for a Monetary Rule," *Newsweek*, Feb. 7, 1972. Reprinted in *There's No Such Thing as a Free Lunch*, op. cit., pp. 77-79. Arguments about active policy making were discussed in Chapter 9.

— of monetary policy. The real interest rate, the nominal interest rate minus the expected rate of inflation, is the rate relevant to determining the level of investment, as we saw in Chapter 6. But a high nominal interest rate, together with a high expected rate of inflation, means a low real rate of interest. Thus monetary policy might be quite expansionary in its effects on investment spending even when nominal interest rates are high. Consequently, Friedman and other monetarists argued, the central bank should not concentrate on the behaviour of nominal interest rates in the conduct of monetary policy.

The second criticism is that attempts to control nominal interest rates might be destabilizing. Suppose that the central bank desired that monetary policy should be expansionary and that the interest rate should be lowered. To achieve these goals it buys bonds in the open market, increasing the money supply. The expansionary monetary policy itself tends to raise the inflation rate. It thus tends to raise the nominal interest rate as investors adjust their expectation of inflation in response to the behaviour of the actual inflation rate. But then the central bank would have to engage in a further open market purchase in an attempt to keep the nominal interest rate low, and that would lead to further inflation, further increases in nominal interest rates, and further open market purchases. The end result is that an attempt to keep nominal interest rates low may lead to increasing inflation. Therefore, Friedman argues, the central bank should not pay attention to the behaviour of nominal interest rates in the conduct of monetary policy,[5] and should, rather, keep the money supply growing at a constant rate.

Each of these arguments on the dangers of conducting monetary policy by reference to nominal interest rates is important. It is indeed correct that real, and not nominal, interest rates provide the appropriate measure of the effects of monetary policy on aggregate demand. It is also true that the central bank could, by attempting to keep nominal interest rates low forever, destabilize the economy. However, once the latter danger has been pointed out, the probability that it will destabilize the economy by operating with reference to interest rates is reduced. The use of interest rates as a guide to the direction of monetary policy does not mean that the central bank has to attempt to keep the interest rate fixed forever at some level. Instead, it may aim each month or quarter for an interest rate target that it regards as appropriate for the current and predicted economic situation.

The monetarist case for concentrating on the behaviour of the money stock in the conduct of monetary policy is a strong, but not conclusive, one. The major weakness in the argument is that the demand for real balances may change over time and indeed has done so. A simple numerical example should help make the point. Suppose that real income is constant, and that the nominal interest rate is constant. Suppose also that the demand for real

---

[5] The details of the argument are spelled out in Friedman's "The Role of Monetary Policy," *American Economic Review*, March 1968.

balances is constant. Then if the money supply grows at, say, the rate of 5 percent, the price level, too, will grow at 5 percent, so that the stock of real balances remains constant. Now suppose, instead, that the demand for real balances is falling by 2 percent per year. Then if the nominal money supply increases at 5 percent per year, the price level has to increase at 7 percent per year to keep the supply of real balances equal to the demand. Thus, shifts in the demand for money affect the rate of inflation, given the growth rate of money. In this example, if the demand for real balances grew at 5 percent per year, 5 percent money growth would not be inflationary at all. These shifts in demand raise the possibility that concentration on the behaviour of the nominal stock may be seriously misleading and inappropriate for the conduct of monetary policy.

The possibility is not purely hypothetical. For instance, in the fourth quarter of 1976, the rate of growth of the money supply fell below the Bank of Canada's target range at a time when real income was rising and interest rates were falling. Under these circumstances, the demand for real balances should, according to the demand for money function of Chapter 7, have been increasing. However, real balances were actually falling at the time, despite the rising real income. This suggests that the demand for money was shifting — that people were reducing their demand for real balances at given levels of interest rates and income. It was appropriate then for the Bank of Canada to allow the supply of real balances to fall. Concentration on the behaviour of the money stock as a guide to monetary policy would have been inappropriate and inflationary.

Given the possibility, and the actual experience, of shifts in the demand for money, we see that the behaviour of the money stock is not a perfect guide to the conduct of monetary policy. Neither is the behaviour of nominal interest rates. However, the behaviour of the nominal money stock and the behaviour of nominal interest rates both provide some information about the direction in which monetary policy is pushing the economy, imperfect as each measure is. Accordingly, the central bank should pay attention to the behaviour of both interest rates and the supply of money in the conduct of its monetary policy.[6]

The Importance of Fiscal Policy

Friedman has frequently, if tongue in cheek, said that fiscal policy is very important. Although we noted earlier that he argues fiscal policy itself is not important for the behaviour of GNP, he does contend that it is of vital importance in setting the size of government and the role of government in the economy. Friedman is an opponent of big government. He has made the interesting argument that government spending increases to match the

---

[6] The argument is worked out in Benjamin M. Friedman, "Targets, Instruments, and Indicators of Monetary Policy." *Journal of Monetary Economics*, October 1975.

revenues available. The government will spend the full tax collection – and some more. Accordingly, he is in favour of tax cuts as a way of reducing government spending.

In the shorter run, Friedman has pointed to the size of the government deficit as one of the variables that does affect the growth rate of the money stock. That is in part due to the central bank's concern over the behaviour of interest rates. When the deficit is large, interest rates tend to rise unless the central bank monetizes the debt, as we saw in Chapter 10. Large deficits, therefore, tend to be associated with rapid monetary expansion, and for that reason have an expansionary effect on the economy. But since there is no inherent reason why a deficit has to be financed by money creation, the link between deficits and expansion is not an immutable one, but rather, a result of the way the central bank behaves. Friedman stands out in arguing that fiscal policy does not have strong effects on the economy except to the extent that it affects the behaviour of money. Thus he has remarked:[7]

> To have a significant impact on the economy, a tax increase must somehow affect monetary policy – the quantity of money and its rate of growth. . . .
>
> The level of taxes is important – because it affects how much of our resources we use through the government and how much we use as individuals. It is not important as a sensitive and powerful device to control the short-run course of income and prices.

The Inherent Stability of the Private Sector

The final aspect of monetarism we consider here is the monetarist view that the economy, left to itself, is more stable than when the government manages it with discretionary policy, and that the major cause of economic fluctuations lies in inappropriate government actions. This view is quite fundamental in that it underlies many other monetarist positions, and it may be the litmus test for distinguishing monetarists from other macroeconomists. It is because this point is so fundamental that a major stage in the acceptance of monetarism occurred when Friedman and Schwartz published their *Monetary History of the United States*. In it they provided evidence for the view that the Great Depression was the result of bad monetary policy rather than private sector instability, arising, say, from autonomous shifts in consumption or investment demand.

Summary: We Are All Monetarists

From the viewpoint of the conduct of economic policy, the major monetarist themes are (1) the emphasis on the growth rate of the money stock, (2) the

---

[7] Milton Friedman, "Higher Taxes? No," *Newsweek*, Jan. 23, 1967. Reprinted in *There's No Such Thing as A Free Lunch*, op. cit., p. 89.

arguments against fine tuning and in favour of a monetary rule, and (3) the greater weight that monetarists, as compared, for example, with Keynesians, place on the costs of inflation relative to those of unemployment.

Although we describe these as the major monetarist porpositions relating to policy,[8] it is not true that macroeconomists can be neatly divided into two groups, some subscribing to the monetarist religion and others to a less fundamentalist faith called neo-Keynesianism. Most of the arguments advanced by Friedman and his associates are technical and susceptible to economic analysis and the application of empirical evidence. Many of those propositions are now widely accepted and are no longer particularly associated with monetarism. As Franco Modigliani has remarked, "We are all monetarists now." He adds that we are monetarists in the sense that all (or most) macroeconomists believe in the importance of money.

Much of the analysis of this book would, a few years ago, have been considered monetarist. For example, we have assumed that Phillips curve is vertical, a proposition that was originally associated with monetarism. We have laid considerable stress on the behaviour of the money stock and less stress on the behaviour of interest rates. We have emphasized that fiscal policy has little long-run effect on inflation. Older readers will doubtless detect other places at which we appear monetarist to their eyes. That is all to the good. If economists did not modify their analyses in the light of new theories and evidence, the field would be barren.

Friedman and his associates have indeed changed macroeconomics. The forceful and persuasive way in which he has emphasized the role of money has changed the views of most economists on the importance of monetary policy. It is always possible that those views would have changed anyway, in the light of the increasing inflation of the last decade. The fact remains, however, that it was Friedman, and not someone else, who hammered away at the importance of money. Fortunately, we are beyond the stage at which it is useful to think in terms of monetarists versus Keynesians.

15-2 GRADUALISM VERSUS COLD TURKEY

Suppose the economy is in full equilibrium with an inflation rate of say 10 percent and that a decision has been made to move to a lower rate of inflation using a monetarist prescription of a reduction in the rate of growth of the money supply. How fast should policy makers try to reach their

---

[8] For a range of views on monetarism, see Karl Brunner, "The Monetarist Revolution in Monetary Theory," *Weltwirtschaftliches Archiv*, 1970; Jerry Stein (ed.), *Monetarism* (Amsterdam, North-Holland Publishing Co., 1976); Franco Modigliani, "The Monetarist Controversy," *American Economic Review*, March 1977; and Thomas Mayer, *The Structure of Monetarism* (New York: Norton 1978).

target? Given the long-run unemployment rate, there is a unique long-run growth rate of money that will satisfy the inflation target. The problem is to know whether, from some initial situation, one should try to proceed to that inflation target at maximum speed — and suffer a large unemployment cost in the transition — or whether, on the contrary, a more gradual approach is called for.

One possibility is that the government commands total credibility with the public and all prices and wages adjust freely. In that case, it is sufficient to announce and implement a reduction in monetary growth to the new long-run target level. The inflation rate will immediately respond because the credibility that the government commands will instantaneously be reflected in a revision of expectations to the new lower rate of inflation. The free adjustability of prices and wages will ensure that the expectations are immediately reflected in actual price behaviour.

It is more likely that the government does not command such credibility, so that expectations continue to be formed — entirely or predominantly — on the basis of past observations of inflation. That case is analyzed in Figure 15-1. The initial equilibrium is at point E, and the long-run target is at point E'. Now we shall examine two strategies which we refer to as *gradualist* and *cold turkey*. A gradualist policy involves an immediate reduction in monetary growth toward the new long-run level, while a cold-turkey policy goes for an immediate reduction in the inflation rate to the long-run level.

The gradualist approach is a compromise. It recognizes that in the

FIGURE 15-1 ALTERNATIVE ADJUSTMENT POLICIES

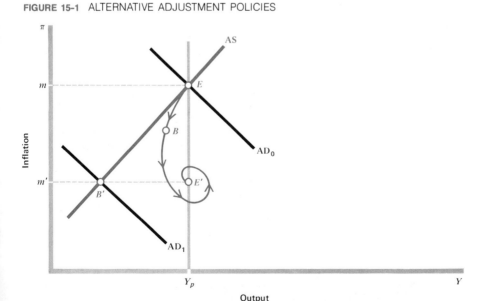

transition to the new long-run equilibrium, unemployment will occur, and that inflation can be reduced faster with a more restrictive policy. The gradualist approach recognizes, too, that more rapid adjustment of inflation will imply higher unemployment. The compromise is to achieve the target of reduced inflation over time.

Figure 15-1 illustrates the two policy options. The gradualist approach is shown by the cyclical adjustment path. Starting at point E, monetary growth with this strategy is reduced somewhat, so that there is an immediate reduction in inflation but also some increase in unemployment because output declines (say, at point B). Over time, the reduction in inflationary expectations shifts the aggregate supply schedule downward and the decline in output and reduction in inflationary expectations shift the aggregate demand schedule down. With this improvement in the inflation-unemployment tradeoff, further reductions in monetary growth become possible until the new long-run equilibrium at point E' is reached. The approach to that equilibrium may well be cyclical,[9] but the outstanding aspect of the policy is not to seek an immediate full achievement of the inflation target.

The cold-turkey strategy immediately implements the new inflation target by sharply reducing monetary growth *below* the new long-run level m'. The strategy is to reduce inflation immediately to the new long-run level. This requires a reduction in the growth rate of money over and above what is appropriate in the long run. This is shown by the shift of the aggregate demand schedule AD_1 in Figure 15-1. The cold-turkey policy immediately moves to point B'. This reduction in output and the sharp increase in unemployment exert a sufficiently deflationary effect to cut down the rate of inflation. From then on the policy faces the problem of building up aggregate demand without raising inflation as the economy moves from B' to the long-run equilibrium at point E'.

How should we evaluate the two policies? Figure 15-2 shows the implications for inflation and unemployment of the two paths. It is apparent that the cold-turkey strategy involves much higher unemployment in the short run. It has the compensating advantage that it achieves the target inflation immediately and that, perhaps, it is a more credible demonstration of policy intent. If the latter were true, it might be argued that expectations adjust faster and that, accordingly, the adjustment process might be faster. By comparison, the gradualist approach chooses adjustment to reduced inflation along a path that involves a lower unemployment rate with the offsetting cost of an inflation rate that declines less rapidly. Also, because the policy reduces inflation only gradually, it may act more slowly in causing people to revise downward their expectations and therefore may lengthen the adjustment process.

---

[9] In principle, a careful economic policy could move the economy from E to E' without a cyclical approach. In practice, a direct approach requires more knowledge of the economy than the policy maker is likely to have.

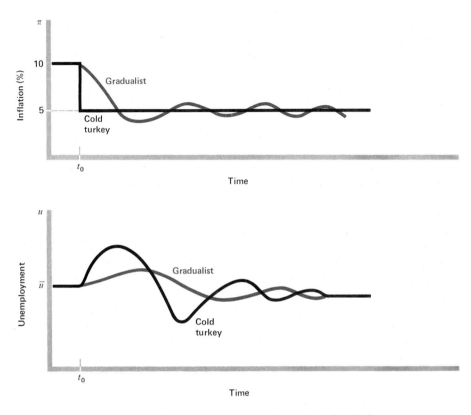

FIGURE 15-2 ALTERNATIVE PATHS OF INFLATION AND UNEMPLOYMENT

In choosing between the policies, the policy maker has to trade off more unemployment now for less inflation. In addition, though, the policy maker has to recognize the lagged effects of monetary policy and must be aware of the possible inaccuracies of predictions or information about the economy.

How is the policy maker to choose among the paths of the type shown? This depends to a large extent on her evaluation of the costs of inflation and unemployment. Someone who is persuaded that the costs of inflation are low would not be willing to incur much unemployment to reduce the inflation rate. Even if such a policy maker agreed that ultimately a lower rate of inflation was desirable, she would not do anything as extreme as is implied by the cold-turkey policy. Rather, she might chip away over time at the inflation rate, slowly trying to move the economy toward a lower rate, but always remaining acutely conscious of the effects of her policies on unemployment. Someone believing that inflation undermines the political fabric of democracy, and that some unemployment does not, would be willing to incur the costs of high unemployment in the short run to rid the country of the curse of inflation. But how to choose?

The discussion of the costs of inflation and unemployment in Chapter 14 suggested that the aggregate costs of cyclical unemployment are relatively easy to measure. However, there are distributional costs of unemployment that are more difficult to quantify. The costs of unanticipated inflation also are largely distributional and equally difficult to quantify. Thus, although economic analysis can help in identifying the costs of inflation and unemployment, it cannot pin them down accurately. Further, the weights given to the losses suffered by different groups of people are likely to vary between policy makers. If it were demonstrated that unanticipated inflation hurt group X and benefitted group Y, that would not guarantee that all policy makers would agree on the costs of unanticipated inflation. Some policy makers would regard damage done to group X as not very costly if not beneficial, and benefits for group Y as a good thing. Other policy makers would doubtless have an opposite view.

This section has raised the question of how fast policy makers should attempt to reach their targets. There is the final question, though, of choosing long-run targets and recognizing that the cost of adjustment may be excessive compared with the benefits. Those who hold this view argue that inflation should be stabilized at the current level, rather than reduced. They contend that a stable rate of inflation removes some, and perhaps most, of the cost of inflation, so that the residual benefits of reducing inflation may look small compared with the adjustment costs.

15-3 MONETARISM AND THE BANK OF CANADA

Prior to the early 1970s, the Bank of Canada's monetary policy was formulated primarily in terms of target levels of interest rates and other measures of the cost and availability of credit. By 1973, the Bank had become dissatisfied with this approach and was beginning to move towards greater emphasis on control of the money supply. In his Annual Report for 1973, Governor Gerald Bouey commented as follows:[10]

> Looking back on the experience of Canada and other countries over a longer period, it is difficult to avoid the impression that from time to time there have been more substantial and persisting departures from reasonably steady monetary growth than would appear in retrospect to have been desirable. Since the lags associated with monetary policy are rather long, the full effects of such departures do not become apparent until well after the event. This helps to explain how they come about. It is not very difficult to understand, for example, that so long as an economy is operating much below satisfactory levels there is a natural tendency to err on the high side so far as rates of monetary growth are concerned. Moreover, in a world where economic forecasting is necessarily imperfect, the temptation is strong in such circumstances to respond to

[10] Bank of Canada, *Annual Report*, 1973, p.7.

troublesome short-run developments by adding somewhat further to the rate of monetary expansion. I believe that the high rates of monetary expansion around the world during the two years leading up to the surge in economic activity in the latter part of 1972 and early 1973 illustrate this basic problem.

In the light of these considerations, I have a certain amount of sympathy with the case that is often made for more stable monetary growth over time, even though I am aware that there are various difficulties involved in such an approach. The Bank of Canada certainly has no intention of basing its operations on any mechanistic formula, but in framing its judgments about the appropriate policy to be followed, it has been giving considerable weight to underlying rates of monetary growth.

Although the governor had rejected the idea of a "mechanistic formula" for monetary growth in 1973, two years later the Bank of Canada moved further towards the monetarist view and announced that it would henceforth follow the practice of establishing target ranges for the rate of growth of the narrowly defined money supply (M1). The initial target was established in late 1975 at 10 to 15 percent a year.

In his *Annual Report* for 1975, the governor stressed the importance of bringing down the rate of inflation and addressed the question of how this should be accomplished:[11]

One answer sometimes given to this question is that the Bank of Canada should do the job through a sharp and immediate reduction of the growth rate of the money supply to a rate approximately in line with the sustainable real growth of the economy. If that were to happen, it is asserted, inflation would readily come to an end.

The trouble with this prescription is not with the medicine but with the dosage, which would be so great that the patient would suffer excessively while it was working. It would sharply curtail the growth of spending on goods and services in the face of continuing large increases in production costs already built into the economy, and this would almost certainly result in extremely weak markets, widespread bankruptcies and soaring unemployment. It must be recognized that the annual rate of increase in average Canadian money incomes that is consistent with price stability is no higher than the trend rate of increase in national productivity, which is usually put at around 2 per cent per year, and we are a long way from that situation. All sorts of existing arrangements, including virtually all wage contracts, are based on the assumption of some continuing inflation. The attempt to force as rapid a transition to price and cost stability as this prescription involves would be too disruptive in economic and social terms to be sensible or tolerable.

Thus the Bank of Canada clearly rejected a cold-turkey policy and opted for gradualism. This strategy was subsequently implemented by successive reductions in the target to the range of 4 to 8 percent established in February 1981 and still in effect in late 1981. As can be seen in Chart 15-1,

---

[11] Bank of Canada, *Annual Report*, 1975, p. 10.

CHART 15-1 TARGET RANGES AND THE MONEY SUPPLY
(*Source*: Bank of Canada, *Annual Report*, 1979)

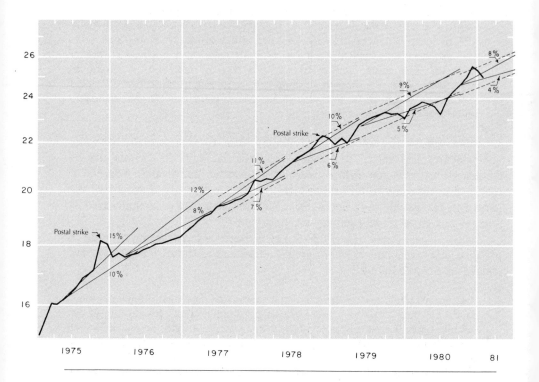

the Bank has generally been successful in keeping monetary growth within the target range.[12]

Since the adoption by the Bank of Canada of a monetarist strategy, the governor has annunciated the philosophy and principles underlying it on a number of occasions. Most recently in a statement before the House of Commons Standing Committee on Finance, Trade and Economic Affairs, the governor put forward three basic propositions.[13] The first reaffirmed the overriding importance of bringing down the rate of inflation:

> For quite a few years now the nature of the major threat to the future economic welfare of the country has been unusually clear. That threat is inflation. The idea

[12] The exceptions have been periods in which the payments system was disrupted by postal strikes as indicated in the chart.

[13] Reprinted in the *Bank of Canada Review*, November, 1980, pages 13-19. The earliest statement was given in an address to the Canadian Chamber of Commerce in Saskatoon in September 1975. This speech has been dubbed the "Saskatoon monetary manifesto" by Thomas Courchene. See T.J. Courchene, *Monetarism and Controls: The Inflation Fighters"* (C.D. Howe Research Institute, 1976).

that some inflation is on balance helpful to the performance of an economy, that inflation is benign — an idea that was never more than superficially plausible but was nevertheless quite popular — is now thoroughly discredited. What has discredited it so effectively is not economic theory but economic experience. The experience of the world economy and the widely varying experience of its national members have shown beyond reasonable question that inflation is malignant. The matter is no longer seriously debated.

As to the role of monetary policy in fighting inflation, the governor stated:

there is one proposition that must never be forgotten, and that is that in a free society no strategy for dealing with inflation will succeed unless it is well supported by firm and continuing control of the rate of monetary expansion in the society. That proposition is, I assure you, as reliable as any general proposition in the whole field of economics. Every central banker in the world knows it to be true, and I doubt that any serious and experienced student of financial affairs would question it. It is a very firm proposition indeed, and anyone who wants to participate responsibly in the debate on how to deal with inflation would be well advised to keep it uppermost in his mind.

In his third proposition, the governor put forward the distinction between real and nominal interest rates:

The basic reason why interest rates are so high is because current and expected rates of inflation are so high. If you make allowance for the current rate of inflation, interest rates are not in fact unusually high. They are not so high as to provide savers with a large real return before taxes or in many cases with a real return at all after taxes. They are not so high as to discourage borrowers who expect continued high rates of inflation.

Thus the Bank of Canada has made a clear commitment to an anti-inflation policy based on monetary gradualism. In doing so, it recognized the consequences not only for the levels of output and employment, but also for the behaviour of nominal interest rates. In his *Annual Report* for 1978, the governor stated:[14]

Whatever their object, however, central bank actions that have the effect of speeding up or slowing down the trend over time in the rate of growth of the money supply have longer run effects on the level of interest rates that can be quite the opposite of the effects produced in the short run. A stepped-up rate of monetary expansion that temporarily lowers interest rates will, if it is sustained, lead eventually to a higher rate of price increase than would otherwise have occurred. With money losing its value more rapidly, borrowers will be less reluctant to incur debt since they can repay in dollars of lesser value, while savers and lenders will for the same reason be more reluctant to provide loans. The consequence of rising inflation will thus be a growing excess demand for

[14] Bank of Canada, *Annual Report*, 1973, p. 14.

credit in relation to the supply which will put increasing upward pressure on interest rates. Thus the eventual result of letting the money supply grow too rapidly is not low interest rates but high interest rates.

If a country wants to have and maintain low interest rates, there is no secret about how to achieve that. Monetary growth must be reduced until it is only just sufficient to finance the expansion in production that the economy is capable of achieving over the longer run without putting pressure on the over-all level of prices, and it must be kept there. The immediate effect of this policy will be to raise interest rates but the longer term effect will be to lower them. The low interest rate countries of the world are the ones that have had the greatest success over the years in resisting the temptation to allow inflationary pressures to be underwritten by excessive monetary expansion. The countries that have experienced less success in controlling the process of domestic monetary expansion have higher rates of inflation and higher interest rates.

15-4 THE FIGHT AGAINST INFLATION, 1975-1980

As discussed in the previous section, the Bank of Canada instituted a policy in late 1975 of gradually reducing the rate of growth of the money supply. At the same time, the government announced a program of wage and price controls to be administered by an Anti-Inflation Board (AIB). The board was given statutory power to control wages and profit margins of private firms with 500 or more employees. Provincial and municipal government wage setting was brought into the program through agreements with the provinces to apply the guidelines established by the federal board. The controls remained in effect until they were phased out beginning in April 1978. Let us examine the performance of the Canadian economy in response to these two policy initiatives.

Wage Settlements and the AIB

The top panel of Chart 15-2 shows the average annual percentage increases in base rates of pay negotiated in wage contracts over the period 1974 to 1980. Prior to the formation of the AIB, wage settlements had risen to nearly 19 percent per year, but during 1976 and 1977 there was a substantial moderation in the rate of increase. However, as shown in the second panel of Chart 15-2, during the same period the seasonally adjusted unemployment rate rose from 6.8 percent to 8.4 percent. To measure the effect of the controls it is necessary to estimate on the basis of historical experience what wage increases would have occurred in the absence of controls given the actual economic conditions experienced.

In a study undertaken for the Economic Council of Canada, Cousineau and Lacroix estimated that the average annual wage increase in major collective agreements would have been 1.7 percentage points higher in the

CHART 15-2   INFLATION AND UNEMPLOYMENT, 1974–1980 (Source: Bank of Canada Review)

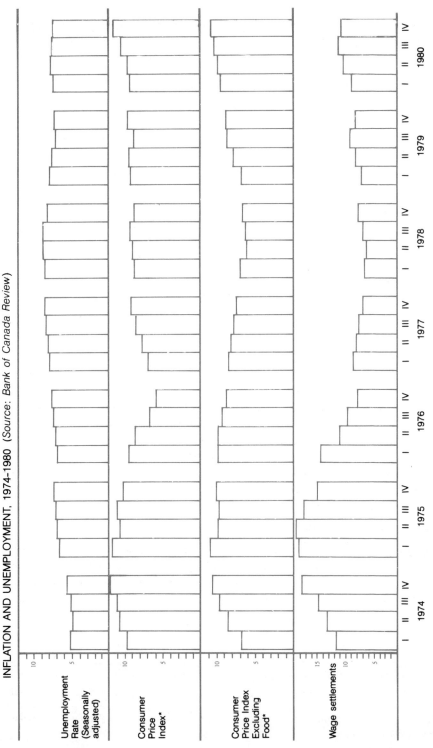

*Percent change over the same quarter of the preceding year.

private sector and 4.3 percentage points higher in the public sector had the anti-inflation guidelines not been in force.[15] In another study, Auld, Christofides, Swidinsky and Wilton concluded that:[16] "in the period of AIB wage controls, union wage settlements in the private and public sectors have been between 2½ and 3½ percentage points per annum lower than the pre-AIB wage structure would predict; by 1977 the cumulative wage affect of the AIB was on the order of 3.2 per cent in the private and 4.6 per cent in the public sectors." Thus it would appear that controls had an impact particularly on public sector wages, but that they were responsible for a limited part of the moderation in negotiated wage increases that occurred.

The Rate of Inflation

The third panel of Chart 15-2 shows the rate of inflation as measured by the percentage change in the Consumer Price Index over the same quarter of the preceding year. During 1976 the rate fell dramatically from the level above 10 percent recorded in 1975 to 5.9 percent. However, a closer look at the components of the CPI shows that very little of this decline in the rate of inflation can be attributed to the AIB controls. A major contributing factor was the sharp decline in the rate of increase of food prices which were not subject to controls.

Since food prices typically exhibit wide variations from year to year, it is common to use the CPI excluding food as a measure of the underlying trend in the rate of inflation. As can be seen in the bottom panel of Chart 15-2, this index shows a slow but steady decline from the fourth quarter of 1975 to the second quarter of 1978 when it fell to 6 percent. Unfortunately in the third quarter of 1978, the downward trend in the underlying rate of inflation was reversed, and by the third quarter of 1980, the CPI excluding food was increasing at a rate above 10 percent, in spite of the fact that the unemployment rate had remained above 7 percent since mid-1976.

Has Monetarism Failed?

The performance of the Canadian economy over the period 1975 to 1980 led some to conclude that the Bank of Canada's policy of restricting the rate of growth of the money supply was misguided.[17] It is argued that the major effect was to slow down the growth of the economy and increase the

[15] See Economic Council of Canada, Fourteenth Annual Review (1977), p. 20.

[16] D. Auld, L. Christofides, R. Swidinsky and D. Wilton, "The Impact of the Anti-Inflation Board on Negotiated Wage Settlements," *Canadian Journal of Economics*, May 1979, p. 209.

[17] See for example the following two studies sponsored by the Canadian Institute for Economic Policy: A.W. Donner and D.D. Peters, *The Monetarist Counter-Revolution, A Critique of Canadian Monetary Policy 1975-1979*; and C.L. Barber and J.C.P. McCallum, *Unemployment and Inflation, the Canadian Experience.*

unemployment rate with very little effect on the rate of inflation. In response to his critics, Governor Bouey made the following statement before the House of Commons Standing Committee on Finance, Trade and Economic Affairs:[18]

> The experience of the past few years appears to have led some observers to conclude that the Bank's approach to reducing inflation has failed. If they mean that progress in reducing inflation is less than the Bank hoped, I agree with them. But if they mean, as I think some of them do, that the Bank's approach was misconceived, then they have misread the history of the period. What they should conclude is that given the economic and financial developments over that period, many of which were unpredictable, it would have been better if the slowing of monetary growth had been less gradual so that it would have had more impact on inflation. That is the moral that should be drawn. In this connection I would point out that the rate of monetary expansion today is very much lower than it was five years ago and although we have arrived at this position through a very gradual process, the impact on total spending can be expected to be much firmer from now on than it was when we started on this path.

Thus the governor's conclusion is not that the monetarist medicine was inappropriate, but that the dose was inadequate. This issue will undoubtedly continue to be the subject of vigorous debate.

15-5 NEW APPROACHES

In this section we consider two developments in macroeconomics in the 1970s, supply management and rational expectations.

Supply Management and TIP

The approach to aggregate supply developed in Chapters 11 and 13 emphasized the role of costs of production in affecting prices. This emphasis suggests that government policies that affect firms' costs can be used to influence inflation directly. For instance, firms pay social insurance taxes for their employees, and pass these costs on into prices. Reductions in these taxes might therefore be expected to reduce the prices charged by firms. At a time when inflation is increasing, it might make sense to reduce the rate of social insurance taxation to offset the increasing inflation.

Such a notion is attractive, but it does leave the question of what other taxes might be used to replace the social insurance taxes and what their effects on the price level might be. We should also note that empirical work has not been able to tie down the effects of changes in these taxes on the

---

[18] See *Bank of Canada Review*, November 1980, p. 17.

inflation rate very precisely. Nonetheless, it is plausible that at least in the short run, reductions in such taxes could reduce the rate of inflation.

The notion of supply management applies also to a variety of new policies that have been suggested to affect prices through tax incentives. TIP—tax-based incomes policy—would offer firms or workers incentives to keep price or wage rises low.[19] For example, in 1978 the Carter administration in the United States proposed *real wage insurance* as a means of reducing the rate of wage increase. The proposal was that unions contracting for a wage increase of 7 percent or less would be compensated by the government for any fall in real wages resulting from inflation in excess of 7 percent; thus, union members would maintain their real wages. For example, if the inflation rate was 10 percent, the government would pay workers who had satisfied the terms set for eligibility for the "insurance" an amount equal to 3 percent of their wages, so as to keep the real wage at the level it would have been had the inflation rate been 7 percent. The payment might be direct or a reduction in taxes. The U.S. Congress did not accept the proposal.

The idea behind real wage insurance depends on the relationship between the rate of wage increase and subsequent price behaviour. If the rate of wage increase can be reduced, then the rate of price increase will fall. Thus, the Carter administration hoped that by setting up incentives to keep the rate of wage increase at 7 percent or less, it would get the inflation rate down, so that the promised insurance payments would be unnecessary. As events turned out, of course, the oil price increase in 1979 provided an extra inflationary force that would have made the scheme very expensive for the U.S. government.

Ingenious as most forms of TIP are, they share a serious failing. The problem is that there does not appear to be any simple form of TIP that could be implemented without creating a bureaucratic mess. It is thus unlikely that TIP will be put into practice, but we are likely to see the supply aspects of taxes discussed here increasingly taken into account in future years in choosing tax packages.

It is also obvious that the reemergence of aggregate supply as an important element in analyses of the economy will lead to an increasing emphasis on policies that attempt to stimulate supply by increasing investment.

We turn next to a second development that can be traced to the inflationary experience of the last decade; the rise of the rational expectations school of macroeconomics.

*The Rational Expectations School

The failure to reduce inflation in the 1970s and the apparent inability of

---

[19] A special issue of the *Brookings Papers on Economic Activity*, that of 1978:2 (Washington, D.C.: The Brookings Institution) is devoted to TIP and similar policies.

macro policy to achieve its goals have led to a reconsideration of the premises of modern macroeconomics. The reconsideration places great emphasis on expectations, on the credibility of policies, and on the limited scope for discretionary stabilization policies. The general emphasis on expectations and the credibility of policies is widely shared. Indeed, we have explained much of the behaviour of the inflation rate and wage increases by appealing to expectations of inflation and the belief that anti-inflationary policies would not be long-lived. But the emphasis and its implications have been taken further by a group of economists who have developed the *rational expectations* approach to macroeconomics. Among the leading members of the school are Robert Lucas of the University of Chicago, Thomas Sargent and Neil Wallace of the University of Minnesota, and Robert Barro of the University of Rochester.[20] Some would add the more eclectic Robert Hall of the Hoover Institution and Stanford University to this list.

The notion of rational expectations itself assumes that individuals use information efficiently and do not make systematic mistakes in their expectations.[21] This assumption is made on occasion by almost all macroeconomists, and its use does not qualify the user automatically as a member of the rational expectations school. One other assumption is made by those we identify as belonging to the school. It is that markets always clear, and that economic agents set wages and prices (given their information) so as to achieve full employment, maximize profits, and maximize economic welfare.

The strongest form of rational expectations has three major implications. The first is that there is no involuntary unemployment. Why? Because anyone who expects to be unemployed, or who is currently unemployed and would prefer to work, can find work by asking for it at a wage below the existing wage. If, at the existing wage, the individual prefers not to work, but rather to continue searching for a job, then the unemployment is voluntary. Of course, the theory recognizes that there is some normal level of unemployment corresponding to individuals who are between jobs or looking for their first job.

If there is no involuntary unemployment, why, then, does the level of output vary? Here the theory points to two factors. The first consists of changes in the level of potential output. The second, more important,

---

[20] For an introduction, see Thomas Sargent and Neil Wallace. "Rational Expectations and the Theory of Economic Policy," *Journal of Monetary Economics*, April 1976. See also Robert E. Lucas, Jr., "Understanding Business Cycles," in Karl Brunner and Allan Meltzer (eds.), *Stabilization of the Domestic and International Economy*, Carnegie-Rochester Conference Series, vol. 5.

[21] In Chap. 13, we discussed the implications of *perfect foresight* for the adjustment of the economy to a change in the money stock, and we showed that in that case, the price level jumped immediately to its new level and output stayed at its full-employment level. Perfect foresight is a special case of rational expectations that holds when there is no uncertainty.

involves mistakes in perceiving the current economic situation. Suppose that individuals do not know the aggregate price level in the current period. Of course, they do know the wage at which they can work. They have to form an estimate of the *real* wage on the basis of the price level they expect to hold during the period. Now, if the price level should turn out to be unexpectedly high, then individuals overestimate the real wage and work harder than they would if they knew the true situation. Thus *unexpectedly high* prices lead to a higher level of output than at full employment. Individuals are working harder than they would at full employment.

This mechanism is very subtle,[22] and it is regarded by some as implausible. It clearly requires that individuals do not have complete information about the current state of the economy. Otherwise, with all markets clearing, the economy would be at the full-employment level of output. Indeed, one of the consequences of the development of the rational expectations school has been a growing emphasis on the information that individuals use and process in making their economic decisions.

The second implication follows closely from the first. It is that the level of output cannot be affected by changes in monetary policy unless those changes are not perceived by individuals in the economy. For, suppose that it is believed and known that the money supply has changed. Then individuals know the price level should be higher, and adjust their prices and wages accordingly so as to produce full employment immediately.[23] If there is a lag in the publication of data on the money stock, individuals will adjust prices to the level of the money stock they expect. If the money stock turns out to be higher than expected, aggregate demand will be higher, and output will rise because of the mechanism, described earlier, in which individuals mistakenly work harder, believing the real wage is above the level at which it currently is. We thus arrive at the most famous proposition advanced by the rational expectations school, that, *with regard to monetary policy, only unexpected changes in the stock of money affect the level of output.*

If only unanticipated changes in the stock of money affect the level of output, then monetary policy cannot affect the level of output except by producing *surprises*. This leads to the third implication: Under these circumstances, there appears to be no role for monetary policy systematically to affect output or unemployment. Any systematic policy, such as increased monetary expansion in a recession (remember that recessions are possible as a result of surprises), would be predicted by market participants, and wages and prices would be set accordingly. Unless the central bank had better information or shorter reaction lags than the market, it could not, according to this theory, have a systematic *real* effect.

---

[22] The mechanism is discussed in more detail, in Robert E. Lucas, Jr., "Understanding Business Cycles," cited in footnote 33.

[23] Recall the application of perfect foresight expectations in Chapter 13 that produced precisely this adjustment.

This theory might seem successful in explaining why monetary policy apparently has little effect on the level of output, but it requires us to interpret changes in output as largely the result of imperfect information. It also has the apparently implausible implication that the central bank should find it easy to reduce the inflation rate. So long as the central bank announces that it will be reducing the growth rate of money, say to zero, market participants should adjust wages and prices accordingly, and the system will remain at full employment but at a lower rate of inflation.

Members of the rational expectations school argue that mere announcement by the central bank of a change in policy would not actually lead to changed expectations, since the central bank will have been pursuing a particular policy pattern for a long time. It would take actions rather than words for market participants to be convinced that the policy had in fact changed. We return to this point below.

Relative Wages, Wage Contracts, and Rational Expectations

The strongest form of the rational expectations theory just outlined, which assumes market clearing in every period and attributes fluctuations to imperfect information, is not widely accepted. There are, however, models that share the basic premise of rational expectations but also recognize economic institutions such as long-term contracts and the importance of the relative wages of various groups in the labour market.[24] Relatively simple amendments here go far in removing some of the least plausible implications of the strong market-clearing form of rational expectations theory.

Suppose we have two-year labour contracts and half the contracts in the economy come up for renewal every year. Suppose further that we start from price stability and that an unanticipated decline in the money stock occurs. If all wages and prices were instantaneously flexible, they would immediately decline in proportion to the fall in money and no real effects would arise. This does not occur, however, if we have long-term contracts that fix nominal wages. With a lowering in the money stock, there is potentially a decline in employment. Unemployed workers whose wages come up for renewal now have the choice of reducing their wages enough to become employed. If they did so, their wages would of course have to fall substantially compared with wages of those whose contract has another year to run. This change in *relative* wages may be as objectionable to unions as the fact of unemployment. Current wages will thus be set somewhere in between the full-employment level and the level of wages on contracts still running. That means wages do *not* adjust immediately to money changes, that is, wages are less than fully flexible. It takes some time until the whole wage structure adjusts. The fact that we have long-term nonsynchronized

---

[24] The discussion here follows a paper by John Taylor. "Staggered Wage Setting in a Macro-Model," *American Economic Review*, May 1979.

wage setting, and that relative wages matter, directly implies the possibility of extended periods of wage stickiness and unemployment.

The model is thus able to explain wage stickiness and unemployment occurring at the same time. It also explains simultaneous wage inflation and unemployment. Suppose there is a contraction in demand, as we have just discussed, and that labour knows that policy will be expansionary in the future. Then those whose wages are currently up for renegotiation recognize that if they set too low a wage, they will be out of line with the wages that will be set next year by a group that will then be facing strong demand. Accordingly, even with the possibility of current unemployment, the prospect of expansionary aggregate demand policies in the future will make current economic slack less effective in dampening wage and price inflation. Rational expectations enter here in that the groups currently setting their wages look ahead and ask themselves what will be the macroeconomic environment in which other groups set their wages next period. If the policy setting next period is expected to be expansionary, this fact will already be anticipated in this year's wages.[25]

The relative wage model, combined with rational expectations, thus has two important features: first, wages are sticky downward in the face of unemployment; and second, wage inflation may persist in the face of unemployment. The extent of persistence is determined by, among other things, the degree to which the policy setting is accommodative or not.

Expectations and Disinflation

What does the rational expectations approach have to suggest about the possibilities of reducing inflation in the Canadian economy? In its most extreme form, the approach would argue that only the announcement of a permanently lower growth rate of nominal money is necessary, but there are few who take such a suggestion seriously. In his *Annual Report* for 1979, Governor Bouey argues that a program of disinflation should be both announced and gradual:[26]

> ... the transition to a declining rate of inflation is much easier if the economic participants have confidence that the policies being followed will succeed. ... The firm commitment of the Bank of Canada to persist with a gradual reduction over time in the rate of monetary expansion is intended both to encourage and to justify confidence in declining inflation in the years ahead. ... It is an orientation of monetary policy that should not be taken lightly; if Canadians effectively resist a gradual reduction in the size of price and income increases they will force a reduction in the growth of employment and output.

---

[25] Similar implications follow if workers are concerned about the real wages they will be receiving in future years, rather than relative wages.

[26] Bank of Canada, *Annual Report*, 1979, p. 8-9.

It is widely recognized that a policy of disinflation would bring about a period of unemployment. In terms of the theory of rational expectations, the slack is needed to show that the central bank is indeed serious about the new anti-inflationary policy. The question is whether economic slack can or should be maintained long enough to reduce the underlying rate of inflation. On this point, Phillip Cagan has commented:[27]

> Market decisions about wages and prices are guided at least in part by rational expectations of the direction of policy. To the extent that prices behave according to the theory of rational expectations, the trend rate of inflation can persist in the face of slack demand, and the proclaimed desire of policy makers to subdue inflation only if they are generally not believed to be capable of translating the desire into effective action. Since the evidence suggests that the economic capability exists, the lack of credibility concerns the political capability. In such circumstances and in view of our past experience, the desire to subdue inflation is obviously not enough and must be confirmed by performance. The conclusion appears inescapable, therefore, that the reduction of inflation requires the maintenance of slack demand, and the less that policy hides an intention to maintain slack, the faster the reduction will be.

Whether the costs of the protracted slack justify the gains in reduced inflation is, of course, the key issue of political economy.

[27] Phillip Cagan, *Persistent Inflation* (New York Columbia University Press, 1979), p. 249.

16

LONG-TERM GROWTH

This chapter discusses long term growth and potential output. In earlier chapters we were concerned with the maintenance of full employment and the behaviour of output relative to the full-employment or potential level of output. In this chapter we shall ask what determines the growth rate of potential output over time. Over long periods, actual output on average stays close to potential output despite short-run fluctuations, so that we will also be discussing the long-run behaviour of actual output.

The question we are asking is brought out by Chart 16-1, which shows the evolution of real output (in 1961 dollars) in the Canadian economy from 1870 to 1980. Over that period, real output grew more than fiftyfold, or at an annual rate of about 3.7 percent. Growth theory asks what factors account for the increase in output over time, and what behaviour an economic system will show along the *growth path* of full-employment output.

In discussing these questions, we go to fundamentals. We step back from the aggregate demand and supply framework and ask how the economy would behave over time if there were always full employment. With full employment, output would be determined by *factor supplies* — by the availability of capital and labour to produce goods. Over time, output would be determined by the growth in factor supplies and by changes in the productivity of factors of production.

This in turn raises the questions of what determines the growth of factor supplies, and how the growth in factor supplies translates into income and output growth. The simple theory we present emphasizes two elements: (1) the production function that relates factor inputs — capital and labour— and the state of technology to output or GNP and (2) the savings rate.

The production function relates growth in factor supplies to growth in output. And the savings rate determines what part of current output is saved and invested (added to the capital stock), and thus results in an increase in the input of capital. Because we assume that output is continuously at the full-employment level, we also assume that any output that is saved is automatically added to the capital stock, and we do not separately discuss the determinants of the rate of investment.

CHART 16-1 REAL GNP IN CANADA
(*Sources*: O.J. Firestone, Canada's Economic Development, 1867-1953; and Statistics Canada, 11-505, 13-201)

Chart 16-1 has already introduced the major questions raised in this chapter: What determines the growth rate of output in the long run? In particular, what made real output in Canada grow at the average annual rate of 3.7 percent over the last 110 years? For many purposes, though, we are interested not in the level of total real output, but rather, in the level of output in relation to population, or in real per capita output.

The average growth rate of per capita income has been about 2 percent per year over the 1870-1980 period. The growth rate of output per head is equal to the growth rate of total output minus the growth rate of population, as shown in Table 16-1. Output per head has increased eightfold over the past 110 years. The average person in 1980 had eight times the amount of output or income at his or her command than the average person in 1870 had. Most of our ensuing analysis concentrates on the determinants of

TABLE 16-1 AVERAGE ANNUAL GROWTH RATES, 1870-1980

Average growth of output	3.7%
Less: Average growth of population	1.7%
Equals: Average growth of output per head	2.0%

Source; See Chart 16-1

output growth per capita. We want to know why per capita output grew to produce the extraordinary eightfold increase over the last 110 years.

There are two central messages from the simple growth theory we study here. (1) The savings rate determines the rate of growth of per-capita output in the short and medium terms. The larger the fraction of output saved and invested, the larger the growth rate of full-employment output. (2) In the long run, the growth rate of output per head depends on the rate of technological change (improvements in methods of production). Total output growth depends on the rate of technological change and the growth rate of the population. In the long run, the savings rate determines only the *level* and not the *growth rate* of the capital stock and output per capita. The higher the savings rate, the higher the amount of capital.

This preview has laid out both the questions to be asked in this chapter and some of the answers. We now turn to a more detailed analysis. In Section 16-1, we introduce the production function, which provides the framework for our analysis. In Section 16-2, we look at the empirical evidence on sources of growth. Here we explain the growth in output in terms of the growth in capital, growth in labour input, and improvements in technology. In section 16-3, we examine measures of potential output in Canada in the postwar period. Section 16-4 turns to growth theory and formalizes the relationships among saving, population growth, and growth in capital. Section 16-5 briefly discusses the question of *limits of growth* that has become an important issue of public concern.

16-1 SOURCES OF GROWTH IN REAL INCOME: THEORY

In this section we ask the question: What are the sources of growth in real output over time? The simple answer is: first, growth in the availability of factors of production and second, improvements in technology. If output is at the full-employment level, then there are only two ways of obtaining an increase in output: (1) to have more factors of production and/or (2) to be able to use existing factor supplies more effectively. The latter possibility means that we are producing more effectively because of either a more efficient allocation of resources or more effective technology.

The Production Function

The preceding remarks can be formalized by writing down a *production function*. A production function tells us how much output or real GNP is produced by given amounts of factor inputs. Denoting real output by Y, capital or machines by K, and the labour force by N, we have

$$Y = AF(K,N) \tag{1}$$

where we treat A as a constant.[1] Equation (1) states that output Y is a function of the inputs of capital and labour. An increase in either input will raise output. We impose a particular property on the production function, namely *constant returns to scale*. Constant returns to scale means that if all inputs increase in some proportion, then output will increase in that proportion. For example, if both capital and labour were to increase by 10 percent, output would increase by 10 percent. With constant returns to scale, the productivity of factors is independent of the scale of production. Constant returns to scale imply that output per head, Y/N, is independent of the scale of operation. Output per head or labour productivity depends on the amount of capital per worker, $k \equiv K/N$. The higher the amount of capital cooperating with each labourer, the more productive the labourer, or the higher is output per person.

Constant returns imply a simple relationship between labour productivity or output per worker, Y/N, and capital per workers, $k \equiv K/N$. The more capital per head we have, or the more capital-intensive the economy, the larger is output per head. We can write this relationship as

$$x = Af(k) \tag{1a}$$

where $x \equiv Y/N$ denotes output per head. We have already noted that in Equation (1a) an increase in the amount of capital per head k will make labour more productive and therefore raise output per worker. We add now the further assumption of diminishing returns *not* to scale but to capital intensity. As we keep raising the amount of capital per head k, labour becomes more productive and therefore output rises. However, the increase in output becomes progressively less. Additional capital cooperating with a given labour force is invariably productive but at a diminishing rate.

In Figure 16-1 we illustrate the properties of the production function that we have discussed so far.[2] In particular, we note that (1) output per head x is an increasing function of capital per head k, which is called the capital-labour ratio; and (2) the contribution to output of progressive increases in the capital-labour ratio diminishes. The latter aspect is captured in Figure 16-1 in the flattening out of the production function.

The contribution of an increase in capital per head to the amount of output per head is called the marginal productivity of capital. We note from Figure 16-1 that an increase in the capital-labour ratio from k_0 to k' raises output by $\Delta x = \text{MPK}\Delta k$. The term MPK denotes the marginal product of capital, which is given in Figure 16-1 by the slope of the production function.

---

[1] The term A used here has no connection with aggregate demand, which was denoted by that letter in other chapters.

[2] The production function was also discussed in Chapters 6 and 11.

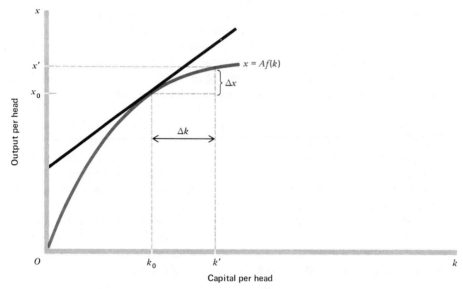

FIGURE 16-1 THE PRODUCTION FUNCTION

The idea of the marginal product of capital is best understood in the following manner. We start off from a capital-labour ratio k_0, where we produce an amount of output per head x_0. Next we have an increase in the capital-labour ratio to k'. Obviously, output per head will increase, and we can read off from the production function that it rises to x'. Thus we have an increase in output of $\Delta x = x' - x_0$ that is brought about by an increase in capital per person of $\Delta k = k' - k_0$. Forming the ratio $\Delta x/\Delta k \equiv$ MPK, we are looking at the increase in output due to the increase in capital or at the marginal product of capital. For sufficiently small changes in the capital-labour ratio we can use the slope of the production function to translate a change in capital into the corresponding change in output. Thus the marginal product of capital is given by the slope of the production function.

Sources of Growth

This exercise has prepared us for a discussion of a first source of growth. We have seen that growth in the amount of capital per head increases output per head. Therefore, one of the sources of long-term growth in output per head is that capital has grown faster than labour and therefore has caused the capital-labour ratio to rise.

A second source of growth is reflected in the constant term A in Equation (1a). Let this term represent the state of technology. An improvement in technology would mean that we could produce a larger quantity of output per head with the same amount of capital per head. Given capital and

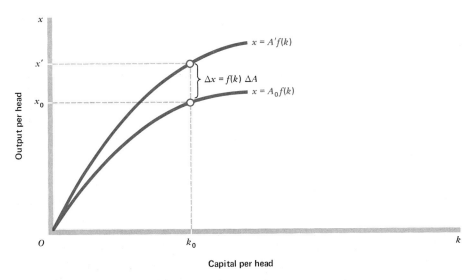

FIGURE 16-2 TECHNOLOGICAL PROGRESS

labour, improved technology raises factor productivity and therefore output. In terms of Figure 16-2, an improvement in technology is shown by an upward shift of the production function and thus a higher amount of output associated with each capital-labour ratio. Our second source of growth in output per head is therefore improvement in technology, or *technical progress*.[3]

We have now seen that there are two sources of growth in output per head: (1) increases in the amount of capital per head, which contribute to output by an amount $\Delta x = \text{MPK } \Delta k$; and (2) technical progress, which contributes to output an amount $\Delta x = f(k) \Delta A$. We can therefore write the total change in output per head as

$$\Delta x = \text{MPK } \Delta k + f(k) \Delta A \qquad (2)$$

If we divide both sides by the level of output per head x, we obtain a much more convenient expression:

---

[3] *Warning*: Technical progress in general implies that more output can be produced with the same inputs. The particular form of technical progress represented by increases in the constant term A in Eq, (1a) implies that the marginal products of both capital and labour increase by the same ratio. Other forms of technical progress imply changes in the *relative* productivities of capital and labour. We choose the form in which A increases for expositional convenience. For more details on technical progress, see R.M. Solow, *Growth Theory* (New York: Oxford University Press, 1970), pp. 33-38 and the very readable treatment in Daniel Hamberg, *Models of Economic Growth*, New York: Harper & Row, 1971 and, Philip A. Neher, *Economic Growth and Development* (New York: Wiley, 1971).

$$\frac{\Delta x}{x} = \theta \frac{\Delta k}{k} + \frac{\Delta A}{A} \tag{3}$$

where the term $\theta \equiv (MPK)k/x$ is capital's share in income.[4] It is capital's share in income because, in a competitive economy, the owners of capital are paid for the services of capital an amount equal to capital's marginal product. Accordingly, the marginal product — the return per unit of capital — times the stock of capital divided by total income, $(MPK)k/x$, is the fraction of income that accrues to capital.

Equation (3) tells us that growth in output per head is equal to growth in capital per head times the share of capital in income plus the rate of technical progress, $\Delta A/A$. To take an example, assume that capital per head grows at the rate of 2 percent. Assume capital's share in income, quite realistically for Canada, is $\theta = 0.3$. Then, if the rate of technical progress is 1.4 percent, the growth rate of output is 0.3 (2 percent) + 1.4 percent = 2.0 percent. In fact, this is approximately the long-term growth rate in output per capita in Canada, as we noted earlier in commenting on Table 16-1.

Growth in capital per head and technology are the only sources of growth in output per head. However, if we are interested in growth of total output — as opposed to output per head — we have to take account of increases in the size of the labour force. If we hold technology constant and hold constant the amount of capital per person but increase the size of the labour force, we expect output to increase. We can use Equation (3) to make this point by recognizing that the growth rate of output per worker is equal to the growth rate of output less the growth rate of the labour force, $\Delta x/x \equiv \Delta Y/Y - \Delta N/N$. Similarly, the growth rate in the capital labour ratio is the growth rate of capital less the growth rate of labour, $\Delta k/k \equiv \Delta K/K - \Delta N/N$. Using these substitutions in Equation (3) yields

$$\frac{\Delta Y}{Y} = \frac{(1 - \theta)\Delta N}{N} + \frac{\theta \Delta K}{K} + \frac{\Delta A}{A} \tag{4}$$

Equation (4) conveniently summarizes the three sources of growth. The growth contributions of capital and labour are weighted by their respective shares in income. Equation (4) implies, as we assumed at the outset, constant return to scale. This is apparent from the fact that, say, a 10 percent increase in both capital and labour will increase output in the same proportion.

---

[4] In more detail, dividing the term $MPK \cdot \Delta k$ in Eq. (2) by x, we have $(MPK \cdot \Delta k)/x$. Now multiply and divide by k to obtain $[(MPK \cdot k/x)](\Delta k/k)$. Now $MPK \cdot k$ is the marginal product of capital times the amount of capital per head, or the amount of income received by capital divided by the number of workers. The derivation of the $\Delta A/A$ term in Eq. (3) is left for the problem set at the end of the chapter.

16-2 EMPIRICAL ESTIMATES OF THE SOURCES OF GROWTH

The previous section prepares us for an analysis of empirical studies that deal with sources of growth. Equation (4) suggests that the growth in output can be explained by growth in factor inputs, weighted by their shares in income, and by technical progress. An early and famous study by Robert Solow of MIT dealt with the period 1909-1949 in the United States.[5] Solow's surprising conclusion was that over 80 percent of the growth in output per labour hour over that period was due to technical progress, that is, to factors other than growth in the input of capital per labour hour. Specifically, Solow estimated for the United States an equation similar to Equation (4) that identifies capital and labour growth along with technical progress as the sources of output growth. Of the average annual growth of total GNP of 2.9 percent per year over that period, he concluded that 0.32 percent was attributable to capital accumulation, 1.09 percent per annum was due to the increase in the input labour, and the remaining 1.49 percent was due to technical progress. Per capita output grew at 1.81 percent, with 1.49 percent of that increase resulting from technical progress.

The very large part of the growth contribution that is taken up by "technical progress" makes that term really a catchall for omitted factors and poor measurement of the capital and labour inputs. Further work therefore turned quite naturally to explore this residual, that is, growth not explained by capital accumulation or increased labour input.

Perhaps the most comprehensive of the subsequent studies is that by Edward Denison.[6] Using data for the period 1929-1969, Denison attributed 1.8 percent of the 3.4 percent annual rate of increase in real output to increased factor inputs. Output per labour hour grew at the rate of 2.09 percent, of which 1.59 percent was due to technical progress. Denison's findings thus support Solow's estimate that most of the growth in output per labour hour is due to technical progress.

The methods used by Denison have been applied to Canadian data for the period 1946 to 1967 in a study done for the Economic Council of Canada. Table 16-2 shows a breakdown of the contributions to growth of real output over this period. Out of an average rate of growth of 4.61 percent, 2.25 percent was estimated to be attributable to growth in factor productivity as a result of technical progress.

Technical progress explains almost half the growth in output, with growth in total factor inputs accounting for the other half of growth. Consider now the breakdown between labour and capital. Here increases in

---

[5] "Technical Change and the Aggregate Production Function." *Review of Economics and Statistics,* August 1957.

[6] *Accounting for United States Economic Growth 1929-1969* (Washington, D.C.: The Brookings Institution, 1974).

TABLE 16-2 SOURCES OF GROWTH OF REAL OUTPUT, 1946-67

Source of growth		Growth rate (percent per annum)
Total factor input		2.36
Labour:	1.24	
Capital:	1.12	
Output per unit of input		2.25
Total output		4.61

Source: Economic Council of Canada, *Seventh Annual Review*, 1970, p.93.

the labour force get a very large credit for their contribution to growth. Why? Because labour grows very fast? The answer is provided by Equation (4), which suggests that labour's growth rate has a relatively large weight because labour's share of income is relatively large. The counterpart is obviously the relatively low share of capital. Thus, even if capital and labour grew at the same rate, the fact that they have different shares in income — labour having a share of about 70 percent and capital having a share of about 30 percent — implies that labour would be credited with a larger contribution toward growth.

In these measurements, the contribution of technical progress includes the effects of improved resource allocation. Here we can think of people leaving low-pay jobs or low-income areas and moving to better jobs or locations, thus contributing to increased output or income growth. An important element is relocation from farms to cities. Also included are the effects of *economies of scale*. This is a bit troublesome because we assumed away economies of scale in deriving Equation (4). Nevertheless as the scale of operation of the economy expands, fewer inputs were required per unit output presumably because we can avail ourselves of techniques that are economically inefficient at a small-scale level but yield factor savings at a larger scale of production.

The major significance of Denison's work, and the work in this area of others, including Simon Kuznets and J.W. Kendrick, is to point out that there is no single critical source of real income growth. The early suggestion by Solow that growth in the capital stock makes a minor, though not negligible, contribution to growth stands up well to the test of new research. Capital investment is certainly necessary — particularly because some technological improvements require the use of new types of machines — but it is clear that there are other sources of growth that can make an important contribution. Furthermore, since for most purposes we are interested in output per head, we have to recognize that we are left with only technical progress and growth in capital to achieve increased output per head. Here we have to ask, What are the components of technical progress? Advances in knowledge stand out as a major source and point to the roles of research, education, and training as important sources of growth.[7]

16-3 POTENTIAL OUTPUT AND PRODUCTIVITY

The idea of potential output became a central concept in macroeconomic policy making in the 1960s. Potential output and the associated concept of the GNP gap provided policy makers with a target for policy setting.

Potential output is a measure of the output the economy can produce when factors of production are fully employed. Using the production function

$$Y = AF(K,N) \tag{1}$$

we obtain a measure of potential output by calculating the level of Y that corresponds to full-employment levels of input K (capital) and N (labour).

Typically, we are interested in both past and future levels of potential output. Past levels of potential output are of interest for judging past macroeconomic performance. Future levels of potential output are useful for guiding policy and for providing a baseline for expectations of future output.

Early estimates of potential output in the United States were made by Arthur Okun. He assumed that potential output corresponded to a level of labour input (N in Equation (1)) that prevailed when unemployment was 4 percent.[8] Although he did not then use the phrase, we would now say that 4 percent was his estimate of the natural rate of unemployment.[9] Okun also assumed that potential output grew at 3.5 percent per year. This estimate corresponded to postwar experience of growth rates of output between periods when there was full employment of labour.

There are two steps in estimating potential output. The first is to estimate the production function, Equation (1), and the second is to estimate the full-employment levels of capital and labour and any other inputs that might be taken into account. For example, recent studies have tried to

---

[7] A collection of useful papers on the sources of growth are contained in Edmund Phelps (ed.) *The Goal of Economic Growth* (New York: Norton, 1970).

[8] Arthur M. Okun, "Potential GNP: Its Measurement and Significance," reprinted in his book, *The Political Economy of Prosperity* (New York: Norton, 1970).

[9] We have not explicitly discussed the meaning of the full-employment level of capital [K in Eq. (1)]. The amount of capital used in production does vary over the cycle as the number of shifts worked, using particular machinery and hours of work, vary. *Capacity utilization*, a number estimated by the Bank of Canada among others, attempts to measure the extent to which capital is being employed. Some standard rate of capacity utilization is typically used to calculate full employment K in (1). Of course, the levels of employment of capital and labour move very much together over the cycle.

incorporate energy as a factor of production, in order to estimate the impact of the energy crisis on potential output.[10]

Projections of future potential output are typically made by calculating the growth rate of potential GNP. For this purpose it is useful to turn to Equation (4), derived from Equation (1):

$$\frac{\Delta Y}{Y} = (1 - \theta)\frac{\Delta N}{N} + \theta\frac{\Delta K}{K} + \frac{\Delta A}{A} \tag{4}$$

Output grows as a result of increases in factor inputs and technical progress. Therefore, to predict potential output growth, it is necessary to predict the full-employment levels of factor inputs and growth rate of technical progress. As mentioned earlier, inputs would include not only capital and labour as in Equation (4), but also factors, such as energy, that might be important.

The growth rate of the labour input depends on the growth rates of the different demographic groups in the labour force and their participation rates — that is, the percentage of each group in the labour force. It also depends on the natural rate of unemployment for each group. The rate of growth of capital depends on future rates of investment. If energy is treated explicitly as a factor, then predictions of the rate of change of energy use have to be made.

Predicting these variables is obviously difficult. For instance, our energy use depends in part on OPEC'S future policy decisions, which we cannot confidently know now. Similarly, investment fluctuates a great deal. And we have also to predict technical progress, which almost by its nature is not firmly predictable.

Because of the complexity of the complete calculation of future output growth using Equation (4), a shortcut is typically taken. Specifically, the productivity of labour, which we denote Z (not to be confused with Z used elsewhere in the book) is measured by

$$Z = \frac{Y}{N} \tag{5}$$

where Y is the level of output and N is the level of labour input. That is, productivity is the *average* product of labour. Now if we turn (5) around, we can write $Y = NZ$ and then see that

$$\frac{\Delta Y}{Y} = \frac{\Delta N}{N} + \frac{\Delta Z}{Z} \tag{6}$$

[10] Robert Rasche and John Tatom, "Energy Resources and Potential GNP," Federal Reserve Bank of St. Louis, *Review*, June 1977; and Jeffrey Perloff and Michael Wachter, "A Production Function-Nonaccelerating Inflation Approach to Potential Output," vol. 10, Carnegie-Rochester Conference Series, Karl Brunner and Allan Meltzer (eds). North Holland, Amsterdam.

The growth rate of output is equal to the growth rate of labour input plus the rate of growth of productivity.

Productivity Growth

Table 16-3 shows a breakdown of the contributions to productivity growth in Canadian manufacturing as estimated by the Economic Council of Canada. The estimates for the subperiods reveal a striking decline in the contribution of factor productivity in the 1970s. This is confirmed in Chart 16-2, which shows a slowdown in the growth of real GNE per person employed after 1973.

This marked decline in productivity growth has been the subject of considerable interest and investigation. In a study undertaken by the Department of Finance, two factors were identified as being significant.[11] About one-quarter of the decline in overall productivity growth was attributed to a fall in productivity in the oil and gas industry. Output per person in this sector declined on average by nearly 10 percent per year over the period 1962 to 1973. Since 1973, employment, particularly in the areas of exploration and drilling, has grown rapidly, while output of oil has declined and output of natural gas has remained close to the 1973 level.

Another 25 percent of the post-1973 decline in productivity growth was attributed to a decline in the growth of the capital-labour ratio. Four other factors were examined but were found not to have had a significant impact. These were: (1) changes in the demographic composition of the labour force, (2) shifts in the share of employment from goods producing to services-producing industries, (3) governmental pollution-abatement regulations, and (4) changes in average hours worked per employee.

[11] Department of Finance, *Recent Changes in Patterns of Productivity Growth in Canada*, April 1980.

TABLE 16-3 CONTRIBUTIONS TO PRODUCTIVITY GROWTH IN MANUFACTURING, 1958-76

Period	Growth rate of output per person-hour	Inputs per person-hour			Total factor productivity
		Capital	Energy	Materials	
1958-76	3.43	.30	.07	2.33	.74
1958-66	3.48	.19	.08	2.32	.89
1967-73	4.26	.35	.07	2.91	.94
1974-76	1.35	.48	.03	1.03	−.18

Source: Economic Council of Canada, *A Climate of Uncertainty*, Seventeenth Annual Review, 1980, Table C-1

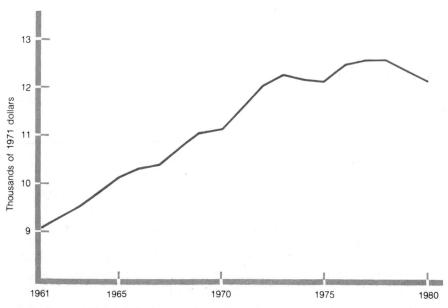

CHART 16-2 REAL GNE PER PERSON EMPLOYED, 1961-1980
(*Source*: Dept. of Finance, *Economic Review*)

*16-4 GROWTH THEORY

In this section we will be concerned with growth of output from a theoretical point of view rather than in terms of the historical record. We ask what determines output growth in the short and long runs. You will see that we have already answered that question when we recognized in Equation (4), that factor growth and technical progress are the sources of output growth. The next step, therefore, is to ask, What determines the growth of factor inputs? We take a rather simple formulation here by (1) assuming a given and constant rate of labour force growth, $\Delta N/N \equiv n$, and (2) assuming that there is no technical progress, $\Delta A/A = 0$. With these assumptions we are left with the growth rate of capital. Capital growth is determined by saving, which in turn depends on income. Income or output in turn depends on capital. We are thus set with an independent system in which capital growth depends, via saving and income, on the capital stock. We now study the short-run behaviour, the adjustment process, and the long-run equilibrium of that interdependent system.

Steady State

We start by discussing the steady state of the economy. Here we ask whether in an economy with population growth and saving, and therefore growth in the capital stock, we reach a point where output per head and capital per head become constant. In such a steady state, current saving and additions to the capital stock would be just enough to equip new entrants into the labour force with the same amount of capital as the average worker uses.

These ideas can be made more concrete by returning to Equation (3), recognizing that we assume zero productivity growth. We therefore have

$$\frac{\Delta x}{x} = \frac{\theta \Delta k}{k} \tag{3a}$$

Equation ($3a$) states that growth in output per head is proportional to growth in the stock of capital per head, $\Delta k/k$. Clearly, to reach a steady state where output per head is constant, we would have to reach zero growth in the stock of capital per head. Our focus is therefore on the determinants of the growth rate of capital per head.

Capital per head, $k \equiv K/N$, grows as current saving provides resources to be invested and added to the capital stock per worker. Capital per head declines to the extent that population growth reduces the amount of capital average workers each have at their disposal.

More precisely, the rate of growth of capital per head is equal to the difference between the growth rate of capital, $\Delta K/K$, and the growth rate of population, $n \equiv \Delta N/N$:

$$\frac{\Delta k}{k} = \frac{\Delta K}{K} - n \tag{7}$$

where we use the shorthand notation n for the given rate of growth of the labour force. Equation (7) shows that capital per head grows if the capital stock grows faster than the labour force. Combining this with Equation ($3a$), we realize that output per head grows if capital grows faster than the labour force:

$$\frac{\Delta x}{x} = \theta \left(\frac{\Delta K}{K} - n \right) \tag{8}$$

where we have substituted Equation (7) in Equation ($3a$).

Equation (8) implies that output per head will be constant when capital and labour grow at the same rate. In other words, we will be in the steady state when output per head is constant because $n = \Delta K/K$. The next step in the analysis is to link growth in the capital stock to income and saving.

The growth rate of the capital stock $\Delta K/K$ is determined by additions to the capital stock, that is, by investment and thus by saving. Additions to the capital stock are equal to investment, which in turn is equal to saving, less depreciation:

$$\Delta K = \text{saving} - \text{depreciation} \qquad (9)$$

We assume that a constant fraction s of income or output is saved. Accordingly, saving is equal to sY. We assume that the depreciation rate of capital is d percent per year, so that total depreciation is at the rate of dK per year. Substituting for saving and depreciation in Equation (9) yields

$$\Delta K = sY - dK \qquad (9a)$$

We have to do some more work on Equation (9a) before we arrive at a final equation that describes the growth process. The further modifications of Equation (9a) are (1) to turn it into percentage change form by dividing both sides by the capital stock and (2) to get into per capita form by subtracting the growth rate of labour from both sides. Undertaking these two operations we have

$$\frac{\Delta K}{K} - n = \frac{sY}{K} - n - d \qquad (9b)$$

We note that the left-hand side is the growth rate of the capital-labour ratio. The right-hand side is made up of three terms. First, we have saving per unit of capital, which is equal to total investment per unit of capital. However, to get to the growth of capital per person, we have to subtract both depreciation and growth of the labour force, which are the remaining two terms in Equation (9b). A final simplification of Equation (9b) is obtained by multiplying and dividing the saving term (sY/K) by the labour force N to obtain $s(Y/N)$ (N/K). This allows us to replace that term by sx/k, using the production function in per capita terms:

$$\frac{\Delta k}{k} = \frac{sx}{k} - (n + d) \qquad (10)$$

or

$$\Delta k = sx - (n + d)k \qquad (10a)$$

Equation (10) is the final form of our growth model. It describes the growth rate of the capital stock in terms of saving behaviour, population growth, and depreciation.

The growth process can be studied in terms of Figure 16-3. Here we reproduce the production function in per capita terms from Figure 16-1. We have added the savings function, which, for each capital-labour ratio, is simply the fraction s of output. Thus, for any capital-labour ratio, say k_0, the corresponding point on the saving schedule tells us the amount of saving per head $sx(k_0)$ that will be forthcoming at that capital-labour ratio.

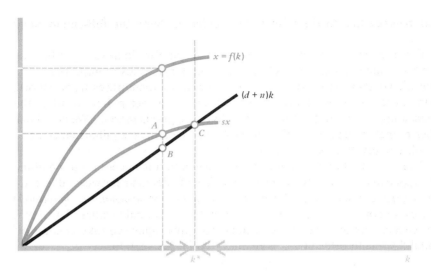

FIGURE 16-3 SAVING, INVESTMENT, AND CAPITAL ACCUMULATION

We know that all saving is invested so that gross investment or gross additions to the capital stock, in per capita terms, are equal to sx_0, given a capital-labour ratio of k_0. We know, too (from Equation (10a)), that the increase in the capital-labour ratio falls short of that gross addition for two reasons:

1   Depreciation reduces the capital-labour ratio, and part of gross investment must be devoted to offsetting depreciation. In particular, if the depreciation rate is d, then an amount dk is required as a depreciation allowance. For example, if the depreciation rate was 10 percent and the capital-labour ratio was ten machines per person, then each year the equivalent of one machine would depreciate and would have to be replaced, that is, 10 percent times ten machines equals one machine.
2   Growth in the labour force implies that with a given stock of capital, the capital-labour ratio would be declining. To maintain the amount of capital per head constant, we have to add enough machines to the stock of capital to make up for the growth in population.

It follows that we can write the investment required to maintain constant the capital-labour ratio in the face of depreciation and labour force growth as $(n + d)k$. That amount of investment is required to maintain constant the capital-labour ratio. When saving and hence gross investment are larger than $(n + d)k$, the stock of capital per head is increasing. If saving and gross investment are less, then we are not making up for depreciation and population growth, and, accordingly, capital per head is falling. We can therefore think of the term $(n + d)k$ as the *investment requirement* that will maintain constant capital per head and therefore, from Equation ($1a$), output per head.

In Figure 16-3 we show this investment requirement as a positively sloped schedule. It tells us how much investment we would require at each capital-labour ratio just in order to keep that ratio constant. It is positively sloped because the higher the capital-labour ratio, the larger the amount of investment that is required to maintain that capital-labour ratio. Thus, with the depreciation rate of 10 percent and a growth rate of population of 1 percent, we would require an investment of 1.1 machines per head per year at a capital-labour ratio of 10 machines per head to maintain the capital-labour ratio constant. If the capital-labour ratio were 100 machines per head, the required investment would be 11 machines (= 100 machines per head times 11 percent).

We have seen that the saving schedule tells us the amount of saving and gross investment associated with each capital-labour ratio. Thus, at a capital-labour ratio of k_0 in Figure 16-3, saving is sx_0 at point A. The investment requirement to maintain constant the capital-labour ratio at k_0 is equal to $(n + d)k_0$ at point B. Clearly, saving exceeds the investment requirement. More is added to the capital stock than is required to maintain constant the capital-labour ratio. Accordingly, the capital-labour ratio grows. Not surprisingly, the increase in the capital-labour ratio is equal to actual saving or investment less the investment requirement and is thus given by the vertical distance AB.

In the next period, capital per head will be higher. You immediately recognize the line of argument we are taking. From Figure 16-3 it is clear that with a somewhat higher capital-labour ratio, the discrepancy between saving and the investment requirement becomes smaller. Therefore the increase in the capital-labour ratio becomes smaller. However, the capital-labour ratio still increases, as indicated by the arrows.

The adjustment process comes to a halt at point C. Here we have reached a capital-labour ratio k^* such that saving and investment associated with that capital-labour ratio exactly match the investment requirement. Given the exact matching of actual and required investment, the capital-labour ratio neither rises nor falls. We have reached the *steady state*. We can make the same argument by starting with an initial capital-labour ratio in excess of k^*. From Figure 16-3 we note that for high capital-labour ratios, the investment requirement is in excess of saving and investment. Accordingly, not enough is added to the capital stock to maintain the capital-labour ratio constant in the face of population growth and depreciation. Thus, the capital-labour ratio falls until we get to k^*, the steady-state capital-labour ratio.

To review our progress so far:

1 Capital and labour are used to produce output according to a production function assumed to have constant returns to scale.

2   To maintain the capital-labour ratio constant, saving and investment have to be sufficient to make up for the reduction in capital per head that arises from population growth and depreciation.

3   With saving a constant fraction s of output, we established that the capital-labour ratio moves to a steady-state level k^* at which output and therefore saving (investment) are just sufficient to maintain constant the capital-labour ratio.

4   The convergence to a steady-state capital-labour ratio k^* is ensured by the fact that at low levels of the capital-labour ratio, saving (investment) exceeds the investment required to maintain capital per head and therefore causes the capital-labour ratio to rise. Conversely, at high capital-labour ratios, saving (investment) falls short of the investment requirement, and thus the ratio declines.

Now we can turn to a more detailed study of the characteristics of steady-state equilibrium and the adjustment process. First, we recognize what a steady-state equilibrium really means. We note that the steady-state level of capital per head is constant, and thus, from the production function, that the steady-state level of output per head is also constant. The steady state is reached when all variables, in per capita terms, are constant. That means that in the steady state, output, capital, and labour all grow at the same rate. They all grow at a rate equal to the rate of population growth, and therefore output and capital remain constant in per capita terms. Note particularly that the steady-state growth rate is equal to the rate of population growth and therefore is not influenced by the saving rate. (Recall that we are assuming no technical progress.) To explore this property of the steady state in more detail, we turn now to an investigation of the effects of a change in the saving rate.

A Change in the Saving Rate

In this subsection we address the puzzling question of why the long-run growth rate should be independent of the saving rate. If people save 10 percent of their income as opposed to 5 percent, should we not expect this to make a difference to the growth rate of output? Is it not true that an economy in which 10 percent of income is set aside for additions to the capital stock is one in which capital and therefore output grow faster than in an economy saving only 5 percent of income?

We show here that an increase in the saving rate does the following: (1) In the short run, it raises the growth rate of output; (2) it does not affect the long-run growth rate of output; and (3) it raises the long-run *level* of capital and output per head.

Consider now Figure 16-4 with an initial steady-state equilibrium at point C, where saving precisely matches the investment requirement. At point C, exactly enough output is saved to maintain the stock of capital per head constant in the face of depreciation and labour force growth. Next

FIGURE 16-4 AN INCREASE IN THE SAVING RATE

consider an increase in the saving rate. For some reason, people want to save a larger fraction of income. The increased saving rate is reflected in an upward shift of the saving schedule. At each level of the capital-labour ratio, and hence at each level of output, saving is larger.

At point C, where we initially had a steady-state equilibrium, saving has now risen relative to the investment requirement and, as a consequence, more is saved than is required to maintain capital per head constant. Enough is saved to allow the capital stock per head to increase.

It is apparent from Figure 16-4 that the capital stock per head will keep rising until we reach point C'. At point C', the higher amount of saving is just enough to maintain the higher stock of capital. At point C', both capital per head and output per head have risen. Saving has increased, as has the investment requirement. We have seen, therefore, that an increase in the saving rate will in the long run raise only the *level* of output and capital per head, as shown in Figure 16-4, but not the *growth rate* of output per head.

The transition process, however, involves an effect of the saving rate on the growth rate of output and the growth rate of output per head. In the transition from k^* to k^{**} the increase in the saving rate raises the growth rate of output. This follows simply from the fact that the capital-labour ratio rises from k^* at the initial steady state to k^{**} in the new steady state. The only way to achieve an increase in the capital-labour ratio is for the capital stock to grow faster than the labour force (and depreciation). This is precisely what happens in the transition process where increased saving per head, due to the higher saving rate, raises investment and capital growth over and above the investment requirement and thus allows the capital-labour ratio to rise.

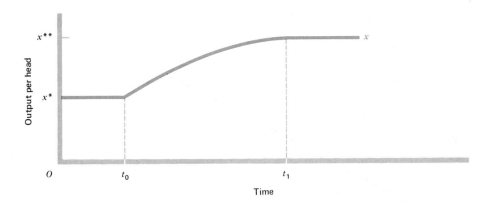

FIGURE 16-5*a* THE TIME PATH OF PER CAPITA INCOME

In summary, the long-run effect of an increase in the saving rate is to raise the level of output and capital per head but to leave the growth rate of output and capital unaffected. In the transition period, the rates of growth of output and capital increase relative to the steady state. In the short run, therefore, an increase in the saving rate means faster growth, as we would expect.

Figure 16-5 summarizes these two results. Figure 16-5*a* shows the level of per capita output. Starting from an initial long-run equilibrium at point t_0, the increase in the saving rate causes saving and investment to increase, the stock of capital per head grows, and so does output per head. The process will continue at a diminishing rate. In Figure 16-5*b* we focus on the growth

FIGURE 16-5*b* THE TIME PATH OF THE GROWTH RATE OF OUTPUT

rate of output and capital. The growth rate of output is equal to the growth rate of population in the initial steady state. The increase in the saving rate immediately raises the growth rate of output because it implies a faster growth in capital and therefore in output. As capital accumulates, the growth rate decreases, falling back toward the level of population growth.

Population Growth

The preceding discussion of saving and the influence of the saving rate on steady-state capital and output makes it easy to discuss the effects of increased population growth. The question we ask is, What happens when the population growth rate increases from n to n' and remains at that higher level indefinitely? We will show that such an increase in the rate of population growth will raise the growth rate of output and lower the level of output per head.

The argument can be conveniently followed in Figure 16-6. Here we show the initial steady-state equilibrium at point C. The increase in the growth rate of population means that at each level of the capital-labour ratio, it takes a larger investment just in order to maintain the capital-labour ratio constant. Suppose we had ten machines per head. Initially, the growth rate of population is 1 percent and depreciation is 10 percent, so that we require per year 11 percent times 10 machines, or 1.1 machine, just to offset population growth and depreciation and thus maintain capital per head

---

FIGURE 16-6 AN INCREASE IN THE RATE OF POPULATION GROWTH REDUCES PER CAPITA INCOME

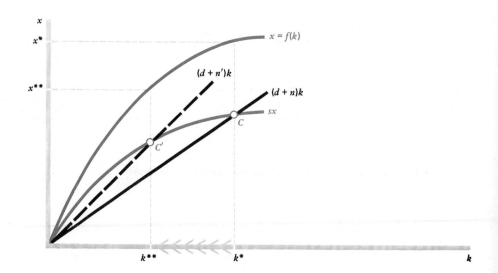

constant. To maintain the capital-labour ratio constant in the face of a higher growth rate of population, say 2 percent, requires a higher level of investment, namely, 12 percent as opposed to 11 percent. This is reflected in Figure 16-6 by an upward rotation of the investment requirement schedule.

It is clear from the preceding argument that we are no longer in steady-state equilibrium at point C. The investment that was initially just sufficient to keep the capital-labour ratio constant will no longer be sufficient in the face of higher population growth. At the initial equilibrium, the higher population growth with unchanged saving and investment means that capital does not grow fast enough to keep up with labour force growth and depreciation. Capital per head declines. In fact, capital per head will keep declining until we reach the new steady-state equilibrium at point C'. Here the capital-labour ratio has declined sufficiently for saving to match the investment requirement. It is true, too, that, corresponding to the lower capital-labour ratio, we have a decline in output per head. Output per head declines from x^* to x^{**}.

The decline in output per head as a consequence of increased population growth points to the problem faced by many developing countries. Fast growth in population, given the saving rate, means low levels of income per head. Indeed, in poor countries one can trace poverty, or low income per head, to the very high rate of population growth. With population growth, saving will typically be too small to allow capital to rise relative to labour and thus to build up the capital-labour ratio to achieve a satisfactory level of income per head. In those circumstances, and barring other considerations, a reduction in the rate of population growth appears to be a way of achieving higher levels of steady state per capita income and thus an escape from poverty.

Technical Progress[12]

So far, we have omitted technical progress from our growth model and simply studied the economy on the assumption of a given rate of population growth and given saving behaviour. In such an economy we saw that the growth rate of output converges to a steady-state growth rate exactly equal to the growth rate of population. As a consequence, in the steady state output per head is constant. In the steady state, saving, investment, and capital accumulation are just sufficient to maintain the capital-labour ratio constant and thereby ensure that output grows at the rate of population growth.

How do we incorporate technical progress in the analysis? First we note that with technical progress we have an additional source of growth. We

---

[12] The treatment is deliberately brief since technical progress in growth theory is a somewhat technical and taxonomic matter. The reader is referred to Robert Solow, *Growth Theory*, (New York: Oxford University Press, 1970) for an exposition of these issues.

would therefore expect that, even with a constant capital-labour ratio, output per head can be growing. In this sense we would expect technical progress — that is, a continuously shifting production function — to add to real growth per head. The next question is whether the economy would actually settle down to steady-state growth. Here the answer depends on the precise form that technical progress takes. If technical progress takes the form of a uniform increase in the productivity of factors so that, at a given capital-labour ratio, output increases in the proportion of technical progress, then a steady state will in general not exist. The economy keeps growing at a rate faster than t..e rate of population growth and at a rate that is *not* constant.

By contrast, if technical progress were *labour-augmenting*, a steady state would exist. Here the idea is that technical progress renders a given labour force more effective. Technical progress of this variety operates as though it increased the growth rate of the labour force. With this special type of technical progress, the economy will indeed settle down to a steady state where output per head grows at a constant rate equal to the rate of technical progress. Thus, technical progress is in fact compatible with steady-state analysis; more important, we see how it contributes to long-run growth in real income per head.

16-5 THE LIMITS OF GROWTH

This section briefly introduces the important and necessarily speculative question of where the economy is heading. The discussion becomes more general and concrete and raises the question of whether limited resources and the pressure of population on scarce land and food will ultimately bring the growth process to a dramatic halt. Are growing economies heading toward stagnation or even disaster?

We have first to raise the question of population and space. The world, being of finite size, cannot accomodate an ever-growing population. It is therefore quite apparent that, unless other planets can be colonized, population growth has to decline. In fact, one of the serious problems of our time is that this is recognized and indeed happening in rich countries that can still cope relatively well with growing populations, while population growth has not been significantly reduced in poor countries. Although space is not yet clearly a problem in these countries, food shortages and poverty are certainly major problems.

The second preliminary point we have to raise concerns food. Even though we recognize that there is still a lot of space in the world to accommodate the physically growing world population, the question of food is a very serious one. Will there be enough food for the 5 billion people who are expected to be in the world by 1990? Experts agree to a significant extent that the food problem is largely a matter of distribution and income inequality, not a problem of the inability of the globe to produce enough food. With the right incentives, food can be produced, but there is the obvious problem that the poor may not be able to afford the costly food that could be produced. These issues are sufficiently important to warrant detailed study, and we refer the reader to an article by Lance Taylor and the references contained in it.[13]

There is a related question that we want to raise here. It is whether, abstracting from food considerations, we expect real income per head to keep growing. The question is whether the world will progressively encounter factors of production in limited supply that prevent continued growth. Factors that are essential to the production process, such as oil and minerals, are *exhaustible resources*, the available stocks of which appear to limit the growth process. This was clearly as true a hundred years ago as today and a question that could have been, and was, raised at that time.[14] With the benefit of hindsight, we would argue that new deposits of these resources have been discovered in the past at a rate much in excess of that at which we have used up resources. If anything, in the last hundred years the supplies of *known* resources have grown. This is the standard retort of the growth-oriented economist. The argument is perfectly valid as a matter of historical record, though it obviously is true, too, that the more we discover, the less there is to be discovered in the future.

A more important challenge to the limits set by exhaustible resources is technical progress. There is no doubt that much technical progress takes the form of inventions and processes that dispense with, or save on, scarce resources used up in production. The expectation or hope, then, is that the same technical progress that in the last century has proved an important source of real growth will continue to keep up real growth in per capita income in the face of limitational factors and exhaustible resources. More particularly, it is hoped and expected that economic incentives will divert resources to inventions and innovations precisely in the field of exhaustible and limited resources and ensure that they will not prove a bottleneck to the growth process.

There is no assurance that the right technical progress will come along and bail us out when coal, oil, and copper run short in supply. Perhaps one should not bank on technological progress, innovation, and ingenuity to help us out. At the same time, it would be irresponsible to dismiss entirely the extraordinary record of technical progress that has contributed substantially to the average growth in real income. There will surely continue to be technical progress. The major problem of social policy then becomes the channeling of resources in the right direction to ensure that research and

---

[13] Lance Taylor. "The Misconstrued Crisis: Lester Brown and World Food," *World Development*, 1975. See also the World Bank's, *World Development Report*, (International Bank for Reconstruction and Development, Washington, D.C., 1980)

[14] See W.S. Jevons, *The Coal Question*, 1865, reprinted (New York: Augustus M. Kelley, 1965).

effort are devoted to solving society's bottleneck problems. The market mechanism itself is a powerful instrument to achieve precisely that purpose, but may in some instances need a helping hand.

There is one further potential contributor to real growth in the face of limited resources. That is *economies of scale*. We have assumed in the previous section that production is subject to constant returns to scale and that productivity of factors is independent of the scale of operation of the economy. This implies that as capital and labour expand, output expands at the same rate without any gains in growth from the fact that the economy has become, as it were, a larger plant. However, it is likely that as the economy expands its use of capital and labour, output expands more than proportionately, even holding the state of technology constant. Like technical progress, economies of scale are a potential counterweight against exhaustible resources. While exhaustible resources tend to put limits to growth, technical progress and economies of scale are sources of growth that help overcome or offset these limitational factors. Again, the only thing one can do is to point to their important role in history and argue that, while nobody can or will guarantee their continued benefit, there will surely be some contribution to growth that we should expect from economies of scale.

The subject of this section is one that cannot have a definite conclusion. This is a controversial question and an important one.[15] The only message we can convey is that, historically, there have been important counterweights to the role of exhaustible resources, and that these will continue to make an important contribution toward growth in real per capita income. That balance is important to bear in mind, and, indeed, to stimulate by the right social policies toward research and invention.

16-6 SUMMARY

1   A production function links factor inputs and technology to the level of output. Growth of output, changes in technology aside, is a weighted average of input growth with the weights equal to income shares. The production function directs attention to factor inputs and technological change as sources of output growth.
2   Growth theory studies the determinants of intermediate-run and long-run growth in output. Growth in factor supplies — labour and capital — and productivity growth or technological progress are the sources of growth. Saving behaviour determines capital accumulation.
3   In Canada over the 1946-1967 period, growth in factor inputs and technical progress each accounted for roughly one-half the average growth rate of 4.6 percent of output.

[15] William Nordhaus. "World Dynamics: Measurement without Data." *Economic Journal*, December 1973.

4   Per capita output grows faster, the more rapidly the capital stock increases and the faster is technical progress. In Canadian history since 1870, output per head has grown at an average rate of 2 percent.

5   There was a marked decline in productivity growth in Canada after 1973. A decline in the growth of the capital-labour ratio and a fall in productivity in the oil and gas industry appear to be the major causes.

6   The concept of steady-state equilibrium points (in the absence of technical change) to the conditions required for output per head to be constant. With a growing population, saving must be just sufficient to provide new members of the population with the economywide amount of capital per head.

7   The steady-state level of income is determined by the saving rate. In the absence of technical change, the steady-state growth rate of output is equal to the rate of population growth.

8   An increase in the growth rate of population raises the steady-state growth rate of total output and lowers the level of steady-state output per head.

9   An increase in the saving rate transitorily raises the growth rate of output. In the new steady state, the growth rate remains unchanged, but the level of output per head is increased.

10   With technical change, per capita output in the steady state grows at the rate of technical progress. Total output grows at the sum of the rates of technical progress and population growth.

11   Limits of growth pose a serious question for continued increases in real per capita income or even the maintenance of current consumption standards. The historical record is one of technological progress that offsets limitational factors and scarce resources. There is no certainty that this offset will continue, but public policy can make a contribution in that direction.

PROBLEMS

1   Which of the following government activities have effects on the long-term growth of output? Explain how they can do so.
   (a) Monetary policy
   (b) Labour market policies
   (c) Educational and research programs
   (d) Fiscal policy
   (e) Population control programs

* 2   The assumption of constant returns to scale in the production function Equation (1) can be summarized as

$$F(bK, \, bN) = bF(K,N) \qquad \text{for any } b > 0$$

Using this fact, derive Equation (1d) from Equation (1) and explain why k is the only determinant of x.

* 3   (a) Use the fact from microeconomics that capital is paid its marginal product to show that θ is the fraction of total income which is paid to capital.
   (b) Derive the $\Delta A/A$ term in Equation (3) from Equations (2) and (1a). Explain why, if $\Delta A/A = 0$, real output does not grow as rapidly as the capital-labour ratio.

* 4   Present and explain the step-by-step derivation of Equation (4), using equation (3) and the formulas leading up to Equation (4).

5   In Section 16-3, we related the growth rate of the capital-labour ratio to the growth rate of productivity. Use equations (4) and (6) to show that

$$\frac{\Delta Z}{Z} = \theta \left(\frac{\Delta K}{K} - \frac{\Delta N}{N} \right) + \frac{\Delta A}{A}$$

Explain why a 1¼ percent fall in the growth rate of the capital-labour ratio would reduce the growth rate of productivity by about 0.3 percent.

6   Draw a figure like Figure 16-3 which indicates the adjustment process when $k_0 > k^*$. How does the adjustment process work? Explain Figure 16-3 in terms of the saving = investment identity (first consider the case when $n = 0$).

7   (a) In the absence of technical progress, what happens to output per head and total output over time? Why?
   (b) What is the long-run effect of the saving rate on the *level* of output per capita? On *growth* of output per capita?

8   Evaluate this statement: "The saving rate cannot effect the growth of output in the economy. That is determined by the growth of labour input and by technical progress."

* 9   Suppose we assume a production function of the form

$$Y = AF(K,N,Z)$$

where Z is a measure of the natural resources going into production. Assume this production function obeys constant returns to scale and diminishing returns to each factor [like Equation (1)].

(a) What will happen to output per head if capital and labour grow together but resources are fixed?

(b) What if Z is fixed but there is technical progress?

(c) Interpret these results in terms of the limits to growth.

*10 Use the model of long-run growth to incorporate the government. Assume that an income tax at the rate t is levied and that, accordingly, saving per head is equal to $s(1 - t)x$. The government spends the tax revenue on public consumption.

(a) Use Figure 16-3 to explore the impact of an increase in the tax rate on the steady-state output level and capital per head.

(b) Draw a chart of the time path of capital per head, output per head, and the growth rate of output.

*(c) Discuss the statement: "To raise the growth rate of output, the public sector has to run a budget surplus to free resources for investment."

11 Use Figure 16-3 to explore the impact of a *once-and-for-all* improvement in technology.

(a) How does technical progress affect the level of output per head as of a given capital-labour ratio?

(b) Show the new steady-state equilibrium. Has saving changed? Is income per head higher? Has the capital stock per head increased?

(c) Show the time path of the adjustment to the new steady state. Does technical progress transitorily raise the ratio of investment to capital?

12 Consider an economy where a baby boom *transitorily* raises the growth rate of population from n to n'. After a few years, the growth rate of population falls back to the rate n.

(a) What is the impact of the baby boom on steady-state output per head?

(b) Show the adjustment process of the economy as the growth rate of population increases and then falls back to the initial level. Draw a time path of the variables shown in Figure 16-5.

13 Discuss the statement: "The lower the level of income, the higher the growth rate of output."

Part 4

17

MACROECONOMICS IN THE OPEN ECONOMY: TRADE AND CAPITAL FLOWS WITH FIXED EXCHANGE RATES

<p style="text-indent: 2em">

This is the first of two chapters analyzing foreign trade and its effects on the economy. It extends the macroeconomics we have learned to open economies — economies that trade with others. International transactions include not only trade in goods and services — Canadians buy Japanese cars and foreign countries buy our wheat, but also borrowing and lending and trade in assets — Canadians buy American stocks and sell bonds to foreign investors. Since Canada exports about 25 percent of national output and makes substantial use of foreign capital to finance investment, transactions with other countries are of major importance in our economy.

This chapter begins with a brief description of the balance of payments accounts — the record of the country's transactions with other economies. Section 17-1 also describes the two basic exchange rate systems — *fixed* and *flexible rate* systems. In the fixed exchange rate system, central banks fix the U.S. dollar price of their currencies and stand ready to buy and sell their currencies at that price. Canada was on a fixed exchange rate from 1962 to 1970 and most other countries were on a fixed rate system from 1946 to 1973, though there were occasional adjustments of exchange rates during that period. In the flexible exchange rate system, the exchange rate is determined in the foreign exchange market and can change from moment to moment.

The rest of this chapter analyzes trade in goods and assets in a fixed exchange rate system. Section 17-2 abstracts from trade in assets and examines the way in which foreign trade affects goods market equilibrium, and the determinants of the balance of trade in goods and services. Section 17-3 examines the effects of devaluation and looks at the financing of deficits. International borrowing and lending and trade in assets are studied in Section 17-4, as are the implications of such transactions for the conduct of monetary and fiscal policy. Chapter 18 presents an analysis of international trade under flexible exchange rates.

17-1 THE BALANCE OF PAYMENTS AND EXCHANGE RATE REGIMES

The *balance of payments* is the record of the transactions of the economy with the rest of the world. There are two main accounts in the balance of payments: the *current account* and the *capital account*. The current account records trade in goods and services, as well as transfer payments. Services include freight, travel, dividend, and interest payments. Transfer payments consist of remittances, gifts, and grants. We talk of a current account surplus if exports exceed imports plus net transfers to foreigners, that is, if recipts from trade in goods and services and transfers exceed payments on this account.

The capital account records borrowing and lending and purchases and sales of assets, such as stocks, bonds, and land. There is a capital account surplus, or a net capital *inflow*, when our receipts from borrowing and the sale of stocks, bonds, land, bank deposits, and other assets exceed our payments for lending and purchases of foreign assets.

Closely related to the current account are certain subaccounts that we mention here for completeness. The *merchandise trade balance* simply records trade in goods. Adding trade in services to the trade balance, we arrive at the *balance on goods and services*. Finally, adding net transfers, we arrive at the current account balance.

The simple rule for balance of payments accounting is that any transaction that gives rise to the disbursement of foreign currency is recorded as a payment. Thus, imports of goods, foreign travel, purchase of foreign stocks and lending to foreigners are all payment items. Conversely, any transactions that give rise to the acquisition of foreign exchange are recorded as receipts. Such transactions include exports of goods and borrowing from foreigners.

The overall *balance of payments* is the sum of the current and capital accounts. If both the current account and the capital account are in deficit, then the overall balance of payments is in deficit. When one account is in surplus and the other is in deficit to precisely the same extent, the overall balance of payments is zero — neither in surplus nor in deficit.

Table 17-1 shows the details of Canada's balance of payments in 1979 and Chart 17-1 shows the movements in the major categories over the past 30 years. The general pattern in 1979 was typical of the past 20 years. There was a surplus on merchandise trade more than offset by a deficit on services and transfers, leaving a substantial overall current account deficit. Much of this deficit was attributable to a large outflow of dividend and interest payments associated with accumulated foreign indebtedness and foreign ownership of Canadian businesses.

TABLE 17-1 CANADIAN BALANCE OF INTERNATIONAL PAYMENTS, 1979 (BILLIONS OF DOLLARS)

	Receipts (+)	Payments (−)	Balance
Current Account			
Merchandise trade	65.2	61.2	
Travel	2.9	4.0	
Interest and dividends	1.1	6.4	
Freight and shipping	3.4	3.1	
Other services and transfers	6.0	9.0	
Balance on current account			−5.1
Capital account			
Long-term capital			
Direct investment	.7	2.0	
Portfolio investment, net	4.1		
Short-term capital, net[1]	4.0		
Balance on capital account			6.8
Change in official reserves			1.7

[1] Includes net errors and omissions.

Source: *Bank of Canada Review*

As shown in Table 17-1, capital flows can be divided into movements of long-term capital and movements of short-term capital. The long-term flows can be further divided into *direct investment* and *portfolio investment*. Direct investment is the item that records changes in nonresident ownership of domestic business and changes in resident ownership of foreign businesses. Thus, direct investment in Canada is capital investment in a branch plant or subsidiary in Canada in which the investor has voting control. Alternatively, it may be in the form of a takeover in which a controlling interest is acquired in a business previously controlled by residents. Portfolio investment, on the other hand, is investment in bonds or a minority holding of shares that does not involve legal control.

In 1979, there was a net outflow of direct investment. Portfolio investment provided the source of surplus on long-term capital, primarily as a result of borrowing by private Canadian corporations, provinces, and provincially owned corporations such as Quebec Hydro. This pattern has been typical since 1975, but is in marked contrast to the fifties and sixties when direct investment accounted for a major fraction of long-term capital inflows.

An overall deficit in the balance of payments — the sum of the current and capital accounts — means that Canadian residents make more payments to foreigners than they receive from foreigners. The foreign currency

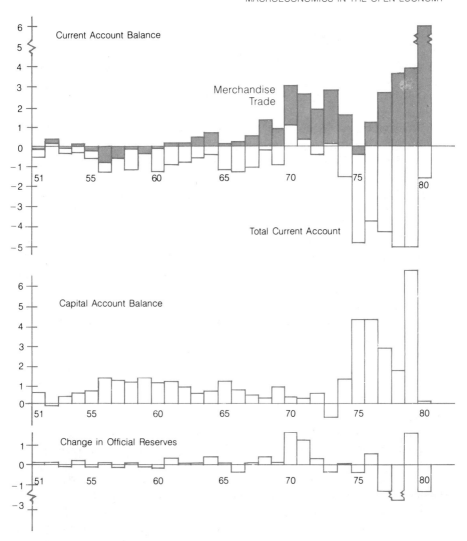

CHART 17-1 CANADA'S BALANCE OF INTERNATIONAL PAYMENTS, BILLIONS OF DOLLARS
(*Source: Bank of Canada Review*)

required to fill the gap is supplied out of the *official reserves* held by the Bank of Canada on behalf of the government of Canada. As can be seen in Chart 17-1, there have been wide swings in the overall balance of payments in recent years. There were very large deficits and losses of reserves in 1977 and 1978, and a large surpluses and accumulations of reserves in 1970 and 1979.

Fixed Exchange Rates

We now return to the way in which central banks, through their official transactions, *finance* balance of payments surpluses and deficits. At this point we want to distinguish between fixed and floating exchange rate systems.

In a fixed rate system, central banks stand ready to buy and sell their currencies at a fixed price in terms of dollars. For example, from May 1962 to June 1970 the Bank of Canada would buy or sell any amount of foreign currency at 92.5 U.S. cents per Canadian dollar.[1] The fact that the Bank was prepared to buy or sell *any* amount of Canadian dollars at this fixed price or exchange rate meant that the market price would indeed be equal to 92.5 U.S. cents. Why? Clearly, nobody who wanted to buy Canadian dollars with U.S. dollars would pay more than 92.5 U.S. cents if they could be gotten at that price from the Bank of Canada. Conversely, nobody would part with Canadian dollars for less than 92.5 U.S. cents if the Bank of Canada was prepared to buy them at that price.

Fixed exchange rates thus operate like any other price support scheme, such as in agricultural markets. Given market demand and supply the price fixer has to make up the excess demand or take up the excess supply. In order to be able to ensure that the price (exchange rate) stays fixed, it is obviously necessary to hold an inventory of foreign exchange that can be sold in exchange for domestic currency. Thus, the Bank of Canada holds *reserves* of U.S. dollars, and gold that can be sold for U.S. dollars, for the purpose of exchange market intervention.

What determines the amount of foreign exchange intervention that a central bank would have to do in the fixed exchange rate system? We already have the answer to that question. The balance of payments measures the amount of foreign exchange intervention needed. So long as the central bank has the necessary reserves, it can continue to intervene in the foreign exchange markets to keep the exchange rate constant. However, if a country persistently runs deficits in the balance of payments, the central bank eventually will run out of foreign exchange, and will be unable to continue its intervention.

Before that point is reached, the central bank is likely to decide that it can no longer maintain the exchange rate, and will *devalue* the currency. In 1967, for instance, the British devalued the pound from $2.80 per pound to $2.40 per pound. That meant it became cheaper for foreigners to buy British pounds, and thus affected the balance of payments. We shall study the way in which devaluation affects the balance of payments in Section 17-3.

---

[1] The Bank of Canada was not committed to maintaining exactly this rate. Under the rules of the International Monetary Fund in effect at that time, countries on fixed exchange rates maintained the value of their currencies within one percent of the stated fixed rate.

Flexible Exchange Rates

We have seen that the central banks have to provide whatever amounts of foreign currency are needed to finance payments imbalances under fixed exchange rates. In flexible rate systems, by contrast, the central banks allow the exchange rate to adjust to equate the supply and demand for foreign currency. If today's exchange rate were 85 U.S. cents per Canadian dollar, and imports from the United States increased, thus increasing the demand for U.S. dollars by Canadians, the Bank of Canada could simply stand aside and let the exchange rate adjust. In this particular case, the exchange rate could move from 85 U.S. cents to a level such as 84 U.S. cents, making American goods more expensive in terms of Canadian dollars and thus reducing the demand for them by Canadians. We shall in Chapter 18 examine the way in which exchange rate changes under floating rates affect the balance of payments. The terms *flexible rates* and *floating rates* are used interchangeably.

Indeed, in a system of *clean floating*, central banks stand aside completely and allow exchange rates to be freely determined in the foreign exchange markets. The central banks do not intervene in the foreign exchange markets in a system of clean floating, and official reserve transactions would, accordingly, be zero in such a situation. That means the balance of payments would be zero in a system of clean floating: the exchange rate would adjust to make the current and capital accounts sum to zero.

In practice during the 1970s, the flexible rate system has not been one of clean floating. Instead, the system has been one of *managed* or *dirty floating*. Central banks have intervened to buy and sell foreign currencies, in attempts to influence exchange rates, and official reserve transactions have, accordingly, not been zero. Chart 17-1 shows that the Bank of Canada has frequently carried out official reserve transactions. The reasons for this central bank intervention under floating rates are discussed in Chapter 18.

Terminology

The use of language with respect to exchange rates can be very confusing. In particular, the terms *depreciation* and *appreciation*, and *devaluation* and *revaluation* will recur throughout this chapter and the next.

A *depreciation* of the exchange rate is a decrease in the value of domestic currency in terms of foreign exchange. Thus, if the Canadian dollar moves from 90 U.S. cents to 85 U.S. cents, we talk of a depreciation of the Canadian dollar. Conversely, an appreciation means that the value of our currency rises in terms of foreign exchange.

A further clarification concerns the difference between devaluation (revaluation) and depreciation (appreciation). The term *devaluation* is used to refer to the adjustment of a fixed exchange rate, such as the sterling devaluation of 1967 from $2.80 per pound to $2.40 per pound. A *depreciation* by contrast, refers to a decrease in the value of domestic currency under a flexible exchange rate system. There is no substantial economic difference between depreciation and devaluation.

Summary

1 The balance of payments accounts are a record of the transactions of the economy with other economies. The capital account describes transactions in assets, while the current account covers transactions in goods and services and transfers.

2 Transactions that give rise to the disbursement of foreign exchange are recorded as payments, while those that give rise to the acquisition of foreign exchange are recorded as receipts. The balance of payments deficit (or surplus) is the sum of the deficits (or surpluses) on current and capital accounts.

3 Under fixed exchange rates, central banks stand ready to meet all demands for foreign currencies arising from balance of payments deficits or surpluses at a fixed price in terms of the domestic currency. They have to *finance* the excess demands for, or supplies of, foreign currency (that is, the balance of payments deficits or surpluses, respectively), at the pegged (fixed) exchange rate by running down, or adding to, their reserves of foreign currency.

4 Under flexible exchange rates, the demands for, and supplies of, foreign currency can be made equal through movements in exchange rates. Under clean floating, there is no central bank intervention and the balance of payments is zero. But central banks sometimes intervene in a floating rate system, engaging in so-called dirty floating.

The remainder of this chapter is concerned with the operation of a system of fixed exchange rates. We begin in Section 17-2 by abstracting from the capital account and dealing only with trade in goods. Section 17-3 examines the reasons for, and effects of, devaluation. Section 17-4 introduces the capital account and discusses the impact of trade in assets on the conduct of monetary and fiscal policy.

17-2 TRADE IN GOODS, MARKET EQUILIBRIUM, AND THE BALANCE OF TRADE

This section is concerned with the effects of trade in goods on the level of income, and the effects of various disturbances on both income and the trade balance — which, from now on, we use as shorthand for the current account. We also examine policy problems which arise when the balance of trade and the level of income require different corrective actions. The section concludes by introducing the important notion of the *policy mix*.

In this section, we shall be fitting foreign trade into the IS-LM framework, which is the basic income determination model of Chapter 4, and which continues to underlie the aggregate demand function used in later chapters. As in Chapters 3 and 4, we assume that the price level is given, *fixed* and that output that is demanded will be supplied. As you no doubt appreciate by now, this assumption enables us to develop the details of the analysis most simply. It is both conceptually and technically easy to relax the assumption, and we shall briefly do so later. But it is important to be clear on how the introduction of trade modifies the analysis of aggregate demand, and for that reason we start from a familiar and basic level.

A word of warning is in order before you start working through the following sections. The exposition here assumes you are thoroughly at home with the IS-LM analysis, and therefore proceeds quite rapidly. However, the material is not inherently more difficult than that of earlier chapters and should, with careful and active reading, be totally accessible.

Domestic Spending and Spending on Domestic Goods

In this subsection we want to establish how foreign trade fits into the IS-LM income determination model of Chapter 4. With foreign trade, part of domestic output is sold to foreigners (exports) and part of spending by domestic residents falls on foreign goods (imports). If we go back to income determination as studied in Chapters 3 and 4, it is apparent that the foreign trade complication will require some modification of our analysis.

The most important change is that it is no longer true that domestic spending determines domestic output. What is true now is that spending on domestic goods determines domestic output. Spending by domestic residents falls in part on domestic goods but in part on imports. Demand for domestic goods that determines output, by contrast, includes exports or foreign demand along with part of spending by domestic residents.

The way in which external transactions affect the demand for domestic output was examined in Section 3-6 of Chapter 3. We provide a reminder by looking at the definitions:

$$\text{Spending by domestic residents} \equiv A \equiv C + I + G \tag{1}$$

$$\text{Spending on domestic goods} \equiv A + NX \equiv (C + I + G) + NX \tag{2}$$

where NX is the trade balance (goods and services) surplus. Spending on domestic goods is total spending by domestic residents, *less* their spending on imports *plus* foreign demand or exports. Since exports minus imports is the trade surplus, or net exports, NX, spending on domestic goods is spending by domestic residents plus the trade surplus.

With this clarification we can return to our models of income determination. We will continue to assume, as in Chapter 4, that domestic spending depends on the interest rate and income, so that we can write

$$A = A(Y,i) \tag{3}$$

As in Chapter 3, we assume for the present that foreign demand for our goods or exports X is given and equal to $\overline{X}$, and that demand for foreign goods, or imports Q, depends only on the level of income, so that $Q = Q(Y)$. As income rises, part of the increase in income is spent on imports, while the rest is spent on domestic goods, or saved.

Now the trade balance is

$$NX \equiv X - Q = \overline{X} - Q(Y) \tag{4}$$

With our assumptions, the trade balance NX is a function only of the level of income. The trade balance is shown as a function of income in Figure 17-1. Imports are small at low levels of income, so that given the fixed level of exports, there is a trade surplus, $NX > 0$. As income rises, import spending increases until we reach income level Y_B, where imports match exports, so that trade is balanced. A further increase in income gives rise to a trade deficit. We can thus write

$$NX = NX(Y,\overline{X}, \dots) \tag{4a}$$

Where $\overline{X}$ denotes the given level of exports and the dots denote the other variables, such as exchange rates and prices, which we hold constant for now. We repeat that, as in Chapters 3 and 4, we assume that domestic prices are given. Here we shall also assume that foreign prices are fixed. These assumptions are relaxed below.

FIGURE 17-1 THE TRADE BALANCE AS A FUNCTION OF INCOME

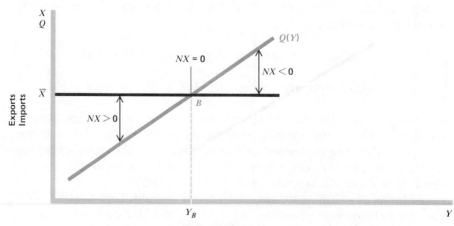

Income, output

Goods Market Equilibrium

There is equilibrium in the domestic goods market when the amount of output produced is equal to the demand for that output. The value of output produced continues to be equal to income, but the demand for domestically produced goods includes net exports:

$$Y = A(Y,i) + NX(Y,\overline{X}, \ldots) \tag{5}$$

Figure 17-2 illustrates the goods market equilibrium condition (5). We still refer to it as a goods market equilibrium schedule, or IS curve, though it is important to recognize that now the trade surplus, or net exports, NX, appears as a component of demand for output. The schedule is downward-sloping because an increase in output gives rise to an excess supply of goods: the increase in income is only partly spent on domestic goods, the rest being saved or spent on imports. To compensate for the excess supply, interest rates would have to decline to induce an increase in aggregate demand. The IS schedule is drawn for the given level of foreign demand $\overline{X}$.

We have also shown, in Figure 17-2, the trade balance equilibrium schedule $NX = 0$. Given exports, we see from Figure 17-1 and Equation (4) that there is some level of income, Y_B, at which import spending exactly matches export revenue, so that trade is balanced. Points to the left of the $NX = 0$ schedule are points of trade surplus. Here income and hence import spending are low relative to exports. Exports accordingly exceed imports.

FIGURE 17-2 GOODS AND MONEY MARKET EQUILIBRIUM

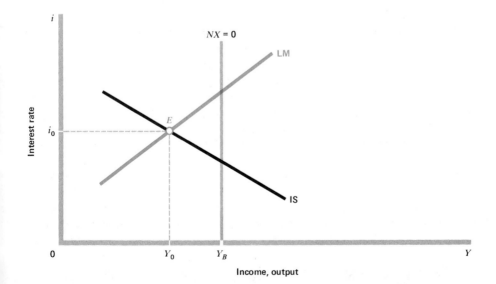

Points to the right of the $NX = 0$ schedule, by contrast, are deficit points. Here income and hence import spending are too high relative to exports for trade to be balanced. Finally, we have drawn, too, the LM schedule, which is precisely the same as in our study of the closed economy.

Equilibrium Income and the Balance of Trade

The next question to address, using Figure 17-2, is where the short-run equilibrium of the economy will be. It will be at point E, the intersection of the IS and LM curves. The reason is: Trade need not be balanced. In the short run, a trade balance deficit can be financed by running down foreign exchange reserves and a surplus can be financed by building up reserves. The assumption then is that the central bank finances the trade deficit by selling foreign exchange and thus maintains the exchange rate at its pegged level in the face of a trade and balance of payments deficit, or that the bank purchases foreign exchange if there is a surplus. We assume the goods and money markets clear sufficiently quickly so that equilibrium is determined at point E in Figure 17-2. As we have drawn the equilibrium, the trade balance is in surplus.

Disturbances

How do internal and external disturbances — shifts in the level or composition of spending or changes in exports — affect equilibrium income and the balance of trade? To answer that question, it is important to remember that both the IS and the trade balance schedules are drawn for a given level of exports, $\overline{X}$.

We can think of three types of disturbances, the effects of which we will briefly analyze in turn: (1) an increase in autonomous domestic spending that falls on our goods, (2) an increase in exports, and (3) a shift in demand from domestic goods to imports. Before going through the exercises, we want to indicate the results we expect to find. There are two results that we should expect. First, any increase (decrease) in spending on our goods should result in an increase (decrease) in equilibrium income. Second, we would expect the trade balance to worsen if domestic income expands, but we would expect it to improve if exports rise or if there is an autonomous decline in imports. It is not so clear how an increase in exports affects the trade balance. Say exports increase and, as a consequence, domestic income rises. This income increase, in turn, raises import spending, and we are not certain whether the net effect on the trade balance is an improvement or a worsening. What we can show is that the net effect is actually an improvement — induced import spending dampens but does not offset the trade balance improvement resulting from an increase in exports.

The Effects of an Increase in Autonomous Spending

With these preliminary remarks, we can proceed to our analysis. First, consider an autonomous increase in our spending on domestic goods, perhaps because of expansionary fiscal policy. In Figure 17-3 we show the effect to be a shift in the IS curve. At the initial equilibrium E, there is an excess demand for goods and, accordingly, the equilibrium income level will increase. The new equilibrium is at point E', where output and interest rates have risen and where we have a reduction in the trade surplus. The expansion in output will have increased import spending, and thus at E' the trade surplus is less than at E. The first lesson is, therefore, that expansionary domestic policies or autonomous increases in spending will raise income but will, too, cause a worsening of the trade balance.

There is a second point worth making, and that concerns the size of the income expansion induced by an expansionary policy. As we saw in Chapter 3, by comparison with a closed economy, we have less of an expansion in an open economy. Multipliers are smaller because induced spending on domestic goods is less. Induced spending is less than in a closed economy because part of an increase in income is now spent on imports rather than domestic goods. Imports are a *leakage* from the domestic multiplier process. Because the spending on imports induced by income increases does not increase demand for domestic output, they reduce the size of the multipliers. Indeed, the larger the fraction of an increase in income that is spent on imports, the smaller the multiplier, because there is relatively little induced spending on domestic goods.

FIGURE 17-3 THE EFFECTS OF AN INCREASE IN DOMESTIC SPENDING

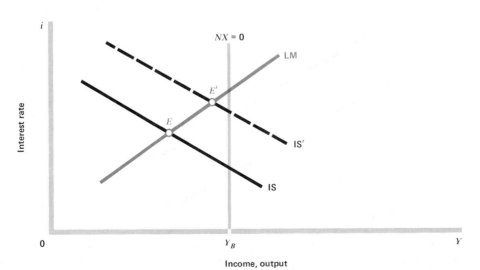

Income, output

The Effects of an Increase in Exports

The next disturbance we consider is an increase in exports. An increase in exports raises the demand for domestic goods and thus shifts the IS curve to the right (to IS'), as shown in Figure 17-4. At the same time, the increase in exports implies that at each level of income the trade balance is improved and that, therefore, the trade balance equilibrium schedule shifts out and to the right. It takes a higher level of income to generate the import spending to match the higher level of exports. Thus, the trade balance schedule shifts to $NX' = 0$. Starting from a position of balanced trade at point E, we find that the increase in exports raises equilibrium income and improves the balance of trade at point E'. The first part is quite intuitive. Higher demand for our goods leads to an increase in equilibrium output. The trade balance improvement, though, is less intuitive. Clearly, the increase in exports by itself improves the trade balance, but the increase in income leads to increased import spending which, it seems, could perhaps offset the direct improvement from the export increase. This is in fact not the case, and we leave the demonstration of that result as a problem.[2]

A Shift in the Composition of Demand

The last disturbance we consider is a shift in demand from imports to domestic goods. You will recognize that this has the same effects as an

[2] See problem 3 at the end of this chapter.

FIGURE 17-4 THE EFFECT OF AN INCREASE IN EXPORTS

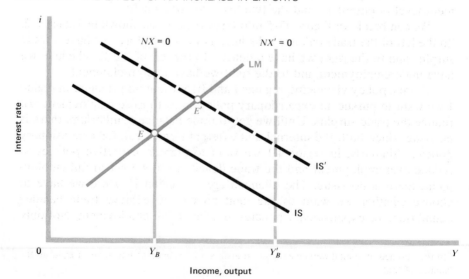

Income, output

increase in exports. It means increased demand for domestic goods and also an improvement in the trade balance.

Internal and External Balance

We have now constructed and used, in Figures 17-2 through 17-4, our basic diagrammatic apparatus for embodying trade in the IS-LM model. We can draw on the analysis of income and trade balance determination to ask about economic policy making. From a policy perspective we would want to be able to achieve both *internal* and *external* balance. Internal balance means that output is at the full-employment level Y_p. External balance is interpreted here as trade balance equilibrium.

It is clear enough why internal balance should be an aim of policy, but why is external balance desirable? In a fixed exchange rate world, balance of payments deficits cannot be maintained indefinitely, as the financing of the deficits requires the country to use its reserves of foreign currency. Such reserves will run out in the face of continual deficits. Hence, a country on a fixed exchange rate cannot aim to run a balance of payments deficit indefinitely.[3] On the other side, a country on fixed rates wants to avoid running a permanent surplus because that causes it to acquire foreign currencies to add to its reserves indefinitely. Since the foreign exchange could be used to buy and consume foreign goods, the country is permanently forgoing some consumption it could otherwise have had, when it chooses to run permanent balance of payments surpluses.

The policy problem is illustrated in Figure 17-5. The problem is that for a given level of exports we may not be able to achieve *both* internal and external balance. In Figure 17-5, we have drawn the trade balance schedule, $NX = 0$, for the given level of exports. We have drawn, too, the full-employment level of output Y_p, and the two lines do not coincide.

We can break up Figure 17-5 into three regions, as shown in Table 17-2. To the left of the trade balance schedule, as we saw before, we have a trade surplus and to the right we have a deficit. To the left of the Y_p schedule, we have underemployment and to the right we have overemployment.

From a policy viewpoint, regions I and III present no problem. In region I we want to pursue an expansionary policy so as to raise employment *and* reduce the trade surplus. Until we get to trade balance equilibrium, there is no issue, since both the internal and external targets call for expansionary policies. Similarly, in region III we want to pursue restrictive policies to reduce overemployment and the trade deficit. Until we get to full employment, there is no issue. The dilemma area is region II. Here we have to choose whether we want to use tight policies to achieve trade balance equilibrium, or expansionary policies to achieve full employment. Not only

[3] In the absence of capital movements and transfers, the balance of payments is equal to the balance of trade.

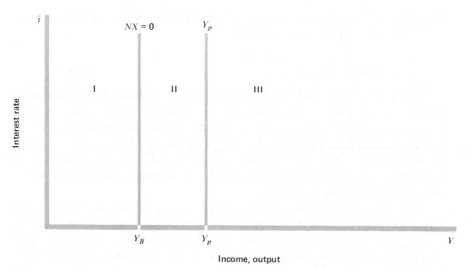

FIGURE 17-5 INTERNAL AND EXTERNAL BALANCE AND THE POLICY DILEMMA

are we unable to reach both targets simultaneously by manipulating aggregate demand, but any attempts to reach one target gets us further away from the other. Such a situation is called a *policy dilemma*, and it can always arise when there are more targets of policy than instruments with which to move the economy towards its targets. In our case we have only one policy instrument — aggregate demand policies — but we have two independent targets — external and internal balance. The policy dilemma that is pointed out by Figure 17-5 can be solved by finding another policy instrument to cope with the multiple targets. It is quite apparent that what is needed is some policy that shifts the trade balance schedule to the right until it overlaps with the full-employment level of output line, Y_p. An obvious policy would be to cut down on imports at each level of income. Such a policy would reduce import spending at each level of income and thus shift the trade balance schedule to the right.

How can we cut import spending? We can use any of a number of tools, among them tariffs and exchange rate changes. Tariffs are excise taxes on imported goods. A tariff would raise the cost of imports to domestic

TABLE 17-2 EXTERNAL AND INTERNAL BUDGET CONFLICT

	I	II	III
Employment	Under	Under	Over
Trade balance	Surplus	Deficit	Deficit

residents and thereby divert demand away from imports to domestic goods. A 10 percent tariff on imported shoes, for instance, makes imported shoes more expensive relative to domestically made shoes, and shifts demand to locally made shoes. A devaluation, as we shall see, would achieve the same effect by raising import prices relative to the prices of domestically made goods. In summary, the point is that if we have a trade deficit at full employment — as is the case in Figure 17-5 — we require a policy that directly affects the trade balance so as to give us trade balance equilibrium at full employment.

The Use of Expenditure Switching and Expenditure Reducing Policies

The argument of the previous subsection needs to be spelled out in more detail to focus attention on a subtle and important point: policies to shift spending from imports to domestic goods generally also affect aggregate demand in the goods market. Accordingly, policies to shift the $NX = 0$ line generally have to be accompanied by policies that adjust aggregate demand.

Figure 17-6 shows a situation in which the level of output in the economy is at Y_{p}, but the balance of payments is in deficit, since the $NX = 0$ line is to the left of Y_{p}. As we saw earlier in this chapter, aggregate demand policies cannot, in this case, both keep us at full employment and reduce the trade deficit. Consider using a tariff which shifts demand from imports to domestic goods. By using the tariff, we reduce import spending and shift the

FIGURE 17-6 THE POLICY DILEMMA WITH A BALANCE OF TRADE DEFICIT

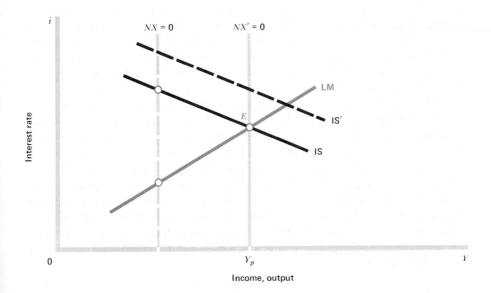

trade balance line to the right until it coincides with the full-employment line.

But the tariff will also effect the demand for domestic goods. The spending which at a given level of income no longer goes to imports goes to domestic goods instead. We are simply *switching* expenditures from imports to domestic goods. We therefore have to use a further policy to offset the expansionary effect of the tariff in the domestic goods market. We could use either monetary or fiscal policy to shift the economy's equilibrium back to the full-employment level Y_p.

The important point, then, is that, in general, it is necessary to combine both *expenditure switching* policies, which shift demand between domestic and imported goods, and *expenditure reducing* (or *expenditure increasing*) policies, to cope with the targets of internal and external balance. This point is of general importance and continues to apply when we take account of capital flows and other phenomena omitted in this section.

Interdependence and Repercussion Effects

The next topic to be taken up in this section is the interdependence of income determination in the world economy. An increase in income in one country (country A), by spilling over into imports, will affect demand for output abroad and thus will lead, in turn, to a foreign expansion in imports from country A. These *spillover effects* in the income determination process have two implications: (1) Countries, in general, cannot decide on appropriate stabilization policies without knowing what policies or income levels will prevail abroad and hence what the world demand for their exports will be. This suggests that coordination of stabilization policy between countries is desirable. (2) One country's income and import expansion spills over to increases in income abroad. But, in addition, the foreign income increase which the spillover induces leads to increased foreign import demand. There is thus a *repercussion effect* that we have so far ignored by assuming that export demand is autonomous. The repercussion effect is the additional effect on country A's income caused by the reaction of foreign countries' income to an initial increase in aggregate demand in country A.

We consider first the problem posed by spillover effects. It is actually a very important one. For example, during the 1975 world recession, some countries, like Germany, were relying on the United States recovery to pull them out of their own recession. How? It was expected that United States monetary and fiscal policies would stimulate the United States level of income and therefore United States imports. With part of United States imports coming from Germany, this would have led to increased German exports. Increased exports, in turn, mean increased income and employment. Thus, a recovery in Germany could clearly have been started off by an increase in exports. For obvious reasons, such a recovery is called an *export-led recovery*.

A critical question in the policy decision to wait for an increase in foreign demand rather than to undertake domestic action must be the size of the impacts of one country's income growth on another country's exports and thus on the latter's income. In the specific context of Germany, the question would be by how much would a 1 percent increase in United States income, say, increase German income. If the number were of the order of 0.5 percent, then United States growth could make an important contribution to German recovery, and disregard of United States policy could lead to serious policy errors.

Table 17-3 provides estimates of the size of repercussion effects and the importance of international linkages. The table, derived from an econometric model of the OECD, shows income multipliers associated with an expansion in one country on that country itself and on other countries.[4] Consider first the case of the United States. An increase of one percentage point in United States autonomous spending would raise United States income by 1.47 percent. What is the impact on selected other countries? Looking at the top row, we find that German income growth rises by about ¼ percent and the same is true for Japan. Thus, the United States expansion does affect these countries, although the size of the effect is not overwhelming. Not surprisingly, the effect on Canada is quite considerable. A United States expansion by 1.47 percent raises Canadian income growth by nearly 0.7 percent. The last entry in the top row of Table 17-3 shows the impact of a United States expansion on industrialized countries as a group. The impact here is to increase the group's combined income by three-quarters of a percentage point.[5]

Consider for comparison a Canadian expansion. The multiplier for Canadian income growth of a 1 percent increase in Canadian autonomous spending is 1.27, about the same as for the United States. The impact on the rest of the world is quite minor, though. The most substantial impact is on the United States (0.06 percent induced income growth) and only 0.03 percent increased growth for Germany or Japan.

What determines the size of multipliers and spillover effects? There are three chief factors to be taken into account in interpreting the multiplier patterns revealed in Table 17-3. First, the size of the country is important. A Canadian expansion, for example, induces only a small percentage increase in United States income because a given dollar change in Canadian income and imports will be only a small fraction of United States income. By

[4] The OECD (Organization for Economic Cooperation and Development) is a grouping of industrialized countries, based in Paris and serving as a framework for international policy discussion. Among the members are the few listed in Table 17-3, plus Italy, the United Kingdom, France, and seventeen others.

[5] Do you see why the relative effect on total OECD income (0.74 percent) of a 1 percent increase in United States autonomous spending is smaller than the relative effect on United States income (1.47 percent)?

TABLE 17-3 THE INTERNATIONAL TRANSMISSION OF
AGGREGATE DEMAND DISTURBANCES

Initiating country/group (1 percent increase in autonomous spending)	Affected country or group (*percentage change in income*)				
	United States	Germany	Japan	Canada	OECD
United States	1.47	.23	.25	.68	.74
Germany	.05	1.25	0.6	0.6	.23
Japan	.04	.05	1.26	.06	.21
Canada	.06	.03	.03	1.27	.10
OECD	1.81	2.38	1.84	2.32	2.04

Source: OECD Occasional Paper, "The OECD International Model," January 1979.

contrast, a given increase in United States income and imports will be a relatively large fraction of Canadian income.

The second important determinant of multiplier patterns is openness to trade. The spillover effects of an expansion in any one country on the rest of the world will be more substantial, the more open the expanding economy.[6]

The third point to note is the extent to which trade patterns are reflected in the multipliers. The United States, for example, benefits relatively more from a Canadian expansion than does Germany. This reflects the fact that Canada has a high marginal propensity to import from the United States in comparison with its propensity to import from Germany.

Table 17-3 allows us to study not only the effects of an individual country's expansion and the induced spillovers but also the effect of a simultaneous joint expansion in all industralized countries. The last row of the table provides the multipliers for this experiment. Clearly, if all countries expand together — each raising autonomous expenditure by 1 percent — the multiplier effects are much more substantial. Each country benefits not only from its own expansion and its repercussion effects through induced expansion abroad but also from the autonomous foreign expansion. Accordingly, the multipliers are around 2 in this case, while being in the range of 1.2 to 1.5 for the case of an isolated expansion.

We can now return to the question of export-led recoveries and ask what contribution United States real growth could have made to Germany.

---

[6] There is, however, an offset to this, since a more open economy (as measured by the marginal propensity to import) will have a smaller multiplier, so that a given demand expansion will induce a smaller increase in imports. The net effect of more openness, though, is to increase the spillover effects. In problem 6 at the end of this chapter, we ask you to check this statement using the standard multiplier model of Chapter 3.

The answer from Table 17-3 is that the impact would not have been large. In the short run, United States autonomous spending would have to increase by more than 4 percent (1/0.23) to raise German income by only one percentage point. The transmission effect in this instance would have been quite small, although for a case like Canada, United States growth is a critically important determinant of Canada's short-run growth performance.

Interdependence, Relative Growth, and the Current Account

The effects of changes in the level of income in one country on income in another, studied in the preceding section, are transmitted through changes in the levels of imports and exports. The spillover and repercussion effects therefore also produce effects on the current account.[7] A country that is growing rapidly will tend to increase its imports relatively fast. The current account of the rapidly growing country will therefore tend to go into deficit.

Such effects were important for Canada in the mid-1970s. Table 17-4 shows the rates of income growth in Canada and the U.S., and the Canadian balance of merchandise trade. In 1974 and 1975, the U.S. economy suffered a more severe recession than was experienced in Canada. American real GNP fell in both these years, while Canadian real GNP continued to grow although at a much slower rate than in 1973. As a result our net exports fell substantially and in 1975 there was a deficit in merchandise trade for the first time since 1960. With the resumption of growth in the United States in 1976 and 1977, our trade balance improved.

A word of warning is needed here. The behaviour of the current account reflects more than relative income growth. Other factors, such as changes in the exchange rate, exogenous shocks such as the oil price increase, shifting

[7] Estimates of current account effects of expansion in different countries are provided in OECD Occasional Paper, "The OECD International Linkage Model," Januray 1979.

TABLE 17-4 REAL INCOME AND THE CANADIAN BALANCE OF MERCHANDISE TRADE

	1973	1974	1975	1976	1977
Real income growth (percent per year)					
Canada	7.5	3.6	1.2	5.5	2.2
United States	5.9	−1.7	−1.3	5.9	5.3
Merchandise trade balance (billions of dollars)					
Canada	2.7	1.7	.5	1.4	2.7

trade patterns due to the emergence of new competitors and the spread of technology abroad, all affect the current account as well. Even so, Table 17-4 is highly suggestive in pointing to Canada's *relative* cyclical performance as an essential determinant of the current account.

External Balance, Money, and Prices

The analysis has been developed so far on the assumption that domestic prices do not respond at all to changes in demand. This is a convenient assumption for expository purposes, but we know it is not realistic. We therefore show now how a more complete model — parallel to the aggregate demand and supply analysis of Chapter 12 — would look in an open economy.

We start by reviewing the main points of Chapter 12. Aggregate demand depends on the level of prices. A higher level of prices implies lower real balances, higher interest rates, and lower spending. In an open economy, the relation is slightly more complicated because now an increase in our prices reduces demand for goods for two reasons. The first is the familiar higher interest rate channel summarized above. The second reason arises because an increase in our prices makes our goods less competitive with foreign-produced goods. When the prices of goods produced at home rise, and given the exchange rate, our goods become more expensive for foreigners to buy, and their goods become *relatively* cheaper for us to buy. An increase in our prices is thus an increase in the *relative price* of the goods we produce, and shifts demand away from our goods towards imports, as well as reducing exports.

In summary, then, an increase in our price level reduces the demand for our goods both by increasing the interest rate (and reducing investment demand) and by reducing net exports — by making the goods we produce relatively more expensive than foreign-produced goods. In Figure 17-7 we show the downward-sloping demand schedule for our goods, D. Demand is equal, as before, to aggregate spending by domestic residents, A, plus net exports, NX:

$$D \equiv A + NX \qquad (6)$$

The demand for domestic goods, D, is drawn for a given level of foreign prices, a given nominal money supply, and given fiscal policy. Remember, too, that the exchange rate is fixed. An increase in the nominal money stock shifts the schedule upward, as does expansionary fiscal policy. We have shown, too, the short-run aggregate supply schedule, Y^s, and the full-employment level of output, Y_p. Initial equilibrium is at point E, where we have unemployment.

Next we look at the trade balance equilibrium schedule, $NX = 0$. An increase in our income raises imports and worsens the trade balance. To restore trade balance equilibrium, domestic prices would have to be lower. This would make the home country more competitive, raise exports, and

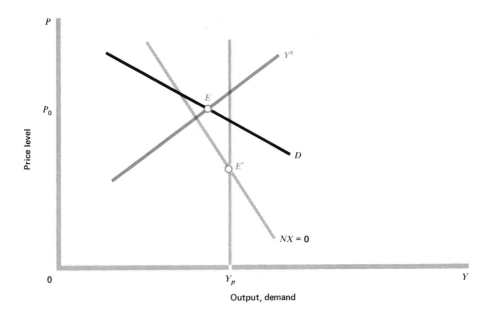

FIGURE 17-7 OPEN ECONOMY MACROECONOMIC EQUILIBRIUM WITH PRICE ADJUSTMENT

---

reduce imports. Thus, we show the trade balance equilibrium schedule as downward-sloping.[8] We assume that it is steeper than the demand schedule for domestic goods. The schedule is drawn for a given level of prices abroad. The short-run equilibrium at point E is one where the home country has a trade deficit. Our prices are too high or our income is too high to have exports balance imports. To achieve trade balance equilibrium, we would have to become more competitive, thus exporting more and importing less. Alternatively, we could reduce our level of income in order to reduce import spending.

The Adjustment Process

Consider next the policy options from an external and internal balance point of view. At point E there is unemployment and a deficit. To restore full employment, we could expand aggregate demand, or else wait for wages and

---

[8] We assume that a decline in prices improves the trade balance. This requires that exports and imports are sufficiently responsive to prices. There is a possibility that a reduction in our price level (which reduces the prices of our exports) lowers our revenue from exports—because the increased sales are not sufficient to compensate for the lower prices. We shall assume that this possibility does not occur. We assume, too, that import spending does not depend on the interest rate.

prices to fall sufficiently to raise the demand for our goods through the interest rate and increased net exports channels. From an external point of view, we have to achieve a decline in income or in prices to restore balance.

Point E' is a point at which we have both internal and external balance. At E', we have full employment and balanced trade. But we cannot get to that point except through a protracted recession that cuts domestic prices sufficiently to shift the aggregate supply schedule down. This adjustment process would indeed occur if the government did not pursue any stabilization policy and simply pegged the exchange rate. The process is sufficiently important to deserve more attention.

Since the central bank is pegging the exchange rate and the balance of payments is in deficit, it must be selling foreign currency in exchange for domestic currency. If the central bank does not undertake offsetting transactions, this intervention in the foreign exchange market will reduce the stock of high-powered money and therefore the money supply. The effect on the money supply could be offset by open market purchases of securities so as to maintain the stock of high powered money at the same level. These offsetting transactions are referred to as *sterilization*.

If we assume no sterilization, then the trade deficit at point E implies that the central bank is pegging the exchange rate, selling foreign exchange to keep the exchange rate from depreciating, and reducing the domestic money stock. It follows immediately that over time the aggregate demand schedule (which is drawn for a given money supply) will be shifting down and to the left. On the aggregate supply side, we remember that unemployment leads to a decline in wages and costs, which is reflected in a downward-shifting aggregate supply schedule. Over time, therefore, the short-run equilibrium point E moves down as both demand and supply schedules shift. The points of short-run equilibrium move in the direction of point E', and the process will continue until that point is reached. (The approach may be cyclical, but that is not of major interest here.)

Once point E' is reached, we have achieved long-run equilibrium. Because the trade balance is in equilibrium, there is no pressure on the exchange rate and therefore no need for exchange market intervention. Accordingly, there is no influence from the trade balance on the money supply and thereby on aggregate demand. On the supply side, we have reached full employment. Therefore wages and costs are constant, so that the supply schedule is not shifting. At point E' we have a combination of relative prices, demand, and employment that gives both internal and external balance. The adjustment of the level of prices ensures that we can have — in the long run — both full employment and trade balance equilibrium.

The adjustment process we have just described is called the *classical adjustment process*. It relies critically on price adjustments and an adjustment in the money supply based on the trade balance. The adjustment process "works" in the sense that it moves the economy to a long-run equilibrium of internal and external balance. However, the mechanism is far from attractive. There is no good case for a protracted recession simply to achieve a cut in prices. A preferable policy is to resort to expenditure switching policies, or to exchange rate changes, as a means of achieving internal and external balance.[9]

The Monetary Approach to the Balance of Payments

How important are monetary considerations in explaining balance of payment problems? Is it true that balance of payments deficits are a reflection of an excessive money supply? These questions must be raised because it is frequently suggested that external balance problems are monetary in nature.

There is a simple first answer. It is obviously true that for any given balance of payments deficit, a sufficient contraction of the money stock will restore external balance. The reason is that a monetary contraction, by raising interest rates and reducing spending, generates a contraction in economic activity, a decline in income, and therefore a decline in imports. It is equally true that this result could be achieved by a tight fiscal policy, so there is nothing especially monetary about this interpretation of remedies for external imbalance.

A more sophisticated interpretation of the problem recognizes the link, examined in the previous section, between the balance of payments deficit, foreign exchange market intervention, and the money supply. The automatic mechanism is for a sale of foreign exchange — as arises in the case of deficits — to be reflected in an equal reduction in the stock of high-powered money. The central bank merely sells one asset (foreign exchange) and buys another (high-powered money). This process will automatically lead to a decline in the stock of money in deficit countries and an increase in the money stock in surplus countries. Given that the money supply is thus linked to the external balance, it is obvious that this adjustment process must ultimately lead to the right money stock so that external payments are in balance. This process was shown in Figure 17-7.

The only way the adjustment process can be suspended is through sterilization operations as we indicated above. If this is done, persistent external deficits are possible because the link between the external imbalance and the equilibrating changes in the money stock is broken. It is in this sense that persistent external deficits are a monetary phenomenon: the central bank actively maintains the stock of money too high for external balance.

The emphasis on monetary considerations in the interpretation of external balance problems is called the *monetary approach* to the balance of

---

[9] An exchange rate depreciation or shifts in demand from imports to domestic goods would shift both the net export schedule and the aggregate demand schedule up and to the right.

TABLE 17-5 BALANCE SHEET OF THE MONETARY AUTHORITIES

Assets	Liabilities
Net foreign assets (*NFA*)	High-powered money (*H*)
Domestic credit (*DC*)	

payments.[10] The monetary approach has been used extensively by the International Monetary Fund (IMF) in its analysis and design of economic policies for countries in balance of payments trouble. We can give the flavour of the approach by describing typical IMF procedure in analyzing a balance of payments problem.

We start with the balance sheet of the monetary authority, typically the central bank, as in Table 17-5. The monetary authority's liabilities are high-powered money, as explained in Chapter 8, but we recognize on the asset side that it can hold both foreign assets — including foreign exchange reserves, gold, and claims on other central banks or governments — and domestic assets, or *domestic credit*. Domestic credit consists of the monetary authority's holding of claims on the public sector — government debt — and claims on the private sector — usually loans to banks.

From the balance sheet indetity, we have

$$\Delta NFA = \Delta H - \Delta DC \tag{7}$$

where ΔNFA denotes the change in net foreign assets, ΔH the change in high-powered money, and ΔDC the change in domestic credit. In words, the change in the central bank's holdings of foreign assets is equal to the change in the stock of high-powered money minus the change in domestic credit.

Now the important point about Equation (7) is that ΔNFA is the balance of payments: recall from Section 17-1 that official reserve transactions, which is all that ΔNFA is, are equal to the balance of payments.

The first step in developing a stabilization policy package is to decide on a balance of payments target, ΔNFA^*. We want to ask how much of a deficit we can afford and then adjust policies to make the projected deficit no larger. The target will be based largely on the availability of loans and credit from abroad and the possibility of drawing down existing reserves. The next step is to ask how much the demand for money in the country will increase. The planned changes in the stock of high-powered money ΔH^* will have to be just sufficient to produce, via the money multiplier process, the right increases in the stock of money to meet the expected increase in demand.

[10] For a collection of essays on this topic, see Jacob Frenkel and Harry G. Johnson (eds.), *The Monetary Approach to the Balance of Payments* (London: Allen & Unwin, 1976). See also International Monetary Fund, *The Monetary Approach to the Balance of Payments* (Washington, D.C., 1977).

Then, given ΔNFA^* and ΔH^*, Equation (7) tells the monetary authority how much domestic credit it can extend consistent with its balance of payments target and expected growth in money demand. Typically, a stabilization plan drawn up by the IMF will include a suggested limit on the expansion of domestic credit.

The limit provides a *ceiling on domestic credit expansion*. The adoption of such a numerical ceiling could be useful in helping the central bank avoid the temptation of expanding its loans to the government or private sector in the face of rising interest rates or government budget deficits.

The simplicity of Equation (7) raises an obvious question. Since all it takes to improve the balance of payments is a reduction in the rate of domestic credit expansion, why not balance payments immediately and always? To answer this question, we need to understand the channels through which the curtailment of domestic credit improves the balance of payments.

Essentially, controlling domestic credit means operating a tight money policy. Consider an economy that is growing and has some inflation, so that the demand for nominal balances is rising. If domestic credit expansion is slowed, then domestically supplied increases in the money stock are lower than the increase in demand, and an excess demand for money develops. This, in turn, causes interest rates to rise and spending to decline. The increase in interest rates tends to improve the capital account and the reduction in spending tends to improve the current account, thus leading to a balance of payments improvement. That is, the monetary approach as used by the IMF relies on restrictive monetary policy to control the balance of payments. But there is a subtle difference between domestic credit ceilings and ordinary tight money. In an open economy with fixed exchange rates, the money stock is endogenous. The central bank cannot control the money stock, since it has to meet whatever demand arises for foreign currency. But it can make "money" tight by reducing the growth of domestic credit. That will imply that the only source of money growth becomes an increase in foreign exchange reserves or foreign borrowing. That means the economy has to go through enough of a recession or rise in interest rates to generate a balance of payments surplus.

The use of domestic credit ceilings is a crude policy to improve the balance of payments. But the simplicity of the conceptual framework, and the apparent definiteness of the policy recommendations to which it leads, frequently make it the best policy tool available, particularly if dramatic action is needed.

Proponents of the monetary approach have also argued that depreciation of the exchange rate cannot improve the balance of payments except in the short run. The argument is that in the short run, the depreciation does improve a country's competitive position and that this very fact gives rise to a trade surplus and therefore to an increase in the money stock. Over the course of time, the rising money supply raises aggregate demand and therefore prices until the economy returns to full employment and external balance. Devaluation thus exerts only a transitory effect on the economy which lasts as long as prices and the money supply have not yet increased to match fully the higher import prices.

The analysis of the monetary approach is entirely correct in its insistence on a longer-run perspective in which prices and the money stock adjust and the economy achieves internal and external balance. It is also correct in arguing that monetary or domestic credit restraint will improve the balance of payments, though the mechanism through which this policy works is more difficult than proponents of the approach typically indicate. The approach is misdirected when it suggests that exchange rate policy cannot, even in the short run, affect a country's competitive position. More important, exchange rate changes frequently occur from a position of deficit and unemployment. In that case, a depreciation moves the economy toward equilibrium. It eases the adjustment mechanism by achieving an increase in competitiveness through an increase in import prices rather than through a recession-induced decline in domestic prices.

Summary

We have covered a lot of ground at a hard pace, and it is worthwhile seeing where we have been and where we are going. In this section we amended our previous analysis to allow for trade in goods. As yet, we have not taken into account trade in assets. We were assuming that the exchange rate was fixed, and that the central bank had enough reserves to meet any demands for foreign currency that might occur as a result of balance of payments deficits. Through most of this section, we assumed that domestic and foreign price levels were fixed. This assumption was relaxed at the end.

The major points were:

1 The introduction of trade in goods means that spending by domestic residents is no longer equal to the demand for domestically produced goods. Some of the demand for goods of our residents goes for imports, and some of the demand for goods comes from foreigners, to whom we export.

2 There is equilibrium in the goods market when the demand for our goods, consisting of spending by domestic residents, plus net exports, is equal to the output of domestic goods, which is equal to the income of domestic residents.

3 In short-run equilibrium, there is no guarantee that trade balances. In our simplest model, there is a unique level of income at which trade balances, and which is not necessarily the income level at which the economy comes into short-run equilibrium.

4 An increase in autonomous demand for domestic goods increases domestic output and worsens the trade balance. An increase in imports reduces domestic output and worsens the trade balance. An increase in

exports increases domestic income and reduces the trade deficit. A shift in demand toward domestically produced goods increases the level of income and reduces the trade deficit, or increases the trade surplus.

5　Because trade does not necessarily balance in short-run equilibrium, there may be a *policy dilemma* in attempting both to move income to the potential output level and to balance trade. An increase in the level of income, to move it closer to potential, may well worsen the trade balance.

6　The use of *expenditure switching* policies, which change the relative prices of domestic and imported goods, combined with *expenditure reducing* policies, can move the economy to full employment with balanced trade.

7　Because foreigners' demands for our goods — our exports — are their imports, and because their imports depend on their level of income, the demand for our goods depends on the foreign level of income. Further, because an increase in their income increases our exports and increases our level of income, and therefore our imports, there are *repercussion effects* by which a change in foreign income eventually induces an increase in the demand for their goods through exports. The size of these interdependence and repercussion effects depends on the relative size and openness of the economy. A small economy may be very dependent on a larger one, but a large economy's level of income does not depend much on the income level in small foreign economies.

8　Once we allow for price flexibility with fixed exchange rates, we use the analytical apparatus of Chapter 12. We see that price flexibility ultimately leads an economy to full employment with balanced trade. The mechanism involves changes in the domestic money supply which occur as the central bank keeps selling foreign exchange to domestic residents in exchange for domestic currency (essentially an open market sale of foreign currency). The falling money stock reduces our prices and therefore improves the balance of trade. Policy can be used actively to bring about adjustments without relying on this automatic and slow-moving mechanism.

9　The monetary approach to the balance of payments emphasizes the central bank's balance sheet identity, Equation (7), which shows that sufficient contraction of domestic credit will improve the balance of payments. The process through which this improvement comes about will require higher interest rates and lower domestic income. We should also note that the link between the balance of payments and the domestic stock of money, which is central to the monetary approach, can easily be broken through sterilization operations by the central bank.

So much for where we have been. In the next section, we compare the alternatives of *financing* a trade deficit by the central bank's drawing down its reserves (or by borrowing) with adjustment through *devaluation*. Then in Section 17-4 we introduce trade in assets, so-called *capital mobility*, and analyze its implications for stabilization policy.

17-3 FINANCING OF DEFICITS AND DEVALUATION

In a fixed exchange rate system, it is possible for the central bank to use its reserves to finance temporary imbalances of payments — that is, to meet the excess demand for foreign currency at the existing exchange rate arising from balance of payments deficits. Other ways of *financing* temporary payments imbalances are also available. A country experiencing balance of payments difficulties can borrow foreign currencies abroad. The borrowing may be undertaken either by the government (usually the central bank) or by private individuals. Although borrowing may be undertaken to finance both current and capital account deficits, we concentrate in this section on the current account.

A current account cannot be financed by borrowing from abroad without raising the question of how the borrowing will be repaid. Clearly, if the counterpart of the current account deficit is productive domestic investment, there need be little concern about paying back the interest and capital borrowed. The investment will pay off in terms of increased output, some of which may be exported, or which may replace goods that previously were imported. The investment would thus yield the foreign exchange earnings with which to *service* (make payments on) the debt. However, problems may well arise in repaying the foreign debt if borrowing is used to finance consumption spending.

Maintaining and financing a current account deficit indefinitely or for very long periods of time is impossible. The alternative to financing deficits is *adjustment* of the current account through policy measures to reduce the deficit. We examined in Section 17-2 one method of adjusting a current account deficit, through the imposition of tariffs. However, tariffs cannot be freely used to adjust the balance of trade, partly because there are international organizations and agreements such as GATT (General Agreement on Tariffs and Trade) and the IMF (International Monetary Fund) that outlaw, or at least frown on, the use of tariffs. Tariffs have generally fallen in the post-World War II period as the industrialized world has moved to desirable freer trade between countries.

Another way of adjusting a current account deficit is to use restrictive domestic policy. In this regard, it is worth repeating that a trade deficit reflects an excess of expenditure by domestic residents and the government over income. In Chapter 2 we showed that

$$NX \equiv Y - (C + I^a + G) \tag{8}$$

where NX is the trade surplus and I^a is actual investment. Thus, a balance of trade deficit can be reduced by reducing spending $(C + I + G)$ relative to income (Y). The trade deficit can, accordingly, be eliminated by reducing aggregate demand, by reducing C, or G, or I. In terms of Figure 17-6, the trade deficit can be eliminated by using restrictive monetary and/or fiscal policy to shift the intersection of the IS and LM curves to the level of income at which trade balances. The costs of such a policy, in terms of unemployment, are obvious.

The unemployment that typically accompanies adjustment through recession and the desirability of free trade, which argues against the use of tariffs, both suggest that an alternative policy for reconciling internal and external balance can be considered. The major policy instrument for dealing with payments deficits in the dilemma situation is *devaluation* — which usually has to be combined with restrictive monetary and/or fiscal policy. A devaluation, as we noted in Section 17-1, is a decrease in the value of domestic currency in terms of foreign exchange. Given the nominal prices in the two countries, devaluation increases the relative price of imported goods in the devaluing country and reduces the relative price of exports from the devaluing country.

Table 17-6 shows the effects of an exchange rate shift on relative prices. Recall that we are assuming that nominal prices in the home currency in each country are fixed. We assume that we (Canadians) produce and export rye whiskey and they (British) produce and export Scotch whiskey. Scotch is priced at £6.00 and rye at $10.00. These prices, in terms of the respective producer's currencies, are assumed to remain constant. Now, at an exchange rate of $2.00 per pound, the relative price of Scotch in terms of rye is $12.00/$10.00 = 6/5, meaning that Scotch costs 20 percent more than rye. Next, consider a devaluation of the Canadian dollar by 25 percent. The table shows that the Canadian dollar price of Scotch rises and that the sterling price of rye declines. Both in Canada and Britain, rye becomes *relatively* cheaper, or Scotch becomes relatively more expensive. The Canadian dollar devaluation lowers the sterling price of Canadian goods and raises the dollar price of British goods. The exchange ratio for Scotch and rye now becomes $15.00/$10.00 = 3/2, so that Scotch now costs 50 percent more than rye. Clearly, the decrease in the relative price of Canadian goods will affect the pattern of demand, increasing both Canadian and British demands for rye at the expense of the demand for Scotch.

TABLE 17-6 THE EFFECT OF EXCHANGE RATE CHANGES ON RELATIVE PRICES

	Scotch Whiskey	Rye Whiskey
Canadian dollar price		
(a) $2.00/pound	$12.00	$10.00
(b) $2.50/pound	$15.00	$10.00
Sterling price		
(a) $2.00/pound	£6.00	£5.00
(b) $2.50/pound	£6.00	£4.00

How does a devaluation assist in achieving internal and external balance? Let us take first a special case of a country that has been in full employment with balance of trade equilibrium, as shown by point E in Figure 17-8. Now let there be an exogenous decline in export earnings, so that the $NX = 0$ schedule shifts to the left to $NX' = 0$. At the given exchange rate and relative prices — that is, prices of domestic goods relative to world prices — the foreign demand for domestic goods is assumed to decline. In the absence of domestic policy intervention, and with fixed rates, the short run and intermediate-run adjustment would be one of a decline in output and income. The IS schedule moves to the left as a result of the fall in exports and the resultant income decline at the point E' lowers imports, but not enough to make up for the loss of export revenue. The net effect is therefore unemployment and a trade deficit.

Next, we ask how the home country can adjust to the loss of export markets. One possibility is for the home country to go through an adjustment process of declining domestic wages and prices as the high unemployment slowly reduces wages or slows down their rate of increase. Such an adjustment would, over time, lower domestic costs and prices as compared with the prices of foreign goods. The home country would gain in competitiveness in world markets and thus restore export earnings and employment. There is no doubt that this is a feasible adjustment process, and, indeed, is the process that would occur by itself, given enough time.

FIGURE 17-8 THE EFFECTS OF A DECLINE IN EXPORTS ON INCOME AND THE TRADE BALANCE

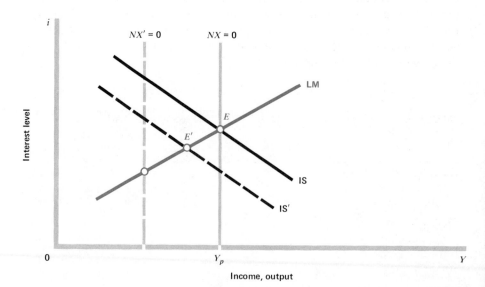

An alternative solution is to recognize that in order to restore full employment and export earnings, the home country must become more competitive in the prices charged for exports and imports. To restore competitiveness, domestic costs and prices have to decline *relative* to foreign prices. That adjustment can occur in two ways: (1) through a decline in domestic costs and prices at a given exchange rate and (2) through a depreciation of the exchange rate with unchanged domestic costs and prices.

The latter strategy has the obvious advantage that it does not require a protracted recession to reduce domestic costs. The adjustment is done by a stroke of a pen — a devluation of the currency. Why would a devaluation achieve the adjustment? *Given* prices of foreign goods in terms of foreign currency (e.g., the sterling prices of British goods), a devaluation, as shown in Table 17-6, raises the relative price of foreign goods. The effect is to induce an increased demand for Canadian goods and a reduction in demand for imports in Canada.

The case we have just considered is special, however, in one important respect. The economy was initially in balance of trade equilibrium at full employment. The disturbance to the economy took place in the trade account. Accordingly, if we could move the $NX = 0$ locus back to the full-employment level of income — as we could with a devaluation — both internal and external balance would be attained. Put differently, the reason there was an internal balance problem of unemployment in Figure 17-8 was the reduction in exports and consequent external balance problem. Both problems could thus be cured through devaluation.

In general, we cannot cure *both* internal and external problems by a simple devaluation. The general case will require expenditure shifting through, say, a devaluation and a policy affecting the level of spending. To make that point, we look at the case of an increase in domestic spending that falls entirely on imports. This is studied in Figure 17-9 where we start from a full equilibrium at point E. The increase in import spending comes entirely at the expense of saving, and consequently there is no change in demand for domestic goods and thus no shift in the IS curve. The trade balance schedule, however, shifts to the left. Since people now spend more on imports at each level of income, a lower income level is required to achieve trade balance. Thus, the trade balance schedule shifts to $NX' = 0$. Now it is apparent that the only effect of the disturbance is to create a trade deficit. There is no counterpart to that disturbance in the domestic goods market.

Suppose, next, we correct the trade deficit by devaluation, thus shifting the trade balance schedule back to the full-employment level of output. This does not solve the entire problem because the devaluation now diverts demand from foreign to domestic goods, and thus the IS curve shifts out and to the right to IS'. The devaluation thus gives rise to overemployment and a deficit at E'. Clearly, we need a further instrument. We need tight monetary or fiscal policy to accompany the devaluation.

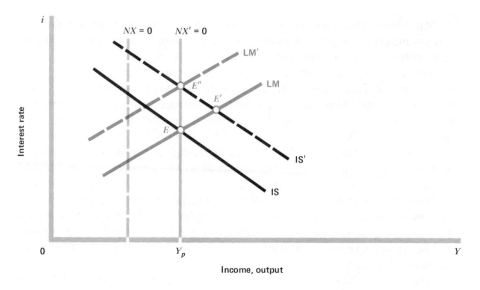

FIGURE 17-9 A DEVALUATION AND TIGHT MONEY TO RESTORE INTERNAL AND
EXTERNAL BALANCE

We show, in Figure 17-9, the use of a tight monetary policy. The monetary tightening shifts the LM curve to LM' and restores full equilibrium at point E''. The point that we have made is that, in general, we need two instruments — affecting expenditure *level* and *composition* — to achieve internal and external balance. A devaluation shifts spending away from foreign goods and toward domestic goods and thus is an important ingredient of the policy mix. A further instrument is required to achieve the proper level of aggregate spending. In Figure 17-9, the level of spending at E' is excessive, and accordingly, either tight money or tight fiscal policy is required to complete the policy mix.

We should not fool ourselves into believing that just because full employment can be maintained, current account adjustment with a devaluation is costless. Current account adjustment involves not only a cut in spending to the level of income, but also, in many instances, a worsening of the *terms of trade* — the price of exports relative to imports. Foreign goods become more expensive, thus reducing the purchasing power of the goods we produce. Therefore our standard of living falls.

Finally, a comment on the role of the exchange rate in a fixed rate system. In the fixed rate system, the exchange rate is an *instrument of policy*. The central bank can change the exchange rate for policy purposes, devaluing when the current account looks as though it will be in for a prolonged deficit. In a system of clean floating, by contrast, the exchange rate moves freely to equilibrate the balance of payments. In a system of dirty floating, the central bank attempts to manipulate the exchange rate while not committing itself to any given rate. The dirty floating system is thus intermediate between a fixed rate system and a clean floating system.

17-4 CAPITAL MOBILITY AND THE POLICY MIX

So far, we have been assuming that trade is confined to goods and services and does not include assets. Now we allow for trade in assets and see the effects of such trade on the equilibrium of the economy and its desired policy mix.

One of the striking facts about the international economy is the high degree of integration or linkage among financial or capital markets — the markets in which bonds and stocks are traded. In particular, the capital markets are very fully integrated among the main industrial countries. Yields on assets in New York and yields on comparable assets in Canada, for example, move closely together. If Canadian yields fell relative to United States yields, there would be a capital outflow from Canada because lenders would take their funds out of Canada and borrowers would try to raise funds in Canada. From the point of view of the balance of payments, this implies that a decline in relative interest rates — a decline in our rates relative to those abroad — will worsen the balance of payments because of the capital outflow — lending abroad by Canadian residents.

The recognition that changes in our interest rates affect capital flows and the balance of payments has important implications for stabilization policy. First, because monetary and fiscal policies affect interest rates, they have an effect on the capital account and therefore on the balance of payments. The effects of monetary and fiscal policy on the balance of payments are limited *not* to the trade balance effects discussed in Section 17-2 but extend to the capital account. The second implication is that the way in which monetary and fiscal policies work in affecting the domestic economy and the balance of payments changes when there are international capital flows. We will examine the monetary-fiscal policy mix that can be used to achieve internal and external balance, and see that capital flows can be used to *finance* the trade balance and thus help in achieving overall balance of payments equilibrium.

The Balance of Payments and Capital Flows

We can introduce the role of capital flows in a framework in which we assume that the home country faces a given price of imports and a given export demand. In addition, we assume that the world rate of interest is given and that capital flows into the home country at a rate that is higher, the higher the home country's rate of interest. That is, foreign investors purchase more of our assets, the higher the interest rate our assets pay relative to the world interest rate. In Figure 17-10 we show the rate of capital inflow *CF*, or the capital account surplus, as an increasing function of the rate of interest. At the world interest rate, i^*, there are no capital flows. If the domestic interest rate is higher, there will be an inflow, and conversely, if the domestic interest rate is lower, there will be a capital outflow.

Next we look at the balance of payments. The balance of payments surplus *BP* is equal to the trade surplus *NX*, plus the capital account surplus *CF*:

$$B \equiv NX(Y, \overline{X}, \ldots) + CF(i) \tag{9}$$

In Equation (9) we have shown the trade balance as a function of income and the capital account as a function of the domestic interest rate. We remember from Section 17-2 that an increase in income worsens the trade balance. We have just learned that an increase in the interest rate raises capital inflows and thus improves the capital account. It follows that when income increases, an increase in interest rates could maintain overall balance of payments equilibrium. The trade deficit would be offset by a capital inflow. That idea is extremely important because it suggests that in the short run we can get out of the internal-external balance dilemma of Section 17-2.

The problem, we remember, was to achieve simultaneously internal and external balance from a position of deficit and unemployment or surplus and boom. The presence of interest-sensitive capital flows suggests that we can run an expansionary domestic policy without necessarily running into

FIGURE 17-10 INTEREST-RESPONSIVE CAPITAL FLOWS

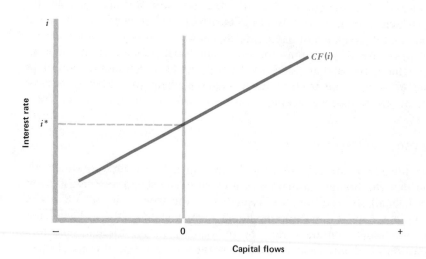

balance of payments problems. We can afford an increase in domestic income and import spending, provided we accompany it by an increase in interest rates so as to attract a capital inflow. But how can we achieve an expansion in domestic income at the same time that interest rates are increased? The answer is that we use fiscal policy to increase aggregate demand to the full-employment level and monetary policy to get the right amount of capital flows.[11]

Internal and External Balance

In Figure 17-11 we show the positively sloped schedule $BP = 0$, derived from Equation (9), along which we have balance of payments equilibrium. To derive the slope of the $BP = 0$ line, start with an income expansion, which raises imports and worsens the balance of payments. To restore balance of payments equilibrium, interest rates have to be higher to attract the capital flows that finance the trade deficit. Thus to maintain payments balance, an income increase has to be matched by a higher interest rate, and the $BP = 0$ line is therefore upward-sloping.

The schedule is drawn for given exports and a given foreign interest rate. The higher the degree of capital mobility, the flatter the schedule. If capital is very highly responsive to interest rates, then a small increase in the interest rate will bring about very large capital flows and thus allow the financing of large trade deficits. The larger the marginal propensity to import, the steeper the schedule. An increase in income worsens the trade balance by the increase in income times the marginal propensity to import. Thus, a high propensity to import means that a given increase in income produces a large deficit and thus requires a large increase in interest rates to bring about the right amount of capital flows to offset the trade deficit. Points above and to the left of the $BP = 0$ schedule correspond to a surplus, and points below and to the right to a deficit. We have also drawn, in Figure 17-11, full-employment output Y_p. The full equilibrium with both internal and external balance is at point E.

We can talk about policy problems in terms of points in the four quadrants of Figure 17-11. Each such point would be an intersection of an IS and an LM curve and the question is how to use monetary and fiscal policy — shifting the IS and LM curves — to get to full equilibrium. Thus, point E_1, for example, corresponds to a case of unemployment and deficit. Point E_2, by contrast, is a case of deficit and overemployment. What are points E_3 and E_4?

---

[11] The idea of the policy mix for internal and external balance was suggested by Robert Mundell in his important paper, "The Appropriate Use of Monetary and Fiscal Policy under Fixed Exchange Rates," *I.M.F. Staff Papers*, March 1962. Mundell's work on international macroeconomics has been extraordinarily important, and the adventurous student should certainly consult his two books: *International Economics*, (New York: Macmillan, 1967) and *Monetary Theory* (Pacific Palisades, Calif.: Goodyear, 1971).

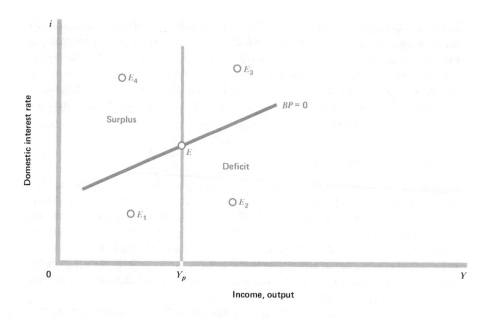

FIGURE 17-11 INTERNAL AND EXTERNAL BALANCE

The Policy Mix

Suppose that the economy is at point E_1. The appropriate policy to produce internal and external balance requires a higher level of employment for internal balance and higher interest rates and/or a lower level of income for external balance.

In terms of the analysis of Section 17-2, there is a policy dilemma at E_1 because employment considerations suggest income should be raised and balance of payments considerations suggest it should be reduced. However, now there is a way out of the dilemma. Suppose we reduce the money supply and thus raise interest rates. To offset the effects of higher interest rates on income, we could use expansionary fiscal policy. Clearly, we would keep income constant and reach balance of payments equilibrium by getting interest rates high enough. However, we can do better. We can use fiscal policy to get us all the way to full employment and use tight money, in the form of higher interest rates, to achieve balance of payments equilibrium. Thus we can get to point E with both internal and external balance.

The lesson we have just derived is that under fixed exchange rates, we should expand income through fiscal policy whenever there is unemployment and use tight money whenever there is a balance of payments deficit. The combination of policies moves us to both internal and external balance. With a situation like point E_4, we want to use the same principle, but the economic conditions are different. Here we have a surplus and unemployment. Accordingly, we need expansionary fiscal policy to achieve full employment and expansionary monetary policy to reduce interest rates. Point E_4 is actually *not* a dilemma situation, since any form of expansionary policy moves us in the right direction with respect to both targets.

We leave it to you to work through the remaining cases and note here merely the principle: Under fixed exchange rates and with capital mobility, we use monetary policy to achieve external balance and fiscal policy to achieve full employment. What is the experience with such a rule? There is little doubt that tight money, for balance of payments reasons, is the oldest remedy in the policy maker's medicine chest. Since monetary policy is a flexible tool, attainment of external balance in the short run through tight money is relatively easy.

Limitations of the Policy Mix

The argument for a policy mix is persuasive, but it overlooks three important limitations. The first problem is that fiscal policy may not be sufficiently flexible to implement the needed policy mix. The discussion of lags in Chapter 9 made the point that the inside lag for fiscal policy is quite long. If fiscal policy cannot be modified readily, then all the policy maker can do is control the balance of payments, *or* employment, through monetary policy. We are back in a dilemma situation, because there are two targets — internal and external balance — but only one instrument — namely, monetary policy. The second point is that a country will typically not be indifferent to the level of domestic interest rates. Even if fiscal policy were sufficiently flexible to implement the policy mix, it would still be true that the composition of domestic output would depend on the mix. Thus, a country that attempts an expansion in aggregate demand, together with tight money, effectively restricts the construction sector and investment spending in general. The notion of a policy mix with monetary policy devoted to the balance of payments therefore overlooks the fact that the interest rate determines the composition as well as the level of aggregate spending.

The final consideration concerns the composition of the balance of payments. Countries are not indifferent about the makeup of their balance of payments between the current account deficit and the capital account surplus. Even if the overall balance is in equilibrium so that one target is satisfied, there is still the problem that a capital account surplus or capital inflow means net external borrowing: our country's debts to foreigners are increasing. Those debts will eventually have to be repaid.

Under a system of fixed exchange rates, there are circumstances under which a country — much like an individual — will find it useful to borrow in order to finance, say, a current shortfall of export earnings. However, continued large-scale borrowing from abroad is not consistent with a fixed exchange rate over long periods. Large-scale borrowing eventually places the country in a position where the interest payments it has to make to foreigners become a major burden for the economy. Faced with the prospect of continued foreign borrowing on a large scale in order to maintain its exchange rate fixed, a country would be well advised to implement adjustment policies that improve the current account balance. Such policies would typically be a devaluation accompanied by restrictive monetary and/or fiscal policy to reduce domestic demand pressures.

17-5 SUMMARY

1   The balance of payments accounts are a record of the international transactions of the economy. The current account records trade in goods and services, as well as transfer payments. The capital account records borrowing and lending and purchases and sales of assets.
2   The overall balance of payments is the sum of the current and capital accounts. If the overall balance is in deficit, we have to make more payments to foreigners than they make to us. The foreign currency for making these payments is supplied by central banks.
3   Under fixed exchange rates, the central bank maintains constant the price of foreign currencies in terms of the domestic currency. It does this by buying and selling foreign exchange at that fixed exchange rate. For that purpose, it has to keep reserves of foreign currency.
4   Under floating or flexible exchange rates, the exchange rate may change from moment to moment. In a system of clean floating, the exchange rate is determined by supply and demand without central bank intervention to affect the rate. Under dirty floating, the central bank intervenes by buying and selling foreign exchange in an attempt to influence the exchange rate.

The remainder of the chapter studies the role of international trade in goods and assets under fixed exchange rates:

5   The introduction of trade in goods means that some of the demand for our output comes from abroad and that some spending by our residents is on foreign goods. There is equilibrium in the goods market when the demand for domestically produced goods is equal to the output of those goods.
6   In short-run equilibrium, the balance of trade may be in deficit. If there is no trade in assets, there may be a policy dilemma in that balanced trade and full employment cannot be attained merely through the manipulation of aggregate demand by fiscal and monetary policy. Expenditure switching policies that change the allocation of spending between imports and domestic goods are needed to solve the problem.
7   Over longer periods, there is an automatic adjustment mechanism in the economy which eventually leads to full employment at balanced trade under fixed exchange rates. A balance of trade deficit leads to a reduction in the domestic money stock which eventually leads to falling

domestic prices that, given the foreign price level, switch spending away from imports and increase foreign demand for our goods. In the long run, domestic wages will also adjust to ensure full employment.

8 However, there are alternative mechanisms for achieving balanced trade without going through an adjustment process involving falling domestic prices. A devaluation, combined with restrictive aggregate demand policies, can lead to balance of payments equilibrium from a situation of trade deficit at more than full employment.

9 The introduction of capital flows points to the effects of monetary and fiscal policy on the balance of payments through interest rate effects on capital flows. An increase in the domestic interest rate, relative to the world interest rate, leads to a capital inflow that can finance a balance of trade deficit.

10 Policy dilemmas can then be handled by combining restrictive monetary policies to improve the balance of payments through higher interest rates and capital inflows, with expansionary fiscal policy to increase domestic employment.

11 However, such policies cannot be used in the long run to maintain balanced payments at the fixed exchange rate. The interest burden of the policies would, in the long run, be excessive, and the exchange rate could not be maintained. If balance of payments deficits are not temporary, then adjustment policies, such as devaluation, with accompanying monetary and fiscal changes, have to be undertaken to correct the imbalance.

PROBLEMS

1 This problem formalizes some of the questions about income and trade balance determination in the open economy. We assume, as a simplification, that the interest rate is given and equal to $i = i_0$. In terms of Figures 17-1 and 17-2, the monetary authorities hold constant the interest rate so that the LM curve is flat at the level $i = i_0$.

   We assume aggregate spending by domestic residents is

$$A = \bar{A} + cY - hi \qquad\qquad 1$$

Import spending is given by

$$Q = \bar{Q} + mY \qquad\qquad 2$$

where $\bar{Q}$ is autonomous import spending. Exports are given and equal to

$$X = \bar{X} \qquad\qquad 3$$

You are asked to work out the following problems:
(a) What is the total demand for domestic goods? The balance of trade?
(b) What is the equilibrium level of income?
(c) What is the balance of trade at that equilibrium level of income?
(d) What is the effect of an increase in exports on the equilibrium level of income? What is the multiplier?
(e) What is the effect of increased exports on the trade balance?

2 Suppose the marginal propensity to save is 0.1 and the marginal propensity to import is 0.2.
(a) What is the open economy multiplier?
(b) Assume there is a reduction in export demand of $\Delta \bar{X} = \$1$ billion. By how much does income change? By how much does the trade balance worsen?
(c) What policies can the country pursue to offset the impact of reduced exports on domestic income and employment as well as the trade balance?

3 It has been suggested that, the smaller the marginal propensity to import, the larger the cost of adjustment to external imbalance. What is the rationale for this argument? Do you agree?

4 It has been argued that a central bank is a necessary condition for a balance of payments deficit. What is the explanation for this argument?

5 Consider a country that is in a position of full employment and balanced trade. You are asked to discuss which type of disturbances can be remedied with standard aggregate demand tools of stabilization:
(a) A loss of export markets
(b) A reduction in saving and a corresponding increase in demand for domestic goods
(c) An increase in government spending
(d) A shift in demand from imports to domestic goods
(c) A reduction in imports with a corresponding increase in saving

Indicate in each case the impact on external and internal balance as well as the appropriate policy response.

* 6 Derive the formula $1/(m + s)$ for the foreign trade multiplier, assuming the demand for imports is $Q = \bar{Q} + mY$. Use the formula to discuss the impact on the trade balance of an increase in autonomous domestic spending. In your discussion, comment on the proposition that the more open the economy, the smaller the domestic income expansion. Comment, also, on the counterpart proposition that the more the economy opens, the more the trade balance worsens. What measures openness? What does this imply about the extent of spillover effects as a function of m?

* 7 Consider a world with some capital mobility: The home country's capital account improves as domestic interest rates rise relative to the world rate of interest. Initially, the home country is in internal and external balance. (Draw the IS, LM, and $BP = 0$ schedules.)

Assume now an increase in the world rate of interest.

(a) Show the effect of the foreign interest rate increase on the BP schedule.

(b) What policy response would immediately restore internal and external balance?

(c) If the authorities took no action, what would be the adjustment process along the lines described by the "monetary approach to the balance of payments"?

* 8 Consider again the case of a country that faces some capital mobility. Here we ask what monetary fiscal policy mix should be pursued to offset the following disturbances:

(a) A transitory gain in exports

(b) A permanent gain in exports

(c) A decline in autonomous spending

(d) An increased rate of capital outflow (at each level of domestic interest rates)

* 9 This question is concerned with the repercussion effects of a domestic expansion once we recognize that as a consequence output abroad will expand. Suppose that at home there is an increase in autonomous spending, $\Delta\bar{A}$, that falls entirely on domestic goods. (Assume constant interest rates throughout this problem.)

(a) What is the resulting effect on income, disregarding repercussion effects? What is the impact on our imports, ΔQ?

(b) Using the result for the increase in imports, we can now ask what happens abroad. Our increase in imports appears to foreign countries as an increase in their exports and therefore as an increase in demand for their goods. In response, their output expands. Assuming the foreign marginal propensity to save is s^* and the foreign propensity to import is m^*, by how much will a foreign country's income expand as a result of an increase in its exports?

(c) Now combine the pieces by writing the familiar equation for equilibrium in the domestic goods market: Change in supply, ΔY, equals the total change in demand: $\Delta\bar{A} + \Delta X - m\Delta Y + (1 - s)\Delta Y$, or

$$\Delta Y = \frac{1}{s + m}(\Delta\bar{A} + \Delta X)$$

      Noting that foreign demand ΔX depends on our increased imports, we can replace ΔX with the answer to 9(*b*) to obtain a general expression for the multiplier with repercussions.

(*d*) Substitute your answer for 9(*b*) in the formula for the change in foreign demand, $\Delta X = m^*\Delta Y^*$.

(*e*) Calculate the complete change in our income, including repercussion effects. Now compare your result with the small-country case. What difference do repercussion effects make? Is our income expansion larger or smaller with repercussion effects?

(*f*) Consider the trade balance effect of a domestic expansion with and without repercussion effects. Is the trade deficit larger or smaller once repercussion effects are taken into account?

10 Use the central bank balance sheet to show how a balance of payments deficit affects the stock of high-powered money under fixed exchange rates. Show, too, how sterilization operations work.

11 Discuss the manner in which income, price adjustments, and money supply adjustments interact in leading the economy ultimately to full employment and external balance. Choose as an example the case where a country experiences a permanent increase in exports.

12 In relation to external imbalance, a distinction is frequently made between imbalances that should be "financed" and those that should be "adjusted." Can you think of a classification of disturbances that give rise, respectively, to imbalances that require adjustment and those that should more appropriately be financed?

18

TRADE AND CAPITAL FLOWS UNDER FLEXIBLE EXCHANGE RATES

This chapter is concerned with flexible exchange rates as an adjustment mechanism both in an individual country and in the world economy. Chart 18-1 shows the fluctuations in the value of the Canadian dollar from 1926 to 1980. Both fixed and floating rates were in effect at various times over this period. Between 1926 and 1929, a fixed rate was maintained

CHART 18-1 THE CANADIAN DOLLAR, 1926-1980
(*Source: Bank of Canada Review, Federal Reserve Bulletin*)

by Canada and most other countries by maintaining convertibility into gold at a fixed price. A floating rate was in effect during the 1930s until the outbreak of World War II when a fixed rate of 90.5 U.S. cents was established. The Canadian dollar was revalued to 100 U.S. cents in 1946 and this rate was abandoned in 1950 in favour of a floating rate. Under the influence of free-market forces our dollar soon rose above 100 U.S. cents and remained there until 1961.

After a rapid downward movement of the Canadian dollar in 1961 and early 1962, the government decided to return to a fixed rate and a value of 92.5 U.S. was established in May 1962. In 1970, the Canadian dollar came under strong upward pressure and a floating rate was adopted again. By 1972, the rate had risen above 100 U.S. cents and was close to 104 cents in 1974. Since then there have been wide fluctuations and the value of the Canadian dollar has been below 90 U.S. cents since 1977.

The plan of this chapter is as follows. We begin with a review of events in the world economy in the 1970s. In Section 18-2 we extend the analysis of Section 17-4 of a Keynesian model with capital mobility and sticky prices to a world of flexible exchange rates. In Section 18-3, we round out the model by looking at a world of flexible prices. The analysis of Section 18-3 leads to a review of the chief determinants of exchange rates. Sections 18-2 and 18-3 are the core of the chapter. Section 18-4 introduces exchange rate measures that are widely used and that deal with the difficulty that the exchange rate of a currency, say the dollar, often appreciates against one currency (for example, the French franc) while it depreciates against another (say, the yen). The question that arises is whether the dollar is on the average appreciating or depreciating, and by how much? In Section 18-5 we review Canadian experience with flexible exchange rates in the 1950s and the 1970s. Sections 18-6 and 18-7 offer some significant extensions of, and qualifications to, the theoretical sections. Section 18-6 discusses exchange rate expectations and international interest rate differentials, while Section 18-7 deals with real wage stickiness and with the important possibility that the trade balance responds perversely to exchange rate changes in the short run — the so-called J curve.

18-1 THE WORLD ECONOMY IN THE 1970s

Most of the major countries of the world moved to a flexible exchange rate system in 1973 as the fixed exchange rate system that had existed since 1945 collapsed. The fundamental cause of the collapse of the fixed rate system — also called the *Bretton Woods system*, after the town in New Hampshire in which the conference setting up the system was held — was the incompatibility of macroeconomic targets among countries.

During the sixties, and again in 1971-1973, some countries, including Britain and the United States, pursued expansionary policies. Other countries — the hard-currency countries, particularly Germany — wanted lower inflation rates than the world economy was experiencing and followed less expansionary policies. With fixed exchange rates, the lower rate of inflation in Germany than in the United States meant that German goods were becoming progressively cheaper relative to United States goods. As a result, Germany ran increasingly large balance of payments surpluses, while the United States (and Britain) had large deficits. Under such circumstances, the countries with large surpluses have to revalue their currencies, or the deficit countries have to devalue, to correct the payments imbalances.

A fixed exchange rate system with free capital flows between countries is badly equipped to deal with revaluations or devaluations that are widely anticipated. To understand this point, we turn to the case of Germany in 1973. There were recurrent rumours in 1973 that the Deutsche mark would be revalued once more.[1] The rumours arose because the exchange rate adjustment of 1971 had not appreciably reduced the United States balance of payments deficit. The belief in an imminent Deutsche mark revaluation led to large capital outflows from the United States and inflows into Germany.

Why would the belief that the mark was about to be revalued lead to a capital inflow into Germany? Suppose people expect the mark will be revalued from 30 cents per mark to 40 cents per mark. A holder of $1 million today could buy DM3.33 million for his dollars at the price of 30 cents each. Then, after the devaluation, he could exchange his DM3.33 million for $1.33 million, receiving 40 cents for each mark. The operation nets a profit of 33 percent. Since there is no risk that the mark will be devalued, there is very little risk in buying it, and hence the belief in impending revaluation leads to large purchases of marks by holders of other currencies. If there is no revaluation, there is hardly any loss, and if there is a revaluation, there is a large profit.

As a result of the expected revaluation, the German Bundesbank had to buy about $10 billion in foreign exchange to meet foreign demands for marks at the existing exchange rate, in the five weeks from the end of January to the first of March 1973. Recall from Chapter 17 that central bank purchases of foreign exchange increase the domestic money supply. Now the $10 billion that the Bundesbank purchased by selling marks amounted to almost 20 percent of the German money supply at that time. Thus, in order to defend the exchange rate, the Bundesbank was being forced to expand the German money supply at an extraordinary rate. The large increase in the money supply in turn created the fear — indeed, the certainty — that the capital inflow would have substantial inflationary effects. The way out was to stop intervening in the foreign exchange market and thus to gain control of monetary policy for purposes of domestic stabilization. But once the

---

[1] The Deutsche mark had been revalued in 1961, 1969, and 1971. In 1971 a number of other currencies also had their exchange rates adjusted.

Bundesbank decided to stop intervening in the foreign exchange market, it left the exchange rate to be determined by supply and demand in that market. That is, it chose to allow a flexible exchange rate regime.

A country which is expected to devalue also faces an intractable problem under fixed exchange rates. In that case, the expected devaluation produces an outflow of capital from the currency. Suppose that the pound was expected to be devalued. Then holders of pounds would buy other currencies in exchange for their pounds.[2] With the Bank of England committed to supporting the exchange rate, it would have to buy the pounds that others were selling. In so doing, it would rapidly reduce its reserves of other currencies and would eventually run out of reserves to exchange for the pounds. Thus it would be forced to devalue.

The general point is that a fixed exchange rate system is not viable if countries pursue policies which lead to different rates of inflation and there is free mobility of capital. The countries with lower inflation rates will eventually have to revalue or those with higher inflation rates will have to devalue. It is thus always clear in which direction there will be a revaluation or devaluation. Capital can flow with little risk and with the promise of large gains in anticipation of exchange rate changes. And, as the capital starts flowing, countries with surpluses are forced to accept increases in their money supplies they do not want, and deficit countries face the risk of running out of reserves.

There were, in the early seventies, increasingly large-scale flows of capital in anticipation of exchange rate changes. The German decision to float the exchange rate in 1973 was merely the particular event which marked the end of the fixed rate system, rather than the fundamental cause of the change of system. The fundamental cause was the incompatibility of the economic policies being followed by different countries.

What is the system that has emerged since 1973? There are three chief characteristics. The first is the formation of *currency areas*. For instance, in 1973, some countries in the European Economic Community (EEC) joined Germany in a currency area with fixed exchange rates that is called the *snake*. The snake is an arrangement, shown in Chart 18-2, whereby exchange rates between partner countries can fluctuate only within narrow limits. However, the exchange rates of all the currencies in the currency area fluctuate relative to the United States dollar. If the small margin of fluctuation within the snake were eliminated, the shaded band in Chart 18-2 would collapse to a fixed rate within the snake — a fixed rate between Dutch guilders and marks, for example — and a floating rate of the mark-guilder relative to the United States dollar.

In 1979 Europe went further in an attempt to create a common currency

---

[2] To see why expected devaluation produces a flight of capital, reverse the example of the expected mark appreciation above.

CHART 18-2 THE EUROPEAN ECONOMIC COMMUNITY SNAKE AND THE FRENCH FRANC IN RELATION TO THE U.S. DOLLAR. (*Source: Organization for Economic Cooperation and Development. Economic Outlook, July 1976*)

area — an area with fixed exchange rates among the members — by setting up the *European Monetary System* (EMS). The EMS is an extension of the snake that includes France and, with special arrangements, Italy and the United Kingdom. Beyond providing for fixed exchange rates between members of the group (within narrow margins), the EMS has worked out a detailed system of intervention and corrective policies should an individual country get out of line with the group. It also provides ample financing for countries that may find it difficult to keep in step with the other members of what is clearly intended to be a low inflation, hard currency club.

The second fact about exchange rate experience since 1973 is also apparent from Chart 18-2. There have been large *fluctuations* in rates in the floating rate period. Movements in the exchange rates between the snake currencies and the dollar have been described as "wild gyrations," and whatever they are called, they have been large. The question arises of where these movements come from and whether central banks should intervene in the market to smooth exchange rate movements.

This leads us to the third fact — *dirty floating*. Rates have in practice not been determined by the free interplay of private demand and supply but have, on the contrary, been significantly affected by official intervention. Central banks have intervened almost daily in the foreign exchange markets to smooth out short-run fluctuations. They well may have also attempted — with some success — to fight longer-run exchange rate movements.

The extent of intervention has increased in the past few years. It is worth noting that in 1978, for example, central banks outside the United States purchased in excess of 35 billion U.S. dollars in attempts to prevent their currencies from appreciating. The intervention was conducted chiefly by the large, industrialized countries. The highest quarterly figure was reported by Japan, which showed a gain in reserves of $10 billion in the last quarter of 1978. This was a time when the yen was appreciating sharply against the dollar and when the U.S. government (on November 1) undertook a substantial stabilization program to shore up the U.S. dollar.

The dirty floating of the period since 1973 obviously again raises the question of why central banks intervene to affect the exchange rate, rather than leave it to the market to set the rate. A final question that is raised by the floating rate regime concerns world trade and capital flows. Prior to 1973, a flexible rate system was viewed with suspicion. The argument was that flexible rates create uncertainty and thus reduce trade and lending in the world economy. The question is important because such an effect, should it occur, would obviously have repercussions at the macro level by forcing countries to be in trade balance. It turns out, though, that world trade did not decline after the move to flexible exchange rates and large payments imbalances continue to be financed through capital flows.

18-2 EXCHANGE RATES AND EQUILIBRIUM OUTPUT

We start with a model of output and exchange rate determination. Our discussion will extend the analysis of Chapter 17, where we looked at income determination in an open economy. In that chapter, we assumed capital mobility, sticky prices, demand-determined output, and fixed exchange rates. Here, we maintain all these assumptions except the last and now allow the exchange rate to be flexible. Our analysis will proceed as follows: First, we shall review the role of exchange rates in determining the relative prices of imports and domestically produced goods and thereby the demand for domestic output. Next, we develop the equilibrium conditions in the goods and money markets and in the external balance. Finally, we use our model to show the implications of monetary and real disturbances for the level of output and the exchange rate. These results can then be directly compared with those for the fixed exchange rate world analyzed in Chapter 17. After making the comparison, we proceed in the following sections to alternative assumptions about capital mobility and to a discussion of longer-term adjustments of prices and output.

Exchange Rates and Relative Prices

A central price in an open economy is the relative price of goods produced in the rest of the world in terms of goods produced at home. If the price of goods we produce falls relative to the price of the goods foreigners produce, then the demand for our goods tends to rise. If Canadian goods become cheaper, then both Canadians and foreigners will tend to buy more Canadian goods and fewer foreign goods. Given income or spending levels, a decline in the relative price of our goods makes us more competitive and, as a consequence, raises *net* exports and creates demand for domestic output.[3]

The price of our goods relative to foreigners' goods is clearly central to the operation of a flexible exchange rate system, and we have to ask how to measure it. We define the relative price as the ratio of import prices to domestic prices, *both measured in the same currency*. Define P^* as the price of goods produced abroad measured in foreign currency (yen per unit), e as the exchange rate measured in \$/yen, and P as the dollar price of our goods. The relative price of foreign goods in terms of domestic goods, *the terms of trade*, is then defined as

$$\frac{eP^*}{P} \equiv \text{terms of trade or relative price of imports} \qquad (1)$$

The term eP^* measures the price of foreign goods in terms of dollars, and P of course measures the price of domestic goods in terms of dollars. If import prices (eP^*) rise relative to domestic prices (P), we say there has been a worsening or deterioration of the terms of trade. For example, the repeated increases in oil prices worsened the importing countries' terms of trade and meant that more units of exports had to be given up to buy a barrel of oil.

We have now defined the relative price of imports or foreign goods in terms of domestic goods and have argued that it is important in determining the demand for domestic output. We consider next the relation between exchange rates and relative prices. Here we make, for the moment, the strategic assumption that both foreign prices, P^*, and domestic prices, P, are given. This implies that the terms of trade move *one for one* with the exchange rate. If the exchange rate depreciates (e rises), then import prices increase in home currency and thus, with our prices given, the *relative* price of imports rises. Exchange depreciation thus raises the relative price of imports or makes domestic goods relatively cheaper. Therefore, exchange

---

[3] We should note, pending further discussion, that we assume that elasticities are large enough for a decline in relative price to raise net exports. We return to this important issue in more detail in Sec. 18-7, under the subheading, "Relative Prices and the Trade Balance: The J Curve."

depreciation leads to increases in net exports and in demand for domestic goods.

The question of the effect of changes of the exchange rate on the terms of trade is a crucial one, to which we return in Section 18-3. We shall argue there that changes in the exchange rate set off forces that in the longer term tend to offset the effects of the initial exchange rate change on the terms of trade. But in the short run with sticky prices, exchange rate changes do change relative prices.

Relative Prices, Net Exports, and Demand for Domestic Output

The demand for domestic output comes from both domestic residents and the rest of the world. We showed in Chapter 17 that we can write demand for domestic goods as the sum of total spending by domestic residents (including spending on imports), A, plus *net* exports or the trade surplus, NX. Domestic aggregate spending depends on interest rates, i, and income, Y. Net exports depend on foreign income, which we take as given, domestic income, and relative prices, eP^*/P.

$$NX = NX(Y, eP^*/P) \tag{2}$$

We recall from Chapter 17 that a rise in income reduces net exports because it leads to increased import spending. In Equation (2) we also include the relative price as an explicit determinant of net exports. A rise in the relative price of imports leads to an increase in net exports because it lowers our imports and raises our exports.

We consider next the equilibrium condition in the domestic goods market. Output is assumed to be determined by demand, and prices are given. Equilibrium requires that output equal the demand for domestic goods or, equivalently, aggregate spending plus the trade surplus:

$$Y = A(i,Y) + NX(Y,eP^*/P) \tag{3}$$

We show in Figure 18-1 the IS schedule that represents goods market equilibrium *given* an exchange rate, say e_0. What happens to the IS schedule if the exchange rate depreciates?

Exchange depreciation will, under our assumptions, raise the relative price of imports or lower the relative price of our own goods. With our own goods more competitive, there is increased net demand arising from increased net exports. Thus, for a given interest rate and income level, exchange depreciation must lead to an excess demand for our goods. To restore equilibrium, output would have to rise or interest rates would have to increase. In Figure 18-1, we accordingly show that exchange depreciation shifts the IS schedule up and to the right. The schedule IS' is drawn for a higher relative price of imports. Conversely, an appreciation and fall in

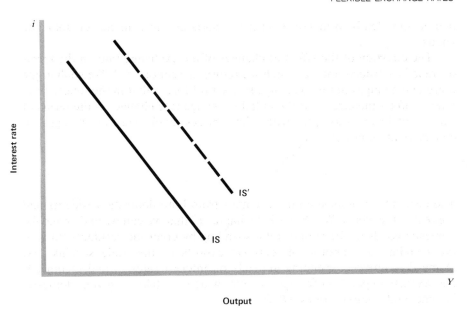

FIGURE 18-1 EFFECTS OF EXCHANGE RATE DEPRECIATION ON THE IS CURVE

import prices would of course lead to an excess supply of our goods and a downward shift of the IS schedule.

We now develop the remaining parts of our model of exchange rate and output determination, namely, the money market equilibrium condition and the balance of payments.

Monetary Equilibrium and Payments Balance

The condition of monetary equilibrium is the familiar LM schedule of earlier chapters. Given prices, P, and nominal money, M, we have a given real money stock, M/P. Equilibrium in the money market requires that the demand for real money balances equal the existing real money stock:

$$\frac{M}{P} = L(i,Y) \tag{4}$$

Real money demand in (4) is a decreasing function of the interest rate and an increasing function of the level of income. The LM schedule is shown in Figure 18-2 for a given real money stock.

We draw on the discussion of capital mobility in Chapter 17 to develop our balance of payments equation. The balance of payments surplus, BP, is equal to net exports, NX, plus the net rate of capital inflow, CF.

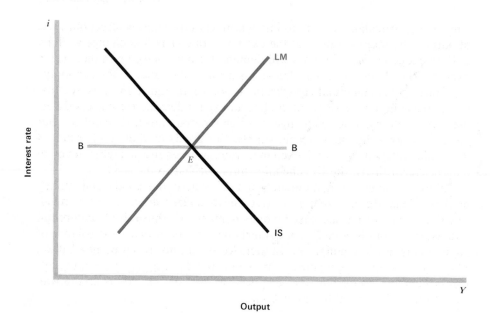

FIGURE 18-2 EQUILIBRIUM OF THE GOODS AND MONEY MARKETS AND THE BALANCE OF PAYMENTS

$$BP = NX(Y,eP^*/P) + CF(i,i^*) \tag{5}$$

We have already introduced the fact that the trade balance depends on income and relative prices. We now have added the rate of capital flow as a function of our interest rate, i, and the given interest rate abroad i^*. If our interest rate increases relative to that in the rest of the world, then there will be a net capital inflow.

For the present, we make the simplifying assumption that capital mobility is very high, so that we can have payments balance only at the world interest rate. If our interest rate were lower, there would be large-scale capital outflows swamping any current account surplus. Conversely, with a higher interest rate than the rest of the world, the capital inflows would swamp any deficit in the current account. We represent this assumption of high capital mobility in Figure 18-2 by a flat BB schedule. Points above it correspond to a balance of payments surplus and points below it to a deficit.

Adjustments to a Real Disturbance

We have now completed our model, represented by Equations (2) through (5) and Figure 18-2, and can ask how the economy will adjust to disturbances. In particular, we want to know how various changes affect our level of output, the interest rate, and the exchange rate. The first change we look at is an exogenous rise in the world demand for our goods, or an increase in exports. The change in export demand is a *real* disturbance to the economy.[4]

Starting from an initial equilibrium at point E in Figure 18-3, we see that the increase in foreign demand implies an excess demand for our goods. At the initial interest rate, exchange rate, and output level, demand for our goods now exceeds the available supply. For goods market equilibrium, at the initial interest rate and exchange rate, we require a higher level of output. Accordingly, the IS schedule shifts out and to the right.

Now consider for a moment point E', where the goods and money markets clear. Here, output has increased to meet the increased demand. The rise in income has increased money demand and thus raised equilibrium interest rates. But is point E' an equilibrium? It is not, because the balance of payments is not in equilibrium. In fact, we would not reach point E' at all. The tendency for the economy to move in that direction, as we show now, will bring about an exchange rate appreciation that will take us all the way back to the initial equilibrium at E.

[4] Disturbances that, by contrast, originate in the money market, are called *nominal*.

FIGURE 18-3 EFFECTS OF AN INCREASE IN THE DEMAND FOR EXPORTS

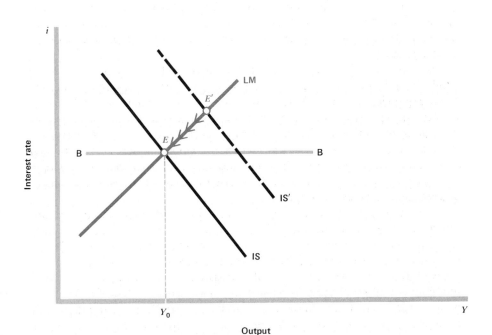

Suppose, then, that the increase in foreign demand takes place and that, in response, there is a tendency for output and income to increase. The induced increase in money demand will raise interest rates and thus will bring us out of line with interest rates internationally. The resulting capital inflows immediately put pressure on the exchange rate. The capital inflow causes our currency to appreciate.

The exchange appreciation means, of course, that import prices fall and that domestic goods become relatively more expensive. Demand shifts away from domestic goods and net exports decline. In terms of Figure 18-2, the appreciation implies that the IS schedule shifts back from IS' to the left. Next, we have to ask how far the exchange appreciation will go and to what extent it will therefore dampen the expansionary effect of increased net exports.

The exchange rate will keep appreciating as long as our interest rate exceeds the world level. This implies that the exchange appreciation must continue until the IS schedule has shifted back all the way to its initial position. This adjustment is shown by the arrows along the LM schedule. Only when we return to point E will output and income have reached a level consistent with monetary equilibrium at the world rate of interest.

We have now shown that under conditions of perfect capital mobility, an expansion in exports has no lasting effect on equilibrium output. With perfect capital mobility, as a result of the increase in export demand, the tendency for interest rates to rise leads to currency appreciation and thus to a complete offset of the increase in exports. Once we return to point E, net exports are back to their initial level. The exchange rate has of course appreciated. Imports will increase as a consequence of the appreciation, and the initial expansion in exports is in part offset by the appreciation of our exchange rate.

We can extend the usefulness of this analysis by recognizing that it is valid not only for an increase in exports. The same analysis applies to a fiscal expansion. A tax cut or an increase in government spending would lead to an expansion in demand in just the same way as increased exports do. Again, the tendency for interest rates to rise leads to appreciation and therefore to a fall in exports and increased imports. There is, accordingly, complete *crowding out* here. The crowding out takes place not as in Chapter 4 because higher interest rates reduce investment but because the exchange appreciation reduces net exports.

The important lesson here is that real disturbances to demand do not affect equilibrium output under flexible rates with perfect capital mobility. We can drive the lesson home by comparing a fiscal expansion under flexible rates with the results we derived for the fixed rate case. In Chapter 17, we showed that with fixed rates, fiscal expansion under conditions of capital mobility is highly effective in raising equilibrium output. For flexible rates, by contrast, a fiscal expansion does not change equilibrium output. Instead, it produces an offsetting exchange rate appreciation and a shift in the composition of domestic demand toward domestic goods and away fron net exports.

We turn next to the analysis of a monetary disturbance.

Adjustment to a Monetary Disturbance

We now show that under flexible exchange rates, an increase in the money stock leads to an increase in income and a depreciation of the exchange rate. The analysis uses Figure 18-4. We start from an initial position at point E and consider an increase in the nominal quantity of money, M. Since prices are given, we have an increase in the real money stock, M/P. At E there will be an excess supply of real balances. To restore equilibrium, interest rates would have to be lower or income would have to be larger. Accordingly, the LM schedule shifts down and to the right to LM'.

We ask once again whether point E' is the new equilibrium. At E', goods and money markets are in equilibrium (at the initial exchange rate), but it is clear that interest rates have fallen below the world level. Capital outflows will therefore put pressure on the exchange rate. The exchange depreciation caused by the low level of interest rates implies that import prices increase, domestic goods become more competitive, and, as a result, demand for our output expands. The exchange depreciation therefore shifts the IS curve out and to the right. As the arrows indicate, exchange depreciation continues

FIGURE 18-4 EFFECTS OF AN INCREASE IN THE MONEY STOCK

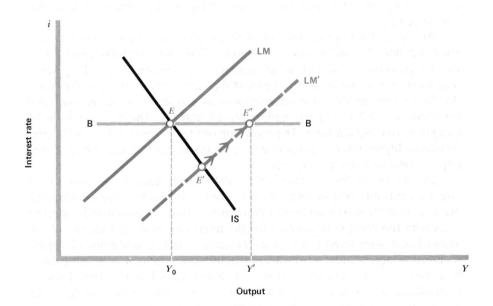

Output

until the relative price of domestic goods has fallen enough to raise demand and output to the level indicated by point E''. Only at E'' do we have goods and money market equilibrium compatible with the world rate of interest. Consequently, there is no further tendency for exchange rates, relative prices, and hence demand, to change.[5]

We have now shown that a monetary expansion leads to an increase in output and a depreciation of the exchange rate under flexible rates. One way of thinking about this result is that with P fixed, an increase in M increases M/P. The demand for real balances is, from Equation (4), equal to $L(i,Y)$. Since i cannot differ from the world rate of interest, Y has to rise to equate the demand for money to the supply. The exchange depreciation raises net exports, and that increase in net exports in turn sustains the higher level of output and employment. One interesting implication of our analysis, then, is the proposition that monetary expansion improves the current account through the induced depreciation.

How do our results compare with those of a fixed exchange rate world? We argued in Chapter 17 that under fixed rates, the monetary authorities cannot control the nominal money stock and that an attempt to expand money will merely lead to a reserve loss as the central bank attempts to prevent the tendency for the exchange rate to depreciate in response to declining interest rates. Under flexible rates, by contrast, the central bank does not intervene and so the money stock increase is *not* reversed in the foreign exchange market. The depreciation and expansion in output actually do take place, given the assumed sticky prices. The fact that the central bank *can* control the money stock under flexible rates is one of the most important aspects of that exchange rate system.

Beggar-Thy-Neighbour Policy and Competitive Depreciation

We extend the analysis of the fixed price variable employment model with a brief discussion of the international implications of exchange depreciation and changes in net exports. We showed that a monetary expansion in the home country leads to exchange depreciation, an increase in net exports, and therefore an increase in output and employment. But our increased net exports correspond to a deterioration in the trade balance abroad. The domestic depreciation shifts demand from foreign goods toward domestic goods. Abroad, output and employment therefore decline. It is for this reason that the depreciation-induced change in the trade balance has been called a *beggar-they-neighbour policy* — it is a way of exporting unemployment or of creating domestic employment at the expense of the rest of the world.

The recognition that exchange depreciation is mainly a way of shifting demand from one country to another, rather than changing the level of world

---

[5] In the problem set at the end of this chapter we ask you to show that the current account improves between E and E'', even though the increased level of income increases imports.

demand, is important. It implies that exchange rate adjustment can be a useful policy when countries find themselves in different stages of a business cycle — for example, one in a boom (with overemployment) and the other in a recession. In that event, a depreciation by the country experiencing a recession would shift world demand in that direction and thus work to reduce divergences from full employment in each country.

By contrast, when countries' business cycles are highly synchronized, such as in the 1930s or in the aftermath of the oil shock, exchange rate movements will not contribute much toward world full employment. The problem is then one of the level of total world spending being deficient or excessive while exchange rate movements affect only the allocation of a given world demand between countries. Nevertheless, from the point of view of an individual country, exchange depreciation works to attract world demand and raise domestic output. If every country tried to depreciate to attract world demand, we would have *competitive depreciation* and a shifting around of world demand rather than an increase in the world level of spending. Coordinated monetary and/or fiscal policies are needed to increase demand and output in each country.

*Imperfect Capital Mobility

The case of perfect capital mobility is extreme, and it probably overstates the speed with which capital moves internationally in response to interest rate differentials. It is therefore important to consider the effects of more moderate capital mobility, or *imperfect capital mobility*. In this case, the rate of capital flows increases as the international interest differential increases, but it remains finite. In equilibrium, interest rate differentials are possible. The larger the equilibrium differential, the larger the associated capital flow and therefore the current account imbalance.

How would monetary and fiscal policy work in a world of imperfect capital mobility? We leave as an exercise at the end of the chapter the demonstration of the following results: First, a fiscal expansion at home raises our interest rate and increases our income. With the higher interest rate, there will be an increased inflow of capital. This implies a deterioration in the current account, since the sum of the current and capital accounts is zero. However, the current account deteriorates by less than the fiscal expansion. There is less than full crowding out, and hence, income rises.

In the case of a monetary expansion, our interest rate falls, income rises, and the current account must improve. We know that the current account must improve since the lower interest rate implies increased capital outflows which, for payments balance, must be offset by an improvement in the current account.

The case of imperfect capital mobility clearly qualifies our earlier results. Now both monetary and fiscal policies are effective and the extent to which fiscal policy can affect income depends on the extent to which changes in interest differentials affect capital flows.

Summary

We have now taken a first look at exchange rate determination under flexible exchange rates. So far, we have studied the role of exchange rates in a world of fixed prices. In this setting, movements in exchange rates change the relative prices of foreign versus domestic goods. An exchange depreciation both raises foreign demand for our goods and moves our own demand away from imports toward domestic goods. The exchange rate thus plays a central role in the determination of macroeconomic equilibrium.

An examination of real and monetary disturbances under flexible exchange rates, fixed prices, and perfect capital mobility gave us the following results:

1 A fiscal expansion leaves output unchanged. The fiscal expansion tends to increase income and raise interest rates. The tendency for interest rates to rise leads to appreciation of the exchange rate as capital is attracted from abroad. The appreciation, by lowering import prices, shifts demand away from our goods and thus offsets the expansionary effect of fiscal policy.

2 This result is the opposite of that derived under fixed exchange rates. The difference results from the fact that under flexible rates, the money stock is exogenous and is kept fixed when fiscal policy changes, while under fixed rates, exchange rate stabilization makes money endogenous and thus accommodates the fiscal expansion.

3 For a monetary expansion, conclusions were also opposite to those for fixed rates. A monetary expansion leads to an increase in income and to exchange depreciation. The tendency for interest rates to fall as a consequence of monetary expansion leads to a capital outflow that causes the exchange rate to depreciate and thereby to raise demand for domestic output.

4 In the case of a fiscal expansion, the induced appreciation of the exchange rate leads to a reduction in net exports, offsetting the increased domestic spending. With a monetary expansion, the depreciation that ensues leads to an improvement in net exports. The trade balance effects of the two policies are thus quite different.

5 With imperfect capital mobility, interest rates can differ internationally and both monetary and fiscal policies can affect the level of output.

The fixed price assumption of this section cannot be expected to hold over long periods. We would not expect wages and prices to stay fixed if there was substantial unemployment or if demand increased when the economy was already at full employment. Therefore we have to expand the model of this section to incorporate the flexibility of prices as well as exchange rates. Still, as in earlier chapters, the analysis of the fixed price case will be needed in understanding the flexible price situation, to which we now turn.

18-3 EXCHANGE RATES, PRICES, AND OUTPUT ADJUSTMENT

In this section we take into account the implications of price flexibility. In particular, we study the effects of price level and exchange rate adjustments on the level of output and the interest rate. To do so, we will have to ask what factors cause the exchange rate and the price level to change.

In the short run, given the exchange rate and the price level, income and the interest rate continue to be determined by the interaction of the IS and LM curves, as shown in Figure 18-5. We also show in Figure 18-5 the BB curve along which the balance of payments balances in the short run. The BB curve is not horizontal, since we do not assume now that capital is instantaneously perfectly mobile. Rather, we assume that the rate of capital inflow increases when our interest rate rises and falls when our interest rate falls. However, we assume that in the long run, capital *is* perfectly mobile. Capital will flow out as long as our interest rate is below the world level and flow in as long as our interest rate is above the world level.

FIGURE 18-5 DETERMINATION OF EQUILIBRIUM, GIVEN THE PRICE LEVEL AND EXCHANGE RATE

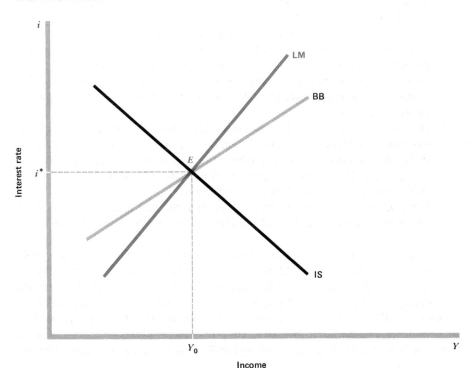

Point E in Figure 18-5 is a position of both short-run and long-run equilibrium. Because the IS and LM curves intersect at that point, we have short-run equilibrium. Because the interest rate is (by assumption) equal to the world level and output is at its potential level, it is also a point of long-run equilibrium, given that the IS, LM, and BB curves pass through that point.

There is one more characteristic of the long-run equilibrium that is not obvious from the diagram. At point E, we assume also that the current account is balanced and there are no net capital flows. The reason this condition is needed for full long-run equilibrium is that if there were capital flows, we would either be increasingly in debt to foreigners or becoming increasingly wealthy by owning more and more foreign assets, and we could not then expect the economy to stay in equilibrium at E. If there was a capital inflow, we would effectively be borrowing from foreigners, becoming poorer over time and thus reducing our consumption. This cannot be a steady state. Similarly, if we were lending to foreigners, our consumption would be increasing over time and the economy would not stay at point E. Thus, in the long run, an economy that is not growing will be in steady state only if the current account balances.

Figure 18-5 shows how the short-run equilibrium of the economy is determined. But if we are not at full employment, and if the interest rate is not at the world level, the price level and the exchange rate will be changing. How? We make two particularly simple assumptions. First, we assume that

FIGURE 18-6 DYNAMIC ADJUSTMENT OF PRICES AND THE EXCHANGE RATE

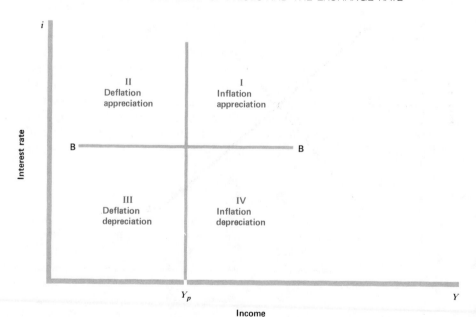

prices rise when output is above potential and decline when output is below potential. Second, we assume that the exchange rate depreciates if the interest rate is below the world level and appreciates if the interest rate is above the world level.

These assumptions are shown in Figure 18-6. The direction of movement of the exchange rate and the price level is shown for each of the four regions in the diagram.

The Adjustment Process

Consider, for example, region I, where we have interest rates above the world level and output above normal. The high interest rate would attract capital, leading to a balance of payments surplus and appreciation. The overemployment in turn leads to rising wages and prices. What adjustments would we expect from the movements in prices and exchange rates?

There are two channels through which changing prices and exchange rates affect interest rates and output. The first channel is the effect of changing prices on the real money stock. With nominal money given, the real money stock, M/P, depends on the price level. Falling prices imply a rising real money stock and rising prices imply a falling real money stock. A falling real money stock, of course, implies rising interest rates and thereby a contractionary effect on aggregate demand.

The second channel is that of relative prices or the terms of trade. Exchange appreciation lowers import prices and thus lowers the relative price of imports. Domestic inflation also raises our prices relative to those of imports. Thus, both appreciation and inflation make us less competitive and therefore reduce the demand for domestic output.

In Table 18-1 we show the direction in which real balances and relative prices move in each of the regions of Figure 18-6. Thus, for example, in region I, inflation lowers the real value of the money stock, and inflation and appreciation both contribute to lowering the relative price of imports. Regions II and IV show a question mark for relative prices (the terms of trade). In region II, the appreciation lowers import prices, but at the same time we have domestic deflation. The movement of relative prices depends on the comparison of the rate at which the exchange rate appreciates and

TABLE 18-1 THE ADJUSTMENT OF REAL BALANCES AND RELATIVE PRICES

	Regions			
	I	II	III	IV
M/P	↓	↑	↑	↓
eP^*/P	↓	?	↑	?

domestic prices fall and is thus ambiguous. We will introduce a further assumption below that will remove this ambiguity.

The next step is to go from the changes in real money balances and relative prices shown in Table 18-1 to the adjustments that they bring about in the goods and money markets. Our discussion uses Figure 18-7, which reproduces Figure 18-6 with a minor change. Consider first region I, with its inflation and appreciation and thus falling real balances and a falling relative price of imports. The inflation reduces the real money stock and thus raises interest rates. The falling relative price of imports implied by appreciation and inflation reduces the demand for domestic goods and thus, together with increasing interest rates, reduces output. Therefore, in region I we have rising interest rates and falling output, as indicated by the arrows. We leave it to you to demonstrate that exactly the opposite arguments apply in region III.

Consider next region II. We have already noted that with deflation we have rising real balances and therefore falling interest rates. There is an ambiguity, however, with respect to relative prices. With deflation and

---

FIGURE 18-7 DYNAMIC ADJUSTMENT OF OUTPUT AND THE INTEREST RATE appreciation, both our prices and import prices are falling, and hence the behaviour of relative prices, eP^*/P, depends on which one falls faster. We resolve that question by the plausible assumption that our prices fall faster, the larger the GNP gap (the further we are to the left of Y_p), and that the exchange rate appreciates faster, the higher our interest rate.

With this assumption in mind, we return to Figure 18-7 to study output adjustment in region II. With a large GNP gap, we have, as noted, very rapidly falling prices and therefore an improvement in competitiveness. The gain in competitiveness, together with falling interest rates, will increase demand and output. Region II*b* corresponds to this case. By contrast, when the GNP gap is quite small, as is the case in region II*a*, we are still losing competitiveness and the falling interest rates are not sufficient to raise demand, so that output is still falling. The broken line HH shows the borderline along which output remains constant by a continuing loss in competitiveness. Again we leave it to you to establish the symmetry of the argument for region IV and to provide the argument for the arrows we have drawn.

An Increase in Exports

We can now use our model to study the effects of an increase in exports. We will use the dynamic assumptions shown in Figure 18-7 to see how the adjustment process works.

Suppose that we start at point E, in Figure 18-8, in full equilibrium and that an increase in exports occurs. For a given price level and exchange rate, the LM schedule stays put and the IS curve shifts outward because of the expansion in demand for our goods. We thus move to a point like A. At A the overemployment leads to inflation, reducing real balances and shifting the LM schedule up and to the left. The appreciation and inflation at A lower the relative price of imports, reducing demand, thus shifting the IS schedule down and to the left.

The successive intersections of the IS and LM schedules, as they shift in response to changes in relative prices and real money, are shown by the adjustment path from A to E. The arrows show the directions in which interest rates and output move.[6]

Starting from point A, with the interest rate rising and output falling, we come to full employment at point C at the border between regions I and II. But at C the interest rate is above that compatible with external balance. Full employment implies constant prices and therefore constant real money, but the continuing appreciation keeps lowering the relative price of imports, thus reducing demand and lowering output. We therefore must move into

---

[6] The path we have drawn is one plausible pattern of adjustment. The exact details of the dynamics, including the question of whether the adjustment is oscillatory, are not of interest here.

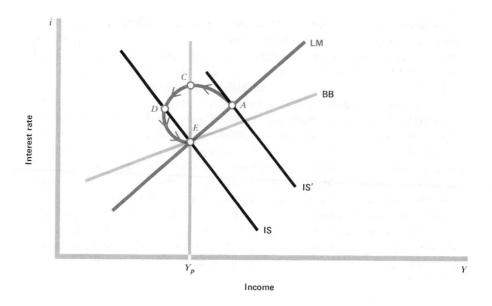

FIGURE 18-8 ADJUSTMENT TO AN INCREASE IN EXPORTS

region II. From here the process continues with falling interest rates and output that still declines beyond point C because appreciation runs ahead of domestic deflation. Only when output has fallen far enough and interest rates have declined sufficiently does the path of output turn around at point D, with a recovery accompanied by still falling interest rates. This phase takes us all the way to point E.

The adjustment process ends when we have returned to point E with the initial stock of real balances and thus the initial LM schedule, and when we are back with the initial IS schedule and an unchanged current account. The increase in autonomous exports has been offset by the effect of a lower relative price of imports that shifts demand away from domestic goods. The long-run effect of increased exports is thus to bring about an offsetting change in the terms of trade. Furthermore, that change is brought about entirely, in the long run, through an appreciation of the exchange rate.

A Monetary Disturbance

We complete the analysis of the adjustment process by studying a money supply increase. In the very short run, the effect of increased nominal money is to lower interest rates. The decline in interest rates and the induced depreciation serve to expand output immediately and thus, in terms of Figure 18-6, move us to region IV.[7] Inflation starts because of the overemployment, and depreciation continues because of the lowering of interest rates. Throughout, real balances are falling and the LM schedule is shifting back up toward its initial position. Output might initially expand further under the impact of depreciation, but soon the level of output has gone far above normal, so that inflation outstrips depreciation and demand starts declining. With declining demand and rising interest rates, the economy moves back to its initial equilibrium.

What is the long-run effect of the monetary expansion? In the long run, the economy returns to full employment and a monetary expansion has no lasting *real* effects. With prices fully flexible in the long run, a monetary expansion leads to an offsetting increase in prices, so that real balances ultimately remain unchanged.

But if prices rise, do we not lose competitiveness in that our goods become more expensive relative to foreign goods? In other words, would we not expect the terms of trade, eP^*/P, to improve as a result of the increase in P? Here the flexibility of exchange rates comes in. The exchange rate depreciates in precisely the same proportion as the price level rises, so that the terms of trade are unchanged and the competitive position of our goods relative to foreign goods is unaffected. Similarly, money and prices have changed in the same proportion, so that real balances, M/P, are unchanged. In long run, then, *money is entirely neutral* and monetary changes are offset by internal inflation and external depreciation.

But note that in the process of adjustment, the monetary expansion does have real effects. During the process of adjustment, output is above its full-employment level, the interest rate is below its equilibrium level, and the balance of payments is in deficit. These real effects of the monetary expansion are a consequence of the less than perfect flexibility of prices in the short run.

Purchasing Power Parity

The long-run neutrality of money discussed above illustrates the potential role of exchange rates in offsetting the effects of changes in the price level at home and abroad on the terms of trade. In the preceding analysis, the exchange rate rose by precisely the right amount to offset the effects of domestic inflation on the terms of trade. That is, the exchange depreciation maintained the *purchasing power* of our goods in terms of foreign goods between the initial and the final equilibrium positions.[8]

An important view of the determinants of the behaviour of the exchange rate is the theory that exchange rates move primarily in response to differences in price level behaviour between the two countries in such a way

[7] You will find it easier to follow this discussion if you draw your own diagram like Figure 18-8.

[8] Of course, the terms of trade were not constant along the adjustment path.

as to maintain the terms of trade constant. This is the *purchasing power parity* (PPP) theory. The theory argues that exchange rate movements primarily reflect divergent rates of inflation. Examining the terms of trade, eP^*/P, the theory maintains that when P^* and/or P change, e changes in such a way as to maintain eP^*/P constant.

PPP is a plausible description of the trend behaviour of exchange rates, especially when inflation differentials between countries are large. In particular, we have seen that the PPP relationship does hold in the face of an increase in the money stock. If price level movements are caused by monetary changes — as they are likely to be if the inflation rate is high — then we should expect PPP relationships to hold in the long term.[9]

But qualifications are necessary. First, even a monetary disturbance affects the terms of trade in the short run. Exchange rates tend to move quite rapidly relative to prices and thus, in the short term of a quarter or a year, we should not be at all surprised to see substantial deviations of exchange rates from the rates implied by PPP. And indeed, the terms of trade do move in the short run, as we shall see in Section 18-4.

The second important qualification concerns the role of nonmonetary disturbances in affecting exchange rates. For example, we saw that an increase in exports improves our terms of trade or leads to currency appreciation at unchanged domestic prices. Or, if we look at an increase in potential output as another example, we will find that the equilibrium terms of trade worsen. To absorb the increased output, demand must rise, implying a decline in the relative price of our goods. Thus, it is apparent that, over time, adjustments to *real* disturbances will affect the *equilibrium* terms of trade. Thus in the longer run, exchange rates and prices do *not* necessarily move together, as they do in a world where all disturbances are monetary. On the contrary, we may have important changes in relative prices. Such changes run counter to the purchasing power parity view of exchange rates.

As an empirical matter, then, PPP views of exchange rates will work well when, as frequently happens, monetary disturbances predominate. Thus PPP is an important explanation of some large exchange rate movements, particularly in hyperinflations. But not all exchange rate changes are caused by monetary disturbances, and PPP does not provide a good explanation for the short-run behaviour of exchange rates.

Summary

In this section we allowed for price flexibility as well as exchange rate flexibility. We assumed that the price level increases when output is above

---

[9] See "Purchasing Power Parity: A Symposium," *Journal of International Economics*, May 1978, for a review of the historical record on PPP.

the full-employment level and that the exchange rate appreciates when the interest rate is above the world level and there is therefore a capital inflow. The examination of real and monetary disturbances under flexible prices and exchange rates gave us the following results:

1   The price level and exchange rate adjustments affect the level of income and the interest rate. An increasing price level reduces real balances, tending to increase the interest rate. Changes in the price level and the exchange rate also affect the terms of trade and thus influence the demand for our goods.

2   An analysis of the dynamic process induced by these effects shows that the economy responds over time to disturbances, such as an increase in export demand or an increase in the money stock.

3   An increase in exports is ultimately totally offset in its effects on real income and the interest rate. However, both income and the interest rate differ from their long-run values during the adjustment process. The increase in exports leads in the long run to an appreciation of the exchange rate just sufficient to maintain net exports constant.

4   A monetary expansion in the long run increases the price level and the exchange rate, keeping real balances and the terms of trade constant. In the short run, though, the monetary expansion increases the level of output and reduces the interest rate, depreciating the exchange rate.

5   Purchasing power parity (PPP) theory argues that exchange rate changes are, in practice, caused by divergences in inflation rates between countries, with the exchange rate changing in a way that maintains the terms of trade constant. This theory is a good predictor of the behaviour of the exchange rate over long periods when disturbances are caused mainly by monetary factors, such as in hyperinflations. But in the short run, monetary disturbances are not neutral, and even in the long run, the exchange rate can change because there are real disturbances. Examples include changes in technology in different countries, shifts in export demand, and shifts in potential output.

We have now completed the core of this chapter. The remaining sections take up a number of issues that extend the basic analysis.

18-4 EXCHANGE RATE CONCEPTS

In this section we discuss two frequently used measures of exchange rates, the *effective exchange rate*, and the *real exchange rate*. These concepts are needed to provide a measure of exchange rate movements in a multiple currency world and to take account of the impact of inflation differentials on exchange rates respectively.

Effective Exchange Rates

The most conventional concept of an exchange rate is a *bilateral* exchange rate, such as the dollar price of yen or of Deutsche marks, or of sterling. In each case we talk about the dollar price of a particular foreign currency, figures we can find in the daily press. If we looked at these rates over any period, we would find, for example, that the dollar had depreciated relative to the Deutsche mark, appreciated relative to the yen, and remained unchanged relative to sterling. How would we summarize such a situation by a simple statement about "the" exchange rate? The concept that has been developed to cope with this problem is the *effective exchange rate index*. This is an index for the dollar price of a "basket" of foreign currencies, each currency being given a particular weight, which we shall discuss. Table 18-2 gives an example of how effective rates are calculated.

In Table 18-2, we assume three foreign currencies: yen, (Y), Deutsche marks (DM), and pounds sterling (£). We assume that the weights attached to these currencies, respectively, are 0.3, 0.2, and 0.5, and thus sum to 1. Suppose now that our base year is 1970. In the base year we set the dollar price of each foreign currency equal to 100, and thus the index equals 100 (= 0.3 × 100 + 0.2 × 100 + 0.5 × 100). Next consider the year 1980 where our hypothetical exchange rates have moved, with the dollar price of the yen rising by 100 percent and that of the Deutsche mark by 200 percent, while the dollar price of sterling has declined by 25 percent. In the second row, we show an index for each of the bilateral exchange rates (200, 300, 75) and th3 effective exchange rate as the weighted sum of these bilateral indexes. The effective exchange rate in our example has risen from the base year level of 100 to 157.5 (= 0.3 × 200 + 0.2 × 300 + 0.5 × 75).[10]

The effective exchange rate index thus serves as a summary measure of the "average" cost of foreign exchange where the nature of the average is determined by two considerations: First, the number of foreign currencies we choose in our basket and second, the weights given to each particular currency. In practice, the commonly used effective exchange rate indexes

---

[10] This is an index of the domestic currency price of foreign exchange so that an increase indicates a depreciation.

TABLE 18-2 BILATERAL AND EFFECTIVE EXCHANGE RATE INDEXES: AN EXAMPLE

	Bilateral rates and indexes			Effective rate index
	Y	DM	£	
1970	$0.0025 = 100	$0.25 = 100	$2.4 = 100	100
1980	$0.0050 = 200	$0.75 = 300	$1.8 = 75	157.5

are based on a basket containing fifteen to twenty of the major currencies. The exact dividing line, as will become clear presently, is not really very important. The important issue is that of weights. We would want an effective exchange rate index to represent a relevant measure of the cost of foreign exchange. Accordingly, currencies of countries which are relatively unimportant in our external trade should receive a small weight and currencies of important trading partners should receive a more substantial weight. This perspective leads to a weighting system that uses bilateral trade flows as a basis. For example, if the United States accounts for 70 percent of our exports and imports, the U.S. dollar receives a weight of 0.7, while Britain is much less important in our trade and may receive a weight of only 0.1 or less.

Table 18-3 shows the effective exchange rate index for the Canadian dollar. The table reveals that the Canadian dollar has depreciated even more in relation to other major currencies than it has in relation to the U.S. dollar. This of course reflects the fact that the U.S. dollar has depreciated relative to other major currencies.

Real Effective Exchange Rates

We have now found a simple summary measure of "the" exchange rate in the form of an effective exchange rate index. The next step is to find a corresponding simple measure of changes in competitiveness, that is, the costs of our goods *relative* to those produced by countries that compete with us in international trade. Such a measure must recognize two important facts: First, we are dealing with a multicountry situation and thus have to use an average measure that is representative of our position relative to our most important trading partners. Second, we must recognize that exchange rate movements do not signal one-for-one changes in competitiveness because they may merely be the counterpart of differing national price level trends. We saw this point in the discussion of purchasing power parity in Section 18-2.

TABLE 18-3 INDEXES OF THE EXCHANGE RATE

	1970	1973	1976	1979
Price of Canadian dollar in:				
United States	96.8	101.0	102.4	86.2
Other Group of Ten Countries[1]	99.3	87.4	102.6	69.5
Total Group of Ten Countries	97.3	97.9	102.5	82.4

Source: Department of Finance, *Economic Review.*

[1] The Group of Ten countries comprise Belgium, Canada, France, Germany, Italy, Japan, the Netherlands, Sweden, the United Kingdom, and the United States, plus Switzerland.

The concept we are looking for is an effective price-adjusted exchange rate index. Such a measure would compare the domestic price of our goods with the "average" price of goods of our competitors measured in our currency. It thus corresponds to a many-country version of the relative price concept, or the terms of trade.

Price-adjusted or *real* effective exchange rates are constructed with the same weighting system as nominal effective rates. The novel point concerns the price adjustment, as we show in Table 18-4.

The first column of Table 18-4 shows the hypothetical development of the Canadian price level as measured by an index such as the CPI. Next, we look abroad. Here P^* shows the development of the foreign price level in foreign currency. Foreign prices in our example rise by 50 percent. The dollar price of foreign exchange, e, rises by 70 percent; thus, the index of the domestic currency price of foreign goods, $eP^*/100$, rises from 100 to 255, reflecting partially foreign inflation and partially the depreciation of our currency. Now what happens to relative prices? The last column shows the ratio eP^*/P. From the base year level of 100, the relative price of foreign goods rises, since the index for 1980 is 127.5. The real rate index shows a gain in competitiveness by the home country.

Where does the gain in competitiveness in our example come from? It derives from the fact that the exchange depreciation of 70 percent exceeds the inflation differential of 50 percent. Thus the exchange depreciation *more than offsets* the inflation differential and leaves the home country with a gain in competitiveness.

We turn next from our hypothetical example to the actual evolution of real exchange rates. Chart 18-3 shows indexes of the nominal and real exchange rate of the Canadian dollar in relation to the U.S. dollar. From 1954 to 1967 similar inflation rates were experienced in the two countries so that the two indexes moved together. The U.S. rate of inflation was above the Canadian rate during the period 1968 to 1971, and this is reflected in a depreciation of the real rate in 1968 and 1969. Following the floating of the Canadian dollar in 1970, there was a sharp appreciation of the nominal rate which dominated the movement of the real rate. From 1972 to 1976, the Canadian inflation rate was substantially above the U.S. rate, and the real exchange rate appreciated until late 1976 when the nominal rate began to

TABLE 18-4 REAL EXCHANGE RATE INDEX: AN EXAMPLE

	Canada	Abroad			Real rate
	P	P^*	e	$eP^*/100$	eP^*/P
1970	100	100	100	100	100
1980	200	150	170	255	127.5

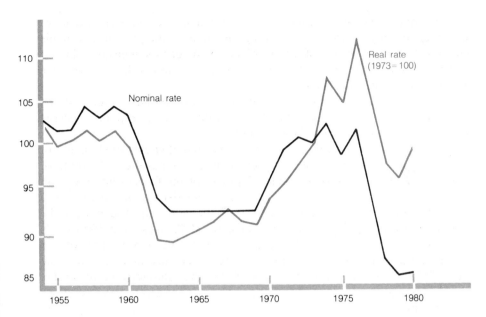

CHART 18-3 NOMINAL AND REAL EXCHANGE RATE OF THE CANADIAN DOLLAR IN
TERMS OF THE U.S. DOLLAR
(*Source*: Dept. of Finance, *Economic Review*; U.S. Dept. of Commerce, *Survey of Current
Business*)

move down. By 1979, Canada's competitive position had been restored to
the 1971 level.

Chart 18-3 is of interest with respect to our discussion of purchasing
power parity. The chart shows both long-term changes in the real exchange
rate and considerable short-term variation. On neither count is the purchasing power parity relationship strong.

18-5 THE PERFORMANCE OF THE CANADIAN ECONOMY UNDER FLEXIBLE EXCHANGE RATES

Over the past 30 years Canada has operated under both fixed and flexible
exchange rate regimes. A flexible rate was in effect from 1950 to mid-1962
and from mid-1970 to the present. In this section we examine the performance of the Canadian economy in these two periods.

The Canadian Economy, 1953-1961

Chart 18-4 shows the performance of the Canadian economy over the period
1953-1961. There was a sharp but brief recession in 1954 followed by an

CHART 18-4 THE CANADIAN ECONOMY, 1953-1961
(*Source*: Dept. of Finance, *Economic Review*; Statistics Canada, 11-206).

investment boom in 1955 and 1956, which resulted in rapid growth in GNP and a decline in the unemployment rate below 4 percent. In 1957 the growth rate slowed and the unemployment rate rose sharply. The entire period from 1957 to 1961 was characterized by slow growth and relatively high unemployment.

The major feature of the balance of payments over the years 1953 to 1961 was the large capital inflow stimulated by the attractive investment opportunities that existed in Canada (See Chart 17-1 on page 487). As can be seen in Chart 18-1 on page 527, the effect of this capital account surplus was to push up the value of the Canadian dollar, which remained above 100 U.S. cents and at times rose as high as 105 U.S. cents. This, in turn, had the effect of reducing exports and increasing imports so that there was a deficit on merchandise trade with the exception of the recession year 1954.

During the boom years, 1956 and 1957, the appreciation of the Canadian dollar acted as a stabilizer and had a desirable dampening effect on aggregate demand. The economy was subject to expansionary real disturbances as represented by the outward shift in the IS schedule shown in Figure 18-3 on page 537. The effect of this is represented by the movement from E to E′ in the figure. At E′ we have a higher value of the Canadian dollar, and therefore we get a deterioration of the trade balance and a movement of the IS curve back towards E.

The question that remains is why did the Canadian economy go through a prolonged period of slow growth and high unemployment during the years 1957 to 1961. There was an effort to stimulate the economy in 1958 and 1959 through expansionary fiscal policy shown by the movement of the cyclically adjusted federal budget balance in Chart 18-4. However, as we saw on page 538, we would not expect fiscal policy to have a lasting effect on income under a flexible exchange rate. An increase in the government deficit leads to a crowding out of private demand in the form of net exports. Clearly, it is necessary for a country with a flexible exchange rate to use monetary policy for stabilization purposes.

How was monetary policy used during this period? During 1958, the money supply expanded at a rapid rate, but this policy was reversed in 1959 and 1960 so that the average rate of growth over the three years was under 3 percent. This was well below the growth in real output, and as a result interest rates rose sharply in 1959 and remained relatively high until mid-1961. Thus, the period 1959 to 1961 was characterized by a very restrictive monetary policy in spite of a clear need for economic stimulus.

The analysis of a monetary disturbance depicted in Figure 18-4 provides an explanation of the behaviour of the Canadian economy during this period. Consider Figure 18-9 in which the point E is assumed to represent equilibrium at the full-employment level of output. The adoption of restrictive monetary policy means the LM schedule shifts up and to the left to LM′ and the economy tends to move to E′ where we have a higher interest rate and output below the initial (full-employment) level. The higher interest rate

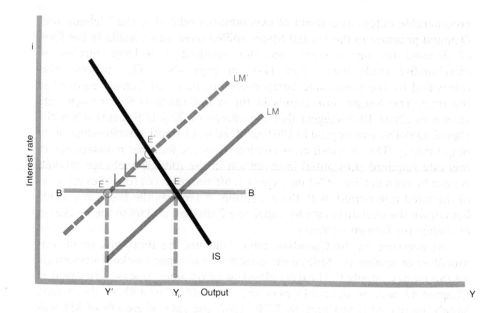

FIGURE 18-9 EFFECTS OF A RESTRICTIVE MONETARY POLICY

and output below the initial (full-employment) level. The higher interest rate induces a capital account surplus and an appreciation of the exchange rate. As a result, the trade account moves toward a deficit position so that the IS curve shifts in and to the left and the economy moves toward E″. This adjustment process is quite consistent with the observed behaviour of the Canadian economy over the period 1959 to 1961.

Thus we conclude that mistakes in monetary policy were largely responsible for the stagnation of the Canadian economy in the late fifties and early sixties. There was indeed considerable controversy at the time, and, in 1960, a group of academic economists called upon the minister of finance to dismiss the governor of the Bank of Canada. Subsequently, there was an acrimonious confrontation between the minister and the governor, and the latter was finally replaced in July of 1961.[11]

The Canadian Economy in the 1970s

The inflation problem of the 1970s has its origins in the second half of the 1960s when the U.S. economy was experiencing boom conditions to a

[11] See H. Scott Gordon, *The Economists Versus the Bank of Canada*, (Toronto: The Ryerson Press, 1961).

considerable extent as a result of expenditures related to the Vietnam war. Demand pressure in the United States spilled over into Canada in the form of demand for our exports, and this resulted in a large surplus on merchandise trade (see Chart 17-1 on page 487). This process was intensified by the favourable competitive position that Canada enjoyed at the time. The longer term trends in the *real* Canada-U.S. exchange rate shown in Chart 18-3 suggest that the choice of 92.5 U.S. cents when the Canadian dollar was pegged in 1962 involved a substantial undervaluation of our currency. This proposition is confirmed by the fact that maintenance of this rate required substantial intervention in the foreign exchange market. As can be seen in Chart 17-1 on page 487, official reserves rose in every year of the fixed rate period, with the exception of 1966, as the Bank of Canada held down the exchange rate by supplying Canadian dollars to the market in exchange for foreign currency.

As pressure on the Canadian dollar built up, the Bank of Canada was unwilling or unable to sterilize the effects of exchange market intervention on the money supply.[12] Thus the classical adjustment process discussed in Chapter 17 was brought into play and the rate of growth of the money supply increased (see Chart 18-5). In 1967, the rate of growth of M1 was nearly 10 percent as compared with an average of about 5 percent between 1960 and 1964. In 1968, the inflationary pressure was intensified by an acceleration of inflation in the United States. As pointed out in Section 18-4 above, the U.S. inflation rate was above the Canadian rate from 1968 to 1972.

The freeing of the Canadian dollar in 1970 provided the Bank of Canada with an opportunity to stem the inflationary pressures. The rate of growth of the money supply was sharply curtailed and the inflation rate eased thereafter. As would be expected, there was a substantial appreciation of the Canadian dollar. However, shortly after the Bank of Canada had freed itself from the restrictions imposed by a fixed exchange rate and made substantial progress in bringing inflation under control, it appears to have become reluctant to exploit the benefits of a flexible rate.

To begin with, the Bank of Canada attempted to resist the appreciation of the Canadian dollar in 1970 and 1971 by intervening heavily in the foreign exchange market. This is reflected in the large increase in official reserves shown in Chart 17-1 on page 487. A substantial appreciation was required to restore the real exchange rate to its equilibrium level, and intervention to prevent this from taking place intensified inflationary pressure in Canada.

The second error in policy was the sharp turnaround in monetary policy that occurred in 1971. Subsequent events indicated that the Bank of Canada overreacted to the slowdown in economic activity and rising unemployment experienced in 1970. As can be seen in Chart 18-5, the rate of growth of M1

---

[12] Sterilization is defined on page 506.

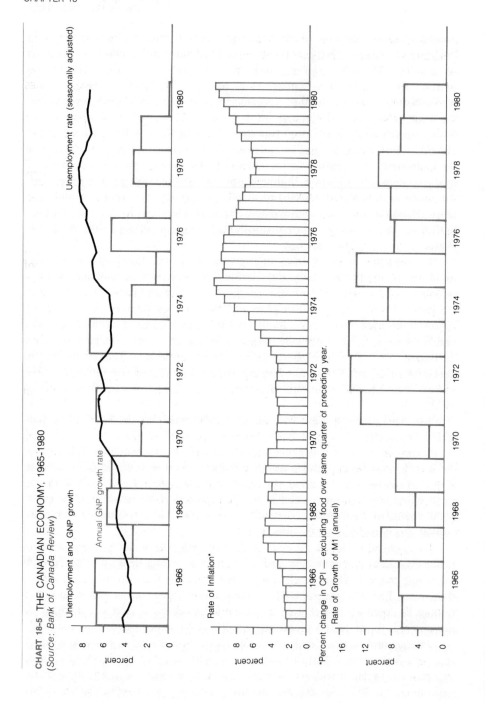

CHART 18-5 THE CANADIAN ECONOMY, 1965-1980
(Source: Bank of Canada Review)

shot up to a level close to 13 percent in 1971 and rose to 14 percent in 1972. In 1973, there was a sharp increase in the inflation rate, and by 1975 the consumer price index was rising at a rate in excess of 10 percent. There was an increase in the rate of inflation in the United States as well but the acceleration was more rapid in Canada. As shown in Chart 18-3, the nominal exchange rate was held close to 100 U.S. cents over the period 1972 to 1976 while the difference in inflation rates lead to a substantial appreciation of the real rate.

In retrospect, it appears that Canada missed an opportunity to avoid at least some of the inflation that plagued the world economy in the 1970s. Monetary policy was immobilized in the late sixties by a commitment to a fixed exchange rate at a time when inflation rates began to rise in other countries. In the early 1970s the full benefits of a flexible rate were not realized, since the Bank of Canada resisted the appreciation of the Canadian dollar. It appears to have been influenced by a misguided concern for the effect of an appreciation on the competitive position of Canada's export industries. This led the Bank to hold down the appreciation by direct intervention in 1970 and 1971, and to stabilize the rate near 100 U.S. cents in 1972 and 1973 by permitting a rapid rate of growth in the money supply. As indicated by the discussion of a money supply increase on page 539, the short-run effect of an expansionary monetary policy is to hold down the exchange rate. However, the longer-run consequence is an increase in prices which restores the competitive position of domestic industries to the equilibrium level. In this case, the monetary expansion induced an overshooting of the price level and an appreciation of the real exchange rate which was reversed by the depreciation that began in late 1976.

A second reason for the mismanagement of monetary policy in the early 1970s was the delayed recognition of the importance of controlling the rate of growth of the money supply. As indicated in Chapter 15, it was not until 1973, when inflationary forces were already entrenched, that the Bank of Canada began to move towards greater emphasis on control of the money supply and explicit target rates of growth were not adopted until late 1975.

18-6 INTEREST DIFFERENTIALS AND EXCHANGE RATE EXPECTATIONS

A cornerstone of our theoretical model of exchange rate determination in Sections 18-2 and 18-3 was international capital mobility. In particular, we argued that with capital markets sufficiently integrated, we would expect interest rates to be equated across countries. How does this assumption stand up to the facts? In Chart 18-6, we show Canadian and U.S. interest rates on 90-day paper. It is quite apparent from the chart that these rates are not equalized. Exchange rate expectations provide the key to squaring this fact with our theory. The bottom panel of the chart shows the interest differential adjusted for exchange rate expectations as reflected in *forward*

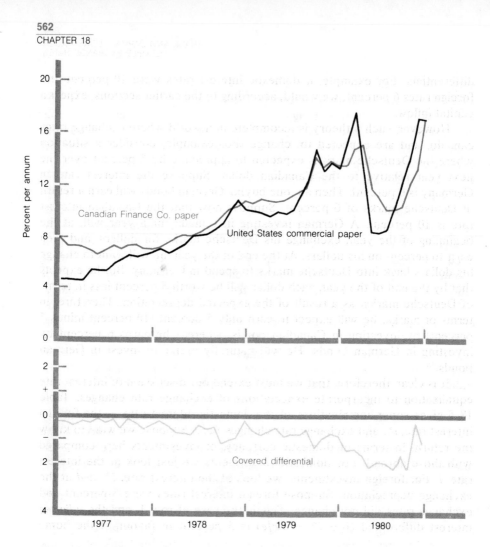

CHART 18-6 INTEREST RATES ON 90-DAY PAPER
(*Source: Bank of Canada Review*)

contracts in foreign exchange. This so-called *covered differential*, which represents the yield difference with no exchange rate risk, is much smaller than the spread between the uncovered rates. Let us examine the role of exchange rate expectations in some detail.

Exchange Rate Expectations

Our theoretical analysis in Sections 18-2 and 18-3 was based on the assumption that capital flows internationally in response to nominal interest differentials. For example, if domestic interest rates were 10 percent and foreign rates 6 percent, we would, according to the earlier sections, expect a capital inflow.

However, such a theory is incomplete in a world where exchange rates can, do, and are expected to, change. For example, consider a situation where the Deutsche mark is expected to appreciate by 5 percent over the next year relative to the Canadian dollar. Suppose the interest rate in Germany is 6 percent. Then anyone buying German bonds will earn a return in Deutsche marks of 6 percent. Suppose now that the Canadian interest rate is 10 percent. A German investing in Canada for a year will, at the beginning of the year, exchange his Deutsche marks for dollars, and then earn 10 percent on his dollars. At the end of the year, he will want to change his dollars back into Deutsche marks to spend in Germany. But he expects that by the end of the year, each dollar will be worth 5 percent less in terms of Deutsche marks, as a result of the expected depreciation. Therefore, in terms of marks, he will expect to earn only 5 percent (10 percent minus 5 percent) by investing in Canadian bonds, whereas he earns 6 percent by investing in German bonds. He will naturally prefer to invest in German bonds.[13]

It is clear, therefore, that we must extend our discussion of interest rate equalization to incorporate expectations of exchange rate changes. Table 18-5 gives some combinations of the domestic interest rate, i, the foreign interest rate, i^*, and exchange rate changes $\Delta e/e$. Suppose we want to know the return, in terms of domestic currency, of investments here compared with those abroad. For domestic investments we just look at the interest rate, i. For foreign investments, we look at the interest rate, i^*, *and* at the exchange depreciation. Suppose foreign interest rates were 5 percent and exchange rates did not change. This is the case of row 1, and the *adjusted* interest differential ($i - i^* - \Delta e/e$) is 5 percent in favour of the home

[13] You should confirm that a Canadian who expects the dollar to depreciate by 5 percent would, given the 6 percent and 10 percent interest rates, also prefer to buy German bonds.

TABLE 18-5 INTEREST RATES AND EXCHANGE DEPRECIATION (*in percentages*)

	Domestic interest rate, i	Foreign interest rate, i^*	Depreciation, $\Delta e/e$	Adjusted interest differential $i - i^* - \Delta e/e$
1.	10	5	0	5
2.	10	15	-5	0
3.	10	15	-2	-3
4.	10	15	-10	5

country. Row 2 considers the case where interest rates abroad are high (15 percent), but where our currency appreciates at the rate of 5 percent or the foreign currency depreciates by that amount. Here the depreciation exactly offsets the higher foreign interest rates and the adjusted differential is zero — what would be gained in interest is lost through the foreign depreciation. Cases 3 and 4 show circumstances where the foreign depreciation falls short of, and exceeds, the interest differential, respectively. Clearly, in cases 1 and 4, we would want to invest in the home country; in case 2 we are indifferent; and case 3 favours the foreign country.

The trouble, of course, is that we do not know ahead of time how the exchange rate will move. We know the interest rates on, say, three-month treasury bills in Canada and the United Kingdom, so that we can compute the interest differential, but we do not know whether the pound will appreciate or depreciate over the next three months. Even if we somehow knew the direction, we would certainly not know the precise amount.

Investors then have to form *expectations* about the behaviour of the exchange rate; that is, in deciding whether to invest at home or abroad, they have to make forecasts of the future behaviour of the exchange rate. Given these forecasts, we would expect that in a world of high capital mobility, the interest differentials, adjusted for expected depreciation, should be negligible. That means that, a country that is certain to depreciate will have interest rates above the world level, and conversely, a country that is expected to appreciate will have interest rates below the world level.

The adjustment for exchange rate expectations thus accounts for international differences in interest rates. These differences are by and large due to differences in inflation rates and are reflected in trend movements of the exchange rate. High-inflation countries have high interest rates and depreciating currencies. We thus have an international extension of the Fisher effect discussed in Chapter 13. The international extension relies on PPP to argue that inflation differentials internationally are matched by depreciation. Our long-term relation then is

Inflation differential $\simeq$ interest differential $\simeq$ depreciation rate

The relation is only approximate because, as we have seen, exchange rates can move independently of prices and also because obstacles to capital flows may create long-term interest differentials.

There is another respect in which the introduction of exchange rate expectations is important and that concerns speculative capital flows and their impact on macroeconomic equilibrium. The point is easily made with the help of Figure 18-10. Here the BB schedule is drawn for a given foreign interest rate *and* a given expected rate of change for the exchange rate, say zero for simplicity. Suppose that we start in full equilibrium at point *E* and that the market develops the expectation that the home currency will appreciate. This implies that even with a lower home interest rate, domestic

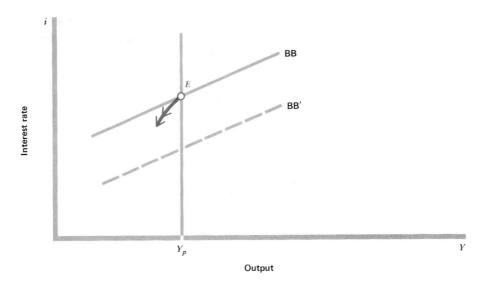

FIGURE 18-10 RESPONSE TO AN EXPECTED APPRECIATION OF THE DOMESTIC
CURRENCY

assets are attractive and so the BB schedule shifts down by the amount of
expected appreciation. Clearly, point E is no longer an equilibrium, given the
shift of the BB schedule to BB', but rather a position of surplus with
large-scale capital inflows motivated by the anticipation of appreciation.
(This might well describe the case of the United Kingdom after awareness of
British oil discoveries spread in the market.) The surplus causes the
exchange rate to start appreciating, and we move in a southwesterly
direction, as indicated by the arrow. The speculative attack causes appreciation, a loss in competitiveness, and consequently, falling output and employment.

This analysis shows that exchange rate expectations, through their
impact on capital flows and thus on actual exchange rates, are a potential
source of disturbance to macroeconomic equilibrium.

*18-7 EXCHANGE RATE CHANGES AND TRADE
ADJUSTMENT: TWO EMPIRICAL ISSUES

In this section we complete our analysis by taking up two important
empirical issues related to the scope for current account adjustment through
exchange rate changes. In our theoretical model of Section 18-2, we
assumed that prices here and abroad were fixed, so that exchange rate
changes affected relative prices one for one. In Section 18-3, by contrast, we

explored a world where prices (and wages) are flexible and full employment is maintained in the long run. In this section, we consider the alternative possibility that wages and prices are flexible but that they may respond to movements in the exchange rate in a way that makes it impossible or at least difficult to change relative prices through exchange rate changes. This issue is particularly important if formal wage indexation arrangements link wage behaviour to import prices and thus to the exchange rate.

The second issue we consider is whether changes in relative prices, assuming that they are possible, will affect the current account in the direction we have so far assumed. The assumption, so far, has been that a decline in the relative price of our goods improves the current account. But the possibility arises that at least in the short run there might be a perverse reaction. With import prices rising, for example, import demand may not decline sufficiently to compensate for higher prices, and thus total import spending (price times quantity) may actually increase. We turn now to these two issues.

Exchange Rates and Relative Price Adjustment

In studying the flexible wage-price model of Section 18-3, we assumed that wages and prices adjust to achieve full employment. Now we consider as an alternative the possibility that prices are based on labour cost or wages and that wages are inflexible in real terms. Suppose that labour wants to maintain the purchasing power of wages or to keep real wages constant. In such a world, changes in the cost of living would lead to changes in money wages, in labour cost, and therefore in prices, which in turn feed back into wages. Two points emerge from this description. The first is that in such a world, we may not be able to get to full employment. Labour may set the real wage too high and, at least in the intermediate run, the full-employment level of output cannot be sustained. The second point is that a process in which changes in prices feed back into wages and from there into prices is one of a *wage-price spiral* that may produce considerable volatility in the price level. Small disturbances can set off quite large changes in the price level.

Suppose, first, that the real wage is fixed in terms of the consumer price index that includes both domestic goods and imports. Let us assume, second, that changes in the consumer price index are fully passed on into wages, and, third, that changes in wages are fully passed on into increased domestic prices. Now assume that starting from an initial equilibrium, there is an exchange depreciation brought about by some short-term, reversible disturbance. The depreciation raises import prices and thereby has a direct effect on consumer prices and wages. To maintain the purchasing power of their wages, workers increase money wages and firms pass on the wage increase into higher prices. Where are we after the process ends? Real wages are constant, which means wages and the price level (a weighted average of the prices of domestic and imported goods) have risen in the same proportion; wage increases have been fully passed on, which means that real wages *in terms of domestic output* are also unchanged. The two results imply that relative prices are unchanged, or that the exchange depreciation is fully matched by domestic inflation.

Of course, this is not really the end because we have to ask how the higher price level affects the macroeconomic equilibrium. To the extent that lower real balances lower aggregate demand, we would have a reduction in employment. To round out our story, we can imagine that the central bank steps in to prevent unemployment by raising the money stock. If nominal money rises in proportion to the price increase, then the full-employment equilibrium, at the same terms of trade, is reestablished but, of course, at a higher level of wages and prices. This is an economy where there is very little stability in the price level because the slightest change in exchange rate expectations leads to actual exchange rate movements that are fully *validated* by domestic wage, price and monetary developments.

A second context in which the idea of sticky real wages is important is that of real disturbances. Suppose our export demand declines permanently because of, say, the introduction of superior technology abroad. To return to full employment, we saw in Section 18-3 that the relative price of our goods must fall so as to encourage foreign demand. But how can the relative price fall? In Section 18-3, we argued that the exchange rate will depreciate, thereby raising import prices relative to domestic prices and restoring our competitiveness. In the present context we have to recognize that import price increases would be immediately matched by wage increases and that these wage increases would be fully passed on into price increases. Relative prices cannot change. The consequences would, of course, be protracted unemployment. Unemployment would continue until the *real* wage declines.

The empirical question, then, is, How flexible are real wages? This is, to an important extent, a question of institutional arrangements. In small open economies with substantial cost-of-living indexation in wage agreements, it may indeed be very difficult to change real wages and relative prices through exchange rate changes. The governor of the Bank of Canada has argued that this problem is of some importance in Canada. For example, in a speech given in November, 1980, Governor Bouey stated:[14]

> In certain circumstances, for example, a significant decline in the exchange value of the Canadian dollar brought about by unusual interest rate relationships between Canada and the United States would not only add almost immediately to the upward pressure on prices and spending but would also, before long, threaten to put increased upward pressure as well on negotiated wage settlements and thus on our on-going costs of production.

---

[14] See *Bank of Canada Review*, November, 1980, p. 10.

Relative Prices and the Trade Balance: The J Curve

We come now to the second issue, the effect of changes in relative prices on the trade balance and the possibility that a depreciation worsens the trade balance. To make this point, we write out the trade balance, measured in terms of domestic goods, as

$$NX = X - \frac{eP^*}{P} \cdot Q \tag{6}$$

where X denotes the foreign demand for our goods or exports and Q denotes our own import quantity. The term $(eP^*/P)Q$ thus measures the *value* of our imports in terms of domestic goods.

Suppose that we now have an exchange depreciation and that in the first instance, domestic and foreign prices, P and P^*, are unchanged. Then the relative price of imports, eP^*/P, rises. This leads to two effects. First, if the physical *volume* of imports does not change, their value measured in domestic currency unambiguously increases because of the higher price. With unchanged physical import volume, Q, higher prices mean increased import spending and thus a worsening of the trade balance. This is the source for the potentially perverse response of the trade balance to exchange depreciation. However, there is an adjustment that runs in the opposite direction. The increased relative price of imports makes us more competitive and shifts demand in volume terms toward domestic goods. This *volume effect* of substitution in response to changed relative prices shows up in Equation (6) in the form of increased export volume, X, and reduced import volume, Q. The volume effects thus unambiguously improve the trade balance.

The question, then, is whether the volume effects on imports and exports are sufficiently strong to outweigh the price effect, that is, whether depreciation raises or lowers net exports. The empirical evidence on this question is quite strong and shows the following result: The short-term volume effects, say within a year, are quite small and thus do not outweigh the price effect.[15] The long-term volume effects, by contrast, are quite substantial, and certainly enough to make the trade balance respond in the normal fashion to a relative price change.

Where does this asymmetry come from and what does it imply about trade adjustment to relative prices? First, the low short-term and high longer-term volume effects result from the time consumers and producers take to adjust to changes in relative prices. Some of these adjustments may be instantaneous, but it is clear that tourism patterns, for example, may take

---

[15] See Michael C. Deppler and Duncan M. Ripley, "The World Trade Model: Merchandise Trade," *IMF Staff Papers*, March 1978.

six months to a year to adjust and that relocation of production internationally, in response to changes in relative costs and prices, may take years. A case in point is increased foreign direct investment in Canada — say, Volvo moving assembly operations from Sweden to Nova Scotia. In the long term, such direct investment leads to reduced Volvo imports by Canada, and thus to an improved trade balance, but such an adjustment takes years, not weeks or months.

The lag in the adjustment of trade flows to changes in relative prices is thus quite plausible. The next question is, What do these lags imply about the impact of relative price changes on the trade balance? Suppose that at a particular time, starting with a deficit, we have a depreciation that raises the relative price of imports. The short-term effects results primarily from increased import prices with very little offsetting volume effects. Therefore, the trade balance initially worsens. Over time, as trade volume adjusts to the changed relative prices, exports rise and import volume progressively declines. The volume effects come to dominate, and in the long run, the trade balance shows an improvement. This pattern of adjustment is referred to as the *J-curve effect*, because diagrammatically the response of the trade balance looks like a *J*.

The medium-term problem of sticky real wages and the J-curve effect are important qualifications to the macroeconomics of flexible rates as spelled out in Sections 18-2 and 18-3. They imply that flexible exchange rates do not provide for instant, costless flexibility of relative prices and trade flows. At the same time, these considerations provide important clues for the interpretation of macroeconomic experiences across countries, particularly in showing why depreciations typically do not lead to improvements in the current account in the short term.

18-8 EXCHANGE RATE FLUCTUATIONS

We asked at the start of the chapter why exchange rates have fluctuated so much in the period since 1973, why central banks have intervened to affect exchange rates, and whether such dirty floating is desirable. The material covered in the preceding sections helps provide answers to these questions.

Before we briefly examine the volatility of exchange rates since the flexible rate system emerged, we should warn you that the discerning eye appears to detect cycles where statistical techniques cannot. It is difficult to establish, from the short experience we have had with flexible rates, that exchange rates under a flexible rate system will indeed cycle in the future. All we can say is that in the past few years, exchange rates have made large movements that were subsequently reversed.

The trend changes in exchange rates observed in Table 18-3 can be largely attributed to divergent inflation rates among Canada and other countries, but there remains the big issue of short-term fluctuations. We showed in Section 18-6 that the mere expectation of a change in exchange rates can lead to an actual change. Some of the movements in rates seen in Chart 18-2 result from expectations of exchange rate changes that reversed themselves. Such reversals are not necessarily a sign that the original expectations were unreasonable. For instance, it appeared during 1978 that the United States wanted the dollar to continue depreciating against other major currencies, particularly the yen and the Deutsch mark. Then, in November 1978, after substantial depreciation had taken place, the United States announced a package of measures designed to reverse the depreciation. The dollar exchange rate actually appreciated in response. Clearly, the new policy reversed expectations about the behaviour of the dollar exchange rate — but that reversal was fully justified by the new information the change in policy provided.

Central banks intervene to affect exchange rates for several reasons. Probably the main reason is the belief that many capital flows merely represent unstable expectations, and that the induced movements in exchange rates move production in the economy in an unnecessarily erratic fashion. The second reason for the intervention is a central bank's attempt to move the real exchange rate in order to affect trade flows. The third reason arises from the effects of the exchange rate on domestic inflation, which we mentioned in Section 18-7. Central banks sometimes intervene in the exchange market to prevent the exchange rate from depreciating, with the aim of preventing a depreciation-induced increase in the inflation rate.

Should central banks intervene in the exchange market? The basic argument for such intervention is that it is possible for intervention to smooth out fluctuations in exchange rates. At one extreme, the argument would assert that any movements in exchange rates produce unnecessary fluctuations in the domestic economy and that exchange rates therefore ought to be fixed. This is the basic argument for dirty floating. The only — and overwhelming — objection to the argument that the central bank should smooth out fluctuations is that there is no simple way of telling an erratic movement from a trend movement. How can we tell whether a current appreciation in the exchange rate is merely the result of a disturbance which will soon reverse itself, rather than the beginning of a trend movement in the exchange rate? There is no way of telling at the time a change occurs, although with the benefit of hindsight, one can easily look at diagrams like Chart 18-1 to see which exchange rate movements were later reversed.

There is one circumstance under which central bank intervention might be desirable. It is clear from our earlier analysis that one of the key determinants of exchange rate behaviour consists of expectations of economic policy. It may sometimes be possible to make it clear that there has been a change in policy only by intervening in the foreign exchange market. This is a case of putting your money where your mouth is.

18-9 SUMMARY

1 Under flexible exchange rates, without government intervention, the exchange rate adjusts to ensure equilibrium in the overall balance of payments. The sum of the current and capital account deficits is zero with floating rates and no intervention.

2 The demand for our goods depends on the exchange rate which, given foreign and domestic prices, affects the relative price of imports versus exports. An increase in the exchange rate — a depreciation — increases the demand for domestically produced goods by reducing imports and increasing exports.

3 When capital is very mobile, so that the interest rate essentially cannot differ from the world rate, fiscal policy becomes totally ineffective in changing the level of income. An increase in government spending merely reduces net exports, with the trade deficit being financed by a capital inflow.

4 Monetary policy — given prices — retains its effectiveness when capital is very mobile. An increase in the money stock leads to a depreciation of the exchange rate and an improved foreign balance, which increases demand for domestic output.

5 If an economy finds itself with unemployment, the central bank can intervene to depreciate the exchange rate and increase net exports and thus aggregate demand. Such policies are known as beggar-thy-neighbour policies, because the increase in demand for domestic output comes at the expense of demand for foreign output.

6 In the long run, exchange rate movements in the absence of real disturbances reflect changes in the price levels in the two countries concerned. A country with a more rapid rate of inflation will find its exchange rate depreciating against the currency of a country which is inflating less rapidly. The exchange rate movements induced by the price level changes merely keep the relative prices of goods produced in the two countries constant.

7 The effective exchange rate is an index of the domestic currency price of foreign exchange. The weights of the different currencies in the basket reflect their relative importance in trade.

8 Real effective exchange rates are an index of competitiveness. The real effective exchange rate index measures the extent to which the prices of foreign goods, adjusted for exchange rate changes, move relative to the prices of our goods.

9 Exchange rate expectations introduce divergences among nominal interest rates internationally. The international interest differential equals the anticipated rate of depreciation when capital is highly mobile. A country that is expected to have a depreciating currency will

have higher nominal interest rates than the rest of the world.

10 A currency depreciation can, in the short run, lead to a worsening of the trade balance. This occurs when the effect of changes in relative prices on the volume of trade is small because adjustments take time. Over time, trade adjusts and the depreciation improves the trade balance. This is called the J-curve effect.

11 Because it raises important prices, depreciation of the exchange rate raises the cost of living and may spill over into increased wage demands. If such spillovers are substantial, then a flexible rate system will have large movements in nominal prices and exchange rate movements may perform poorly in bringing about relative price changes.

12 Since the 1973 beginning of the flexible rate system, there have been substantial fluctuations in exchange rates. These movements are hard to explain. They affect the allocation of resources. A central bank which wants to intervene to smooth out the fluctuations has to know when an exchange rate change is going to be reversed and when it is permanent. For this reason, foreign exchange intervention to smooth out exchange rate fluctuations is extremely difficult.

PROBLEMS

1 Explain why the belief that a devaluation is imminent makes a devaluation more likely in a fixed exchange rate system.

2 Why do you think countries were reluctant to move away from the system of fixed exchange rates during the late sixties and early seventies, even though it was by then not operating very well? Also explain what "not operating very well" means.

3 Explain why an expansionary fiscal policy "beggars our neighbours" less than direct intervention by the central bank in the foreign exchange markets to depreciate the exchange rate.

4 Assuming there are no capital flows, explain how an increase in the domestic interest rate (which we have assumed fixed, so far) affects the level of income and the exchange rate. How could the domestic interest rate be changed?

5 (a) What are the terms of trade?
  (b) Why does expansionary policy affect the terms of trade in a floating exchange rate system?

6 Assume that capital is perfectly mobile, the price level is fixed, and the exchange rate is flexible. Now let the government increase purchases. Explain first why the equilibrium levels of output and the interest rate are unaffected. Then show whether the current account improves or worsens as a result of the increased government purchases of goods and services.

7 Assume that there is perfect mobility of capital. How does the imposition of a tariff affect the exchange rate, output, and the current account? (*Hint:* Given the exchange rate, the tariff reduces our demand for imports.)

8 Explain how and why monetary policy retains its effectiveness when there is perfect mobility of capital.

9 Consult the *Globe and Mail* or some other newspaper which has foreign exchange rates listed on its financial pages. For some countries, such as Britain and the United States, you should find future prices listed. This is the price to be paid today to receive one unit of the foreign currency in the future. A 30-day future price for the pound sterling, say, is the price paid today to receive £1 30 days from now. Explain why the future prices are not generally equal to the spot prices — the price paid today to receive the foreign currency today. See whether you can explain the difference between the relationship of spot and future prices for the pound and U.S. dollar, respectively.

10 Assume you expect the pound to depreciate by 6 percent over the next year. Assume that the Canadian interest rate is 8 percent. What interest rate would be needed on pound securities — such as government bonds — for you to be willing to buy those securities with your dollars today, and then sell them in a year in exchange for dollars? Can you relate your answer to this question to your answer to problem 9?

11 What considerations are relevant for a country deciding whether to borrow abroad to finance a balance of trade deficit, or to adjust?

12 Explain the purchasing-power-parity theory of the long-run behaviour of the exchange rate. Indicate whether there are any circumstances under which you would not expect the PPP relationship to hold.

13 This problem deals with the current account effect of an expansion in the money

stock, given prices, perfect capital mobility, and flexible exchange rates.

(a) Given the interest rate, i^*, the real money stock, M/P, and the money market equilibrium condition

$$\frac{M}{P} = kY - hi$$

solve for the equilibrium level of income, Y_0, that is compatible with monetary equilibrium.

(b) Consider next the goods market equilibrium condition:

$$Y = A(Y, i) + NX$$

Let $A = \bar{A} + cY - bi$. Substitute for $i = i^*$ and the equilibrium level of income from 13(a). What is the equilibrium value of the trade balance, NX?

14 Suppose capital is imperfectly mobile, so that the higher the interest rate at home, the higher the rate of capital inflow, but that the flows remain finite. Then we can write the balance of payments as

$$BoP = NX\left(\frac{eP^*}{P}, Y\right) + K(i,i^*)$$

where K denotes the net rate of capital inflow and i^* is the given foreign interest rate.

(a) Suppose the exchange rate adjusts to maintain payments equilibrium. Then $BoP = 0$ and the current account surplus equals the capital account deficit:

$$NX\left(\frac{eP^*}{P}, Y\right) = -K(i,i^*)$$

Suppose the goods market is *also* in equilibrium so that

$$Y = A(i,Y) + NX\left(\frac{eP^*}{P}, Y\right)$$

Substituting for the current account in the goods market equilibrium condition yields

$$Y = A(i,Y) - K(i,i^*)$$

Show this equation graphically in i, Y space and interpret it.

(b) Also draw an LM schedule in the same space and interpret the intersection point.

(c) Show now the effect of a fiscal expansion in the home country on interest rates, income, and the current account.

(d) Show the effect of a monetary expansion on income, interest rates, and the current account.

(e) What can you say about the exchange rate in cases 14(b) and (c)?

15 Suppose in year 1 we have price levels $P = 100$ and $P^* = 100$. Suppose next that in year 2 the respective price levels are $P_2 = 180$ and $P_2^* = 130$. Let the exchange rate initially be $2/£.

    (a) If there were no real disturbances between year 1 and year 2, what would be the equilibrium exchange rate in year 2?

    (b) If the terms of trade eP^*/P had deteriorated between year 1 and 2 by 50 percent, what would the exchange rate be in year 2?

16 This problem draws on the discussion of stabilization policy and beggar-thy-neighbour policy in Section 18-2. Suppose we have two countries with full-employment output levels of Y_p and Y_p^* at home and abroad, respectively.

    (a) Draw a diagram with actual output levels, Y and Y^*, on the axes. Draw also lines corresponding to potential output levels. Label the resulting four quadrants I, II, III, and IV.

    (b) Identify for each of the quadrants the state of demand in each country as boom or recession.

    (c) Which policies can be pursued when output exceeds potential in each country? When output exceeds potential in one but falls short of potential in another?

    (d) In which quadrants are beggar-thy-neighbour policies particularly dangerous? Where is coordination of policies essential?

Index